A MAN OF CHANGE

A STUDY OF THE POLITICAL
LIFE OF BORIS YELTSIN

YELTSIN
CENTER

GLAGOSLAV PUBLICATIONS

A MAN OF CHANGE

A STUDY OF THE POLITICAL LIFE OF BORIS YELTSIN

Authors:
professor and doctor of history M.R. Zezina,
prof., doctor of history O.G. Malysheva, D.Eng.Sc. F.V. Malkhozova,
prof., doctor of history R.G. Pikhoya

Material by the following was used:
doctor of philosophical sciences V.A. Boikov,
doctor of history A.D. Kirillov, G.M. Kayota

Edited:
prof., doctor of history R.G. Pikhoya

Translated by Huw Davies

© 2015, Glagoslav Publications, United Kingdom

Glagoslav Publications Ltd
88-90 Hatton Garden
EC1N 8PN London
United Kingdom

www.glagoslav.com

ISBN: 978-1-78437-936-0

A catalogue record for this book is available
from the British Library.

CONTENTS

PART 2. MOSCOW. FROM THE CENTRAL COMMITTEE OF THE CPSU TO THE 1ST CONGRESS OF PEOPLE'S DEPUTIES OF THE USSR

*"The main accomplishment of my life is done.
Russia will never return to the past.
From now on Russia will always move ahead only."*
– Boris Yeltsin

Dear reader,

Presented for your attention is the political biography A Man of Change, celebrating the life and heritage of Russia's first democratically elected leader, Boris Yeltsin.

Supported and promoted by The President B. Yeltsin Centre Foundation, this book is a gift to the libraries of the United Kingdom and is the fruit of the combined efforts of a team of researchers whose aim was to compile a comprehensive collection of facts pertaining to the late President.

This book is believed to be of importance to British historians working in the field of Slavic Studies, for it contains details of Yeltsin's childhood and upbringing, education and ambitious career in politics, and an overview of Yeltsin's role in the formation of the new state after the collapse of the Soviet Union.

The President B. Yeltsin Centre Foundation strives to contribute to worldwide engagement in a pro-active dialogue, facilitating social and political change that would strengthen ties between all members of the international community, including the United Kingdom and Russia. By examining the history of political reforms in Russia under Boris Yeltsin's leadership and Yeltsin's influence on international politics, including the policies of the United Kingdom among others, as explored in A Man of Change, The President B. Yeltsin Centre Foundation offers a unique opportunity for an intellectual discourse in the best interest of both nations, and hopes to promote the peaceful resolution of issues related to Russia's interaction with the rest of the world.

Sincerely,
The President B. Yeltsin Centre Foundation

FOREWORD

The aim of this book is to study the political biography of the first President of Russia, Boris Nikolaevich Yeltsin. The objectives of this study are as follows:

- to reveal a range of historical source material which makes it possible to create a scientific biography of the first President of Russia;

- to analyze the social, economic, political and ideological factors which influenced the formation and development of the political views of Boris Nikolaevich Yeltsin;

- to investigate the factors which determined how Boris Nikolaevich Yeltsin's world-view evolved

- from his worldview defense of and continuation of the Communist ideology to his gradual rejection of it and transition to an anti-Communist stance.

The authors strove, as far as they were able, to base their conclusions on documentary evidence — both evidence that was already in circulation among academics and evidence that was used to study this subject for the first time.

We analyzed documents related to the history of the Yeltsin family from the late 19th century to the start of the 1930s, up to the period of 'dekulakization' and the family's exile, which are held by the State Archive of the Sverdlovsk Region (SASR) and the Shadrinsk State Archive of the Kurgan Region (SSAKR). The SASR holds documents related to Boris Yeltsin's work as a civil engineer, and about the influence he had, as secretary of the Sverdlovsk Regional Committee of the CPSU, on the activities of numerous government organizations, charities and businesses in the Sverdlovsk Region.

Extremely valuable information about Boris Yeltsin's activities as director of the department of construction, and as secretary and first secretary of the Sverdlovsk Regional Committee of the CPSU are held by the Center for Documentation on Non-profit Organizations of the Sverdlovsk Region (CDNOSR). This set of documents also contains information on practically every aspect of the activities of the regional committee of the CPSU, as the political and state center for regional government and the implementation of national policy in a regional context.

Information about Boris Yeltsin's activities as director of the department of construction in the CPSU's Central Committee, as secretary of the Central Committee, as a prospective member of the Politburo of the CC of the CPSU and as first secretary of the Moscow city committee was found in documents from the secretariat and Politburo, held by the Russian State Archive of Recent History (RSARH), in the minutes of Politburo assemblies and elsewhere, which reflected the attitude of the country's most senior political leaders toward Yeltsin.

A large number of documents about Yeltsin's practical activities as first secretary of the Moscow City Committee of the CPSU were deposited in the vaults of the Central Archive for the socio-political history of Moscow (TsAOPIM).

Documents containing detailed information about the course of the elections for the Congress of people's deputies of the RSFSR, the activities of the Congresses and the Supreme Soviet of the Russian Federation, the presidium and the committees and commissions of the Supreme Soviet are held at the State Archive of the Russian Federation (SARF).

His time in office as President between 1994 and 1999 has not been documented nearly as well. Anyone seeking to conduct research into this subject must have recourse to publications containing the directives and orders issued by the President, statistics from the State Statistics Committee, material from the Central Electoral Commission and the President's state of the nation addresses. A significant set of documents about the President's activities, which gives us an important insight into the reasons why decisions were taken, is held by the Archive of the President of the Russian Federation. This material (transcriptions of Security Council assemblies and meetings held by the President and his Administration, analytical notes) cannot yet be accessed by researchers under current legislation.

The researcher is required to consult the press as an additional source of information. The newspapers contain a diverse range of articles about the latest sensational stories that are considered newsworthy at that specific time by the publication in question. The information contained in periodical newspapers tends, as a rule, to reflect the party line — not necessarily in the direct, organizational sense (although such cases are not infrequent).

The press reflects the various shades of public opinion in the country[1] including the differing attitudes toward President Yeltsin. It is also important as a historical source which reflects less concrete facts than stereotypes and notions which were commonly held in society at the time in relation to those in power.

The appearance of a vast stream of autobiographical literature and memoirs, unprecedented in the history of Russia, is an extremely recent phenomenon in historiography. The very fact that those involved the political process, and the decision-makers in it, feel this need to put on record, in their memoirs, the role they played in the recent past, testifies to their understanding of the importance, and magnitude, of the changes which occurred in our country at the end of the 20th century.

Memoirs had become so much more than a story about the past. They could now be used as a political weapon and form part of a campaign manifesto. This peculiarity of memoirs was exploited by Boris Yeltsin in 1989 when he wrote his book *Against the grain*, but this does not render the author's view of the state the country was in, or his analysis of the crisis in the system in the USSR of the late '80s, any less important; the same can be said of the publication, in this book, of an extremely important document — a letter to Mikhail Gorbachev requesting permission to resign, dated September 1987.

A huge number of memoirs by the leaders of the Soviet government were published in the '90s, after the collapse of the USSR.[2] Given the disparity between many assessments of the recent past, the information provided by those who wrote memoirs gives us a fuller understanding of the position of the Soviet leaders, contrasting as it did with that of the Russian authorities which came to power following the elections in 1990.

The 'Russian assessment' of the events which took place at the end of the 20th century is set out first and foremost in the memoirs of President

---

1   This can be seen by comparing publications such as Sovetskaya Rossiya, Zavtra, Izvestiya, Moskovsky komsomolets, Moskovskiye novosti.

2   A.N. Yakovlev: Prologue. Collapse. Epilogue. M., 1992; L.A. Onikov: The CPSU: anatomy of the collapse. The view from inside the CPSU administration. M., 1996; K.N. Brutents: What didn't work out. A few partisan notes about perestroika. M., 2005. S. N.I. Ryzhkov: Ten years of huge jolts. M., 1995; V.I. Vorotnikov: It was like this...Notes from the diary of a member of the Politburo of the CC CPSU. M. 1995; V.V. Grishin: *From Gorbachev to Khrushchev*. Political portraits of five general secretaries and A.N. Kosygin: Memoirs. M., 1996; A.S. Chernyaev: Six years with Gorbachev. Based on diary entries. M., 1993; M.S. Gorbachev. His life and reforms. Book 1. G. Shaknazarov: The price of freedom. M.: Rossika, 1993; V.A. Medvedev: On Gorbachev's team. A view from the inside. M., 1994; V.I. Boldin: The fall of the pedestal. Lines about the portrait of M.S. Gorbachev. M.: Republic, 1995; Y. Prokofiev: Before and after the ban on the CPSU. The memoirs of the first secretary of the MCC CPSU. M., 2005; A. Lukyanov: In the whirlpool of the Russian disturbance. (Thoughts, dialogs, documents). M., 1999; Y.K. Ligachev: Perestroika: ideas, results and defeats and lessons. M., 2005 and other editions.

Yeltsin[3] as well as in those of members of his Administration[4] *The Yeltsin Era*, which was written by some of President Yeltsin's aides, examines the course of events in Russian political history, starting in the late '80s. The book's authors were directly involved in the events they describe. It provides an insider's view from people who were biased, who did not simply execute orders but had their own distinct position, and were part of a team. They acknowledge and admit oversights and errors made by the executive, and by Yeltsin himself, and express regret about the things they failed to achieve. Of particular interest are the passages about how political solutions were thrashed out, how Yeltsin behaved in particular situations, how he managed to shape his interaction with political opponents, what his style of working was and how the president felt about those in his inner circle.

The far-from-straightforward process of bringing democracy to the country, which was triggered by *perestroika* (the process of 'restructuring'), was described in the works of one of the key Russian politicians between the late eighties and the mid-nineties, Sergei Alexandrovich Filatov. He worked at the Supreme Soviet of the RSFSR in the early '90s, before taking charge of the President's Administration, then the public movement in support of Boris Yeltsin in the presidential elections in 1996. The range of subjects discussed by S.A. Filatov is extremely diverse: from general issues of parliamentarianism, to the relationships between politics and economics, the government and the opposition, ties with the regions, the art of governance and maintaining approval in society, to more personal, yet topical issues, such as the work he did in the president's 'team', and so on.[5]

The views of the President's political enemies are set out in a large number of memoirs. R.I. Khasbulatov, who was initially an ally of Boris Yeltsin's but later became one of his most bitter enemies, produced a 7-volume treatise in which he set out his own personal view of the country's development from the '80s onwards.[6]

Khasbulatov has nothing positive at all to say about Yeltsin's activities as head of the Supreme Soviet. When he writes about working with Yeltsin, the

---

3   B.N. Yeltsin: Against the Grain. M., 1990; same author: The Presidential marathon. — M., 2000; same author: Notes by the president. M., 2006

4   L.Y. Sukhanov L.: Three years with Yeltsin. A first adviser's diary. Riga 'Vaga', 1992; V. Kotikov: A love-story with the President. Notes by the pres-secretary. M., 1997; S.A. Filatov: On the road to democracy. M., 1995; Same author: An open secret. M., 2000; Yeltsin's Era. Sketches from a political story. M.: Vargius, 2001 — 816 p. Authors — Yeltsin's advisers, 1992-1998: Y.M. Baturin, A.L. Ilyin, V.F. Kadatsky, V.V. Kostikov, M.A. Krasnov, A.Y. Lifshits, K.V. Nikiforov, LG. Pikhoya, G.A. Satarov.

5   S.A. Filatov: On the road to democracy. M., 1995; Same author. An open secret. M., 2000.

6   R.I. Khasbulatov: The 4th Republic: from Yeltsin's non-state to Putin's state. In 7 volumes. Vol. 1: The 'loosening' of the Soviet Empire — the USSR. M.: A training manual, 2009. - p. 240. Vol..2.: Operation 'Thunder'. Preludes to the fall of the USSR. – M.: A training manual, 2009. - p. 236 (publication not yet banned)

author proves unable to contain the sense of wounded pride and frustrated ambition that has built up inside him.

Of all the memoirs written by Boris Yeltsin's political opponents, the publications of greatest value are probably the diaries of V.B. Isakov[7]. Their value, in our opinion, can be attributed to two circumstances. Firstly, the diary format provided a record of the specific circumstances surrounding the preparations for the first Congress of people's deputies, and the disputes at the presidium of the Supreme Soviet of the RSFSR. Secondly, V.B. Isakov published a large number of documents in his memoirs related to political history in the period 1990-1993.

The memoirs of A.V. Korzhakov, the head of Boris Yeltsin's personal security team, must also be noted. Korzhakov was close to Yeltsin but from 1996 onwards was among his opponents. Without troubling the reader with an assessment of the ethical qualities of this man who was 'attached' to the president, this 'aide-de-camp', whose professional duties required that he keep the private life of the "protected individual" secret — a requirement to which Korzhakov, without question, fails to adhere — we must observe that his memoirs contain a host of facts which are important for the purpose of reconstructing the political biography of Boris Yeltsin[8].

An analysis of the potential of memoirs as source material always involves criticism of the source, taking into account all the factors which influenced the authors and how they reached their verdicts on the events of the past.

The authors made the conscious decision to avoid reaching a verdict on the body of historical work on the subject of Boris Yeltsin as a political figure. There is a simple reason for this. Any historiographical essay coming before the main body of the text would be seen as a way of imposing a particular point of view on the authors. We shall therefore confine ourselves to a simple list of the most important studies on this issue, a list which will certainly not include all the books published on this issue, of which there is a vast number.[9] The authors are of the belief that this book will merely open up the

---

7   V.B. Isakov: Chairman of the Soviet of the Republic. Parliamentary diaries 1990-1991. Yekaterinburg, 1997

8   A. Korzhakov: Boris Yeltsin: from dawn till dusk. M., 1997

9   Aron L.: Yeltsin. A revolutionary life. N.Y. 2000;

Colton T.: "Moscow politics and the El'tsin Affair" The Harriman Institute Forum 1, no/6 (June 1988), Pp.1-8.;

Colton T.: Yeltsin. A Life. N.Y. 2008;

A.S. Barsenkov: An introduction to modern Russian history 1985-1991 Lecture series. M.: Aspekt Press, 2002;

V. Baryshnikov: Chinese political scientists on the 'Yeltsin era'. The problems of the Far East

academic investigation into the biography of Boris Nikolaevich Yeltsin and that new books will doubtless appear which will examine the history of the first President of Russia, as well as a large number of related subjects — to name a few:

- the reasons for the fall of the ideas of communism and the Communist Party of the Soviet Union in Russia;
- the circumstances which led to the collapse of the USSR;
- the market reforms in Russia: causes and consequences;
- the Soviet and Russian political elite at the turn of the century;
- the fate of the Soviet Army and the security services during the political transformation of the Russian state and society;
- the journey from an atheist state to cooperation with the church. The peculiarities of the 'Russian concordat'...

The list of problems seems almost endless.

We have no doubt that this book will provoke arguments and debate.

What we are presenting is our own vision of this political biography. It is founded on the approaches and principles of professional historical science.

We hope that those who follow in our footsteps will remain true to these principles as well.

No. 1. 2001 D. Boffa: From the USSR to Russia. The story of an incomplete crisis. 1964-1994. M., 199 Y. Gaidar: Days of defeats and victories. — M., 1996;

A.D. Kirillov: The Urals: from Yeltsin to Yeltsin (a chronicle of political growth, 1990-1997). Yekaterinburg, 1997;

A.D. Kirillov, N.N. Popov, B.A. Kirillov: The political Urals: history and the modern era: Parties. Elections. Deputies. Yekaterinburg, 1999 A.L. Litvin: The Yeltsins in Kazan. Kazan, 2006 B.D. Minaev: Yeltsin. M., 2010;

O. Moroz: 1996: How Zyuganov didn't become president. - M.: OJSC Rainbow Publishing House, 2006. Perestroika. Ten years on. (April 1985 – April 1995). M., 1995 R.G. Pikhoya: Moscow, the Kremlin, power. 40 years after the war. M., 2007;

R.G. Pikhoya: Moscow, Kremlin, power. Russia on the cusp of the new millennium. 1985-2005. M., 2007; R.G. Pikhoya: The Soviet Union: a story of power. 1945-1991. Novosibirsk, 2000;

R.G. Pikhoya, A.K. Sokolov: The story of modern Russia. The crisis of communist power and the birth of the new Russia. The late 1970s — 1991 M.: ROSSPAN, 2008; V.V. Sogrin: The political history of modern Russia. 1985-2001: from Gorbachev to Putin. M. 2001;

V. Soloviev, Y. Klepikova: Boris Yeltsin. Political metamorphoses. M.: VAGRIUS, 1992 L. Shevtsova: The Boris Yeltsin Regime. M., 1999 V.N. Shevchenko: Day-to-day life at the Kremlin under the Presidents. M., 2005;

A.V. Shubin: The paradoxes of perestroika. The USSR's missed opportunity. M., 2005

PART I. THE URALS

Chapter I
Childhood. Landowners

The Yeltsin clan hails from the Trans Urals region, from the southern areas of the Tobolsky district, land that was occupied during the second half of the 17th century, mainly by peasants from the Verkhotursky district.[10] In terms of their social make-up, they were emancipated black-*sokha* peasants from the 17th century who were later attached to state-owned plants, and from the start of the 19th century — state peasants who never experienced serfdom.

"These lands are fertile, generally speaking..., both districts, (Kamyshlov district and Shadrinsk — *author*)" — wrote P. Slovtsov, a man who conducted research into Siberia in the early 1840s, "Shadrinsk more so than Khamyshlov, hover between lofty, merry valleys... These districts are deemed to be suitable places in which to house factories, and when the harvest fails in the Western districts of the province of Tobolsk, they are separated from their surplus...Consequently, the harvest there has at times, both now and in the past, been 7-10 higher than the crop."[11]

---

10   A.A. Preobrazhensky: The Urals and Western Siberia in the late 16th century and early 18th century. M., 1972. pp. 78-81

11   P. Slovtsov: A historical survey of Siberia. Second volume, 1742 to 1823. Spb., 1844. P. 250. The fertility of areas 7 and 10 in the Shadrinsk and Kamyshlov districts, with a typical sowing rate of 2 centners per hectare of sowed field, was between 14 and 20 centners per hectare.

A. N. Zyryanov, a reporter for the Russian geographical society during the reform years who lived in the Shadrinsk district, observed that this district was predominantly used for agricultural purposes: "it has been famed since days of yore for its fertile soils and the richness of the land...bad harvests are a rarity here, and are merely the exception that proves the rule. The fertility of our land can doubtless be attributed to the clumpy, crumbly soil which predominates in all the localities in the town of Shadrinsk. ...The soil here is of such good quality that despite a century of being worked by agricultural laborers, it has not lost any of its strength, and has thereby particularly caught the eye of its owner"[12].

There were Yeltsins in several villages near the town of Basmanovo, in the Shadrinsk district, around the settlement of Butka, which was founded in 1676.[13]

There were many Old Believers among the people living in this district, as befitted a place where all the characteristic traits of traditional farming have been preserved[14]. There were 22,127 Old Believers in the Shadrinsk district in 1913, out of a relatively small overall population.

The Yeltsins (the surname is spelt Ельцин in Cyrillic; the alternative spellings Елцын and Ельцын crop up in the archives prior to the 1930s) are mentioned in records books and tax inspectors' reports from the mid-eighteenth century onwards as residents of the town of Basmanovo in the district of Shadrinsk. There were Yeltsins in several villages around the town of Basmanovo, in the Shadrinsk district, 20 versts (just over 21 km in today's terms) from the settlement of Butka.[15]

There is not a great deal of information about the Yeltsins to be found in the documents held by the State Archive of the Sverdlovsk Region, which holds data about the local self-governance of the reformed town of Basmanovo.[16]

---

12   A.N. Zyryanov: Providence in the Shadrinsk district of the Perm governorate. Shadrinsk, 1997.

13   Address book-calendar and commemorative book for the Perm governorate for 1905. Perm, 1905. P. 74

14   Sketches from the history of the Old Believers in the Urals and the adjoining territories. Yekaterinburg, 2000. P. 109. In the Butka Sloboda and the villages around it there were mass self-immolations by Old Believers in the mid-18th century. See: N.N. Pokrovsky: Protests against feudalism by the Urals-Siberian Old Believer peasants in the mid-18th century. Novosibirsk, 1974. P. 235, 237, 242-243

15   D.A. Panov: Generational paintings by the peasant clans of Yeltsin and Starygin. 1996. Manuscript. P. 2-4. (From the collection held by the B.N. Yeltsin Urals Center).

16   This is a typical problem for Russian archivists — the 'recycling campaigns', when sources which seemed unimportant were destroyed on mass; studies of the Yeltsin family are rendered all the more difficult by the fact that in the 19th century the village of Basmanovo was constantly changing its administrative status. In 1918 Basmanovo was the center of Basmanovo town in the Shadrinsk district of the Perm governorate; in July 1919 it was in the Shadrinsk of

The earliest recorded information about Boris Nikolaevich Yeltsin's forefathers that I discovered was contained in the lists of officials in the town and village council for the town of Basmanovo for 1893.[17] They include references to Ignat Yekimov Yeltsin, aged 28, who would later become the grandfather of the future President, and Ignat Yeltsin's cousin Pyotr Savvin Yeltsin, aged 25.

It is worth mentioning that the petty officer for the municipality, his deputy (and prospective replacement), the chairman of the municipality and the eight municipal judges were all illiterate.[18]

More detailed information about Boris Nikolaevich Yeltsin's relatives is contained in the list of home-owners in the Basmanovo village community. A total of 324 houses were recorded in the village.[19] The village assembly documents from 1908, containing the names of home-owners who were entitled to vote, listed Yekim Savvich Yeltsin and his son, Ignaty (Boris Yeltsin's grandfather), Pyotr Savvich Yeltsin, Pyotr Lukich Yeltsin and Ilya Lukich Yeltsin, Viktor Yevdokimovich, Mikhail Yevdokimovich and his son Pyotr, and also Andrei Mitrofanovich Yeltsin and Mikhail Grigorievich Yeltsin.

The Urals village experienced the revolution and the civil war, suffering heavy losses as it did so. The area of land on which crops were sown in 1922 was 68% smaller than it had been in 1916, the number of horses had fallen by 48%, there was 63% less large cattle and 68% less small cattle, and the number of pigs had fallen by no less than 90%. The structure with which areas of land were sown had changed and deteriorated and less wheat was grown.[20]

---

the Yekaterinburg governorate. In late 1923 the Shadrinsky district was abolished and part of its territory joined the Shadrinsk district in the Urals Region. A section of the old Basmanovo town became part of the Butinsk district. Basmanovooe became the center of the Basmanovo Village Council for the Shadrinsk district of the Urals Region. Under a Central Executive Committee directive dated 1934, the Urals Region was split into three regions — Sverdlovsk, Chelyabinsk and Obsk-Irtysh, and Basmanovo village became part of the Okunevsk district of the Chelyabinsk Region. In October 1938 Basmanovo village, by then part of the Butka district, was handed over to the Sverdlovsk Region. Basmanovo, along with Butka, later became part of the Talitsky district of the Sverdlovsk Region. For historians and archivists this means that legal documents about the agricultural family of the Yeltsins, covering a relatively short period, turn up in at least three regions, due to the policy of collectivization: the Sverdlovsk, Kurgan and Chelyabinsk Regions, as well as the Kazan, Perm and Berezniki Regions and a host of Moscow archives. See: The administrative and territorial dividing up of the Kurgan Region (1917-2004), Kurgan. 2005. P. 10-12, 14, RSFSR. The administrative and territorial dividing up as of 1st January 1972, M., 1972, p. 291

17   The State archive of the Sverdlovsk Region. Hereinafter — GASO, f. 203, op. 1, d. 388, l. 28.

18   Same ref., l. 44-45

19   Same ref., l. 19-22

20   Material on the dividing up of the Urals Region into districts. Tome 4. Long-term five-year plans for the development of the core sectors of the economy in the Urals Region, 1922-23 — 1926-27, Yekaterinburg, 1923. P. 4.

Judging by the documents that have survived, the Yeltsins did not fight either for the reds or the whites. Ignat Yekimovich Yeltsin's large family was quite well-to-do. In a list published in 1920 of people who paid the state natural tax in the Shadrinsk district of the settlement of Basmanovo, in the village of Basmanovo, there is a record of Yeltsin, Ignaty Yekimov, whose family consisted of 7 people. I.Y. Yeltsin had planted crops on 6 tithes and had to pay 20 poods of rye in tax, or 15 poods if he elected to pay in wheat. The amount of tax owed by I.Y. Yeltsin was among the highest of all the tax-payers in Basmanovo. I.Y. Yeltsin[21] had to pay full tax and was categorized as 'well-off'. The material status of I.Y. Yeltsin — the grandfather of the future President — was roughly equivalent to that of the average Siberian peasant family at the turn of the century. According to the calculations made by a historian from Novosibirsk named L.M. Goryushkin, 35.1% of peasants had between 4 and 9 tithes, whilst 26.7% had 9 tithes or more.[22]

Heads of household had to sign to confirm that they had been made aware how much tax they owed. I.Y. Yeltsin was illiterate. One of his fellow-villagers, Ivan Bersenev, signed the document on his behalf.[23]

Later, in 1934, the chairman of the Basmanovo Village Council, in response to a request from the OGPU (the Associated State Political Directorate – the precursor to the KGB), reported that Ignat Yekimovich Yeltsin, father to Nikolai and Andrian Yeltsin, who had been arrested in Kazan, had once owned a watermill and a windmill, a threshing-machine, a reaping-machine, five working horses and four cows, owned 5 hectares of land and had leased and cultivated up to 12 hectares. He also stated that in 1924 Ignat had divided the estate into three parts — in all likelihood for his two eldest sons, Ivan and Dmitry, with one part for himself.[24]

There is indirect evidence suggesting that in around 1924 Ivan Yeltsin began to manage some land of his own, separate from that of his father. The minutes of the presidium of the Butka district executive committee, for the Shadrinsk district of the Urals Region, in 1925, contain the names of dozens of agricultural laborers who were fined for chopping down trees in the forest without permission. Among them were Feoktist Yekimovich Yeltsin, Ivan Yeltsin's uncle, and Ivan Ignatievich Yeltsin himself. The fact that the data about the division of property by Ignat Yekimovich Yeltsin coincides with the information about his son Ivan chopping down trees in the forest may be interpreted as a sign that this was when Ivan began building his house.[25]

---

21   Thenceforward the surname Ельцын was spelt Ельцин in official documents.

22   L.M. Goryushkin: The Siberian peasantry at the turn of the century. The end of the 19th century — start of the 20th century. Novosibirsk, 1967.

23   GASO, f. p.-718, op. 1, d. 14

24   A.L. Litvin: The Yeltsins in Kazan. Kazan, 2006. Pp. 24-26

25   The Shadrinsk state archive of the Kurgan Region. Hereinafter — SSAKR. F. P-209. Op. 1. D. 329. L. 363-365

Also of note is the fact that Ivan Yeltsin worked for the Village Council between 1924 and 1928 and even served as its acting chairman when the man who held this position went on holiday in 1926.[26] He had managed to procure himself an initial education.

Thus, in the years following the revolution, the affairs of Ignat Yeltsin and his family were going decidedly well.

The sizeable Yeltsin clan included the following residents of the Basmanovo settlement: Vasily Petrovich Yeltsin, a member of the town council, an illiterate, poor man who tilled the land, was not a member of the party and had been employed since 9th November 1923[27]; in the village of Porotnikovo, Fyodor Stepanovich Yeltsin, Stepan Nikolaevich Yeltsin, Kiprian Spiridonovich Yeltsin, Nikita Ivanovich Yeltsin, Stepan Dmitrievich Yeltsin and Yakov Mikhailovich Yeltsin; in the village of Konovalovo, Stepan Dmitrievich Yeltsin, Filip Vasilievich Yeltsin, Yeremey Ivanovich Yeltsin, Alexander Spiridonovich Yeltsin[28] and Ivan Mikhailovich Yeltsin.[29]

The material status of the clan's various members varied considerably. Among the residents of the Porotnikovo Village Council, Nikita Ivanovich, Stepan Dmitrievich and Alexander and Fyodor Stepanovich Yeltsin had the right to vote taken away from them, but it was returned to them in October 1925, when Yakov Mikhailovich Yeltsin had the right to vote taken away from him as well.[30]

In the time of the New Economic Policy, elements of local self-governance which were rooted in the past continued to be part of life in the Trans-Urals village. These traditions had now been adapted to suit the Soviet way of doing things, however. There was a practice of holding assemblies of the Butka district executive committee *in situ*, with dozens of local residents attending the meetings. At one of these meetings, held on 19th December 1926 in the village of Porotnikovo, 67 people from the "disorganized population of the village of Porotnikovo" — of 'society', as the chairman of the Butinsk district executive committee, Ovchinnikov, described them in the old style — were present, in addition to the district bosses and members of the Porotnikovo Village Council.

Ovchinnikov spoke to the people about the technical agricultural measures which had been introduced, and added that the residents had a sufficient number of horses and cattle, but that most of the horses were elderly and the cows were not very mobile; he said that there were not enough agricultural

---

26   SSAKR. F. P-209. Op. 2. D. 51. L. 79. See also: The Autobiography of N.I. Yeltsin. 22nd March 1953 From the collection of documents held by the Urals Center for B.N. Yeltsin.
27   SSAKR. F. P-209. Op. 1. D. 73. L. 46
28   SSAKR. F. P-209. Op. 1. D. 205 l. 309-310
29   SSAKR. F. P-209. Op. 1. D. 205. L. 143
30   SSAKR. F. P-209. Op. 1. D. 329. L. 24-27

implements, because such things were expensive, and that it was essential that long-term loans be secured in the district so that machinery could be procured. Ovchinnikov warned that "our district ranks almost first in terms of the amount of forested land, and also ranks first in terms of the amount of forest stolen. Particularly in the Porotnikovo Village Council, in the village of Konovalova," and he added that the community must hire someone to guard the forest. According to Ovchinnikov, the horse-breeding exhibition, at which 18 horses had been exhibited, had not been a success.

He reported that the lending partnerships were not doing a good job, and were too small.

Other members of the 'community' contributed to the discussion. They complained about the shoddy work done by the medical orderly, and the lack of funding for refurbishment of the school in the village of Konovalovo.

A Deputy in the Village Council named S.D. Yeltsin said: "I would be interested in finding out what the discount was on agricultural tax for dead crops, and how it was applied? Because some citizens were given a discount, whilst others weren't. As regards the common agricultural tax of 43 rubles per tithe. ... As I see it, that's not quite the right way to do it. Take the Smolinsk and Kataratskiye lands, for example — they give a much bigger harvest than ours, in the Porotnikovo Village Council. In future, it is essential that the agronomist conduct an inspection of the soil in our arable land to find out how fertile it is (in comparison) with other Village Councils."

Another member of the district executive committee, S.K. Samokhvalov, also spoke about the flaws in the taxation system. "I must comment on the fact that the same agricultural tax is imposed on all craftsmen, which does not seem quite right, since craftsmen earn more from their crafts than agricultural laborers earn from working the land." He expressed support for what Yeltsin had said: "Some citizens in the Porotnikovo Village Council are upset by the fact that their land is not bringing in much profit. I share their views, and I would add this: it's quite true that the land in Porotnikovo will never provide the same sort of harvests as those enjoyed by the citizens of the Kataratsky Village Council."[31]

Life went on as normal in this Trans-Urals village, with its back-breaking agricultural labor and its occasional moments of happiness. In 1925 the Urals region produced and handed over to the state more bread than was supplied by all the other regions of the country with the exception of Ukraine. Nikolai Ignatievich Yeltsin was involved in this feat — he was the director of the grain-reserves shops (the stores) in the Basmanovo Village Council from 1926 to 1928.[32]

---

31   SSAKR. f. P-209. Op. 2. D. 51. L. 66-67.

32   Personal staff records sheet of N.I. Yeltsin. 11th October 1948. From the collection of

But this life was to come to an end.

A new policy: the elimination of the Kulaks as a class

In December 1927 the 15th congress of the All-Union Communist Party of Bolsheviks (VKP(b)) was held; the congress voted in favor of a policy of collectivization. A huge number of books have been written about the circumstances which led to the government altering its attitude toward the countryside. First and foremost I would highlight the studies and extremely important publications of documents by V.P. Danilov.[33]

The 15th congress of the All-Union Communist Party of Bolsheviks set itself the objective of launching an attack on the Kulaks, the 'grasping fists'. At this stage, the main form in which this attack took place was the new system of taxation. For the so-called Kulak-owned areas, a progressive tax of between 5% and 25% of income was introduced. The Kulaks were supposed to pay 8 times more than the poor or 'middling' for a single hectare of land, 21 times more for a hired laborer, and 30 times more for their own land.

This change to the taxation system brought about the start of a degradation of the economy in the countryside. Large land holdings began to shut down production due to the impossibility of making a profit. Production of agricultural produce began to decline almost immediately.

The consequences of this were as might have been expected. A process of 'self-dekulakization' began. (See table 1)

Table 1. Agricultural production levels in the Urals region, 1926-1929.[34]

As a % of the previous year	1926–27 agricultural year	1927–28 agricultural year	1928–29 agricultural year
Total area sown	107.1	99.1	95.3
Total cattle (large)	106.1	102.8	101.6

Statisticians from the Urals Region observed: "the past year, 1927-1928... has been marked by the emergence of a series of negative trends: slowdowns,

documents held by the Urals center for B.N. Yeltsin.

33   V.P. Danilov: The evidence is in the documents. From the history of the countryside before and during collectivization, M., 1989. (Co-editor and co-writer); The collectivization of agriculture in the USSR // The history of the USSR. 1990. No. 5; The Soviet countryside as seen through the eyes of the VChK-OGPU-NKVD. 1918-1939. Documents and material in 4 volumes. / V.I-3. M., 1998 — 2003. (Co-editor and co-writer); The tragedy of the Soviet countryside. Collectivization and de-kulakization. Documents and material in 5 volumes. 1927-1939. / Vols.I — 5. M., 1999-2004. (Co-editor and co-writer).

34   Control figures for the economy of the Urals Region for 1928-1929, Sverdlovsk, 1929. P. 17

growth coming to a standstill, and even reductions in grain production." Reductions in the area of land on which crops were planted were observed primarily on those holdings which had 8 hectares or more. The biggest reduction in the area of land on which crops were sown in 1928 took place in the central and southern Trans-Urals region — a reduction of 8.3%, statisticians observed[35].

"The area of land used for crops and large horned cattle has fallen in the last two years, and the main explanation for this is the fall in production among the richest people in the countryside and the generally unfavorable market conditions for grain production and butter-making," the authors of the statistical report concluded.

In order to overcome the growing negative trends in the village, and the shortage of grain, which was growing worse, the authorities dramatically strengthened repressive measures against the peasants. In January 1928 Stalin set off in person for Siberia to take part in the grain production process. His visit only served to strengthen his belief that the difficulties being experienced in grain production could be put down to resistance on the part of the Kulaks - to 'Kulak saboteurs'. In a telegram from the Central Committee dated 14th January 1928 on the strengthening of grain production measures, signed J.V. Stalin, he demanded: "we must strike out against the hoarder and the grasping-fists at once, we must arrest the speculators, the little Kulaks and all the others attempting to bring disorder to the market and the pricing policy we will be unable to isolate the speculators and the Kulaks in the market, unable to achieve a decisive turning-point on the front-line of grain production."

The so-called Urals-Siberian method of self-taxation was introduced by the tax services from the spring of 1929 onwards. Its introduction was to be accompanied by direct supervision and pressure from local party agencies and Soviet agencies, but was disguised using decisions made by local assemblies and the demands of the poor and 'middling' peasants. In parallel to this, wealthy peasants were denied the right to vote and expelled from their co-operatives and from the local Soviet agencies[36].

The Trans-Urals countryside was not exempt from the things that were going on in the rest of the countryside.

On 16-17th February 1929, the Shadrinsk district committee of the VKP(b) held an assembly for the district's party activists.

Grain production was the main item on the agenda. The annual plan for 1928 was only 55% fulfilled as of 11th February. The situation was even worse

---

35   Review of the state of farming in the Urals region, 1927-28. Sverdlovsk, 1928. P. 1-2, 19
36   N.Y. Gushchin: 'Dekulakization' in Siberia (1928-1934): Methods, stages, socio-economic and demographic consequences. See: memorial.krsk.ru/Articles/1996Guscshin/02.htm

in particular areas. The plan was only 43.08% fulfilled in Kargopol, 52.26% fulfilled in Shadrinsk and 53.90% fulfilled in Butka.[37]

During the discussions, various approaches were put forward as to how grain production policy ought to be implemented in the countryside. Which was more important — financial interest or political expediency?

The secretary from Kargopol, Timofeyev, complained that poverty usually acted as an incentive for the grain production workers, but that was not helping. The financial levers were not operating. Grain had been produced, but it was being tightly held on to and distributed very slowly. The well-off are saying: give us 5 poods, but then another one arrives, and his needs must be seen to.

The Butka secretary Patrakeyev protested: "I think that if we're going to intersperse the grain production methods by 75% with emergency measures, we won't get very far." In Patrakeyev's opinion, however, the peasants were not particularly afraid of fines, either. "In the Butka district the financial levers have no effect as far as grain production is concerned, because the peasants earn money from the work they do on the side." A financial boycott of the peasants would not work, in Patrakeyev's opinion, because "he (the peasant) will sell 20 poods in the city and get some goods in exchange."

Partakeyev's views were echoed by the Shadrinsk party activist Fominov, who warned that instead of handing over grain the peasants were taking geese to the Shadrinsk market, selling it and paying their taxes out of the money they earned.

Ogurtsov, who represented the Urals district committee of the ACP(b) at this meeting, observed that the peasants simply had nothing to buy in the local co-operative, and therefore had no incentive to sell grain here, at home. "When I arrived from the District," he said, "I was...told that in these areas manufactured goods were in decay, and that in the co-op stores and on the shelves of consumer society there was nothing but rats (Basmanka, Kalinovka). The staff of the co-op have completely given up lately..."

As for 'grain recruitment', as he put it, this was being done by Komsomol members aged 14-15. "In my opinion this is wrong, for the wealthier peasants are already turning a deaf ear on us. ...There is a trend towards estrangement between the poor and the middle peasants, particularly with those delivering grain. ...

A journalist named Beloglazov, who edited the newspaper, was the most radical of all. "Comrade Gendel is wrong when he says that depriving the kulak of industrial goods has no effect on him. All we need to do is deprive him of all products, everywhere...the Red wagon trains must be condemned

---

37   Center for the documentation of public associations in the Sverdlovsk Region — hereinafter CDPASR f. 4, op. 7, d. 221,

once and for all for the time being, because the kulak can hide under a branded wagon train carrying 5-10 poods." He also had something to say about the co-operative owners, who, in his opinion, did nothing but get drunk.

Attempts to ban trade in grain and leave the city without grain, whilst preventing the party committees from organizing 'red convoys', provoked strong opposition from one of the people attending the meeting. Beryukhov (Chetkarino) said that he didn't share Beloglazov's view that the party cell ought not to organize red wagon trains. "What are you suggesting — are the kulaks to organize them?" he asked, though the answer to this was obvious.

He then complained that the district had made plans for 16% of grain surpluses to be confiscated, and that for our district it was planning to confiscate 31%.

Beryukhov also raised another issue which turned out to be central to the discussions: the attitude toward manpower. He said that the most decisive measures possible — right up to removal of their party membership card — must be taken against communists with large reserves of grain.

People protested. The grassroots workers needed to be supported. Last year 38 workers had been removed from their positions; if we are to go on like that, soon we will have no workers left.

The dispute went on. Another speaker talked about the chairman of the Village Council in the Kargopol district. He was a communist, had 6 horses, 5 hens, 14 tithes, had refused to give a single pound to the state, was discrediting the state...

Summarizing the intermediary results of the assembly, the chairman of the Urals Regional Executive Committee, M. K. Oshvintsev, set the problems of the Urals region in their nationwide context. He said that in 1928 "Ukraine and the Caucuses had had...a huge crop failure last year..., as a consequence of which the grain production plan for the Urals had been increased from 42 million poods to 49 million poods." He talked about the importance of grain production for industry, demanded that the assets of the countryside be mobilized, warned of a forthcoming purge of the workforce and called on people not to count on administrative measures as a cure.

Equipment owned by the aforementioned local leaders was quickly installed in the regions. On 29th March 1929 there was an extraordinary meeting of the Butka district executive committee (RIK). It began with the following statement: "taking account of the complete lack of grain products in the local market, the supply of food (and flour) for the laborers and servants is to be continued from the Butka credit cooperative.

Bring the above to the attention of Okrik and the Okrtorgotdel.[38]

---

38   SSAKR. F. P-209. Op. 1. D. 674. L. 81

At the same meeting, the issue of approving directives from the general assemblies of land associations on the adoption of self-taxation was discussed.

The presidium of the RIK approved these directives. "Given that there were no breaches of the law, the directives from the general councils, on the adoption of self-taxation by the land associations of Danilovo, Beregovo, Borovushkino, Porotnikovo, Nepeino, Kazakova and Bulatovo are to be approved. The land department shall monitor performance." One cannot help noticing the choice of wording here: "there were no breaches of the law this year" — it appears as if the members of the RIK were attempting to reassure themselves.

The lengthy minutes for this meeting contained a point about a review of petitions made by citizens to have their right to vote restored. Listed among those who had had their right to vote taken away were some residents of the village of Konovalovo, Ivan Ignatievich Yeltsin — formerly a deputy in the Basmanovo village council, and Stepan Dmitrievich Yeltsin, who had been a deputy in the village council not long before this, and who had taken an active interest in the taxation system in 1926. His petition to have his right to vote restored was rejected.[39]

In July the presidium of the Butka RIK fined dozens of agricultural laborers for concealing crop harvests from the taxman. Among them was Filip Vasilievich Yeltsin, who was fined 7 roubles for concealing a harvest covering an area of 0.25 hectares.[40]

In the summer of 1929 the country's leader issued a series of directives in the field of agriculture[41]. Kulaks were banned from joining collective farms, and collective farms which they were involved in creating were declared "false collective farms".

J.V. Stalin formulated the specific provisions of his policy on the kulaks and collectivization in his speech at a conference of Marxist-agrarians on 27th December 1929.

"This is why we have effected a transition in recent times from a policy of limiting the exploitative tendencies of the kulaks to a policy of eliminating the kulaks as a class. (J.V. Stalin's italics — Author's note).

Well, what are we to do with our policy of de-kulakization, can de-kulakization be permitted in areas where there is collectivization throughout? ... The question is absurd! ...

---

39   SSAKR. F. P-209. Op. 1. D. 674. L. 83
40   SSAKR. F. P-209. Op. 1. D. 674. L. 132-133
41   See: Transcripts of Politburo meetings, 1923 — Vol.3. 1938, M., 2007. Pp. 83-118

Now we have the opportunity to launch a decisive attack on the kulaks, to break their resistance, to eliminate them as a class and replace them with production by means of collective farms and state farms. Now, de-kulakization is being carried out by the masses of poor and middle peasants themselves, who are carrying out collectivization in all areas. ... That is why it is absurd and ill-advised to talk about de-kulakization now. No tears are shed for the hair once the head has been chopped off.

Another question seems equally absurd: can the kulak be permitted to join the collective farm. Of course he must not be allowed to join the collective farm. He may not join it, for he is the sworn enemy of the collective farm movement.

I think I have made myself clear."[42]

The spike of state policy had now been turned against the well-off peasants — the kulaks. Documents were hastily drawn up about the "elimination of the kulaks as a class", and the rates of collectivization in various regions of the country were determined. A Politburo commission was set up, with Molotov in charge, "to draw up measures in relation to the kulaks." The commission's members included the first secretary of the Urals regional committee of the VKP(b) I.D. Kabakov. The total number of kulaks facing exile under the first and second categories throughout the country rose to 210,000 families.[43]

From the point of view of the Urals Directorate of the OGPU, the 'Urals quota' of deportees was clearly insufficient. "We consider it essential to raise before you the issue of increasing the figures for those deported from the Urals to 15,000 households, since the 5000 households given for the Urals does not in any way satisfy current requirements in terms of purging the region of the kulak and counter-revolutionary White Guard and criminal element... The Urals regional committee also insists, in accordance with the material it has related to the study of the countryside, also insists, categorically, on an increase in the figures for deportation to 15,000 households."[44]

The quota requirements for Sverdlovsk were met. On 5th February 1930 a directive from the Urals regional committee was adopted on the eradication of petitions by the kulaks in connection with mass collectivization.

As political solutions within the union developed, the Urals regional committee adopted a special directive on the eradication of kulak farms in the Urals region.[45]

---

42   J.V. Stalin: The issues of Leninism. 11th edition M., 1947. P. 292-293
43   The tragedy of the Soviet countryside. Collectivization and de-kulakization. Documents and materials Volume 2. November 1929 - December 1930. M. P. 15.
44   The tragedy of the Soviet countryside. Collectivization and de-kulakization. Documents and materials Volume 2. November 1929 — December 1930. M., 2000. P. 144
45   CDPASR, f. 4, op.7, d. 445, ll. 103

The kulaks were split into three categories:

Category 1 — counter-revolutionary kulaks, who were to be arrested with immediate effect;

2 — the wealthiest kulaks and semi-landowners, who were to be deported to the north of the region;

3 — the rest of the kulaks, who were sent to live on poor-quality collective farm land.

Up to 5 thousand people were to be banished in the first category, and up to 15 thousand in the second.[46]

The numbers in the third category were not counted.

The authorities were creating a legal basis for de-kulakization. On 16th January 1930, two directives were passed into law: the Directive of the All-Russian Central Executive Committee and the Council of People's Commissars 'On measures to counter the sale of agricultural equipment, working and useful cattle, by agricultural farms which are members of collective farms and other agricultural and manufacturing associations', and the Directive of the Central Executive Committee (TsIK) and the Council of People's Commissars (SNK) 'On measures to counter the theft of cattle', which became both the instrument of and basis for repression. The executive district committees allowed land to be taken away from the accused, as well as cattle and farming implements. In addition, kulaks were to be brought before the courts, "and the court may sentence them to imprisonment for up to two years, and may in addition exile them from the territory in question, at its discretion."[47]

This Directive was the weapon that played a decisive role in wiping out the well-off peasants. Its introduction also marked the start of the fall of the peasant clan of the Yeltsins, and of the well-to-do, entrepreneurial peasanthood of the Trans-Urals.

On 2nd February 1930, at an assembly of the Butka district executive committee, the de-kulakization campaign began.

First of all their property was seized.

The first issue on the agenda at the assembly was described as: "Inventories of the property owned by Kulak farms, to check whether there is a need for alienation due to failure to pay taxes and dues." "It was decreed," read the

---

46   CDPASR, f. 4, op. 8, d. 54, ll. 104-107
47   The story of collective farm law. Collected legislation of the USSR and RSFSR 1917-1958 T.1 1917- 1936 M., 1959. P. 163

minutes of the presidium, "that, in light of the fact that the farms listed below are stubbornly refusing to hand over the taxes and fees owed by them, that part of their property, as set out in the inventories, be transferred to the collective farms via the district lending partnership.

There followed a long list of peasants from the Zarubino, Kataratskoe, Butka, Smolino, Gorokino and Kazakova Village Councils.

This was followed by persecution in the courts. A separate point in the legislation read:

"The farms listed below, for deliberately destroying cattle, seeds and property, winding down production and refusing to take part in events organized by Soviet power, shall be punished by the courts on the basis of the Directive of the TsIK and the SNK dated 16th January 1930, and shall have all or part of their property confiscated."

The lists below this text contained the names of the peasants who were the very first victims of de-kulakization. I am going to re-print this list in full. For the Nizhny-Derevensk Village Council: Ivan Savich Zavertkin, Fyodor Matveyevich Koksharov; for the Basmanovo Village Council: Filip Alekseyevich Aksyonov, Tit Pavlovich Shabunin, Glebov Aleksander An. (sic!), Vasily Yegorovich Staryn, Ignaty Yekimovich Yeltsin, Glebov Vasily Stepanovich; for Kalinovo — Mikushin Guryan Khrisanfovich, Stepanov Savva Lukyanovich; for the Butka Village Council — Zemerov Ivan Fedotovich, Sorokin Andrei Yudich, Ryzhkov Ivan Yakovlevich, Zemerov Dimitri Vidonovich, Zemerov Afanasy Prokopievich; for the Zarubino Village Council: Oblasov Fyodor Naumovich, Telminov Ivan Yemelyanovich, Sanochkin Filaret Yevstigneyevich, for the Porotnikovo Village Council — Yeltsin Nikita Ivanovich, Porotnikov Andriyan Filippovich, Porotnikov Mark Vavilovich.[48]

Ignat Yekimovich Yeltsin and his brother-in-law, Vasily Yegorovich Sarygin, were de-kulakized. Their offspring — Nikolai Ignatievich Yeltsin and Claudia Vasilievna Starygina — got married.

The evictions began shortly afterwards. The procedure used was as follows. First came the decision by the poor peasants' assembly in the village council, then this was approved by the agenda of the presidium of the Butka district executive committee, and thereafter — by the Shadrinsk area executive committee.[49]

A total of 1300 families were evicted from the Shadrinsk district.

---

48   SSAKR, f. p-209, op. 1, d. 806, ll. 91-95
49   SSAKR, f. p-209, op. 3 d. 93, l. 59

If a missive from the Urals district committee of the ACP(b), entitled 'On the progress of efforts to liquidate the kulaks as a class. (For the months of January and February)', dated 7th March 1930 — after Stalin's famous article about how the country was 'Giddy with success' — is anything to go by, there were countless abuses during the process of de-kulakization. Rather than being registered, property was stolen (that was what happened in the Butkino district, specifically), items were confiscated by members of the de-kulakization commissions, felt boots (valenki) were confiscated, along with fur coats, fur hats, and food; even children had the clothes taken from their backs in spite of the extreme cold; there was drunkenness in the homes of the de-kulakized, and they stole everything they could get their hands on — from gold watches to the last children's smocks.[50]

Exile

The deportations from the Shadrinsk district began in February 1930.

According to the OGPU reports, 844 families were banished, 3 489 people in total, 1177 husbands, 1173 wives and 1139 children.[51]

V.P. Biryukov, an extremely well-known local historian and resident of Shadrinsk, and someone who always demonstrated his loyalty to the Soviet authorities, wrote in his diary, in February 1930: "A few more words about the food. There are hardly any potatoes...There is hardly any feed for the cattle either...

... The people who have been de-kulakized are left in nothing but rags and sent to Shadrinsk, from whence they will be expelled. No-one will tell me where they send them from there.

... My brother's wife, Arkasha...told me she had overheard the head of the Shadrinsk unit of the State Political Division, Movshenzon, complaining about the fact that women and children were being sent in the cold.

... According to Liza, they even took away a pregnant woman who was about to give birth, despite her protestations. She gave birth during the journey; the baby was left in the nearest village, and the mother travelled to Shadrinsk and was taken to hospital. It is utterly horrific. Equally horrific is the fact that, according to S.S-ch, when the de-kulakized people from the village of Mishagino were sent to Shadrinsk, they brought along four lads who had

---

50   CDPASR. F. 4. Op. 8. D. 241. L. 2-7
51   For reports about the deportation of kulaks from the Shadrinsk district see: CDPASR, f. 4, op. 8, d. 101, ll. 14

frozen to death. It is entirely possible that there are many others who shared the same fate, because they often pack people off with barely any clothes on them at all."[52]

Under the classification system of the Urals regional committee, Ignat Yekimovich Yeltsin's family was de-kulakized in the second category, as "the wealthiest kulaks and semi-landowners", and accordingly they were "supposed to be exiled to the north of the region." Ignat Yeltsin was exiled to Nadezhdino, and his brother-in-law Vasily Yegorovich was sent to the north of the Urals.

Collective farm workers

Ignat Yeltsin's sons — Ivan, Dmitry, Nikolai, Andian and their sister Maria — remained in exile "in the third category" — they could stay in their home district but had to give up all their property. They went from owning a mill to working in one and having to clean it and keeping the milling going. They were employed at the Red May collective farm in Butka.[53]

Life wasn't easy at the newly-erected collective farms, either. In December 1929 and January and February 1930 the local authorities went from organizing animal-rearing and grain partnerships to creating communes; there was a conviction that the commune was the way forward in the Shadrinsk district.[54]

On the collective farmers' farms they banned poultry, as well as cattle. It reached a point where in some collective farms women had their heads forcibly shaved, so that their hair could be submitted as recyclable material.[55]

Understandably, actions such as this on the part of the authorities provoked strong protest. A report by the Shadrinsk District Committee of the ACP(b) about anti-Soviet activity, arson and terrorist acts demonstrating kulak activity, dated 25th April 1930, said that "recently, particularly throughout the month of April, a particularly intense (handwritten) surge in actions against the collective farmers, representatives of power in the village and peasant activists, on the part of the kulaks and anti-Soviet elements." On 6th April, during an attempt by the commune's senior command to take cattle away, they were chased away by a crowd of women, and on 8th April, when 9 members of the commune and a policeman went back for the cattle again, about 100 women gathered together, led by the wives of those who had been

---

52   F. GASO P.-2266, Op.1. D. 1373. L. 11-14
53   T. Colton: Yeltsin. A Life. N.Y. 2008. P.20
54   CDPASR, f. 4, op. 8, d., d. 492, l. 1 ob.
55   CDPASR. F. 4. Op. 8. D. 104. L. 30

de-kulakized, and when the cattle were taken away, these women picked out the horses, spat in the eyes of the commune members and shouted: "You all ought to be shot, you thieves, tramps, jailbirds etc." (5 of the de-kulakized people were arrested — the investigation is being led by the SPU). Rumours spread in the countryside that there would soon be an end to Soviet power, that Stalin had bottled it and changed his policy, but that in any event the cossacks would soon come, and they would teach the people who had taken part in the de-kulakization a thing or two."[56]

A famine began. In the summer of 1930 the agencies of the OGPU announced that "in the districts of Troitsk, Ishim, Kurgan, Chelyabinsk, Shadrinsk and Tyumen, which suffered from crop failure last year, there is an urgent need for food. The reserves of food in these areas are utterly inadequate in terms of meeting the needs of the hungry. Numerous cases of the consumption of substitute foods, disease and intumescence have been recorded, against the backdrop of the famine. In a host of places, incidents involving the killing of dairy cattle and the grinding of seeds and grain, to for use as food, have been recorded."[57]

In the subsequent years, 1931 and 1932, the situation grew even worse. According to the OGPU report, in the Urals "in December 20 collective farms in 10 districts were gripped by production difficulties, in January this was true of 146 collective farms in 18 districts, and in February — 202 collective farms in 22 districts. There were a number of instances of the consumption of surrogates, animal corpses, and grass, and as a result — bloated stomachs among collective farm workers and occasional cases of death. There is mass poverty in 5 districts as a result of difficulties in production."[58]

It is no accident that in 1932 specifically, on 7th August, the famous 'Law on three wheels' was passed — Directives from the TsIK and the SNK of the USSR dated 7th August 1932 'On the protection of property owned by state companies, collective farms and cooperatives and the strengthening of community (socialist) property'.

The famine prompted people to flee the countryside, with its collective farms, to the cities, where there was a demand for manpower. By this time Nikolai Ignatievich Yeltsin's family included a son named Boris. With the new-born baby, Nikolai, his wife Claudia Vasilievna and Nikolai's brother Andrian fled to Kazan, where they found work at a construction site for an aeroplane factory. At their new workplace they were paid a salary and given rations.

---

56   CDPASR, f. 4, op. 8, d. 135, l. 4-6
57   The tragedy of the Soviet countryside. Collectivization and de-kulakization. Documents and materials. Vol. 2. November 1929 — December 1930. M., 2000. pp. 473-474
58   Documents and materials Vol. 3. End of 1930-1933. M., 2001. P. 319-320

As experienced joiners (for millers this went with the territory), they found work at the site. This was just the start of the long and tortuous process of the urbanization of an ancient peasant clan.[59]

The birth certificate

That was the name of the first document Boris Yeltsin ever received. On 14 February 1931 an employee of the Butka Registry Office filled in a standard form with the number 26/11 at the top. Written on the form was the following: Surname: Yeltsin. Given name — Boris. Gender — male. Date of birth — 12th February 1931 Parents: father: Yeltsin, Nikolai Ignatievich, age — has turned 24 (that was how it was phrased!). Nationality — Russian. Profession (position, occupation, trade etc.) agriculture. Social status (1. worker, 2. servant, 3. landlord, 4. family member, 5. no fixed profession or 6). Number 3. landlord was underlined. Mother — Yeltsina, Claudia Vasilievna, has turned 22, Russian, profession — agriculture, social status — housewife.

This standard document is striking in the internal disparity between its form and its content; it is a snapshot which records something which is mutable, undergoing a transformation or is set to disappear in a few short moments. The only sense in which Nikolai Yeltsin and his wife were landowners was in the old, statistical sense. Landowners had been abolished, eliminated as a class. It was for this reason that Boris's birthplace was not his parents' native village of Basmanovo, where his parents had owned land, but Butka. Agriculture, as a profession, had been replaced by a different one altogether: collective farmer.

There is absolutely no doubt whatsoever about his date of birth: 12th February.[60] Within the family, however, and on all his other documents in later life — from his passport and party membership card to official biographies of him — a different date is stated: 1st February.

How could such a shift have occurred? As I see it there is a simple explanation for this. In addition to the official Soviet document, the fact of a baby being born in a well-off peasant family was always recorded in the main family book. This was something that was present in practically every household, and which lay in a red corner under the icons, covered with an embroidered handkerchief — a psalter containing a menology — a calendar in which the

---

59   No documents containing direct reports of the exile have been discovered to date. Details about the exile were obtained by B. Minaev in an interview with N.I. Yeltsina. See: B. Minaev: B.N. Yeltsin. M., 2010.

60   Another child was born on the same day as him — Anatoly Gomzikov. His birth was recorded on the same form as that of Boris Yeltsin.

head of the household regularly made entries whilst out in the field — at what point in the year the first snow had fallen, on which day there had been a strong storm, when significant family events had taken place — weddings, births, deaths. These entries on the pages of the psalter served as a family manuscript and chronicle, which provided a faithful record of the peasant clan.[61]

The system of recording family events on the pages of the church calendar broke down in 1918 — the very first year under Communism. On 24th January 1918 the Council of People's Commissars of the RSFSR adopted a 'Decree on the introduction into the Russian republic of a western-European calendar'. Under this decree, the date immediately following 31st January was not 1st February, but 14th February. Consequently, in order to transpose a date of birth from the Soviet calendar to the church calendar, certain adjustments had to be made. These adjustments were essential in order to work out the date of birth under the church calendar. The adjustments were not made by experts on historical chronology, but by peasants who did not know all that much about the difference between the Gregorian and Julian calendars. Inevitably, mistakes were occasionally made. Thus 1st February was considered to be Boris Yeltsin's date of birth under the church calendar, his family birthday, which would later became his official birthday.

The deportees

A clear idea of the circumstances in which the dekulakized peasants were living, after being exiled to the north of the Urals (including Ignat and Anna Yeltsin and Vasily and Afanasia Starygin — the two sets of grandparents to the new-born child, Boris Yeltsin), can be gleaned from material from a commission led by V.G. Feigin, a board member of the People's Commissariat of Agriculture of the RSFSR and the deputy People's Commissar for Agriculture. Feigin visited the village of Gremyachinsk, near Usva, in the Kizelovsk district, and the Usva mines.

Reporting on 4th August 1931 on the work done by the commission in the Urals regional committee of the VKP(b), Feigin attempted to place new emphasis on the situation faced by the deportees. He wrote that they had been "sent to an isolated corner, not a place that could be used for agricultural purposes." And he added that now "the question had to be asked as to what was the most rational agricultural use of it."[62]

---

61   And not only the peasants. Pushkin's comic tale *The story of the town of Goryukhin* contains an anecdote about a retired officer named Ivan Petrovich Belkin who comes across some ancient calendars.

62   CDPASR, f. 4, op. 9, d. 53, l. 19

The relocated people were seen first and foremost as a workforce. A workforce from which the maximum had to be extracted. Consequently, it was essential to exclude any irrational use of it. Farming efficiency was at the top of the list of things Feigin and his commission have to assess. It is therefore unacceptable, in his opinion, that there is a situation in which the elderly and sick are sent out to work in forestry, whilst the able-bodied do nothing. It is a bad thing that salaries go unpaid for up to a year or more. People are getting by on rations, "so there is no incentive for them to earn big salaries... No incentive for them to earn big salaries is being created".[63] The money is "not going where it ought to be going." "It was not just the agricultural men who were at fault, it was the ban imposed by the commandant's office, stating that these people had been deported and that nothing needed to be taken into account."

Things were particularly bad as regards the housing situation. The people exiled are banned from chopping down parts of the forest themselves in order to build their own homes. The situation as regards housing construction is disgusting. There is a ban on chopping down trees to build houses in the forested areas. For those exiled to the north (!) there were wooden huts without stoves. In the Usva mines they are building two-storey barracks for 420 people which are going to have two stoves, two cookers and four toilets. "Imagine a situation in which 210 people have to cook their dinner on a single cooker!" — Feigin wrote in exasperation.[64]

In the commission's opinion it would be a good idea to get the exiled settlers to provide for themselves. It would therefore make sense to allow the exiled to have their own gardens — or else the authorities "will once again be required to go through all the bother and fuss of providing food etc., without being able to use children (!)." The older children had to work in the garden.

For the little ones, things were even worse. "The little children died, there are only 6-8 children aged one year or over left, who are able to eat bread, and who don't need milk as much as the smaller children; they manage to survive, although they look in a very bad way. The slightest scratch results in them getting swollen bumps...blindness, trachoma and other illnesses are rife. Feigin went on: "At the distribution point, where new groups arrive, and where we saw little children, they will doubtless die, there is no milk, they look awful."

There are no medical services at all. Feigin clarified his concerns: "I am raising this issue not only from the point of view of concern for their lives, but from the point of view of production capacity." According to his information, 30-40% of those exiled had become disabled, with boils on their arms and legs.[65]

---

63   Same reference. L. 19 ob.
64   Same reference. L. 20 ob.
65   Same reference. L. 21-21

They weren't fed or given medical attention, but were forced to work — quite literally on pain of death. If the production quotas weren't met, the men had to sleep in an unheated bathhouse for 30 nights on end, and the women for 8 nights; during the day they were sent out to work. Some people were even shot for failing to meet the quotas.[66]

The director of the government commission reports on these horrors in a coldly objective way, informing the party's regional committee about it, and his greatest concern is that resources — manpower — are being used inefficiently!

The other man present at the regional committee meeting, Razkazchikov, indulges in a more emotional and, if you will, humane assessment of the situation. He reports that the exiled kulaks were often punished several times over for breaking the rules just once: they would be deprived of their rations, then put on the same rations as those who were unfit to work; they would have certain foods "from the commandant's product line" taken away from them or have their days off taken away. "The upshot is that a man has to work like an animal; though even the animals are allowed a bit of rest and get looked after."[67]

During the meeting a form of classification system for exile and the exiled settlers was proposed.

The first group was for those who had been forced to do agricultural labor. They were "not too bad at all at managing agricultural matters."

"There was another type of resettled kulaks as well: those who worked in forestry. This was the hardest task of all. Worst of all is the service, and worst of all is supply and a little-known sector to us. ...

And, finally, *the deported peasants working in industry. This was a group with special privileges. It is seen as good fortune to end up in this group.* (My italics. — the author) At the construction sites there are special re-settled peasants who live in better conditions than the main workers in the mines."[68]

Many people tried to flee the special settlements. In 1934 Ignat Yeltsin was listed among those who tried to get away.[69] The battle against escape attempts

---

66   Same reference. L. 22

67   Same reference. L. 22 ob. The information provided by the Feigin commission is fully supported by the special reports from the OGPU for the summer of 1931: there was a lack of housing, the deportees were being put up in vegetable store rooms or brick outhouses, there was no food, people were eating grass, bark and wood, and the guards regularly got drunk, behaved violently and stole from the deportees. See: The history of Stalin's GULAGs. The late 1920s and first half of the 50s. Volume 5. The deportees in the USSR. M., 2004. P. 156-160

68   CDPASR, F. 4. Op. 9. D. 53. L. 53 ob.

69   A. L. Litvin: The Yeltsins in Kazan. Kazan, 2006. P. 26

became a constant concern of the authorities; the OGPU for the Urals region reported on 12th June 1930 that:

"1) In all the points to which kulaks have been exiled, a circular surety was introduced, with a senior person allocated to each *desyatok* and responsible for supervising the *desyatok* (group of ten people) entrusted to them and immediately reporting back on any incidents or attempts to escape. Due to the introduction of mutual responsibility, subscriptions have been confiscated both from the group of kulaks and from the older *desyatoks*.

2) In areas where there are exiled kulaks, measures have been taken to entice the locals to help search for escaped kulaks, with a reward of 30 roubles paid to anyone who finds them. Moreover a 100 rouble fine is imposed on captured kulaks for attempting to escape.[70]

Compared to this, the position in which Nikolai Ignatievich Yeltsin's family found itself, after having essentially fled to Kazan to the 'construction site of communism' — the site that would later become the Tupolev aviation plant — was incomparably better. First of all, there was a desperate need for manpower at the construction site, and this created a certain sense of security (an illusory one, as would later become clear); secondly, he and his brother Andrian, who were both good carpenters, were given a room each in the barracks at Aviastroi. There were no windows or doors, admittedly — but that could be rectified. Thirdly, they were paid and kept fed at the construction sites. Fourthly, a large construction site required well-qualified, intelligent workers, and Nikolai Yeltsin became a team leader for a brigade of carpenters, and his brigade performed well.[71] In Kazan, Nikolai Ignatievich Yeltsin signed up for evening classes at the construction school, and began working and studying.

But Nikolai and Andrian Yeltsin, like their comrades in their brigade — most of whom had also been de-kulakized — did not manage to become residents of Kazan. They were taken away, as people used to say in Russia at the time. In April 1934 the Yeltsin brothers were arrested.

Other members of the brigade were arrested too. Word had reached them that 'anti-Soviet' conversations had been taking place in the brigade, specifically — people had been complaining about the poor quality of the food in the dining room, and about the lack of desire to sign up for loans. But the most important thing of all was that they had been de-kulakized.

---

70   The history of Stalin's GULAG. The late 1920s and the first half of the 1950s. Volume 5. The deportees in the USSR. M., 2004. P. 124-127

71   This subject was investigated in more detail in the book: A. L. Litvin: The Yeltsins in Kazan. Kazan, 2006. P. 22-62

Those arrested did not consider themselves to be guilty of anything, and were charged by the Extraordinary assembly under article 58-10 of the Criminal Code of the RSFSR; the brothers were sentenced to three years each in the corrective labor camps and were sent to communism's next great construction site — to Dmitlag, to work on the Volga-Moscow canal, the direct descendant of the White Sea-Baltic canal[72] — where they joined up with 190,000 prisoners.

What made the situation so horrific for Nikolai Yeltsin's wife was that she was left alone with a three-year-old child, literally on the street. The once-great Yeltsin-Starygin clan had been swept away into exile and into the camps. To have made the journey there — into exile — would have been tantamount to a death sentence for her son, three-year-old Boris. She was saved by a medical orderly who happened to be in the same prison cell as Nikolai Vasily Petrovich Petrov, born in 1878. At Nikolai's request, he took in Klavdia Vasilievna Yeltsina and her son Boris and gave them shelter. They spent three years living with the Petrovs – until Nikolai Yeltsin returned from Dmitlag.[73]

Berezniki

In 1935 Nikolai Yeltsin's elder brother Ivan was arrested, convicted and sent into exile. He had been charged with 'sabotage' and was sent from the collective farm to exile at the construction site of the Berezniki Chemical Combine.[74]

We can learn about the Berezniki of the early '30s from the memoirs of Varlam Shalamov, who was exiled there in 1929. "Soon Berezniki was overcome by an influx of prisoners of all kinds — deported kulaks, people from the camps, re-settled collective farmers — under the major procedures which had been initiated...The soda plant itself, the one formerly known as Salve, became part of the Berezniki chemical combine, became one of the giants constructed in the first five-year plan — the Bereznikhimstroi, which brought together hundreds of thousands of workers, engineers and technicians — both Russian and foreign. At Berezniki there was a village for foreigners, ordinary exiled peasants, the deportees and the people from the camps. As many as ten thousand camp workers came out to work in one shift. It was a construction site with an incredibly fluid workforce turnover, where, each month, three thousand volunteers would be taken on based on written or oral contracts and

72   The White Sea-Baltic canal named after Stalin. The history of construction. Edited by M. Gorky and others. M., 1934. S.

73   A.L. Litvin: The Yeltsins in Kazan. Kazan, 2006. Pp. 53-57

74   Aron L. Yeltsin: A revolutionary life. N.Y. 2000. P. 6

four thousand people would attempt to flee. This construction site has yet to be properly described."[75]

One of the people who informed on N. Yeltsin, a former farmhand, told an employee of the OGPU: the kulaks in the brigade had taken all the positions of leadership, and the poor ones weren't being allowed in. The kulaks were getting their hands on vouchers for better food more often. His words were backed up by the OGPU's reports: former kulaks tended to become *desyatniks* (in charge of a group of ten people) or brigade leaders. These people, who were intelligent and able to work, had finally become needed by the system, which was now forced to use their labor. Despite official policy, which continued, even there in the camps, to harrass former kulaks as 'class enemies', and to contrast them with the so-called 'class friends' of the power of the 'thirty-fives' — those convicted under the criminal code.[76]

The new 'focal point' for the Yeltsins was the construction site of the Berezniki chemical combine — yet another 'great construction site of socialism'. The first person to end up there was the eldest of Ignat Yeltsin's sons, Ivan. Following Ignat Yeltsin's death, his widow Anna also moved to the site. Dmitry, Nikolai and Andrian Yeltsin also travelled here. Claudia Vasilievna Yeltsina's mother and father, Vasily and Afanasiya Starygina — who survived their time in exile — also made the journey to the construction site.

And there, among the hustle and bustle of people, the building site, and everyday business, the Yeltsins took shelter. The peasant clan had been broken.

At the end of the book *The White Sea — Baltic canal named after Stalin*. The story of its construction, dedicated to the 17th congress of the VKP(b) and published with the editorship and direct involvement of Maksim Gorky, there is the remarkable line: The practical experience at Belomorstroi is one of the things that provides evidence of the fact that we have moved into an era in which we have a classless society."[77]

I couldn't have put it better myself.

---

75   V. Shalamov: Galina Pavlovna Zybalova/Collected works in 4 volumes V. 2. M., 1998. P. 307-320

76   It was thus in accordance with the order GULAG No. 190736 on the use of records of working days at the camps. On 30 June 1931, for criminals who were fulfilling the quotas, 3 days in exile were recorded as 4, and for the dekulakized — 4 days were recorded as five. See: The history of Stalin's GULAG. The late 1920s to the first half of the 1950s. Volume 3. The economy of the GULAGs. M., 2004.

77   The White Sea-Baltic canal named after Stalin. The history of construction. Edited by M. Gorky and others. M., 1934. S.

The 'socialist settlement'

In 1937 the whole Yeltsin family gathered together at Berezniki. The six-year-old Boris was now reunited with his father after an absence of almost three years; Boris also saw his grandfather Vasily, a bearded joiner and carpenter, for the first time, and his grandmothers: his mother's mother, Afanasia, and his father's mother, Anna. His recognized his uncles — Ivan, Dmitry and Andrian.

At that time, Berezniki was rapidly turning into not only the country's biggest centre for the chemical industry but also a model socialist city, one of the new cities whose very existence was supposed to demonstrate the achievements of socialism, and the new lives of its residents.

Berezniki was at once a new city and one of the oldest cities in the Urals. This city was 'assembled' in 1932 following a directive from the All-Russian Central Executive Committee out of the extremely old cities founded in the 16th and 17th centuries. And what cities they were! From the city of Usolye, the capital of the 'famous line of the Stroganovs' — the richest people in Russia in the 16th-17th centuries, who were descended from a clan of black-sokha peasants, to the Stroganov town of Eagle City — the town from which, in 1580, the Cossacks had launched their assault led by Yermak. It was from here that the conquest of Siberia began. Alongside these towns was the alpine city of Dedyukhin, a cosy and resilient place whose residents had customs and traditions which had developed over many decades.[78] There were also a series of workers' settlements which sprang up around the sources of salt: Veretie, Lenva, Ust-Zyryanka, Churtan, and the Berezniki railway station, from which the new city took its name.

Next to Berezniki was Solikamsk, from whence, in the 16th and 17th centuries, the warlords governed the Priuralie; here stood the ancient temples and stone palaces of the wealthy people of Solikamsk, who had made their fortune by extracting and trading in salt.

In the late 19th and early 20th centuries, the traditional sources of wealth in this northern region — salt, wood and fish — were augmented with new ones. In 1883 the merchant I.I. Lyubimov built Russia's first ever soda plant. Next to the plant a village was built which contained residential houses, a school, a hotel and a theatre. Amid the old Russian architecture and estates of the 19th century was a town about which Boris Pasternak, who visited it in 1916, wrote that the plant and the village next to it was a "small industrial Belgium."

---

78   For a remarkable account of aspects of the lives of citizens of the Urals Region in the mid-19th c. see: D. Petukhov: The mountain city of Dedyukhin and environs // West Russian geographical society. Spb., 1863. Vol. 4. S.17-80

The colossal sources of potassium salts, the ability to arrange production of ammonium and nitric acid, approved for use in agriculture, and also the extraction of magnesium and sodium predetermined the future development of the town known as Berezniki.

The most important construction site for the new city was the one at the Berezniki chemical combine. The combine was supposed to become a giant of industrialization, in every sense of the word. Its construction was supervised by the people's commissar of industry, Sergo Ordzhonikidze. From the very outset this construction project was supervised by, and involved the direct participation of, OGPU agencies.

K. Paustovsky, who spent time in Berezniki as a reporter for ROST in 1931, recalled: "There were prisoners working at the construction site. The construction project seemed to me to be outlandishly enormous. It consisted of various plants: a sulfuric acid plant, a caustic acid plant and several others, featuring an electric power plant and what seemed like a whole nation-state of large colourful pipes.

Night had come to this polar region. At first I wandered through the darkness among the trenches, the piles of bricks, the slabs of cement, the driveways, the iron reinforcements for the concrete, the gigantic frames, the farms, the half-finished buildings, enclosures and diggers.

… It was December — the darkest month of all in the North. At first, I didn't like those long nights. Voices speaking in various languages rang out in the morning frost (there were a lot of British and German experts among the men building the combine, called over from overseas), the runners of sleighs went whistling by, and occasionally snow could be seen pouring down from the gloomy skies by the light of the powerful lanterns.

From time to time the reddish glow of the Northern lights, wispy and fleeting, could be seen. The local residents called them 'flashes and fire-bolts'. The latter name was very appropriate for these fiery lights, which pulsated randomly like flames.

And beyond the edge of the construction site the night lay so heavy, and in such a deep sleep, that it was like a huge creature which has gone off for its winter hibernation in the wild hills, the impassable hills, the escarpments of the mountains. There the gigantic fir trees of the Urals stood like black pagodas, and on starry nights the treetops seemed to touch the stars.

But there was rarely a starry sky over the construction site that winter — there was too much smoke and fumes on the ground, of all colours and hues — from canary-yellow 'foxtail' to violet, brown, red, white and bluish-black smoke. The sky was constantly filled with smoke."[79]

---

79   K. Paustovsky: A tale about life. Books 4-6 M., 2007

The New Year was organized based on common plans. Back in 1932 the task of drawing up plans for the social city of Berezniki was given to the Uralhyprogor institute. In 1935 the scientific and technical soviet of the people's commissariat of petrochemicals defined the main parameters of the future city. It was designed to accommodate 135,000 people and was supposed to become the second-largest city in the Perm district, behind the capital, Perm. For the project, special construction institutions were created: Khimstroi and the 2nd potassium mine, which were under the control of the head of Glavkhimstroi.

You have to take your hat off to them, and praise the high quality of the planning for the project. The engineers strove to arrange the residential construction project in such a way as to minimize the negative impact of emissions from the production sites. The regional sanitary inspectorate demanded that the engineers take into account negative past experiences at a series of plants in the Urals — (Karabash, Kirovograd, Krasnouralsk), which back then, in the '30s, had already come up against problems such as gas contamination and poisoning of the surrounding forests with manufacturing waste.

The city was intended primarily to house buildings with 1-2 floors, and mighty public buildings were supposed to be built against this backdrop: a Palace of culture, a food combine, a hospital and a polyclinic, an urban communications hub, the Khimik stadium and the general schools No.1 named after Pushkin, No. 2 named after Gorky, No. 3 named after Kalinin and No. 4 named after Ostrovsky. Banks of brick buildings with 3-5 floors were built along the city's main axis — from the Chemical combine to the Palace of Culture. Squares and parks sprang up throughout the city, including a site that was compulsory for primary cities in regions, though not in districts — a Central Park of Culture and Leisure. As much as 30 square m. of green spaces were to be built per head of the population of Berezniki.

Water pipes, a sewage system, an energy supply and waste treatment processes were also built — all the things which make a city a city.[80]

The fact that good architecture was combined with, and to a certain extent built through the forced labor of prisoners, was seen as something entirely commonplace and normal.

Life in a new place

Nikolai Yeltsin's family finally had a place of their own. After the corner of the Petrovs' house in Kazan, which had been their salvation but nevertheless

---

80   O.D. Gaisin: The experience of planning the sots-city of Berezniki (1930s-1940s)

belonged to someone else, they now had a room of their own in a hut. Before long a second son was born — Mikhail, a brother to Boris. A sister was born in 1944. "We were housed in a hut — it was typical of what they used to build in those days, and what you still sometimes see today: it was wooden, had a boardwalk, and was extremely draughty," B.N. Yeltsin recalled in 1989. "There was a shared corridor and 20 tiny little rooms; there were no creature comforts, of course — the toilet was outside, as was the water, which we got from a well. We were given a few things, and we bought a goat. By that time I already had a brother and a dear little sister. And there we were, all six of us, including the goat — lying on the floor, squeezed up against one another."[81]

His father had a job to do, however. Nikolai Yeltsin, a man with both experience and qualifications, worked as a setter, a master and a foreman. Significantly, he had also completed three years at the construction technical college. There was a lot of work around for people in the construction industry.

Life was getting better. Between 1935 and 1937, people's incomes went up one-and-a-half times. In 1937 and 1938 the government reduced the price of 80-90% of industrial goods and food products, by between 5 and 16%. The prices of so-called collective farm goods fell sharply as well.[82] The card-based system had been cancelled.

They lived the same way as everyone else. And everyone was like them. "Strange to say," Yeltsin recalled, "in those difficult conditions people were somehow friendly to one another. Considering there was no soundproofing... people didn't even know what that word meant back then, by the way — there was no such thing — and if there was a bit of a party going on in one of the rooms — a name-day, or a wedding, or what have you — they would put the gramophone on, there were 2 or 3 records shared by all the residents of the huts, as far as I recall, and I especially remember the song 'Schors is marching with the flag, the commander of the regiment...' — and all the people living in the huts would sing along. Any arguments, conversations, big rows, secrets, laughter — all the neighbors would hear them, everyone would know everything."[83]

The children went along to the first year of school, with all the other children. They were all the same. They were all equal. They had teachers who told them about the bright future of the socialist Motherland. They watched films about Chapayev. They listened to stories about the flight made by Chkalov — Stalin's falcon — across the ocean in a Soviet plane, to America. They knew that there was a red flag on the North pole, because Soviet explorers had discovered it, and had been the first in the world to do so.

---

81   B.N. Yeltsin: Against the Grain. M., 1990

82   I.N. Levicheva: The problems of monetary circulation in the USSR in the late 1920s — 1930s //The Reporter of the Bank of Russia. M., 2007.7 March (№ 13(957). P. 37-43

83   B.N. Yeltsin: Against the Grain. M., 1990

Boris started school in 1939, when he was eight — a year older than his peers. At that age, an extra year can make a big difference. This big, strong lad was destined to become the ringleader of the children's antics, which often bordered on the unacceptable.

When the war broke out, the family was unable to avoid the hardships of military existence. The father was left at the construction site. Manufacturing was expanding. Berezniki was one of the most important centres of Russia's military industry. Without nitric acid, nitrates and ammonium nitrate there would be no explosive substances and the army would have no gunpowder. Ammunition was manufactured at Berezniki, metal nitrate was produced here, and grenades were built...Boris's younger brother, Agnat Ignatievich Yeltsin, went to serve in the war and was killed in action.

30,000 evacuees arrived in Berezniki, the site of the remarkable Leningrad theatre of the young audience member. Battalions of construction workers — so-called *stroibaty* — were moved here, consisting of Germans from the Volga region, relatives of the victims of oppression, and Latvians, Lithuanians and Estonians who had not been accepted in the army. A large prisoner-of-war camp was built in Berezniki in 1945.

The family subsisted on rations. Boris's father, as someone who had worked for a company in the chemicals industry and was therefore allowed to supply 'category-one products', was allowed 800 grams of bread a day and 800 grams of sugar a month. His dependants — Boris's mother and the children — were entitled to 400 grams of bread a day and 600 grams of sugar a month.[84] That was what their rations should have been, in theory. In practice rations were often delayed and might be reduced. Bread could be bought at the market, but there a kilo of bread cost 200-250 roubles, and Boris's father was on a salary of 800-1000 roubles a month.

The family had the goat as a back-up, and the children were given goat's milk. In the summer, Boris and his mother reaped hay for the collective farm and were given a portion of the hay, both for their own daily needs and to sell on, so that they could buy bread.

The father

Boris's father managed to achieve the almost impossible: in 1944 he built a house of his own, in the 8th district of Berezniki, at 27 Sadovaya Street. Having a house of their own meant that the Yeltsins now had a garden,

---

84   Collection of the most important orders and instructions on issues related to the card system and normalized supply. M., 1943

potatoes, herbs, and the ability to feed the children and have enough for themselves as well. Given that the harshest years of famine throughout the country, and in Berezniki in particular, were 1944-1946, having your own garden could be your salvation. And it was their own home, which Nikolai Yeltsin could now enjoy living in after fifteen years of being shunted about from one hut to another.

Nikolai Yeltsin was a talented man.

He had managed to break out of a dekulakized village, and a camp, and simply tear those pages out of his biography. And he did so quite literally. Neither on his personal employee record sheet, filled in on 11th October 1948,[85] nor in his autobiography, written on 22nd March 1953[86] was there any reference to his arrest and trial or his time working at the Dmitlag camp. On his personal record sheet he stated that from 1930 to 1935 he had worked at the construction site for the Kazan aviation plant, and that between 1935 and 1937 he was foreman at Kinopromstroi, also in Kazan; in his autobiography he extended the duration of his stint at the aviation plant to 1936, and wrote that he had begun working at Khimstroi, in Berezniki, in 1937. Fortunately there were no employee records books prior to 1939 (they were only introduced in January 1939), and it was therefore difficult to check records about people's employment in the '20s and '30s.

In response to a question on the personal records sheet, "Have you ever been brought before a court of law?" he answered "No", and wrote in his autobiography: "I was not a victim of persecution."

The fact that he *had* been persecuted was known by all those whose job it was to know such things — so why 'open himself and his family up' to interrogation by 'vigilant citizens'?

The builders had a slightly vulgar joke — an in-joke in the profession. When asked "what's your job?" they would reply "I'm a dog," and that meant a technician. They described themselves as dogs because they had to run around the building site, shout at the workers, the staff hired from other industries, the planners...Nikolai Ignatievich Yeltsin was a man with an essential role in the construction process. He worked as a technician, a setter, a foreman and a senior foreman — i.e. the man directly responsible for organizing the construction process. N.Y. Yeltsin was awarded a medal 'For outstanding work during the Great Patriotic War'. A photograph of Nikolai Ignatievich Yeltsin was put in the Book of honor of trust No. 1 Sevuraltyazhstroi in the Regional Economic Council for Perm.

---

85   Personal sheet for personnel records of N.I. Yeltsin. 11th October 1948. From the collection of documents held by the Urals Center for B.N. Yeltsin.

86   The Autobiography of N.I. Yeltsin. 22nd March 1953 From the collection of documents held by the Urals Center for B.N. Yeltsin.

The young engineer I.A. Neverov, who was subordinate to N.I. Yeltsin in 1958, when Yeltsin was a foreman at SU-4 in the Bereznikikhimstroi trust, recalled: "When I arrived at the building site, Yeltsin was already a tough old nut, with vast experience of life. He was a demanding boss — very demanding, I would say."

But N.I. Yeltsin was not only an organizer who knew what he was doing and a demanding manager.

He thought of his work as his own personal affair. He was forever coming up with new ideas, trying to perfect his methods and looking for ways to cut costs on labor, materials and resources. In 1952 N.I. Yeltsin was presented with an award for his invention and rationalization methods by the Ministry of construction.[87] He was sent to the Exhibition of the achievements of the national economy of the USSR as a foreman who had introduced rationalized methods in the late '50s. Records of his numerous proposals on how to rationalize production, which were put into practice in the '50s and early '60s, have survived. He proposed changing the foundations under the arches of the stores, and improving the roof...These proposals alone would lead to savings of around 6000 roubles in 1961 prices, and the remuneration was approximately 250 roubles.

His son, Boris Nikolaevich Yeltsin, recalled: "Father was always inventing things. To give you an example, he dreamed of inventing a bricklaying machine — he would sketch it, draw blueprints for it, then think up other features, do some calculations, and draw blueprints again; it was nothing more than a pipe-dream, really. To this day no-one has invented such a machine, regrettably — although whole institutes are racking their brains over it, to this day. He told me all about it: what sort of machine it would be, and how it would work: how it would lay the bricks, and the cement, then wipe off the excess; how it would move around — he had it all worked out in his head, and sketched it in his blueprints, but he didn't manage to make the concept a reality."[88]

The son

A strict disciplinarian in the workplace, Nikolai Ignatievich was strict at home too, particularly towards his eldest son, Boris. "Father's main tool when it came to our upbringing was the belt, and when I did something wrong he used to give me a good hiding."

---

87   Production specifications for the old style of production at Khimstroi, in Nikolai Ignatievich Yeltsin's Sevuraltyazhstroi trust. From the collection of documents held by the Urals Center for B.N. Yeltsin.

88   B.N. Yeltsin: Against the Grain. M., 1990.

The belt may not have had much pedagogical merit, but it must be said that Boris often provoked his father's rage by his actions. During the war years the young miscreant often indulged in the sort of behaviour that had his father reaching for the belt — on one occasion he and some friends poisoned their German teacher, the poor woman (O, the poor German teachers of that era! The things they had to put up with all over Russia from their brutal pupils, who didn't differentiate between their German teachers and the German soldiers!)

Then there were the deadly games in which the kids swam in the Zyryanka river while rafting. And the fights, in which whole districts would be pitted against one another. There were dangerous games involving weapons which had been handed in to be repaired, or in the plant's re-melting furnace; there were experiments with armaments dragged out of the stores, which were manufactured right there in Berezniki.

There was an incident in which a grenade was taken apart. This particular act of curiosity nearly cost Boris his life. The grenade's fuse exploded, injuring his left hand: two of his fingers became infected and had to be amputated.[89]

Did he deserve to be torn apart for such behavior?

Boris Yeltsin was a good student, however. In 1945, when he was in the 6th grade, he joined the Komsomol. His school-years coincided with the war, with a sense of the dignity of the Motherland, a sense of his debt to her; "everything for the front, everything for Victory" was more than a slogan, it was part of the younger generation's social psychology. A sense of his own dignity, of echoing the behavior of the soldiers on the front line, of his forefathers, who had worked for days on end to achieve Victory. And faith in justice. It is worth noting that each of these attributes was encouraged and supported by the propaganda of the day.

His faith in justice and honor, coupled with his sense of his own worth, prompted the 15-year-old Boris Yeltsin to do something that could almost be described as political, the first such act of his life. In 1946, during the graduation ceremony following completion of the 7th grade, Boris requested the floor — in the presence of the parents, the teachers and all the other schoolchildren. After thanking the school and his teachers, as it might have been expected that he would, Boris began to talk about their previous head of year. He said that she had insulted the pupils, humiliated them and forced them to work at home.

A row erupted.

---

89   Same reference. S.

Boris's punishment was swift in coming. He was excluded from the school and given what was known as a 'wolf's ticket' — a certificate confirming that he had completed 7th grade, with a codicil stating that he was not allowed to join the 8th grade.

But Boris Yeltsin of the Komsomol felt he was in the right, and considered that his actions were in line with how a Komsomol member ought to behave. Didn't the films made in those days show young Komsomol members standing up and exposing inadequacies? Didn't the newspapers call on them to fight back against failures and suffering? He went to the offices of the party's district committee, Education Department and city committee — and eventually got what he wanted. He was allowed back into the education system, but transferred to a different school — school No. 1 named after Pushkin.

Yeltsin was in luck. It was a good school, and an old one, considering how young the city was.

He had an outstanding head of year — Antonina Pavlovna Khonina, whom Boris Yeltsin still remembered with fondness and gratitude forty years later. It was a boys' school, one of the ones built in the country after the war.

His head of year, A.P. Khonina, recalled: "I started at the Pushkin school in the fall of 1946. It was an all-boys' school. How interesting I found it to work with them! There's no time to sit around yawning at a place like that, you have to be ready to answer questions every minute of the day. I was entrusted with the role of being head of year for class 8 A until they left the school in 1949. They were wonderful lads, each one better than the next, full of beans, bright, and ever so talkative. These are the names of my first year-group at that school: Mark Belov, Viktor Nikolin, Serezha Molchanov, Robert Zaidel, Vitaly Scherbakov. Borya Blokh, Slava Kukushkin, Lenya Suslov, Vasya Nasedkin, Volodya Titov, Igor Dovgy... And among them was Boris Yeltsin, a tall, stately, serious boy. He would stare straight at you; he was attentive, and smart. He was good at sports. Boris never broke the school rules, couldn't stand lies and contested arguments hotly and convincingly. He was an avid reader and loved poetry. When answering questions he would look at you from under his brow, ever so slightly. He was a persuasive speaker, and emphasized the important points, without adding any empty words.

Even then you could tell he had a strict nature and a fiery temperament. He was genuinely well-disposed toward his comrades. Children were different back then, of course. This was just after the war, and times were hard, but the children were friendly and quick-witted, there was no anger or spitefulness. I can remember assemblies which they organized and led themselves, where they worked to rectify mistakes they had made! And what interesting evenings they would arrange! They would put on plays, read poetry, argue about books. The girls from the all-girls' schools, the Ostrovsky school and the Gorky school, were always keen to come and visit us — the boys treated them with great respect."[90]

The boys were conscientious in their studies. It was a tradition that was very important to this academic group — to study hard. Of the 19 school leavers from this group, four were awarded medals — two gold and two silver.[91] Boris didn't win a medal — he finished with two *chetvyorki* [the second-highest grade, four out of five].

Boris Nikolaevich Yeltsin's time at the Pushkin school also gave him something else that was very important to him: sport. Sport consumed boundless amounts of energy and instilled rivalry in him, in the form of sporting competition. Boris Yeltsin practised sport furiously and religiously. "I was immediately captivated by volleyball," he wrote in his memoirs, "and could have played it for days on end. I liked the fact that the ball was obedient to me, that with an incredible leap I could retrieve a ball that looked like a lost cause. I also liked skiing, gymnastics, track and field, decathlon, boxing and wrestling — I wanted to do it all, to be able to do absolutely everything. But eventually volleyball won out, and I started to play it really seriously."

The Pushkin school's volleyball team won the city championships. Boris Yeltsin was the team's captain. Each member of the winning team was presented with a watch. "For little boys in the post-war era, this was as exciting as if their peers nowadays had been given cars," one of Yeltsin's classmates, S.F. Molchanov, recalled.

In the summer of 1948 the class went on a field trip to the banks of the river Yaiva. The northern taiga, where the dense forest turns into a bog, where the earth is covered by a layer of half-rotten tree-trunks and every step requires effort, and where there are no external landmarks — became a bridge too far for the group. The adventurers lost their way, fell into the bog, and drank the water, sucking the filthy slurry through cloths. There was an outbreak of typhoid.

Luckily the kids were found, but they were ill for almost the whole of the first quarter of the year, and had to stay at home. The final-year pupil Boris Yeltsin, who had completed the academic programme pretty successfully, was suddenly faced with a new problem which he had not seen coming at all. Under the regulations of the Ministry of national education, self-study at

---

90   From the memoirs of A.P. Khonina. See: http://www.perm1.ru/perm/YWhg67pTq7/info.html

91   From the memoirs of S.F. Molchanov, a classmate of B.N. Yeltsin. See: http://www.perm1.ru/perm/YWhg67pTq7/info.html

home — external schooling — was prohibited. "I went to school to sit the exams, and they told me that there was no such procedure — that home-schooled pupils could not join school leavers, and that I was free to go. Once again I had to go down a familiar route, the one I had taken before: the district committee, the Education Department, the city committee. By that time I was in the city volleyball team. Fortunately, people knew who I was — that I was a city schools' champion in several different sports, and a regional volleyball champion. To cut a long story short, they allowed me to sit the exams as an external pupil — admittedly, I didn't manage to get straight 5s, I was given a four in two subjects. That was the baggage I had to take to university," B.N. Yeltsin later wrote of this episode.

Boris Yeltsin was 18 years old. He was the first Yeltsin to obtain a full middle education. His grandfather had been illiterate, whilst his father had an incomplete middle special education. He lived in a city which was changing and growing more lovely before his very eyes. His father was a respected man, a construction engineer, and through the efforts of his father and his comrades the city was growing and factories and mine-shafts were being built. The powers that be had given him an education and the opportunity to take up sport. These particular powers that be seemed to him to be just. It was thanks to them that he had found protection at a difficult time.

Yes, he was aware that his relatives had been dekulakized, and he remembered his early childhood in Kazan. But that had been an injustice, something that the authorities had admitted was a mistake. Mistakes such as this were acknowledged in the Short history of the VKP(b), in textbooks about the history of the USSR and in Sholokhov's *Virgin Soil Upturned*. Nowadays these mistakes had been rectified! There were no disputes or doubts as to the justice of the aims and objectives these days. "I genuinely believed in the ideals of justice which the party stood for," B.N. Yeltsin recalled.

His next task was to decide where to continue his studies. His boyhood dream of studying at the ship-building institute had been replaced by a conscious decision to enrol at the faculty of construction at the Urals Polytechnic Institute. There were numerous good reasons for doing so. His father had been a civil engineer, so it was a profession with which he was familiar. There was a direct rail link between Berezniki and Sverdlovsk — this was also an advantage.

Boris Yeltsin was to become the first member of his family to go through higher education.

Chapter 2
The construction worker's career

The student majoring in 'civil and industrial construction'

To the young man from the provinces, Sverdlovsk seemed like one huge, oversized construction site. Apartment blocks stood beside the railway station in the city center, and towering cranes could be seen in the city's outskirts. Boris used to take the tram to get to the eastern part of the city. As he passed under the railway bridge he glimpsed a wonderful panorama of Vtuzgorodok, rising up out of the wilderness. The first thing that caught his eye was the huge building on the little hill at the top of Prospekt Lenina. The building was adorned with a portico featuring columns and the crest of the USSR on the frontispiece.

The institute itself came into being in accordance with a decree from the Council of People's Commissars of the RSFSR, signed by V.I. Lenin on 19th October 1920. Under this document, a state university was founded in the city that was still known as Yekaterinburg at the time, consisting of six institutes, including a polytechnic. The complex financial and economic situation in the country meant that there was no choice in the 1920s and '30s but to change the form and profiles of universities and their component parts. The inadequate funding had an effect on the number of students being taught, although this figure went up year on year. Whereas 17 students graduated from the Urals Region Polytechnic Institute in 1925, 64 young experts graduated from it in 1928.

The huge demand for experts in the construction industry meant that there was no choice but to set up a special faculty in 1929. Its initial objective was to provide fast-track retraining for technical experts and workers, so that they could fill vacancies among engineering and technical employees in the medium and higher chains of the construction industry. Specialists were also required in order to construct the Urals-Kuzbass metallurgical complex and build metallurgical and engineering plants in the Urals. The student acceptance procedures were simple, too: first of all the faculty accepted people who had been 'delegated' to study by party committees, Komsomol committees or professional unions. Among these so-called delegates were people who had no grasp of mathematics, let alone physics, foreign languages and the other subjects taught in schools.

In 1930 the Urals Region Polytechnic Institute was split into nine separate institutes according to sector, including an institute for the construction sector. Five years later the government acknowledged that this had been a mistake. The institutes were turned into faculties of the URPI once again, but it was now referred to not as a polytechnic institute but as an industrial one — a word which better reflected the policy of the VKP(b) at the time.

The merging of the separate institutes was to some extent made easier by the construction of a special complex of buildings in the eastern sector of Sverdlovsk. The complex was completed in 1939. The academic buildings housed faculties which had their own auditoriums and laboratories. Alongside them were halls of residence for the university's students and staff. There was also a canteen, a student club and several sports halls. The complex was known as Vtuzgorodok, which translates as 'Technical College village', which was more or less accurate. The facilities at the Urals Region Industrial Institute were the envy of staff at other universities in Sverdlovsk, not just in the '30s but thereafter as well.

The institution entered a new phase of its development after the war. In 1948 it was given a new name — the Urals Region Polytechnic Institute named after S.M. Kirov — UPI. New faculties sprang up at the institute to cater for cutting-edge fields in science and technology — a physico-technical faculty (in 1949) and a radio-technical faculty (in 1952). A faculty of architecture was also set up at the UPI, in 1947.

By then the construction faculty had become very much a traditional one. According to Boris Yeltsin's former classmates, there was hardly any competition for places there. The faculty was not considered a prestigious place to study. The bursary of 280 roubles that its students were given was the lowest of all the UPI's faculties. The potential earnings of these future technicians and foremen did not seem at all enviable. There was a wealth of applicants for the faculties of metallurgy, chemistry and engineering, however.

In addition to their exam results, a decisive role in determining whether or not students were admitted to the construction faculty was played by the grades they received on their matriculation certificates. Yeltsin had an average grade of 4.57 on his certificate, and a score of 5 in maths.

The construction faculty, which was celebrating its 20th anniversary that year, also offered two other specializations: 'Water supply and sewage systems' and

'Heating and ventilation'. Yet to the son of a foreman from Berezniki, the specialization 'industrial and civil construction' must have seemed like the most important one of all, the one with the strongest 'construction-oriented' focus.

On 17th July 1949 Yeltsin submitted his application to the admissions commission. Matriculants at the construction facility had to sit no fewer than nine (!) exams.

The exam marathon began with a an essay. 1st August — good. 3rd August — mathematics — written algebra — excellent.

5 — mathematics — written geometry — excellent. Oral mathematics — excellent.

Overall grade for mathematics — excellent. 10th August — drawing — good.

12th August — mechanical drawing — good.

14th August — oral Russian — excellent.

16th August — oral physics — good.

17th August — foreign language, oral — excellent.

He passed all the exams. On 25th August 1949 Boris wrote to the UPI's director (as the person in charge of the institution was referred to in those days) requesting that he be given a place at the construction faculty specializing in ICE (industrial and civil engineering).

Boris Yeltsin was awarded a place.

Anyone who has been a student at one time or another can attest to the feeling one gets on receiving a positive response from the admissions commission. It is as if there is suddenly a pair of wings on your back, and you want to fly into the air and shout at the top of your voice: "I'm a student!" But then, just like after any other celebration, the next working day arrives, and all that passion dissipates after the first few lectures. Being at university is a far cry from being at school — the students realised that right from the outset.

"At school we had grown accustomed to the idea that every day you might be called to the front or asked a question, but there you had to keep on top of everything yourself, and what was the end result: there had been 15 medal-winners among us when we matriculated, but after the first two exam sessions most of them had to drop out, and there were only two left," recalls Yeltsin's classmate Y.Y. Permyakov.[92]

---

92   V. Sutyrin: Boris Yeltsin and the Urals Polytechnic Institute. Yekaterinburg, 2009. P. 58-60.

This 'school syndrome' did not affect Yeltsin, however. At the end of the first term all but one of his grades was a five, and he completed the second, third and fourth terms with straight A's. "He studied hard," his former classmate N.A. Viselova confirms. "It came to him easily, but he devoted a lot of time to his studies anyway. He was a workaholic — he only slept for four or five hours a day."[93]

Boris had no need to spend any extra time working on his memory or diligence, it goes without saying. By his very nature he could not be left to rot among the mediocre students, let alone the stragglers. In addition to the subjective reasons for this, there were also objective ones. One under-achieving student managed to lose his entitlement to a bursary in the course of a single semester — whereas those who excelled were awarded higher stipends. The group was by no means impartial about the success of their fellow students: having people who got poor grades in one's class was seen in the faculty as a 'disgraceful phenomenon'. For that reason anyone who was falling behind was immediately given a bit of help in mastering the topic in question.

The dean of the faculty of civil enginering was a legendary figure to his students. And this was not only because of the fact that Stanislav Andreevich Rogitsky, a doctor of technical sciences, was considered an academic of global renown and had recently been made an associate member of the Academy of construction and architecture of the USSR. His students saw him as both a father-figure and a friend. In his memoirs, entitled 'The Team of our Youth', A.N. Yuzefovich observes: "The bursaries weren't enough for us, it goes without saying. And one day, during a seminar, Stanislav Andreevich said to the group:

'How come you're all so down in the dumps today, then?'

'We aren't down in the dumps, Stanislav Andreevich — we're hungry. We have to wait another two days till we get our bursaries, and our pockets are empty, we've got nothing to buy food with.'

'Group captain! Come round to see me after today's lessons.' And he paid our bursaries out of his own pocket."[94]

Another of P.M. Rogitsy's pupils, Bogdashin, had this to say about his teacher: "He used to read lectures on construction mechanics, the theory of elasticity and materials' resistance in an utterly selfless way, like a grouse in mating season, without paying attention to anyone or anything. With genuine delight, carefully explaining the most complicated material, and covering the blackboard with an endless stream of equations, he would murmur a little

---

93   Same reference. P. 58.
94   A.N. Yuzefovich: The team of our youth. Perm, 1997. P. 23.

song to himself quietly, jumping back from the board from time to time to admire the beauty of his theoretical solution, and exclaiming: "O-ho, how striking!" or "Gosh, how *very interesting..*!" It was as though, whilst cut off completely from the outside world during his lectures, he had a remarkable ability to see his audience and sense what they were thinking. He was capable of suddenly spinning round, when no-one was expecting it, and getting the attention of Rita Buchelnikova, who was sitting chatting to the students on either side of her, with a single sentence: "Buchelnikova, did you get all that?" Rita — and indeed all of us — had understood everything, of course. And it was a bit of an awkward moment."[95]

Once they had received their degree certificates, and become first-rate specialists and directors, they would always maintain that they had "got really lucky as regards their lecturers". Professor Konstantin Trofimovich Babykin had no academic qualifications, yet was known and deeply respected in the architects' community. He had designed several buildings in Sverdlovsk which had been named architectural monuments, and the central building of the Ural State Technical University was one of his works. The students saw in their professor "a pedant and an aristocrat". Konstantin Trofimovich came to his lectures on architecture "in a stern black suit, with a waistcoat and an immaculately white shirt. Always polite, calm and collected, and somewhat slow, he would hold his fat 'architect's pencil' with great elegance." He would begin his lectures, incidentally, with "a practice session on how to sharpen a pencil in the correct manner". Babykin was also remembered for his flawlessly pure speech, in which there were no vulgarisms or crutch words, and his respectful attitude towards his students.

Professor Boris Alexandrovich Speransky, who lectured on metal constructions, always used the polite form of address when talking to students, and used both their first name and patronymic. Could it be that Yeltsin picked up this habit from him, as a young student? In whatever role he went on to have in later life, Boris Nikolaevich would never switch to using the overly pally, familiar form of 'you' when talking to people of various ranks and ages, and would never call them by their first name alone. There was something of Babykin in him, too: his strict, elegant clothes, his dapper haircut, his desire to enunciate clearly without resorting to vulgar expressions.

Another unforgettable character was the geodesy lecturer, Nikolai Nikolaevich Mazurov, who "was very proud of the fact that in his youth he had worked for the famous V.K. Arseniev, the ethnographer, writer and researcher into the Far East." He was very meticulous, demanded exceptional accuracy from his students in their calculations, and did not suffer any shoddy work. "Mazurov was so principled and uncompromising in his affairs that on several occasions

---

95   P.M. Bogdashin: What is this life of ours? B/m. 1998. P. 21-22.

he sent his own daughter, who studied in our faculty, out of the examination hall",[96] P.M. Bogdashin observed in his book 'What does our life amount to?'" These aspects of Mazurov's character — his principles and uncompromising nature — were also observed in Yeltsin by his peers.

The dean's assistant, Y.V. Voronin, combined strictness and kindliness. Her former students recall that on one occasion she subjected a student who had got a poor grade in theoretical mechanics, and who had therefore lost his bursary, a stern talking to: "She referred to his father, who had died in the war, and mentioned the fact that he had his mother to take care of. And then she handed a permit to retake the exam to him and said, in a threatening tone: "Try not to flunk it this time!"[97]

Why make a secret of it, they did of course have lecturers who gave them grief, and subjects that they hated, such as 'The tenets of Marxism-Leninism' and 'The art of warfare'. There were more good examples that stayed in their minds than bad, however. "Well-educated, attentive to their interlocutor, with flawless mastery of Russian speech and technical terminology — that was the image of our tutors that stayed with us," A.N. Mogilnikov asserts in his book 'This all happened to me and the country'. Mogilnikov had been another of B.N. Yeltsin's classmates. "If only a tiny portion of that moral and cultural richness stayed with us, we would have to thank fate for making our paths cross with such people."[98]

But is it not the case that exceptional professors sometimes have bad students? They say every family has its black sheep, after all. Surprising as it may seem, this saying does not apply to the group with whom Boris Nikolaevich was studying. The guys and girls, not yet spoilt by life, realised that the most important task for them now was to acquire knowledge, in order to become genuine engineers. They could not, of course, conform to a 'standardized' model: each had their own character, particular interests and talent. Unlike the other faculties, in which some of the students were former soldiers who had gone off to test themselves on the front-line, the other people on their course were almost all of a similar age and came from the school benches. Felix Plekhanov was the only first-year student who had managed to graduate from technical school and had had a little bit of practical experience in the construction industry. The only problem was that "he found the theoretical side quite hard, and had trouble holding a pencil in his big hand."

Shura Reifschneider was slightly older than the rest of the students. His party trick was his ability to recite by heart the popular tales by Ilf and Petrov, *The Twelve Chairs* and *The Golden Calf*, as a result of which his fellow students

---

96   P.M. Bogdashin: What is this life of ours? P. 28.
97   Same reference.
98   A. Mogilnikov: It happened like this for me and the country. Yekaterinburg, 2000. P. 17.

forever associated him with the character Shura Balaganov. Reifshneider, incidentally, was from a family of Germans from the Volga Region, who had been deported to the north of the Sverdlovsk Region. By way of an exception, Reifschneider was allowed to study at the Ural State Technical University, but he was obliged to appear before the security services every month with a report "confirming that he was all present and correct" in Sverdlovsk. Due to his being an "unreliable" character, he had not been allowed to train in the military academy. Be that as it may, "Shura was respected by the students and tutors for his serious nature, reliable appearance, kindly sense of humor and assiduousness in his studies. He studied very well and was often given an increase in his allowance."

The second "suspicious character" was Aleksei Dyakov, the son of Russian emigrants from China. His father, a journalist, had been sentenced under the notorious 58th article for a book he had written about the fate of his compatriots during the Civil War and as emigrés, and he met his end in a labor camp. Dyakov spoke good English and was well-read, chiefly in technical literature, which his fellow students would only look at during lectures. Dyakov passed all his higher math exams in his first year at the university. "It transpired that he knew more about nuclear physics than the students at the recently-opened physics and technical faculty at USTU, which was frightfully fashionable and terribly secretive. With his mastery of absolutely all of the technical disciplines, Aleksei was forever dazzling us with his fantastical projects and calculations, such as some sort of spaceship, for example (this was in the fifties, don't forget!), with the help of which he, Dyakov, would be able to smash the sun to smithereens. Often he would use what seemed a sufficiently well-argued chain of evidence (which we would confirm) to lead us, step by step, to the conclusion that all the angles inside a triangle were obtuse, "just like the one in our faculty," he would add, referring to the triangle formed by the party organization, the Komsomol organization and the professorial organization. On occasion he would even demonstrate that two times two was five, and come up with other such tricks, taking advantage, in an obvious and impudent way, of glaring gaps in our knowledge." That was the impression left by the faculty's phenomenon by P.M. Bogdashin. At the same time, he noted: "He was an incredibly quiet student, he wouldn't hurt a fly; he was totally consumed with science, and never got involved in sporting events, helping to unload railway cars, student parties or making counterfeit tickets to the new year's eve party at the institute. He would joke about the people who insulted him, and tried to be witty at their expense, in a condescending and non-malevolent way..."[99]

There is no student body that does not include such wits and jokers. Yasha Olkov was known for his amusing pranks. On one occasion he announced

---

99   P.M. Bogdashin: What is this life of ours? P. 49-50.

that he was going to sell some spare tickets to a concert by "leading soloists from the Italian opera: the colorful soprano Caniafora Seribella, the tenors Mirulius Lakrimans, Poria Vapararia and others." Naturally, there were plenty of people who wanted to catch a glimpse of these foreign musical stars, and were prepared to spend whatever money they had left in their wallets to do so. The following day Olkov appeared in the lecture hall with a ticket... drawn onto some plywood. It emerged that Yakov had pulled a fast one on the students who had missed the latest lecture on wooden structures. The names of the "Italian singers" were none other than the names of types of fungus which destroy trees.

Everyone thought of Pasha Bogdashin as not only a celebrity in their year group but throughout the whole university. Admittedly, his fame did not come to him straight away. Pavel's passionate love of motor-sport had become clear during the first year. He spent all his downtime in the university's workshops, making his own motorbikes. As Pavel Mikhailovich recalled, the "powerful, highly maneuverable vehicles he made, which were not typical of the time," enabled him to "get a long way ahead of his sporting rivals and, in just three years, go from being a complete novice to a master of sport, and become a very popular character at the university and beyond it." After starting off with victory in the city-wide competitions, Bogdashin went on to achieve podium finishes in national and international competitions. He came back from the DOSAAF (Volunteer Society for Cooperation with the Army, Aviation and Fleet) championships with the title of champion and two coveted prizes — a TV and a leather motorcycle suit. The KVN-49 television was the sixteenth television in a row to be invented in Sverdlovsk. One can imagine how valuable it must have seemed at the time, but Pavel, without much pause for thought, sacrificed it "on the altar of the group", since he lived in a hostel. "They installed it in our lecture hall (it captured the imagination of the students: 'The constructors have got a TV!')" Bogdashin wrote in his book. They made an unusually shaped antenna themselves and put it on the roof of the faculty of construction. The TV screen measured 100x140 mm, so they clubbed together and bought a special lens filled with glycerine, the size of a modern-day TV, to put in front of it. The first screening attracted an auditorium full of people, led by professor Babykin, who sat down reluctantly and suspiciously on the high-backed drawing stool prepared for him in front of the television set. Then the fuss died down, mainly due to the poor quality of the programs made in those days by the amateur television center, and the TV disappeared somewhere."[100]

On one of those days the group went off to sit a Strength of materials exam. The deafening roar of a motorbike prompted everyone to glance out of the window. Bogdashin went hurtling past them. And suddenly, right before

100   P.M. Bogdashin: What is this life of ours? P. 71.

everyone's eyes, the motorcycle went crashing into a tree, and Pavel flew into the air. The group rushed over to him. The first thing that caught their eye was his torn leather jacket and his hands, which were covered in blood. Pavel was brought to his senses and taken to the medical point; his motorcycle, which had hardly suffered any damage, was taken away. Anxious about their comrade, the students headed back to the examination hall. Before long Bogdashin appeared at the door, to everyone's surprise, with his arms tied up in bandages. After finding out about what had happened, the sentimental professor Rogitsky offered the "poor lad" a grade of 'four' without having to sit the exam. That evening, the group found out that Pavel had gone straight from the university to Uktus, on his motorcycle, where the city championships were being held — and had returned in triumph as champion.

What about Yeltsin, though — in what way did he stand out from the crowd? Was he known for his exemplary grades, or his unusual height? He would often be called "lanky", in response to which Boris would reply: "I'm not lanky, I'm tall." It wasn't this that attracted the attention of his classmates, though. N.A. Vilesova recalled: "Right from the outset he showed himself to be a true leader. And he never lost his charm, his naturalness, his ability to be cheery at all times, and occasionally slightly mischievous. His convication that what he was doing was the right thing to do — that instantly drew people to him. Both the lecturers and his fellow students. And at the same time he would always listen carefully to criticisms that were made of him, and was not afraid to admit to his mistakes. He would hear people out, think things over, form an opinion and then express it."[101] A friend of Yeltsin's, M.L. Karasik, recalled: "Boris was a good man, benevolent and amiable. I never saw him smoking, and he never swore. He wasn't greedy when it came to money... When we were students, it was tough trying to get presents; we were invited somewhere for someone's birthday, and he brought along his transistor radio (he used to have one like that), and gave it away as a present. Everything he did was from the soul, he never did anything rashly, everything was carefully thought through."[102]

In his memoirs, P.M. Bogdashin describes Yeltsin as follows: "The current president of Russia was an ordinary lad from the countryside, with the fate that the majority of us shared...A distinctive character trait of his was that he was always energetic in his actions, and had an innate desire to be a leader. It would be wrong to say that this desire to lead was his raison d'être: it was simply that his dedication to his goals, energy, mobility, capacity for work, unpretentiousness, and simply his healthy organism, which demanded dynamic growth, placed him among the leaders in those affairs to which he was drawn. He was always a lad with 'drive', as they say nowadays, and he did

101   V. Suturin: Boris Yeltsin and the Urals Region Polytechnic. P. 58.
102   Same reference. P. 62.

not become a leader through agitating for it, by means of eloquent speeches or by relying on the support of any official agencies — no, he simply rolled up his sleeves and threw himself into fighting for the issue or cause which happened to interest him at that particular moment."[103]

What made Pavel Mikhailovich describe Yeltsin as "an ordinary lad from the countryside"? Perhaps it was a simple mistake. Or perhaps, being from Sverdlovsk, he thought of the provinces as "the countryside" — as people often do. Without question, Yeltsin sensed, in his early days as a student, how far behind he was in his intellectual development, by comparison with his peers from the big city. It was no accident that he decided spend a sizeable chunk of his measly allowance on a subscription to the expensive Great Soviet Encyclopedia, and begun studying the articles it contained. After passing his exam on the tenets of Marxism-Leninism with a 'five' (the top grade), Yeltsin to all appearances limited his exploration of politics to that success. He was not drawn to this field of activity at all. His fellow classmates recall that they were often invited to talks at the workers' collectives, where lectures and reports were read out, but that it was usually the girls that took up these invitations — the guys would try to get out of them under various pretexts.

Naturally, dissident ideas of any kind were the last thing on any of their minds at the time. When the 'leader of all peoples and times' died, the students mourned his passing, along with the rest of the nation. On this day of shared grief, "professor Bychkov read out his lecture on concrete assembled structures in a halting voice, with tears in his eyes. Breaking the chalk, he wrote some equations on the board which were barely legible, amid a deathly hush in the lecture hall and the occasional bit of sobbing by the girls."[104]

Afterwards the group decided, of its own accord: on the day of comrade Stalin's funeral they must lay a wreath on his coffin. They made haste to procure a wreath and two tickets to Moscow. Since all of them wanted to go, they cast lots. Zina Shabalina and Raya Akhtyamova were the 'lucky ones'. The perceptive rector of USTU, meanwhile, issued an order categorically banning trips to the capital during the leader's funeral. Anyone breaching the terms of this ban faced the threat of exclusion from the institute. The group interpreted the rector's actions "as an attack on the holiest of holies — paying one's final respects to a beloved leader", and the delegates set off by train to Moscow in secret. The others awaited their return anxiously and with impatience. The most anxious student of all was probably the group's captain, Volodya Fomichev — it was his job to cover for the two girls' absence. On their return, Zina and Raya recounted how they had managed, via an incredible effort, to get into Red Square with the wreath, where they had

103   P.M. Bogdashin: What is this life of ours? P. 54-55.
104   A.N. Yuzefovich: The team of our youth. P. 46.

heard all the speeches delivered from Lenin's mausoleum, and had liked the ones by Molotov and Beria the most.

No-one gave a moment's thought to Stalin's cult of personality. They were all concerned by one thing only: who was going to become the next leader? They were free to ponder this over and quietly discuss it, aware that they would have no bearing on the decision — and nor would the entire Soviet people. Far better to stick to "one's own affairs". The young Yeltsin certainly couldn't complain that he wasn't being kept busy. One the one hand he had his studies, and on the other — he had sport.

The interest he had shown in sport during his school years might perhaps have diminished had he ended up in a different environment, but in the circumstances pertaining in Sverdlovsk and at the institute, it grew stronger. The city was full of passionate fans of the local football team, Uralmash, and the ice hockey team from the House of officers; in the national and international sports competitions, everyone would support the Russian speed-skaters Tatiana Karelina and Rimma Zhukova, the weightlifters Arkady Vorobiev and Nikolai Samsonov, the boxer Alexander Zasukhin, the athlete Sergei Sukhanov, the gymnast Liliya Nizmutdinova and other local stars. The cult of sport flourished at the USTU, as well. Teams from the polytechnics and student sports teams presented a serious threat to the strongest sports collectives in the city and the region. Taking up sport was considered a matter of prestige at USTU. And Boris was not the only one who loved it.

Sports training was obligatory for Soviet students, and Yeltsin soon became the organizer of all the sporting events throughout the faculty: cross-country skiing and ski races, relays, swimming galas and, of course, volleyball matches.

At first the volleyball team didn't want him — after all, he had two fingers missing on his left hand. After training avidly, though, he made into the team for his year-group, then the faculty team, and then the first team for the whole Urals polytechnic. He became one of the best volleyball players at the university.[105]

He joined the team on trips to the Baltic states, the Volga region, Moscow, Leningrad, Georgia and Azerbaijan. What was it that made volleyball so appealing? Boris Minaev, in his book about B.N. Yeltsin, provides an answer to this question. "Volleyball is a team sport, in which the role of the on-court leader is invaluable. Someone must always "take the lead", changing the course of the game through sheer willpower. This 'someone', the team's leader, was always him of course. His magnetic presence on the court - and not just his imposing height, quick reactions, powerful leap, 'thumping' blows — became the decisive factor in determining victory."[106]

---

105   For further details see: B.D. Minaev: Yeltsin. M., 2010. P. 27
106   Same reference. P. 28.

"Volleyball had a huge following," recalls S.S. Naboichenko, the rector of USTU-UPI for many years. "There was a volleyball court next to every student hall of residence, where 2-3 teams would try to improve their game. There was a gradation in the courts, as well: some were for the weaker teams and some were for the elite teams, representing the 5th, 9th and 10th corpuses. Even for the amateur games huge crowds of fans would gather. Not to mention what it was like at the official tournaments...! Unmissable events in the university's volleyball calendar were the 7th November Cup, the May cup, and the inter-faculty championship during the Spartakiade. These were the most popular games for the spectators: there was so much emotion, so much cheering for one's faculty. I experienced all this at first hand: if you won a meet, you would be carried aloft to the halls of residence, let into the showers without having to queue, and the girls in the canteen would give you tea and jam... If you lost there would be cries of "shame on you", you would be ridiculed, and you'd have to stand in line for the shower room."[107]

Pavel Bogdashin, who was often one of the spectators, wrote the following: "We loved going to the sporting events when Boris was playing, along with Nolik and Volodya Dorofeyev from the older group, because, as well as the moral support which our warriors needed, we got genuine pleasure ourselves from these matches, from contemplating the sportsmen themselves, dashing about the court with incredible leaps, and boundless energy...Boris played volleyball beautifully, with a certain recklessness, with an indestructible will and desire for victory. Robust, springy as a spring, excited, with fire in his eyes, he was a wonderful sight at those moments...naturally, the groups of fans, in addition to the noise and commotion as they shouted their approval and support for their teams, would excel with their witty comments, and would not shy away from shouting things out about the other team...Boris, as the captain and strongest player, bore the brunt of the sarcastic and hurtful chants, which were designed to put him off and demoralize him. All of this backfired, though: Boris was ferocious, and filled with healthy sporting enmity; he would gather up all his willpower and focus it on achieving victory, showing an infectious desire to take risks and drawing his team-mates to him. When he went up to the net, his attacks, which were accompanied by a sort of 'boar-like' exclamation, were unstoppable. He struck the ball like a cannon, and directed his blows accurately; if one of them happened to hit a spectator who had got too close to the court, it would send them flying."[108]

Yeltsin was acknowledged as the No. 1 player in the faculty team, without question. It was no accident that his opponents would set themselves the task, before the game, of 'cutting him out' of the game, and not letting him 'get stuck in'. A range of tactics were used to counter the threat posed by Yeltsin:

---

107   S.S. Naboichenko: Meetings with B.N. Yeltsin. Yekaterinburg, 2009. P. 43.
108   P.M. Bogdashin: What is this life of ours? P. 55.

when he was on the back line, his opponents served the ball into his area; when he was on the front line, they tried to make it as difficult as possible for him to return the serve or have the ball set up for him; and they tried to win as many points as possible whilst he was at the rear of the court.[109]

To many onlookers, it seemed as though Boris saw the game as "his raison d'être". He was on fire on the court, and, by all accounts, "was very demanding in terms of the quality of passes, and told people off (sometimes adding a few insults) when they made mistakes. Woe betide anyone sending him a pass that was under-hit, too short, or too far away from the net."

One time, though, when he was in the third grade, there was an unfortunate incident: "...my beloved volleyball," Yeltsin wrote, "very nearly sent me to an early grave. "There came a point when, whilst training for six to eight hours a day and catching up with my studies at night — I wanted to get straight grades of 'outstanding' in the exams — I clearly overdid things a bit. And as luck would have it I got a throat infection, I had a temperature of forty degrees, and yet I still went to training — and my heart couldn't take it. I had a pulse of 150 beats per minute, and felt weak; I was taken to hospital. They told me to stay in hospital, and that my heart might recover in four months — or else I would end up with a heart defect. I escaped the hospital after just a few days — some of the guys tied some sheets together to form a rope and I climbed down from a top-floor window and went back to Berezniki, to my parents' place..."[110]

To cut a long story short, on 27.03.1952, B. Yeltsin, a student from group S-370, was excluded on grounds of ill health and sent on an academic holiday, and on 13th September of that year, by order of the rector of UPI, Prudensky, he was brought back to the university in the third year, in group S-376. He was now some way behind his former classmates. Moreover, Boris had failed to learn his lesson. He continued to live at the same pace as before. He not only played volleyball but also coached the faculty teams, in return for which he received the small salary paid to coaches on top of his allowance.

Yeltsin, the Komsomol member, also had some social obligations: he was in charge of the sports office in the faculty of construction. It was not in his nature to see himself as a leader on paper only, and to shirk his orders. And how could he even contemplate doing so, when there was such an intense battle for the championship between the faculties?! His classmates, L.A. Vidineeva and M.K. Batsulova shared the following view: "Boris, who had the ability to draw people around him, infecting them with energy and enthusiasm, attracted everyone to the faculty's sporting and social life."[111]

---

109   S.S. Naboichenko: Meetings with B.N. Yeltsin. P. 44.

110   B.N. Yeltsin: Against the grain... P. 36-37.

111   V. Suturin: Boris Yeltsin and the Urals Region Polytechnic. P. 62.

The biggest sporting event of all at the university was the athletics relay, for which the top prize was awarded by the UPI newspaper 'For the industrial staff cadres', which was held on 9th May — Victory Day. The preparations for it were 'all-encompassing' in nature, since the organizing committee took into account not only victory at the finish-line but also the aggregate results of everyone taking part. Not everyone in the faculty of construction got involved in the sports groups, and it was therefore decided that daily morning exercises should be introduced for those living in student halls. These began at 7am, when the students were woken up by a bugler. The piercing, upbeat sound of the bugle would interrupt their sweet slumbers, and some found this very annoying. Shura Reifschneider, who had no interest in sport, could not restrain himself and "had a chat with the bugler which ended with the phrase 'I'll shoot you down like a dog'". This 'disturber of the peace' had to relocate to the floor below — but the sound of the bugle could still be heard, wherever he was. In order to escape him, Shura and Pavel Bogdashin used to put their mattresses up on the door before the morning performance and sleep on their bed-springs.

'Mobilizing the troops' was not the sports office's only task. It also had to divide the team's members up in the best possible way over the various stages. To this end it was important to know what the 'enemy' was planning, and 'spies' were sent over to the enemy camp to try and find out. Boris would always put himself forward for the main heat, for the strongest competitors. The civil engineers had a strong women's team. The only problem was that the other faculties had strong, experienced male and female runners as well. The prestigious award for 'Mass participation' would almost always be won by the faculty of construction, however.

Its victories were met with universal celebrations, with many people joining in the festivities. "The team from the faculty of construction," N.A. Vilesova recalled, "had its own uniform — yellow tops and white shorts. Our girls, including Naina Girina, used to sew the team's emblem onto each shirt at night. During the relay, the team would be cheered on by groups of supporters led by the teachers; they would stand along each section and, without a care for the strain on their vocal chords, urge the athletes on to victory. When this victory was achieved, everyone would be praised, but special mention was made of the fact that "Boris had done so much."[112]

A comparison of the grades achieved by Yeltsin each semester reveals that they fell dramatically after the fourth semester. In the fifth, sixth and seventh semesters, there was a single 'good' in each semester among all the 'outstandings', and by the final semesters — the eighth and ninth — grades of 4 ('good') were predominant. The cause of this was volleyball. In 1954 Boris

112   V. Suturin: Boris Yeltsin and the Urals Region Polytechnic. P. 52.

was selected for the regional team, Burevestnik (Sverdlovsk), which played in 'A' group (the top league) in the championship of the USSR. He began to go on trips to various cities within the Union for away matches, which caused systematic disruption to the academic process. As a result, his teachers made greater demands of Yeltsin, feeling that volleyball was distracting him from his studies. They believed that Yeltsin might one day be an "outstanding academic". Back in the third year, according to S.S. Naboichenko, "B. Yeltsin had tried his hand in the initial stages of involvement in science, getting involved in the student science society (SNO). He enjoyed solving complex, unusual tasks related to construction mechanics and the theory of elasticity, and calculating the size of girders. Under the guidance of professor A.A. Antipin, and in conjunction with his classmate A. Lavochkin, he proposed formulae for working out the planning marks and volumes of trenches and embankments."[113]

Science did not win out, though. Volleyball did.

It is difficult to form an opinion as to what Boris Nikolaevich thought of the military training given to the future engineers. The students were traditionally not fond of the military faculty, although it got them out of having to do military service in the army. Some of his classmates were critical of the "training in the trenches" and the university's military faculty, which "took a whole day out of the students' week". They were forced to learn the military charter by heart, and drive military vehicles. At the annual summer camps they slept in tents, on wooden boards. They had their meals in the soldiers' canteen, and "the food was so miserly and of such poor quality that they were constantly wondering where they might find something to eat, although the students were by no means gourmets," P.M. Bogdashin wrote. And yet he admits: "Once we had put on our shabby uniforms, and learned to curse the tailor and show off, we sensed that we had got close to something great, important and overpowering."[114]

At first, the reservists were trained — the sappers. "A sapper's work was interesting to us and at the same time made us feel some sense of inner protest and alarm...Besides our semi-starving existence and slavish dependence on our commanders, our position was also rendered more complicated by the fact that the officers were fresh out of the military academies, and were young lieutenants. They were our peers; they were not particularly well-educated, but had already had a taste of the intoxicating power and boundless might of army discipline..."[115]

The witty students poured scorn on the soldiers with their intellect, and went so far as to demand that they account for their "unlawful actions". One night

113   S.S. Naboichenko: Meetings with B.N. Yeltsin. P. 15-16.
114   P.M. Bogdashin: What is this life of ours? P. 3.
115   Same reference. P. 32.

there was considerable alarm. A kerfuffle had begun in the darkness and someone had been wounded with a bayonet — so seriously that he had to be taken for medical treatment. For the others, a long assault march began, over many kilometers, weighed down by their ammunition. Many felt their legs giving way. When they arrived at some trenches and the command 'halt' rang out, it seemed as though the torture had ended. Fifteen minutes later, though, they were ordered to man the trenches and ready them for a tank attack. "We had no strength left by that point," P.M. Bogdashin recalled, "our hands were shaking with hunger and fatigue; sitting at the bottom of the trench or lying down, we were shouting out and knocking our fists against the walls, occasionally throwing clumps of earth into the air, we continued to "reinforce the defences"...The tanks of the 'enemy' eventually appeared. It wasn't a very nice feeling — in fact it was a pretty awful one. The steel monsters came crawling along, firing blanks in our direction; the air was thick with black smoke, the roar of the engines and clouds of dust. A tank regiment was clearly on the move…".[116] The attack was warded off with a few explosives. The tanks crossed the trenches with ease, showering the sappers sitting in them with clumps of earth. A few minutes later they returned to the rear and then, after 'smoothing over' their positions once again, disappeared over the horizon. Was it all over, at last? No, a command was barked out: "Lay some mines in the area where the tanks might come through!" "Since we could only have been lifted out of that trench with a jack screw," P.M. Bogdashin wrote, the commanders found a very simple solution to the problem: they threw explosive canisters containing tear gas into the trench...We flew like falcons out of the trench and began to lay the mines, cursing the "enemy", our commanders, the war, and the enemy laying siege of the Socialist camp, making up our minds to dedicate the rest of our lives to keeping the peace."

Then, in the next year, someone decided that the sappers should be retrained as tank-drivers. They liked this idea: they had been entrusted with powerful vehicles with fascinating mechanisms, armaments and communications systems. And they liked the commanders, too: they were "experienced people, men of few words; they were respectful of our engineering-based approach to troubleshooting, which had already made itself felt, and our analysis of the situations which arose; they made no attempt to suppress these things."[117]

During the lessons, everyone tried to learn the theory, but the practical lessons were more appealing. At a tank training ground outside Nizhny Tagil they were taught how to fire rounds from a tank and a machine gun, in the daytime and by night. They drove fearful vehicles around the gusty locality. When the military groups were formed, Boris Yeltsin was assigned the role of a tank commander. On one occasion his team, consisting of Mogilnikov,

---

116   Same reference. P. 34.
117   P.M. Bogdashin: What is this life of ours? P. 41.

Sakharov and Lavochkin, went out onto the course and failed to come back. It later emerged that by an oversight they had driven the vehicle into a ditch full of water, and got stuck. "They were lucky," A.N. Yuzefovich recalled, "that the tank didn't get completely flooded, because they had left the fuel for the tank on the bank of the river. It was at this point that they were forced to demonstrate the ability to use their initiative. They were helped by some comrades in other tanks, who had turned back to help the stricken crew. Three tanks came up one after another and hauled the unlucky crew out of the ditch, like a radish out of a vegetable patch."[118]

This was how Yeltsin, who would go on to be a member of the Military Council for the Urals military district, and later the Commander-in-chief of the Armed Forces of the Russian Federation, was introduced to the "harsh reality of life in the army, its hardships and deprivations". Who could have predicted what was to follow, back then?! They would return from the summer camps with all manner of adventures, stories and memories to recount, and with a whole new set of anecdotes and legends about life as students in the army, which caused a lot of laughter in the halls of residence and smoking areas.

The UPI had one of the best auditoriums in Sverdlovsk. Films were shown there for the students, with free admission. In addition to concerts put on by the student art groups independently, famous artists also performed there, such as A. Vertinsky and G. Vinogradov, as well as students from the Sverdlovsk conservatoire, B. Shtokolov, I. Arkhipova, Y. Gulyaev and others. The famous symphony orchestra of the Sverdlovsk symphony hall also performed on the stage numerous times, conducted by M. Paverman. The famous fiddler I. Bezrodny performed Kabalevsky's violin concerto with the orchestra. "The student auditorium, which was not particularly worldly wise, was profoundly affected, and forced the violinist to play several encores, amid thunderous applause," A.N. Mogilnikov recalled.

Occasionally, particularly after they had just received their allowance, the students organized cultural excursions to theaters in the city. They were drawn to the theater of drama by the acting of the people's artist of the USSR B. Ilin and the actors M. Tokarev, B. Molchanov and K. Maksimova. Boris Yeltsin particularly enjoyed going to see operettas, with their classic music performed by A. Marenich, M. Viks, G. Dybcho, P. Yemelyanova, A. Matkovsky and others.

His personal preference was for the music hall, although his access to it came via gramophone records or on so-called 'ribs' — X-ray sheets which were used to make sound recordings. The students' idols were K. Shulzhenko, L. Utyosov, Yves Montand and also A. Vertinsky and P. Leshchenko, both of

---

118   A.N. Josefovich: The team of our youth. P. 34-35.

whom were held in disgrace at the time. To the accompaniment of their songs, dance evenings were held on Saturdays, on the second floor of the hall of residence. Poetry by the university's poets Senchenko and Oborina was recited. The song *Little flames*, composed by a student from the faculty of construction, I. Filatova, was a great favorite.

"In the spring, when it was warm, and we had met up to go out for a stroll until it got late," A.Y. Pavlova recalled, "we would go to the canteen first of all, and order something sweet — jam donuts, or pancakes. And then we would go and listen to the nightingales. In the area where the presidium of the Urals Division of the Russian Academy of Sciences now stands, there was a forest, and it used to have nightingales in it..."

Would it be possible to imagine a student life without parties? The excuse for them was usually that it was someone's birthday. The call would come, saying "let's all add something to the pot," and the guys would head off to the shops, whilst the girls prepared some simple appetizers. Today, Boris Nikoalevich's classmates recall these banquets fondly:

"We used to drink on the public holidays, but we didn't let it get out of hand. We just wanted to have a lot of fun, that was all. They used to sell *Slivyanka* in those days, and *Volzhskoye krepkoe*; there was vodka too, of course, and champagne. We ate caviar, and salmon — this was typical food for us, even students could buy it. We had trouble getting our hands on smoked sausage, though..."

"And with beer it was like this: when a student was celebrating his birthday, he wouldn't buy vodka, only beer. We lived on the 4th and 5th floors, and on the first two floors were families. We borrowed a crossbeam from them, and three buckets. We went out to the tram ring - there were some beer stalls there. We bought three buckets' worth of beer, went back to block 6, and celebrated the birthday...There was plenty of beer in those days..."

The students got together not with the sole purpose of getting drunk, but to have a good time: to 'muck about' and sing and dance. Boris had mastered the art of playing the wooden spoons to accompany songs — and this remained his favorite musical instruments throughout his later life. "He was pretty good at that," said N.A. Vilesova, recalling her student days...Once, on one of my birthdays, when we were about to have tea, I brought out a three-liter teapot from the kitchen. Boris declared: "That's not enough for me, I'm going to drink thirteen glasses — but I must have some lemon with it." And when I brought in the five-liter teapot, he put a whole lemon in his glass and started pouring out the tea. He started drinking it and counting how many glassfuls he had drunk. That was how he fooled us...And as for why he did that — I had told him that my grandfather had been a tea-drinker, and that he had once put a towel round his neck and drunk thirteen glasses...I'll let you into a frightening secret. Boris's favorite type of candy was pink and white fudge. For him that was the best present to get."[119]

Naturally, the guys had their own particular interests — masculine ones. Occasionally they indulged in a trip to a fancy restaurant, or, when they were feeling exhausted, went to the bathhouse to have a beer and enjoy the sauna."

Money was always tight, despite the fact that they managed to make a little bit on the side by unloading railway wagons.

Boris Nikolaevich recalled that he had once been struck by the idea of going on a trip around the country — at that point he had not even laid eyes on the sea yet. And during the summer holidays, "without a copeck to my name, and with the bare minimum of clothes, only my tracksuit trousers, sneakers, shirt and straw hat," he left Sverdlovsk. No-one had heard of the concept of hitch-hiking back then. Yeltsin travelled "mostly on the roofs of railway cars, sometimes on the tambour, or on the footboard, or occasionally on a lorry. On occasion, of course, the police would stop me, and ask: where are you off to? I would say I was headed for Simferopol, for example, to see my grandma. What street does she live on? I always knew that every city had a Lenin Street, so I would never get caught out by that one. And they would let me go...But I set myself the following task: I would travel by night, and arrive in a town — I always chose cities that I knew, of course — and then I would spend a whole day looking around, sometimes two. I would spend the night in a park somewhere, or at a station, and then continue my journey on the roof of a railway car..."[120]

He had a stroke of luck in Zaporozhe. A colonel he happened to bump into told the traveller that he was trying to get into university — and that the only trouble was he "didn't know the first thing about mathematics." The young student immediately offered his help, but set two conditions: the man must work a 12-hour day and feed him well. The two sides both fulfilled their sides of the bargain. The tutor "was able to eat my fill for the first time in a long time, and even put on a bit of weight."[121]

The 'customer', for his part, kept pace with the lessons, and as Boris later found out, passed the entrance exams for math and enrolled as a student. The tutor himself did his work and went back to the university, filled with memories and stories to tell, and having seen with his own eyes that "broad is my native land, it boasts many forests, fields and rivers", as the poet once said. He had not found out just how much more freely a person was able to breathe in this land than in other countries, though.

---

119   V. Sutyrin: Boris Yeltsin and the Urals Region Polytechnic. P. 39, 64.

120   See: B.N. Yeltsin: Against the Grain. P. 30.

121   B.N. Yeltsin: Against the Grain. P. 31.

Boris had found out something else, however: wherever he was, and however good life was there, his soul always yearned for his homeland, and missed his customary habits and his friends and comrades. During his time at the university, his halls of residence became a home from home, and his classmates were like a second family. Mutual benefit was key in their relationships with one another. They shared everything that could be shared: anyone who was hungry would be given food, anyone who was in need would be given support, the depressed were cheered up, and the homesick were cajoled into having fun.

In later life they would never forget hall of residence No. 6 on Komintern Street. Looking back on his time there, A.N. Josifovich wrote: "Suddenly you hear a scuffle of feet in the corridor, and someone trying to play Chopin's funeral march on the balalaika. You would jump out into the corridor and see a little procession: at the front of it a pillow was being held up, and behind it there was an 'Orchestra' consisting of a single balalaika player.

What's going on?

We're holding a funeral for a bedbug!

You involuntarily join up with this procession, and wait for other people who've had their interest piqued to join you, picturing how much fun you're going to have once all this is over."[122]

Communal living did not prevent friendship groups from forming within the group, most of which were quite small, and would usually consist of three people, with a girl always included. That's how it was. There were various 'triangles', for example: Fyodorov — Taran — Chipushatanov, Reifschneider — Gorbunova — Bogdashin, Yeltsin — Girina — Lavochkin. They did not become completely introverted, of course. They recall how on one occasion, Boris decisively suggested, to the group consisting of Arnold (Nolik) Lavochkin, Volodya Anisimov, Naya Girina, Lyusya Vidineeva and Rita Batsulova: "Let's live as a 'collective farm'." I've had enough of the girls feeding us! From now on us guys are going to contribute to the catering costs." Everyone present expressed their support for the idea, but Yeltsin ended up being elected as the chairman of this collective farm. Boris devised a charter which had to be adhered to by all the 'collective farmers':

"1. The 'collective farm' is created voluntarily on the basis of friendship and sympathy. It has a total of 6 members.

2. The duties are to be divided up as follows: the chairman is Boris; the chancellor is Lyusa; the nurse is Naya; the secretary is Rita; the brigadier is

---

122   A. Josefovich: The team of our youth. P. 50-51.

Nolik; the peculator of the collective farm's benevolence is Vova.

3. Lectures may be attended without passes.

4. Members may only go to the cinema, the theater and sporting events once a week at most.

5. Visits to the bathhouse are to take place on Saturdays.
Money will be allocated for this purpose. The boys are to drink beer, and the girls — red wine.

6. We will celebrate public holidays and the birthdays of members of the collective farm and close friends.

7. Etc.

Passed at a general meeting of the 'collective farm'. November 1952."[123]

There was a reason why the author of the charter had jokingly described V. Anisimov as "the peculator of the collective farm's benevolence". Volodya had made so bold as to eat a roll bought for the collective farm all on his own, without permission. He and Arnold used to accompany the chancellor, Lyusa, on trips to buy food at the store, or potatoes and vegetables at the market. Naya was responsible for cleanliness and order in the bedroom. Rita was involved in organizational events and entered them into the agenda.

Everyone knew about the collective farm in the faculty, although nobody supported the initiative. The others were probably able to get along on their own, or else lacked people with initiative, like Yeltsin.

It is hard for today's students to imagine what life was like for those in their position in the 1950's. As they see it, students in the fifties had no knowledge of the "sweet fruits of civilization". Young people were indeed very different in those days. Looking back on their youth, which was now so distant, Yeltsin's classmates L.A. Vidineeva, M.K. Batsulova, M.L. Karasik and Y.A. Permyakov recall:

"To us, everything was novel and interesting: the studying, the leisure time, making new friends among our classmates. We were quite fearful of the older students, and they turned their noses up at us a bit. One time two tall, handsome boys came into our room. They were Misha Ustinov and Borya [Boris] Yeltsin. They had come to see two girls they knew from Berezniky — Rita Yerina and Alya Kozneva. We were introduced to them. We were a bit shy at first, and reserved. As time passed, other boys came to see us as well, as well as them, and it was interesting and a lot of fun." "Looking back, I'm

123   V. Sutyrin: Boris Yeltsin and the Urals Polytechnic Institute. P. 31.

quite surprised at what pure friendships we had. There was no advantage to be had from it, nothing — it was founded entirely on thinking well of one another."[124]

"In the past, if a boy and a girl made friends, then it really was a genuine friendship on a personal level, and not what it is understood to mean nowadays...It would be like this: a boy would come up to a girl: "Let's be friends." "All right." And we were friends for three years."[125]

"The trio of Reifshneider, Gorbunova and Bogdashin sat at the same table right up until we graduated, and they were very close. These two strapping young lads, who were almost twice her height, had taken a liking to Lida Gorbunova, a tiny, nymph-like Sverdlovsk girl, who was always tastefully and fashionably dressed. And she was clearly fond of them, too. The two of them, who remained no more than friends to her right up until graduation day, would ward off other guys, who perhaps had firmer intentions as regards Lida, with their grenadier-like appearance."[126]

And yet none of the students was lacking in innate emotion. Sympathies and likings began to grow into love. The weddings began in the third year. Reifschneider got married to his girlfriend in Leningrad, without telling anyone. Others found love within the faculty, at the university. The first 'home-grown' married couple was Sasha Yuzefovich and Rita Razdyakonova. The weddings themselves were prepared by means of joint efforts, and, of course, with the students devising various scripts and scenes. At the Pavlovs' wedding, Yeltsin, who was a bachelor, played the role of father of the bride.

He played the role of matchmaker with aplomb at the wedding of another of his friends, M. Karasik. By the time they finished their studies, many of the students had families, and everyone was waiting for Boris to follow suit.

Yeltsin's chosen one studied in a parallel course in a group of future experts in water supply and water technology (purification), whom the civil engineers nicknamed the 'fecal riffraff'. On this subject A. Yuzefovich recalls, in his book: "...we did not yet realise that this group of plumbers amounted to a bouquet of potential brides — for some reason it consisted mainly of girls." It was in this "bouquet" that Boris found his Naya — Naina Girina, a girl from Orenburg. How had she managed to bewitch him?

According to her friends, "Naya was known for her friendly nature and amiability. It was impossible to rile her, and she was always able to resolve any conflicts in the group of girls. She was always well turned out, with her hair

---

124   V. Sutyrin: Boris Yeltsin and the Urals Polytechnical Institute. P. 34.
125   Same reference.
126   V. Sutyrin: Boris Yeltsin and the Urals Polytechnical Institute. P. 29.

nicely combed. She was liable to miss a whole hour of lectures at the university just to make sure that she arrived looking attractive. She loved dancing, and went to the dance evenings, where she had no trouble finding dance partners. Her classmates tried to make overtures to her, but she remained loyal to the "collective farm". It was easy to make friends with her."[127]

This was how our protagonist described it: "In the whirlpool of that hectic student life, our own particular friendship group took shape: six guys and six girls. We lived side by side, in two big rooms, and met up almost every evening. Naturally, some of the guys fell for the girls, and there were some that I liked as well, but gradually, in our big group of student friends I began to notice one girl in particular more and more — Naya Girina. She had been born in the Orenburg Region and was registered on her birth cerificate as being called Anastasia. But her parents called her Naya, Naina. She had therefore not used to being called by her given name...She probably ought to have just got used to it, but instead she went to the Registry Office and changed the name in her passport to Naina. I preferred the name Anastasia. For a long time after that I addressed her not by her name, but by saying: "girl".

She was always modest, amiable and tender in some way. This was a very good match for my indefatigable nature. Our mutual liking for one another gradually grew, but we didn't let it show, and even when we kissed it was only on the cheek — just like with all the other girls. There were no fervent declarations of love. And our platonic relationship went on like that for a long time, although on the inside I was aware that I had fallen in love, and felt a strong love for her, and that there was no getting away from that fact. I remember that the first time we declared our love to one another was during the second year, on the gallery in the foyer, in front of the university's ceremonial hall. And we kissed next to one of the columns, and not on the cheek this time, but properly..."[128]

Relationships such as these were known as "pure love". It was the foundation on which strong families brought up their sons and daughters, it was what the classic works of literature called for, and it was what was taught in films, shows and songs. Pure love had become the guarantee of a strong family, which would remain intact until the spouses' dying day. The Yeltsins were not the only ones who remained forever loyal to one another: their classmates did, too.

Boris and Naina had different temperaments and interests, but theirs was a case of physical similarity in which there was a coming together not of two positive fields, or of two negative fields, but of two opposing fields,

127   V. Sutyrin: Boris Yeltsin and the Urals Polytechnical Institute. P. 30.
128   B.N. Yeltsin: Against the Grain. P. 74-75.

a positive and a negative, resulting in the creation of energy. The energetic, driven Boris, with his fiery nature which sometimes boiled over and love of his work, had a strong need for the calm, amiable, rational, homely Naina. They tied the knot a little later, after graduating, and were to remain faithful to one another for the rest of their lives. Neither of them would ever forget that column at the UPI, behind which, hiding from the gaze of strangers, they stole their first kiss.

The time of lectures, exams and practical sessions, which had at first seemed so endless, was coming to an end. In his final report, Yeltsin had 7 passes, 21 grades of 'outstanding' and 11 grades of 'good'.[129] Next up was his presentation of his degree project. And as Yeltsin admitted, he had had to do this work in just one month, rather than the three and a half months which were allocated for it: "I had been away all the time, the national championships had been on, and were reaching their climax, and the team was moving from place to place. When I got back to Sverdlovsk, there was just a month left before I had to present my degree project."[130] In the end, the manager of his degree project, the chief engineer from Urals Steel Construction, professor S.S. Krupennikov, was pretty concerned for his charge. In his report he felt obliged to note: "He was very late setting to work on his project, but his impressive mental powers, good preparation and capacity for work enabled him to get his work finished and present his project on time." Conclusion: "B.N. Yeltsin is capable of working successfully in production or for developers. The overall grade for his project is 'outstanding'.[131] His work 'Project for an aerial cable car along the bank of a coal mine and a project for the organization of work to build it' was awarded a similar grade by the state examination commission.

Before being given their degree certificates, all the graduates were given character references which they were obliged to present at their future place of work. These were signed by the 'triumvirate': the dean of the faculty of construction, the secretary of the Komsomol organization and the chairman of the office of the professional union. They assessed Yeltsin as follows: "... During his time at the university he never got anything less than outstanding or good grades in all academic disciplines. Comrade B.N. Yeltsin played an active part in community work and did a great deal to enable the successful development of sport among the students in the faculty; he was a serious, able student who showed initiative; he did not always work systematically. After graduating from the university comrade B.N. Yeltsin could take charge in his own right of the production of construction and installation work, as part of the erection of civil and industrial buildings."

Reading this document, one cannot help but linger over the remark "did not always work systematically". The authors were probably referring to the

---

129   S.S. Naboichenko: Meetings with B.N. Yeltsin. P. 23.
130   B.N. Yeltsin: Against the Grain. P. 33.
131   S.S. Naboichenko: Meetings with B.N. Yeltsin. P. 31.

incident which occurred in the fifth year, when Yeltsin was late handing in a report after a practical session on production, and consequently had his allowance taken away. Another possible explanation is that they were referring to the frequent occasions on which he left class to go and take part in sporting events.

Does it really matter? The main thing was that he had his degree in his hands — he was a civil engineer! He was offered the chance to stay on and work at the faculty: it would be a prestigious position and one with a future — a post-graduate degree, a dissertation, a degree, a job as a teacher at the UPI! Yeltsin turned the offer down without a moment's hesitation.

He had other ideas: he wanted to get into professional sport.

Boris took this news to the dean of the faculty of construction, G.P. Dorosinsky, at a time when the graduates were already being allocated jobs. After hearing him out, the dean openly rebuked this "deserter": we teach you, and the state spends money on you, so as to end up with specialists, but they decide they want to go and play sports! In a word, Boris got the message: he had to go and work at a construction site, and justify the degree he had been given.

He left the Urals Polytechnic with more than just a degree. In addition to knowledge, the university had tempered him very well for the life ahead of him. Yeltsin's strength of spirit and determination to achieve victory were fed by his sporting exploits.

University had been a new environment for him, which he had made his own, becoming acquainted with metropolitan culture, theaters and concert halls. Within the university campus Yeltsin found out the true value of the collective and of friendship, to which he would remain true throughout his life, as would his classmates, who never abandoned Boris in any situation throughout the rest of his life.

All these challenges were still to come, however.

The construction site

In the summer of 1955, Boris Yeltsin, a student at the faculty of construction at the Urals Polytechnic Institute, was awarded a grade of 'outstanding' for his degree project on the subject 'Project for an aerial cable car along the bank of a coal mine and a project for the organization of work to build it'. In his comments on the project, a reviewer for the chief engineer of the Sverdlovsk directorate of the trust Urals Steel Construction, K.A. Mukhamedeev, stated that "the volume and quality of the work done on this degree project indicates the author's high level of theoretical knowledge." A comment by his academic supervisor, professor Krupennikov, in addition to a high assessment of the work that had been done stated that "B.N. Yeltsin will be able to work successfully in production or for developer organizations." This signified that a well-trained specialist was set to join the ranks of civil engineers in the Urals. At his own admission, the idea of a career in politics did not even enter the young graduate's head at the time: his objective was to acquire serious mastery of the practical skills of a civil engineer.

The first entry in Boris Yeltsin's record of professional service was made at the Nizhny-Isetsk construction department of the Urals Heavy Piping Construction trust. Even at this early stage, however, he let his character shine through, rejecting the role of foreman that was offered to him. He would later give the following explanation for this: "...I thought it would be a big mistake to take charge of a construction site, and of people, straight away, without getting a feel for it in person...So I decided to spend a year mastering 12 different professions in construction. A different one every month."[132] As a result of his stubbornness and perseverance, he managed to achieve what he had planned: Yeltsin tried out the professions of bricklayer, concrete mixer, carpenter, joiner, glazier, plasterer, painter and decorator, crane operator and several others.

Just like the hero of the tale by P.P. Bazhov — the writer most closely associated with the Urals and an unusually popular man in those years — Yeltsin tried one profession after another, attempting to grasp the "heart of the matter".

B. Yeltsin's path up the career ladder was impressive. 1955-57: specialist, 1957-58 — foreman, 1958-60 — senior foreman of construction division No. 11 of the Yuzhgorstroi trust in the city of Sverdlovsk.

Joining the Communist Party

In 1960 an important event occurred in Yeltsin's professional career. He was appointed chief engineer, and soon afterwards — head of the department of construction. In addition to his understandable rise up the career ladder of the civil engineer, his political status was also changing, whether he wanted it to or not. Chief engineer of the construction department — that meant he was in the *nomenklatura*. It may only have been the district *nomenklatura* — but that still counted!

---

132   B.N. Yeltsin: Against the Grain. P. 37.

He was appointed chief engineer at the Yuzhgorstroi trust, but he would also have to get through an interview with the party's district committee. Henceforward, furthering his career path would require him to join the party. He was approved as head of the construction department at the district committee's bureau. The higher the position, the higher the level at which it was approved: first it was the regional committee's registry *nomenklatura* or main *nomenklatura*, and thereafter — the relevant levels of the *nomenklatura* of the Central Committee of the Communist Party of the Soviet Union (CC CPSU)...Membership of the party had become an essential factor in professional management activity. The party committees were attentive in making sure that potential managers become party members.

But what exactly was going on in the party at the time? I shall make a number of preliminary remarks.

In the '50s some important, symbolic changes occurred in the party and the state. On 5th March 1953 Stalin died, and on 9th March he was buried. At the funeral ceremony, Khrushchev, Malenkov, Molotov and Beria all delivered speeches from the steps of the Mausoleum, each of them swearing their loyalty to the Lenin-Stalin cause. In July 1953, however, Beria was declared a spy and a criminal. He was put on trial at a Plenum of the CC CPSU first of all, before being brought before a closed court and then executed. Malenkov and Molotov, along with the Politburo members Voroshilov, Kaganovich and Bulganin — these names were known by every schoolboy in the USSR — and their close associates were revealed to be an "anti-party group" in the summer of 1957.

Stalin's reputation took a blow too. On 25th February 1956, the day after the official end of the 20th congress, N.S. Khrushchev delivered his so-called 'secret speech'. In the speech, which shook the delegates at the congress to the core, the first secretary of the CC CPSU told of the illegal repression and persecution of innocent people, and the executions without trial, responsibility for which lay firmly at the feet of Stalin and his immediate entourage. On 5th March the Presidium of the CC passed a directive 'On familiarization with the speech by N.S. Khrushchev, 'On the cult of personality and its consequences', at the 20th party congress', which stated the following:

"1. Propose that the regional committees, district committees and Central Committee of the communist parties in the Union republics make known the speech delivered by comrade N.S. Khrushchev, 'On the cult of personality and its consequences', at the 20th party congress, to all communists and Komsomol members, and also to the workers, employees and state farm workers who are not party members.

2. The speech by comrade Khrushchev must be sent out to the party organizations with a stamp saying 'not to be printed', after removing from the cover the stamp 'top secret'.[133]

The text of the 'secret speech' was read all over the country. Discussing it was forbidden. Many organizations found they were unable to abide by this rule however. A huge row erupted — why was it that this had been allowed to happen in our country? Where had the Politburo been? What lessons did the party intend to learn from the bitter experience of the past?

In Sverdlovsk, at the UPI, the debate was brought up at a Komsomol conference by a student named Nemelkov. His views were supported by many students, but the party leaders were unable to put up any resistance. The political row was so great that information about the events in Sverdlovsk found its way into a letter from the CC to the party organizations, under the characteristic heading 'On the strengthening of the political work of party

organizations among the masses and the curtailing of the attacks by anti-Soviet, hostile elements."[134] The letter was prepared by a commission from the Presidium of the CC CPSU, led by the CC secretary and candidate member of the Presidium, L.I. Brezhnev.

The aforementioned letter contained the following definitions: "hostile actions are being covered up with false words about criticism and self-criticism, and slogans about a struggle 'for democracy'." ... Furthermore, there are also some 'communists' who, under the guise of being members of the party, and under the banner of the struggle against the consequences of the cult of personality, are slithering towards adopting anti-party stances, and allowing demagogic attacks to be made against the party, and throwing into question whether or not it has chosen the correct line. ... It is a dangerous and unacceptable state of affairs, when the party organizations behave passively, and often pass over these facts, ...they are not putting up any organized resistance to the anti-party and demogogic speeches and are not taking any decisive measures to curtail the activities of the anti-Soviet, hostile elements."

Word of the events in Sverdlovsk spread to all the other higher education institutions — discussions which bordered on demonstrations took place at the Urals university and at the Sverdlovsk pedagogical institute. Dozens of students were expelled and lost their entitlement to continue their studies.

By this time Yeltsin had already become a specialist at the construction site. One can't help thinking that it was lucky he graduated from UPI in 1955 rather than in 1956, and that he was unable to take part in the discussions about Stalin at his home university.

---

133   Same reference.
134   RGANI. F. 89. Op. 6. D. 1.

It is highly unlikely Yeltsin spent much time pondering the fact that in 1958 the first secretary of the CC CPSU, Khrushchev, also became Chairman of the Council of Ministers of the USSR. This signified that the party administration was now more important than the bodies of state governance.

One thing is for sure, though. The criticism of Stalin and of the repression which took place in the 1930s became a form of political rehabilitation, albeit an indirect one, for the persecution of his family and of the millions of people who had been 'de-kulakized' in the '30s. The country was now going through a period of economic growth. It was a period of Soviet dominance in the space race, new industrial concerns and the mastering of new technologies.

Social politics was changing. For the first time, the authorities were voicing the slogan: a separate apartment for every family. The generation which had grown up in huts and communal apartments was hoping to receive its own separate apartments, with hot water, a bathroom and a kitchen. It was the civil engineers who were going to solve this problem. And Yeltsin was one of them.

In 1960 chief engineer Yeltsin was given the chance to become a member of the CPSU. Getting into the party by one's own efforts was not easy. The main sources from which the ranks of the party were compiled were, first and foremost, workers and peasants. Historically the CPSU had been seen as the party of the workers, but the weight they carried within the party was not very big: the workers were not joining the party because it didn't give them any benefits or advantages whatsoever.[135] Another route to accelerated membership of the party was the Soviet army. Soldiers in their second and third years of service could become party members fairly easily, and this, in turn, helped them when they enrolled at senior academic institutions. The most common method of receiving a party membership card, though, was by working in an elected position in the Komsomol. The Komsomol — 'the party's loyal assistant' — opened up a route to the party administration, and became a crucial source for the recruitment of the party rank and file.

Yeltsin never worked "in the Komsomol". He did not take up the opportunity to apply to join the party at the moment when his time in the Komsomol came to an end, on the eve of that deadline, when he was about to turn 28, i.e. in 1958-1959.

The offer to become a member of the party was made to him based on his professional position, and taking into account the expected career path of a civil engineer with the potential to direct projects.

---

135   The first secretary of the Sverdlovsk Regional Committee, B. Yeltsin, warned in 1977 that "the party does not accept enough workers as members — in the Upper-Isetsk, Oktyabr and Kirov district committees." — CDPASR. F. 4. Op. 84.D. 3. L. 54

He was accepted as a candidate member of the party in March 1960. Yeltsin himself later stated that he had genuinely believed in the ideals of justice which the party advocated.[136]

At an assembly of the communists in the directorate and at a meeting of the trust's party committee in March 1960, the future candidate for membership of the party, Yeltsin, was assessed based on his business and actions. And, it must be said, those present had nothing but good things to say about him. Even the man in charge of the Yuzhgorstroi trust, N.I. Sytnikov, with whom Yeltsin had developed a somewhat "strange" relationship right from the outset,[137] confessed: "Comrade Yeltsin, Boris Nikolaevich joined us after graduating from the polytechnic institute in 1955. There is nothing but positive things to say in relation to comrade Yeltsin's work; he began as a joiner, and he is now chief engineer in the construction and installation directorate. Comrade Yeltsin is a young, growing comrade." Admittedly, he did not shy away from remarking: "In addition to the positive feedback, it should be pointed out to him that he is a little blunt and rude at times, for his age. He must take cognizance of this. I propose that he be accepted as a candidate member of the party."[138]

The proposal by N.I. Sytnikov was seconded by N.S. Dzhanenko, who had perceived in Yeltsin the quality of a good specialist, and Y.N. Bostandzhieva, who, though she gave a positive description of Boris Nikolaevich, nevertheless expressed the wish that she would not "observe any presumption in him".[139]

P.D. Rybakov, who recommended Yeltsin, observed that in the construction directorate "Boris Nikolaevich is successfully taking charge of work to introduce state-of-the-art manufacturing methods, and is studying Marxism-Leninism at university." The decision was passed unanimously.[140]

The acceptance as a candidate member of the party of chief engineer Yeltsin was accompanied by a series of party punishments. After just three months Yeltsin was reprimanded for an accident which resulted in three workers being injured. The reason was that neither the joiner nor the foreman had checked the timber prepared by the carpenters, and they had given way when some bricklayers had tried to walk across them. A month later he was ordered to "appear for punishment due to shortcomings in his production and administrative activity." Judging by order No. 77 dated 10th June 1960, these shortcomings were expressed in the fact that chief engineer B.N. Yeltsin, and the head of the directorate G.A. Mukhin, "were unable to provide specific

---

136   Same reference. P. 43.
137   For further details see: B.N. Yeltsin: Against the Grain. P. 41-42.
138   CDPASR. F. 2992. Op. 6. D. 527. L. 8.
139   CDPASR. F. 2992. Op. 6. D. 527. L. 8.
140   Urals Region center for B.N. Yeltsin. (UCBNY). The personal matter of B.N. Yeltsin. F. 1. Op. 1. D. 12. P. 12.

details of the nature of the damage and the reasons which had caused poorer performance in the management statistics based on the value of the works, as contrasted with data from the report compiled in 1959."

In November of that year, both directors were given two reprimands each "for allowing the deadline for completion of work to be missed" and "for allowing costs on materials to get too high".

The punishments were meted out in equal proportion, but the level of demand for them was different. The head of Construction Directorate No. 4, G.A. Mukhin (Yeltsin's immediate supervisor) was fired. B.N. Yeltsin was appointed head of the construction directorate.

Head of the construction directorate

The relentless stream of reprimands directed at Yeltsin was a kind of initiation into the etiquette of Soviet governance, at both state and party level. The intention was not only to punish him but to educate him and teach him how to manage something himself.

This was the template for governance, and Yeltsin the young communist was mastering it by being the subject of it. A month after his promotion his trial period as a candidate member came to an end, and he wrote a standard application to the party organization: "I hereby request that you accept me in the ranks of the Communist party of the Soviet Union, since I wish to be one of those struggling actively to build communism in our country. I believe I am ready to join the party."[141]

In March 1961 the bureau of the CPSU's district committee accepted B.N. Yeltsin as a party member. The young communist Yeltsin was presented with his party membership card amid great fanfare. The first few days of his time as a party member were spoilt by a party punishment: he was given a stern reprimand which was recorded in his registration card. The bureau of the party's Sverdlovsk city committee, when the results of the year were announced, decided in favor of extending the deadline for the construction of a boarding school (this was the reason why Yeltsin's predecessor as head of the construction directorate was fired) "to discourage the others from the habit — give Yeltsin a stern reprimand, to be recorded in his registration card."

On this occasion Yeltsin tried to appeal against what he saw as an unjust decision. In his memoirs, he wrote: "I walked up to the lectern and said:

---

141   Urals Region center for B.N. Yeltsin. F. 1. Op. 1. D. 12. P. 13.

'Comrades, members of the bureau..., you must understand that I was given my party membership card just yesterday. Here it is, hot off the press. And today you are proposing that I, as someone with just one day's experience as a communist, be given a stern reprimand which will be recorded in my registration card for failing to complete a boarding school. There are some civil engineers here, they will confirm that commissioning it was simply out of the question. But no, you refused: so as to discourage the others... This came as a serious blow."[142] He had trouble dealing with this incident. And although the reprimand was annulled a year later, the record of it stayed in the registration card of the communist Yeltsin right up until his party documents were replaced in 1973.

When one reads *Against the grain*, one gets the sense that the individual who annoyed its author the most was the trust manager M.I. Sytnikov (in the book his surname is distorted and written as Sitnikov). There are almost three pages of memoirs dedicated to him, including an extremely negative description with the suggestion of a personal insult. The nature of his relations with this man was clearly too painful for Yeltsin.

For the record we shall point out that people who knew Mikhail Ivanovich would take issue with much of what Boris Nikolaevich said. They knew Sytnikov to be a "strong manager who maintained strict discipline". In their opinion, Mikhail Ivanovich had taken a dislike to Yeltsin's behavior — his wrangling, his constant desire to express his "personal opinion", his independent-spiritedness and his disrespectful tone when speaking to his elders.

It seems that the director of Yuzhgorstroi wished to break his subordinate, by whatever possible means. He had messing with the wrong guy, though! As subsequent events would show, Yeltsin was a man who did not just obey orders unquestioningly, and had a stiff resolve.

Without going so far as to act as judge and jury regarding this complex relationship, let us observe that M.I. Sytnikov, who had at his disposal substantial administrative resources, used these resources against Yeltsin in full measure. How else are we to explain the fact that in the space of just one year, the manager of the trust reprimanded the cheeky young director 17 times. Yeltsin recalls that, refusing to accept such a prejudiced attitude, on 31st December one year he gathered together these "conclusions on work done during the year", went into his office, bashed them on his desk and said: 'If you reprimand me once more next year, I'll kick up a fuss about it. You've been warned.' On 2nd January I was reprimanded over the fact that we didn't go to work on 1st January. 1st January was a public holiday, a day off, but

---

142   B.N. Yeltsin: Against the Grain. P. 43.

our manager still felt that we ought to have been at work. I decided to fight back against this reprimand, and went to all the appeals institutions. I had it annulled. And after that he was more cautious."[143]

M.I. Sytnikov attempted to get Yeltsin dragged before the courts for keeping inaccurate financial reports, and to remove him from office for assisting the party's city committee, but received no backing for this,[144] which attests to the manager's prejudiced view of his employee. The allegations he made were not upheld.

This 'undeclared war' continued, however. The press, which was 'independent' at the time, tried to intervene. The thirteenth construction directorate, which Yeltsin was in charge of, became the object of criticism from all sides. The leader in this regard was the newspaper *The Sverdlovsk constructor*.

The newspaper's columnist R. Mizin, in his report *Simply an apartment block*, made some acerbic comments regarding the construction of a show apartment block made by SD-13. Specifically, rebuking those in charge of construction for their inability to organize supplies of concrete and solution on time, wrote: "Directorate No. 13 has somehow managed to get through its entire life without having so much as a small concrete solution hub of its own. There is talk here all the time of late supplies and poor quality solution at the Nizhny-Isetsk plant. All the directorates, of course, are having to pay the price for this. The others, though, have built small hubs for themselves, and are able to take off solution as and when they need it — so that complaints don't matter. The civil engineers here, by contrast, even when starting construction of a huge block, did not bother to do a little bit of auxiliary management, which would have been such a help on another day…".[145] We shall avoid commenting on the author's tone and poisonous criticism of the directors at SD-13: suffice to say that the article had clearly be written at someone's orders.

Confirmation of the fact that the author's criticisms had clearly been forced out of him was the fact that before long the journalist's claims were refuted in convincing fashion by an impartial third party — the head of the planning department, I. Semukhin. An article published in the same newspaper reached the following conclusion: "A significant resource in terms of the future reduction in the value of construction would be the eradication of small, semi-home-made concrete and solution installations, the losses caused by which in 1961 amounted to 357,000 rubles."[146]

Criticism, naturally, does not make life easy. It is most irritating of all, however, when it is misplaced. Yeltsin foresaw the consequences of using

---

143   B.N. Yeltsin: Against the Grain. P. 41-42.

144   Same reference.

145   *Sverdlovsk construction worker*, 28th February 1962.

146   *Sverdlovsk construction worker*, 13th June 1962

home-made materials and insisted that order be restored in the centralized supplies of construction materials. As he saw it, increased productivity by the workforce was to be achieved not by making the workforce sweat but through the broad-based introduction of machinery — primarily new machinery. The facts themselves attest to this. The successful introduction of new technology was precisely the reason why Construction Directorate No. 13 was awarded the biggest trust premium — 300 rubles, and its boss (Yeltsin) was given a 50 ruble bonus.

The order regarding the trust dated 6th March 1962 read: "For the completion of measures to introduce new machinery in full-assembly and production line construction, and construction for show, as regards mastery of the built-up coating method, in the third quarter of 1962, an award is hereby given to: the head of construction directorate No. 13, comrade B.N. Yeltsin amounting to 75 roubles... His contribution to "achieving the best performance in terms of reducing work-related injury rates."[147]

These achievements by Yeltsin the manager by no means signified, though, that he had finally been crossed off the 'blacklist'. Soon, in another article entitled 'Negligence multiplied by disorder', yet another accusation was made against him. The authors of the article — V. Churakov, a senior engineer from Stroibank, and T. Akselrod, a senior inspector, literally thunder at the leadership of CD No.13: "The things we encountered when we inspected the work done by construction directorate No.13 (the director of which is comrade Yeltsin and the chief accountant is comrade Rabinovich), goes beyond any normal ideas about negligence and carelessness. The insertion of clauses into contracts, the frittering away of resources, and a careless approach to construction materials have become a method of working here, and huge losses have become part of a system, to which both the head of the directorate and his subordinates have become accustomed."

Allegations such as this can send shivers down one's spine — they create a whiff of criminality. But the accusations boiled down to the fact that there had been failings in the construction directorate regarding the documentation on decommissioned construction materials. "At one of the sites, 23 cubic meters of reinforced concrete went missing. It transpired that an unscrupulous foreman, whose job it had been to decommission them the year before, had simply forgotten to do so. Also discovered in the complex management by comrade Yeltsin were 185.2 cubic meters of wall panels, which had been used long, long ago to erect buildings Nos. 34 and 6, literally a stone's throw from the directorate...The long list of materials which were overdrawn included, for example, 458 kilograms of pigment and 610 kilograms of linseed oil. These were indeed nowhere to be found. These materials had been put towards

---

147   Urals Region center for B.N. Yeltsin (UCBNY). The personal matter of B.N. Yeltsin. F.1. Op.1. D. 12. L. 21.

resurfacing the floors and walls in a dormitory in the boarding school in building No. 12…".[148]

The list of "unacceptable practices" such as this is long, but on reading it one can't help wondering: why was such a fuss kicked up about it? No-one had stolen anything, and there were objective reasons for the losses. Admittedly, not everyone at the directorate had familiarized themselves with the records books, there was no disagreeing with that. The oversights in the bookkeeping provided an excuse for the directors to bring the boss of CD No. 13 before the courts.

Boris Nikolaevich recalled these judicial proceedings as follows: "The claimant on behalf of the trust was the chief accountant, and, accordingly, I was the respondent. There I was sitting on the bench in the district court, testifying that there was nothing underhand or criminal in all this. Fortunately, the intelligent judge was probably about forty or fifty years old. In his summing up, he said — and I quote: 'In the actions of any manager there may, or indeed must, be an element of risk. The important thing is that this element of risk should be justified.'" In this instance, the risk in Yeltsin's actions was indeed justified. The court therefore found in favor of Yeltsin and decided that all court costs were to be paid by the claimant, i.e. by the Yuzhgorstroi trust. "This came as a mighty blow to the

chief accountant, and to the manager; the court somehow inspired me with this decision, as well."[149]

One can't help thinking: if such a large-scale attack against the director of one of the construction directorates at a major industrial city had been sustained for such a long period, how could it incorporate all these "explanations", "exchange of testimony" etc., with the performance of their direct obligations?

He withstood all these attacks and blows in silence, on his own, biting his tongue in consternation. He never complained to his wife — why spoil her mood? But Naya understood what was going on in her husband's soul without him needing to say anything. The expression on his face, and his mood, said it all. At such times she would find the right thing to say, which would act as a soothing medicine. The mood of the head of the household improved, and the family treated the wounds he had sustained at work.

The staff at the construction directorate also gave their backing to their boss, and had faith in his plans and actions. Boris Nikolaevich gave more of himself to them than to his family. Often, during the night-shifts, he would drive out to the facilities, not just to keep an eye on what was going on but to boost morale and have heart-to-heart conversations with his staff. He recalled about

---

148   *Sverdlovsk construction worker*, 16th July 1962
149   B.N. Yeltsin: Against the Grain. P. 42.

such incidents: "...it doesn't seem like much — driving to see his women's team during the night-shift and chatting to them about this and that, and doing a few jobs — sticking up the wallpaper, painting the windows — but it improved my mood and that of the girls no end. And it helped with what we were doing, too — I found out some details, about problems which didn't seem particularly serious, but which, if the director wasn't aware of them, would have grown into huge, unsolvable ones. Mirrors for the women's staff quarters, badges to reward a job well done, and other gifts purchased for the professional unions — sometimes using his own money — all this created an entirely different kind of atmosphere between the boss and his employees."[150]

He was well aware of his staff's needs, but unfortunately was not able to help them in every regard — far from it. There was not enough housing, and it was extremely difficult to secure places in kindergartens (as it still is today, incidentally). Some people were unable to go on holiday because it was impossible to get hold of rail tickets during the holiday season; others didn't have the time to stand in a long queue at the furniture store, and so on. What could the boss of the construction directorate do about that, besides express his sympathy? As for the fact that payment of salaries was occasionally delayed, he admitted he was to blame — he had not gone to the bank manager (the bank often suffered from a shortage of currency) ahead of time, to persuad him to make the payments.

Yeltsin's style of management, moreover, which took shape in those years, could certainly not be described as 'softly-softly'. He was the first to admit this. "People said my style of management was rough. And that was true. I demanded strict discipline of my staff and expected them to stick to their word...A job done professionally and to a high standard would not go unrewarded, and by the same token failures and sloppy work would not go unpunished. If you had given your word, then you ought to stick to it — and if you didn't, then you must answer to people."[151] This is Yeltsin all over, with his desire to get the best out of people and demands that his staff submit to his orders.

His respect for others and the stern demands he placed on them were not mutually exclusive methods of management, and the sensible combination of them would inevitably lead to success. Documentary evidence of this is provided in the shape of a character reference signed on 16th August 1963 by the boss of the Sverdlovsk city construction directorate, V. Bushkov: "In his time as head of the construction directorate, comrade B.N. Yeltsin showed himself in a positive light, and adopted an honest and conscientious approach to his work. The directorate under his control went from being behind all

---

150   B.N. Yeltsin: Against the Grain. P. 46.
151   B.N. Yeltsin: Against the Grain. P. 45.

the others to being one of the leaders. In 1962 this directorate executed the plan under the general contract at 105.5%, and through its own efforts — at 106%. In the first six months of 1963 the plan under the general contract was executed at 136%, and through its own efforts — at 112%, and labor efficiency stood at 103.4%.

Comrade Yeltsin has been playing an active part in life in the community, and is a deputy in the Chkalovsky district council. A man of great personal discipline, who is exacting with regard to himself and his subordinates, restrained on the ideological front, and with a resilient spirit, he enjoys considerable authority among the workforce."[152] And readers should not be troubled by this series of set phrases in the language of officialdom — this was the standard language of the day. Moreover, the wording chosen in this particular description of Yeltsin was in accordance with the truth.

The question arises as to why this description was signed not by Boris Nikolaevich's direct supervisor but by his supervisor? The reason is simple: M.I. Sytnikov was still striving to rid himself of this overly wilful employee, by fair means or foul. The then secretary of the party committee at the construction trust, A.I. Vinogradov, recalled: "I often had to intervene in their arguments. The question of whether or not Yeltsin should be sacked came up on several occasions. We, the members of the party committee, were against the idea. We thought of him as a young man with great potential. It had become such a big issue that complaints were made against me in the party's regional committee. The committee decided that I was right, however, and that put an end to it."[153]

An opportunity to separate the two opposing managers presented itself in August 1963, when Yeltsin was relieved of his duties as head of CD No. 13 due to his appointment as chief engineer of the Sverdlovsk housing construction combine. And this company, with its workforce of many thousands, was in the same league as the biggest construction trusts.

The housing construction combine

Boris Nikolaevich interpreted this transition to a 'new stage' of his career not as some sort of reward but as a challenge. He knew that the current director of the HCC trust had reached retirement age, and a replacement needed to be found. Yeltsin, who was 31 at the time, looked set to become his natural successor in the near future.

---

152   Urals Region center for B.N. Yeltsin (UCBNY). The personal matter of B.N. Yeltsin. F.1. Op.1. D. 12. L. 15.
153   From the film *Boris Yeltsin. The making of a leader.*

It was thought, at Glavsreduralstroi and Sverdlovskgorstroi, that Yeltsin would be ideally suited for the role of being a director at one of the biggest construction organizations in the region's center. The bosses of Glavsreduralstroi, who were extremely experienced people, knew that he would have learned his lessons after all those reprimands. Yeltsin was independent, highly qualified and successful. He had been through the school of Soviet management and mastered its methods in full. He had been 'knocked in', and in Russia, someone like that is worth their weight in gold.

The combine performed an entire range of house building services, from preparing assembled reinforced concrete parts at the reinforced concrete plant, to the construction, finishing and commissioning of housing. Its workforce included, in addition to the plant, 4 construction directorates (including CD-13), and of these, one specialized in installing boxes of residential housing. The structure itself was organized in 1962 and was considered young and not yet fully-formed. The HCC was supposed to become the new face of the construction sector, however. The housing construction combine was supposed to introduce industrial technologies into the construction sector, thereby significantly accelerating residential construction in Sverdlovsk.

In his new role, Boris Nikolaevich Yeltsin subjected himself to his previous working regime — "from dusk to dawn", without giving up his night-time "excursions" around the construction sites. He once again stayed true to the principle of "see everything, know about everything".

The former editor of *The Sverdlovsk construction worker*, V.F. Dvoryanov, described the following episode: "I had occasion to meet him face-to-face for the first time when he was already chief engineer at the housing construction combine. I was working as a reporter at the time, and it was my job to interview him. I was tasked with telling our readers about how the housing combine, set up fairly recently at the large-panel housing construction trust and the plant for reinforced concrete goods was enhancing the quality of construction, and how there was a war being waged against malfunctions, mismanagement and the need for corrections.

After calling Boris Nikolaevich in advance, I agreed to hold a meeting with him, which he decided would take place at 7 am. I remember being surprised at the time that a director began his day so early. Later on, though, when I got to know this larger-than-life, original man better, I realised that this was simply his *modus operandi*."[154]

Let us put to one side the reporter's personal impressions from this meeting; instead let us merely quote what B.N. Yeltsin said to him during the course of their conversation: "If you dig a little deeper, there is one particular

---

154   V.F. Dvoryanov: Landmarks of fate. Yekaterinburg. 2006. P. 196.

circumstance that cannot fail to be mentioned. We have the concept of straightforward solutions drilled into us — and in my view this concept is damaging. It tells us that the brigadier is always right — and so on down the pecking order. It is as if every aspect of our citizens' lives has been provided for, he has no need to think about his own fate, he has been made to fit into a system of simple solutions. We have unlearned the habit of thinking with our own minds…".[155] Let's face it, expressing such 'seditious' ideas at the time — to a representative of the media, no less — was something that by no means every director was able to do. Yeltsin was, however. Evidently, "thinking with his own mind" was a distinctive characteristic of Boris Nikolaevich. His work and position demanded as much of him on a daily basis. If the opposite was true, what sort of director would he have been? And who could have filled his shoes when it came to solving a whole host of diverse problems?

Another person who had an interesting conversation with Yeltsin, in 1964, was O.V. Minyukhin, a professor at UPI and expert on the economics of construction. Minyukhin, who went on to become an important engineer and developer, recalled that he and Y.P. Rozhkov, an economist in the field of construction who had once taught Yeltsin, were once invited by the chief engineer of the recently created HCC, Yeltsin, to conduct an analysis of the housing construction combine's losses as a result of poorly built assembled structures at the plant. The investigation came to an end in 1965. Yeltsin studied the academic report in person. (The meeting between the client and the executives had taken place, incidentally, in the HCC building, in 11 pm).

The proposals made by the academics were implemented in the HCC's work.[156]

The state of affairs at the HCC, meanwhile, was complicated. In 1963 the city had expected to get 104,000 square meters of housing from the HCC, but in 10 months only 40,000 square meters had been commissioned. A bit of basic math tells us that the remaining 60,000 meters had to be done in the two remaining winter months. It was practically a case of mission impossible. But can a plan be implemented at any price? "Doing a slap-dash job won't be good enough," Yeltsin said. "Is it really acceptable if 30% of the housing commissioned by the housing directorates is assessed as 'good' and not a single project is assessed as 'outstanding'?[157]

In 1964 the chief engineer introduced measures to improve the quality of major residential housing projects. Under these plans, brigades who focused on the end product were set up, and advanced methods of installation were introduced. That year, 70% of the apartment blocks commissioned by the

---

155   Same reference. P. 196.
156   From the archive of the Urals Center for B.N. Yeltsin.
157   *Sverdlovsk construction worker*, 18th January 1964

workforce were assessed as 'good', whilst CD-13, where Yeltsin had learned his trade, achieved 90%.[158]

1965 brought another upward step in the administrative and management career of Boris Nikoalevich Yeltsin. He was appointed head of the housing construction combine (HCC). And here, in this new setting, he began actively struggling for new, advanced methods of organizing management and labor to be implemented. A large article on this subject printed using the civil engineers' printing press, and signed by B. Yeltsin, Y. Kopylov, the chief engineer, V. Imshenetsky, the chief technical expert and M. Kuznetsov, the head of the department of labor and salaries, had a powerful effect. The methods of scientific organization of labor (SOL) proposed by the authors enabled an increase in 1965 in the number of apartment blocks constructed from 4.6 blocks a month to 7 a month (based on blocks with 60 apartments). As a result, 120,000 square meters of housing was commissioned, of which more than 80% was assessed as 'good'. Revenue went up by 23.7%.[159]

In his new position, with more powers at his disposal and more opportunities open to him, Yeltsin flourished. The annual results for 1965 were remarkable: under the state plan, the combine was to commission 120 square meters of housing, but it completed substantially more — 132,500! Rather than resting on his laurels, however, Yeltsin wrote an article entitled *A good result but a hard lesson*. "We did not manage to achieve any rhythm in our work this year," he wrote, "particularly as regards the housing that we built, as we did in previous years." Here are the figures. The year 1966 begins. In the first two months we failed to complete a single apartment block. In March, no fewer than 12 apartment blocks were completed before the quarter ended. Now for the second quarter. In April we completed 5 apartment blocks, but in May — none at all. In June, at the end of the quarter, we completed 9 apartment blocks. And things went on like that...This is no way to work, of course. It doesn't create the right conditions for work, either. When faced with this sort of rush work, the workers are under a colossal amount of strain, which cannot continue for long..."[160]

Changes to the rhythm of work during the construction of residential housing would become Yeltsin's personal goal the following year. And, unaccustomed to backing down, he would achieve this goal. In November 1967, he reported, again in *The Sverdlovsk construction worker*: "By the October public holiday[161] we had completed 80% of the housing out of the total area set aside for residential housing which had to be built during the course of the year. In

---

158   Same reference. 11th January 1965
159   *Sverdlovsk construction worker*, 16th April 1966
160   *Sverdlovsk construction worker*, 11th January 1967
161   The October public holiday was the main state public holiday in the USSR; it marked the October Revolution in 1917 and was held on 7-8 November.

10 months the people of Sverdlovsk obtained almost 109,000 square meters of housing. This is all the more pleasing given that in the one-and-a-half months that remained we would not be required, as we had been in previous years, to carry out rush projects in order to fulfil the state plan. What helped us to achieve this success was the fact that we managed to keep up the tempo we had adopted at the start of the year. Seven apartment blocks a month — we kept that rhythm going throughout that entire time. And on the last few days before the celebrations marking the 50th anniversary of October, we constructed a 60-apartment building in five days.

Yeltsin had managed to streamline the work of the HCC dramatically — within the combine's structure there was now a special department responsible for the first stage of construction. This initial stage, which had previously been a weak point, had now been sorted out. Architects were brought into the HCC who were able to liven up the standardized buildings, and the work done by the Moscow HCC No.1 was studied carefully, and various methods of organizing production were introduced in Sverdlovsk.

Meanwhile the director of the HCC built a leisure center for his staff at Beloyark, a sports club at one of the halls of residence, three children's combines and a health center.[162]

The Sverdlovsk HCC, led by Yeltsin, became the leader in mass residential construction not only in the region but also in the country. At the start of 1966, as always happened after the latest five-year plan had come to an end, the time came to reward those who had excelled, and the bureau of the party's regional committee proposed Yeltsin for the award of the Order of Lenin — the highest state award in the USSR. The regional committee backed this proposal.

But then something unforeseen occurred. During the 23rd party congress, on the night of 30th March 1966, a five-storey large-panel apartment building which was nearing completion, and which had been built by the HCC, where B. Yeltsin was the director, came crashing to the ground during the night. A special commission later found that this was due to a lack of quality in the way the foundations were put in. This work had been done not by the HCC but by a subcontractor. They had prepared the concrete in winter, the solution had not set, and in the spring it had started to move, together with the entrance hall of the as-yet unfinished building. Fortunately no-one was killed or injured. Nor could the blame be laid directly on the director of the HCC. He was asked to step up supervision of the work done by subcontractors.[163]

---

162   Y.V. Kopylov (memoirs). In V. Lipatnikov's book, B. Yeltsin and the DSK. Yekaterinburg, 2007

163   Y.P. Ryabov: My 20th century. M., 2000. P. 33.

Yeltsin's name remained on the list of nominees for awards. Rather than the medal for the order of Lenin, however, he was to receive the 'Badge of Honor' — the lowest in the hierarchy of Soviet medals.

In 1968 the HCC began the transition to the 'B' series, which the State Construction Department of the USSR had not declared suitable for construction work in cities until the mid-'70s. Yeltsin set the task of completing the transition to this system in 1969. And, in addition to the production of the former type of reinforced concrete goods, the forming equipment at the reinforced concrete plant began to be replaced.

France through the eyes of Yeltsin the civil engineer

The almost unthinkable happened. In May 1966 Yeltsin was sent off to France. The firm Construction consortium Paris-2 had invited a group of Soviet civil engineers to pay them a visit. The head of the Sverdlovsk HCC, Boris Nikolaevich Yeltsin, was among those invited.

When he returned home after this trip, Yeltsin reported, in an article in *The Sverdlovsk construction worker*: "Our days were absolutely jam-packed. We would go to bed at three am, then at seven they served us breakfast and the excursions began. The itinerary had been drawn up in advance and included a familiarization visit with Paris, its culture and architecture and, of course, first and foremost, with the Consortium. Our attempts to gain an in-depth insight into the construction methods used, the everyday lives of the workers and the work of other construction firms were not met with any enthusiasm on the part of our hosts, who were polite but not very forthcoming."

Yeltsin continued his article, though, in the capacity of an organizer of construction, an engineer who had studied the methods used by his French counterparts with respect and interest. "Work is conducted on each bit of infrastructure by approximately 20 firms with narrow specializations, who have signed agreements with the contractor firm, which does not carry out any work in its own right. Projects are always completed on time. A significant contributing factor to this is the system of penalties. If work is completed a day after the deadline, the subcontractor receives 10 percent less than the contract price. If the work is two days late there is a 30 percent deduction. The same procedure is used in the provision of materials to subcontractor companies.

These are ordered by the companies themselves (the general contractor plays no part in this) and the suppliers are penalized mercilessly for the slightest delay...The construction team's labor is paid for on time and, it goes without saying, the quota must be fulfilled.

The workers receive a monthly bonus which is in effect a component part of their salary...the construction teams' labor is mechanized effectively. We particularly liked the mechanization of the finishing work and surveying works. The mechanisms used are in exemplary condition and are even color-coded using special 'construction' colors: yellow and red.

Finishing work is never done manually. Both the paint and the plaster are applied to the surface using special pneumatic mechanisms. Interestingly, special mechanisms are used for each type of surveying work. There is one mechanism for digging cable tracks, another for filling them in, a third for digging trenches and so on." The director of the biggest housing construction combine in the Middle Urals was fascinated by such exotic phenomena.

Boris Nikolaevich "managed for a short while to get away from our hospitable hosts and get to know the directors of the famous Camus firm, which was constructed large-panel residential housing in France and six other countries." Yeltsin wrote: "in the new-build areas the firm sets up housing construction combines, which manufacture all the concrete goods required for housing construction"; "at the construction sites there is hardly any plastering work done on products at all — they all arrive almost completely prepared for use;" by contrast with our practices, the French do not take the earth that has been dug up away from the construction site but use it to create an artificial landscape; construction workers in France are not required to wear any special protective clothing.

What else was he surprised by? "The French installation workers, who always have the materials they need to hand, can erect a storey in 5-7 days, and whole apartment blocks are constructed in three to eight months, and the directors of the firms are quite happy with this kind of time-frame."

In Sverdlovsk construction work was conducted more quickly by that time. It was unthinkable that commissioning of an apartment block might be delayed artificially, because every apartment block and every apartment had to be completed in accordance with timetables maintained by professional committees and local committees, and approved by the party committee and the administration. Yeltsin draws the following conclusion: "here we can see the essence of a capitalist company, which depends entirely on demand, market prices and so on."[164]

He told the combine's workforce about what he had seen and learnt. The people envied him for having been able to take a look at the 'wild West'. They found it hard to believe the stories he told them: "When you walk up to the front door of the building, it opens of its own accord to let you through.

---

164   *Sverdlovsk construction worker*, 11th and 15th June 1966

You walk into the building and the door closes automatically behind you. The photocells are even equipped with water dispensers. We tried to find the taps but there was no sign of them — it turned out all you had to do was put your hand under the pipe and the water would come gushing out of its own accord...The apartments at Paris-2 are magnificent, too — two-bedroom, three-bedroom and six-bedroom apartments, with floor space of between 49 and 220 square meters. The walls of the bedrooms have fabrics draped over them, and the apartment is comfortably furnished, with tastefully selected furniture, so that the owners can enjoy all these creature comforts the first time they open the door."

This sounded like pure fantasy! "Who is this all for though, you might ask?" Yeltsin asked, raising a finger. "Can ordinary French workers move in at Paris-2, in this kingdom of comfort? We asked how much the new apartments cost. A three-bedroom apartment, albeit in instalments paid over twenty years, costs 35,000 rubles in our money, and a six-bedroom one costs 65,000. It was clear that this paradise was not intended for the typical Parisian, who would have to stay in his overcrowded district."[165]

For a Soviet director, it was a matter of honor to have some social infrastructure for one's company. It was common to have a house of culture, leisure center and pioneer camp of one's own. The fact that the contents of this estate affected the value of products did not seen as a serious issue. And what was even harder to understand was that the capitalists, who were capable of building quickly and well, took their time over completing the apartment blocks. They were capable of completing construction in a couple of months but would drag it out for seven months, until some buyers were found.

Naturally, in the Soviet Union as a whole, and in Sverdlovsk in particular, where people would wait to receive free apartments from the state, it was hard to imagine apartment blocks standing empty like that.

In the space of ten years Yeltsin had completed the journey from being a young specialist to becoming the director of an extremely big and forward-thinking construction company. He had become a hardened man of the system; much was expected of him, and for his part he demanded a great deal from his subordinates. He worked very hard and demanded the same of other people. He knew why he was building homes for people. He wanted them to be built quickly and well, and for his workers to earn money and be able to enjoy good living standards.

He was a man of ideas who would go on to become a man of action.

---

165   *Sverdlovsk construction worker*, 11th June 1966

Chapter 3
The Sverdlovsk regional committee

In April 1968 Yeltsin was invited to have a chat with the first secretary of the Sverdlovsk region party committee, Yakov Petrovich Ryabov. Y.P. Ryabov made Yeltsin the following offer: "Boris Nikolaevich, you and I have known one another for some time now. I don't mind telling you that the regional committee has studied your candidacy from every possible angle. You are an exemplary director, you have organized your workforce well, and your performance in terms of output has been outstanding. In community life you have shown the positive side of your character, and you are a member of the party's city committee and a deputy on the city Council. We held a consultation and decided to offer you the opportunity to take part in the work of the party, on a professional basis. The position we are offering is head of the department of construction in the Sverdlovsk regional committee of the CPSU."

Yeltsin wrote in his memoirs that this offer did not come as a very great surprise — "I was engaged in work in the community constantly. But I accepted the offer without much enthusiasm. I had done well during my time as director of the combine: the workforce always fulfilled the plan. I had enjoyed my work on the whole, and my salary was pretty good...And yet in the end I agreed to it. I wanted to try something new."[166]

There are two points to make here: heads of department in the party's regional committee earned significantly less than the director of the HCC. Research has shown that in the '60s and '70s a number of employees in the party administration (instructors and heads of department) were paid salaries that were comparable to workers' average monthly salary, or were even lower. This meant that a wide circle of potential candidates for roles within the party administration were far less attracted to roles in the party administration from a material point of view.[167]

---

166   B.N. Yeltsin: Against the Grain. P. 46.
167   P.Y. Kuznetsova: The evolution of the regional administration of the CPSU as a social group. (1965–1985). 22.00.04

That was how things stood. First of all, though, the offer was one that was hard to refuse. He was a member of the *nomenklatura*. If he rejected the offer it might lead to serious problems, punishment by the party and removal from his job, all the more so given his desire not to have anything else held against him — he had been rebuked enough times already. Secondly, a job in the regional committee would entail a fair amount of prestige. In addition to the modest salary and bonuses — unpaid leave amounting to a month's salary — he would also have the opportunity to climb the career ladder. Yeltsin was competitive and ambitious by nature; he was also focused on his goals and had a huge capacity for work. And for working for the good of other people. This had also become part of his character. This was in line with the objectives the party had declared, incidentally.

And in terms of his lifestyle, the move to the regional committee would allow him to get a slightly bigger apartment, and the family was growing bigger.

A character reference on Yeltsin as a director, for the transition to a new place of work, was signed by the secretary of the Sverdlovsk regional committee of the CPSU, F.M. Morshchakov, who knew Yeltsin well, held his practical qualities in high esteem and had helped him out on several occasions when he was in difficulties. The character reference tells us that Yeltsin "...has shown himself to be an able and proficient engineer, and a good organizer of production processes. The workforce at the housing combine managed by comrade B.N. Yeltsin operates effectively, fulfilling the plans for residential construction in the city time and time again...Comrade B.N. Yeltsin has made a sizeable personal contribution to the technical mastering of large-panel housing construction. At his instigation and with his direct involvement, a progressive technology of production-line construction of large-panel housing was devised and introduced, ensuring that infrastructure is completed on time; the working conditions have been improved significantly and there have been savings with regard to material resources...

Comrade Yeltsin has been actively involved in the community life of the workforce, was elected a member of the combine's party committee, and speaks to the workers, engineers and technical staff regularly on political matters and issues related to production...Comrade Yeltsin is a member of the Sverdlovsk city committee of the CPSU, and a deputy in the city council."[168]

Thus, at the age of thirty-seven, Yeltsin's life changed dramatically. He had to give up his career in management for a career in the party, one which would later take him to the very top of the tree — head of the Russian state.

The workers at the housing combine were far from thrilled when they heard the news of his promotion. They were sorry to part company with him. At a farewell dinner with the directorate's staff, Boris Nikolaevich looked at those

---

168   CDPASR. F. 161. Op. 41. D. 145. L. 11-12.

present and said: "I thought you would all be glad to see the back of me, yet you have all spoken so warmly..."[169] Indeed, those present meant what they said that evening — this is clear from the memoirs of Yeltsin's colleagues in the 2000s. What memories of him did they take away?

Some of the company's veterans shared these memories.

Svetlana Andreevna Zinovieva, who had worked in the administration of the HCC since the day it was founded, said: "Let me put it like this: we worshipped Boris Nikolaevich. He was unlike all the other directors — in a good way. He was tall and handsome, and, most importantly of all, very well-read when it came to matters of construction. He found it impossible to give up on anything or put it to one side. Yes, people were afraid of him, but they respected him for his sense of justice and attentiveness toward people. He knew all the names and faces of the members of the construction brigades. He demanded discipline from everyone, and forced everyone to put everything into what they did; and he worked hard himself, in a selfless way...If he spotted some spilt concrete or broken glass at the construction site there would be no mercy — the foreman would have part of his wages deducted. And Boris Nikolaevich knew how to thank people properly for the work they had done, as well. Not just out of the HCC's budget, incidentally, but sometimes out of his own pocket. He would always keep his word: if he had promised to give a construction brigade an apartment, he meant it — the apartment would be handed over at the end of the quarter."[170]

Valery Semenovich Nudel, an Honored Architect of Russia, and laureate of the Council of Ministers of the USSR, said: "I met him in 1964: Boris Nikolaevich was the chief engineer at the combine, and I was a workshop director at the reinforced concrete plant, which was part of the HCC. He would often visit the plant and walk around the workshops, and rather than asking questions he would set challenges; but he always asked: "What do you need in order to get the job done?" And if he promised something, he would always keep his word...In 1967 I was appointed chief engineer at the plant, and Yeltsin was the director of the HCC by then, so we began to meet regularly to discuss issues related to output...

At least twice a week there would be meetings in his office to discuss issues at the plant. Occasionally we would sit there until 10 or 11 at night. We would discuss all the subtleties of the technical refurbishment of the plant's manufacturing facilities. To be honest, these issues fell under the remit of the chief engineer in terms of their status and level of importance, but Yeltsin wanted to be kept abreast of all the key issues, and that was what differentiated him from the others — he wanted to get to the bottom of everything... Here's

169   V. Lipatnikov's book, B. Yeltsin and the DSK. Yekaterinburg. 2007. P. 27.

170   Same reference. P. 26.

another example. A miniature district had taken shape around the plant — the Komsomol district — and our club was a wooden building, no more than a hut. We tried to persuade the authorities to improve it but there was nothing doing. Boris Nikolaevich took the decision: a club with room for 320 people must be built, using funds set aside for major repairs. It was a clear breach of the rules, but he assumed all responsibility for it."[171]

Galina Dmitrievna Chernushkina, the former head of the department of labor and salaries at the HCC, said: "Boris Nikolaevich took personal charge of staff recruitment. His piercing, attentive gaze made a lasting impression on me, as did his questions: where had I worked, when had I graduated and what did I study, where did I live? I sensed at once how stern this new director was, and how demanding he was going to be...He chatted to everyone, sought to recruit people who were highly educated, and sent people skilled in practical work to do some training. There was great prestige about getting a job at the HCC...to tell the truth, some of the specialists, on hearing that he was planning to visit their facility, would hide from him. They knew they would be caught red-handed: the previous week they had promised to finish decorating an entrance-hall, for example, but hadn't done so, and Yeltsin would remember..."[172]

Anatoly Aleksandrovich Volynsky, a veteran of the HCC and a merited architect of Russia, recalls: "It was no accident that the HCC became a serious training ground for workers engaged in construction and industrial manufacturing. Just like Boris Nikolaevich, many engineers and technical workers had successfully managed to climb the career ladder. Former chief engineer Y.V. Kopylov became the chief engineer of the association Soyuzstroikonstruktsiya, and N.L. Bievets took charge of the main directorate for the construction industry within the Ministry of heavy construction of the USSR. V.S. Nudel was the deputy director general of 'High-dispersal metallic powders' and A.A. Kopachev was in charge of the general contractor directorate of Uksstroi. USTU-UPI educated the young replacement for the head of the Technology of construction manufacturing faculty, G.S. Pekar, and the faculty's professor, V.B. Yezhov. I could go on..."[173]

As regards Yeltsin's qualities as a man, Volynsky observed that he "worked hard on self-improvement, not only on the professional front, I noticed, but also as regards culture. In my opinion his incredible capacity for work was achieved at the cost of sleepless nights. It was clear even at that stage that this focused young man would go far." He commented, as did many others, on Yeltsin's phenomenal memory: "...even at that stage there were rumors

---

171   V. Lipatnikov's book, B. Yeltsin and the DSK. P. 31-32.
172   V. Lipatnikov's book, B. Yeltsin and the DSK. P. 63.
173   Same reference. P. 51.

circulating about it," — he was excellent at remembering names and numbers. He could remember the details of any report, no matter how many financial statistics it contained."[174]

Sergei Ivanovich Peretrutov, the former director of CD No.13, who succeeded Yeltsin in the role: "Boris Nikolaevich was precise in what he did: he was never late to meetings and did not tolerate tardiness on the part of others. I remember that the head accountant of the combine once went into his office and said: "Boris Nikolaevich, can I borrow the car to go to the bank?" But Yeltsin wanted to drive to a meeting somewhere. He pulled his wallet out of his pocket and gave some money to the chief accountant: "Take a taxi."[175]

A phase in Yeltsin's career had come to an end.

This architect of housing was now set to become the architect of a region.

Head of department at the regional committee

On 12th April 1968 Boris Nikolaevich Yeltsin walked into the building of the party's regional committee as director of the Housing construction combine, but came out of it as head of the department of construction in the regional committee of the CPSU.

B.N. Yeltsin owed the start of his career in the party to the party leader in the region — Yakov Petrovich Ryabov.

Y.P. Ryabov was the second secretary of the regional committee — another new man in the administration of the regional committee. He was without question a remarkable individual. Three years Yeltsin's senior and of low birth[176], he had begun work in 1942, when he was just a boy, as a turner, miller and driller at Uralmash, the main plant for the manufacturing of the famous T-34 tanks.

This young lad had achieved the feat of procuring an education in 'Planning, manufacturing and testing of diesel tank engines' by attending evening classes.

---

174   V. Lipatnikov's book, B. Yeltsin and the DSK. P. 17-18.

175   Same reference. P. 42.

176   I surmise that the Ryabov family, just like the Yeltsin family, were badly treated during the years of collectivization. There is some indirect evidence of this in the discrepancy in the data available about his place of birth — some reports state that he was born on 24.03.1928 in the village of Shishkovo in the Ruzaevsky district of the Mordavian ASSR, whilst others claim he was born in the village of Salkovo in the Pervomaiskoe district of the Yaroslavl Region. The fact that his parents were at a construction site in Uralmash in the '30s also bears a resemblance to the Yeltsins' time at Berezniki.

After graduating from technical school after the war, he was transferred in 1946 to factory No.76, and later to the Urals turbine engine factory, a concern with extremely advanced technology at the time. There he worked in the construction office and attended evening classes at the Urals Polytechnical Institute, from which he graduated in 1952, and later worked as a head of department at the special construction bureau, deputy director of a workshop and manager of a workshop.

Ryabov's career in the party began after that, and his most important achievements were his qualities as a specialist in production and an organizer. For the Sverdlovsk Region, which was filled to bursting with industries, mainly defence companies, this was an essential move. His career path was as follows: secretary of the plant's party committee (from 1958 onwards), 1st secretary of the district committee, 1st secretary of the Sverdlovsk city committee of the CPSU, and from 1966 onwards 2nd secretary of the Sverdlovsk regional committee of the CPSU. In 1971 he replaced Konstantin Kuzmich Nikolaev, a veteran of the party apparatus, who had been in charge of the defence department of the Sverdlovsk regional committee during the war, and who after the war had chaired the regional executive committee, in the role of first secretary of the regional committee of the CPSU.

Ryabov had been a master of sport and regional champion in wrestling in the past. This was another area of common ground with Yeltsin. Having served in the war and gone through the harsh school of the party apparatus, Y.P. Ryabov was known for his tough character and unrestrained use of language.

Later, when asked by a reporter why he had proposed Yeltsin for a role in the party, Yakov Petrovich said: "He was like me in some ways. Energetic, obstinate. I met him in 1963. He was head of the construction directorate, and built purification facilities for manufacturing industries and the city. He worked effectively and tirelessly. We proposed him as chief engineer of the housing construction combine, and eighteen months later as a director at the HCC. ...When I was elected as second secretary of the regional committee, I sensed that I wasn't drawn to being a head of department: my age and ill health were both making themselves felt. I invited Boris to do the job."[177]

Yakov Petrovich recalls that he had to hold off a fair few "attacks" from his friends and acquaintances. "They started telling me about his love of power, ambition, desire to acquire power by any means...In response I said to them: 'Thank you for telling me this; so he wants to make a name for himself and get ahead — this is news to me though. How do you rate him in terms of doing his job, though?' They would stop to think this over. Then they would say: 'There are no concerns on that score — he'll do whatever it takes to fulfil his bosses' orders.'

177

'In that case I'll take him under my wing; I've got enough knowledge and experience, strength and willpower to make him work in the right way. If I notice him getting ideas above his station, I'll put him in his place…'."[178]

Yeltsin was to benefit from his time under the tutelage of Ryabov, who made great demands of his subordinates. Ryabov, the first secretary of the Sverdlovsk regional committee, knew how to get others working and did a huge amount of work himself.

In the space of seven years, B.N. Yeltsin became the party director of construction for the whole of the Sverdlovsk Region. The daring approach he brought to construction spread throughout both the capital of the Mid Urals and the region. He later wrote with pride, in an article in the newspaper *The Urals worker*: "In Sverdlovsk (and not only in Sverdlovsk) there are new buildings of which the citizens are proud. The Cosmos cinema, the Urals Palace of culture, the House of political enlightenment, the Palace of culture in Pervouralsk, the Palace of culture of construction workers in Nizhny Tagil…Contemporary in their style and defined by their painstaking design and beautiful finish, they will please everyone and attest to the high level of professional mastery among construction workers in the Urals."[179]

But Yeltsin also had to deal fairly often with problems related to poor quality construction and failures to fulfil plans in relation to industrial construction — in a word, he was the party's foreman. As Y.P. Ryabov admitted, Boris Nikolaevich "might at any time report back on the state of affairs at one construction site or another, and when he did so he would go into a lot of detail and quote the figures."[180]

At 37, Yeltsin was the youngest member of the regional committee's team of directors. The age gap did not make itself felt, however — only one of the heads of department had turned fifty, and the others were 45 or younger.

It was an administration like any other. There were cliques within it, friendships and feelings of antipathy, disagreements and rivalries. That was how it was, and it will remain that way.

The same thing had been seen in the Sverdlovsk regional committee. Influential figures were the forty-year-old head of the organizational department, Boris Markovich Markushkin, and Konstantin Alekseevich Sotnikov, the head of the general department, a veteran of the administration and a man who had worked for the regional committee for twenty-three years. These two

---

178   Y.P. Ryabov: My 20th century. P. 35.
179   *The Urals Worker*, 11th June 1971.
180   From a conversation between G.M. Kayeta and Y.P. Ryabov.

departments had a special place within the regional committee's structure: they organized the work it did, kept registers of the *nomenklatura* and all related problems, prepared drafts of documents and were responsible for issuing numerous decisions made by the regional committee.

From 1959 onwards the department of engineering industry was led by Vyacheslav Yakovlevich Baev, defence man and erudite, who was nicknamed the 'walking encyclopedia'.

Yeltsin befriended the head of the department of science and academic institutions, Aleksei Afanasievich Dobryden. They had graduated from UPI at the same time, albeit from different faculties. The engineer and metallurgist Dobryden, after graduating, switched to science and became a candidate of technical sciences, and professor in the faculty of the theory of metallurgical processes. Like Boris Nikolaevich, Aleksei Afanasievich joined the regional committee without a single day's experience of working for the party. He showed signs of erudition and unfeigned intellect. Conversing with this man was always interesting and insightful.

The regional committee's heads of department formed a kind of 'clan'. The whole of the party apparatus was unofficially divided up into four categories: secretaries, heads of department and their deputies, heads of sector and instuctors, and service staff. This same system was repeated even in the canteen, which had three lunch rooms, one of which was for the instructors, service staff and guests, who were not allowed into the other two. On Fridays the lower-ranking staff were given their 'rations' in the canteen, and the higher-ranking ones had food delivered to their homes. The secretaries rented dachas for their families on Lake Balty, and heads of department were given rooms in the village of Maly Istok. The two groups traditionally celebrated public holidays and birthdays among their own close circle.[181]

The first secretaries of the party's regional committee, Y.P. Ryabov and B.N. Yeltsin, developed a good working relationship. Yeltsin was probably impressed by Ryabov's businesslike approach, assertiveness and love of innovations.

An important event for Yeltsin which took place in 1971, when Ryabov was appointed first secretary of the regional committee, was the planning for an assembly of the State committee for civil construction under the State Construction Department of the USSR and the State Construction Department of the RSFSR. At this assembly the new general plan for

---

181   From a conversation between G.M. Kayota and F.M. Blokhin, the former deputy head of department of organizational and party work in the Sverdlovsk regional committee of the CPSU.

Sverdlovsk was reviewed and approved. It did not allow the satellite towns to merge with the regional center in the future, thereby transforming it into a "sprawling city, of the kind which usually cause no end of problems for residents." New industrial firms were to be built 60-100 km from Sverdlovsk. Taking into account future problems with transport, the plan stipulated that expressways would be built, which would circumvent the densely populated parts of the city, and the construction of an underground metro system along two axes: north to south, and south-west to north-east. The south-western section of the regional capital was to be the site of "the biggest scientific center and university complex in the country.

According to the developers' calculations, by 2000 the population of Sverdlovsk should reach 1,350,000, and in order to house these people 11 million square meters of housing will be required, 5.7 million of which will be built in the old part of the city. Half of all the new buildings will be nine-storey apartments, 10 percent will have between 12 and 16 storeys and 40 percent will have 5 storeys. The five-storey apartment blocks will look markedly different from the ones built in the '60s. They have a very attractive architectural design, and feature rubbish chutes, convenient interior layouts of the apartments, spacious kitchens and bathrooms, cupboards and built-in wardrobes."[182]

In order to make this plan a reality, not only would Ryabov and Yeltsin need to do a serious amount of work, but so would the rest of their team, and some parts of it remain pure fantasy to this day. At the time, however, those who had initiated the plan believed that these ideas could be turned into a reality and that they were capable of making that happen.

As the years went on there was a sense that Boris Nikolaevich had got stuck in a rut, and that there was nowhere left for him to go within the regional committee apparatus. As Y.P. Ryabov recalled, "the first secretary of the Kostroma regional committee, Y.N. Kostromin, invited Yeltsin to accept the role of secretary. Yeltsin canvassed my opinion. I said to him: "If you want to do it, go and do it — but what makes you want to leave a regional committee like ours, you've got good career prospects here as well." A second offer was made by I.T. Novikov, the chairman of the State Construction Department — to take up a role as his deputy. I said: "Look, it's your decision, but I've got big plans for you."[183]

In January 1971 Konstantin Kuzmich Nikolaev, having reached retirement age, was sent off for a well-earned holiday. Waiting in line for the role of first secretary of the regional committee was the second secretary, Ryabov, and the secretary of the regional committee, G.V. Kolbin. The two men were

---

182   *The Urals Worker*, 23rd June 1971.
183   Y. Ryabov: My 20th century. P. 38

roughly the same age and had had similar careers. The CC CPSU expressed a preference for the second secretary. Gennady Vasilievich moved into Ryabov's office, and in 1975 he was given a promotion and sent to Georgia as second secretary of the republic's Central Committee.

Ryabov proposed that the head of the department of engineering, V.Y. Baev, be chosen as the successor to Kolbin, but Baev categorically rejected the offer. Y.A. Korovin was appointed second secretary of the regional committee. On 15th April 1975, the plenum of the regional committee elected B.N. Yeltsin secretary of the regional committee — the position vacated by Korovin — and appointed him a member of the regional committee's board. He was charged with overseeing all construction and landscaping work in the region and on the roads, and overseeing the construction industry and the wood processing and forestry industries. In his new role he had already become a political figure in his own right.

Back in 1971 Ryabov had proposed that Boris Nikolaevich pick a new deputy with the potential to take up the role of head of department. Yeltsin chose the chief engineer at the planning institute, O.I. Lobov, as his candidate. Lobov, a calm and level-headed man who was not very talkative, was well liked by the first secretary. He was the right age, 34, and he was a candidate of sciences. In a word, he was a comrade with a bright future ahead of him. But this particular comrade bristled at the suggestion: "I don't want to work for the party!" Ryabov received a call from the chairman of the State Construction Department of the USSR, Novikov, and asked him to keep his hands off Lobov: "I'm not going to let you have him, you know." This last threat prompted Ryabov to take decisive action. He engaged the help of the Central Committee department to help solve the matter, and Lobov was transferred to the regional committee. Over the last three years Lobov had shown how suitable he would be for the role, and he was therefore seen as more suitable than anyone else to take Yeltsin's place in the department of construction.

It was a successful appointment. In 1975 the region's construction workers made a significant breakthrough, achieving the highest rates of growth in the whole of the ninth five-year-plan.

Secretary Yeltsin, who was responsible for construction, continued to relate to construction matters as his own personal affair, and according to Ryabov took any criticism of construction workers very much to heart, particularly those made by the Glavsreduralstroi, seeing them as a personal insult...He drew his own conclusions but they did not last long. At one construction site, when the two men were alone together, Yeltsin ventured to say: "Yakov Petrovich, perhaps it's fair to say, after all, that I sometimes dig a hole for myself, and don't always behave with tact towards those who cause a project to go wrong. Pressure is the only thing that works with these people, though.

But perhaps the pressure I put on is not always exerted properly." This was how Boris won me over and calmed my fears. He had restored control over his relationships with people."[184]

There were others who held a different view, however — one of the first secretaries of the district committee said: "It must be said that during his tenure as secretary of the regional committee, Boris Nikolaevich tried his best to keep his emotions in check, and few people were aware what a trying temperament he had."[185]

The first secretary of the regional committee

In 1976 Y.P. Ryabov was appointed secretary of the party's Central Committee and ordered to take charge of the defence industry. This set a precedent for the Sverdlovsk party organization. In 1962 the first secretary of the Sverdlovsk regional committee, A.P. Kirilenko, was transferred from Sverdlovsk to Moscow to take up a position as first deputy on the Board of the Central Committee for the RSFSR, and as a member of the Politburo.

Y.P. Ryabov now faced a difficult decision: who to recommend for the post of the region's most senior party leader. He later recalled: "There weren't many people to choose from. They wouldn't let us take Kolbin back. Korovin was an excellent, honest and conscientious man, but he had a weak character and problems with his health. There was also A.A. Mekhrentsev."[186] After pondering over this small group for a short while, Ryabov lingered over Yeltsin: "he is eager to work and good at his work, sufficiently strong-willed, and he'll be able to get everyone working. He knows the region well and the local people know him. ...

Yeltsin was approachable. He was capable of forcing people to work and got plenty of work done himself. And he learned a great deal from me. It was me that taught him what he knows."[187]

At the time, Yeltsin was in Moscow, at a month-long course at the Academy of social sciences, organized by the Central Committee. During one of these lectures the course leader, Korolyov, announced that Yeltsin was expected at the Central Committee at 11 o'clock. Such an unexpected turn of events could only mean one thing: something was going to change dramatically in his life; as for whether this change would be for the better or for the worse, it would become clear later.

---

184   Y. Ryabov: My 20th century. P. 40.
185   I.I. Potapov: Our fate was different, p. 171.
186   Same reference.
187   L.M. Mlechin: Boris Yeltsin. P. 44.

Yeltsin was invited to the Central Committee's offices on Staraya ploshchad, for an interview with the CC secretaries I. Kapitonov, who was in charge of staff issues, and A. Kirilenko, the secretary for industry, and M. Suslov, the secretary for ideology. None of them said anything specific to Yeltsin. He was asked all manner of questions, and his answers were listened to attentively. It was an audition.[188]

The General Secretary of the Central Committee, as Ryabov later recalled, was surprised by his choice. He asked: "Why are you recommending Yeltsin? After all, he isn't second secretary, he isn't a deputy in the Supreme Soviet, we don't know him here at the CC. I.V. Kapitonov gave me the resumé of the second secretary of your regional committee, Korovin."[189]

Ryabov explained his conclusions and Brezhnev gave his consent.

Eventually Yeltsin was taken to the Kremlin to see Brezhnev himself. The General Secretary to a liking to the tall and reliable Yeltsin, and informed him that the Politburo had recommended him for the role of first secretary of the party's regional committee. "All this came as a surprise to me, of course: it is a very big region, and the party organization was very big...I said that if the Politburo and the region's communists put their trust in me, I would work to full capacity, as hard as I possibly could."[190]

Few people knew it at the time, but another candidate was also considered for the vacancy in Sverdlovsk. The Central Committee also summoned Leonid Fyodorovich Bobykin — the director of the party organization for the city of Sverdlovsk, for an interview. Unlike his rival, Bobykin knew the way the party operated like the back of his hand, having worked in the party's district committee and city committee.

Recalling this, V.M. Manyukhin, who at the time was second secretary of the Sverdlovsk city committee, wrote: "I was told: go and meet Bobykin at the airport and don't tell anyone about it. I arrived at the airport, and O.I. Lobov's car was waiting outside the special area for deputies — he was there too. I asked him who had been appointed by the Politburo as our first...I went on torturing Oleg Ivanovich a little longer, and began to sense that he didn't know either. Then I suggested: whoever gets out of the plane first — that'll be the first secretary. The plane landed, the gangway was put in place, the door opened, and standing there was...L.F. Bobykin. I glanced at Oleg Ivanovich — he had grown pale. Bobykin, popping out onto the gangway, adjusted his coat and stood leaning against the exit. And then Yeltsin came down the steps looking powerful, with the gait of a stocky bosun. Behind him came

188   See: L.M. Mlechin: Boris Yeltsin. P. 44.
189   Y.P. Ryabov: My 20th century. P. 54.
190   B.N. Yeltsin: Against the Grain. P. 51.

Bobykin. The expression on my companion's face began to change slowly, until it was eventually lit up by a smile. We congratulated Boris Nikolaevich on his appointment, although he was not particularly forthcoming about it to us, feeling that the plenum of the regional committee had not yet taken place."[191]

Literally a few days later, on 2nd November 1976, there was a plenum of the regional committee in Sverdlovsk, where the issue of the first secretary of the Sverdlovsk regional committee was discussed. In his speech to those present, Y.P. Ryabov remarked that "lately the Central Committee, when replacing its senior management staff, has followed the principle of promoting local employees. This practice has proved to be effective. The regions now have teams containing good organizers, many of whom can be put in management roles. This was particularly true of the Sverdlovsk party organization. It is well known that it has been an ideal place in which to prepare people for important roles within the party and in Soviet life.

One need only point to the work done by the members of the party's regional committee, literally in the last eighteen months to two years, many of our excellent activists and members of the regional committee have been promoted — G.V. Kolbin, who is second secretary of the Central Committee in Georgia, comrades N.I. Ryzhkov, G.Y. Ovchinnikov and M.I. Neumin, who are deputy ministers in major industry ministries in the USSR, comrade S.V. Bashilov, who is a member of the collegium of the State plan for the USSR and others."[192]

It is worth noting that Y.P. Ryabov himself had by that time been elected secretary of the Central Committee.

As he presented his candidate for first secretary of the regional committee, Ryabov stressed the following: "When looking into the matter of the first secretary of the regional committee, the Central Committee was also guided by the need to select a worthy, authoritative, knowledgeable leader here, in the region. The board of the regional committee has considered this issue and unanimously recommends, for the role of first secretary of the regional committee, comrade B.N. Yeltsin..." He expressed his conviction that "B.N. Yeltsin will justify the faith placed in him, will not let the regional party organization down, and with his dedicated, wholehearted work will justify the faith shown in him."[193]

---

191   V.M. Manyukhin: A leap backwards. Pakrus Publishing House, Yekaterinburg, 2002. P. 34-35.
192   CDPASR. F. 4. Op. 88. D. 12. L. 4.
193   CDPASR. F. 4. Op. 88. D. 12. L. 4.

According to I.I. Potapov, who was present at the plenum, everyone felt that the Politburo's decision "was unexpected. Usually the candidates proposed for this post had risen through the ranks of the party, but in this case the person didn't know what the primary, district and city party organizations were, and had only been in office as a secretary of the regional committee for a year, but since the Central Committee was proposing Yeltsin for the job, then we had to go along with it.

Only a handful of them were aware what had been discussed at the plenum which had taken place the previous day. Some of its members, such as the secretary of the regional committee in charge of ideology, L.N. Ponomarev, were categorically against the candidate proposed by Y.P. Ryabov, citing Yeltsin's peevish character and the fact that he was underprepared for the role of first secretary. Ryabov paid no heed to his comrades."[194]

During the plenum, nobody dared express any doubt about whether the Politburo had made the right decision. "The vote," B.N. Yeltsin recalled, "was unanimous, as was always the case. I was congratulated, and I requested the floor, and gave a short speech in which I set out my agenda for the future. And the main idea in it was an extremely simple one: we must show concern for people first and foremost, and the people would always respond to our good work by working harder."[195]

Yeltsin recalled: this is still my credo today."

That same day, the Central Committee secretary Ryabov handed over the office he had previously occupied, with everything in it, to his successor, and headed off to the capital. And Boris Nikolaevich Yeltsin was left in charge of a huge region, an area bigger than some foreign countries. Henceforth, at his own admission, he was "accountable for everything". Whatever happened in the region, he would be the first person to face questions.

It should be noted, though, that his tasks in the role of first secretary of the party's regional committee were immeasurably more wide-ranging. Yeltsin began his activities in this role with a reshuffle among his staff, with the goal of creating "his own team".

Yeltsin found himself among some three thousand people who embodied real power in the country.[196]

---

194   I.I. Potapov: Our fate was different. P. 171-172.
195   B.N. Yeltsin: Against the Grain. P. 52
196   R.G. Pikhoya: The Soviet Union: a history of power. 1945-1991. Novosibirsk, 2000. P. 6-8

The Sverdlovsk Region

In order to get a sense of the scope of Yeltsin's duties as first secretary of the regional committee, we shall give an overall description of the Sverdlovsk Region within the system of governance of the USSR.

The area which B.N. Yeltsin had been entrusted with governing is known geographically as the Mid Urals, and is known in the administrative and territorial breakdown of the country as the Sverdlovsk Region.

In the mid-'70s the Sverdlovsk Region covered an area of 195,000 square kilometers. As of 1st January 1976 the population of the area stood at 4,416,000. There were 44 cities in the region and 95 workers' villages.

84.4% of the region's population lived in the cities. The population of Sverdlovsk was 1,211,000, Nizhny Tagil was home to 396,000 and Kamensk-Uralsky had a population of 188,000.[197]

In terms of industrial potential, the Sverdlovsk Region was in third place in the country behind the Moscow Region and the Leningrad Region: it was home to the country's biggest mining, metallurgy and engineering companies.

Industry. At the heart of the Sverdlovsk Region's economy was heavy industry. Of all the sectors of industry, the ones that were able to compete at nationwide level were engineering, ferrous and non-ferrous metals, industrial construction materials, forestry and the wood processing industry.

There were more than eight hundred industrial concerns in the region. These produced 80% of the union's output of asbestos, 40% of its freight wagons and 17% of its steel piping. 11 million tonnes of steel was smelted in the region each year. Industrial products were exported to 82 countries around the world. The annual amount of capital investment was in excess of 2 billion rubles.[198]

But the production lines had grown outdated. Industry in the Urals had a 250-year long history. The biggest plants in the Urals had been built in the 1930s, during the process of industrialization; it was in this period that equipment purchased overseas — in Germany and the USA — was installed at the factories. During the Second World War, machine tools from Western areas of the country were evacuated to the Urals for safekeeping. A third major refurbishment took place in the factories in the late 1940s, when machinery was supplied to the USSR from Germany as part of the system of reparations.

---

197   CDPASR. F. 4. Op. 89. D. 212. L. 67.
198   CDPASR. F. 4. Op. 89. D. 212. L.67; Op. 87. D. 225. L. 1.

As the years passed, the machinery became out of date. New investment was required. The task of updating the industrial potential came to the forefront of economic planning.

Another problem was that the raw materials base for industry had got worse. In 1965, 85% of the needs of the metallurgical plants in the Urals were met using local resources, whereas in 1980 this figure was down to 50%. Ore was imported from Kazakhstan, the Kursk source and the Kola Peninsula. The journey took 8-10 days.

As regards non-ferrous metals, the situation was similar. The smelting plants in the Urals were only able to provide 10-30% of the ore required. Raw material was imported from Central Asia, the Altai and the North Caucasus, and even from overseas countries. The sources of coal in the north of the Sverdlovsk Region proved to have been largely exhausted.

There was not enough electric power, despite the fact that some powerful new power units had been commissioned at the Chelyabinsk power plant and the South Urals and Troitskaya coal-fired power plants. In the Sverdlovsk Region, the Reftinskaya coal-fired power plant was commissioned. In the mid-'70s the world's biggest power unit was installed at the Beloyarsk nuclear power plant, with a BN-600 fast neutron reactor. Some small power plants were built as well, but these did not provide enough electric power. There was a worrying shortage of energy resources.[199]

The Urals region continued to boast the world's biggest mining and metallurgy complex. The level of concentration of industrial output in the city was 2-3 times higher than the national average. This had its drawbacks. This region had a higher concentration than any other of firms which had an extremely negative impact on the environment, and also of potentially dangerous manufacturing techniques, including companies in the defence sector. In terms of the aggregate amount of work done in the region involving radiation and technogenic work, the Urals region was unparalleled in the country and indeed the rest of the world...[200]

In terms of emissions, the Urals was the leading region in Russia. It produced more than 450 kg of gas and steam waste a year per head of the population, and in the Sverdlovsk region the figure was 600 kg per annum. The industrial centers in the Urals region were among the cities with the highest levels of atmospheric pollution in the country.[201]

---

199   CDPASR. F. 4. Op. 89. D. 212, p. 67-69
200   Engineering and ecological problems of the Urals Region. *Engineering ecology.* 1995. No. 1. P. 46.
201   See: same ref. P. 49

It was the job of the first secretary to be accountable for the state of industry in the region.

In late 1968 and early 1969 Uralplan, the body which coordinated administrative and financial activity in the Urals region, was abolished. Gosplan (the State Planning Committee) and the Center for the economic scientific research institute (CESRI), meanwhile, set up a sector for the improvement of the manufacturing power of the Urals Economic Region.

The liquidation of the Sovnarkhozies (Councils of National Economy) and the transition from a territorial-based principle of governance to a sector-specific one, objectively increased the role of the party's regional committees and executive committees in coordinating issues related to the regional development of companies subordinate to multiple central ministries.[202]

To a certain extent, scientific coordination functions in the preparation of proposals related to planning were taken on by the recently created Institute of economics at the Urals scientific center. The Institute was led by the former secretary of the regional committee (prior to 1971), M.A. Sergeev, who in 1976 had become an associate member of the Academy of Sciences of the USSR. The Institute prepared for the regional committee, and for subsequent transfer to the government, 'Proposals as to the general timetable for the development and deployment of the manufacturing power of the Urals economic region in 1976-1990,' and 'Prospects for the development of the minerals and raw materials base in the Urals'.

Sergeev was strongly in favor of reconstructing industrial companies in the Urals region, and this conviction was supported by the regional committee.

In the Urals as a whole, as in the rest of the country, the '70s and '80s saw a slowing down in economic growth which seemed unstoppable. Companies' activities were regulated by dozens of performance indicators and hundreds of regulations passed down from above. Remuneration for labor was not directly tied to results. The economic system, which was founded on economic growth, had rejected scientific and technical breakthroughs, meaning that it was unprofitable to use them.

Under these circumstances, the party administration acted as bodies responsible less for political governance than for economic governance. In *Against the grain*, B.N. Yeltsin sought to answer the question: was this a good thing or a bad thing? He wrote: "It was only in recent times that we began to think about the negative role played by interference in the economy on the part of the party. At that stage both the economists and, to an even greater extent, the party employees thought of this as entirely in the normal run of

---

202   The regional executive committees, the Councils of deputies of laborers, the electoral bodies.

things. I thought so too, and I found it entirely natural to be summoned to several district committees of the party simultaneously, to attend meetings; admittedly I tried, of course, to get out of having to go to all of these meetings, but the fact that they were taking place, and that during them, with the help of rewards and penalties and so on, numerous economic problems and other problems were resolved — that was the essence of the system's existence and it did not provoke any concerns or objections on my part."[203]

The question of whether this was a good thing or a bad thing is irrelevant now. That was how it was, and it could not have been any other way.

Agriculture

The Sverdlovsk region is an industrial region. The number of people working in agriculture in 1977 was 153,800, i.e. just 3.8% of the region's population. The rural population was rapidly growing smaller. Between 1960 and 1970 the population in the countryside fell by 85,000. There was a chronic shortage of staff with specialist knowledge, machine operators and livestock breeders.[204]

The official statistics did not take account of the fact that in the Sverdlovsk Region, just as in the rest of the country, most of the population were involved in agriculture in some capacity or other.

Workers and employees of planning institutes took part in reaping hay, students in years 1-3 were sent off to help with the potato harvest each September — a practice which had gone on for decades — and in the districts schoolchildren in the 5th grade and above were sent out to harvest potatoes. Excursions by organizations from the cities — from the procurator's office and the police to teachers from higher education institutions — would pick cabbages, carrots and other vegetables in the fall. Trucks and other vehicles were mobilized and used in agricultural, manned by drivers from institutions and organizations.

Just as in the other regions in the country, most of those who worked or taught in the cities were required to help in the provision of food in some capacity. Thousands of people, from all walks of life, would leave their workplaces on getting the command and drive out into the fields and vegetable plots to "rescue the harvest".[205]

The extent to which the country's working population was used in the so-called 'battle for the harvest' took on such proportions that the Central

---

203   B.N. Yeltsin: Against the grain...P. 43.
204   CDPASR. F. 4. Op. 89. D. 212. l.77
205   For further details see: The Yeltsin era. Sketches from a political history. M., 2001. P. 38-39.

Committee issued a directive 'On cases of workers being taken away from their workplaces in manufacturing without justification', on 30th January 1984.

The Sverdlovsk regional committee conducted an analysis in November 1983 on the removal of workers from their positions in the production process and on overtime. The results revealed that the region's workers were being invited to work to help provide their bosses with assistance in preparing animal feed and gathering the harvest, commissioning construction facilities, landscaping and ensuring cleanliness and good order, and the packing away of vegetables for storage. An average of around one percent of the total working time of all the workers in the region (6.9 million working days) was lost on all manner of distractions and other pursuits.[206]

At so-called 'gardens' — plots of land outside the city — people planted potatoes for their families, along with vegetables, blackcurrants and raspberries, to use as stocks during the long winter in the Urals region.

At every industrial concern of any size, there were auxiliary farms which often had the status of factory workshops. This practice had come about during the war, when survival had depended on being able to grow one's own food supplies. After the war the practice continued to exist. These were the same potato fields in which most of the work was done by workers from the factory and the hothouse, and the harvest resulting from which — fresh cucumbers — could be given as gifts to women on 8th March, if their husbands were able to get hold of them at their particular firm. The idea of being able to buy fresh cucumbers in winter in a typical store in Sverdlovsk was pure fantasy in the '70s and '80s.

There was a shortage of meat and meat-related products, however. It was a shortage that refused to go away, and the Sverdlovsk region depended directly on the funds set aside for meat, which had to be obtained from the union's central government; since these funds were not very sizeable, they had to be coaxed out of the authorities.

It was the regional committee's job to do this coaxing.

All of this 'assistance to the bosses', accompanied by the enormous economic losses and jitters, came up against fierce resistance in the regions and forced the authorities to resort to the tried and trusted methods of party leadership: summonses, excoriating criticism and bonuses. The fearful orders and directives were fulfilled from a formal point of view, but the situation as regards foodstuffs became all the more depressing with each year that passed.

---

206   See: CDPASR. F. 279. Op. 106. D. 59. L. 10-12, 21.

During Boris Nikolaevich Yeltsin's tenure at the helm of the Sverdlovsk Region (1976 — April 1985), there were more than 200 meetings of the regional committee's board. On 175 occasions the issues discussed at these board meetings concerned agriculture (in 1976 alone, agricultural matters were on the agenda for the regional committee's board on 33 occasions). By way of comparison: in the same period, issues related to ideological work were discussed 146 times, issues related to industry — 118 times, science, culture and healthcare — 58 times, construction — 36 times and transport — 23 times.[207]

The way people lived and the food they ate

In the Urals Region, the amount of investment in the social sector — that is to say education, healthcare, culture and trade — was lower than the average figure in the RSFSR, and had been falling for some time. As a proportion of the total amount of investment in the region, the social sector received 18.5% between 1971 and 1975, and 16.4% between 1976 and 1980. The corresponding figures for the rest of the RSFSR were 20.7% and 18.2%. In the Urals Economic Region (UER), the amount of investment in social infrastructure in the '70s and '80s per 10,000 people stood at 80% of the national average.

A report from the statistics directorate, entitled 'On the key indicators for the quality of life of the population of the Sverdlovsk Region' and received by the Sverdlovsk Regional Committee of the CPSU in August 1977, stated that the average salary in 1976 was 160 roubles a month. The statisticians had found that for every 100 households there were 64 sewing machines, 79 TV sets, 62 refrigerators and 70 washing machines.[208]

The fact that Y.P. Ryabov had left for Moscow meant that the supply of food to the region became a lot more complicated. Ryabov had been very successful in securing funds. When he left, the region's standing among the country's supplier networks was weakened. The results of this soon became apparent. Whereas in 1975 there had been an average of 60 kg of meat and meat-related products coming into the region per head of the population, in 1976 this figure was down to 57 kg.[209]

This may not seem like much of a reduction, but it is put into context by another report which was prepared for the regional committee in 1978. The

---

207   These calculations were made by the author on the basis of: Lists of the matters examined at meetings of the board of the Sverdlovsk regional committee (1976-1984). Yekaterinburg. 2006. P. 4-47.

208   CDPASR. F. 4. Op. 88. D. 207. L.2

209   CDPASR. F. 4. Op. 88. D. 207. L.12

report states: "There is currently no trade in meat in the region. A limited range of smoked sausages are available in the shops. These are available — though they are not always on the shelves — in some of the industrial cities. Consumption of meat products in the region amounted to 1.904 million tonnes in 1977, and it is anticipated that the same amount will be consumed in 1978".[210]

A bit of basic arithmetic — dividing up the so-called "consumption of meat products", i.e. 1.904 million tonnes, by the population of the region in 1977, which was 4.416 million people — tells us that there was an average of 41.3 kg of meat products coming into the region per person per year. And that meant that supplies of meat-related products had fallen by almost a third since 1975.

The report goes on: "In many of the cities in the region there are delays in the supply of milk and butter, and the amounts supplied do not last a whole day. There is hardly any curd and there is a severe shortage of dairy goods. The amount of animal fats set aside for 1978 is 3234 tonnes lower than the amount consumed in 1977, and the amount of rennet cheese is down by 4550 tonnes. Supplies of frozen fish are adequate, and it can be bought throughout the region. The range of products available is extremely limited however (capelin and minnow), and does not satisfy demand among the public... In retail and public catering there is a shortage of sugar-based confectionery, particularly coated chocolates...In 1978 there have been drastic reductions compared to 1977 in the supply of a range of industrial products...".[211]

It is hardly surprising, therefore, that anyone going to Moscow on business would spend the last day of their stay in the capital (the train to Sverdlovsk left in the evening, which worked in their favor) doing the rounds of the shops, to buy a few kilos of meat, or, failing that, frozen chicken, or saveloy, or perhaps some Moscow caramel, or, if there was a public holiday coming up, some oranges or even something as outlandish and exotic as a pineapple — in other words, things that simply weren't available in Sverdlovsk, or in most other cities in the Russian regions.

There were at least two options open to the regional committee and its first secretary, Yeltsin, in terms of rescuing the situation as regards the provision of foodstuffs to people in the region.

The first was a traditional one, and was to be expected from the region's leaders. They could demand funds in Moscow for foodstuffs (meat first and foremost) and industrial products for the people.

---

210   CDPASR. F. 4. Op. 89. D. 212. L. 67,81
211   F. 4. Op. 89. D. 212. L. 81.

That same year, 1977, Yeltsin wrote to the Chairman of the Council of Ministers of the USSR, A.N. Kosygin, asking him to increase supplies of meat. His letter contained a request for help and outlined the measures being taken by the region to improve the situation.[212] Letters were also sent to the Chairman of the Council of Ministers of the RSFSR, M.S. Solomentsev[213], the deputy Chairman of the Council of Ministers of the USSR, N.K. Baibakov[214]...

It was clear however that meat production needed to be set up within the region, and Yeltsin took the decisive step of creating new meat production sites. Traditional forms of agriculture were unable to provide rapid growth, so it was decided that livestock and poultry farms would be built.

In November 1977, the first secretary of the regional committee, Yeltsin, and the chairman of the Sverdlovsk Executive Committee, A.A. Mekhrentsev, wrote to A.N. Kosygin requesting that he begin construction of poultry farms along the same lines as the Kekav poultry farm in Latvia, so that chickens could be reared.[215] The first poultry farm was to be built in Nizhny Tagil, a centre for the metallurgy and defence industries.

Poultry farms such as this began to be built not only in Nizhny Tagil but also in other cities in the region.

The regional committee of the CPSU secured renewed funding for the construction of dairy complexes for 800 cows at the Loginovsky state farm, and for 1200 at the Rezhevskaya state farm.[216]

The Laisky pig-farming complex was constructed outside Nizhny Tagil.

The regional committee demanded that the major plants build auxiliary companies using their own resources. The results were seen 3-4 years later. Chickens went on sale in the shops. The range of dairy products available improved. Beef remained as hard as ever to come by in the shops. But supplies of foodstuffs to those living in the region began to improve noticeably. Clear evidence of this could be seen in the fact that people from the Chelyabinsk and Perm regions began travelling to Sverdlovsk to buy food — not least those chickens.

It was a success story. It did not go unnoticed by the region's residents.

---

212   CDPASR. F. 4. Op. 89. D. 58. L. 78-79
213   CDPASR. F. 4. Op. 89. D. 58. L. 94-95; F. 4. Op. 92. D. 110. L. 68-69; F. 4. Op. 92. D. 110. L. 70-71.
214   CDPASR. F. 4. Op. 92. D.110. L. 5
215   CDPASR. F. 4. Op. 80. D. 76. L. 107.
216   CDPASR. F. 4. Op. 89. D. 58. L. 42

Yeltsin also attempted to penetrate traditional agricultural technologies. Prior to his appointment as first secretary, in August 1976, he had become familiar with the work done by the Urals Science and Research Institute of Agriculture (URALNIISKHOZ), and the institute's testing fields situated not far from Sverdlovsk.

G.A. Romanov, who at the time was the deputy director of UralNIISKhoz for science, recalls: "When he visited the institute Boris Nikolaevich familiarized himself in great detail with the results of the work done by the deparments of agriculture, grain cultures and feed production, as well as the advanced technologies for preparing feeds for livestock rearing. He was particularly impressed by the alfalfa crops, which had yielded more than 360 hundredweight of greenery per hectare. ... They were equally impressed by the crops of highly resistant barley, which had yielded 70 hundredweight per hectare. ... He drove from the experimental fields to the experimental production farm (EPF) Istok, famous for its herd of dairy cows, which had supplied a yield that was unprecedented in the Urals Region — 6 000 kg of milk a year".[217]

The problem of providing foodstuffs remained the most tortuous of all, right up until the final days of his period in charge of the region. True, he managed to secure tonnes of butter and meat from Moscow "ahead of the public holidays in November" or "for the May 1st public holiday", but that was hardly a solution. The direct supplies of fruit and vegetables from the south did not help.

The region had to resort to regulating and dividing up the meat among the population. Since there was no beef available on the open market, it might as well be divided up among the people in equal proportions, using a system of vouchers. This was at least a more honest approach, and meant no-one could claim that people with time on their hands could buy it, whilst those who were at work were unable to do so.

In addition to this, poultry could now be bought in the shops again.

"Manual control", as they say nowadays, remained an important means of influencing what was going on in the region. The events of autumn 1978 would remain etched in the memory of those living in the region. Extremely heavy downpours began at the end of August. The rains continued in September. Tractors got stuck in the soil, which had become swollen by the water. The potato diggers couldn't drive into the fields.

To rescue the harvest, the potatoes had to be planted manually, using pitchforks. And that required a huge amount of manpower.

---

217   From an interview with the merited agricultural worker G.A. Romanov.

They could have taken the usual approach: send out orders to the district committees, which would forward them to the companies, create head offices and so on.

Yeltsin did things differently. In the course of the day it was announced on the radio and television that first secretary Yeltsin was going to speak on the regional TV and talk about the potato crop. At the time it was unheard of for politicians to do this except when going through the rituals of state occasions. As a rule, the country's leaders only appeared on the nation's TV screens on 1st May and 7th November. For the first time ever a party boss was due to speak on the TV about an issue that was genuinely causing problems for people.

Within two hours of the start of his TV address, an image appeared on the nation's TV screens: limp-looking fields, people wrapped up in coats and plastic capes, struggling to pull their boots out of the dirt, and tractors stuck in the mud. And endless rain, rain, rain...

Yeltsin did not talk for long. He said there was a risk that the region might be left without potatoes. And that if people didn't muck in and help, before long there wouldn't be anyone left to help. He asked the people living in the region to go out into the fields and help themselves.

The next day the rain turned to snow. But on Saturday and Sunday, the days on which Yeltsin had asked for people's help, almost 90,000 people went out into the fields.

They had believed what Yeltsin said. This was a direct result of his three years in charge of the region.

Construction

Construction was also on the agenda for first secretary Yeltsin. More than 50 major suppliers to construction organizations, including Glavsreduralstroe from the Ministry of Heavy Construction of the USSR, with a program of over 600 million roubles' worth of construction and installation works, the Uralenergostroi trust from the Ministry of Energy of the USSR, and 6 trusts from the Ministry of Installation and Special Construction of the USSR. The region contained contractor construction organizations in the shape of trusts and special directorates at over 30 ministries and institutions in the USSR and the RSFSR.

A particular style of party-managed construction had developed in the Sverdlovsk Region back in the mid-1970s. At the start of each year the office of the party's regional committee drew up a list of the most important construction sites (no more than 15, as a rule). The list included major industrial and agricultural complexes, as well as housing and social infrastructure.[218]

The issue taken most seriously of all was that of perfecting the way construction was organized and managed. The party leadership gradually accumulated a certain amount of experience and drew conclusions on the factors which were slowing down the future development of capital construction projects.

These reasons were related to both the internal procedures and the external ones, which did not satisfy the requirements for the contemporary working conditions of construction organizations.

The example cited was the planning process used by the major industrial complexes. "It often lasts 5-8 years, and it is revealed at the start of construction that the machines used in construction have grown incredibly out-dated, as has the whole technological process on occasion. And during the course of construction the developers begin releasing indexed blueprints, the cost of the facilities changes, and most importantly of all, this hinders the developers as they attempt to go about their work as normal".[219]

The party leadership in the region began to direct criticism and complaints at Gosstroi USSR (the State Committee of the USSR for Construction Issues), claiming that "Gosstroi USSR must review its approach to the issue of qualitative assessments of planning solutions, and also force the planning institutes to take the precaution, in their solutions, of including in the plans the documents required for computerized planning and control, and plans for how work will be carried out on the construction of major industrial complexes."[220]

Other problems were cited too. One of them was "...the evil practice of unbalanced planning." A system had been established in which the funds allocated for metals, wood, cement and other resources were allocated at the level of 85-95% of the amounts planned. This forced the party's regional committee, led by its secretary Boris Yeltsin, to decide each year whether or not to provide an additional allocation of fittings, pipes, softwood logs and so on.

The institutional disunity among the developers did a great deal of damage to capital construction projects. It sapped people's strength, broke up the construction industry's production base and led to huge costs that were

---

218   See CDPASR. F. 4. Op. 87. D. 225. L. 18
219   CDPASR. F. 4. Archive 87. Matter 225. P. 48.
220   Same ref.

unrelated to production."[221] Yeltsin sought a solution and hit upon one: it occurred to him to create a conglomerate for construction and installation work in the region, based at the allocation organization Glavsreduralstroi.

As revealed by a comprehensive note prepared by the regional committee, 'The experience of the party leadership in capital construction in the Sverdlovsk region': "...the problems raised would seem to have no relation to the work of the party, but when the staff structures and economic performance of the construction organizations are analyzed, one can clearly see in them — relative to other sectors — a worsening in terms of qualifications, education, salary and so on. And one cannot help but be concerned by this and want to look for the reasons for this phenomenon."[222]

B.N. Yeltsin seized every opportunity he could to bring in radical improvements to the quality and completion times for capital construction projects entrusted to him in the region, and among other things he strove to enlist support from the 'center'. He succeeded in arranging a meeting on this issue with the deputy chairman of the Council of Ministers of the USSR, Veniamin Emmanuilovich Dymshits. At the end of the conversation the regional committee prepared several proposals on how to improve the activities of the Main directorate for construction in the Mid Urals Region (Glavsreduralstroe) in the Ministry of Heavy Industry of the USSR.

The biggest cause for concern was the fact that although the amount of capital investment was increasing each year, the construction organizations within Glavsreduralstroi were not growing, and this led to delays in the construction tasks which had been scheduled. The reasons for this phenomenon were cited: "...the exhaustion of the resources in the production base, the insufficient supplies of materials and machinery, the large turnover among developers and a host of other factors."[223]

Concerned by the state of affairs which had arisen, the Sverdlovsk regional committee of the CPSU requested a review of proposals on how to develop and strengthen the construction organizations within Glavsreduralstroi, which would make it possible to create a model construction organization at the site.[224]

Dymshits tasked a minister from the Ministry of Heavy Industry, comrade Goldin, with "reviewing the questions posed by the Sverdlovsk regional committee of the CPSU and informing comrade Yeltsin about the results."[225]

221   CDPASR. F. 4. Op. 95. D. 257. P. 118-119.
222   CDPASR. Facility 4. Archive 95. Matter 257.. P. 50.
223   CDPASR. Facility 4. Archive 89. D. 76. L. 74.
224   See: same ref.
225   See: same ref. L. 71.

The response, which was signed by the Minister's first deputy A.A. Babenko, was fairly formal. Alongside vague promises to "conduct reviews", "continue working with the relevant organizations to resolve matters related to additional allocation of resources…" etc, it expressed disagreement with the Glavsreduralstroi assertion that "…the reasons for the poor performance by the Head Committee in 1976-1977 were the issues left unresolved by the aforementioned organizations, and nothing else. At the same time it contained a recommendation that all efforts be directed towards making the maximum possible use of internal reserves."[226] It was hard to imagine anything other than that, all the more so given that the people of Sverdlovsk had been so bold as to criticize the aforementioned organizations, a rare occurrence in those days.

The following facts indicate the scale of construction work in the Sverdlovsk region at the time: during the course of the 10th and 11th five-year plans (1976-1985), the same amount of resources were used up as in all the previous years of the Soviet Union's existence. This vast region amounted to a gigantic construction site. Industry in the Urals region was expanded and reorganized, social infrastructure was improved, and agriculture was in dire need of new facilities.

Boris Yeltsin himself proudly recalled: "In the seventies alone 900 new sites were put into operation [in the Sverdlovsk region]…and approximately 25 billion rubles of capital investment was secured. The first line of the water supply system for the Sverdlovsk industrial district, from the Ufa river, was put into operation; the Bogdanov gravel plant began to produce its first output; the universal beam mill at the Nizhny Tagil Iron and Steel Works was tested; and the people of Sverdlovsk were given the unique building of the state circus and many other buildings.

For many people, housing remained the biggest problem of all. A huge number of complaints and requests about this particular issue were sent to the party's regional committee. After achieving a record in residential construction in the early '80s of over 2 million square metres a year, the region found it difficult to break away from the past — the ugly huts of the 1930s and '40s.

Boris Yeltsin, who knew the construction industry inside out, did a great deal to ensure that the best decisions were taken at the right time. Take his famous 'battle against the huts', for example. Yeltsin himself took an extremely dim view of "these dilapidated hovels, ridden with drafts." By his own admission, as someone who had spent ten years of his life living in one, his memories of these wooden huts, designed to hold 10, 15 or even 20 families, stirred up difficult emotions within him. It was not right for people to be living in such conditions in the twentieth century.[227]

---

226   CDPASR. Facility 4. Op. 89. D. 76. L. 70.
227   See: B.N. Yeltsin: Against the grain…P. 64.

The people living in the huts wrote letters to all the courts complaining about the unbearable conditions. One of the letters, sent from residents of a hut in Khimash and addressed to a deputy in the Supreme Soviet from this district, the secretary of the Central Committee of the KPSU A.P. Kirilenko, contains some truly astounding facts. *"We, the residents of hut № 13, Shlakoblochnaya Street, are living in abominable conditions. There are currently 29 families in the hut, sharing a single kitchen, with a single tap and a single basin. The hut was built in 1945 by prisoners of war. It has fallen into disrepair, and is in a terrible condition. The plaster is falling off the ceiling, rain comes into the rooms when it rains and in the spring, the fittings and joints are rotten, there are huge cracks in the floor...Water flows straight from the sink onto the floor, and the floor is always wet...And the scariest thing of all: there are around 20 children aged between 2 and 14 living in the hut... How long must we suffer in this hut, in these unbearable conditions, with 2 families trying to find a way to live in rooms measuring 13 square metres...".*[228] The numerous complaints sent by people in the region to the various courts and authorities, including to the press, were fruitless. This prompted them to seek help from their member of parliament.

A letter was taken to the Central Committee to be screened and then sent to Sverdlovsk to be examined *in situ*. The resolution written in response to this letter, contained in a letter written by hand by Boris Yeltsin, has survived to this day: "Visit the site on 21st March at 10.00. Invite leaders from the city, the district, the plant, the trust and the regional committee. B. Yeltsin."[229] The case of this hut, and the other huts on Shlakoblochnaya Street, ultimately had a positive outcome. All of the residents (356 people) were given more acceptable housing.[230] Yet for many thousands of families, the problem remained unsolved.

A ten-year government program was in place for rehousing people from the huts. Yeltsin set himself more lofty obligations: bringing this situation to an end ahead of schedule, once and for all.

Based on calculations made at his request, it became clear that in order to rehouse people living in huts in the Sverdlovsk region once and for all, approximately 2 million square metres of housing would be needed — as much as the region constructed in a year.

It was not an easy decision to make. As Boris Yeltsin himself admitted: "On several occasions in my life as a political leader I have had to take difficult decisions, some of which have worked out not too well, and some of which have worked out badly. What's more important — getting people out of those

---

228   CDPASR. F. 4. Op. 98. D. 161. P. 18, 20.

229   Same reference. L. 16

230   CDPASR. F. 4. Op. 98. D. 16. L.14.

huts and freezing all the queues for housing for a year, or letting people go on suffering in inhumane conditions for another decade, but being able to give housing to the people in the queues?"[231]

The office of the party's regional committee decided to freeze the queues for housing and to rehouse the people living in the huts in new-build housing. It was an extremely unpopular move which upset thousands of people, including company directors, and the authorities were inundated with complaints. Yeltsin stood firm, however. He managed to secure the support of his predecessor, the secretary of the CC CPSU A.P. Kirilenko, and of the prime minister A.N. Kosygin.

"That was exactly how it happened," he would later write. "Company directors complained, protested, sent me letters, but we went on taking down one hut after another, then moved into the districts where the huts were, broke them down, destroyed them, and a year later all the former residents of the huts moved into new, comfortable apartments."[232]

He would later talk with undisguised pride about this "victory of local significance". In an article written by the first secretary of the Sverdlovsk regional committee of the CPSU, B.N. Yeltsin, for the newspaper *Soviet Russia*, we find the following: "The decision we took was a risky one: we faced the task of moving almost two thousand families to new-build housing, on an unplanned basis. We tried to be as cunning about it as we could: we asked for government loans, built housing by the industrial method, postponed resettlement by a year for those who were able to wait...We took this step because unless we did so, unless we just got on with it, we would never have been able to sort out a problem that had gone on for forty years. There were a few tears and arguments, of course. But we got through it. And six thousand souls benefited from our disorder. Similarly we intend to go on the attack against the others as well, as decisively as possible. That is the only way! Otherwise the Urals would be unable to cope, unable to overcome these age-old afflictions which are preventing us from being able proudly to consider ourselves a region that is a "pillar of the state."[233]

This passage is typical of Yeltsin: "get stuck in", "go on the attack", "the only way!". The complex character of the 'region's boss' had been forged and tempered in the harsh conditions of everyday life in the Urals.

The look of the Urals region's capital city was gradually changing. The new buildings of the state circus and the Palace of chess were put up, the Theatre of Opera and Ballet was rebuilt, and the October cinema — an architectural monument — underwent restoration.

---

231   See: B.N. Yeltsin: Against the grain...P. 64.
232   B.N. Yeltsin: Against the Grain. P. 65.
233   CDPASR. F. 4. Op. 106. D. 97. L. 147

Construction work began on the metro. It was not initiated by Yeltsin; instead, it was thought up in accordance with the general plan for the development of Sverdlovsk. A plan is all well and good on paper, but making it a reality is another matter entirely. The State Planning Committee didn't award any funding for the construction of the metro. Where would they able to get hold of the millions of roubles needed? They could only be allocated by decision of the Central Committee's Politburo. The politburo was against 'excesses' of any kind. Boris Yeltsin appealed directly to Brezhnev. The General Secretary agreed to hear him out. Yeltsin would later write about this meeting: "Knowing how he operated in those days, I had prepared a note in his name, so that all he had to do was impose his decision. I went in, we talked for literally five to seven minutes...he couldn't bring himself to write the resolution himself. He turns to me and says: "Why don't you dictate what I should write." Naturally, I began dictating: "Explain the situation to the Politburo and prepare a draft Politburo directive on the construction of the metro in Sverdlovsk." He wrote down what I had said, signed it, and gave me the piece of paper. Yet, aware as I was that documents were always prone to getting lost, and disappearing, I said to him: "No, call your assistant in please." He invites his assistant into the room, and I say to him: "Order him first of all to register the document, and secondly to carry out your order officially: "Send to all the members of the Politburo." He did this as well, without a word, the assistant picked up the papers, we said our goodbyes, and soon Sverdlovsk received the Politburo's decision regarding the construction of the metro."[234]

On 28th August 1980 the people building the metro began their work, and on 19th April 1984 the first tunnel was completed, between the stations Kalininskaya and Ordzhonikidzevskaya.

Yeltsin considered transforming the regional center into a modern city, albeit one that had no skyscrapers but lots of tall buildings. The first of these was the multi-storey 'candle' building on October Square, to which agencies from the regional committee of the CPSU and the regional Council were to be moved. Plans to erect it had been made in the past. Yeltsin was not satisfied by the plans, but he did not manage to get them altered. He did manage, however, to accelerate the process of construction. By approving the words of Sverdlovsk's former chief architect, G.I. Belyakin, the first secretary of the party's regional committee, who knew whereof he spoke, 'interfered' not only in the course of construction itself, but also in the creation of the city's architectural image. At his initiative, on-site meetings of the town planning board were held regularly, with members of the party's regional committee in attendance, in order to review ongoing and future tasks. "When Yeltsin inspected the areas of residential housing which had already been built in Sverdlovsk, in the vicinity of Zhukov Street, he went against the opinion

---

234   B.N. Yeltsin: Against the Grain. P. 67

of those behind the construction of the city center, by proposing that the construction work be put on hold. Many people, including various figure in authority in the region and the city, couldn't make sense of this proposal, but after a bit of hesitation they decided to call a halt to construction work. Today no-one has any doubt that Yeltsin's decision was the right one to take."[235]

The first secretary of the regional committee was involved in resolving several 'trifles', such as the landscaping of the bridge over the city dam, the installation of a 'gallery of glory' for the Uralmash heavy machinery production facility, and the erection of a monument to the legendary spy, Hero of the Soviet Union N.I. Kuznetsov. Sverdlovsk's literary quarter became a major visitor attraction, with its museum of writers from the Urals Region and its original Chamber Hall.

One of Yeltsin's dreams remained unfulfilled: his plans for the construction of a memorial to the heroism of those from the Urals Region lost during the Great Patriotic War were impeded by his transfer to Moscow.

The regional party organization in figures. And that's not all

Before moving on to the issue of the local 'team' and the apparatus of the Sverdlovsk party organization, we shall first provide a general outline of the group who made up the region's Communist Party. Between 1938 (when the borders of the Sverdlovsk Region were defined) and Yeltsin's appointment as director of the regional party organization, membership of the region's party organization increased six-fold, and the number of rank and file party workers grew by 8.5 times. The overall level to which the communists were educated increased dramatically: the proportion who had completed school and held a degree had risen from 17% to 62%.[236]

As of 1st January 1980 there were 236,668 people in the regional party organization (for the sake of comparison, there had been 138,319 members in 1960, i.e. an increase of 58.5%), grouped together in 4630 primary and 6068 branch organizations, and 7463 party groups.[237] They were led by 63 city and district committees within the party.[238]

In 1980, the party's social make-up, in terms of the numbers of laborers and agricultural workers, was as follows:[239]

---

235 G.I. Belyankin: My city and I. Yekaterinburg, 2005. P. 172.
236 See: CDPASR. F. 4, Op. 89. D. 1. L.3.
237 CDPASR. F. 4. Op. 95. D. 131. L. 84.
238 CDPASR. F. 4. Op. 95. D. 114. L.7.
239 Compiled by the author on the basis of: CDPASR. F. 4. Op. 95. D. 190. L. 5.

Social Status	Number	%
Laborers	78,370	33.1%
Agricultural workers	3,145	1.3% of which 67

White collar workers	106,897	pensioners
Students	2,200	45.2%
Unemployed	46,056	0.9%
		19.5%

The level to which the region's communists were educated, in 1980, was as follows:[240]

Higher education	52,686
Incomplete higher education	4,731
Secondary education	100,113
Incomplete secondary education	48,074
Primary education	28,046
No primary education	3,018
PhD	302
Post-doctoral students	2231

The table shows that the number of party members with higher education, or incomplete higher education, was less than 25%, and the number with secondary and unfinished secondary education was over 62%; almost 12% had primary education and 1.2% had no education at all.

Over 55% of the communists were aged between 26 and 50, whilst almost 40% were over 50.[241] The party organization was growing old. This could not but cause consternation among party leaders.

The ranks of the region's communists were genuinely multicultural. People from 80 different nationalities had party membership cards. The reason for this was clear: during the first five-year plans, many plants had been constructed by people from far-flung corners of the country, and on top of which there had been mass evacuation during the Great Patriotic War...[242] Incidentally, there were no ethnic clashes at all, neither among the communists nor among non-party members, in the Sverdlovsk Region.

---

240   CDPASR. F. 4. Op. 95. D. 190. L. 5.
241   CDPASR. F. 4. Op. 95. D. 190. L. 5.
242   For this data see: same ref.

A comparison of data about the party organization in the Sverdlovsk Region with data regarding the rest of the country reveals a few more of its distinctive characteristics.[243]

For example, party membership was growing more slowly in the Sverdlovsk Region than in the rest of the country (6.8% and 8.4%, respectively), fewer candidates were putting themselves forward for membership of the party (3.4% and 3.7% respectively), and the number of agricultural workers in the party was extremely low compared to the rest of the country. Whereas in the rest of the country 12.8% of the party's members were agricultural workers, in Sverdlovsk the equivalent figure was almost ten times lower — 1.3%. The proportion of party members among each category of citizen (laborers, agricultural workers and members of the intelligentsia) was lower in the region than in the party as a whole. It stood at 4.8% as against 6.5%, 8.2% as against 8.7% and 18.2% as against 22%, respectively.[244] Of particular concern was the fact that the number of party members among laborers and agricultural workers was firmly on a downward trajectory. In 1971 they had accounted for 9.9% and 6.2% respectively, and in 1977 — for 9.5% and 6.0%.[245] And this despite the fact that these categories of Soviet citizen were given special preference when applying to be members of the CPSU.

There were fewer party members among representatives of science, education and healthcare than in the rest of the country in 1980. In the Sverdlovsk Region, fewer members of the Komomol than the average numbers for the rest of the country strove to bind their lives and careers inextricably to the Communist party. The nucleus of the party, in the Komsomol, was two times smaller than elsewhere, whilst the average age at which people joined the party was higher than in the USSR as a whole. The number of communists among the region's pensioners was also very different in the region than in the country as a whole (19.4% and 13.8%, respectively). 4.3% fewer communists in the region than elsewhere had higher education, incomplete higher education or secondary education.

The number of people thrown out of the party in the region were shocking, too. The reasons were many and various: drunkenness, hooliganism, moral and domestic degradation, theft, embezzlement, breaches of party or state discipline. Among those excluded from or leaving the party, the proportion of laborers in the region was 60%.[246] All this undoubtedly provided a basis for criticism of the region's party leadership from the party centre – the CC CPSU.

---

243   Data entered for the period 1975-1979. See: CDPASR. F. 4. Op. 98. D. 192. L. 12-13.
244   CDPASR. F. 4. Op. 98. D. 192. L. 12.
245   CDPASR. F.4. Op. 89. D. 1. L. 8.
246   CDPASR. F.4. Op. 89. D. 1. L. 13.

And although by some measures the region was slightly ahead of the overall statistics (number of laborers joining the party, number of laborers in the CPSU, number of communists working in the national economy and even the number of women in the ranks of the CPSU), the situation as a whole did not change this very much.

It must not be forgotten that there were objective reasons which, whether the party liked it or not, reduced the party's authority among the masses and lessened their desire to join its advance ranks. These factors include the permanent decline in quality of life, the chronic shortage of foodstuffs and essentials, and instances of abuse of authority and immoral behavior by party bosses, which had become known to many. The party's authority was on the wane.

The party organization was continuing to grow old. Whereas in 1956 the average age of the communists was 41 years old, by 1977 it had risen to 45 and was continuing to grow.[247]

The first secretary of the party's regional committee spoke with particular concern in one of his addresses about the fact that the requirements imposed on those joining the CPSU were falling, thanks in part to those giving recommendations regarding candidates for CPSU membership. For the party organizations it was important to provide a 'plan' for recruitment of laborers, and for that reason they turned a blind eye to 'certain failings'.[248]

Another worrying symptom — a form of 'acid test', which indicated how much influence the party had lost among the masses — was the number of people thrown out of or expelled from the CPSU. Moreover, whilst some were excluded under paragraph 8 of the CPSU's charter (for failure to pay membership fees), roughly the same number were excluded under paragraph 16 (failure to pass the selection process). The number of these sorts of cases was growing every year. It was a very alarming signal and testified to a fall in the CPSU's authority.

Boris Yeltsin attempted, as he put it, to talk frankly and openly about these problems to the first secretaries of the party's city committees and district committees. He admitted that this was not a case of him instructing them what to do in one or another situation, but a "chat from which I could take a great deal that was useful, as first secretary of the district committee. Everyone concluded that these meetings are mutually enriching."[249]

Incidentally, after 'testing out' this crucial form of interaction with his fellow ideologists — 'informal conversation', Yeltsin armed himself with it and

---

247   CDPASR. F.4. Op. 89. D. 1. L. 10.
248   See: CDPASR. F.4. Op. 89. D. 1. L. 11.
249   See: same ref. L. 22.

would go on to use it in his work in the future. Yeltsin mocked the activities of certain party organizations as things which were only being done for show — these included the Verkhne-Pyshminsk city committee, which had set up "a city party head office led by the first and second secretaries of the CPSU's city committee, for the purpose of refurbishing a bathhouse. Almost all employees in senior positions must be approved by the head office's members. In eleven points of the directive there are orders regarding the allocation of people and materials, etc., etc. Surely," asked Yeltsin, "this issue could have been delegated to the city executive committee, its various services, and the city's administrative organizations? It is clear that this could have been done and should have been done... And the party's city committee...ought to have focused its attention on the most important issues."[250]

There were also cases of a different kind, when the party committees took it upon themselves to carry out roles which were purely administrative, and approved tasks for their Soviet and administrative directors.

This was standard procedure. It was used by Yeltsin himself, although he also criticized the use of it for trifling matters. When discussing the matter of the work done by the North Urals city committee of the party, at a meeting on 20th April 1979, Yeltsin admonished the local party organization for having examined the issue 'On the unsatisfactory performance of the cash plan by the city division of the State Bank of the USSR in 1978'. There was nothing party-specific about this decision whatsoever. "And there was nothing that could be said on the matter," Yeltsin said, "because this issue is one that falls entirely within the competence of the city council."[251]

The new first secretary's 'team' had taken shape. The man elected second secretary of the regional committee was L.F. Bobykin, with whom, incidentally, Yeltsin had had a complex relationship during his time as director of the HCC. Ideological matters were dealt with by V.A. Zhitenyov, who in the past had been first secretary of the Sverdlovsk district committee of the Komsomol. The first secretary of the party's city committee for Nizhny Tagil, Y.V. Petrov, took up the post of secretary for construction, which had previously been held by Yeltsin. N.M. Dudkin kept his post as secretary for agriculture.

Nine of the fifteen heads of department were replaced, one after another. Remaining in their posts were V.Y. Baev, F.M. Yelokhin, V.S. Kashpurov, A.I. Letov, V.P. Mazyrin and V.I. Tsepennikov. Joining the leadership of the other departments were the Soviet and party-oriented practitioners A.G. Zhdanovich, I.A. Osintsev, V.A. Titov, Y.A. Tomashov and N.M. Tishkin.

---

250   CDPASR. F.4. Op. 89. D. 1.. L 23.
251   CDPASR. F. 4. Op. 95. D. 89. L. 46.

The former director of the regional committee's department of construction, O.I. Lobov, was appointed to the most important post in the construction complex in the Central Urals region — the boss of Glavsreduralstroi.

The leadership of the Sverdlovsk regional executive committee changed hands as well. The general director of the Kalinin plant, Anatoly Alexandrovich Mekhrentsev, was appointed to this position. Mekhrentsev's CV was flawless: he had been a fighter pilot during the Great Patriotic War and an engineer; he held a PhD in technical sciences, had won a State Prize, and was a Hero of Socialist Labor. In his 'Confession' Yeltsin writes: "I was aware of his superior qualities as an individual, his erudition, his ability quickly to grasp what was going on, and not to get out of his depth in any situation — and that he was relatively young. I offered him the role. At first he said no, then he promised to think it over. And I put a lot of pressure on him! In the end he agreed, and set to work." Yeltsin was convinced he had not been mistaken about this candidate. ... "I believe it was the best decision I could have made. He gradually began to make progress, and then, in my view, became the strongest chairman of the regional executive committee in all the regions in our republic."[252]

The practice of putting one's own people in key posts was par for the course. It is one of the principles of senior level management — surround oneself with people who were not your superior just a matter of days ago, who will not call your seniority into question, who will be accustomed right from the outset to looking up at you.

Yeltsin later recalled: "thus the first 'Yeltsin team' gradually took shape — a powerful, creative one. It was a group to be reckoned with. We devised programs in all the key areas — programs that were serious, in-depth and carefully thought through. Each program was read out in the office of the party's regional committee and then put into action. We held open sessions and closed sessions. At the closed sessions each person would make representations about ongoing issues, including any complaints in relation to me. I intentionally created a businesslike, open setting, so that any criticisms addressed to me would be seen as a normal part of our working activities, although I didn't always accept the criticism — it dented my pride somehow — but I tried not to let those feelings get the better of me."[253]

After Bobykin's transfer to Moscow, the first secretary of the Sverdlovsk city committee of the CPSU, V.M. Manyukhin, was elected as his replacement, as tradition dictated. Viktor Mitrofanovich was a man with a large amount of experience of working in manufacturing, the professional unions and the

252   Same reference
253   B.N. Yeltsin: Against the Grain. P. 5 paras 2-53

party. Yeltsin enjoyed good relations with Manyukhin on both a personal and professional level.

In 2002 V.M. Manyukhin wrote: "…given my extensive experience of working with Boris Yeltsin, I can honestly say…, working with him was difficult, but he certainly knew how to work. He didn't patronize people about anything, didn't seek to put organizations of lesser standing in their place, and bravely went about seeking solutions for problems, particularly in terms of the socio-economic development of Sverdlovsk, with its population of one-and-a-half million. I don't remember an occasion on which he didn't support at least one of the city's initiatives. Yeltsin…considered the matter of staff training one of the most important of all. Particularly during the first stage of his work. He tried to apply his principles to the established procedure and *modus operandi* within the party's staff services…

He felt that in order to be able to hold down a position within the party organization, it was not essential to go through, as they said in those days, the school of practical and theoretical party training. Secretaries of regional committees ought not to have to go through such a long period of preparation: first be elected secretary of the party committee, then of the district committee, the city committee, and only after then — the regional committee. He considered all these steps extraneous. Instead, he felt that a promising administrative leader ought to be chosen, someone who was respected at the plant, generally from among the directors, chief engineers and their deputies, and promote them to being secretaries of the party committee, district committee, etc.."[254]

To talk of "promoting" these people was one thing; in practice, Yeltsin found it quite difficult. When the time came to replace the first secretary of a city committee or district committee, he would drive out to the site in question. He would go out there with a particular person already in mind. The candidates he suggested usually turned down the offer, however. They rarely stated their main reason for doing so, but Yeltsin could always put his finger on it: a comrade in the post of director received a salary of 500-700 roubles, and he was being asked to move voluntarily to a salary of 250 roubles. The potential candidate's argument was effectively: "go and try it on with someone else."

Only none of them were able to make Yeltsin change his mind. Citing 'party duty', he would 'break' anyone who opposed his views. After convincing his chosen candidate to stand, the first secretary of the regional committee would always meet local activists and find out their opinion on who they wanted to see in charge of the party committee. On occasion, the name of the candidate Yeltsin had in mind wouldn't even come up, but in such cases Yeltsin would stand firm, and the plenum would 'obey' him.

---

254   V.M. Manyukhin: A leap backwards. P. 26

There was strict delineation of duties between the secretaries. Thus first secretary Yeltsin was in charge of the department of organizational and party work (responsible for the communists' personal affairs and staff recruitment), the general department (in charge of documentation) and the party commission. In addition to this, the first secretary was also in charge of 'defence work'[255], and carried out 'overall management of the regional Committee of state security, as well as the companies in the 'secret' cities of Sverdlovsk-44 and Sverdlovsk-45.

In terms of importance, the first secretary of the regional committee was naturally followed by the second secretary. He was responsible for heavy industry and defence industry, transport, communications, engineering and financial and administrative activity, and also for the work of the planning organizations and the head office during the campaigns to provide assistance to the village.

Next in the hierarchy was the secretary for promotional activities and propaganda, who patronized scientific organizations, academic institutions, cultural and administrative bodies, the branch of the Academy of Sciences, sport, healthcare and social issues.

The fourth secretary was in charge of construction and the manufacturing of construction materials, work in the community, the allocation of housing, and the wood and paper manufacturing industries.

Finally, the fifth secretary was responsible for agriculture, light industry and food industry, and companies involved in agricultural engineering and trade.

By the end of the '70s almost two thousand members of the party organization (regional, city and district committees) had been relieved of their duties, 1192 of whom had held positions of responsibility within party agencies.[256] The leaders of the party took the issue of improving the quality of the responsible employees within the party agencies extremely seriously. The quality of the personnel improved dramatically. Particularly big changes took place among tutors — the key decision-makers in the party apparatus. The number of tutors with higher education rose by a factor of two and a half between 1969 and 1979, whilst the number of experts on the national economy almost doubled.[257] The regional committee imposed similar tasks related to the formation of the administration on the district and city party committees, as well.

---

255   In this regard B.N. Yeltsin, a member of the Military Council of the Urals military district was awarded the rank of colonel in 1978.
256   See: CDPASR. F. 4. Op. 95. D. 89. L. 5.
257   See: CDPASR. F. 4. Op. 95. D. 89. L. 5.

Things were a little different there, however. And whereas all the secretaries of the region's city committees and district committees had been through higher education, only 90% of the department directors and 78% of the tutors had degrees. There were staff in official positions in six of the region's party committees, who had not even been through secondary education.[258] Increasing the level of education and professional training of employees in official positions would become one of Yeltsin's constant preoccupations. As a result this level gradually went up.

It must be said, admittedly, that most of those who had been 'put forward' for such jobs did not last long. After doing it for two to four years (to coincide with the elections), they would ask to be released and given roles in manufacturing. There was no sense in holding back 'temporary' employees such as this by having recourse to party discipline. Those who were given backing tended first and foremost to be the people for whom work within the party had become a profession. This team contained the first secretaries of the city committees L.T. Belavin (Asbest), M.I. Khomyakov (Bogdanovich), I.S. Makhmutov (Verkhnyaya Salda), S.A. Zhdanov (Kamensk-Uralsky), V.F. Trenikhin (Karpinsk), A.I. Savchenko (Krasnouralsk), A.I. Khabarov (Krasnoufimsk), N.M. Tishkin (Krasnoturinsk), P.I. Sergeev (Kushva), E.B. Iskhakov (Novouralsk), N.A. Matveenko (Revda), S.A. Vinogradov (Severouralsk), N.K. Chechenin (Serov), and from among the secretaries of the district committees — M.P. Repenko (Oktyabrsky district of Sverdlovsk), V.K. Vasiliev (Artinsky), P.Z. Sysolyatin (Achitsky), P.D. Mingalyov (Slobodoturinsky), V.A. Shilin (Sysertsky), V.D. Syukosev (Shalinsky), V.V. Malyshkin (Talitsky).

Sverdlovsk and Nizhny Tagil played a particularly important role in the region and in its party organization. Their leaders were frequently replaced for one and the same reason — staff were plucked from here to be put forward for the regional and central agencies.

Nizhny Tagil is the second most highly-populated city in Central Urals, with a population of 450,000. It has some extremely powerful industrial enterprises. It has many thousands of people working in construction. All over the city there are local directors in charge of sizeable management agencies, plus party committees, professional committees and Komsomol committees.

Using the authority afforded by his high office, particularly after he became a deputy in the Supreme Soviet of the RSFSR, the first secretary of the Nizhny Tagil city committee, N.A. Talalayev, requested assistance from the central agencies and ministries, and a great deal of progress was made. When the first secretary of the party's regional committee, Boris Nikolaevich Yeltsin, found out about this, he began reprimanding Talalayev, saying that such

---

258   Same reference. L. 8-9.

wilfull behavior was unacceptable. Before seeking help from Moscow, he ought at least to have consulted the regional committee. In response Nikolai Alexandrovich, with a guilty smile on his face, said cunningly:

"Boris Nikolaevich, I can see what huge issues the regional committee is burdened by, and you personally are burdened by. Why add Tagil's problems to all that, if I can solve them by myself?"[259]

Yeltsin, it seems, understood this approach and accepted it.

Often, when meeting party leaders from the cities and the districts, the first secretary of the regional committee not only took an interest in the status quo and in the real problems that were affecting the city — he also set them an exam of his own devising. And he was not always satisfied with the knowledge displayed by those 'examined' in this way. On one occasion he concluded: "Many first secretaries have either no knowledge at all, or very shaky knowledge, of economic issues, the principles of working with human resources, issues related to acceptance of new party members, and the latest advances in agriculture. Strange as it may seem, the secretaries do not understand issues related to trade, discipline in the workplace and loss of working hours (and this includes the secretaries in charge of ideology)."[260]

Yeltsin was quick to introduce punishment — in this sense he had learned the lessons of his time as a student of the party.

And he also tried not to let his own team be punished by others. Although at times, even the first secretary of the regional committee found that his ability to protect them was hampered.

The chairman of the Council of Ministers of the USSR, N. Tikhonov, took a strong dislike to the director of Uralmash, Y.N. Kondratov. In all likelihood he was annoyed by the numerous requests coming in from the plant director, supported by the regional committee, asking that the enterprise by restructured. The friction between the two men led to personal hostility towards the director of Uralmash on the part of Tikhonov, and this enmity was matched by the other man. Eventually Yeltsin summoned Kondratov to his office and declared openly to him:

"Yury Nikolaevich, you've somehow managed to upset Tikhonov big-time, he's insisting that you be removed from your role as director. I don't think I need to explain to you the significance of the opinion of a member of the Politburo of the CPSU's Central Committee. In light of these circumstances, I wish to propose to you an honourable transfer to the role of deputy chairman of the regional executive committee."[261]

---

259   See: The Generals of industry. Collected notes. Yekaterinburg, 2009. P. 368.
260   CDPASR. F. 279. Op. 1. D. 136. L. 38.
261   See: The Generals of industry. See above. P. 194

It is worth noting that Tikhonov had an axe to gring not only with Kondratov, but with Yeltsin too — as would become clear in 1985, when Tikhonov was the only member of the Politburo to express reservations about Yeltsin's appointment to the Central Committee as head of the department of construction.

Kondratov was left with no option but to agree to the move. Before long it was down to him to find a solution for a problem which might have affected every single person living in the Sverdlovsk region. The last few months of 1978 would be remembered for record low temperatures. On the eve of 1979, the temperatures displayed on the thermometers installed around the city fell below minus 40. The plunging temperatures very nearly resulted in a disaster at the Beloyarsk nuclear power plant forty kilometres east of Sverdlovsk. Due to the closing of the electricity cables, the roof of the plant's turbine hall caught fire. The fire began to spread. There was a very real threat of a nuclear disaster — and this was long before the tragic events which were to unfold in Chernobyl. Yeltsin and Mekhrentsev tasked Kondratov with dealing with the emergency. He was forced to take risky decisions on the ground, at the site of the accident. Preparations were made behind closed doors for an evacuation of local residents.

The technical measures proposed by Kondratov and the engineers of the Beloyarsk nuclear power station were unprecedented in the USSR. After hearing about this over the telephone, the chairman of the Council of Ministers of the USSR, A.N. Kosygin, warned: "If people end up dying, Kondratov will be responsible." "It was Gulyaev who passed that on to me," Yury Nikolaevich recalls. "I told him that Kosygin was a long way from the site, whereas we were there, close to the reactor. And that unless we cooled it down, it would be very bad news for all of us."[262]

At around eight in the morning on 31st December, the temperature of the reactor began to drop. And by midnight the situation had been made safe. The Middle Urals region saw in the New Year joyfully, without the faintest inkling of what lay in store for it.

For the expertise he displayed in warding off the disaster, Kondratov was awarded the order of the October Revolution.

In addition to this, in Sverdlovsk just as in other regions, the leaders of the regional committee strove to adhere to the 'protocol used in the capital', particularly when it came to meetings with visitors from Moscow and from abroad. The first secretary of the regional committee began to be accompanied to the airport, and met there when arriving from foreign trips, by a cortège of

---

262   Generals of industry. See above. P. 187

cars containing his colleagues — just as happened in Moscow. A helicopter was used for excursions around the region. In Sofia Kovelevskaya Street a special luxury hotel was built, which was given the same name as the Central Committee's hotel — the Oktyabrskaya (October). At the professional union's Palace of Sport, a box was set aside for board members of the party's regional committee.

Yeltsin's requirements with regard to adherence to a 'dress code' of sorts were made known. Administrators who were invited to the regional committee for the first time to meet the 'first official', and who were ignorant of the established 'etiquette', would turn up in shirt-sleeves, without ties or jackets. On seeing such 'wilfulness', Boris Nikolaevich immediately sent them off to "get dressed properly." It was forbidden to attend a meeting of the regional committee's board with the buttons of one's jacket undone. At the same time, Yeltsin remained fairly demanding when it came to the directors of Soviet and administrative bodies of all levels. On one occasion, during a visit to the Karpinsk cotton-spinning plant, he spoke to the plant's director. The latter was standing in front of the first secretary of the regional committee with his hands in his pockets — his customary pose. Yeltsin deemed this far too 'lax', and gave him a sharp reprimand, telling him to "adopt a more dignified appearance." The director, looking flustered, began to stumble and give answers that bore no relevance to the questions he was asked, which only served to increase the ire of his distinguished guest.

And yet however that may be, nobody could accuse Boris Yeltsin of putting up barriers between himself and the people. The people did not see the head of their region's communist party as a leader of some sort, or, worse still, as a lord and master. He mingled with the masses confidently and eagerly, and never evaded questions from ordinary laborers.

Yeltsin would not hear of any favors being granted to his family, either. One of the doctors at the special hospital which provided services for the region's leaders revealed that the wives of senior party bosses, if they did not wish to work, used to try and persuade the doctors to give them a disability note for at least the second category. And the doctors would oblige. One day, when Yeltsin's wife Naina fell ill, the doctor treating her "suggested to Yeltsin: 'perhaps we ought to let your wife claim disability? She'll be able to stay at home all day.' Yeltsin (and I witnessed this with my own eyes) said to her in no uncertain terms: 'If Naina Iosifovna genuinely has a claim for disability because of her illness, then give one to her. If not — then under no circumstances give her one.' Yeltsin turned out to be the only secretary of the regional committee I can recall who did not wish a 'disability' on his own wife."[263]

---

263   See: *Komsomolskaya pravda*, 25th November 1997

The first secretary used to come along to agricultural and 'Lenin' *subbotniki* (community tidying-up events held on Saturdays) in civvies and muck in with everyone else. He would choose the site for the administration's own *subbotnik* himself. In April, everyone went along to the construction site for a future hospital complex. In the '80s, that was all the hospital for the disabled and war veterans was. The hospital's head doctor, a well-known regional manager S.I. Spektor, wrote: "I often took pleasure in citing the example of the first secretary of the regional committee of the CPSU, Boris Nikolaevich Yeltsin, who had himself taken part in a *subbotnik* once, when we were building the main hospital...The people had liked that. And he had liked it himself. He was there side by side with the people, and he probably felt an extraordinary sense of unity with those veterans who had won the war, and who, though already growing physically weak by then, remained spiritually strong..."[264]

Yeltsin also introduced another informal means of developing the collective spirit. This keen sportsman and volleyball player decided to encourage the regional committee's secretaries, heads of department and instructors involved in his favorite pastime. Some authors have claimed that he forced absolutely everyone to play volleyball, and this is not correct. Nothing of the kind ever took place — only those who were genuinely keen on the sport used to go along to the sports hall. Part of the appeal, of course, was that they would be able to contest matches in Yeltsin's team, which consisted of secretaries and members of the regional committee's board. And it was in fact a very strong team — after all, its members had 'learnt their trade' not only in that particular sports hall but also at Yeltsin's summer residence in Baltymsk. The 'secretaries' seldom lost, and when they did, Yeltsin's disappointment was liable to make him extremely angry.

As a general rule, the secretaries of the regional committee — particularly the first secretary — could only dream of being able to enjoy some down time. A detailed schedule was compiled for the entire working day, every week: where to be, what to do, who to hold talks with...The working day officially began at nine in the morning. Yeltsin would always arrive at eight. He would start his day with a visit to the hairdresser's — first secretaries had to make sure their appearance was flawless. This habit of needing to maintain a smart and tidy appearance was to stay with him throughout his life. Years later, the press-secretary of the President of the Russian Federation, V. Kostikov, recalled: "Usually the President took great care to make sure that he looked dignified, not to say elegant. He demonstrated particular — I would go so far as to say excessive — concern for his haircut. And whenever he walked past a mirror in the Kremlin, he would always take the opportunity to have a quick look at himself."[265]

---

264   S.I. Spektor: I love you, people! Yekaterinburg, 2010. P. 195.
265   V. Kostikov: A love-story with the President. Notes by the press-secretary. M., 1997.

At eight o'clock the press department delivered a 'summary' of the publications of the central newspapers in the Sverdlovsk Region, with a brief summary of their contents. If any 'burning issues' came up, he would read about them in the original. After that the 'daily grind' of meetings, assemblies, conversations and telephone calls would begin…Everything was supposed to be brought to an end by 6pm, but as a rule Yeltsin was never able to get home any earlier than about nine or ten in the evening. Yeltsin favored trips out into the region over his official duties — out there he could see "life being lived". Even when he was ill he did not let his poor health prevent him travelling around the region.

Yeltsin gave no quarter to members of party or state agencies who were accused of taking gratuities, abuse of office, or seeking to make personal gain from their official position.[266]

By the start of the '80s the party system in the Soviet Union, including its administrative body, was failing with increasing frequency. That same dissolution 'from above', which had given rise to a free-for-all and mass abuses for a particular section of the party administration, had begun — a phenomenon which would ultimately lead the party to a loss of authority among the masses and, ultimately, to the collapse of the entire Soviet-Communist system.

At this stage Boris Nikolaevich Yeltsin was still trying to resist the downward spiral towards a loss of morals among senior officials and party members. In February 1983, at a party assembly of the regional committee's administration, he took the floor and read from a large report 'On the moral countenance, personal responsibility and sense of discipline among senior party staff in the light of the requirements of the 26th congress of the CPSU, and the tasks facing the communists in the administration of the party's regional committee'.

He spoke as frankly as he possibly could at the assembly about the idea that "whichever issue we are trying to resolve, whichever enterprise we are seeking to undertake, the most important issue facing us is that of personnel."[267]

Yeltsin himself, who had not yet lost hope of altering the status quo as regards the top chain of party and state employees by improving the quality of work with personnel, tried to make use of all the powers at his disposal as a leader within the party. In 1981-1982, at a plenum of the party's regional committee, these issues were discussed 9 times; they were also examined at 35 plenums

---

P. 166.

266   CDPASR. F.4. Op. 95. D. 13. L. 16, 66, 68; Op. 92. D. 269. L. 63; F. 279. Op. 1. D. 130. L. 127, 24, 25, 30; F. 279. Op. 1. D. 136. P. 33, 34.

267   CDPASR. F. 279. Op. 1. D. 136. L. 24.

and board meetings of the party's city and district committees, and at many assemblies of the region's communists.[268] These efforts did not lead to any serious results. The party continued to be eaten away at by moral turpitude both in its upper echelons and among its grass-roots members.

In 1982, the region's prosecution services brought cases against a total of 573 officials for deceiving the state, violating laws regarding the protection of socialist property or allowing sub-standard products onto the market.[269]

Yeltsin continued to insist that "it is becoming more and more important that our personnel achieve a state of *moral* maturity (B.N. Yeltsin's italics — *Auth.*)." In order to demand unimpeachable behavior from others, it is essential first of all to have this quality oneself. "It was well put," he added, "by one of the secretaries of the party's district committee: 'People judge us secretaries less by what we say at the despatch box than by how we conduct ourselves in everyday life.' This is fully and entirely applicable to any leader."[270]

Boris Nikolaevich Yeltsin conducted himself properly during his time in office as secretary of the CPSU's regional committee.

He displayed talent and enthusiasm in the way he went about organizing the work of the party's administration.

He managed to maintain and slightly improve food supplies to the region, at a time when this was proving impossible in most of Russia's regions.

He was conscientious in his defence, before the union's leadership, of the idea that the amount of social support afforded to the people ought to be proportionate to the contribution made by the Sverdlovsk Region to the nation's economy — the third largest economy after Moscow and Leningrad.

He defended the 'idea of communism' at every possible opportunity.

He loved hunting and would often go out on hunting excursions with his comrades in the regional committee.

At the same time, he was a man with plenty of common sense and a strong awareness of his personal responsibility.

A secretary such as this was a blessing to the residents of the region and a subject of envy for their neighbors.

---

268   CDPASR. F. 279. Op. 1. D. 136. L. 25.
269   Same reference. L. 31.
270   Same reference.

Keep them fed. Keep them clothed. Provide for them. Unsolvable tasks

The top-down system of management which had been built up within the system of Soviet *nomenklatura*, when extended to cover the planning and distribution system, meant that the buck stopped with the first secretary when it came to providing supplies for the region's people. Securing funding, organizing the region's own production of consumer products — that was the job of the administration of the regional executive committee, the city executive committee, the district executive committee and the relevant party agencies — but organizing this entire bureacratic machine, checking it and monitoring it, and, if absolutely necessary, requesting help from the region's neighbors in Moscow — that was his concern, and that was what he was asked to do.

In 1976 there was 57 kg of meat and meat-related products per head of the population, 321 kg of milk and dairy products, 257 eggs, 119 kg of bread, 130 kg of potatoes and 82 kg of vegetables.

It was all very well counting it all up, but how could people get their hands on it?

Queues had become an integral part of life. People didn't buy food when they wanted it, but whenever meat and other foodstuffs which were in short supply were 'thrown out' onto the shelves in the shops. Since this process usually took place right in the middle of the working day, the only people who were able to buy food were those who were able to get to the shop-windows during the daytime. People who were at work were unable to get their hands on meat, curd, smetana or cheese. This situation resulted in calls from all sides for the authorities to bring in cards and vouchers, so that working people would be able to buy the kilogram of meat to which they were entitled each month!

People found they were lacking the bare essentials. The Sverdlovsk Region received less per head than the average for the rest of Russia — 9 roubles and 54 kopecks less leather shoes, 12 roubles and 47 kopecks less clothing and bed-linen, and 4 roubles and 82 kopecks less knitted garments.[271]

Boris Yeltsin wrote to the chairman of the Council of Ministers of the RSFSR, M.S. Solomentsev, on 14th November 1978, that "sales of leather shoes in the region are down 3.9%." Sales of clothing and bed-linen were also down, as were sales of knitted underwear, tights and socks, soap, cars, confectionery and fish; but for products such as silks, outer knitwear, furniture and jewellery, sales went up significantly less than in the RSFSR as a whole.

---

271   For further details see: CDPASR. F. 4. Op. 92. D. 110. L. 68.

Well-founded complaints were coming in from the public about the lack of ladies' toiletries, bed-linen and children's cotton underwear, and a host of other mass-consumption products."[272]

Yeltsin, when requesting help in increasing the amount of funding for industrial products, highlighted to senior figures in the party the fact that "in recent years the amount of funding allocated to the region for a host of industrial goods has satisfied demand among the people at the level of 50-60%. There has been major disruption to sales of cotton and linen fabrics, children's underwear and knitted underwear, ladies' toiletries, tights and socks, bed-linen and a host of other mass-consumption products. Numerous complaints have been coming in from people in the region about the fact that these products are not available on the shelves."[273]

The letters were almost carbon copies of one another. The numbers were the only things that changed. The shortage of goods had come into effect.

The industrial firms' auxiliary companies could not save them. In total there were around 400 such auxiliary companies. Huge efforts were put into the construction of the dairy and pig-feed complexes mentioned previously. Teams of engineers from the Ministry of medium-level engineering, which had been responsible for creating the nuclear weapon and the closely related companies run by the Ministry of Energy, were sent over to help construct them.

Agricultural production in the region, by means of the workforce from the cities, was monitored on a constant basis.

Yet the situation, which had improved as regards certain small details (specifically it became easier to get hold of poultry) had essentially remained the same. In letters to the Council of Ministers of the RSFSR with expressive titles such as 'On improvements to the supply of meat and dairy products for the people of the Sverdlovsk Region', 'On improvements to the supply of animal rearing products to the people of the Sverdlovsk Region' and others, it was reported that "more than 700,000 people (roughly 30% of the working population in the region) work in the ferrous and non-ferrous metals industries, down mines, on the railways, at petrochemicals plants and in various other sectors with dangerous and difficult working conditions. Moreover, due to the harsh climate and high levels of air pollution and pollution of the water basins, the people of the Middle Urals region had to put up with less favorable living conditions. For this reason, the Academy of medical sciences of the USSR recommends increasing the regulatory norms for the consumption of meat products. However, due to the specific conditions in which the region's

---

272   CDPASR. F.4. Op. 92. D. 110. L. 68.
273   Same ref.

economy has grown, it does not seem as though it will be possible to improve supplies to the people without an increased donation from the Republic's budget."

It was a cry for help from the regional authorities.

One got the impression that the regional authorities, having set up and repaired the management apparatus, had fallen into a vicious cycle whilst trying to improve matters for the public. The more the authorities stepped up their efforts, the more any possible solution to the problems of supply seemed to vanish over the horizon.

It was no coincidence that Boris Yeltsin, in his address to the Central Committee, referred to the numerous complaints coming in from the public to the authorities about vitally important issues. Analyses of the letters coming in from citizens, and of the information contained in them, were for him an important source of objective information about the true state of affairs. A huge number of these letters have survived in the archives. In some of them one can hear a cry for help in a very literal sense, despair, and fierce criticism directed at those in authority at every level. A study of their contents, and of the prevailing mood in society in that period as a whole, has been the subject of our independent research. We wish to take the liberty of pausing for thought over one such letter.

The letter was written by a man named Ilya Ignatievich Ivanov, who hailed from Sverdlovsk. It is of interest first and foremost because it was sent to Boris Yeltsin's home address. The man who wrote it only knew the street name and the number of the apartment block in which the first secretary's family resided. The apartment number and the words 'letter received by addressee' were carefully added, in pencil, by the postman. The servants refrained from throwing it away, although it was clearly of an unofficial nature, and instead passed it on to its intended recipient. Boris Yeltsin not only read the letter in its entirety — something that must have been a painful experience — but also took it to the regional committee, registered it and forwarded it for review. The envelope still bears the recipient's home telephone number, which suggests that Yeltsin was contacted by telephone about the letter's contents. We will now ask the reader to be patient and reproduce the text of this letter in full.[274]

"Dear Boris Nikolaevich!

What is going on? Where are we currently headed? How can there possibly be talk of communism as things stand? Who believes in this communism? Absolutely no-one. When we were younger, we had such strong faith in the bright future! We were so hopeful that something good would happen! And

---

274   The spelling in the letter has been left as it was in the original.

what are we to do now? Our living conditions are getting worse and worse. We have nothing but problems all around us. Those who work face constant calls to work and work, and work more efficiently. And what are people getting in return? Absolutely nothing! Our money has lost its value, you can't buy anything with it. You could draw up a list as long as your arm of all the everyday good that are no longer available on the shelves. Not to mention the problems with foodstuffs.

What do we see happening here in the Urals Region? Products which we make with our own hands are being packed off to all corners of the world! And the people are breaking their backs! So why must these people constantly suffer such hardships? Why don't you go and have a look around the shops yourself after work one evening? Surely you can see that there's absolutely nothing to eat? And what huge queues there are for the small amount of food that sometimes goes on sale! Why don't you draw up a contract for the supply of fruit from the republics in the south? After all, so much of their fruit and veg goes to waste. Where can our children go to enjoy a healthy diet? They are simply not getting enough nourishment...

If only you could hear some of the jokes the people are telling about Brezhnev and our government! And the thing is, they're spot on, they paint an accurate picture! The people hate Brezhnev, the young people have no respect for him, and mock him. The press and the radio are nothing but a talking shop, all you hear are slogans and phrases. If one were to give an entirely honest and just description of exactly how the average worker lives in our country, it would be deemed 'anti-Soviet propaganda' in our language. There is so much disorder and chaos in this country that to an outsider looking in it might well come across as being a fiction, a bit of slander against Soviet reality. And all this is down to the irresponsible behavior of our leaders.

And how bad things are when one gets ill! How hard it is to arrange an appointment with the doctor! All the appointments take place during the daytime, there's no chance of being seen in the evening after work, you always have to take time off work, which makes your bosses get all jittery.

Right now you're probably thinking that I'm just a nit-picker, who only sees the worst of everything. But just imagine for a minute that's not the case. The things I have written about in this letter are on everyone's lips. You can hear all this in the workplace, among your friends, or on public transport. And they are saying that this socialism of ours is just a front, and that we have poisoned the whole planet with our false socialism, whilst here at home we've got nothing but chaos and mess in the country...

Is it really the case that with all your power, you are unable to show concern for the Urals? After all, we are known as 'the Urals — the region that props up the state', the 'working Urals', etc. So we ought to be taking care of our people. We have a poor climate, and hardly any sunlight, warmth or fruit. We provide heavy industry for the country — but what we need are foodstuffs, fruit and warm clothing. Why is it that in the country's southern and western republics people live lives that are so much better? That's how they see it, too — that we don't so much live as merely exist, we never see anything good, all we have is work and cares...They have stopped importing fruit to us altogether. And what little is still sent here is consumed before it's left the central stores, bypassing the shelves in the shops.

And I'm well aware that once you've read this, all you'll do is screw up your eyes angrily.

Many people are already saying there ought to be a second revolution. How can we go on living like this? Why don't we introduce a system in which basic foodstuffs are allocated based on vouchers? After all, in Tyumen they distribute meat using vouchers. Whereas here there's only enough meat for one portion between three, and other people never lay eyes on meat at all.

Surely it is not too late to change our system?

I am sending this to your home address, because letters like this never get through to you at the office.

Yours faithfully, I. Ivanov."[275]

Vouchers were in fact introduced. Yeltsin managed to organize seasonal fairs for agricultural produce from Central Asia in the Sverdlovsk Region, and these markets began to take place. I. Ivanov's letter does not seem to have played any direct role in this. It was a relatively accurate reflection of public opinion at the time — opinion which had given rise to the depressing joke: "in 1980 they promised us communism, but organized the Olympic Games".

People's attitudes were changing. Yeltsin simply began listening to them earlier than anyone else.

The most unusual step taken by the regional powers was probably the decision to allow the opening, at the Shuvakish railway station, not far from Sverdlovsk, on the line between the region's two biggest cities — Sverdlovsk and Nizhny Tagil — of a gigantic flea-market, to which anything and everything for which there was demand (and there was demand for absolutely everything) was imported, from all over the Soviet Union: radio sets, records from the West, anoraks from Japan, mohair wool from India, cosmetics from Poland, jeans from Vietnam...

---

275   CDPASR. F. 4. OP. 98. D. 149. L. 96-97.

Every Sunday the suburban train to Shuvakish was heaving with people, and thousands thronged through the glade set aside for the market.

The start of the 'era of openness'

If we were to divide Boris Yeltsin's time in office as the first secretary of the Sverdlovsk regional committee into its key stages, it would be easy to divide up his activities into two stages. The first would include the time he spent getting used to the role, the steps he took to resolve the most important problems facing the region — above all the problem of food shortages — and the fact that he set up his own sustainable system of management, which was turned in, by means of nomenclature mechanisms, on the first secretary himself. In theory this would be sufficient for an entire term in office as first secretary. In early 1981, at the 26th congress of the CPSU, Boris Yeltsin was appointed a member of the Central Committee — the CC CPSU. Later that year, however, a new stage of his activities began which was completely out of the ordinary for such a high-ranking official in the party.

His career as a political figure had begun. As he issued instructions to the departments of science, propaganda and agitation of the CPSU's regional committee, asking them to arrange meetings with students from Sverdlovsk, collect questions from the students and teachers and prepare answers to them, the idea that he would henceforth be not only a party leader, but a national one, could not have been further from his thoughts. A regional leader, that is to say — for the time being at least.

So what exactly happened? Not a great deal, on first glance. There had always been a tradition of senior figures in the party speaking at plenums, conferences, triumphal assemblies and meetings with the community marking various occasions — usually anniversaries. They would be driven out to various enterprises, state farms and collective farms, construction sites and military bases and meet some of the directors, and occasionally some rank-and-file civilians too. They would ask questions and listen to the answers they were given. They were asked questions, too. For decades, the regional newspaper *Urals worker* had prepared, for the regional committee, summaries of the letters coming into the editorial offices, which contained a wide range of complaints and questions. Lecturers from the regional committee of the CPSU were given direct instructions to collect questions and inform the party leadership. Up to a hundred letters of complaint were received by the regional committee and dealt with by the letters department every day.

In April 1981 it was announced that the first secretary was going to hold a meeting with teachers and students. Large boxes shaped like pillar boxes were installed inside the university, the UPI, the Institute of Mining, the Institute of Pedagogy, the conservatoire, the University of Forestry, the Institute of Agriculture and other institutes of higher education, so that the students could post questions to the first secretary.

Yeltsin did a tour of the institutes along with his assistant V. Ilyushin, then was driven to the university, walked into the lecture hall, where a lecture on philosophy was under way, listened until the speaker had finished his lecture, then put in an appearance in the museum of ancient books along with the university's rector, where he spent a long time looking at some ancient books, most of which were written by the Old Believers, then discovered, to his surprise and obvious satisfaction — one might almost say with a possessive satisfaction — that Sverdlovsk was home to some of the rarest printed publications in the world, which had been produced several years before Ivan Fedorov's famous *Apostle* in 1564, went into the student dining room — where, to the rector's amazement, tablecloths had suddenly been put on the tables, chatted to the rector and his staff about the tasks facing the university — and left. The same pattern was repeated in a host of other universities and institutes, the only difference being that each university showed off its best assets.

With the exception of the more exotic elements of these visits, such as the lecture on philosophy, this too more or less fitted into the template for a visit to an institute of higher education by a minister or a senior party leader — whether in Sverdlovsk or in Moscow.

But thereafter things did not follow the pattern that had been repeated for decades.

The questions from the students had been collected. There were almost a thousand of them. The regional committee's administrative office had been tasked with sorting them into groups, analysing them and preparing draft answers, including suggestions as to how the issues raised could be solved.

In May 1981, one and a half thousand students and teachers, from 16 institutes of higher education in Sverdlovsk, gathered together at the Palace of Youth. Boris Yeltsin began with a few ritualistic opening remarks: "A 50,000-strong brigade of students...you are our future, you are a powerful force, a force which in tomorrow's world will provide us with experts for the national economy, and which will play a key, decisive role in developing technological progress, science, culture and our society as a whole. When the 21st century arrives, you will be flourishing. So it is fair to say that your gaze, as you look at me in this hall today, is the gaze of the century to come...."

After this preamble the bit everyone had been waiting for began — the answers to the questions. New questions had come flooding in, in addition to the ones prepared in advance. They were brought into the presidium from the hall by the bucket-load. It was later calculated that a total of 1074 questions were submitted.[276]

The meeting lasted five and a half hours. This was the moment when Yeltsin the polemicist was revealed; when he showed himself to be a person capable of holding and audience and inspiring unquestioning and obvious sympathy. He answered the questions, he thought about his answers right before the eyes of the audience, and people sensed that he was seeking to provide an answer all of his own, rather than one which had been prepared in advance in case this question came up.

The audience forgave him for his evasive answers, allowed for his official position and the limitations that came with it, and had no difficulty identifying the need to read between the lines in some of his answers. Here is a short excerpt from the transcript:

"Question. Why is it that no young people want to live in rural areas?

Answer. B.N. Yeltsin. To be so categorical about it is probably not quite right, after all — 'don't want to'...'none of them want to'...it's not the case that none of them want to. Young people are staying in the countryside, of course a lot of the girls face problems, serious problems. The young men have jobs for which they can stay, they can be mechanics, but unfortunately there aren't too many professions for girls — ones that appeal to them enough. The girls are therefore leaving in their droves, and naturally the young men are following them. Now, as for how we can bring the two of them together, how we can halt the exodus of girls, so that the young men stay put as well — we are currently weighing this up, but it's not as straightforward as you might think.

Question. Uralobuv is making sub-standard, ugly shoes for the shops, but exporting high-quality shoes. So does that mean we're not allowed to wear shoes that are as good as those worn by people in other countries?

Answer. B.N. Yeltsin. Well first of all I should point out that I'm wearing shoes made by Uralobuv too, albeit ordinary, mass-produced ones. They aren't too bad at all, incidentally — at least, they're pretty solid and I didn't buy them overseas, but here, in the department store. Uralobuv turns out 11 million pairs of shoes a year, half of which are sold in our region; 55% of its shoes are for children. In recent years it has expanded its range and the quality has been somewhat improved, let's say...Over 400 types of shoe have been re-certified and manufactured using the state mark of quality — that's 15% of the total number of models — and these are the ones which you will struggle to find today.

---

276   The student meridian. 1981. No. 11

Question. What do you intend to do to improve the way the Shuvakish market is run? (laughter inside the hall)

Answer. B.N. Yeltsin. It has already been brought to my attention that the students refer to this place as 'the herd'. It truly is an ulcer on the body of the hard-working city of Sverdlovsk. We must try to bring some order to the Shuvakish market. We must build a road to the market, organize a paid parking lot (laughter inside the hall), strengthen the fences and introduce a special system of entry. We must destroy the radio products which are being sold there illegally, and then make sure that anyone selling anything must indicate the price, by hanging a price-tag around the product, 30 roubles, 20 roubles, etc. Next — in the past it was very hard to bring illegal tradesmen to justice, because while the person was being brought to Sverdlovsk he would either flee, or the judge would change his mind, or the policemen arresting him would decide to have him put on trial right there, on site — they have *in situ* trials operating there these days. It all happens straight away — the moment they find two dodgy records — he's a speculator, they have a trial, and that's it...he's banged up (laughter and applause inside the hall).

A question. A question. We are students from the Urals State Economic University.[277] Our canteen is really dirty, you often see flies on the food, and cockroaches crawling along the floor and the tables. The food is cooked in a sub-standard way, it's not appetizing at all, there's no real choice, the staff are really slow, sometimes the dishes are all the same as each other.

Answer. B.N. Yeltsin. I went to your university's canteen today, along with my comrades, but clearly I made a tactical error — yesterday, at eleven o'clock in the evening, I gave my colleagues a bit of warning. As for what's written down here — there was nothing of the kind. There were no cockroaches, we checked; we went to look at the food, there was a huge heap of pastries, they were hot, I felt them. There was a range of juices, tea, cucumbers, tomatoes (loud laughter inside the hall),[278] a choice of three main dishes, including beef stroganoff, no less. Religiously, I specially took away a menu. I'm not going to point him out now, but among you is comrade Boris Stepanovich, of the Regional directorate of public catering."

Yeltsin's performance on stage, and, specifically, his answers to the questions from the hall, caused a genuine sensation in Sverdlovsk, at a time when sensations were few and far between.

The most striking thing was that the man in charge of the region was a normal person, to whom people did not find it difficult to relate. He was

---

277   SINKh — The Sverdlovsk Institute of National Economy
278   The reason for this laughter was that finding tomatoes in Sverdlovsk in 1981 was as difficult as it was to find violets in the forest in E. Schwartz's fairytale. The directorate of public catering had managed to do so.

aware of the conditions in which people were living, he realised that there was a shortage of goods, that people were being swindled at the shops and conned by caterers. He was trying to make life better for them. People trusted him. And he was just an all-round great guy!

The second thing people noted was the first secretary's desire to meet all the key groups of the population in person: workers at the factories, writers, the people behind party propaganda, journalists, pensioners... This created an enormous number of problems for the administrative agencies of the regional committee and the regional executive committee. They had to analyse thousands of questions, prepare draft answers, and, most importantly of all, find positive solutions to the problems about which Yeltsin was being informed, and which, thenceforth, came under his strict, personal control. Understandably, this did not go down well with the administrative office, which now had to cope with new, burdensome duties.

The other great thing about Yeltsin was the fact that when admitting responsibility for something, he would always publicly name the person who, in his opinion, was guilty of an oversight, or who had performed badly.

There were other things of note, too. Yeltsin had been the first person to converse openly with a huge audience of some 1500 people. His experience as an athlete helped him to feel at ease on the stage, just as he had once been at ease in the sports hall. His knowledge of management, of the role of first secretary, his instinctive desire for power and his charisma gave him the ability to hold sway over people's moods. This was quite possibly a revelation for the man himself, as much as anyone. He had become a leader — not only in terms of his official position, but in his very essence; not only as a result of his appointment among the nomenclature, but also because he talked about the issues which were affecting millions of people, and didn't gloss over them, as the official propaganda always did.

I wish to point out here that as soon as Yeltsin began these meetings with the general public, the level of conflict between him and the other secretaries of the regional committees, who were unable or unwilling to hold such meetings — and were sometimes afraid of them — began to rise, negligibly at first, and then to an increasingly noticeable extent. Even at that stage, accusations of demagoguery and populism hung in the air among his party staff.

Why had Yeltsin undertaken what was, if not a violation, then a clear departure from the rules governing the behavior of a party secretary? Why had he chosen an audience which was not comprised of party and administration members, or members of the Komsomol? This is probably the most important question of all, the answer to which will enable us to understand his subsequent political activity.

It seems to the authors that even in those days, right at the start of the '80s, Yeltsin had a sense — before he actually came to this understanding, and formulated it for himself — that it was impossible to govern the region by relying solely on an obedient staff. That only mass popular support could, if not rescue him from innumerable difficulties, then at least give people an understanding of the authorities' behavior. And as for the idea that his (and the party's) plans coincided with the plans of the people — he doubtless never called that into question.

Yet there were others who did. And their doubts would come bubbling to the surface during meetings with the first secretary. Some unexpectedly pointed questions, on issues of fundamental importance, were posed to Boris Yeltsin on 7th April 1982 at a meeting with the heads of the departments of social sciences and teachers, and ideologists from the region's higher and middle special educational establishments — in a word, the people who, to use the terminology of the day, were on the 'ideological front-line'.

The most difficult question and unexpected question of all was this: why had the Sverdlovsk Region been awarded the title in a socialist inter-regional competition marking 60 years since the USSR was founded, and been named the best region in the Urals? If things were as they were in the Sverdlovsk Region — masses of problems providing the people with what they needed, vouchers and cards, a chronic shortage of everything — did this mean others had it even worse?

And this was followed by another question: was this the end product of sixty years of the USSR?

The questions differed from one another, but they were all awkward, and could not be dealt with by the standard, stock responses. "Why are we seeing a constant disparity in our national economy?" i.e. why are the plants working for their own interests, and for the good of industry, rather than to satisfy the ordinary needs of the people?

"Why was the 26th congress of the CPSU so obsequious towards Leonid Brezhnev, and why didn't Yeltsin react at all to the excessive praise that was heaped on the general secretary by the local leader from Krasnodar, S. Medunov?"

"Students often wonder: 'Why was Uzbekistan awarded the order of Lenin, and comrade Rashidov the order of the October Revolution, when one in four enterprises in the Uzbek SSR is failing to meet its sales targets?'",

"Why have we not established a communist party of the Russian Federation?"[279]

---

279   CDPASR. F.4. Op. 101. D. 87. L. 11-14.

These questions were coming from the very section of the party which ought to have been explaining the party's policy, and which could clearly see the inherent contradictions between the words they heard, the ideological dogma and the reality of life.

There is another aspect to these questions as well. When asking them, the university teachers were putting their faith in Yeltsin. They could only be asked of a man who was himself concerned about the country's destiny. And they could only be posed in the particular atmosphere which prevailed in the Sverdlovsk Region following the famous meeting with local students.

Yeltsin conscientiously set about arranging meetings with people from all social and professional backgrounds, and of all ages, as the months went by. He had not yet seen the pensioners, though. He had not yet seen people living in small towns and villages. And then he hit upon an idea: to organize a meeting 'live on air', via the regional television, involving everyone living in the region. The meeting was scheduled for 18th December 1982.

The journalist G. Kaeta, who at the time was editor-in-chief of the newspaper *The Urals Worker* and was on the board of the regional committee, would later recall: "I was required to get directly involved during the preparatory period, and therefore to this day I can still feel the 'horror' which gripped the regional committee's staff and the region's Soviet services. We received 4090 letters on 1037 different issues! How could we give precise, concrete and, above all, concise answers to all of them? How much information would we need to collect, how many papers would we have to trawl through? We didn't know where to start. …We devised answers for groups of questions on similar issues, and decided to put the most awkward ones "on one side". Yeltsin objected straight away: "Deal with the awkward ones first!"[280]

G. Kayeta wrote: "On the evening of 18th December, it was as if the whole region was sitting in front of the TV; those who were unable to catch it demanded that re-runs be shown. Nobody had ever heard such frank and open debate with the region's most senior official."

Yeltsin began his TV address by saying: "It will doubtless have come to your attention via the mass media that the party's regional committee has of late been holding a lot of meetings...with people working in industry, teams of engineers, people rearing animals, technicians at zoos, milkmaids, propaganda experts, students, teachers from social science faculties, leaders of pioneer groups, those working in education and healthcare. These conversations have varied in nature and involved audiences of various sizes: 12, 15 or 25 people, occasionally 1500 people, such as the meeting with the students, for example.

---

280   G. Kayeta: Boris Nikolaevich Yeltsin. The Urals period of his life. Yekaterinburg. 1996. P. 22-23.

Yet they had one thing in common: they have all been held in an atmosphere of strong trust and they have been extremely open. Practically all the questions which have been asked by our comrades have been answered."

And the first question he began answering was that same one again: "we're facing a lot of drawbacks in the region, a lot of oversights, problems, and, it must be said, failures and so on. …And then suddenly, after all this, the Sverdlovsk Region is declared the winner in the all-union socialist competition marking 60 years since the establishment of the USSR, and is given the Red Banner of the Central Committee of the CPSU, the Council of Ministers of the USSR, the Council of Trade Unions and the CC of the Komsomol. It begs the question, how can this be? On the one hand there are so many failings, and yet on the other, we are the only region in the Urals to receive a Red banner. It seems to me, comrades, that we oughtn't to couch the question in those terms. First of all, it is a competition, and all the figures achieved by the competing regions are compared with one another, that's how it works. That means that the Politburo, the party's Central Committee, the government and the Council of Trade Unions, as well as the Council of Ministers and the CC of the Komsomol, have recognised our results as being the best, better than all the other regions in the Urals, let's say."

This response did not quite get to the heart of the matter. The region was better...because its results had been better. And yet he had noticed this question, and opened with it!

"In short," Yeltsin continued, "what I want to say is that it is our belief that the Red banner is always awarded for good reason, but that we are on no account trying to paper over our failings. I am going to go into this in more detail when I answer your individual letters. And for our part, of course, with all the work that we do, including by the party's regional committee, we are trying first and foremost to draw people's attention to our efforts to get rid of these failings, so as to make this crucial year, 1983 — to make it better than the two previous years, 1981 and 1982, because in many ways it is going to go further than the successes achieved during the five-year plan as a whole."

Next came answers to the most topical question of all — that of the 'food program'.

Yeltsin revealed that the region had adopted a food program of its own. "Naturally, when devising this program we took into account the particular nature of our region — and it is indeed a special region. Firstly, in terms of the volume of industrial output it is the biggest region in the country. The density of industrial output here is 4.6 times higher than the level throughout the Russian Federation and the country, and the region has a population of 4.5 million people, in a region with an area of 194,000 square kilometers.

...But most importantly of all, given such density of industrial output, we have companies in absolutely all of the ministries and institutes — the region is unique in this sense as well. Yet it is unique in the region in the sense that here...only 6 percent of the working population are employed in the agricultural sector. In neighboring regions this figure stands at 20, 25, 30, 40 or 50%. Here it is just 6%. And this 6% must somehow make every effort to implement the Food program for all of the 4.5 million people living in the region. That is no easy task, it has to be said."

Looking at this objectively, Yeltsin had said nothing new. These self-same arguments had been used by both him and his predecessors when they were asking the Union of Ministers and the CC for additional food supplies. When they were expressed by someone appearing on a TV screen, however, these arguments took on a new meaning: why had a region produced iron and titanium, tanks and rockets, and parts and pipes for the oil industry, for which there was such a strong need in the country at the time, was not getting supplies from the national budget which were proportionate to its contribution to the economy, including food supplies?

The first secretary of the regional committee went into great detail about the measures being taken in the Sverdlovsk Region to ease the problems with the supply of food. These involved the construction of new animal rearing complexes, auxiliary farms for industrial enterprises, and assistance for the village at citizens' expense. Yet the situation, Yeltsin said, remained complicated.

The transcript of his TV address contains the following passage:

"Many people in Sverdlovsk are wondering what the specific prospects are for 1983, in terms of improving the supply of meat and dairy products to Sverdlovsk and the other cities.

Supplies of milk in 1983 — and this is a firm commitment — are going to improve. As regards supplies of meat. Here things are rather more complicated. It is made more complicated by the fact that we only produce 40% of the meat for the Sverdlovsk Region ourselves, whilst the remaining 60% is donated to us. There are, of course, many complexities and difficulties here. And the more we increase our understanding of meat production, the more we will be able to see reductions in the amount donated. Therein lies the key to understanding that the provision of meat products to the people of the Sverdlovsk Region does not depend on us alone. We must, without question, increase meat production, because this improves the provision of resources to us, but this does not solve the issue of supplies. This year we are going to consume 215,000 tons of meat and meat-related products. 215,000 tons. May I remind you: in 1970 we consumed 140,000 tons — 140,000."

Yeltsin quoted a letter he had received from the Artemovsk district, which had contained the line: "We are keeping a cow — without it we would be struggling."

This letter, and the questions posed in it about the situation faced by individual subsidized farms, prompted Yeltsin to declare from the screen: "It must be acknowledged that insufficient attention was given to this issue in the 1960's. It was felt that we would be able, via the state sector, to provide the whole population with sufficient food supplies within the next 20 years or so, let's say. But lately the party's Central Committee has adopted a series of directives designed to activate the work we are doing and draw particular attention to citizens' private farms. In our region, with the exception of the last 2 years there has been a constant fall in numbers of the following per head of the population: cows, pigs, sheep etc. ...At the moment we have slightly more cows per head of the population this year than we had last year.

The public are adding to the numbers significantly from their own private auxiliary farms."

"Comrades, the next section of our program," Yeltsin said, turning to the camera, "involves your questions on retail, which are very, very difficult for me."

After that, quoting the letters he had received, he listed the items which could not be found on the shelves at all and the ones which were in short supply. There were no cotton fabrics and there was no bed-linen. The letters contained requests that sales of bed-linen be organized "to order", i.e. simply on presentation of cards. "This is a huge issue, and a very topical one," Yeltsin said. "It is a question we are asked wherever we go — in the warehouses, on the farms, at companies, at organizations; sometimes we go into the shops and they surround us and bombard us with questions." After lengthy discussions about the fact that most of the cotton was being used to meet the needs of industry, to hospitals, or to children's institutions, the first secretary admitted: "Of course people get angry, and I get angry too, and I insist on finding out where the blame lies among the regional agencies, and identifying my own personal blame before you, for the fact that we can't solve this problem, and yet for the time being it doesn't seem possible that we can solve it... As regards selling cotton fabrics and bed-linen in exchange for coupons. On several occasions we discussed how little it would be, and the fact that it would simply be inconvenient to sell..., we don't have the ability to effect a transition to selling goods, including bed-linen, on a coupon-based system."

Yeltsin replied and explained why it was not possible to buy Krona batteries, ordinary scissors, teapots...

He reported that "the tension has been removed in the retail of cosmetic and household soap, toothbrushes, toothpastes, things are better as regards electric lightbulbs, and certain ladies' toiletries, and there has been a rise in sales of mass-consumption products, even lipstick — so for women in particular the problem has been dealt with."

On the one hand this indicated that the head of the region was aware of the problems the people were facing and was trying to deal with them, but on the other hand people had involuntarily become convinced that the root of the problem did not lie in the mistakes made by the bosses or the craftiness of retailers. Behind the list of decisive measures for the manufacture of teapots at the Bogdanovich and Systertsk factories[281] there had been a simple idea — or perhaps, error — within the economic system itself, which was now beyond the control of the people who were supposed to be handling this economy...

There was a need to seek out the simplest possible answers to the most difficult questions, all the more so given that this was what most of his audience were expecting.

So there weren't enough cabbages, potatoes or carrots on the shelves? In that case he ought to agree to the suggestion contained in a collective letter from staff at the Sverdlovsk instrument-manufacturing plant — to buy up potatoes, beets, carrots and cabbages in the Beloyarsk district, where the instrument-manufacturing plant (which produced extremely technical electronic hardware for the army) collected the harvest each year. "On their way home after work, many people would have agreed to buy vegetables straight from the fields. So they ought to be brought to the city in the same vehicles in which they arrived.

Which, it may be said, is an entirely proper proposal, very much so, and moreover it does not contradict any of our directives or laws, and we are making use of this proposal and are trying in 1983 to arrange sales of this kind."

---

281   I shall quote this section of the speech. It is typical of him. "First of all — teapots. Well, they have built an enormous porcelain factory in Bogdanovich, and there's a porcelain factory in Sysert; they produce wonderful dinner services, and teapots — they are part of these dinner services too..., but since they get broken more quickly, it's hard to find them anywhere after that. And I would go so far as to say that this reason is so petty that it hurts. It is more profitable for the company to produce a whole dinner service than a single teapot, which is 3 times bigger than a plate in terms of volume, but costs the same as a plate to buy. After hearing your questions, some of which, I have to say, were not expressed very politely, we shall look at this issue; I would say it has not yet been fully dealt with, but we will get to the bottom of it. This year 500,000 teapots are going to be manufactured by the Bogdanovich porcelain factory, including 50,000 by the factory in Sysert. A minimum target has been set — we shall come back to this issue — of producing 700,000 teapots in 1983, and by 1985 a million teapots will be produced each year. I think a million teapots a year ought to be enough to satisfy demand."

"Comrades (there followed a long list of surnames) are asking for sales of meat and smoked sausage products by order to be arranged, the way they are with animal oil. We spent a long time discussing this matter yesterday, in accordance with your letters. And in the end we decided to take this step. As of the first of February 1983 sales of smoked sausage have been introduced in Sverdlovsk based on orders of 1 kg a month for each resident."

There had been abuses within the house management services which distribute the coupons for cream: "We are currently taking emergency measures along with the city, this has already been announced to the Sverdlovsk city committee, to the party, and the city executive committee, and closer ties will be established between the internal affairs agencies and the house management services.

I would ask that you give your opinion as soon as possible, in February, as to what exactly went on. Ought we to continue to use this system in the future, or did we do something wrong. It is down to you to determine the answer to this."

Yeltsin talked about the scale of residential construction in the region, which was genuinely impressive, and about the construction of kindergartens, schools, hospitals and clinics, and about the fact that a circus and a children's theatre had been built in Sverdlovsk, as well as a Palace of Young People and numerous swimming pools...

In addition to this he gave extremely detailed answers to criticism directed at transport arrangements in the districts where construction was under way, and the problems associated with landscaping of new districts, and issued orders from the TV screen to the chairman of the Sverdlovsk city executive committee.

Announcing the start of construction work on the metro, Yeltsin said "the technical plan has been approved, that the first line would run from Uralmash to 1905 Square, that construction work had begun, and that a special bridge unit had been created, and that we had already gone down into the first mine, that bridge engineers were working very intensively, and that the plan for the current year had been fulfilled. For the following year, 1983, approximately 5.5 million roubles had been allocated, which will, without question, be poured back into the economy." And he noted, not without a hint of bitterness: "Of course we wish it could be built more quickly, so that we could ride on it before we become pensioners, but that is going to depend on how many centralized resources are allocated to us by the government and the State plan for the USSR."

The installation of telephones and telephone stations, messages from veterans and people with disabilities, the age-old problems of having to wait to be given housing, the status of discipline in the workplace and the battle against drunkenness — this is by no means an exhaustive list of the questions and answers touched upon in Boris Yeltsin's address, which took up over two hours of screen time.[282]

The first secretary of the regional committee allowed himself the indulgence of quoting the following letter, too: "Comrade Yeltsin, in the year in which you took office as first secretary, the region lost both its football team and its ice hockey team. What are you going to do to make sure that football and ice hockey survive in Sverdlovsk?"

"I understand," Yeltsin replied, "that, as Leonid Brezhnev wrote in his memoirs, first secretaries are held accountable for everything — little things, medium-sized things and big things — and that means that I am accountable for the fact that Uralmash has failed in the football, and for the fact that Avtomobilist was relegated from the top league. I must admit that I have probably not spent enough time on this issue in person, and nor have the staff of the party's regional committee who are directly responsible for handling this area. We had an in-depth look at what happened, and we spoke about it to the coaches, the responsible officials from the party's regional committee, from the regional executive committee and from the regional union of professionals. This is what we think: we want to see Automobilist in the top league within two years, and we want to see Uralmash in the first group within two years. Although it won't be easy to make that happen. There are a great many issues involved here."

This came across as impertinent and fairly irresponsible.[283] But at the same time it sounded like the sort of thing a real fan might say, and was provocative in a sporting sense.

He then touched on another subject — this time one that was extremely serious. This was the problem of directors being held accountable for the results of their activities, the problem of directors' moral countenance. After some providing some information that was becoming of this subject about the educational level of the "senior director personnel", listing the people in the region who were held in esteem, and declaring that "the vast majority of our directors are by their nature independent, courageous, and demonstrate initiative, modesty and concern for the issues which affect the whole country," Yeltsin moved on to the crux of the matter.

---

282   The transcript of the televised address on 18 December 1982 is quoted based on a record autographed by the then adviser to the first secretary of the Sverdlovsk regional committee, V.V. Ilyushin. The transcript is kept in the collection of the B.N. Yeltsin Center in Yekaterinburg.

283   The football team Uralmash did not get into the top Russian league until 1990.

"I am not going to conceal it," he told the region's people from their television screens, "...lately there has been a large increase in the number of letters sent in to the party's regional committee, including letters addressed to me in person, about abuses of position by administrative leaders, their personal conduct, their conceit, instances of bureaucracy, lack of restraint and rudeness...

With great regret I must inform you that 573 people in official positions, i.e. people in authority, have been punished for deceiving the state. ...43 directors were given severe punishments, 88 directors were relieved of their responsibilities for failing to cope with their work, and 117 members of staff in directorial roles were expelled from the party, this year and last year alone. ...

It isn't pleasant, of course, to read that you are driving around in black *Volgas* with zeroes on the license plates, but when it's you that's okay, but then also your wives, relatives, children and so on are also being driven around.

I had a meeting recently with a group of school principals. There were 14 of us here in my office, and they were telling me, with a strong sense of bitterness, that it is simply extremely unpleasant, not to mention the damage it does, when so many schoolchildren are dropped off at the school gates by black *Volgas* assigned to their fathers. It is simply extremely damaging to the psyche, firstly of the child who is being dropped off, and also to all the other pupils, who see that this child is getting a ride to school for some reason, whereas I have to take the tram.

This causes a huge amount of damage to the psyche. And it is my belief that here in our region we must take the following line: we must state that it is unacceptable for anyone to be driven around in a car, unless the official to whom the car is assigned is present in the vehicle. It is unacceptable."

"Comrades," Yeltsin said, bringing his TV address to an end, "I understand that not all of you are satisfied by my answers. I shall do all I can to ensure that satisfaction levels rise throughout December and January, and perhaps February, when we will be dealing with some of these issues, and you will get the answers you want. And it may be that the issues will be resolved, and you will understand that they have been resolved without the need for more answers. In closing I must say that these letters taken together, with their 4090 signatures, give me a strong idea of the typical Urals resident, the typical citizen of Sverdlovsk. And this typical citizen is, as you know, resolute in their intentions, strong, and without doubt desiring success for their affairs, for their home region, their company, their street, their yard, their city...someone who wishes, of course, to do all he can to make life better for the people of Sverdlovsk. And I am convinced that the people of the Urals are sufficiently resilient that no ill winds, of whatever nature — particularly insignificant ones, and including ideological ones — will ever perturb them."

It is the authors' belief that this TV address was designed to set out Yeltsin's entire program.

Whilst demonstrating ideological loyalty, in practice Yeltsin nonetheless went beyond the acceptable boundaries of behavior for someone in a position of authority.

Let us now list these departures from the norm.

He allowed the people living in the region to become acquainted with the same arguments in defence of their social and economic rights which had previously only been used by the authorities in the region. Thus the public became party to the discussion about issues related to the place of the Sverdlovsk Region — which was ranked third in terms of its industrial potential — within the system for the distribution of social welfare.

He openly identified the problems and indicated how the authorities intended to go about solving them, determined the levels of accountability — what the regional committee was supposed to be doing and was doing, and what the other local authorities were doing or not doing (and did not neglect to name the individuals responsible), gave a clear hint as to where the boundary lay between the region's capabilities and the remit of the state plan, the Council of Ministers and the CC.

He called on the people themselves to get involved in solving some of the problems, stating that the regional committee would lend its support to this activity.

Those in power, according to Yeltsin, must be under the constant supervision both of those in power and of the citizens on whose behalf they serve.

He spoke of the need for there to be constant contact between those in power and the people.

And, finally, he revealed, probably unintentionally, how powerful television could be as a tool for propaganda and mobilizing people.

It is not hard to see the continuation of these provisions, which were first formulated in Sverdlovsk, later on, in Yeltsin's activities as first secretary of the CPSU's Moscow city committee.

For the record let us point out at this stage that this degree of openness on the part of the first secretary of the CPSU's regional committee was not to everyone's liking — far from it. The one-time secretary of the CC CPSU and former party leader in the Sverdlovsk Region, Yakov Ryabov, would later write: "...he sensed that he had become the *Boss* (his italics — author) in the region and began this false game, playing with the people like a pharisee, looming large from their TV screens for between 90 minutes and 2 hours at a time, answering questions and publicly 'ruffling a few feathers' among the officials in the region, the cities and the districts."[284]

Ryabov had himself ruffled a few feathers in his time. But he had always done so within a close circle of people who were directly responsible for getting things done. And he was equally aware himself that he was a boss. He was a strong person with a strong will — so strong, indeed, that he openly argued with Marshal Ustinov, a member of the Politburo, about issues related to the country's defence policy. And he also spent a lot of time and genuine effort looking into problems related to raising the status of the Sverdlovsk Region.

Ultimately he was unable to rely on the support of the people, however. And his sacking, which was both unjust and undeserved, became no more than a brief episode in the history of late Soviet history and a complicated period in his life. He was never able either to forgive or forget his successor, who was both more successful and, frankly, had a better feel for the times.

The start of the 'era of openness', which had been initiated by Yeltsin, was going to have considerable significance for him as a politician. He was a man people were going to hear about throughout the country. S.A. Filatov, the head of the first President of Russia's administration, later confessed: "The first time I noticed Yeltsin was when he was working for the Sverdlovsk regional committee of the CPSU. They had just launched a new program on the TV - meetings between TV audiences and senior officials in the regions. By the standards of the day it was something new and progressive, and a whole series of programs like that began after the one with Yeltsin. It was clear that the man on the screen was a party functionary, but at the same time a lot of people were impressed by his disarming openness, energy, his knowledge of the subject, about which he was able to talk at length."[285]

Yeltsin, the first secretary of Sverdlovsk, had become a political giant of Russia-wide dimensions.

Ideology rears its head

The Sverdlovsk was not only an extremely large industrial hub and a cultural centre boasting theaters and concert halls, around fifteen institutes of higher education, the Urals scientific centre, a powerful publishing house and a number of literary journals. In the late 1970s there was a journal called *Urals*, approximately 100,000 copies of which were printed with each edition.

---

284   Y.P. Ryabov: My 20th century. P. 56.
285   S.A. Filatov: An open secret. M., 2000. P. 421-422.

The magazine often featured articles by Viktor Astafiev, Boris Ruchiev and Lyudmila Tatianicheva. The journal later had a literary criticism section which was one of the best in the country.[286]

In May 1980 the secretary for ideology on Sverdlovsk's regional committee, V.A. Zhitenev, invited a tutor from the department of philosophy at the Urals University, V.P. Lukyanin, to pay a visit to the regional committee. He was a well-known literary critic and one of the regular feature writers for *Urals*. The secretary of the regional committee proposed that he take charge of the journal and become its editor-in-chief. Lukyanin fended off his advances, saying that the role of an administrator was not for him, and that he had no knowledge of the mechanics of the publishing industry.

Zhitenyov rejected this, saying that all the technical work related to the publishing of the journal was carried out by the publishing house.

Below is a brief extract from a conversation mentioned in one of V.P. Lukyanov's articles.

"'Vladimir Andreyevich, whatever makes you think it would be a good idea to appoint me? After all, you'll have to remove me from the post again in two or three months' time — all you'll have done is ruin my reputation for no good reason.' …

'And secondly,' I went on insistently, 'I'm bound to go making ideological errors…'

He started laughing:

'What nonsense! We understand perfectly well that there's no place for dogmatic thinking these days — that fresh, bold approaches are needed. We'll be here to support you.'

That's the progressive kind of guy he was. At first it seemed to me as if he was as good as his word even on that score: right from the outset we allowed ourselves a little 'indulgence' of some kind or other, and no-one made any complaints against us.'"[287]

For all V.P. Lukyanin's obvious irony, the fact remains that during his tenure as editor-in-chief he succeeded in changing the journal's editorial policy, turning a regional publication into something that was of genuine interest to the whole country. A series of stories and novels were published in the journal

---

286   L.P. Bykov, N.L. Leiderman: Literature in the Urals in the 1960s-70s // Literature in the Urals. — Yekaterinburg, 1998. — P.268
287   V.P. Lukyanin: The period of ice-breaking. The Urals on the eve of perestroika // The Urals, 2008, №1

which touched on the problems of an individual's personal responsibility when subject to pressure from the authorities, and the problem of where to draw the line when seeking a compromise with them — such was the theme of A. Romashova's story *Diophantine equations*, which was set in the late classical era, and N. Shut's novel *The rat-catcher*, which was recommended to the journal by the translator Nora Gall. The novel centred around the fate of a person who risked their life to rescue children from occupied France in 1940. It seems fair to subscribe to the view expressed in literary circles that both A. Romashov's story and N. Chute's novel foretold the 'air of penitence' which was a feature of Russian literature in the 1980s.[288]

The incident which really made the journal's name, however — and it was one that was not without controversy — occurred in 1982-1983, when a novel called *The bronze mastiff*, by K.Y. Lagunov, a novelist from Tyumen, was published, in the final three editions of the journal for the year 1982, followed up immediately by the a story by N.G. Nikonov entitled *The Old Man's Mountain*.

K. Lagunov regularly wrote for *Urals*, and often wrote sketches for the journal about the achievements of those in the oil and gas sector[289]. His new novel, however, though it recycled material he had used in the past, was about something completely different. The protagonists of *The bronze mastiff* were the 'gas and oil generals', the very men who, ten years later, were to become known as oligarchs and 'new Russians', who had their own distinct moral code, and what was practically an 'anything goes' approach, with absolutely all forms of local authority subservient to their will. There was nothing else like it in the literature of the day! It was in many respects a prophetic novel.

Readers got drawn into the novel, and the journal was passed on from one avid reader to the next.

K. Lagunov's novel was imbued with a little bit of extra controversy — of local significance — as a result of its setting, which readers had no trouble identifying and 'relating to a particular place' — Gudy, where the action was set, was clearly meant to be Nady, a centre for the extraction of gas in the Yamalo-Nenetsk Autonomous Region; readers recognised not only the scenes in which the action was set, but also the characters. Naturally, the Tyumen Regional Committee was furious and appealed to the 'powers that be' requesting that they introduce a bit of order on the ideological front.

---

288   S.B. Khodov: The aesthetic position of the Russian regional journal (based on material from the magazine "The Urals" (1958-1998). SPECIALITY 10.01.01. — RUSSIAN LITERATURE. Abstract of a dissertation competing for the academic title of doctor of philological sciences. YEKATERINBURG 1999

289   K. Lagunov: also wrote the first novel in Russian literature about the peasant insurrections in Western Siberia

N. Nikonov's story *The Old Man's Mountain*[290] fitted in naturally with the context of the 'rural prose' of F. Abramov, V. Rasputin, V. Belov and V. Astafiev.

It was a lyrical tale about an artist who lands up somewhere beyond the Urals, in a village in the middle of nowhere, tranquil and rurified, and finds that the former way of life has been completely destroyed — drunken people, voices yelling through tape recorders, and an abandoned, almost overgrown quarry... And the only person who had tried to keep aspects of rural life alive was an old man who had once been 'de-kulakized', and who was therefore hated by everyone in the village.

Keep in mind that these stories were published in 1982 and early 1983.

They coincided directly with a new campaign designed to "strengthen ideological discipline". On 30th June 1982 a directive from the CC CPSU was published in *Pravda* 'On the creative ties between literary and arts journals and the practical work of building communism'. The directive directed criticism at the works published in the journals, in which "the portrayal of the events of Russian history, the socialist revolution and collectivization contains serious departures from the truth of what happened. Certain publications contain prejudiced, superficial judgments about modern life...whose authors demonstrate a confused world-view, and an inability to examine social phenomena from a historical point of view, from clearly defined class positions."[291]

Given that a directive such as this had been published, the party's regional committee was *obliged* to discuss the issue of the literary journals.

On 24th May 1983 the office of the Sverdlovsk regional committee debated the following issue: 'On the work of the *Urals* publication, designed to enhance the ideological and artistic level of its readers, in the light of the demands made by the 26th party congress and the CC CPSU directive 'On the creative ties between literary and arts journals and the practical work of building communism'.'

The directive was written in a style that remained true to party traditions: "on the one hand, on the other hand."

On the one hand, the *Urals* journal was "performing a particular role as regards the implementation of the decisions of the 26th party congress, in both May and November (1982), the Plenums of the CC CPSU, the directives of the

---

290   V. Lukyanin: How the writer Nikolai Nikonov encroached on the Soviet regime // Urals, 2006, No. 12.
291   *Pravda*. 1982. 30th July

Central Committee of the CPSU 'On the creative ties between literary and arts journals and the practical work of building communism' (1982), and strives to interpret, in art and prose, the problems of the modern world, and of the socio-economic lives and communist education of laborers," which was confirmed by a long list of stories which had been published in the journal.

On the other hand, "the editors of the *Urals* journal were guilty of serious failures and oversights in terms of the themes covered by the publications, and had not been sufficiently thorough in the work they had done with authors to raise the level of their works from an ideological and artistic perspective."

Yet the harshest criticism of all was reserved for "a series of works in which there were no clearly defined ideological standpoints at all, and which were weak in an artistic regard."

The works in question were K. Lagunov's novel *The bronze mastiff* and N. Nikonov's story *The old man's mountain*.

"The protagonists of K. Lagunov's novel, above all the people in charge of constructing the mainline gas pipe," the regional committee's directive reads, "are portrayed as people who are on a downward spiral, morally disreputable, money-grubbers and drunks. The author adds no depth to his portrayal of the workers but spares no effort when describing the masters who are their 'scourge'. In N. Nikonov's work, the results of collectivization are questioned. The life of a modern village is portrayed in hues which are far from optimistic, and far removed from the creative tasks which society has managed to solve."

The first point in the Sverdlovsk regional committee's resolution read: "Acknowledge that the work carried out by the editorial office of the *Urals* journal to increase the ideological and artistic level of the works published in it does not satisfy the requirements of the 26th party congress and the directive from the CC CPSU."

This stern criticism was not followed by any official sanctions, however. "For the oversights and failures committed in the course of his work, and for publishing a series of sinful works, the communist editor-in-chief, comrade V.P. Lukyanin, and the secretary of the party organization, comrade Y.A. Gorbunov, deserve severe punishment from the party; however, taking into account the discussions held at the board meeting of the CPSU's regional committee, this shall be limited to a warning."

This was the most lenient of all possible forms of punishment. The editor-in-chief, V.P. Lukyanin, remained in his job, and the editorial team was left unchanged. Stories would later abound about the regional committee's board meeting: V.P. Lukyanin, a talented journalist and editor, acquired a sort of 'martyr's halo', and pieces were written about this incident in the 1990s by both the Spanish journalist Pilar Bonet and the journalist Pavel Gutiontov, who worked for *Izvestiya*.

The fact remains, however, that the journal survived, and that the regional committee, after making a few threats, did not deal out any real punishment.

The ideological problems were resolved without any heads having to roll, and without any of the oppressive measures by means of which 'ideological management' had been achieved in the not-too-distant past.

A new appointment: off to Moscow
The move to Moscow

Following the death of Leonid Ilyich Brezhnev, some long-awaited changes began to take place at the very top of the party. The older generation, consisting of Brezhnev's peers, was dying out, and began to be replaced by new faces. From 1983 onwards, approximately 90% of the regional committee secretaries and communist party secretaries in the union's republics were replaced over the course of a few years.[292]

In Moscow, a whole team of graduates of Stavropol came hot on the heels of Gorbachev — Murakhovsky, Razumovsky, Polozkov. N.I. Ryzhkov was sent from Sverdlovsk to Moscow and appointed director of the economic department of the CC; Y.K. Ligachev, the first secretary of the Tomsk regional committee, was also brought in — he was to be responsible for the recruitment of senior staff within the CC.

Y.K. Ligachev, in turn, was appointed to a position in Tomsk, and had to leave his position as first secretary of the Soviet district committee of the CPSU in Novosibirsk. This was the official name for Akademgorodok. This region was weaker than the Sverdlovsk Region from an industrial point of view, but it had oil of its own, a nuclear centre which was secret at the time, and the oldest university in Siberia. The appointment paid dividends. He busily set about helping physicists in Tomsk, got involved in protecting crafts and trades in the old part of Tomsk, and made skiing competitions and compulsory cross-country skiing pretty much an obligatory part of life for all the civil servants in Tomsk. He was known for his refusal to tolerate drunkenness. He was one of the regional committee secretaries who enjoyed the respect of his region's citizens.

---

292   N.I. Ryzhkov: Ten years of huge jolts. M.: The association 'Books. Enlightenment. Charity', 1995. S.75.

Now, in Moscow, he selected for the ranks of the Central Committee only those regional committee secretaries who were going to satisfy his expectations. Ligachev, who himself hailed from Siberia, made no attempt to hide his obvious interest in Yeltsin. He must have found the high expectations Yeltsin had of his team — which he had demonstrated under Brezhnev — particularly appealing. Under the new general secretary, Yury Andropov, this quality proved to be particularly in demand.

In January 1984 Ligachev was a guest of honor at the party conference for the Sverdlovsk Region, where an election was to be held. The conclusion to the first secretary's report was fully in keeping with the spirit of the times: it called on every member of the party "...to keep in mind, above all else, that he was a fighter on behalf of the party, that for him there was nothing more important than the common interest, and that it was his calling to set the tone and serve as an example in all he did."

In order to assess the qualities of Boris Yeltsin (a member of the CC CPSU since 1981) and "dispel some doubts" regarding his suitability for a transfer, Y.K. Ligachev, an authorized spokesman of the new General Secretary, Mikhail Gorbachev — one of the men of the "new way of thinking" — set off for Sverdlovsk. Moreover, the secretary of the CC CPSU Y.P. Ryabov, who had worked with Yeltsin for an extensive period, recommended his candidate to M.S. Gorbachev for an invitation to Moscow.

This offer may have come as a surprise to Yeltsin, but in the corridors of power in Staraya ploshchad, the idea of transferring him to Moscow had been mooted even before Gorbachev came to power. There is an entry in the diary of V.I. Vorotnikov which states that during a conversation which took place on 2nd June 1984, Gorbachev talked about the need to improve the way construction and transport were managed in the CC, and that it might be a good idea to have a CC secretary responsible for this subject area, as was the case in the big regions.[293] Yeltsin's surname did not feature in the diary entry, but in all likelihood he was precisely the man Gorbachev had in mind: a professional engineer and constructor with plenty of experience of managing operations in the sector and the party, and on top of that someone whom he knew well.

The story goes that Ligachev was given a tour of all of the region's success stories and achievements. These included the reconstruction of the Sverdlovsk opera house. The regional committee's car pulled up outside the theatre. Yeltsin and Ligachev stepped out of the vehicle. Ligachev stopped the first passer-by — fortunately for him it was a bustling area. Pointing at Yeltsin, he asked:

---

293   V.I. Vorotnikov: It was like this...Notes from the diary of a member of the Politburo of the CC CPSU. M.: 'The Council of veterans of book publishing' SI-MAR, 1995. P. 43.

"Do you know who this man is?

The woman replied that of course she did, it was Yeltsin, and added: "Why? Have you come to take him away to Moscow?"

Rumors about a possible transfer to Moscow for Yeltsin had been circulating in the city for some time, and were not inspiring much pleasure.

Yeltsin did not seem too happy about it either.[294]

The situation in which he found himself was far from straightforward. On the one hand he was a senior figure in a region where he knew, if not everything, then a great deal. Where he had an active administrative board which had been tried and tested, as well as colleagues and friends. Where he enjoyed the support of the people.

In some ways, the transfer to Moscow was almost inevitable. His predecessors Kirilenko and Ryabov had left for the capital. But they had been appointed to such senior positions as secretaries of the CC CPSU. To agree to anything else would be seen as a loss of status.

A move to Moscow would mean uncertainty. The people were different, the way they related to one another was different. He would go from being head of a region to merely being part of something, a cog in a different bureaucratic machine. He could not but be concerned by what had happened to Y.P. Ryabov, who had suffered after having to make such major adjustments in the capital, for all his — Ryabov's — desire to do what was best for the country.

Yet Yeltsin was 55 years old. He was capable of doing a great deal. He was honest. He understood that the keys which unlocked the solutions to most problems tended to be kept not out there in the regions, but in Moscow, inside the Garden Ring.

And in any case, if he said no, who else was there?

In early April 1985 he received a call from a candidate for the Politburo, V.I. Dolgikh. In fulfilment of a directive from the Politburo of the CC CPSU, he suggested that Boris Nikolaevich move to Moscow, to join the party's Central Committee as director of the department of construction.[295] Yeltsin turned down the offer. The level of department director within the CC clearly didn't correspond to the level of a secretary of the party organization in one of Russia's biggest regions.

---

294   See: An interview with S.D. Alekseev. [Video record]. Quotation no.: L.N. Snegirev. See above. P. 35.
295   B.N. Yeltsin: Against the Grain. P. 70.

The next day Yeltsin received another call, this time from the 'political heavyweight' Ligachev, who was a member of the Politburo. He spoke insistently and decisively, calling on Yeltsin to obey party discipline. The latter could find no way to object when faced with such arguments.[296] The decision to transfer him to Moscow was taken. On 12th April 1985, at the dawn of *perestroika*, Yeltsin became a member of the new 'team', which had declared a new direction for the country.

In the best traditions of the principle of 'democratic centralism' (further confirmation that big politics was something that was 'fixed' in the Kremlin, and that the opinion of the grass-roots members counted for nothing), the members of the party organization in the Sverdlovsk Region present at the 7th plenum of the Sverdlovsk regional CPSU organization did not hear about Boris Yeltsin's new posting until 19th April 1985.

The first issue on the agenda at the plenum was an administrative matter. A report was read out by P.A. Smolsky — the deputy director of the department of organizational and party work within the CC CPSU. In his speech he expressed his opinion that it would be a good idea to promote Boris Yeltsin. It is appropriate to reproduce the text of his speech in full, in order to dispel any possible misreadings of the reasons behind Yeltsin's transfer to Moscow, which are often encountered in numerous memoirs. One of the things he said was: "Allow me, by order of the Central Committee of the party and the board of the regional committee of the CPSU, to report on the essence of the administrative issue which we must consider and decide upon today. This issue concerns the first secretary of the party's regional committee in Sverdlovsk. By the decision of the Politburo of the CC taken on 11th April 1985, Boris Nikolaevich Yeltsin was approved as the director of the department of construction within the CC CPSU.

This position, as you are well aware, is a senior role and one that brings with it a considerable amount of responsibility. The problem of capital construction — of which an enormous amount is taking place in our country — demands constant attention and serious engagement on the part of the party.

In this regard, it was taken into account that Boris Yeltsin is a well-trained, experienced and selfless worker. Significantly, he is a civil engineer by training, and worked in civil engineering and in a management capacity here, and with you in Sverdlovsk, for 13 years; he has worked for the party since 1968 — i.e. for 17 years already. In his time he has been director of the department of construction and secretary of the party's regional committee, and for 9 years he was in charge of your party organization in Sverdlovsk. This is one of the biggest organizations in the party, and has been a battle-ready and reliable outpost of the CPSU; Boris Nikolaevich spent many years working for your

---

296   See: same ref. P. 71.

organization and did a great deal to develop the economy, science, culture, the region and, it is fair to say, made a worthy contribution to the work of the party organization, and to your affairs in general. He is a member of the CC CPSU and a deputy in the Supreme Soviet of the USSR, which is also significant. There can be no doubt that the experience he gleaned here will stand Boris Nikolaevich in good stead for the work he does in the future. It is fair to say that the huge trust which the Central Committee and the Politburo of the CC have placed in Boris Yeltsin also represents trust in your party organization as a whole, and in your staff."[297]

The decision to release B.N. Yeltsin from the post of secretary of the regional committee of the party was adopted unanimously in accordance with the rules in effect at the time. Little could this Moscow civil servant have known, whilst reading this pre-prepared speech before the plenum, that in one regard his words would prove to be almost prophetic. This concerned the experience Yeltsin had picked up in the Urals, and the idea that it would provide him with a firm foundation for his work in the future.

Boris Nikolaevich himself took with him to Moscow all his experience as a civil engineer and a manager for whom there was no such thing, and could be no such thing, as 'trifling' issues. Of course, the rapid rise to the top which awaited him in the capital, and the huge tasks related to the re-equipping of Russia during his tenure as President, are of incomparably larger scale than anything he was required to do in the Sverdlovsk Region. Yet his qualities of a leader — a stubborn, at times brutal one, who was able to think several steps ahead of the game, and admitted to any miscalculations or mistakes — had taken shape during his time in the Urals.

Even before the start of the 'Moscow period', whilst preparing material for the supplement *And carry faithfulness down the years* in *Soviet Russia*, intuitively sensing the difficult political destiny which was in store for him, he was to write, in confidence: "The clash between the old and the new always gives rise to conflict. But it seems as though it would be wrong on my part to divide people up along traditional lines — into 'progressives' and 'conservatives'. Our lives require that we combine within ourselves both the restless of the reformer, and constant creativity. There would not be much use in an innovator who was incapable of putting on the brakes on time, and reinforcing a victory — nor, indeed, in someone who was well-grounded and stable but did not sense the moment when his affairs had run their course. The clash of the old and the new is therefore taking place more frequently now not in the relations between people, but within the soul of the protagonist himself, who must decide whether to hurl himself into battle once again, or whether the peace that has been achieved last as long as he possibly can...And — why try to

---

297   CDPASR. F. 4. Op. 11. D. 4. L. 2-3.

deny it — in this clash it is not always the new, the progressive forces, that win out."

And he added: "They say that the people in the Urals Region are ambitious... We don't deny it: after all, ambition for ambition's sake is a different matter, but our ambition, here in the Urals Region — it is the pride of experts who know the true value of themselves and their abilities. And that is something of which we can only be proud...".[298]

The road to Moscow, where a new chapter of Yeltsin's life would begin, was opening up before him. He would leave behind his little homeland, his childhood, his youth, and his experiences whilst becoming the person he was. He would be accompanied to the capital by the baggage of his experience as a leader, his management style and his methods.

...

After the plenum of the regional committee, during which Yeltsin was relieved of his duties as first secretary of the regional committee, a farewell dinner was held for the secretary of the regional committee. Many of Yeltsin's close friends and co-workers gathered for the dinner. As was customary, they drank a toast. Mikhail Grigorievich Kryukov, the first secretary of the party's Nizhny Turinsk regional committee, the secret district Sverdlovsk-45, turned to Yeltsin and said: "You know what, Boris Nikolaevich, in Moscow you'll either start a revolution or end up losing your head." "I'd rather it were the former," Yeltsin said, looking a little troubled.[299]

---

298 CDPASR. F. 1. Op. 1. D. 14. L. 155, 159.
299 Based on the memoirs of the second secretary of the Nizhneturinsk city committee, N.A. Volgin.

PART 2.
MOSCOW

FROM THE CENTRAL COMMITTEE OF THE CPSU TO THE 1ST CONGRESS OF PEOPLE'S DEPUTIES OF THE USSR

Chapter 4
Director of the construction department, secretary of the CC CPSU

On 12th April Yeltsin set to work in Moscow. He was familiar with the construction industry and had accumulated a lot of practical experience. But for him, a natural born leader, fitting into his new role was no easy matter. Instead of dealing with the problems of a large region, he was forced to deal mostly with paperwork. His dealings with the General Secretary were limited to telephone calls. He was not used to being subordinate: ever since his first few years on the construction site he had been a leader — a head of section, then of the board of management, then director of the residential construction combine. After just over nine years as a 'regional boss', he now found himself playing the role of a small cog within the apparatus of power, in which, as he put it, "the mechanism of subordination, of a strict party-based hierarchy, is taken to absurd extremes."[300]

---

300   B.N. Yeltsin: See above P.93

Yeltsin found it hard to make an impression in this new system of relationships, and his behavior may have seemed alarming at times. The knowledge that this was only going to be a temporary role was the only thing that saved him from starting conflicts.

He did not have to wait long for a new appointment. On 29th June, at an assembly of the Politburo of the CC, several major changes were made. First of all the fate of the post of Chairman of the Presidium of the Supreme Soviet of the USSR, which had been left vacant following the death of Chernenko, was determined. Gorbachev proposed A.A. Gromyko for this role. Gromyko kept his status as a member of the Politburo, but due to his new role he relinquished the position of foreign minister, which he had held since 1957. E.A. Shevardnadze was proposed as the new minister of foreign affairs.

It was also decided that G.V. Romanov would be relieved of his duties as a member of the Politburo and a secretary of the CC, who was considered a potential rival to Gorbachev. He was formally asked to retire, and he stated that he was doing so "on health-related grounds". The man proposed as a replacement for Romanov, who had been in charge of the defense sectors of industry, was L.N. Zaikov.

When arguing in favor of Yeltsin being appointed to the post of secretary of the CC responsible for construction, Gorbachev talked about the problems facing the industry — the huge amount of unfinished construction projects and the fact that capital investment had been frozen: "We have started to take steps to solve this problem, and as you know we have brought in a series of major directives. We have strengthened this sector by bringing to Moscow the director of the construction department, comrade Yeltsin, who was formerly first secretary of the party's regional committee in Sverdlovsk and has valuable experience in the field of construction. Perhaps we could see him as a secretary of the CC CPSU who, whilst remaining head of his department, could deal with construction issues at the level of secretary of the CC CPSU?" The general atmosphere of consensus was suddenly disrupted by N.A. Tikhonov. But how will he fare in his new role?

Gorbachev. I can see why you might ask. But comrade Yeltsin has plenty of experience: he worked as a foreman, chief engineer, head of a construction trust; he was chief engineer, then head of the Sverdlovsk housing construction combine. He then worked for the party's regional committee in Sverdlovsk. So he knows this sector very well and has a lot of experience of working for the party.

Tikhonov. That's as maybe, but I haven't yet got a real sense of what sort of man he is.

Ligachev. Comrade Yeltsin went about his business with enthusiasm, and has worked in a series of ministries; people have felt drawn to him.

Dolgikh. Comrade Yeltsin knows how to go about building relationships with the ministers. He has got strong contacts with the party's regional committees. After getting to know him fairly well, I didn't discover any weaknesses in his character.

Gorbachev. There is a lot to be done in the construction sector. We need someone with energy.

Tikhonov. Construction is our weakest area.

Solomentsev. We must propose comrade Yeltsin as a secretary of the CC. He will grow into the role. He ticks all the boxes: the right education, practical experience as an engineer in the construction sector. He's a man who will go places.

Gorbachev. I raised this question specifically in order to encourage an exchange of views. I wanted to test my own feelings and find out what my comrades thought. So what are we going to do? We are going to propose that comrade Yeltsin be elected a secretary of the CC at the plenum?

Members of the Politburo. Yes, we must formally make this the Politburo's decision."[301]

Tikhonov's criticism of Yeltsin at that meeting probably ended up working in Yeltsin's favor. The members of the Politburo were aware of the fact that relations between Tikhonov and Gorbachev were strained, and that they were often at loggerheads. He had been the fiercest opponent of the idea of strengthening Gorbachev's standing, and had adjudged the former secretary of the Sverdlovsk regional committee to be a supporter of the General Secretary and one of his henchmen.

There may also have been another basis for Tikhonov's discontent: an age-old conflict between Yeltsin and Tikhonov regarding the director of Uralmash, who was mentioned above.

The next issue to be decided, following the decision to appoint Yeltsin, was the election of the secretary of the CC and director of the department of defence industry, under the first secretary of the Leningrad regional committee, L.N. Zaikov. The man appointed to replace him was Y.F. Soloviev, who at the time was working as minister of industrial construction in the USSR. Tikhonov was extremely critical of this appointment as well, but Zaikov did not let this get in his way.

---

301   Archive of the President of the RF. Minutes of the Politubro assembly. 1985, 29 June. P. 1-9.

Tikhonov's time was running out. On 26th September 1985 the Politburo decided that he should resign "on health-related grounds". The post he left vacant — that of chairman of the Council of Ministers of the USSR- was occupied by N.I. Ryzhkov.

The fact that Yeltsin was now joining the party elite was accompanied by marked changes in the family's life. The Yeltsins moved from the dacha they had shared with Lukianov, who at the time was also a department director in the CC, to the dacha which had previously been occupied by Gorbachev. The dacha was incredibly luxurious.

The family now had their own household staff: three chefs, three waiters, a maid, a gardener with a team of his own, and a security team. The senior member of the security team also acted as an errand boy for the family.

The Yeltsins, like the other families of the top brass, were able to receive medical care at special clinics equipped with state-of-the-art technology, do their shopping in special shops and have their clothes made at special workshops; they received 'Kremlin' rations, for which they only had to pay half the actual value. The head of the family was given use of a ZIL with a special communications system, whilst the other family members were assigned a Volga.

During his short stint as secretary of the CC, Yeltsin travelled around the country a great deal, visiting many places in the Moscow and Leningrad Regions, the Far Eastern Region, Turkmenia, Armenia and the Tyumen Region. These trips had a purpose to them. He got to know the country better, expanded his outlook on the country, met new people and was able to accumulate a wealth of experience through his travels and encounters. This leader at regional level was slowly but surely beginning to make his mark at a new, national level.

Perhaps the most memorable of his excursions was his trip to Tashkent for the plenum of the Uzbekistan party CC, which opened his eyes to a great many things. Yeltsin arrived in the republic whilst the investigation into the so-called 'cotton case' was in full swing. Begun under Andropov, the investigation led to senior officials in the republic being exposed for having taken bribes. On 20th March 1985 the former deputy minister of the interior in Uzbekistan, Kakhramanov, was arrested. A series of arrests began which essentially affected the whole of the party and state elite in Uzbekistan. The republic was riven with unrest. As soon as word got out that the CC secretary was coming over from Moscow, throngs of people gathered at the hotel where he was due to stay. The guards refused to let them in, but Yeltsin said he was prepared to hear the people out.

In the space of two days he heard a huge number of stories, which seemed improbable yet were all too real, about bribe-taking in the senior ranks of the party in the republic. Yeltsin was shocked by the picture that had been painted. Furthermore, he was handed documents which provided evidence of bribe-taking by the new first secretary of the republic's communist party, Usmankhodzhaev. On his return to Moscow, Yeltsin took these documents to Gorbachev and filled him in on all the details of what he had heard. Gorbachev's reaction was not what Yeltsin was expecting: he grew angry and said that Yeltsin had got it wrong, that Usmankhodzhaev was an honest communist, but that he had been forced to try to take on the bribe-takers, and the old mafia was therefore compromising him with falsified accusations and pronouncements.[302]

The Tashkent episode was in many ways typical of Yeltsin. No matter what position he was in — secretary of the regional committee or secretary of the CC — he was never a cabinet leader. His trip to the plenum of the CC of Uzbekistan did not entail any 'drop-in sessions' for the public whatsoever, but if people wanted to meet him, Yeltsin would make no objection. He would take in everything he heard trustingly and in an emotional manner, and was willing to act on what he heard straight away. It is quite possible that the other factor at play, in addition to the documents which exposed Usmankhodzhaev's bribe-taking, was Yeltsin's famed intuition. The upshot was that Usmankhodzhaev, like so many other senior officials in the republic, was removed from office and held accountable for his misdemeanours.[303]

On 22nd December 1985 Yeltsin was appointed to a new role. He was summoned to an assembly of the Politburo, where it was proposed that he take charge of the party organization for the city of Moscow. Yeltsin would later recall: "I found it hard to accept that job. And not because I was afraid it would be difficult: I realised full well that I was being used, with the aim of toppling Grishin's team."[304] A new man was needed, someone who had no ties to Moscow and was sufficiently decisive and bold.

During K.U. Chernenko's brief tenure, V.V. Grishin had been seen as a potential successor to him in the role of general secretary. Considerable efforts were made after Gorbachev came to power to undermine Grishin's standing. Preparations for the toppling of the all-powerful Moscow leader had been going on for almost a year. Y.K. Ligachev worked harder than anyone to try to bring this about. On his orders, the print media — in particular the pages of the newspaper *Soviet Russia* — were filled with criticism of the problems facing the people of Moscow in retail, housing and utilities. In 1985 the

302   B.N. Yeltsin: See above P. 102-103.
303   Note by detectives for matters of special importance at the General procurator's office of the USSR, T.Kh. Gdlyan and N.I. Ivanov to the CC dated 11 November 1986. See: RGANI. F. 89. Op. 24. D. 18.
304   B.N. Yeltsin: See above P. 109-110

political leaders in the Moscow region began to be replaced. The first secretary of the Moscow regional committee, V.I. Konotop, and the chairman of the regional executive committee, Pestov, were asked to retire.

V.I. Vorotnikov recalls that on 13th December 1985 Gorbachev complained to him that a large number of letters of complaint were being sent to the CC about Grishin, and that at party meetings and in the unions there was much grumbling about his snobbery, the fact that he was making a show of being busy, and the fact that he was more interested in slogans than doing anything useful. Gorbachev reported that he had already spoken to the other members of the Politburo about the need to replace Grishin.[305] All sorts of rumors circulated about Grishin: people tried to accuse him of various machinations, but the law enforcement agencies did not find any compromising material against him. When Yeltsin joined the Moscow City Committee, the safes inside the first secretary's study were empty.[306]

On 23rd December 1985, half an hour before an assembly of the Politburo, Grishin was summoned by Gorbachev.[307] (In their respective memoirs Grishin tells us this meeting took place on 19th December, whilst Yeltsin says it took place on 22nd December. The most likely explanation is that Gorbachev held two meetings — one with Grishin only, and the second with Yeltsin and the members of the Politburo). After telling Grishin that the city committee had received complaints about the work of the organizations in Moscow, Gorbachev offered to give him his notice. It was an unexpected offer, given that there was still a month and a half to go before the party conference in the city. But the issue of the appointment of the first secretary of the city committee was decided by the Politburo.[308]

The only people present at the assembly were members of the Politburo, CC secretary Razumovsky, who was responsible for party staff, and Yeltsin. Gorbachev told them that he had had a difficult conversation with Grishin, and that the latter had been forced to write a letter in which he requested permission to retire and be appointed as one of the advisors to the Presidium of the Supreme Soviet of the USSR.

He then added: "If you have no objections, comrades, then I could take part in the work of the plenum of the Moscow city committee of the CPSU myself [officially, the first secretary of the Moscow city committee could only be relieved of his duties by a plenum of this city committee]. Let us turn now

---

305   V.I. Vorotnikov: It was like this...Notes from the diary of a member of the Politburo of the CC CPSU. M.: 'The Council of veterans of book publishing', SI-MAR, 1995. P. 80.
306   B.N. Yeltsin: See above P. 111
307   APRF. F.3. Op. 73, D.1242, L.1-3
308   V.V. Grishin: From Khrushchev to Gorbachev. Political portraits of five general secretaries and A.N. Kosygin. Memoirs. M.: ASPOL, 1996. P. 294-296.

to the subject of the candidates for the role of first secretary of the Moscow city committee of the CPSU. This issue concerns the party organization in the capital. It would therefore be advisable to recommend for this role someone from the CC CPSU, with experience of working for a major party organization and sound knowledge of economics, science and culture. It has been proposed that comrade B.N. Yeltsin take on the role... I have spoken to comrade Yeltsin. He understands the standing and significance of the party organization in Moscow, and the difficulty and complexity of the role of first secretary... A capital city represents a huge challenge. It is an administrative and economic centre, and a scientific and cultural hub.

A future adviser to Gorbachev, A.S. Chernyaev, wrote the following diary entry on 23rd January: "Today is a happy day for the whole of Moscow: Grishin has been sacked at long last, and Yeltsin has replaced him."[309]

First secretary of the MCC CPSU

The very next day, on 24th December 1985, Yeltsin was elected first secretary at a plenum of the Moscow City Committee. There was no discussion about his candidacy at all. Yeltsin took charge of the biggest party organization, for a city, in the country. On 1st January 1986 the capital's party organization officially had 1,120,400 members, 58.6% of whom were white collar workers and 45% of whom were laborers. In the USSR as a whole the party had more than 19 million members.[310] Moscow also led in terms of the number of communists per head of the population. Throughout the country as a whole 9.7% of the adult population were members of the party, whilst in Moscow this figure stood at 16.5%.[311]

It was an honor to take charge of a party organization such as this, but it was also an endlessly complicated challenge, all the more so given that the capital was constantly under close scrutiny by the Kremlin. In his capacity as first secretary of the Moscow city committee, he encountered the innumerable problems faced by this gigantic city, many of which came as a surprise to him. During his 18 years in charge of the city, Grishin had succeeded in making sure that no-one interfered with Moscow's affairs. Officially, there were no problems in Moscow at all: in fact it was almost the 'archetypal communist city'. And this was true, if one were referring to the lives of the small percentage of Muscovites who were part of the *nomenklatura* — not just the official list of civil servants working for the party and the state, whose appointments had to be approved on a compulsory basis by the party agencies, but also a small

309   A.S. Chernyaev: Six years with Gorbachev. Based on diary entries. M., 1993. P. 63.
310   TsAOPIM F.4. Op.220. D.1363. L.37.
311   TsAOPIM F.4. Op.220. D.1365. L.80

number of people employed in the arts and science, in the police and in retail, who were bound to the *nomenklatura* by ties which, though not always visible to the untrained eye, were nonetheless very strong. These people lived in nice apartments (by Soviet standards), enjoyed good healthcare and enough goods to buy in the stores.

But then there was Moscow the megapolis, the city of millions, fenced off from the Moscow mentioned above by the police posts and the concierges in the entrance halls, by the 'personal' cars provided by the party and the 'halls for official delegations', as the Soviet brand of VIP waiting rooms at stations and airports were referred to. There was also the Moscow in which every fourth resident was officially on a waiting list for housing, and hundreds of thousands of temporary workers, hired to do all the most unglamorous jobs in the capital, and waiting ten to fifteen years for the right to be considered Muscovites and receive the notorious 'registration'. For this other Moscow there were poor-quality clinics and hospitals, long lines in the stores, streets that were not kept clean, communal flats and 'Khrushchevkas' — apartments with kitchens measuring 3.5 square metres.

In Moscow, just as in other parts of the country, people were longing for change, and the arrival of Yeltsin, with his clearly defined stance on things, his stark assessment of the current state of affairs in Moscow and in the country as a whole, and his proposals on how to change the situation, was greeted with optimism.

Yeltsin's work in his new role began with the preparations for the 26th city-wide party conference. Although Gorbachev had given a generally positive assessment of Grishin's work at a plenum of the MCC in December, the CC issued an edict demanding that a conference be held where the prevailing atmosphere would be one of sharp criticism aimed at the shortcomings of the previous head of the city committee, in order to provide an example of the process of *perestroika*.

For Moscow, the new political year began on 24th January 1986, with the city-wide party conference and Yeltsin's address to it. Whilst working on his report, Yeltsin had met dozens of people, visited various enterprises in the capital, analysing their working environment, and attempted to find the ideal solution as to how they could emerge from the crisis in which they found themselves. His address to the conference lasted two hours. After the long years of seeing Grishin at the despatch box at city-wide conferences, some bitter truths about the harsh reality in the nation's capital were finally spoken at the city-wide party conference: "the average annual rate of industrial output has fallen 3 times by comparison with the 8th five-year-plan. Average annual growth in industrial output has fallen from 5% to 1.3% — several times lower than in the rest of the country. ...there is a shortage of housing — in 1985 almost 300,000 sq. km of housing which was due to be constructed was not built.." Yeltsin talked about cases in which people had had the wool pulled over their eyes, as a result of which a whole series of buildings had had to be left off the statistical reports.[312]

Chernyaev, one of Gorbachev's aides, wrote in his diary: "In terms of how symptomatic it was of the times, and of how it reflected the depth and scale of change, this speech was on a par with the 20th congress of the CPSU. It was on a par with it both in terms of the spirit of it and in terms of what was actually said, and the advent of some genuinely new standards for people's lives and activities. There were huge lines at the kiosks where *Moskovskaya pravda* [the newspaper which printed the text of Yeltsin's speech] was on sale."[313]

As Yeltsin later recalled, "When I had finished, Gorbachev said to me: 'A powerful breath of fresh air has just been felt.' But there was no smile of encouragement on his face when he said it, he said it with a neutral expression on his face."[314]

Gorbachev was concerned about how the voting was going to go. As he would later write in his memoirs, "the Moscow party membership was pretty furious about the fact that they hadn't found a worthy candidate for the party organization in the capital, and had brought in an 'outsider'. But there was no interference in the elections."[315]

After the conference, a decision was taken with regard to it at a meeting of the Politburo on 30th January 1986, which spoke in sharp tones of "serious shortcomings in the work of the party's city committee and the city's party organization." Grishin asked for the appraisals of his work to be made more objective: after all, the Moscow organization had been under constant supervision by the CC like no other organization, and the MCC's criticism was therefore indirectly aimed at the CC as well. But his proposal was rejected.[316] After the conference widespread criticism began to appear in the media about everything that had been done in Moscow under Grishin.

The 27th congress of the CPSU

One month later, Moscow's new party leader addressed the party congress. The 27th congress of the CPSU opened on 25th February 1986. People looked forward to the congress and to the program that Gorbachev was going

312   Moskovskaya pravda, 25th January 1986.

313   A.S. Chernyaev: See above. P. 63-64.

314   B.N. Yeltsin: See above P. 111

315   M.S. Gorbachev: His life and reforms. Book 1. P. 292.

316   V.V. Grishin: From Khrushchev to Gorbachev. Political portraits of five general secretaries and A.N. Kosygin. Memoirs.

to announce. On the whole, the speech made by the general secretary lived up to these expectations. It began with an acknowledgement of the problems and shortcomings in the party's work — something that was seldom seen in such documents. "For a period of many years, not only for objective reasons but also, above all, for a reason of a subjective nature, the practical measures taken by the party and state agencies have lost touch with the requirements of the times and of life itself. Problems related to the country's development have multiplied at a faster rate than they have been solved. Inertia and staleness in the forms and methods of management, reduced dynamism at work, the growth of bureaucracy — all of this has done considerable damage to our various ventures. Stagnation has crept into the life of society. The situation called for change, but in the central party agencies and out in the regions a specific way of thinking has begun to take the upper hand: how to improve the state of affairs without changing anything. But it doesn't work that way, comrades... We must not put off the task of finding a solution to the problems we now face. Such an attitude would be too costly for the country, the state and the party. Let us spread this message loud and clear!"[317]

The text of the speech was not without internal contradictions, and at times gave the impression of being a 'patchwork quilt', in which the former, traditional appraisals were combined with attempts to interpret the world in a new way.

As regards domestic policy, the growth strategy for the country was related to an acceleration of socio-economic growth. What was new was the fresh approach, announced by Gorbachev, aimed at union with the press. "Of fundamental importance to us," he said at the congress, "is the question of expanding *glasnost*... Without *glasnost* there is no possibility of democratization, political creativity among the masses, or their involvement in governance... At other times, when the issue of *glasnost* is raised, we have to endure calls for people to be more careful as regards what they say about our shortcomings and failings, and about the inevitable difficulties which crop up in any form of human endeavor. There can only be one response in such cases, and it is the one Lenin gave us: what communists need, at all times and under any circumstances, is truth... For that reason we must make glasnost a fail-proof system."[318]

Yeltsin's speech was third on the agenda for the General secretary's address, after the chairman of the Council of Ministers of the RSFSR, V.I. Vorotnikov, and the first secretary of the CC of the communist party of Ukraine, V.V. Shcherbinsky. It was an indication of the status enjoyed by the first secretary of the capital's city committee that he spoke immediately after the representatives of two of the largest republics in the union.

---

317   Material from the 27th party congress. M., 1986. P. 4.
318   Same reference. P. 60.

Yeltsin's speech would live long in many people's minds. He asked the sort of questions which had occurred to anyone who had given any serious thought to the state of affairs in the country: "Why do we discuss the same problems again and again at every congress? Why has the word 'stagnation', which clearly has no place here, cropped up in the party's lexicon? Why is it that for so many years we have been unable to tear out of our lives the roots of bureaucracy, social injustice and abuse of position? Why is it that even now the calls for radical change are getting lost in the inert layer of good-for-nothings with party membership cards?"

Yeltsin felt that the reasons had to do with personnel: "...there are a host of senior party figures who lack the courage to give a prompt and objective assessment of the situation, and of their own personal role, to say what needs to be said and weigh up each issue or action — both their own actions and those of their co-workers, and the aforementioned directors — not from an opportunistic point of view but from a political one."

His criticism of the CC came across as bold: "the structure of the CC's departments has become almost a carbon copy of the ministries." Many people in the departments have simply forgotten what party work truly entails. Everywhere we see a doubling up of the State Plan and the Council of Ministers. We get choked up trying to approve resolutions on simple issues for years...it is abundantly clear that the department of administrative and party work is overloaded. It deals with every issue under the sun — railway cars, animal feed, fuel. All this is, of course, important. Yet the party personnel is an issue that is more important than anything else. And it was in this work that there were oversights. (Applause.) The staff of the party were not very well-known within the department. The supervision of their work was poorly executed. Many people were not given a core assessment on time. And how else can we explain the shortcomings which were allowed to be made in a host of party organizations in the country's regions, territories and republics? Is it really the case that nobody in the CC CPSU could see the turn things had taken in Uzbekistan, Kyrgyzia and a host of regions and cities, where there was, let's be blunt about it, a rebirth among the staff cadres? (Applause.)."[319]

Yeltsin spoke openly of the mistakes made by the country's leaders: "...it begs the question: what were the reasons, who is to blame? Well, who if not us, the members of the party's Central Committee? It is clear that at times we simply lose a little of the vigilance we owe the party. ...The fact that those in power are unimpeachable, and that the leader cannot be held to account; the 'double standards' in our lives today — all this is intolerable and inadmissible."[320] Specific proposals were put forward, too: a proposal to devise,

---

319   27th Congress of the Communist Party of the Soviet Union, 25th February — 6th March 1986, Transcript vo. 1 M: Political literature publications, 1986 P. 142
320   27th Congress of the Communist Party of the Soviet Union, 25th February — 6th March

within the CC, a system of periodic reporting by all senior managers at all levels, including reports by the secretaries of the CC CPSU to the Politburo or the plenums of the party's Central Committee, and also to cancel "benefits for managers at all levels" wherever they were "not justified".[321] This last slip of the tongue essentially gave the lie to the idea that there was going to be an end to the privileges enjoyed by the *nomenklatura*. After all, it was the leaders themselves who determined what was justified and what wasn't. Yet in this form Yeltsin's words, spoken from the despatch box at the congress, sounded pretty revolutionary.

Immediately after the congress the Politburo was given a makeover: Boris Yeltsin, Y.F. Soloviev, the secretary of the Leningrad regional committee and N.N. Slyunkov, the first secretary of the CC of the communist party were named as prospective members. The following were elected secretaries of the CC CPSU: A.P. Biryukova, who had spent many years working in senior positions in the Soviet unions, A.F. Dobrynin, the USSR's ambassador in Washington for many years, V.A. Medvedev, who was also appointed head of the Central Committee's department for communications with the communists and party workers in socialist countries, G.P. Razumovsky, who had held on to his position as head of the department of administrative and party work. A.N. Yakovlev was appointed secretary of the CC CPSU for ideological matters.

On 13th March 1986 a new delineation of responsibilities among the party's senior leadership was approved at a meeting of the Politburo. Gorbachev took charge of issues related to organizing the work of the Politburo, key issues in domestic and foreign policy, the division of staff groups, general issues related to the economy, defence and national security, external trade and also a number of Central Committee departments: the administrative-party department, the general department, the economic department, the department of administrative bodies, the international department, the department of communications with communist parties in socialist countries and the department for work involving foreign staff cadres, and management of affairs. Gorbachev went far further than Andropov — the latter only took charge of organizing the work of the Politburo, key issues in foreign and domestic policy, defence and external trade, delegating many issues to his second secretary Chernenko.

Second secetary Ligachev, by contrast, was given far less to do: organizing the work of the secretariat of the CC CPSU, ideological work, issues related to science and culture and management of the agricultural and industrial complex. He was supposed to monitor the departments of propaganda,

---

321   27th Congress of the Communist Party of the Soviet Union, 25th February — 6th March 1986, Transcript vo. 1 M: Political literature publications, 1986 P. 144

scientific and educational institutions, culture and agriculture. A strict and ambitious man, who was used to giving orders, he now found himself in an ambiguous position: ideology was being dealt with by two CC secretaries simultaneously — Zimyanin and Yakovlev, and the latter was among Gorbachev's inner circle, and to him Ligachev's opinion made no difference. The same thing had happened in the field of science and culture, which had previously been under the control of Medvedev, who was also a member of Gorbachev's inner circle. Yet the field of agricultural and industrial output was in any case linked to the previous experiences of the secretary of the CC CPSU for agriculture over many years. A delineation of responsibilities such as this could only signify one thing: Gorbachev had no wish to have a strong second secretary, and potential rival, working close to him.

By decision of the Politburo, issues related to the development of engineering, the defence and chemicals industry, and construction were made the responsibility of Zaikov; heavy industry, energy, transport and communications fell within Dolgikh's remit; and light industry and trade were given to Biryukova. Dobrynin was in charge of the CC's international department; Zamyanin was responsible for issues related to science, education and healthcare; Medvedev was responsible for ties with other socialist countries; CC secretary Nikonov was in charge of agriculture; Razumovsky was responsible for work involving party staff; Yakovlev was put in charge of ideological work within the party, foreign policy propaganda and the development of culture and art.[322] A notable feature of this division of responsibilities is the obvious doubling up of functions. Far from being a mistake, this was in fact a fundamental principle of Gorbachev's staff policy: his favored approach was to create structures within the party management which competed with one another. Of itself, this principle called for a strong leader at the very top of the power structure.

On the same occasion, at the meeting of the Politburo, Gorbachev touched upon two other important issues. Firstly he insisted upon the right to existence of the private sector: "We still have a fear of work that is done by individuals, and a fear with regard to private ownership," Gorbachev stated. "Let's not allow this fear to undermine the state farms! For if we do, socialism will find itself under threat..! We must incorporate unusual approaches into what we do. So a private entrepreneur might make some headway somewhere. What of it? Have we not preserved any shreds of Leninist wisdom, so as to be able to cope with such things?"

The second consideration to cause strong consternation for Gorbachev was the fact that he had been forced to acknowledge that responsibilities had had to be divided up between the centre and the regions. "Let them scratch their

---

322   Archive of the President of the RF. Minutes of the Politubro assembly. 13th March 1986

head over these issues in the regions. And not blame everything on the Soviet powers. And let it not be thought that if there's nothing in the shops in town A or town B, Moscow must be to blame..."[323]

The staff cadres

The most important and difficult thing of all, for someone coming in from the outside, was to pick a team he could count on. Yeltsin did not have any of his own people in Moscow, and he was concerned that Grishin might try to hold on to his henchmen by putting forward men of straw. Yeltsin was not schooled in cabinet machinations, but did everything he could to expurgate the city committee's board of anyone who had worked with Grishin.

According to Y. Prokofiev[324], by mid-February of 1986 Yeltsin had accused him of pusillanimity with regard to the staff cadres, and said that they had to be more active in their efforts to replace Moscow staffers.[325]

He was quick to replace the team of aides. He brought in from Sverdlovsk V.V. Ilyushin, who had worked with Yeltsin in 1980.[326] He also appointed as an aide A.N. Tsaregorodtsev, who had worked in this position when Yeltsin was still in Sverdlovsk.[327] These aides also performed the role of speech-

323   A.S. Chernyaev: See above. P. 72.

324   Yury Anatolievich Prokofiev — at the time Yeltsin joined the MCC as head of the department of trade, from 1986 onwards — secretary of the Executive Committee of the Moscow Council, from 1988 — secretary, second secretary, from 1989 — first secretary of the MCC, from 1990 — member of the CC, member of the Politburo.

325   Y. Prokofiev: Before and after the ban on the CPSU. The memoirs of the first secretary of the MCC CPSU. M., 2005. P. 64.

326   Viktor Vasilievich Ilyushin (born 4 June 1947 in Nizhny Tagil) After graduating in 1971 from UPI, worked as a Komsomol in Nizhny Tagil; and for the Sverdlovsk regional committee VLKSM from 1975. From 1980 — deputy head of the Sverdlovsk regional committee's Organizing Department, assistant to the first secretary of the regional committee B.N. Yeltsin. Transferred to Moscow in 1985. Graduated from AON CC CPSU in 1986. From 1987 — instructor at the CC, March to October 198 — adviser in the CC Popular-democratic party of Afghanistan. From 1990 — director of the secretariat of the Chairman of the Supreme Soviet of the RSFSR, B.N. Yeltsin, and one of his closest advisers; from July 1991 — director of the secretariat of the President and the Administration of the President of Russia. From May 1992 — first assistant to the President. 1996-1997 – first deputy Chairman of the RF Government on social policy. From 1997 — chairman of the Board of directors of OJSC Gazprom-Media.

327   Aleksei Nikolaevich Tsaregorodtsev (born 1950) Graduate of UPI, Komsomol member from 1973 onwards, first secretary of the Sverdlovsk regional committee of the VLKSM from 1980. From July 1984 — adviser to the first secretary of the Sverdlovsk regional committee of the CPSU, B.N. Yeltsin (from April 1985 — Y.V. Petrov). From July 1985 — secretary to the CC Secretary B.N. Yeltsin. From January 1986 — adviser to the first secretary of the Moscow city committee, B.N. Yeltsin. From September 1986 — head of the department for general affairs, MCC CPSU. From November 1987 — deputy Vice-Rector for administrative

writers for him. The first secretary of the MCC was supplied with a security detail consisting of three people. He established friendly relations with one of his bodyguards, A.V. Korzhakov,[328] which were to endure for many years.

Yeltsin replaced all the MCC secretaries, reducing their number from 7 to 6 (enabling Yeltsin to refer to a 14.3% reduction in one of his speeches).[329] Yeltsin invited V.G. Zakharov to take up the position of second secretary of the city committee.[330] The following were elected secretaries: O.A. Korolev for industrial issues, A.A. Nizovtseva for social issues, I.D. Pisarev, L.I. Matveev, L.N. Spiridonov. The following were elected members of the MCC: Y.S. Karabasov, M.D. Polushchuk, V.V. Shiryaev, V.T. Saikin, N.E. Chelnokov, A.V. Malyshev and L.V. Petrov, and the following were elected candidates — Y.A. Prokofiev and S.A. Smirnova.[331]

Matters of personnel were often resolved in brutal fashion. In the very first meeting with the chairman of the executive board of Mossovet, V.F. Promyslov, Yeltsin demanded that he bring him a letter of resignation by 12 noon the next day. When Promyslov failed to show up he received a call from the first secretary of the city committee: "I would suggest that you do this the easy way — after all, there are other ways of doing it..." 20 minutes later Yeltsin had Promyslov's letter of resignation on his desk.[332] This style of operating was in stark contrast to the "careful approach to personnel" which had been adopted during the Brezhnev era, and, naturally, caused deep discontent among the ruling elite. Strictly speaking, the first secretary of the MCC had overstepped his authority — the chairman of the executive board of Mossovet was an elected position. He was not acting in accordance with

and management work at the Institute of social sciences in the CC. From June 1990 — adviser to the Chairman of the Supreme Soviet of the RSFSR B.N. Yeltsin. From July 1991 — director of the secretariat of the Vice-president of the RSFSR, A.V. Rutskoi.

328   Alexander Vasilievich Korzhakov — graduated from the All-Union juridical institute in 1980; 1970-1989 — worked at the ninth Directorate of the KGB (security for senior party and state figures). Provided security for the disgraced B.Yeltsin after being sacked from the KGB. After Yeltsin was elected a deputy, began working at the reception of the chairman of the Committee of the Supreme Soviet of the USSR for issues of construction and architecture (B. Yeltsin). Then served in Yeltsin's personal security detail. From 1990 — head of the department of security for the Chairman of the Supreme Soviet, head of the President's Security Service; from 1992 onwards — major-general. 20 June 1996 — fired from all roles. 1997-2000 — deputy in the State Duma of the RF. Author of the book 'Boris Yeltsin: from dusk till dawn' (M. 1997). From January 2000 — member of the deputy bloc The Fatherland is All Russia, deputy chairman of the Committee of the State Duma for defence. Doctor of economic sciences.

329   Central archive for socio-political history of Moscow (hereinafter TsAOPIM) F.4. Op.220. D. 1362. L. 16

330   On 5 October Zakharov was dismissed, and Y. Belyakov was elected in his place. In *Against the grain*, Yeltsin refers to him as A. Zakharov, clearly in error. (B.N. Yeltsin, See above P.112). In material for the plenum published in Moskovskaya pravda — V. Zakharov.

331   Moskovskaya pravda. 1986. 26 January.

332   B.N. Yeltsin See above P.112.

the norms of formal law, however, but within the context of the natural order which had taken shape, whereby the director of the party organization was to all intents and purposes in charge of the city. It had been like that in Sverdlovsk, where he had been the boss of the region, it had been like that in Moscow during Grishin's tenure, and it was thus in every Soviet region.

In order to destroy for good the ties which had been formed within the party and state structure during the Grishin era, Yeltsin resorted to unusual measures. He rejected all four of the candidates for the role of chairman of Mossovet, who had been put forward by various cliques within the city's ruling class, and chose a suitable candidate by himself. As Yeltsin later recalled, he was driven there in a ZIL, walked around the warehouses from 8am till 2 in the morning, met ordinary workers, experts, party activists, constructors and heads of department, met the general director V.G. Saikin, and tried not to miss the slightest detail: how he spoke to the workers, his subordinates and the directors. Once the new candidate had been approved by Gorbachev, on 4th January 1986 Saikin was appointed chairman of Mossovet. Y. Prokofiev was appointed secretary of the executive committee of Mossovet.

By order of the first secretary of the MCC, almost all the secretaries in the district committees were sent off on business trips to various cities so that they could pick up some experience.[333] Yeltsin replaced twenty-three of the party's first thirty-three district committee secretaries, i.e. 70% (he put the figure at 60% in *Against the grain*). Most of them left with some form of punishment from the party, such as the second secretary of the Oktyabrsky district committee, Danilov, who was removed from office for having built himself a 'lordly' apartment in an apartment block.[334]

The replacement of the personnel in the party and state administration was not confined to Moscow. The revolution in terms of personnel spread throughout the whole country. A total of 66% of first secretaries in the regional committees were replaced throughout the country. Yet within the context of a single city — all the more so a capital — the replacement of personnel was a painful process.

The news reports about the retirements of party leaders sounded like casualty reports from the front-line. 5-6 reprimands were made at each board meeting of the MCC. On 24th July the first secretary of the Brezhnev district committee, Tikhonkov, was fired; the first secretary of the Frunzensky district committee, Gryaznov, went on 27th August, and the directors of the Department of Internal Affairs, the Department for the Committee for State Security, and the heads of the central boards. The suicide of the first

---

333   RGANI. F.2. Op.5 D.34 L.74.
334   TsAOPIM F.4. Op.220. D. 1362. L.25.

secretary of the Kiev district committee, Korovitsyn, who had been relieved of his duties and been dealt a harsh punishment, sent shockwaves through the ruling elite.

Occasionally the district committee would intercede on behalf of its director, but Yeltsin went ahead with his plans regardless. Y. Prokofiev recalled one such case involving the first secretary of the Leningrad district committee, I.V. Shakhmanov. Yeltsin had brought up the issue of whether or not to relieve Shakhmanov of his duties, but the district committee did not lend him its support. Then all the staff of the city committee were sent out into the district to collect compromising material on Shakhmanov, so that the members of the district committee could be convinced of the need for him to retire. And once again the district committee did not let Shakhmanov go. Then the Board of the Moscow City Committee, under pressure from Yeltsin, announced that the plenum of the Leningrad district committee was "not yet mature enough to be able to take independent decisions", and that the Board of the MCC was therefore relieving Shakhmanov of his responsibilities of its own accord. A similar thing happened to Grafov, the secretary of the Timiryazev district committee.[335]

Yeltsin began working in Moscow in the same manner as he had been accustomed to working in Sverdlovsk. And his *modus operandi* was in stark contrast to that of Grishin. Unlike his predecessor, Yeltsin strove to be in the limelight and to talk directly to the people, and paid a lot of attention to the mass media. He visited the editorial offices of *Moskovskaya pravda*, after which the editor-in-chief was replaced. V. Markov of *Pravda* was replaced by M.N. Poltoranin,[336] with whom he managed to establish strong informal relations. With the support of the first secretary of the MCC, *Moskovskaya pravda* began publishing controversial stories which frightened a lot of people and put them on their guard. A great deal of fuss was created by the sketch *Carriages at the gates*, about the private cars in which dignitaries dropped their children off at school and then, at the end of the day, the parents would take their bosses' children to their homes.

There was a stormy reaction to articles which appeared in *Moskovsky komsomolets* about drugs, prostitution and organized crime. The newspaper had become more popular, and its print-run had risen from a hundred thousand to a million.

M. Poltaranin later recalled, in an interview: "What did I find surprising about Yeltsin? His frankness. I had occasion to talk to party bosses quite a

---

335   Y. Prokofiev: Before and after the ban on the CPSU. The memoirs of the first secretary of the MCC CPSU. M., 2005. P. 66-67.

336   M.N. Poltoranin — in 1990-1992 — minister of print and information in the Russian government, in 1992 — deputy chairman of the government.

lot...They always kept other people at a distance, and put up barriers between themselves and strangers; even during frank conversations with them you had the sense: that's where the line is — I can't go any further. With Yeltsin it wasn't like that. With him you could go as far as you wanted in those days, you could break down all his doors... "[337]

Y. Prokofiev, a member of the MCC administration, wrote about the peculiarities of Yeltsin's style in his memoirs: "...if people spoke openly to him, his reaction was more positive than when they tried to be cunning and evasive: like a wild beast, he could sniff out uncertainty, knew when the tone people adopted with him was not quite right, and was always on his guard. All it took was a slight delay in replying and straight away he would ask: 'Why are you taking so long to answer?' I would sometimes reply: 'Boris Nikolaevich, I'd rather give an accurate answer than one that has been ill-thought-through.' If he asked you who you thought should be appointed to a particular position and you named someone straight away, the person you mentioned would be given the job the very next day. If you said you needed time to think it over, he would start to think it over himself— about whether to give the person the job or not."[338]

The members of the city committee were wowed by the new first secretary's phenomenal memory and impressed by his independence. As Y. Prokofiev recalled, Yeltsin had no fear of those in power. He was capable of taking unusual decisions, regardless of who might look down on them, and how they would express their disapproval. He sought, and generally found, ways out of situations which could not be solved using the tried and trusted methods.[339]

The first secretary's inner circle included the city committee secretaries Y. Belyakov, Y. Karabasov, the head of the department of State Security Chelnokov, the chairman of Mossovet, Saikin, the head of the City Directorate of Internal Affairs, and Poltoranin. They used to meet every Monday morning in Yeltsin's office to plan the week ahead.[340]

There was a mixed reaction to the new first secretary in the nation's capital. Muscovites greeted him with enthusiasm and were hopeful that change would not be long in coming. Reports of him travelling on public transport and going to the shops were the talk of the town, and were embellished with all sorts of details; the idea that he was a man of the people — someone who fought against the privileges enjoyed by the elite and the excesses of civil

337   Quoted by: V. Andriyanov, A. Chernyak. The lonely tsar at the Kremlin. Boris Yeltsin and his team. Book 1. M.: CJSC Pravda newspaper, 1999. P.51
338   Y. Prokofiev: Before and after the ban on the CPSU. The memoirs of the first secretary of the MCC CPSU. M., 2005. P. 65.
339   Y. Prokofiev: Before and after the ban on the CPSU. The memoirs of the first secretary of the MCC CPSU. M., 2005. P. 66.
340   V. Andriyanov, A. Chernyak, See above. P.53

servants — took shape in the public consciousness. The ruling elite treated Yeltsin with caution and animosity. He was alien and unpredictable, he broke down the working traditions which persisted, and he mercilessly got rid of anyone whom he deemed to be 'putting the brakes' on *perestroika*.

The problems facing Moscow

On many counts Moscow was lagging further and further behind the regional centres. Whereas in 1975 the capital had been ranked fifth in the country in terms of the amount of capital investment, by 1985 it was in 44th place. In terms of the construction of housing Moscow had plummeted from second to 58th place.[341]

One of the most serious problems in Moscow was the acute shortage of housing. The city's population stood at 8.7 million, which was 1.1 million more than the calculations under the general plan adopted in the early 1970s. This was due to the appeal of the capital, the above-average amount of goods that were supplied, and the fact that temporary manpower was brought in.

Laborers from other cities began to be enticed to Moscow in the 1970s due to the shortage of manpower at certain enterprises where the working conditions were harsher than elsewhere. Every year 70-80 thousand people[342] went to Moscow for temporary work. These workers were given temporary residence rights in Moscow and a bed in a hostel. These laborers were predominantly young people who had broken away from their customary environment, had no families and lacked qualifications, and dreamed of making a living in the capital. To ordinary Muscovites, these people were second-class citizens. Most of the temporary workers, however, managed, by resorting to half-truths and lies, to become Muscovites on their own account and joined the waiting lists for housing.

The waiting list for an apartment contained the names of 2 million people. Of these, 512,000 were on the waiting lists at the district councils (i.e. they had less than 5 sq. m. per person), and 300,000 were on the waiting list at their place of work (less than 7 sq. m. per person). Some 1 million people, most of whom had been born in the city, lived in shared apartments. The situation was particularly difficult in the shared flats in the centre of the city, which housed as much as 65% of the population of Moscow. 28,000 people owned apartments in decrepit apartment blocks which were due for demolition.[343]

---

341   TsAOPIM F.4. Op.220. D. 1362. L. 19.
342   TsAOPIM F.4. Op.220. D. 1362. L. 21.
343   TsAOPIM F.4. Op.220. D. 1362. L. 4.

In addition to its permanent residents, Moscow was also home to approximately three million people during the summer months and two million during the winter. The city's transport system could not cope with this huge burden. There was severe overcrowding on the metro: the norm was 4.5 passengers per square meter but the average in Moscow was 7.5, and rose even higher during the rush hour.[344] Construction of the new lines on the metro was running behind schedule. 60 km of new lines which were contained in the general plan had yet to be built. In 1985 the situation as regards food supplies to the city grew worse. As much as 60% of the potato crop went to waste due to poorly organized storage and processing, and also due to the fact that in the suburbs of Moscow, types of potato were grown which did not hold up to long-term storage. In terms of the degree of mechanization and the technologies used to store potatoes, Moscow's storage centres were 15 years behind those in Leningrad. The quality of the produce in Moscow was low, and was often worse than in the other regions. Average consumption of dry milk in Moscow stood at 37%, and up to 60% in the summer months. In the rest of the RSFSR this figure stood at around 8.5%. Only 54% of the capital was used for retail — not including the 2-3 million migrant workers.[345]

Grishin's administration had ruined relations with the rest of the region. Moscow therefore received more produce from the neighboring regions than from the suburbs. Allotment co-operatives could have provided a significant boost to the supply of food to the people of Moscow, but they were developing at a snail's pace. There were 637,000 people registered in Moscow on the waiting list for allotments. In 1985 two thousand hectares of allotments were made available, when demand stood at 50 hectares; in 1986 five to six thousand hectares were made available.[346]

Most of the problems in Moscow echoed those faced by the country as a whole, and it was impossible to solve them within the context of a single city. Some changes were made, however. The decision was taken to transfer out of Moscow enterprises which were polluting the city, and which manufactured products which were exported out of the capital. Plans were drawn up to move numerous institutions out of the centre in order to turn the vacated premises into shops, theaters, museums and restaurants.

The flow of manpower into the capital was halted, and 1500 new shops were opened; trade fairs were regularly held and crime levels fell. Cleaning days were organized every Friday, and due to the lack of yard-sweepers, experts were brought in to help keep the city clean.[347]

---

344   TsAOPIM F.4. Op.220. D. 1362. L.7.

345   TsAOPIM F.4. Op.220. D. 1362. L.12.

346   TsAOPIM F.4. Op.220. D. 1362. L.15...

347   V. Soloviev, Y. Klepikova: Boris Yeltsin. Political metamorphoses. M.: VAGRIUS, 1992. P.67-68.

The city was also 'purged' of its criminal elements. The law enforcement agencies carried out raids in various districts, going into yards, cellars, attics and derelict apartment buildings. Sleazy haunts frequented by alcoholics, parasites and drug addicts were shut down, several criminals who had been the subject of nationwide manhunts were captured.

Yeltsin's efforts to fight corruption were met with resistance — it was as if he had come up against a brick wall. A large number of facts were gathered, and letters came flooding into the MCC about bribes being taken in retail and by the police. The claims were investigated, officials were replaced, and Yeltsin did the rounds of the shops and canteens, monitoring the import and distribution of products.

Such 'hands-on management' was not very effective, however. The methods which had worked in the Sverdlovsk Region, where he had been the all-powerful lord and master, did not work so well in the capital, where the first secretary of the city committee and Politburo candidate was one of the top-ranking officials, but was by no means the top dog. It was not within his power to destroy the strong ties and dubious relationships which had formed in the capital over many years. At the time he did not realise that the whole system, which had given rise to food shortages and corruption, needed to be destroyed.

The following episode from Yeltsin's memoirs is a case in point. "The scene takes place in a food store; there are several packages containing cold meats in the director's office. 'Who are these for?' 'Depends who ordered them.' 'So anyone can put in an order, can they?' Silence. At that point we start trying to get to the bottom of it with the director. He is forced to admit that the orders are distributed on a hierarchical basis, to the district executive committee, the Ministry of Foreign Affairs, the district party, the municipal ministries etc., and that they are all different — in terms of weight, product range and quality."

As a result of the fight against corruption, approximately 800 senior officials in retail were brought before the courts in the space of just over a year.[348] The directors of the department of internal affairs and the KGB were replaced, as were their deputies and numerous bosses from the most important directorates etc.

The purges also affected the 'untouchables' — staff from the foreign affairs and foreign trade ministries, and also the Moscow State Institute of International Relations. This was related to the change of leadership at the top of the Ministry of Foreign Affairs, of which E.A. Shevardnadze was put in charge in July 1985.

---

348   B.N. Yeltsin: See above P.117; TsAOPIM F.4 Op.220. D. 1362. L.25.

The meeting with the propagandists in Moscow on 11th April 1986

One of Yeltsin's first speeches in Moscow was made at the House of political enlightenment on 11th April 1986 to a group of propagandists. Of all the duties within the party organizations, this was the one that involved the largest number of participants. There were some 122,000 propagandists and 250,000 agitators in Moscow.[349] The party had an entire system of 'ideological education', based on an extensive network of all manner of circles and seminars for the study of classic political works, party documents, and external and domestic policy. Leadership of these circles and seminars was usually assigned to the most well-educated party members, for whom this work was their full-time job within the party. Thus most of the people who attended the meeting with the first secretary of the MCC were representatives of Moscow's intelligentsia, from all sorts of different fields.

A great deal of significance was attached to this event, and thorough preparations were made for it. A group of consultants was set up, which included secretaries and heads of department in the MCC, directors from the Moscow city executive committee, and bosses from the Municipal department of internal affairs and the Department of state security. A run-through and dress rehearsal were held on the eve of the meeting. Yeltsin was present, as were the MCC secretaries Pisarev, Korolev and Nizovtseva. Approximately two thousand people gathered together in the hall.

Yeltsin gave a speech about the current state of affairs in Moscow, but the climax of the meeting was set to be the question and answer session. Around 200 questions had been prepared in advance, and roughly the same amount were asked from the hall. Yeltsin knew how to get an audience on his side. Right at the start of the meeting he set the tone for a relaxed and frank discussion by saying: "I promise to answer all your questions honestly. I'll stand here as long as I can, and we'll see whether I outlast you or you outlast me."[350] He loved public speaking and was good at it: he was able to get a sense of the audience's mood and was able to alter his approach on the fly during his speeches. His experience of 'going out among the people' to interact with them, in Sverdlovsk, served him well in this regard.

Yeltsin's speech testified to the fact that in his three and a bit months as first secretary of the MCC he had managed to get a strong sense of the problems the city was facing. He had visited 29 of the city's industrial enterprises, and had met representatives of the intelligentsia (Y. Bondarev, N. Mikhalkov and D. Kabalevsky, among many others — he listed about fifteen names).

He spoke in great detail and with proficiency about pertinent issues — housing, public transport, the dacha co-operatives, trade. Yeltsin said that

349   TsAOPIM. F.4. Op.220. D. 1362. L. 2.
350   TsAOPIM F.4. Op.220. D. 1362. L. 4.

he went to the shops himself and sometimes went to the markets, and that he often rode on public transport in the outskirts of the city, where the major enterprises were located. His overall conclusion — "we cannot go on living like this"[351] — was almost identical to the name of a famous film by S. Govorukhin which was released in 1990.

So how were we to live, if not "like this"? Yeltsin told them in great detail about what he had already managed to achieve in terms of supplying the city with food and making the public transport system more effective. The former leaders of Moscow city council had prohibited the construction of stalls in the city on the pretext that they spoilt the city's appearance, but Yeltsin proposed that summer markets be set up selling fruit and vegetables. He reached agreements with the secretaries of all the republics in the union about the construction of trade centers in Moscow. He asked the government to give the capital two new state-of-the-art sausage factories, and promised that the smoked sausage produced at the factories "would smell of meat". He managed to secure a contract for the construction of a frozen food factory with a capacity of 200,000 dishes per shift. (at the time Moscow had a similar undertaking with a capacity 10 times less powerful).[352] He proposed that co-operative trade be developed, in order to push down prices in the Moscow markets. A construction program had already been drawn up for 33 co-operative stores, one for each district, the last of which was supposed to be launched in 1988. He talked about the need to commission 45 km of metro lines in the 12th five-year-plan and open 20 new stations, and also mentioned the city committee's decision to reject temporary workers.

The manner and style of working of the party's new leader in the capital were in sharp contrast to those of his predecessor. In each area of his activity, the MCC secretaries who were personally accountable were identified: trade issues — Nizovtesva, transport — Korolev. Noticing that there were no fold-out easels attached to the chairs in the hall, and that the members of the MCC were therefore not taking any notes during the assembly, Yeltsin immediately called up to the stage the MCC's head of affairs, Chubarov, and demanded that he replace the chairs by the end of the year.

90% of the notes sent up to the stage were written anonymously, but Yeltsin nevertheless promised to answer all of them. His answers were fluent and confident, and often humorous. In response to a note which read: "They say Yeltsin takes the metro. But we've never seen him on it..." he replied: "...I'm still a 'young' Muscovite, not everyone recognises me yet. If *everyone* recognised me, they might be too shy to ask me to hand their money to the driver on the bus, or stamp their ticket for them when it's crowded."[353]

351   TsAOPIM F.4. Op.220. D. 1362. L.9.
352   TsAOPIM F.4. Op.220. D. 1362. L.13-14.
353   TsAOPIM F.4. Op.220. D. 1362. L.10.

Generally speaking, Yeltsin was seen as a next-generation party leader, energetic, businesslike and reliable, and eager to interact with his audience. He may have come across as provincial to the capital's intelligentsia, with his primitive artistic needs, and a little bit naive. He went to the theater rarely and only when his duties required him to do so, and the only books he was able to say he had read were Y. Bondarev's *The bank*, V. Ardamatsky's *The trial* and A. Chakovsky's *Victory*. In response to a question about his daily regime, Yeltsin said that he worked from 8 in the morning till midnight, slept for 4 hours and worked on himself between 5 and 7 in the morning.[354]

This 'work on himself' became the subject of many barbs among the capital's snobs.

Meetings with the MCC's first secretary such as this one were held in the House of political enlightenment on numerous occasions. Each time Yeltsin was bombarded with questions, and each time he patiently and dutifully answered them.

From Chernobyl to Hamburg

On 1st May Yeltsin stood atop the Mausoleum in the Red Square for the first time. In the photos in the newspapers this tall, handsome man, in his light-colored suit, stood out among the rest of the party leaders. That evening he flew to Hamburg to attend the Eighth congress of the German Communist Party. This was his second visit to the West (the first had been his trip to Paris in 1966 as part of a delegation of Soviet engineers) and his first visit whilst in such a senior position in the party and as the leader of a small delegation. He was joined by V.N. Golubeva, a weaver who was famous throughout the country and who had twice been named a hero of socialist labor (in 1986 she was appointed director of the Ivanovskaya weaving factory) and first deputy director of the international department in the CC, V.V. Zagladin.[355] The trip proved to be a difficult one.

A week earlier, an event had occurred which was to throw a shadow over all other political news from around the world: at 1:23 am on 26th April 1986 there was an explosion at the fourth power unit at the nuclear power plant in Chernobyl, 100 km from the Ukrainian capital, Kiev.

A government commission was set up and an evacuation began in the town of Pripyata, which was located near the power plant.[356] There was a blackout

---

354   TsAOPIM F.4. Op.220. D. 1362. L.29.
355   Moskovskaya pravda 1986. 2 May.
356   N.I. Ryzhkov: Ten years of major upheavals. M.: The association 'Books. Enlightenment. Charity.' 1995. S.165-167.

about the incident in the Soviet press, radio and TV — both the central ones and the local ones. It was not until the evening of 28th April, following an assembly of the politburo, that the first official report about the accident at the Chernobyl nuclear power plant came out. It gave no clear indication at all about what had actually happened. The report published the following day, under the headline *In the Council of Ministers of the USSR*, contained just 19 lines.

It was reported that "...the accident took place in one of the buildings of the 4th power unit and led to the destruction of some of the structures within the reactor building, damage to the reactor building and a leak of a certain amount of radioactive matter. The three other power units have been restored and repaired and are currently being used as back-up. Two people died in the accident. Initial steps have been taken to deal with the consequences of the disaster. At present the levels of radiation at the power plant and in the adjoining areas have been stabilized, and essential medical aid is being provided to the victims...".[357]

The "leak of a certain amount of radioactive matter" was in fact a leak of as much cesium-137 as you would find in three hundred nuclear bombs, all as powerful as the one which the Americans dropped on Hiroshima. The chairman of the State committee for meteorology and monitoring of the environment in the USSR, Y.A. Israel, later announced at the Supreme Soviet of the USSR that the levels of radiation following the accident had been relayed on a daily basis to the Politburo, the CC CPSU, the Council of Ministers of the USSR and the republics, and the regional executive committees since day one. But that did not get in the way of the celebrations marking 1st May. In Kiev, Chernigov, Minsk, Gomel, Smolensk and Kursk, and in the cities and districts, demonstrations took place attended by thousands of people, and lasting several hours, as well as popular *gulyaniya* (processions through the streets) under the warm spring sun. It was not until 14th May 1986 that Gorbachev gave a television address on the situation.

The dearth of information gave rise to a huge number of rumors and speculation. Increased levels of radiation were registered in a host of European countries, leading to a state of near-panic among the public. Reports of thousands of victims were published in the newspapers. Addressing the congress in Hamburg, Yeltsin, understandably, could not possibly keep silent on the matter. He was required to talk about Chernobyl again when questioned about it in numerous interviews. His comments went further than the official reports.

It transpired that Yeltsin was the first senior Soviet official to visit the West after the accident at Chernobyl, and he became the primary source of

357   Pravda, 29 April 1986

information for the Western press. Journalists from leading TV companies and leading information agencies, newspapers and magazines inundated him with questions at press-conferences. In general Yeltsin confined his remarks to the directives issued by the Politburo, declaring that the scale of the disaster had been exaggerated in the West. The Soviet leaders feared that the countries in the West would demand compensation for the environmental and material damage caused by the explosion at Chernobyl. As the *International Herald Tribune* reported, he gave a speech on 5th May in which he was "sharply critical of Moscow's ideological enemies for spreading false rumors about the accident". At the same time, many newspapers noted that Yeltsin's answers were out of kilter with the reports coming out in TASS. The weekly newspaper *The Observer* concluded on 4th May 1986 that "not a single one of the comments made by Yeltsin has been reported by the Soviet mass media."[358]

The trip to Germany was Yeltsin's first taste of international activity. In addition to the communist party congress and the press-conferences, the week-long visit included meetings and negotiations with politicians: Yeltsin met the prime minister of North Rhine-Westphalen, Johannes Rau, the leader of the German SDP in Lower Saxony, Gerhard Schröder, and of the West German Bundestag, Philipp Jenninger, and the leaders of a number of charities and parties.[359] The West German politicians were keen to get to know this man whom Gorbachev was now promoting, and Yeltsin acquired the skills required to take part in international meetings, which were to prove useful to him in the future.

The day-to-day activities of the secretary of the city committee

The first secretary of the MCC had a very busy schedule. On top of the meetings he had to attend — assemblies of the MCC board, the Politburo and the secretariat of the CC CPSU — Yeltsin was constantly travelling around the city and familiarizing himself with what various enterprises were doing. In October 1986 he told an interviewer from the Yugoslav magazine NIN that 3-4 days before the end of each month he drew up a schedule on which he wrote down all his duties for the month ahead. With a considerable amount of time still left in the year, he had visited almost 60 enterprises.[360] These had included the Filevsky Bus and Trolleybus depot, the Khrunichev automobile manufacturing plant, the Salyut construction office, the Research and manufacturing center Research Center in Zelenograd, the embroidery association *Moskva*, the Moscow plant for automated production lines

358   TsAOPIM. F.4. Op.220. D. 1695. L.5
359   Moskovskaya pravda 1986. 8 May
360   TsAOPIM. F.4. Op.220. D. 1695. L.27

named after the 50th anniversary of the USSR, the *Colossus* manufacturing association, the Mosfilm film studio, the Moscow meat combine, the *Microsurgery of the eyes* complex, the S. Ordzhonikidze Moscow machine-tool production plant, the Hammer and Sickle metallurgical plant, the Vladimir Ilich Moscow electromechanical plant, the Lenin komsomol automobile plant, the Institute of cardiovascular surgery, and many, many others.

Yeltsin threw himself into his activities with his customary gusto, which the regional committee had come to know so well. Essentially, the first secretary's work centered around making sure that the city was able to keep functioning. They had to decide a huge number of practical issues related to the public transport system, the construction of housing, the arrangement of housing for medical staff, supplies of food and the arrangement of trade. When he visited the various enterprises, Yeltsin strove to gain an insight into every detail of their work. Each of his visits was prepared in great detail by the administration of the city committee, in conjunction with the directors of the enterprises, and recommendations were drawn up on how the working processes could be improved, the implementation of which was monitored strictly.

Many of the first secretary's instructions regarding the outcomes of his visits to these enterprises were implemented swiftly. When Yeltsin toured retail and catering establishments in a number of Moscow districts for a second time, he noticed a number of improvements.[361] Some of his specific, one-time orders had been carried out as well. By way of example, technical college No. 178 in the Oktyabrsky District had been formally attached to the *Prodtovary* concern. A branch of deli №8 had been turned into a business in its own right, the timetable for supplies of smoked sausage to the shops had been altered, with more delivered in the afternoon.[362] In the micro-district adjacent to the Town-planning office for the local area, transport links had been improved and a store had opened selling baked goods.[363] In May 1987, at the request of staff from the Vladimir Ilyich Moscow electro-mechanical plant, the sale of German blenders from the German store Leipzig was introduced.[364] In July 1987, in accordance with the orders of the first secretary of the city committee, 2 electronic scales were installed in store No. 6 in the Gagarin health center.[365]

Trouble-shooting such as this did not alter the general state of affairs in the city, however. Difficulties in providing supplies to the city were mounting. In the 1970s, due to the worsening shortage of foodstuffs, order tables were

---

361   Moskovskaya pravda, 18 May 1986
362   TsAOPIM. F.4. Op. 218 D. 39. L. 63.80.
363   TsAOPIM. F.4. Op. 218 D.40. L.1.
364   TsAOPIM. F.4. Op. 218 D.67. L.66.
365   TsAOPIM. F.4. Op. 218 D.67. L.88

introduced at various companies and educational institutions. In theory they were supposed to make it easier for people to buy goods which were in short supply, and avoid having to stand in line at the stores. Whether or not these orders were fulfilled depended to a large extent on how close the director was to the Soviet distribution system — in other words, to bribery. As the shortage of goods grew worse, the orders for ordinary citizens began to grow noticeably "thinner on the ground". Furthermore there were not many of them, and there was not enough for everyone. At the ZIL plant in Moscow, for example, one food order was made for every three employees. According to data from Glavtorg for March 1987, the food stores prepared a million orders each week, but this only satisfied approximately half of the total demand.[366]

Most of the problems which needed to be solved went beyond the jurisdiction of the municipal leaders or were strictly related to manufacturing. For example, when visiting one of the country's finest shoe manufacturers, the Paris commune factory, in February 1986, the first secretary of the MCC discussed with its senior staff the need to introduce automated leather tailoring, and provide the factory with high-quality card thick enough to be used to make packaging.[367] It was proposed that an international association be created for the sewing of shoes, involving the Paris commune factory; the embroidery factories in Moscow asked for help procuring scissors from Czechoslovakia and complained about their suppliers. In March 1987 a letter was sent to the MCC from the director of Vympel, in which he said that it would be impossible for the clothing factory to fulfil the plan for the first quarter due to the fact that for certain product lines — fabrics, collars and furniture — supplies had fallen as low as 25%.[368]

An analysis of the reports on the implementation of the first secretary's orders reveals that most of them were either not carried out or were impossible to carry out. After his visit to the Apakov tram depot on 26th August 1986, for example, Yeltsin proposed enlarging the depot, so that the tramlines emerged onto Mytnaya Street and Apakov Drive. The response from the Moscow GlavAPU implied that it would make no sense to reconfigure the depot like that — the cost of laying down the communications and knocking down the residential buildings would be too high.[369]

Moscow city council's executive committee agreed to Yeltsin's proposal to introduce a cashless system of payment for journeys on public transport, but felt that it would be premature to introduce such a system, since it would require a huge amount of preparatory work.[370]

---

366   TsAOPIM. F.4. Op. 218 D.66. L.19.

367   TsAOPIM. F.4. Op. 218 D. 38. L. 5.

368   TsAOPIM. F.4. Op. 218 D.66. L. 53, 57.

369   TsAOPIM. F.4. Op. 218 D. 38. L. 24.

370   TsAOPIM. F.4. Op. 218 D. 38. L. 43.

The sole outcome of Yeltsin's visit to the depot that was of any practical use was the handing over to the firm of a residential apartment block which was undergoing major refurbishment and was commissioned in the 4th quarter of 1987.[371] This proved to be a false dawn in terms of improving the living conditions of the workers at the depot, however — there was over a year to wait before the building would be ready. The promises to the effect that the work of Moscow medical and sanitary unit No.32 would be improved and retail of industrial goods at the depot expanded seemed even more doubtful.[372]

Yeltsin was asked about housing every time he met workers at Moscow's various enterprises: during a visit to the First Moscow radio parts plant on 11th March 1986, at a meeting at the Institute of nuclear power on 4th April 1986 and at the Nauka aggregate plant on 19th May that year.[373]

For all this, some advances in the life of the city were made during Yeltsin's time in office. For the first time, kindergartens with their own swimming pools were built. The first such kindergarten was due to be commissioned in the Kuntsevsky district in the first quarter of 1987,[374] and 5 stores for the union republics were opened.[375] There was an expansion in on-site retail. In 1985 this form of retail was in place at 133 companies. On 15th April 1986 the directive from the Department of Trade 'On the procedure for organizing on-site retail at industrial firms in Moscow', which was to affect 244 companies (218 industrial firms, 11 transport firms, 8 construction firms and 7 academic ones).[376] On 17th September 1987 the directive from the CC CPSU and the Council of Ministers of the USSR, 'On measures to improve the quality of medical assistance to the people and perfect the work of the healthcare institutions of the city of Moscow', was adopted.[377]

There were even more measures in the pipeline: to build two meat processing plants which operated using imported equipment, construct a frozen meals plant, and expand the network of own-brand shops. By decision of the executive committee of Moscow city council dated 20th January 1987, 17 smoked sausage workshops were due to be built in Moscow in the 12th five-year-plan, each with a capacity of 5 tonnes per shift and 3 similar workshops at the existing firms.[378]

During the course of the year which followed Yeltsin's departure from the MCC, the heads of department wrote detailed notes about the progress made in implementing his instructions following his visits to Moscow's various enterprises. For the most part these were works of fiction, such as, for example,

371   TsAOPIM. F.4. Op. 218 D. 38. L. 33.
372   TsAOPIM. F.4. Op. 218 D. 38. L.47.
373   TsAOPIM. F.4. Op. 218 D. 38. L.117, 124, 130.
374   TsAOPIM. F.4. Op. 218 D. 38. L.7.
375   TsAOPIM. F.4. Op. 218 D.38, 13.
376   TsAOPIM. F.4. Op. 218 D.40. L.84.
377   TsAOPIM. F.4. Op. 218 D.66. L.118.
378   TsAOPIM. F.4. Op. 218 D.65. L.1.

the "program of administrative and technical measures to increase the quality of smoked sausage goods" which was adopted by the Research Institute of the meat industry in conjunction with the association Mosmyasprom.[379]

For all the first secretary of the MCC's energy and stubbornness, it proved impossible to put the plans that were drawn up into action. Yeltsin believed that a change of personnel, personal accountability, a conscientious approach and a critical outlook would help to alter the situation within the management structures and lead to the first tangible results in terms of solving the city's problems. The revolution in personnel, which affected not only the management bodies but also various organizations and institutions, turned into a huge game of leapfrog. In 1986, 3 directors of district food exchanges were replaced, as well as 36 headteachers and their deputies. In a third of these cases the grounds stated were that they had failed to cope with their work.[380]

But the replacement of the Grishin administration with a new one did not lead to any real results. The winds of change blowing through the administration boiled down to an overhaul of the terminology and slogans used, and an expansion of the obligatory critical passages in the administration's fictional reports and speeches. When he studied the material from the plenums of the district committees, Yeltsin could see that nothing had changed, and that the same shortcomings were being criticized again and again, rather than those responsible for them. The personal criticisms essentially related to minor details: of one person it was said that he "lacked the required level of equanimity and sensitivity in his interaction with people", of another party worker it was said that he "never asked the workers for advice", and a third person "had forgotten all about an individual approach to working with people". The secretaries of the district committees remained completely untouched by the criticism.[381]

In a speech at an assembly of the GUVD on 25th July 1986, Yeltsin acknowledged that in the course of the last six months, nothing had changed. There had been no genuine reduction in crime. Spontaneous markets, known as *tolkuchki*, were popping up all over the city. The MCC had been inundated with letters about police inaction in the face of breaches of the law. As he saw it, the reason for this was that "those in charge are being slow to readjust their working processes in the light of modern requirements".[382]

Yeltsin was encountering the same problems in the city that the general secretary was encountering on the level of the country. In August 1986, during a trip to the Far Eastern Region, Gorbachev publicly accused the middle chain in the

---

379   TsAOPIM. F.4. Op. 218 D. 39. L.79

380   TsAOPIM F.4. Op.220. D.1364. L.20.

381   TsAOPIM F.4. Op.220. D.1364. L.22-23.

382   TsAOPIM F.4. Op.220. D.1365. L.27

country's system of governance of shortcomings and sabotage. He would later write in his memoirs that the "great and the good in the civil service were, whether by instinct or deliberately, ignoring perestroika".[383] In a speech to members of the Politburo following his return from the Far Eastern Region, Gorbachev first coined the slogan "hit out at the staff headquarters."[384] He complained that the press were hushing up the failings, that the people were growing nostalgic about Andropov, and that a reshuffle was needed among the party staff. "People are willing to take part in perestroika," he said, "but they're already questioning whether it might not lead to the collapse of the union." The style adopted by the local organizations has not changed, it is still conservative."[385] Gorbachev was sharply critical of the union ministries, the government's economic services and the party administration. In his opinion there was no political opposition in the country representing those who opposed perestroika; instead, there was only conservatism and stagnation.

The Central Committee plenum of January 1987

The issue of staff cadres was put off until the plenum of the CC in January 1987. On 19th January, the day before the plenum, a draft version of Gorbachev's speech was discussed during a meeting of the politburo. It contained two key pieces of news. The first was that communists would now be able to elect their 'first' leader, in open elections with more than one candidate: from the secretary of the primary organization to the secretaries of the regional committees and the organizations in the republics. In theory, these elections had always existed. In practice, however, the leaders of all the party organizations, from the top down, conducted their elections not by means of a direct vote but, depending on the size of the party organization, at a meeting of the party board, the party committee, the board of the regional committee or the Politburo, 'approving' the appointments in what was essentially a rubber-stamping by the next most senior party agency. The second innovation was that the process of the elections now fell within the remit of public supervision. The fact that candidates could now be openly criticised was a means of checking whether or not those standing for office within the party adhered to the ideas of 'perestroika'. The leaders of the CPSU were hoping to rely on public opinion, as expressed in the press, and on the voices of rank-and-file communists as a tool with which to conduct a 'purge' of the staff cadres, and to instigate this purge by means of open elections.

During the Politburo assembly a dispute broke out about a particular phrase in the speech, which stated that "the CC CPSU and the country's leaders,

---

383   M.S. Gorbachev: His life and reforms. Vol. 1. P. 305.
384   Same reference. P. 109.
385   Vorotnikov, V.I. See above. P. 108-109.

primarily for subjective reasons, failed to recognise on time, or in full, the need for change, and the danger that society would face growing crises..."[386] What exactly were these subjective reasons? Which members of the CC CPSU had been slow on the uptake, and had failed the spot the need for change? These were not rhetorical questions — far from it — and it was proving impossible to translate them into philosophical reality.

Yeltsin had some serious criticisms of the speech. Below is a short excerpt from his speech:

"Yeltsin:

Firstly: the evaluations of the current state of perestroika have been slightly exaggerated. The circumstances within the staff cadres are such that it would be dangerous to let optimism take hold. Some members of the party are not ready for revolutionary change. We would be better off thinking of this current period as a time of new forms of work which will lead to perestroika.

Secondly: The assessment of the 70th anniversary. It is eagerly anticipated. We must have the courage to state, without mincing our words, that both the last Politburo and the CC are to blame for the slowing-down of it.[387] It is far better to give specific assessments of the current course of perestroika, for specific areas: for specific territories and major organizations.

Thirdly: with regard to the guarantees of success. The guarantees which are stated are the socialist configuration, the Soviet people, the party. Yet these have been around for the last 70 years! So they are in no way guarantees that we will not return to the past. They are instead a basis for guarantees. The guarantees in fact stem from the themes mentioned at the end of the speech. And the most important of these is the process of democratizing every field of life.

Fourthly: there is a huge contrast between the assessments of the pre-April (prior to April 1985) and post-April periods. The post-April assessment contains no self-criticism at all directed at the leaders of the party and the country. It is worth noting that the staff cadres are deeply struck by this...And at many levels there has been neither a revamp, nor perestroika. The criticisms contained in the report are all directed downwards."[388]

---

386   V.A. Medvedev: On Gorbachev's team. P. 45.

387   Of the members of the former Politburo, the one described as being 'stagnated', Gorbachev, Gromyko, Shcherbitsky, Aliev, Solomentsev and Vorotnikov were in the new Politburo, and Shevardnadze, Dolgikh, Demichev and Chebrikov were candidate members.

388   In the Politburo...According to notes taken by Anatoly Chernyaev, Vadim Medvedev, Georgy Shakhnazarov (1985-1991). Compiled by A. Chernyaev. Pakrus Publishing 2nd ed. M: Gorbachev-Foundation, 2008. P. 124-125

There were more than ten points in the list of criticisms; Yeltsin spoke for a long time, and Gorbachev even attempted to stop him at one point. Yeltsin's darts of criticism were aimed at Gorbachev himself, and at his 'perestroika'.

Naturally, they were met with resistance. E.A. Shevardnadze attempted, not without a degree of cunning, to absolve himself and his colleagues in the Politburo of responsibility, by declaring that "there was no collegiate responsibility in the Politburo in those days, decisions were taken by a small group of people, side-stepping the Politburo";[389] in the discussion which followed, people were advised not to "stir up the past".

Gorbachev himself spoke out against the idea of reducing everything to an assessment of previous members of the leadership, and previous members of the CC, when forming assessments of the past. "It is important that we draw political conclusions and learn lessons for the future," he declared. In Gorbachev's opinion, the slow speed at which perestroika was taking place was down to mistakes in the staffing policy and in the management structures.[390]

In conclusion, turning to Yeltsin, Gorbachev came out with the remarkable line: "We do not support you, although we approve of your activity."[391] This remark, which was essentially absurd, was a Freudian slip which revealed the true nature of his attitude towards Yeltsin. Yeltsin was necessary as the broom with which to sweep Grishin's lot out of Moscow, but his exacting nature and stubbornness were surplus to requirements in the Politburo.

Needless to say, Gorbachev did not accept a single one of the fundamental criticisms made by Yeltsin. And when he gave his closing remarks, it sounded as if he was reprimanding a naughty schoolboy. That was precisely how Yeltsin interpreted his comments. He felt oppressed and bothered: "I'm a relatively young member of the Politburo. This has been a lesson for me. I think it is a timely one."[392] This was no easy admission for a man of such ambition. This was followed by a comment from Ligachev: "That is the hardest thing of all — to get used to the idea that you, too, might have to take one on the chin."[393] It was not in Yeltsin's nature to get used to being boxed around the ears. And he was in no mood now to shoulder arms and abandon his beliefs.

Gorbachev could not forgive Yeltsin for his speech. The day after the Politburo assembly, he called Vorotnikov and told him that Yeltsin's methods were to play games with personnel, make promises and shake up the staff cadres, and that the situation in Moscow was not changing for the better...[394] The dispute in the Politburo was suddenly of a fundamental nature. Whereas until recently

389   V.A. Medvedev: See above. P. 45.
390   M.S. Gorbachev: See above. P. 309.
391   In the Politburo...P.129.
392   In the Politburo...P.129.
393   In the Politburo...P.130.
394   V.I. Vorotnikov: See above. P. 46.

Gorbachev and his 'intellectual circle', led by Yakovlev, had been more radical than anyone else, there was now someone in the Politburo who had taken the liberty of criticizing its approach, and insisting that it take measures which were even more radical. Gorbachev was forced to wage a war on two fronts. The duo of Gorbachev and Yeltsin had begun to fall apart. Yeltsin had lost the man who had supported him and been his political ally.

He had no intention of taking a backward step, however. In his address to the plenum, Yeltsin essentially repeated the same things he had said at the assembly of the Politburo: "It is my belief that following the report and comprehensive analysis, absolutely everyone must be assessed as regards their ability to implement perestroika, right down to the members of the Central Committee, particularly the leaders...a fundamental assessment must be made of the major errors that were made." He proposed "establishing an age restriction and a cap on the amount of time that could be spent in office in a single role for administrative and other leaders," including the staff of the party administration.[395]

The plenum which was held on 27th-28th January 1987, entitled 'On perestroika and staff policy', featured one of the biggest political events of the day. It was at this plenum that it was decided to hold open elections — both in the party and in the Soviets — and to hold the first party conference since the war. There were changes of personnel, too: D.A. Kunaev was expelled from the Politburo; and M.V. Zimyanin was expelled from the CC. A.N. Yakovlev became a candidate member of the Politburo, and A.I. Lukyanov and N.N. Slyunkov became secretaries of the CC CPSU.

Yeltsin had a growing sense, meanwhile, that perestroika was stuck in a rut: little had changed in Moscow, the new style of management and policy of state verification of quality were not coming to the rescue, and a host of enterprises which had crossed over to self-financing were faltering. Addressing a session of the Moscow city council, he acknowledged bitterly: "There have been no tangible changes either in the allocation of housing, in trade, in healthcare or in transport."[396] The reasons for these failures are to be found in the poor level of skills in the staff cadres, the lack of a proper system of work between the district committees and the companies, and the passive nature of many deputies.[397]

After the January plenum, the barrage of criticism within the party organization in Moscow took on the proportions of a tsunami. The biggest victims were the secretaries of the district committees, whilst the board members of the MCC, who had to give personal reports at the plenum of the city committee, also

---

395   RGANI. F.2. Op.5 D.34 L.75.

396   Moskovskaya pravda 15 March 1987.

397   B.N. Yeltsin: 'Act insistently and decisively' Report to the plenum of the MCC, 21 February 1987 //Moskovskaya pravda. 23 February 1987.

suffered. Concluding his public admonishing of the MCC board members I.D. Pisarev and V.P. Scherbakov at the plenum on 30th May 1987, Yeltsin gave them the following piece of advice: "accept what I am saying without taking offence, feeling stressed or letting ambition cloud your judgement."[398] Just a few months later this same advice might well have been directed at him.

The first secretary of the MCC believed that some personal criticism would whip the city and district leaders into shape. For the civil servants who had grown used to the quiet life during the years of 'stagnation', however, the increased exactingness of the new 'city boss' caused irritation and strong resistance. Addressing a meeting of the Moscow city council, the director of a Science and Research Institute, Y.O. Adamov, said: "There are no areas of life which are not subject to criticism in Moscow these days, but some of these areas have already been transformed into areas thick with artillery fire, to such an extent that if a good person crops up and there are hopes that this person will work effectively, we are too hasty in expecting results from him, and we don't give him a chance to show what he can do."[399]

Moscow was on the receiving end of criticism from the central media, and this was bound to be hurtful to Yeltsin. At a plenum of the MCC on 8th August 1987, he said, seeking to reassure himself as much as anyone else: "It inspires feelings of bitterness, of course, to read and hear all this. And yet we must remember at all times that in the current circumstances this is a necessary, entirely normal state of affairs. There are a lot of sores on the face of the city, and we need to lance these boils — life will be easier that way."[400]

He could see that he was losing support both in the Kremlin and in the MCC. Under the circumstances, a single uncertain step might be used against him. The catalyst for these events was the first unauthorized mass rally by the historical and patriotic association *Pamyat* (Memory), which was held on 6th May 1987 in Moscow on the square commemorating the 50th anniversary of October (now known as Manezhnaya Square).

The meeting with Pamyat

The *Pamyat* society was an unregistered charity with a nationalist agenda.[401] The rally was attended by approximately 300-400 people shouting slogans

---

398   Moskovskaya pravda 31 May 1987.
399   Moskovskaya pravda 31 May 1987.
400   Moskovskaya pravda, 9 August 1987
401   The Pamyat (Memory) association emerged in 1982 on the basis of the Society of Book-lovers at the Ministry of Aviational Industry of the USSR; from 1986 onwards it was called the historico-patriotic association Pamyat (in honor of V. Chivilikhin's novel Pamyat). The association was led by D.D. Vasiliev from 1985 onwards.

such as 'Down with the saboteurs of perestroika', 'Give Pamyat the status of a historical and patriotic association', 'We demand to see Yeltsin or Gorbachev' and 'Restore Poklonnaya Hill'. The chairman of the Moscow city council, Saikin, drove to the square, but the demonstrators refused to disperse and demanded to see either Gorbachev or Yeltsin.

The crowd grew in size and the directors of the Department of Internal Affairs were in two minds about whether or not to break it up. The decision taken by the first secretary was an unusual one: he agreed to meet the demonstrators and even suggested a choice of three possible meeting points: the House of Soviets, the party's city committee or the House of political enlightenment. The leaders of Pamyat opted for the House of Soviets. The meeting with Yeltsin was held in a huge hall which could hold almost a thousand people. The participants in the rally talked about the fact that historical monuments in Moscow were being destroyed, the Americanization of culture, the fact that architects, in their efforts to put up a new monument, had effectively destroyed Poklonnaya Hill, which had served as one of the historic symbols of the capital. Interestingly, Pamyat's leaders laid the blame for all this at the feet of the "enemies of perestroika".

Some of their ideas and thoughts seemed to Yeltsin to make perfect sense: the need to take care of the Russian language, the problem of the perversion of Russian history, the need to protect monuments to the past, and so on. Yeltsin confessed that under the General Plan for the development of Moscow in 1935, more than 2000 historic monuments had been destroyed, but he took issue with the demonstrators, arguing that there were still around 9500 monuments in Moscow and that the amount of restoration work that was being done had doubled. He thought it over and was in two minds about what to do with Poklonnaya Hill and with the monument to Victory which was to be put up there; he said that it was down to the Moscow city council to determine how the rallies would be organized.[402]

This meeting, the only reference to which in the press was a short piece in *Moskovskaya pravda*,[403] resonated throughout Moscow. For the first time ever, the secretary of the city committee had listened to the demands being made on the streets; for the first time, a representative of the authorities had made direct contact with protesters.[404]

---

402   V. Soloviev, Y. Klepikova: Boris Yeltsin. Political metamorphoses. M., 1992. P. 59-62.
403   The name of the Pamyat association is not mentioned. The only thing mentioned is the first secretary's meeting with "a group of Muscovites assembled on the square of the 50th anniversary of October, and then at the Moscow Council." See: Moskovskaya pravda 7 May 1987.
404   The last occasion when a party leader spoke to protesters was when A. Mikhoyan visited Novocherkassk in 1962. This conversation ultimately ended in the demonstrators being fired on ruthlessly, resulting in many deaths, arrests and prison sentences.

Yeltsin's meeting with the protesters put him in an extremely vulnerable position. A dangerous precedent had been set. One of the capital's official halls served as a useful site in which to arrange an impromptu debate, involving people who made no secret of the fact that they were inclined to oppose the authorities. Pamyat's reputation among the Moscow intelligentsia as a nationalist, anti-Semitic organization (a reputation which was entirely justified, incidentally) cast a shadow on Yeltsin as well.

According to V. Soloviev and Y. Klepikova, who wrote one of the first biographies of Yeltsin, his meeting with Pamyat was a strategic error. He had overestimated the importance of this organization, which was to all intents and purposes controlled by the Committee of State Security. The demonstrators' demand to meet Yeltsin and rejection of talks with Saikin stemmed directly from the instructions they had received from their patrons. They intended to sully Yeltsin's reputation and put him in a compromising situation. Soloviev and Klepikova examine this provocative act by Pamyat in the context of the conflict between Yeltsin and Gorbachev, which had begun in the spring of 1987.[405]

This interpretation does not come across as particularly convincing. If the rally on Manezhnaya Square had been provoked by the state security forces with the aim of harming Yeltsin's reputation, its organizers would probably have waited for the first secretary of the city committee to sanction the use of armed force to disperse the crowd. All the more so given that all the legal bases for doing so were in place: the organization was not registered, the rally had not been authorized, and it was disrupting the traffic.

The leaders of Pamyat were completely unprepared for the meeting with Yeltsin. When they were demanding a meeting with Gorbachev or Yeltsin, it is highly unlikely they were seriously expecting a senior party leader would actually come out and meet them. After all, they had not drawn up any specific demands whatsoever for the party leaders. The issues which were discussed at the meeting — safeguarding the Russian language and Russian history, and protecting Russian monuments — were an attempt to draw Yeltsin into a debate, rather than demands for anything from the authorities.

Yeltsin agreed to meet the demonstrators because he was not afraid of talking to large audiences. As the 'boss of the city' he considered himself duty-bound to hear people out, without stopping to think about whether doing so would compromise him in any way.

---

405   V. Soloviev, Y. Klepikova: Boris Yeltsin. Political metamorphoses. M.: VAGRIUS, 1992. P.65-66.

Yeltsin at the Politburo of the CC CPSU
("We don't support you, although we approve of your actions")

Following his election as secretary of the CC, and then as a candidate for membership of the Politburo, Yeltsin ascended to the very top of Russian politics and threw himself into the life of the Soviet political elite. Assemblies of the Politburo were held every week. They began at 11 o'clock in the morning and lasted between 5 and 9 hours.

There was a strict hierarchy within the Politburo which determined the entire matrix of relationships within the party's most senior body, as well as a formal order for going into the assembly hall, an order determining the places in the hall and even an order governing everyone's places at the dining table during the break. Yeltsin, who was used to the more democratic methods employed by the regional committees, was not keen on this — particularly given that in his capacity as secretary of the CC he was part of the third, lowest category, the so-called 'sky-residents', whilst when he became a candidate for membership of the Politburo he joined the second category.

Assemblies of the Secretariat, led by Y.K. Ligachev, took place every Tuesday. The division of obligations between the Politburo and the Secretariat was fairly perfunctory. The Secretariat usually examined the less important issues, whilst the most serious matters were discussed at joint assemblies of the Secretariat and the Politburo. Yeltsin, who had been a head of department at the CC for almost six months and had seen the administration at work from the inside, was of the view that the administration was running the show, and that the members of the Politburo were often merely taking part in the discussion for the sake of form.

Initially Yeltsin did more listening than talking during the assemblies, but after a while he gradually began to make his voice heard. Whenever he felt that an issue was being decided in an incorrect way, he would object — and he would be fairly insistent about it. He would generally tend to have disputes with Ligachev and Solomentsev.

In his memoirs Yeltsin described the characteristics of his colleagues in the Politburo. They are of considerable interest, because they tell us not only about the people with whom he was required to work, but also about Yeltsin himself.

Yeltsin felt as if he was a representative of a new, younger generation. When seen alongside the 77-year-old A.A. Gromyko and the 73-year-old M.S. Solomentsev, Gorbachev and Yeltsin, both 55, and N.I. Ryzhkov, 57, were indeed relatively young. Most of the Politburo seemed to Yeltsin to be the remnants of the old guard from the Brezhnev era. A.A. Gromyko, Yeltsin felt, "had a poor grasp of the situation in the country, and was living out his life in some sort of isolated world which he himself had created." To Yeltsin, the generals V.M. Chebrikov and D.T. Yazov were no more than "products of the old system". Yeltsin described the latter as a limited man and a committed fighter. He felt that Aliev, the first secretary of the communist party of Azerbaijan, and Shcherbitsky, the first secretary of the communisty party of Ukraine, had both been indecisive during their time in the Politburo, and had sat on the fence with regard to Gorbachev's actions.

Yeltsin did not see any strong characters coming through among the younger generation, either. Though he praised the qualities of N.I. Ryzhkov with regard to the handling of affairs, Yeltsin considered him a poor organizer, particularly in light of the growing economic chaos in the country.

Yeltsin had good things to say about V.I. Dolgikh, describing him as one of the most professional and efficient secretaries in the CC. In his opinion, Dolgikh was notable for his systematic approach, his balanced approach to decision-making and his relative independence. The pair sat next to one another at assemblies of the Politburo (probably because they were sitting in alphabetical order rather than as the result of any particular friendship) and often had frank discussions about the problems facing the country and how they were being resolved.

Yeltsin reserved his most flattering remarks for A.N. Yakovlev, as "the most intelligent, sensible and far-sighted politician."[406]

Of course, Yeltsin's appraisals were written three years after he left the Politburo, and the scathing criticism to which Yeltsin gave voice at the plenum in 1987 affected his relations with his former colleagues. An exception was Yakovlev, who also spoke out against Yeltsin in October 1987. At the same time, it is clear that Yeltsin began to form his opinion of his colleagues once he was already working with them.

Yeltsin could not help noticing the contradictions between the members of the Politburo. These contradictions had always been there: they would argue about what needed to be done, and how it was to be done; they would rival one another for influence and power; there would be disputes between the members of the Politburo who had been in charge of the Council of Ministers of the USSR and the RSFSR, and their "curators in the party"; and on top of this there were complex relations between individuals at play. At a Politburo assembly held on 27th October 1986, during a discussion about the letters which had been received by the CC CPSU, a genuine political debate flared up, during which the differences of opinion on the restructuring of the "older

---

406   For more details see B.N. Yeltsin: See above P. 140-146.

generation", in the shape of Gromyko and Gorbachev's team, were brought into sharp focus.[407]

After making the journey from his home region of Sverdlovsk to the Kremlin, and reaching the summit of Russian politics, Yeltsin (against most people's expectations, perhaps) did not run up against any particularly powerful or notable characters. With one or two exceptions, he didn't even feel that his colleagues in the Politburo merited much respect. In light of this, his confidence in his own powers increased, and he behaved more actively, although he did not feel at home in the Politburo. He refrained from getting drawn into discussions about ideological matters, and instead raised pointed questions primarily about practical and political matters. Far removed from behind-the-scenes back-stabbing, and direct and open by nature, Yeltsin did not strive to establish strong informal relations and win friends, but instead waited for people to take note of the work he was doing in Moscow. His only hope was that he would secure the support of Gorbachev.

Gradually, however, Yeltsin, who by nature had a strong sense of the psychological context of relationships, began to feel a certain tension and some sort of alienation from his colleagues in the Politburo. In the assemblies Gorbachev began to suggest in passing, with increasing frequency, that all was not well in Moscow. There were several serious clashes with the second-most important person in the party — Ligachev — about tax exemptions and privileges, and about the directive on the struggle against drunkenness and alcoholism. Ligachev demanded that the brewery in Moscow be shut down, and that a halt be called to sales of all spirits — and even of dry wines and beer. Later, in his book *Against the grain*, Yeltsin dismissed the campaign against alcoholism as "poorly organized and absurd", and said it had been conducted without taking the social and economic consequences into account.[408] Naturally there was nothing he could to sabotage its introduction in Moscow, however. Production of strong, ordinary wines was brought to an end in the capital, whilst production of dry wines, dessert wines and vintage wines fell by 40% compared to 1985.[409]

During the discussions in the Politburo, Ligachev could count on support from Solomentsev, whilst Gorbachev played a game of 'wait and see'. Further tension was added to the relationships between the members of the politburo by Yeltsin's speech at the assembly on 9th January 1987, during a debate on the draft version of Gorbachev's speech about staff cadres for the January plenum.

---

407   AP RF, Working record of the Politburo meeting. 27 October 1986
408   B.N. Yeltsin: Against the grain. P.126
409   TsAOPIM. F.4. Op. 218 D.38. L.9.

The plenum of the CC CPSU, on economic concepts related to 'perestroika', had been prepared in June 1987. A group of academics and employees of the CC administration had done some preliminary work in the suburban residence in Volynsk; the group had included the famous economists Aganbegyan, Abalkin, Sitaryan, Petrakov and Popov. The essence of the economic transformations consisted in increasing companies' financial independence, which had become possible, according to its authors, following the adoption of the law about companies, which, in turn, ought to lead to significant changes in the way the economy was managed. At the same time it was proposed that he reject centralized state supplies and begin to convert defence companies, and that he reorganize the banking system. Permission was granted for the creation of co-operatives.

At a Politburo assembly on 22nd June, the day before the plenum, various opinions were expressed about the forthcoming economic reforms. Yeltsin made a hard-hitting speech in which he declared that the plenum, and certain government directives in particular, had not been sufficiently well prepared. V. Medvedev, when recalling this incident years later, wrote that in his heart of hearts he agreed with Yeltsin, but that there was no way they could postpone the plenum.[410]

Yeltsin did not hold back at the plenum either: unlike the other speakers, who spoke mostly about specific economic problems, Yeltsin once again brought up the issue of the need to reform the entire system of party-and-state governance: Two years have passed since perestroika began, and it has not gone very far...Nothing has changed within the Secretariat of the CC — there is still an abundance of paperwork and administrative tasks. It is essential that we create political agencies and liquid committees in order to reduce the administrative workload within the ministries and agencies, and introduce an institute of party agencies within the CC. We must restructure the party as a whole, and not just each party agency."[411]

The plenum in June did not change anything at all. The economic problems had grown and the prevailing mood in society was becoming ever more politicized. Below are some of the messages which were written down on the election slips during the elections in Moscow for the local Soviets of people's deputies in the summer of 1987, the first open elections in six decades of Soviet rule:

"When will they stop mincing their words? When will they start operating in accordance with the directives of the CC CPSU?"

---

410   V.A. Medvedev: On Gorbachev's team. P.51-52.
411   In the Politburo...P.195-196.

"Order number one was to appoint people who are not members of the party to senior roles, but the communists have revealed themselves to be thieves from top to bottom."

"As long as we have a one-party system, no good will come of it."

"We request that you to speak out in defense of the patriotic movement, the Pamyat society."

"Power should be in the hands of the Soviets, not the party." "Bring the troops home from Afghanistan."

On 6th August, at a Politburo assembly at which all the issues on the agenda were discussed, Yeltsin brought up the fact that "individuals of an extremist persuasion" were attempting to organize demonstrations and rallies in Moscow, under various pretexts, and demanding that the Moscow city council determine the rules governing them. The grounds for asking this question was a riotous demonstration by Tatars from the Crimea. The assembly of the Politburo came to an end, and no solution was adopted on this issue. Gorbachev merely said: "In theory this ought to be adopted. Prepare some proposals."[412] Gorbachev's words are related in more detail in the notes written by A. Chernyaev, V. Medvedev and G. Shakhnazarov. The General secretary said that "the right to hold demonstrations and the rules governing how they are held" needed to be determined by the local Soviets. And, importantly, without mentioning Yeltsin by name, he effectively expressed his support for what Yeltsin had done during the Pamyat demonstration: "we must go out to the people and by so doing isolate the extremists."[413]

In early September the rules governing the way rallies were held were approved by the Moscow city council. This document — the first document in Soviet history to in effect allow a right enshrined in the Constitution to be made a reality — was adopted at Yeltsin's initiative. And it was Yeltsin who suffered as a result. The initiative taken by Moscow caused extreme discontent in the Kremlin.

At an assembly of the Politburo on 10th September, Ligachev gave a hard-hitting speech: "Why didn't Yeltsin examine this issue with the board of the MCC? Who discussed it, and with whom?" From the point of view of the Politburo members who supported Ligachev, Yeltsin's culpability was abundantly clear: without consulting the Politburo he had dared to establish a standard for the entire USSR — for such was the precedent that Moscow of course set.

---

412   V.I. Vorotnikov: See above P.152.
413   In the Politburo...P.217

A commission was formed comprising Vorotnikov, Yeltsin, Lukyanov and Razumovsky, which was tasked with discussing the issue with experts from the Ministry of Justice and the Ministry of Internal Affairs and preparing a draft Directive from the Presidium of the Supreme Council 'On the procedure for the organization by socio-political organizations of mass-participation events: rallies, demonstrations and processions'.[414]

The October Plenum of 1987: 'The Yeltsin affair'

In the Politburo Yeltsin felt isolated, and he found it increasingly difficult to work. He interpreted the criticism directed at him by Ligachev not as an attack but as a concerted attempt at harassment. The final straw was the Politburo assembly on 10th September 1987, when the issue of the unauthorized decision taken by the Moscow city council about the procedure for holding rallies was discussed.

On 12th September Yeltsin sent a letter to the general secretary, who was on holiday in southern Russia, in which he asked for permission to tender his resignation. This was probably the first and only instance, in the entire history of the CPSU, of such a high-ranking party leader, who was not incapacitated, voluntarily relinquishing his position. If the rationale behind this extraordinary and emotional act was that Gorbachev would not let him go, but would instead promise to support him, then it was a rationale of childlike naivety. However that may have been, it was certainly an act of desperation. If he were to retire, Yeltsin would be burning all his bridges, and would only be able to count on a return to his previous profession — that of a civil engineer.

Yeltsin wrote: "...I always tried to express my own personal opinion, even if it was not an opinion that was shared by others. As a result I found myself getting into an increasing number of awkward situations. Or to be precise: I turned out to be unprepared, with my whole style, directness, and background, for being a member of the Politburo... The party organizations proved to be right at the back of all the events which mattered. Here there was practically no... perestroika... These comments were carefully thought-through and designed to sound revolutionary. The implementation of them, however, in the party — the same old party, concerned as ever with happenstance and order of precedence, preoccupied with trifling matters, bureaucratic, an approach that was very audible on the outside. This is where the gulf opened up between the revolutionary talk and party affairs, which were far removed from a political approach... In my opinion, Yegor Kuzmich [Ligachev] does not have a system or a culture in his work. His constant references to his "experiences

---

414   V.I. Vorotnikov: See above P.153-154.

in Tomsk" are already becoming difficult to listen to...In relation to me, after the plenum of the CC in June, and taking into account the Politburo assembly on 10th September, I can find no other words for the attacks he has made than coordinated harassment. The decision of the executive committee regarding the rallies is a municipal matter, and was decided in the correct way. I do not understand the role of the commission that was set up. ...I find the attitude of some of my comrades in the Politburo of the CC depressing. They are intelligent and have therefore been quick to be 'restructured'. Yet are they really to be believed? It is convenient to have them around, and, if you'll forgive me, Mikhail Sergeevich, it seems to me as if they are becoming convenient for you, too...

I, on the other hand, am an inconvenience, and I realise this. I also understand that it's not easy to find solutions with me...

In future, given the current situation in the staff cadres, the number of issues which have to do with me is going to grow, and this will impede you in your work. With all my soul, I would not want this to happen...These are a few of the reasons and motives which prompted me to turn to you with this request. It is not a sign of weakness or cowardice on my part.

I hereby request that you relieve me of the position of first secretary of the MCC CPSU and of my obligations as a candidate for membership of the Politburo CC CPSU. I ask that you consider this official notice. I do not feel that it will be necessary for me to address the plenum of the CC CPSU directly.

Yours sincerely,
B. Yeltsin
12th September 1987."[415]

The letter was not only a request to tender his resignation — it was also a political document. The grounds that Yeltsin had given for his resignation was the fact that he did not see eye to eye with party policy — which involved trumpeting perestroika so loudly when in fact nothing had changed — and when Ligachev spoke, he did so first and foremost as a symbol of the adminstration's unchanging nature, its unwavering stance. It was a document full of disappointment, and of unrealised hopes for reform of the country; it was payback for having had faith in Gorbachev. It was a letter which contained great personal courage — a blind courage which bordered on desperation. Achieving high office in the party was an incredibly difficult thing to do. Losing it, and finding oneself ejected from a close circle of "party peers", would transform him into an outlaw, a political miscreant, whom law-abiding careerists would give a good kicking for years to come.

---

415   B.N. Yeltsin: See above. P. 12-14.

It is worth noting that as he burned his bridges, Yeltsin used a whole series of arguments which must have offended Gorbachev. Gorbachev must have detected an implied criticism in Yeltsin's assertion that he, with "his directness, his particular background", did not wish to work in the Politburo. A row erupted. Gorbachev tried to transform it into a "family" affair.

Yeltsin called Gorbachev in the Crimea to find out what would happen following his letter; Gorbachev prevaricated and suggested returning to the issue after the October public holidays, and asked him not to raise the issue of his retirement.[416] In the company of a close circle of advisers, Gorbachev complained: "He's not happy with how perestroika's going, with the work of the Secretariat, and with plenty more besides. Start examining the issue of relieving him of his responsibilities in the Politburo. He's made a mess of things in Moscow, and now he's looking for someone to blame."[417] Gorbachev chose not to reply to Yeltsin's letter. He would have to wait to see what the outcome was.

Everything continued as it had before. Yeltsin continued in his position. On 19th September 1987, large-scale festivities were organized for City Day for the first time.[418] Yeltsin laid a wreath on the mausoleum and walked up to the tribune above it. This did not go unnoticed: the tribune on the mausoleum was intended for the senior leadership of the country, not the city. On 25th September there was a meeting with propagandists in Moscow. On 4th October Yeltsin organized a meeting of the party group before an assembly of the Moscow city council. An atmosphere of sharp criticism prevailed throughout the entire session.

During a Politburo assembly on 15th October, when a draft version of Gorbachev's speech marking the 70th anniversary of the October revolution, Yeltsin addressed the assembly, speaking calmly and assuredly. All his comments were essentially about the need to talk in more detail about the party's activities between February and October, the fact that the Bolsheviks had seized power in the Soviets, the need to provide more precise assessments of Lenin's peers in the Politburo, and talk more forcefully about the party's organizational activities. It appeared that Yeltsin had no intention of confining himself to the historical section of the speech, and wished to continue. His final remark was: "And then we must say — what do we have, as we arrive at this 70th anniversary?" But Gorbachev, sensing the discord in his tone, cut

---

416   A.S. Chernyaev: Six years with Gorbachev. Based on diary entries. M.: Publishing group Progress, Culture. 1993. P. 175.
417   V.I. Boldin: The fall of the pedestal. Lines about the portrait of M.S. Gorbachev. – M.: Republic, 1995. P. 326-327.
418   The decision to adopt this was passed by the MCC on 7 January 1987 on Yeltsin's suggestion. Since then, City Day has been celebrated every year in Moscow on the first weekend in September.

him off, saying: "We are on the right path: of that we can be sure as we reach the 70th anniversary...! If things were different we would stray off course."[419] The outpouring of words from the general secretary enabled the discussion to sidestep the dangerous area to which Yeltsin had nearly brought it.

The plenum opened on 21st October 1987. On the agenda was the following item: 'Issues related to the 70th anniversary of October and several ongoing challenges.'[420] Gorbachev gave a speech to the plenum. This was probably one of the greatest speeches of his political career. It featured a powerful introduction about historical events, based largely on new documents from the Politburo's archive and on attempts to reach a new understanding of the country's development; this was followed by critical remarks — appropriate a speech of this nature — of the "as yet modest successes achieved by perestroika", and specific criticisms directed at the heads of ministries and departments, secretaries of regional committees and of the CC administration.

After the report, Ligachev, who was chairing the plenum, asked: "Are there any questions? No." Vorotnikov, who was in the presidium at the time, recalled the following detail: "In the first row, where the candidate members of the Politburo were sitting, B.N. Yeltsin put his hand up somewhat hesitantly, then put it down." Gorbachev: "I see that Yeltsin has a question." Ligachev: "Let's decide on the matter, are we going to open the floor?" Various people responded: "No". Ligachev: "No!" Yeltsin started to get to his feet, then sat back down again. Gorbachev once again said: "Comrade Yeltsin seems to have some sort of statement to make."

Ligachev brought the assembly to an end. This had not been part of Gorbachev's plan. He *insisted* that Yeltsin address the plenum. To Yeltsin in fact want to address the plenum? Let us make so bold as to express our own personal view: *he did not want to.* Furthermore, *he was not prepared to give his speech,* and was not intending to make a speech, because Gorbachev had intentionally warned him that Yeltsin's tendering of his resignation would only be looked at *after* the plenum. And for that very reason Gorbachev tried to force Yeltsin to speak, supposing that Yeltsin's extemporising would fail to have any effect, whereas the criticism of Yeltsin would be far more convincing.

Under pressure from Gorbachev, Ligachev gave the floor to Yeltsin.

Yeltsin's speech, which was muddle-headed in many ways, for the most part echoed what he had said in his letter to Gorbachev:

"...first and foremost we ought to reorganize the work of the party committees in particular, and of the party as a whole, starting with the Secretariat of the

---

419   In the Politburo...P.249-250.

420   The transcript of the plenum was published. See: Izvestiya CC CPSU. 1989. No. 2 P. 209-287. For working versions of the transcript se: TsAOPIM F.4. Op.220. D.1790

CC, as was said at the Plenum of the CC in June. I must say that since then, although five months have passed, nothing has changed as regards the style in which the Secretariat of the CC works, and the style in which comrade Ligachev operates."

"…we are currently sensing the free-form nature of our attitude to perestroika. At first we were incredibly enthusiastic about it — it lifted our spirits…after the CC plenum in June, people sensed a faith of some sort beginning to wane…It would seem to me, therefore, that on this occasion we ought perhaps to be more careful about when we proclaim the actual results of perestroika over the next two years."

"There has been a certain increase lately, from some members of the Politburo, in singing the praises of the General Secretary — from certain permanent members of the Politburo. I feel that now, of all times, this is simply inadmissible. Now, of all times — when the most democratic relations possible are being formed, and when we are establishing relationships based on trust between one another, comradely relations and comradeship towards one another. It is inadmissible…We simply cannot let this happen. We must not let this happen. I realise that right now this is not causing any particular, inadmissible, so to speak, lapses in our work, but nevertheless the first signs of such an attitude are in evidence, and it would seem to me that this must of course be prevented in the future. And one final thing (Pause). It seems that things are not working out for me on the Politburo. For a variety of reasons. Clearly, my experience, and other factors, perhaps, and the lack of certain support in some quarters, particularly from comrade Ligachev, I would emphasize, have led me to the conclusion that I must raise the issue of my being relieved of my responsibilities and duties as a candidate member of the Politburo. I have handed in notice to this effect, and as for the view that the first secretary of the party's city committee is going to take on this, this will be decided, it seems, by the plenum of the party's city committee."[421]

Yeltsin had taken the liberty of giving an assessment of the course of perestroika; moreover, he had asserted, confidently, that perestroika was not bringing the country the results which had been anticipated. In the context of the upcoming festivities — the 70th anniversary of the October revolution — and Gorbachev's emotional speech, this came across as nothing short of counter-revolutionary talk. This seems to have been the outcome desired by Gorbachev, who wanted Yeltsin to be subjected to excoriating criticism in public.

Yeltsin's entire speech takes up *less than two pages* of the minutes of the assembly.[422] In the debate which it triggered, he had *48 pages of accusations*

---

421   TsAOPIM F.4. Op.220. D.1790 L.1-2.

422   Izvestiya CC CPSU. 1989. No. 2 P. 239-241.

levelled at him. First to take the floor was Ligachev, who asserted that none of what Yeltsin had said bore any relation to the truth, and that his claim that the Soviet people's faith in perestroika was on the wane was a serious political mistake. The chairman of the committee for national supervision, S.I. Manyakin, dismissing Yeltsin's speech as a sign of political immaturity, reminded those present that he had been slow to join the party, that there was no need to over-dramatize the events which had taken place, and that "this is a natural trial and a rightful final act" for Yeltsin,[423] and that it was the "final nail in the coffin". The first secretary from Astrakhan, L.A. Borodin, after reminding those assembled that he had begun his career in the party under Stalin — and taking no small pleasure in doing so — accused Yeltsin of being a deserter. According to V.K. Mesyats, the secretary of the Moscow regional committee, Yeltsin's crime had been his "originality": he did not chair the plenums of the city committee in the way he was supposed to, and he held meetings with foreign journalists and diplomats. Yeltsin was not spared criticism from the men from his home-town, either, who had once worked with him in Sverdlovsk: Y.P. Ryabov, N.I. Ryzhkov, G.V. Kolbin.

The chairman of the KGB, Chebrikov, gave a speech that was well-founded and carefully thought through, with pointed remarks. His speech gave the impression of having been prepared in advance. By all accounts this was indeed the case, and the chairman of the KGB knew the script of the plenum in advance, and that Yeltsin was going to get a good kicking.

There was no small amount of sacrilege in the speech, too: Yeltsin was more concerned with himself than with the party, the country or Moscow. "You have not taken to the people of Moscow, Boris Nikolaevich. Had you taken to Moscow, you would never have taken the liberty of pronouncing such a speech from the tribune today." Chebrikov accused Yeltsin of having failed to sort out the problems in Moscow, and said that his speech was designed to pour cold water on what was being written by hundreds if not thousands of analysts in the West.[424]

A.N. Yakovlev also addressed the assembly, reading what seemed to be a text which had been prepared in advance. Yakovlev gave a precise assessment of Yeltsin's speech: "politically misguided and morally vacuous. It is wrong from a political perspective because it stems from an inaccurate assessment of the situation in the country, from an inaccurate assessment...of the views held by the Politburo and the Secretariat of the CC CPSU... And immoral... because you have put your personal ambitions and private interests above the common interests of the party..." In his opinion, Yeltsin had been distracted by a leftist-revolutionary phrase and by his own personality.[425]

---

423   Same reference. P. 243
424   Same reference. P.261-262.
425   Same reference. P. 262-263.

Shevardnadze, after praising Gorbachev's speech in an expressive and elegantly phrased manner, also hit upon a fitting description of Yeltsin's speech. "How would I describe it? Various terms have been used to try and do so: conservatism, for example. The term I would add would be: primitivism. Yet the most appropriate way of saying it — and this is probably the one that has been used to describe it the most — is that he has been irresponsible. He has been irresponsible with respect to the party, the people, his friends and colleagues, and his comrades in the Politburo." "But you will not succeed," Shevardnadze went on, turning to Yeltsin, "in setting the Central Committee on a collision course with the Moscow city party organization. No, you shan't succeed!" and a round of applause broke out among those present at the plenum.[426]

Gorbachev read out the final outcome of the assembly. He was on the point of giving the floor to Yeltsin, but did not have the patience to hear him out, cut him short, and in the end began to speak himself. He announced in his speech that Yeltsin had sent him a letter, whilst he was on holiday in the south of Russia, in which he had tendered his resignation, but that they had agreed to postpone the matter until after the October public holidays. Gorbachev maintained that Yeltsin had broken their agreement by speaking at the plenum. There followed an outpouring of accusations directed at Yeltsin.[427]

As a result, Yeltsin's speech at the plenum was recognised as having been "politically mistaken" by a special directive. The Politburo of the CC CPSU and the party's Moscow city committee were instructed to "reconsider the issue of B.N. Yeltsin's application to be relieved of his responsibilities as first secretary of the MCC CPSU, taking into account the views which had been expressed at the plenum of the CC."[428]

The flood of accusations which came crashing down on Yeltsin were a serious blow for a man who was going through such a serious internal crisis at the time. In his closing speech at the plenum of the CC, he repeated his request that he be allowed to resign, but later changed his mind. The plenum of the MCC was postponed until the festivities were over. As first secretary of the MCC, Yeltsin chaired a meeting of the board of the city committee. On 28th September they discussed the course of the preparations for the 70th anniversary of October,[429] on 29th September Yeltsin, in his role as leader of the Moscow party organization and a deputy, spoke at an assembly of the Supreme Soviet of the RSFSR.[430] His life seemed to be going on as normal — but that was merely how it looked on the surface.

---

426   Same reference. P. 265-267.
427   Same reference. P. 280-286.
428   Same reference. P. 287.
429   Moskovskaya pravda 29 October 1987
430   Moskovskaya pravda 30 October 1987

His internal condition was reflected in his address at the next Politburo assembly, on 31st October. He looked lost, and was not as self-assured as he usually was: "...I am prepared to continue working, we must stay on the path towards perestroika." I admit that I have taken on far too much and that I am to blame in that regard. I am yet to identify what exactly it is that I am guilty of, yet to get a genuine sense of what it is. Since the middle of 1986 I have been feeling a strong psychological strain. I ought to have been open about this and taken it to my comrades in the city committee, and in the Politburo. But I let my ambition get in the way. And that was my biggest mistake. I am willing to speak to Yegor Kuzmich, Alexander Nikolaevich and Georgy Petrovich (Razumovsky) on a one-to-one basis. My comrades in the city committee have remained loyal to me, and are asking me to stay, although they have also criticized me for what I said in my speech."[431]

A.S. Chernyaev, one of Gorbachev's aides, put his finger on the condition Yeltsin was in. In a letter to Gorbachev written whilst the words spoken at the Politburo assembly on 31st October were still ringing in his ears, he wrote: "First and foremost it is an outpouring of emotion: I am giving it my all, he is saying, without a thought to my own welfare (and this is indeed the case), I am attempting to get something done here in Moscow, this city which has become so lazy and stuck up, so stagnant, and in return I am merely getting knocked down — and in coarse form, in public, at the Secretariat. As for his ambitions, generally speaking we can forgive him for them..."[432] In Chernyaev's opinion, by tendering his resignation at the plenum, Yeltsin had been reckoning on them not 'daring' to accept it; he was relying on his popularity in Moscow and thinking of the undesirable reaction there would be in the West, where his resignation would be portrayed as a 'backward step' in the progress made by perestroika. Chernyaev felt society would interpret Yeltsin's retirement as a victory for the forces of conservatism, and would dent Gorbachev's authority. And ultimately it did exactly that.

Yeltsin sent a letter to Gorbachev in which he asked to keep his post as secretary of the party's city committee,[433] but by then it was too late. The decision had been taken, but they did not hurry to announce it. In spite of the new policy of *glasnost* (openness), the texts of the speeches made at the plenum were kept quiet. Rumours spread throughout the country.

The party leadership, meanwhile, was noisily celebrating the 70th anniversary of the October revolution. On 2nd November a triumphal assembly was held at the Kremlin's Palace of congresses, at which Gorbachev gave

431   In the Politburo...P.269
432   A.S. Chernyaev: See above P. 176.
433   V.I. Boldin: The fall of the pedestal. Lines about the portrait of M.S. Gorbachev. M.: Republic, 1995. P. 328.

a speech entitled 'October and perestroika: the revolution continues'. On 5th November a triumphal assembly was held by the city authorities in Moscow. Yeltsin opened the assembly and gave a speech marking the anniversary.[434] And then came the climax of the festivities: on 7th November there was a huge military parade in honor of the celebrations, a rally by Muscovites, and then a reception in the Kremlin in the evening. In his capacity as a candidate member of the Politburo (the decision to relieve him of his duties had not yet been taken), Yeltsin took his place on the tribune above the mausoleum alongside the other leaders, and attended the celebratory reception, although, as he would later write, he was in an "ultra-bad" mood.[435] It is not hard to imagine why he used this particular word. Standing out there in public, amid the hustle and bustle of the festivities, he felt like an outlaw. After all the things that had been said against him, his colleagues in the Politburo refused to speak to him and avoided him. The coldness shown to him by his colleagues was compensated for to an extent by the warmth shown to him by V. Yaruzelsky and Fidel Castro.[436] Yeltsin had got to know Castro well in March 1987, when he had stopped off in Havana on his way to Nicaragua.[437]

The two weeks that followed the ill-fated October plenum of the CC were probably the most difficult of Yeltsin's life. It was as if the ground had been pulled out from under him. He regretted what had happened, but there was nothing he could do to fix it. The experience of having to await his sentence, against the backdrop of this celebratory atmosphere, made his condition unbearable.

On 9th November, on the first day back at work after a series of public holidays, it was announced that Yeltsin had attempted suicide. In his office — or to be more precise, in the living room next to his office, he stabbed himself in the chest with a pair of scissors. The scissors were designed for opening envelopes and had long, sharp blades; they plunged into one of his ribs and slid across his chest, leaving a deep incision and causing huge loss of blood. In his memoirs, Gorbachev claimed that Yeltsin had "simulated an attempt at suicide."[438] We shall pass over this remark, leaving it on Gorbachev's own conscience.

Gorbachev summoned the members of the Politburo to an emergency session. Yeltsin was taken to hospital and given sedatives. But in the doctors' opinion his life was not in danger. After discussing all this information, the members of the Politburo decided that the issue of Yeltsin's position had to be

---

434   Moskovskaya pravda, 6th November 1987
435   B.N. Yeltsin: See above P. 180
436   B.N. Yeltsin: See above P. 180
437   Moskovskaya pravda, 5th March 1987, 7 March 1987.
438   M.S. Gorbachev. His life and reforms. Tome 1. P. 374.

raised immediately. "I spoke to him in person on the telephone," Gorbachev wrote. "In order to save him from having to talk about a subject which could hardly bring him any pleasure, I said straight away that I was aware what had happened, and that I could imagine what sort of state he was in. We therefore needed to agree on a day and hold a plenum of the MCC."[439]

It was at this point of the conversation that Gorbachev told Yeltsin that he — Yeltsin — would no longer be allowed back into politics. The next day, on 10th November, the matter of who was going to replace Yeltsin in the role of first secretary of the Moscow city committee was decided. The man appointed was L.N. Zaikov. The minutes of the Politburo assembly reveal what Gorbachev said at the time:

Gorbachev. Firstly it must be said that Yeltsin undertook what was essentially an attack on perestroika, and demonstrated a failure to understand either the pace at which it is taking place or its true nature. Furthermore, from the standpoint of a demagogue he brought into question the activity of the Politburo and the Secretariat. And in connection with this it must be said that the plenum was unanimous in condemning him for all this. This is probably going to be set out in more detail than I can provide at this stage. Generally speaking, there is a need to separate out what deserved condemnation from a political point of view, and then move on to the second part, the part which concerned his application to resign, so to speak. To point out that he was not supported, although at first there was some support, during the initial phase, when the slogans were being chanted. But when the moment to act arrived, he did not have the stomach for the fight. Those are the two positions, which balanced one another out. And here's another question for the council. We interpreted Yeltsin's speech as an attack on the Politburo and an attempt to stir up trouble in the plenum, and disorientate it as regards the manner in which the Politburo operates. What do you think, ought we to talk about this when we set out the situation?

Demichev. No, we ought not to.

Gorbachev. It seems to me this would illustrate his adventurist nature. But then the question arises: why were we so quick to hold a plenum of the CC. Everyone realises that he could equally well have raised the issues he had in the Politburo. But he decided to do so at the plenum, making various hints. This caused consternation among the members of the CC, and they stood up to him. We ought not, therefore, to try to avoid this issue in the information we release, lest it seem as if there is some sort of powerful opposition force at play. At the end of the day, he is simply an adventurist. So shall we explain all of this in our explanation?

---

439   M.S. Gorbachev. His life and reforms. Tome 1. P. 374.

Members of the Politburo. We are in favour."[440]

Yeltsin's exclusion from the senior echelons of the party ended up having a completely different political meaning, however, from the one on which the organizers of this campaign were counting. In the recent past, an attempt to settle scores such as this had indeed led to a person being forced out of politics. On this occasion it had the opposite effect. After tendering his resignation and being removed from his position, Yeltsin was rapidly transformed into a political figure who operated outside the rules governing political life which existed in the country.

On 10th November the first demonstrations began by people who were unhappy about Yeltsin's dismissal. Leaflets began to be published in defence of him, as well as placards; on the 17th, an attempt was made at the MCC to put together a petition to return Yeltsin to office and publish his speech at the plenum of the CC CPSU; on 19th November the MCC CPSU began consultations with the leaders of the unofficial movements about ending the campaign in support of Yeltsin;[441] rallies and strikes took place throughout the Urals Region.

Yeltsin's speech soon became the stuff of legend, with all manner of plausible, colourful details added; apocryphal texts ascribed to Yeltsin appeared. These texts, which varied in length from 2 pages to 30 pages, were copied out by hand and reprinted using typewriters, then passed from one person to the next, in some cases for money. Various versions of "Yeltsin's speech at the plenum" were published in emigrant newspapers and some Western ones — *Le Monde* (Paris), *The Observer* (London), *US News and World Report* (New York) and *Die Zeit* (Hamburg).

Yeltsin's speech became part of contemporary mythology. Just as could be expected under all the laws of social psychology, people put words into Yeltsin's mouth — and they put in whatever they wanted to hear:

"I find it hard to explain to an ordinary factory worker why it is that in his seventieth year of having political power, he is required to stand in line for sausages which contained more than just meat, whilst our tables are laden, during the festivities, with sturgeon and caviar, which we were easily able to obtain at a place which he would not even be allowed to get near";

"...the amount of bureaucracy in most of our ministries hasn't fallen at all, and in the Agricultural industry it has in fact gone up! That's what is slowing us down! It's there that perestroika is coming unstuck! It's there that all those good intentions are getting bogged down in bureaucracy. Things are not

440   AP RF. Minutes of the Politubro assembly. 12th November 1987
441   The modern political history of Russia. (1985-1997). Vol.1. Timeline. M., 1997. P. 116-118.

getting any better as far as trade is concerned, either. I was reporting to you, comrades, about how things stand here in Moscow. Little has changed since then, and those self-same civil servants from the ministries are covered by thieves from the bazaar."[442]

It was said that Yeltsin had criticised Gorbachev's wife, Raisa Maksimovna, who accompanied her husband wherever he went — even when he was shown round battleships, which had traditionally been no-go areas for women under Russian military customs. It was claimed that he had personally requested that Gorbachev prevent his wife from interfering in his work, and calling him every day with instructions. Comments about the need to bring Soviet troops out of Afghanistan were also attributed to Yeltsin.

Members of the Moscow intelligentsia began to discuss the various extravagant ways in which Yeltsin might have taken his leave. Some of them speculated that he had conspired with other discontented members of the Politburo, but that they had lost their nerve at the last moment and decided to keep quiet. Others supposed that any agreement was imaginary, any conspiracy fictitious, and that they had simply wanted to get rid of Yeltsin. Others still claimed that Yeltsin had lost his mind or that he was suffering from cancer.[443]

Yeltsin was being transformed into a leader for all those who were discontented in the country, a political enemy of the very party in which, until very recently, he had been one of the men at the helm. In a country in which there were no opposition parties at all, Yeltsin had become the leader of a movement that would take shape in the future. A leader of the opposition had come into being. There were people who were unhappy, and who were eager to join the opposition. The battle-lines had thus been drawn for the intense political struggle and political confrontation which were to take place over the coming years, for the kinds of political processes about which the men behind the 'Yeltsin affair' could not even have imagined.

Yeltsin was taken out of hospital to attend the plenum of the Moscow city committee, which opened on 11th November 1987. He wrote in his memoirs that he felt awful — "I felt dizzy, my legs were shaking, I could barely speak, my tongue wasn't doing what I told it to do."[444]

Gorbachev himself took charge of the plenum. He described Yeltsin's actions as an attempt, at a critically important moment politically, to take the work of the CC plenum in a different direction, by declaring his own unique stance on a number of issues. Even fiercer criticisms were heard in

---

442   Referendum. Journal of independent opinions, 1987-1990. M., 1992. P.159-160.
443   V. Soloviev, Y. Klepikova: Boris Yeltsin. Political metamorphoses. M.: VAGRIUS, 1992. P. 76.
444   B.N. Yeltsin: See above P.181.

the speeches made by members of the MCC: "this was far from being a mere mistake, it was a calculated stab in the back for the party's Central Committee (calculated in terms of timing, among other things), and its Politburo, with the aim of reaping ambitious political dividends," "a betrayal of perestroika" (F.F. Kozyrev-Dal); "a piece of political adventurism, a treacherous stab in the back against the party, at a carefully chosen time and place and with a calculated aim" (L.I. Matveev); "an attack on the party's leaders, the Moscow party organization, and its authority", and a sign that he was "hoping for disunity" (V.A. Zharov).

Gorbachev would later write that the atmosphere at the plenum had been heavy, and that "elements of vengefulness and malice had crept into a number of the speeches", and that "all this left an unpleasant after-taste." The general secretary could not help but admit, however, that "Yeltsin demonstrated resilience," and "comported himself in a manly way".[445]

Yeltsin addressed the plenum in contrite fashion, and admitted that his "actions had been simply unpredictable", that he agreed with the criticisms levelled against him, but that "he had had no malicious intent, and that his speech was not meant to reflect a political line of any kind".[446] He assured the plenum that he had always been true to the "general party line", and the decisions of the 27th congress: "I am a firm believer in perestroika and in the idea that however difficult it might be to bring about, it will triumph in the end. It is quite another matter that — and in this regard there were certainly different nuances in our appraisals of it — it is seeing different levels of success in different regions and even within different organizations."

The decision taken by the plenum read that Yeltsin was relieved of his duties as first secretary and as a member of the MCC's board "for the serious shortcomings on his part during his tenure in charge of the Moscow party organization." There was hardly a mention of any specific shortcomings at all during the discussion, however.

On 12th November, the following day, Gorbachev brought up the issue of the coverage of the MCC plenum in the press during a meeting of the Politburo. He proposed that Yeltsin's speech be described as "an attack on perestroika", "a failure to understand its tempo and nature", and "an attempt to bring disorder to the work carried out by the Plenum." As far as Yeltsin's resignation was concerned, Gorbachev felt it necessary to point out that Yeltsin had no support to rely on, "although at first he had had some support, during the initial phase, when the slogans were being chanted. But when it came down to it, they had not had the stomach for the fight." It was important to the general secretary to convince everyone that there was no opposition, that Yeltsin was no more than an adventurist.

---

445   M.S. Gorbachev. His life and reforms. Book 1. P.375.
446   For the transcript of the plenum see *Moskovskaya Pravda*, 12 November 1987.

All this came too late to be of any use politically, however. In the mass popular consciousness, the image of Yeltsin as a man who had suffered for a just cause had already taken shape. Rallies in support of Yeltsin were held all over the country, with people in his native Sverdlovsk proving particularly active. In December 1987, at an unauthorized rally in Sverdlovsk, the first secretary of the regional committee of the CPSU, Y. V. Petrov, was required to explain to those assembled why it was that Yeltsin had had to endure such "oppression". It should be noted that in the mass public consciousness in the Russian provinces, Yeltsin was thought of as a defender of the people, and in no way as a leader of the anti-communist forces or as a leader of democratic organizations.[447]

---

447   A. Kirillov, B. Kirillov: The Sverdlovsk bear // Rodina 2001. No.11. http://www. istrodina.com/rodina_articul.php3?id=269&n=14

Chapter 5
A return to front-line politics

A new role

The role of first deputy chairman of the Ministry of Construction, at the level of minister, was created especially for Yeltsin. After the criticisms levelled at him at the October plenum of the CC and the November plenum of the city committee, the appointment of a leader who had been punished — all the more so one who had been such a huge critic — to such a senior role in Moscow, and the fact that he was allowed to keep his status as a candidate member of the Politburo and secretary of the CC, seemed illogical. It seemed as if this decision had been influenced by Yeltsin's extremely depressed state whilst he was in hospital, on the one hand, and that on the other hand it was an attempt to smooth over the consequences of removing Yeltsin from the MCC. He remained a member of the CC CPSU and a Soviet minister — this was intended to forestall any potential activity as a member of the opposition. Yeltsin found out about this new appointment before the Moscow plenum, and it no doubt influenced what he said in his speech.

Gorbachev recalled what they said to each other over the telephone: "Yeltsin was trying to buy himself some time, and was feverishly seeking some sort of plan B. Then, when we started discussing the idea that he might work in the Ministry of Construction as a minister, the conversation took on a more businesslike tone."[448] A.V. Korzhakov recalled that "Yeltsin was awaiting a call from Gorbachev. And the call from Gorbachev eventually came through. I took the receiver over to my boss's bed and left the room. Through the door I could hear Yeltsin speaking with what sounded like a deadened voice. Gorbachev offered him the role of deputy chairman of the Ministry of Construction, at the level of minister of the USSR. Without thinking it over for very long, Boris Nikolaevich agreed."[449] Indeed, Yeltsin could not possibly have hoped for a better offer. He was returning to the construction sector, with which he was so familiar.

---

448   M.S. Gorbachev. His life and reforms. Book 1. P.374.
449   A.V. Korzhakov: Boris Yeltsin: From dawn to dusk. M.: Interbook publishing house, 1997. P.66.

On 8th January 1988 Yeltsin set to work in his new role. L. Sukhanov, who was a senior expert in the Ministry of Construction, and who became an aide to Yeltsin,[450] recalled the alarm that was caused by the new deputy chairman's arrival. The traffic was closed off along Pushkinskaya Street and Moskvin Street, and the nearest entrances to apartment blocks and side-streets were cordoned off by security guards whenever the government cortege drove up to the Ministry of Construction building (nowadays the building is home to the Soviet of Federations of the Russian Federation). Yeltsin marched into his new office, accompanied by his bodyguards. His doctor arrived from the special clinic, along with the deputy department director and a dietician responsible for ensuring that the candidate member of the Politburo followed a balanced diet. The office was furnished with a first aid kit and a desk with a built-in alarm system.[451]

The Ministry of Construction, whose director at the time was Y. Batalin, a man from Sverdlovsk, was considered a wealthy organization. Since the mid-1980s there had been a procedure in place for financing of planning work on a contractual basis. Companies were able to use cashless funds to pay for research and development, and to pump them into cash. Salaries at planning institutions had gone up several times over.[452]

Yeltsin's role within the Ministry of Construction had been specifically introduced for him, but without any specific tasks being assigned to him. On paper, he was in charge of three units: the scientific and technical unit, the planning unit and the regulations unit. A different first deputy — Bibin — dealt with the key ongoing issues. The new role did not suit Yeltsin's character. In the autumn of 1988, during a meeting with students at the Higher Komsomol School, Yeltsin was asked whether he was satisfied by his work at the Ministry of Construction. He said that he was not satisfied by it — "instead of lively, dynamic work with other people, I've been given an office, and I sit there shuffling papers."[453]

As a minister and first deputy of the chairman of the Ministry of Construction, Yeltsin was supposed to attend meetings of the Council of Ministers, but

---

450   L.Y. Sukhanov: Lev Yevgenievich — (1935-1998) graduated from the Moscow architectural and construction college in 1955, and from MISI in 1966; in 1955 he took up a job at the Central scientific research institute Proyektstalkonstruktsiya, in various roles; 1978-1988 — senior expert in the Department of type-based planning; 1988 onwards: worked with B. Yeltsin as an adviser to the deputy chairman of the Ministry of Construction of the USSR, and adviser to the chairman of the Committee of the Supreme Soviet of the USSR on issues related to construction and architecture (1989-1990), adviser to the Chairman of the Supreme Soviet of the RSFSR (1990-1991); 1994-1996 — coordinator of the Public chamber under the President of the RF.

451   L.Y. Sukhanov L.: Three years with Yeltsin. A first adviser's diary. Riga 'Vaga', 1992. P. 33, 37.

452   V.I. Vorotnikov: See above. P. 154.

453   RGANI. F.89. Op.8. D.29. L. 5.

these meetings merely irritated him. After turning up at two meetings, he decided they were a waste of time and didn't show his face at them again.[454]

Yeltsin now had some free time — and this, for someone so active, could have proved fatal. At the plenum in February 1988, he was relieved of his obligations as a candidate member of the Politburo. He remained a member of the CC, but was no longer entitled to a ZIL or a security detail. The decision had come as no surprise, and was taken without much discussion, alongside a series of decisions on other matters,[455] yet for an individual who had not yet recovered from a severe bout of depression, it came as a huge blow. As Sukhanov recalled, Yeltsin, as someone who was "hyper-sensitive, was greatly pained by these first blows dealt by fate, and felt awful throughout January and February,"[456] and when he turned up at work after the plenum, his face was utterly devoid of any expression.[457]

Yeltsin felt as though he was in a vacuum, as if a circle had been drawn around him and everyone was staying on the outside of it: they were afraid of coming into contact with him. He had a sense of being in the hands of fate. An 'ice age' of alienation was taking shape, consisting of invisible lines and subtle psychological nuances, and, just occasionally, there would be a burst of outright hostility. He would later recall: "At the plenums of the CC, and the other meetings, when there was nowhere to hide, our leaders greeted me with reluctance, and with some sort of caution, with a little nod of the head, letting it be known that whilst I was alive and well, that was merely how things stood nominally, and that politically I no longer existed, politically I was a dead man."[458] He observed the May Day celebrations that year not from the Mausoleum but from a position lower down, alongside the ministers, the heads of committees, and the secretaries of Moscow's district committees.[459]

He suffered from insomnia and constant headaches, and his nerves were shredded. In *Against the grain*, he confesses that he was not always able to restrain himself, and sometimes took it out on his family: "My wife and kids tried to comfort me somehow, and distract me. And I could sense that, and it would set me off... They had a hard time of it with me in those days."[460]

His salvation came in interaction with people. At that time, all telephone calls, good wishes on a public holiday or celebration, and invitations to the theater or to a concert were gratefully received. Journalists called him and came to see him as well. He gave interviews to APN and Ogonek, but they

---

454   B.N. Yeltsin: See above P.142.

455   V.I. Vorotnikov: See above, P.192.

456   L.Y. Sukhanov L.: See above. P.38. 46

457   L.Y. Sukhanov L.: See above. P.40.

458   B.N. Yeltsin: See above P.185.

459   L.Y. Sukhanov L.: See above. P.48-49.

460   B.N. Yeltsin: See above P.186-187.

were never published. As Ogonek's editor-in-chief, V. Korotich, explained: they weren't allowed to print them.

Foreign journalists tried to talk to him too, not directly but via the State television and radio of the USSR. In connection with the party conference coming up in the summer of 1988, a number of TV companies, including the BBC, CBS and ABC asked for interviews with Yeltsin. Some pointed questions were asked. Yeltsin said of his relations with Ligachev that they shared identical views on strategy — as regards the decisions of the congress, and the challenges of perestroika — but that they had different views on tactics and social justice, and that he did not like Ligachev's way of working. When they broadcast their program, journalists from CBS edited one of his answers. A huge scandal erupted. At one of his press-conferences, Gorbachev said that Yeltsin had to be dealt with, if he had forgotten what party discipline was, and that he was still, for the time being, a member of the CC. There followed a summons from the chairman of the Commission for party supervision, Solomentsev, so that Yeltsin could explain his actions.[461]

He still had to carry out his duties as a deputy in the Moscow city council. In his electoral district, Ramenki, people were well-disposed towards him. During his time as secretary of the city committee, he helped with the construction in the micro-district of a supermarket, a clinic, a kindergarten with a swimming pool and a school. Yet his powerful socially-inclined temperament demanded a wider plane than Ramenki could offer. All the more so given that he sensed he had people's support — a large number of letters were sent to him at the Ministry of Construction.[462]

The 19th All-Union party conference, scheduled to take place in the summer of 1988, was an opportunity to make himself noticed once again. The six months which had elapsed since that telephone call had shown that Yeltsin had been right when he had said that perestroika was stalling. Economic hardships were worsening, national and territorial problems were rearing their heads, and there was growing discord among the senior political leadership. Decisive individuals were required, who were prepared to shoulder the burden of responsibility. Yeltsin sensed that his moment had come.

The 19th party conference

Yeltsin's candidacy in the elections for delegates at the party conference was supported by a number of major industrial concerns. Each time they

---

461   The 19th All-Union conference of the Communist Party, 28 June — 1 July 1988: Transcript. In 2 vols. M.: Politizdat, 1988. Vol.2. P.55-56.
462   Sukhanov L.Y. L. See above. P. 43.

voted, however, he was sifted out by the more senior party agencies. He enjoyed particularly strong support in Sverdlovsk. Under pressure from the workforce of the biggest plants in the city — the Uralmash, Verkh-Isetsk and electromechanicals plants, as well as Uralkhimmash, Pnevmostroimashiny and many others, the Sverdlovsk regional committee took the decision to recommend Yeltsin. Battles broke out on this issue at the plenum of the party's regional committee. When the workers threatened to go on strike, and the plenum was still unable to make a decision, the CC decided to take a step back. Since the electoral campaign in Sverdlovsk was nearing its end, Yeltsin was included on the list of candidates from Karelia, where the plenum had not yet taken place. Thus Yeltsin found himself among the thirteen delegates of the 19th party conference from the Karelia party organization. According to Sukhanov, the reason for this was the small detail that the delegation from Sverdlovsk was supposed to sit in the front few rows, whilst the delegation from Karelia was supposed to sit on the balcony.[463]

Yeltsin had prepared thoroughly for his speech at the conference; he had written the text himself, and was constantly making amendments to it. His advisor, Sukhanov, counted 15 different subjects in it.[464] It was moment of great responsibility for him. He would be making his first public appearance after a long 'conspiracy of silence', and people reacted to it in a variety of ways: some watched him with curiosity, others averted their eyes, but from some quarters there were words of support.[465]

The key issue at the conference was the forthcoming reform of the political system. Gorbachev, sounding fairly optimistic, announced that the country's leaders had managed to halt its gradual slide towards crisis in the economic, social and spiritual spheres.[466] He said that the slow progress of economic reforms was linked to conservative attitudes in the government administration.[467] This led to the following conclusion: in order to transform the economic situation in the country, there was a need to reform the political system which had taken shape during the Stalinist era. Gorbachev identified the excessive intrusion by the state into public life as a serious shortcoming in the political system of the day. The general secretary saw a possible way out in "clearly delineating the functions of the party agencies and the state agencies", and making the Soviets genuine agencies for governance of the people.[468]

463   L.Y. Sukhanov L.: Three years with Yeltsin. A first adviser's diary. Riga 'Vaga', 1992. P.52.
464   L.Y. Sukhanov L. See above. P. 54.
465   B.N. Yeltsin See above P.201-202.
466   The 19th All-Union conference of the Communist Party, 28 June — 1 July 1988: Transcript. In 2 vols. M.: Politizdat, 1988. Vol.1. P. 19.
467   The 19th All-Union conference of the Communist Party, 28 June — 1 July 1988: Transcript. In 2 vols. M.: Politizdat, 1988. Vol.1. P.31.
468   The 19th All-Union conference of the Communist Party, 28 June — 1 July 1988: Transcript. In 2 vols. M.: Politizdat, 1988. Vol.1. P. 49.

At the same time it was proposed that the roles of chairman of the Soviet and first secretary of the party agency be combined. Reform of the political system involved the creation of a Congress of people's deputies as the highest body of state power.

For the first time, Gorbachev was forced to acknowledge that "certain deformations" had taken place within the party itself, which had led to "the loss of many democratic Bolshevik traditions". Some of the party workers, and even the committees, had been expressing conservative views. He talked about the need for a radical restructuring of the way the party worked, democratization of the party's internal life, and an updating of party ideology.

The debate about the report was intense. Criticism was heard from the floor of the conference of the government administration, right up to the CC, and there were many who did not support Gorbachev's proposal that the roles of director of the Soviet and the party committee be combined; many criticised the gushing praise of glasnost, and some proposed that a two-party system be introduced, as a guarantee against the cult of personality. In terms of the volume of criticism expressed, the 19th party conference went slightly further than what Yeltsin had indulged in doing at meetings of the Politburo and the plenums of the CC.

Yeltsin sent several messages to the presidium asking to be given the floor, but to no avail. On the final day of the conference he realised that there was nothing for it but to take the floor by storm. Lifting his red delegate's warrant above his head, he strode right up to the presidium, tall, powerfully built and visible from every corner of the hall.

It had been known long before the conference that Yeltsin intended to take the floor. According to one of Gorbachev's aides, V. Boldin, Yeltsin was the main focus of the intelligence agencies' interest prior to his election to the Supreme Soviet of the USSR, and this information had been reported directly to the general secretary.[469] Needless to say, the work Yeltsin had done on the theses in his speech could not go unnoticed. On the eve of the last day of the conference, the second secretary of the MCC, Y. Belyakov, put in a call to its first secretary, Y. Prokofiev, on L. Zaikov's orders, and asked him to speak out against Yeltsin at the conference if the latter took the floor.[470]

The "storming of the despatch box" was a dramatic sight. With his warrant in his raised hand, Yeltsin walked up to the presidium, went up three steps, walked over to Gorbachev and, holding out his warrant, and looking him

---

469   V.I. Boldin: The fall of the pedestal. Lines about the portrait of M.S. Gorbachev. – M.: Republic, 1995. P.334.
470   Y. Prokofiev: Before and after the ban on the CPSU. The memoirs of the first secretary of the MCC CPSU. M., 2005. P.133.

right in the eye, said in an unwavering voice: "I demand to be given the floor, or to have the matter put to a vote by the whole conference." Shouts were heard from the delegates in the hall: "give the floor to Yeltsin." Finally, Gorbachev muttered: "Sit in the front row." Yeltsin sat in the front row, on the corner next to the aisle.[471]

He began his speech by responding to the attacks on him made in some of the speeches, then moved on to the key issue — the process of democratization within the party. Essentially he said the same things that he had said at the October plenum of the CC: perestroika needed to be commenced in the party, and the party was lagging behind as far as perestroika was concerned. The preparations for the conference, and the elections, had only served to convince him all the more of the fact that the highest level of the administration was not being reorganized.

On the subject of reform of the political system, he proposed that a mechanism be created which could provide genuine rule by the people and prevent the possibility of rule by a single, all-powerful leader. The proposal to combine the roles of first secretaries of the party committees and of the Soviet agencies was, for Yeltsin (as it was for many at the conference), both unexpected and hard to understand. Yeltsin thought that a nationwide referendum ought to be held on this issue. With regard to the elections he emphasized that they ought to be direct and all-encompassing, and held by secret ballot. A limit of 2 terms should be imposed on all those in elected positions. An age limit of 65 should be introduced.[472]

These proposals fitted in quite naturally to the discussions on the issue of reform of the political system. After that, however, Yeltsin brought up his favorite hobby-horse: he raised the question of the government's responsibility for the state the country was in: "They're saying now that Brezhnev alone is to blame for the stagnation. But what about the people who were in the Politburo for 10, 15 or 20 years each, and are still in it now?"

"Why was Chernenko put forward even though he was sick at the time?" These were the kinds of awkward questions he was asking. "Why was the Committee of Party Monitoring, when handing out punishments for relatively minor breaches of the norms of life in the party, afraid — and why is it still afraid — to hold to account senior leaders from the republics and the regions for taking bribes, for causing millions of rubles' worth of damage to the state and so on...? It is my belief that certain Politburo members, who deserve blame as members of a collegiate body, and in whom the CC and the

---

471   For more details see B.N. Yeltsin See above P.203-205; V. Boldin. The fall of the pedestal P.335-336.
472   The 19th All-Union conference of the Communist Party, 28 June — 1 July 1988: Transcript. In 2 vols. M.: Politizdat, 1988. Vol.2, P.56-57.

party have invested their trust, must answer these questions: why have the country and the party been brought to the state they are currently in?[473]

Yeltsin switched from the past to the present: "What is happening at the moment is that the policies introduced by the directors of the governing bodies are, essentially, unquestioned — they are beyond criticism and beyond the control of the masses, even today." "...certain prominent party leaders have got embroiled in corruption, bribery and underhand dealings, have lost all sense of propriety, moral purity, modesty and party comradeship. The moral disintegration among the upper echelons of the party, during the Brezhnev era, took hold in many regions, and we must not underestimate this or talk about it in simplistic terms. The rot, it would seem, set in deeper than it is commonly thought, and the mafia — I know this judging by Moscow — definitely exists."[474]

There was more to come — Yeltsin proceeded to take aim at the privileges bestowed on the *nomenklatura*: "We must at long last abolish the food 'rations' for the so-called 'hungry nomenclature', prevent elitism in society, and prohibit, both in real terms and in form, the word 'special' from our vocabulary, because there is no such thing as a special communist." "I propose that the administration of the regional committees be reduced by 2-3 times, of the CC — by 6-10 times, and that the branch departments be abolished."[475]

After this furious philippic, the conclusion to Yeltsin's speech came as a surprise to everyone. He asked the conference to grant him political rehabilitation following what had happened at the October plenum of the CC. There was a stir in the hall, and he conceded: "If you believe that there is not enough time for that, then that is all." But he was allowed to continue: "... My speech at the Plenum in October was adjudged to have been a "political mistake". But the issues that were mentioned there, at the Plenum, have been brought up by the press on numerous occasions... I feel that the only mistake I made in my speech was the fact that the timing of it was wrong — just before the 70th anniversary of October."[476]

After the lunch break, there was supposed to be a debate on the decisions made at the conference. But what happened was a repeat of the October plenum. As if to order (and it was probably exactly that!) the delegates at the conference took the attack to Yeltsin.

473   The 19th All-Union conference of the Communist Party, 28 June — 1 July 1988: Transcript. Vol.2, P.58.

474   The 19th All-Union conference of the Communist Party, 28 June — 1 July 1988: Transcript. Vol.2, P. 59, 60.

475   The 19th All-Union conference of the Communist Party, 28 June — 1 July 1988: Transcript. Vol.2, P.61.

476   The 19th All-Union conference of the Communist Party, 28 June — 1 July 1988: Transcript. Vol.2, P.61.

G.I. Usmanov (the First secretary of the Tatar regional committee): "With his actions and conduct, Yeltsin is not helping to increase the authority of the party or of our country, as he gives interviews to all sorts of foreign agencies, left, right and center. They are taking him under their wing, and he is helping to increase his own authority."[477]

Ligachev Y.K.: Yeltsin the communist has started to go down the wrong path. "I would hasten to point out that, whilst he was secretary of the party's city committee, he never attended the meetings of the Secretariat...

And the following may seem hard to believe, but it's a fact: whilst he was in the Politburo, and attending Politburo meetings — and the meetings last 8-9 or 10 hours each — he hardly took part at all in discussions about vitally important problems in the country, or in decision-making on issues which the whole country was waiting to hear about. He chose instead to keep quiet and sit it out. This may seem monstrous, but it's a fact."[478]

The only person who spoke out in support of Yeltsin was his fellow Sverdlovsk native, the secretary of the party committee from the Kalinin engineering plant, V.A. Volkov: "Yes, Yeltsin is a very difficult person, he has a difficult personality; he is a very strict person, at times, perhaps, even brutal. But this person, during his time in office in the party organization in the Sverdlovsk region, did a great deal to enhance the authority of the party worker and of the party, and was someone who always backed up what he said by his actions. For that reason he still possesses a great deal of authority among ordinary people. I believe that the Central Committee inflicted a damaging blow to its own authority when it chose not to publish the material related to the October plenum."

This last sentence was greeted with applause.[479] Soon afterwards, however, Gorbachev read out a note which had been brought up to the presidium: "The delegation from the Sverdlovsk region party organization fully supports the decision of the October (1987) Plenum of the CC CPSU regarding comrade Yeltsin. No-one gave comrade Volkov permission to speak on behalf of the delegates. His speech has been roundly condemned. From the first secretary of the party's regional committee, Bobykin, on behalf of the delegation."[480]

The delegates from Moscow exacted revenge for things which had upset them in the past. N.S. Chikirev (the General director of the NGO The

---

477   The 19th All-Union conference of the Communist Party, 28 June — 1 July 1988: Transcript. Vol.2 P.64-65.

478   The 19th All-Union conference of the Communist Party, 28 June — 1 July 1988: Transcript. Vol.2 P.86.

479   The 19th All-Union conference of the Communist Party, 28 June — 1 July 1988: Transcript. Vol.2 P.102

480   The 19th All-Union conference of the Communist Party, 28 June — 1 July 1988: Transcript. Vol.2 P.105.

S. Ordzhonikidze machine-tool plant) said: Yeltsin spent 6 hours at my plant, and came up with a single criticism — one which I find entirely unjustified, and inadequate.[481]

I.S. Lukin (the First secretary of Moscow's Proletarsky district committee): "The attempt to force through perestroika led, in Moscow, to the party organization being literally broken... The first secretaries of the Kuibyshev, Kiev, Leningrad district committees, and many others, have not only left, but were to all intents and purposes left broken and spiritually destroyed. Your soulless attitude to people manifested itself in the extremely high turnover among the party staff. The main thing has to do with your style of operating — your desire to be liked by the masses. Your number one method is to drive a wedge between the party committee and the working class and intelligentsia."[482]

It is worth noting that nobody objected to Yeltsin *per se*. The focus was on old bones of contention and certain character traits. It was therefore all the more difficult for Yeltsin to have to put up with the hail of admonishments and accusations.

Gorbachev alone, in his closing remarks, acknowledged that what Yeltsin had said, insofar as it touched on certain specific problems, was in keeping with the speech and the discussions. But when he began telling the story of the "Yeltsin affair" in more detail, Yeltsin could not restrain himself, and piped up with the comment: "On the whole I agree with the assessment of my comrades in the CC. I undermined the CC and the Moscow city organization by speaking today — it was a mistake."[483]

The Central TV broadcast the 19th conference to the whole country. Against all expectations, the public dressing down of Yeltsin, at the conference, had the opposite effect to what the party leadership had been hoping for. The Ministry of Construction was inundated with thousands of telegrams and letters offering support to Yeltsin. "People offered me honey, herbs, raspberry jam, massages and so on and so forth, to help me get better and never get ill again. I was advised not to pay attention to the stupid things people were saying about me, because no-one believed them anyway. People were demanding that rather than get embittered I should continue to fight for perestroika."[484]

---

481   The 19th All-Union conference of the Communist Party, 28 June — 1 July 1988: Transcript. Vol.2 P.103.
482   The 19th All-Union conference of the Communist Party, 28 June — 1 July 1988: Transcript. Vol.2 P.104.
483   The 19th All-Union conference of the Communist Party, 28 June — 1 July 1988: Transcript. Vol2 P.183.
484   B.N. Yeltsin See above P.217-218

A breach of the information blockade

Many journalists from Russia and overseas wished to meet this disgraced politician, and Yeltsin was eager to let them interview him. The resulting material was never published in the Soviet press, however. Even the flagship publication of the perestroika media, Ogonyok, steered clear of publishing an interview with Yeltsin which had been pre-prepared for publication. Ogonyok's editor-in-chief, Korotich, explained the thinking behind this to foreign reporters: "There were several bits in the interview which put me in an awkward position.

Firstly: The large number of criticisms aimed at the other members of the party's CC. Logic would dictate that I would have to interview them as well, and ask them to write responses to these criticisms. That would have been pretty difficult at that particular time.

Secondly, it would have put Yeltsin himself in a pretty awkward position. He talks about how his wife goes to the shops and has to stand in line, and makes this sound like an achievement. If we were to publish that in a country in which the majority of people have to stand in line, we would hardly be likely to enhance Yeltsin's authority...

I asked for some work to be done on the material, and for more details to be given about a positive agenda — as first deputy of the Chairman of the Ministry of Construction of the USSR. I think that we will eventually publish the interview with Yeltsin..."[485]

The conspiracy of silence was broken on 4th August 1988, when an interview Yeltsin had given to Alexander Olbik was published in two Latvian newspapers, *Sovetskaya molodyozh* and *Yurmala*.[486] It was reprinted by approximately 140 publications throughout the country. In some regions, by order of the regional committee, the entire print-run of the newspapers which contained the interview with the disgraced politician was destroyed.

The level of interest in Yeltsin in society, as someone who had dared to challenge the System, was huge. Since the interview had resonated so powerfully, it is worth pausing for a moment to consider the circumstances surrounding its publication, and its contents. What exactly had Yeltsin said that had won him the trust of millions of people? What sort of views and

---

485   Moskovskiye novosti 17 July 1988.
486   Alexander Olbik — member of the Latvian Union of Journalists and Union of Writers. Worked for several years at the biggest Russian-language newspaper Sovetskaya molodyozh, where he was in charge of the department of industry. Later worked for the weekly city newspaper Yurmala. Has written the following books: What's round the corner? (1990), Wild bees on the sunny riverbank (1991), Three years with Yeltsin (1992), The emissary matter (1993), The Doublet (1993), The collapse of Baltiya bank (1995) and others.

ideas about the country's problems, and about what needed to be done to fix them, did Yeltsin have?

Olbik gave more details about the meeting which was to become a turning point in his journalistic career. It had taken place soon after the party conference, whilst Yeltsin was on holiday at the government health resort Riga bay. On 22nd July he went to the tennis stadium in Lielup, where a Davis Cup tie was being played between the USSR and the Netherlands. In one of the breaks between sets, the journalist summoned up the courage to go over to Yeltsin and request an interview. The next morning they met up at the health resort where Yeltsin was staying.[487]

They talked about the growing number of problems the country was facing: the fall in the esteem in which socialism was held, the need for revolutionary change within the political structure of society, in economics and in the social sphere, the gulf between the slogans bandied about so vociferously and real life, and the privileges enjoyed by the party nomenclature.

In effect Yeltsin was saying the same things that he had said almost a year earlier on 12th September 1987, in his letter to Gorbachev, and at the 19th party conference.

The fact that when it came to perestroika, the party was talking the talk but not walking the walk. "Let's face facts: so far, other than the action taken by the mass media and the intelligentsia, there has been no sign of any other eye-catching advances. Or at least there have been very, very few of them."[488]

The fact that there was a need to appreciate the current quality of life among the people: "...I believe it is essential that we set aside a period of two to three years, in which a host of key issues concerning the welfare of the people must be resolved." And to make them a reality, whatever happens. This will provide very strong support, as you put it, for the spirit of the people, and will strengthen their faith in perestroika. The people need to be provided with plenty of good-quality food and clothing, given a firm roof over their heads, and convinced of the fact that once we have set out on the process of democratization, there is no going back..."

These words were lent added weight by the fact that, during his tenure as director of the Sverdlovsk regional committee, and then of the Moscow city committee, Yeltsin had in effect been in charge of meeting the everyday needs of the people, had organized fairs on days off in Moscow, and had devised residential construction programs and developed transport networks in the city.

487   http://bookz.ru/authors/ol_bik-aleksandr/ebn/1-ebn.html
488   Here, and henceforward, quotations from the interview are cited as they appear in the book: Alexander Olbik. Boris Yeltsin's Baltic vector http://bookz.ru/authors/ol_bik-aleksandr/ebn/1-ebn.html

Referring to his time in office in Moscow, Yeltsin stressed that he had always tried to find out how the people were living from the inside, and to meet people in a natural setting: "I had to drive around the clinics, sit there awaiting my turn for several hours at a time — luckily the people of Moscow didn't know me from Adam at the time — and talk to people. They had timed sessions — some district doctors would only spend a maximum of five minutes with each patient. What can you get done in five minutes? Not a great deal, other than destroy for good people's willingness to believe in their doctor, the system of healthcare as a whole and, ultimately, the principles of social justice."

"Yes, I did indeed travel on public transport, and let me tell you this: it is an extremely labor-intensive thing to do. If, for example, I wanted to go to a factory of some sort, I would mark out in advance the route which the factory workers usually took. For example, the bulk of the factory workers from the Khrunichev plant set off from Strogino. At six in the morning I would get on the bus, then take the bus to the metro, then get on another bus and by seven I would be at the entrance to the building. And I didn't just stand about waiting for the director to arrive — I went into the workshops and the canteen. And then when people began talking about the "hellish" difficulties of public transport, I could see exactly where the workers were coming from."

In 1988 the word 'populism' had not yet gone into common parlance, and the idea of 'being out amongst the people' was taken at face value, and enabled Yeltsin's popularity to grow. All the more so given that he came across as an emotional and sincere man who was at pains to do what was best in his affairs and for his country. People were drawn to his conviction and his exacting standards with regard to himself and those around him: "...There was another thing I could never forget, as well: if you are going to demand something of another person, you must be twice as demanding with regard to your own self. It's true that when I was first secretary of the Moscow party organization I used to work from 8 in the morning until midnight. And I demanded that others give their all for the cause. Many were not up to the task — some of them were recalcitrant, and began to accuse me of being brutal. I believed, however — and I still do — that we cannot get through perestroika without a bit of self-sacrifice. And in that sense I must admit that I am strict, in some ways — even excessively demanding, perhaps — but certainly not brutal."

When Yeltsin spoke out against the privileges enjoyed by the *nomenklatura*, there was a dramatic response among the people. He had brought this subject up at the 19th party conference, and expanded on it in the interview: "There are some sections of the population between which there is no proper balancing of their salaries. Some work harder but earn less, whilst others live off 'benefits' from the state. I find this unjust. If there is a shortage of something in society, then everybody ought to be feeling its absence. The director of Agroprom, who has luxury foods delivered to his residence, will never be able to put his heart into promoting the Food program. As far as he's concerned the issue was sorted out long ago."

For Yeltsin, the fight against privileges and perks in 1988 was a struggle for "socialist justice": "Socialist justice is in no sense a utopia, as some have tried to portray it. If it does not reign supreme, then sooner or later this will cause discontent among the people. They will lose faith in the party and in Soviet power. And in socialism in general."

For Yeltsin, "socialist justice" was about more than receiving fair remuneration for labor, in accordance with the socialist principle of the distribution of wealth. It was a wider concept, which incorporated civil freedoms: "The principles of socialist justice are measured not only by how many rubles you have, and whether or not you've got a dacha or a luxury holiday. That is also important, of course, but I want to talk about something different. We have strangled the individual from a spiritual point of view. He now finds himself under pressure from the over-blown powers-that-be, from directives, orders which cannot be gainsaid, and an infinite number of government decrees and so on and so forth. We have taught people how to be strangled and suffocated as one, rather than to think and feel as one. Is that justice? When we hold a vote, there are bound to be 100% in favor, or as good as; if we are asked for a show of hands, then everyone to a man is 'in favor'. It is shameful that the word 'pluralism' came into our language from the lexicon of our ideological enemies."

Yeltsin postioned himself as a communist: "Us communists — whom do we serve? We serve the people — in no event should it be the other way around." He refers to himself as a Leninist. "Sometimes people said to me: calm down a bit, show a little more restraint, that way you'll seem more reliable. Personally, I don't understand this. Lenin was a very emotional, passionate man, and yet that didn't prevent him from finding solutions to almighty challenges. And we are his students. And it is an absurdity to describe oneself as a Leninist yet have a heart as cold as ice."

Yeltsin does not criticize the policy of the party or of Gorbachev, and does not propose any specific measures which could be taken to solve these problems. He does not consider himself an opponent of the political course on which the country is currently being steered — an updating of socialism. What is moving about his interview is that he talks about the divergence between the slogans chanted so loudly and the reality of life, and believes that the wonderful ideals of socialism are capable of being made a reality.

A serious struggle was sparked off around the publication of the interview with Yeltsin. The editor of Yurmal, Avar Baumanis, was summoned to the Yurmalsk city committee and 'strongly advised' not to publish the interview.

When the city committee's conclusions were ignored, the attempts to 'persuade' him not to publish were elevated to the level of the Central Committee of the Communist Party of Latvia. But there was no unanimity in the CC: some of its members were categorically against the idea of interviewing the disgraced politician Yeltsin, whilst others were tempted by the idea of spoiling Gorbachev's mood.

On the evening of 3rd August the Latvian edition of the newspaper *Yurmal* was printed. It was a local paper in a resort town, and as such did not attract much attention, but things were a little more complex when it came to the Republic's newspaper for young people. At 8.30pm a representative of Glavlit walked into the office of the editor-in-chief of *Sovetskaya molodezh*, Svetlana Fesenko, who had approved the idea of publishing the interview. It was a critical moment, because, once he had ascertained that no approval had been given by anyone, the civil servant left, and nobody knew what he would do next. No bans on publishing the interview ensued, however. The Russian edition of *Yurmal* was printed that night, as was *Sovetskaya molodezh*.[489]

The next day 300,000 copies of the newspapers containing the interview with Yeltsin were snapped up at newspaper stands.

The publishing of the interview played a very significant role in helping to quash the rumors about Yeltsin. Some extremely gloomy rumors started to spread — it was said that Yeltsin had suffered a heart attack, that he had shot himself in an act of desperation, or that KGB agents had fired radioactive particles at him. Evidence of the reaction to the publication of the interview can be found in numerous letters which were sent in to the editorial offices of *Yurmal* and *Sovetskaya molodezh*.

A letter from Eleonora Shtoff, of Leningrad, contained the following passage: "I wish to express my support for Yeltsin, my conviction that his political views are correct, particularly as regards his unequal battle against the system, in which we have a newly emerging class of party and administrative bureaucrats. My friends and I feel complete solidarity with his stance: unless we take away the privileges enjoyed by this class that has taken shape, perestroika will die a death, because people will stop believing in it."

An article was written in the newspaper *Kalibrovschik* (from Magnitogorsk) which read: "We had heard all sorts of things about this interview, and in October (1988) one of us managed to visit Sverdlovsk, and go to an exhibition of non-formalist artists, where this interview is proudly on display. Everyone reads it. The publication responsible for this is the weekly newspaper *The Far-eastern academic*, which reprinted a conversation with Yeltsin from the newspaper *Yurmal*.

---

489   Alexander Olbik: Boris Yeltsin's Baltic vector http://bookz.ru/authors/ol_bik-aleksandr/ebn/1-ebn.html

In December 1988, when Gorbachev was preparing for a visit to the USA, the interview was published in the Agency for Political News's magazine *Sputnik*, which had a readership beyond Russia's borders. The interview was supplied in a bound issue, as an 'urgent dossier'. As one can well imagine, the decision to publish was taken by the man at the very top. Gorbachev was loathe to come across as someone who was clamping down on glasnost in the eyes of American society. He might be asked, at any press-conference, what was going on with Yeltsin, and why were the mass media saying nothing about him.

But things did not go according to plan at all. In December 1988 there was a powerful earthquake in Armenia; Gorbachev was forced to cut short his visit to the USA, and the tragedy in Spitak took over the front pages of the world's newspapers.

The meeting at the Higher Komsomol School on 12th November 1988

In November 1988 Yeltsin was invited to speak to students at the Higher Komsomol School, under the CC of the All-Union Leninist Young Communist League. The invitation had come from the secretary of the Komsomol committee at the Higher Komsomol School, Yury Raptanov, and had been approved, of course, with the director of the school and with supervisors from the CC ALYCL. Sitting on the stage alongside Yeltsin were the rector and provost of the HKS, the secretaries of the party committee and the committee of the ALYCL school. Such a level of interest in the disgraced politician testified to the fact that the Komsomol elite had come out from under the iron grip of the party's tutorage, and were seeking new coordinates by which to be guided in the future.

Yeltsin was in his element once again: for four hours non-stop he took questions from the audience in a hall where there was standing room only.[490] As was his wont, Yeltsin asked the audience to ask him about anything they liked, saying that there would be no time limit to worry about. Judging by the minutes of the meeting, the audience was in an extremely benevolent mood. The students at the HKS were interested in hearing about everything — from Yeltsin's personal passions and tastes to his opinion on issues related to the building of socialism. Most of the questions contained nothing new or unexpected for him, and to some extent or other touched upon his previous interviews and the speeches made at the 19th party conference.

Among the core questions which are important in terms of understanding Yeltsin's theoretical ideas, one that was of particular note was "what sort of

---

490   Sukhanov L.Y. See above P.68-69.

society are we building and did we build; if it is socialism, then what sort of socialism is it". Yeltsin replied that only one of the key component parts of socialism had been achieved — the transfer of the ownership of property to society. The slogan 'updating socialism' was therefore inaccurate: you can only update things which have already been created, "whereas we are simply building socialism".[491] In this respect, Yeltsin's assessment of which stage had been reached in the construction of socialism in the USSR was similar to the one expressed by Y.V. Andropov in his time.

Yeltsin gave contradictory answers when asked about introducing a multi-party system. On the one hand he said that they would need to effect a transition from a single party system to a two-party system in the future, "so that we do not repeat what happened in the past - the cult of Stalin."[492] On the other hand he talked about the complexity of introducing a multi-party system: "traditions and so forth have dictated that none of this is particularly straightforward."[493]

It's worth highlighting the following, incidentally: anyone who raised the issue of a multi-party system in 1988 — particularly in public — was committing a real act of sedition.

Yeltsin's hero in politics was, without question, Lenin. For that reason he considered any campaign against the first leader of the socialist state out of the question.[494]

Excerpts from this meeting were then published in HKS's newspaper. The only other publication with a mass readership to publish details of the meeting with Yeltsin at HKS was the Perm-based newspaper *Molodaya Gvardiya*, which printed it under the headline 'A politician or an adventurist'.[495]

The election campaign of 1989

The project for reform of the political system, which was discussed at the 19th party conference, began to be implemented when the Supreme Soviet of the USSR brought in two laws: 'On amendments and addenda to the Constitution (the Primary Law) of the USSR' and 'On the elections for people's deputies of the USSR'. Under these amendments, the highest legislative body in the land would be the Congress of people's deputies of the USSR, and, in the intervals between congresses, the Supreme Soviet of the USSR, whose members were

491   RGANI F.89. Op.8. D.29. L.7-8.
492   RGANI F.89. Op.8. D.29. L.36.
493   RGANI F.89. Op.8. D.29. L.64
494   RGANI F.89. Op.8. D.29. L.39.
495   L.Y. Sukhanov See above P.71

deputies elected to it and which operated on a permanent basis. The congress was created as a direct continuation of the congresses of Soviets, which had existed between 1917 and 1936. This circumstance was underlined by the particularities of the make-up of the congress. A third (750) of the deputies were elected based on territorial district, the second third — based on national and territorial district, and the final third were chosen from the all-union social organizations — the CPSU, the Komsomol, the professional unions, the Academy of Sciences of the USSR, and the unions of writers, artists, designers, philatelists and so on.

As a rule, the deputies from the social organizations were elected unopposed. The example for this was set by the 'front-line of perestroika', the party's Central Committee. At the January plenum of 1989, where elections were held for the people's deputies from the CPSU; the delegates at the plenum were given a list of one hundred people to choose from. As for who had compiled this list, and why it contained those particular candidates rather than anyone else — none of that was discussed, and this was a source of irritation as much for those attending the plenum as for anyone else.[496] This list of a hundred candidates had been selected in advance by G.P. Razumovsky, a CC secretary who was close to Gorbachev, and carefully 'filtered' by Gorbachev himself, who was reluctant to get personally involved in the election campaign in his usual constituency.[497] In radical democratic circles, this interpretation of the right to vote was the subject of much mirth: the deputies from the CPSU were immediately dubbed the 'red hundred'. As for Gorbachev, he put a somewhat different spin on things: "I was convinced then, and I am convinced now, that it was the right thing to do to put forward 100 candidates for the 100 seats allotted to the CPSU. We could not allow a situation to arise in which certain senior figures in the party at the time failed to get elected. This would have led to them immediately being opposed to the reforms, either openly or in secret... Our estimates showed that if we had included, let's say, 103-105 names on the list, the candidates who would have been 'black-balled' the most would have been Ligachev, Ulyanov and Yakovlev. If we were to add 10 candidates to the list, the majority of the Politburo would not have made the cut..."[498] To the former General Secretary it was neither here nor there that this approach was not at all in keeping with the democracy that he was proclaiming so loudly.

In spite of all the delays, the election campaign was the most democratic in the whole of Soviet history. The assemblies of voters were given the genuine right to promote their own candidates, heated campaign debates were held, and

496   V.I. Vorotnikov: This was how it was...P. 245-246.
497   V.I. Boldin: The fall of the pedestal. Lines about the portrait of M.S. Gorbachev. M., 1995. P. 338-339.
498   M.S. Gorbachev. His life and reforms. Vol. 1. P. 424.

the candidates' manifestos were discussed. The elections became a powerful factor in terms of politicizing the population. For the first time in many decades, people were now legally able to express opinions which differed from the officially approved ones. The nature of the letters to the CC had altered considerably. Whereas in the past they had generally written about personal problems and asked for help solving them, it was now common for them to touch on socio-political problems.[499] People had a genuine sense that it was within their power to bring about some sort of change.

The election campaign divided the candidates into two large groups. One of them contained people who had the backing of the CPSU administration, whilst the other consisted of people with a variety of political views: advocates of social democracy and market economists, popular journalists and so on. Their opposition to the party apparatus turned into a powerful support for voters.

Yeltsin received messages from several dozen territorial districts — Yakutia, Sverdlovsk, Novosibirsk, Krasnoyarsk, Karelia, the Far East and Murmansk, to name but a few — informing him that he had been selected as a candidate to be a people's deputy of the USSR. Of particular importance to him was the support of Moscow, where six districts voted in favor of selecting him: the Kuntsevo district, the Gagarinsky district, the Voroshilov district, the Cheremushki district, the Sverdlovsk district, the Oktyabrsky district and also Zelenograd.[500]

Yeltsin now had a chance to effect a return to front-line politics through the front door, and he decided to stand for election. A team of advisers began to take shape: Muzykantsky, Demidov, Shimaev, Mikhailov, Garnak. His first official authorized representative was A. Muzykantsky. A total of 10 authorized representatives were registered, and roughly the same number worked for him on a voluntary basis.[501] He was helped in his work by a campaign team consisting of V. Lantseva, L. Sukhanov and the journalists M. Poltoranin, P. Voshchanov and V. Yumashev.

Work began on the election manifesto. Had Yeltsin's views evolved in some way? What ideas did he intend to put forward to voters? In this respect, the second interview he gave to A. Olbik, on 29th December 1988 — three months before the election — is of considerable interest.[502]

499   RGANI. F.2. Op.5 D.227. L.6 ob.
500   Alexander Olbik: Boris Yeltsin's Baltic vector http://bookz.ru/authors/ol_bik-aleksandr/ebn/1-ebn.html
501   L.Y. Sukhanov L.: Three years with Yeltsin. A first adviser's diary. Riga 'Vaga', 1992. P.78.
502   For the text of the interview see: Yurmala, 16 March 1989, Alexander Olbik. Boris Yeltsin's Baltic vector http://bookz.ru/authors/ol_bik-aleksandr/ebn/1-ebn.html

One of the subjects he touched upon in his conversation with the journalist was the issue of whether the ideology needed updating. This question was already being widely debated in society, particularly after the February plenum of the CC in 1988, when Gorbachev had admitted that there was a need to reevaluate the past once again and express the theoretical basis for the prospects of this "new phase in the building of socialism". At the 19th party conference, the writer Y. Bondarev likened perestroika to an airplane which was up in the air, but whose pilots were now unsure where to land it.[503] But the problem was not just that they couldn't see a runway anywhere. It was not entirely clear where the plane had come from in the first place. The official interpretation of Soviet history, as set out in the textbooks at school and university, was creaking at the seams under pressure from the stories coming out about so-called 'white stains' and 'black holes'. A re-evaluation of history, of elemental force had begun; rubrics about history had appeared on the pages of the magazines and newspapers; public lectures about Soviet history attracted huge audiences.

Ideology was not Yeltsin's favorite subject area. He was a practical man by inclination, education and temperament, and not a theoretician. When asked by a journalist "where are we headed?" however, he gave an extremely detailed response, which included brief forays into history and was delivered with feeling. It was immediately apparent that he had thought long and hard about this issue. Yeltsin spoke of the need to re-examine the ideological dogma: the path to the future was blocked by lies and all sorts of dogmatic junk, and there was quite a bit of work to do if we were not to get lost in the scrap-heap of the past. So who was it that had blocked the way ahead with all this "ideological junk"? According to Yeltsin, it was the result of "entire universities, huge departments, which were writing all kinds of nonsense, for which they would have to pay dearly." Yeltsin came up with some extremely unflattering epithets: These "Lysenkovites of ideology, dogmatists," "dyed-in-the-wool perverters of the ideas of Lenin and Marxism in general" were well aware that all their dissertations, all their monographs, all their knowledge, right down to their academic works, are so much nonsense.

It begs the question who is going to pay for this army of dogmatists, whose interests it was serving, but this question did not come up.

For Yeltsin, the ideal which the party ought to be aiming for was "Leninist socialism", the "democratic route", which had been "torn to pieces" in 1929 by Stalin. Democracy had been still-born, and the seeds of a political dictatorship — an authoritarian-state socialism — had been planted. In Yeltsin's opinion, socialism had not yet been constructed in the USSR. Other than the fact that

503   The 19th All-Union conference of the Communist Party, 28 June — 1 July 1988: Transcript. In 2 vols. M.: Politizdat, 1988. T

property was now owned by the public, none of the real elements of socialism were in place at all — or else they had been retouched to such a degree that it was impossible to make them out. The slogan 'updating socialism' was therefore inaccurate, because you could only update something that was already in existence, whereas "we are still at the stage of building socialism".

A large section of the interview was dedicated to economic issues. Yeltsin felt there was a need to give a clear definition of the party's place in society, and outline the "core areas where it would strike". Specifically: trade and public catering, ensuring that the country was well supplied with goods for public consumption, and the service industry. Yeltsin identified the need to create "an economic mechanism, with the help of which it would be possible to regulate the relationship between supply and demand", and he proposed to secure the funds for this by taking money, a little at a time, from the budget for the space program, the defence budget and the budget for industrial construction. For all the economic naivety and political bankruptcy of such a proposal (he was essentially talking about reducing the party's activity to solving tasks of a purely administrative nature), the thinking behind it was the realisation that the deficit was eating away at the economic system, and that every effort had to be taken to overcome it.

Yeltsin talked about issues which spoke directly to the hearts of readers: the poverty in which people were living, the abject poverty facing pensioners, the shortage of medicines in the pharmacies, the shortage of foodstuffs and the poor quality of the food on the shelves. The heartfelt nature of what he said and his occasional exaggerations only served to make what he said even more convincing: "we are vegetating, stuck behind the times without a glimmer of hope", whilst "there are piles of diamonds and gold all around us"; "people are having to eat semi-toxic potatoes, fruit and vegetables"; "we are being forced to consume what makes us rich as a nation: we are giving away our most precious resources in exchange for bread — oil, gas, wood and gold. What are we going to do when these reserves run out?", "socialism is belied by the abject poverty in the country".

So what sort of measures had to be taken in order to solve these problems? Yeltsin gave a critical assessment of the outcome of the first steps towards economic reform. The introduction of cost accounting and self-financing had only led to an increase in prices — concerns had begun to sell what was in their interests to sell, and cheap daily essentials had vanished from the shelves because they could not be manufactured for a profit. The co-operatives, for all the positive impact they had had, had created additional difficulties with consumer products.

Yeltsin identified a link between the prospects for economic reform and the transition towards a market economy: "we will not be thinking up anything new, anything other than normal product and monetary relations." In his opinion, the idea of a market economy did not contradict socialism.

A considerable number of contradictions can be seen in what Yeltsin said, and they contain no clearly thought-through plan of action. For him, socialism meant ensuring that property was owned by society and at the same time bringing in product-for-money relations. He talks about "Leninist socialism" as some sort of ideal, and yet at the same time says that we have idolized Lenin for too long. He is cautious on the issue of having a multi-party system: "I'm not saying we are ready for a different party to be introduced, but equally it would be naive to say: what do we need a second party for, given that we already have criticism of the party, of ourselves?" He is "in favor of creating popular movements, but only on condition that they actually set themselves the goal of battling for perestroika, and that the methods they use in this battle do not contradict their agendas."

Whilst being critical of the situation in the country and the course of perestroika, Yeltsin does not want to fall out with Gorbachev permanently. He owns up to his mistakes and failures: "I did not make full use of the assistance which Gorbachev, and the Politburo, could have provided. Assistance with the problems in Moscow, that is."

Yeltsin's ideas and reasoning were reflected in his campaign manifesto. The core provisions in it could be summarized as follows:

- the highest legislative body in the land must reflect the will of the people as regards solving all the fundamental issues and hindering the taking of decisions and directives which may be unnecessary or, on occasion, damaging. Every single political, governmental and societal organization, without exception, must be subordinate to it by law — including the party;

- people's faith in the triumph over bureaucracy, corruption and social injustice must be strengthened by means of a host of legislative acts;

- the deputies must be governed by a moral framework featuring the following: honesty, propriety, working fearlessly and without being indifferent, being principled, and serving the people selflessly. To this end there was a need to create a mechanism in the Supreme Soviet of the USSR, which would act as a guarantee for society that recidivist features of the past, such as authoritarian rule and the cult of personality, would not be possible; toughen up the fight for social and moral injustice. Strive to achieve a situation in which there were equal opportunities for all citizens (from the ordinary worker to the head of state) in terms of provision of services, state education and medical services;

- to this end, switch the focus of the Fourth Main directorate of the Ministry of Health of the USSR and the service staff nomenclature, to the section of society with the poorest protection;

- bring an end to the privileges of various kinds — special rations, special allocations and special services. Regulate people's contribution to society only by means of their salary, by means of the ruble, which should have identical buying power for every section of society;

- the greatest danger was that an elitist and bureaucratic layer would form in society, which could only be fought against by means of a decentralizing of the political and administrative system and by removing the privileges enjoyed by the elite;

- in society there were clearly all the hallmarks of an extremely deep-rooted crisis in the party, in economics and in the spiritual sphere, and a lack of social justice. Specific people must bear responsibility before the people for the mistakes which had been made;

- it was essential to have supervision over the new, highest body for popular power over the party (which must be deeply principled and democratic), and the demand from its leading core for the mistakes which had been made and bringing people to account. Only by going down this road would it be possible to update society and reach a situation in which the people genuinely had power.[504]

B.N. Yeltsin conducted a powerful election campaign. The numerous meetings and rallies were portrayed in a film about Yeltsin which was made by the Central studio of documentary films scripted by V. Yumashev. In the spring of 1989 a contract was signed for the publication of an autobiography entitled *Against the grain*, with the involvement of the literary agent Nurenberg.[505] The manuscript had to be ready by October. Yeltsin's popularity was on the up. Each speech he gave attracted thousands of people, and the meeting with him in Sverdlovsk was broadcast directly to the square for the crowds who had gathered in front of the huge Palace of culture.

A huge number of questions were asked, as had become customary. Yeltsin was more circumspect in his answers than he had been in the interview. He said that he was not putting himself up against Gorbachev, and that he fully supported the general secretary on strategic issues in domestic and foreign policy.[506] As far as the issue of having a multi-party system was concerned, in his opinion the law about young people ought to make allowance for creating organizations to run in parallel to the Komsomol, but that it was too early to

---

504   TsAOPIM. F. 4, Op. 220 D.1790 L.34-43.
505   L.E. Sukhanov. See above P.184.
506   TsAOPIM. F. 4, Op. 220 D.1790 L.45.

create parties, and "we are not ready for that, either from an organizational stand-point or psychologically."[507] He was negative about the attempts made by the Baltic republics to leave the USSR.[508] When asked about freedom to enter or leave the USSR, the answer he gave was extremely vague: "this issue shall be examined on a separate basis with respect to each individual."[509] He saw no need to introduce private property available for rent.[510]

Of the two hundred official invitations to stand as a people's deputy which he had received from many cities throughout the country, he chose Moscow — the city with the largest electorate and the most prominent place in the country. If he were to be elected in Moscow, where the influence of the Central Committee and the KGB ought to be felt more strongly than anywhere else, it would really throw down the gauntlet to the system.

32 candidates had been registered in the Moscow national and territorial district, including some rivals to be reckoned with: the singer L. Zykina, the cosmonaut G. Grechko and the director of the ZIL car plant, Brakov. He won his first battle at the district assembly on 21st February in the Column Hall in the House of Unions, where 10 candidates spoke, each from their own individual platform. There were two winners: the General director of ZIL, Y. Brakov (577 votes) and the minister from the Ministry of Construction of the USSR Boris Yeltsin (532 votes). The cosmonaut G. Grechko withdrew his candidacy and declared his support for Yeltsin.

The party *nomenklatura* used all the resources at its disposal not to allow Yeltsin to win the elections. Speaking out against him now was a factory worker from the Vladimir Ilyich plant, V.P. Tikhomirov. He was one of the people's representatives on the Central Committee, and had been specially chosen for a new attack on Yeltsin that would have a powerful effect. At the CC plenum in March 1989, dedicated to the elections for people's deputies from the CPSU, Tikhomirov put it to Yeltsin that some of the things he had said had brought Soviet power and the state into disrepute. He cited the rally of the Democratic Union, held on 12th March in Moscow, where the slogans chanted had included 'The October coup was a counter-revolution. People's freedom was taken away', and 'Don't believe what the state's leaders say'.[511] "What are we to understand by it, Boris Nikolaevich," Tikhomirov asked, "when you speak in favor of a multi-party system, submission on the

507   TsAOPIM. F. 4, Op. 220 D.1790 L.47.

508   TsAOPIM. F. 4, Op. 220 D.1790 L.56.

509   TsAOPIM. F. 4, Op. 220 D.1790 L.57.

510   TsAOPIM. F. 4, Op. 220 D.1790 L.61.

511   In V. Vorotnikov's diary the Democratic Union is mistakenly referred to as Democratic Russia (see: V.I. Vorotnikov It was like this... P.251). In actual fact, Democratic Russia, in its capacity as an association of political forces in favor of carrying out reforms in Russia was only set up in 1990. It has nothing in common with theDemocratic Union (one of whose leaders was V. Novodvorskaya).

part of the parties to the Soviets, and organizing a new youth organization as a counter-weight to our Komsomol organization." Gorbachev piped up with the comment: "Comrade Yeltsin's political position is drifting, it would seem, in the wrong direction."[512] He could equally have levelled this criticism at himself — his own position had 'drifted' somewhat as well, and it is highly unlikely he could have given a convincing answer if asked what the 'right direction' was.

Yeltsin himself did not know which direction he ought to be drifting in, either. He had a job to do: to win the election against the will of the general secretary, to overcome all the obstacles and barriers which had been put in his way.

When he met the electorate and addressed rallies attended by thousands of people, he was supposed to say what people wanted to hear. Meetings such as this on the eve of the elections sometimes went on for up to 5 hours, and Yeltsin had to answer 300-400 questions. He had a wonderful ability to sense his audience's mood, and since the idea of having more than one party was already hanging in the air, he could not pass over this subject in silence.

In response to Tikhomirov's attacks, Yeltsin immediately brushed off accusations that he had ties with the Democratic Union: "I have no idea what sort of organization it is, what its charter says, or what it does." And this seemed to be true.

As he set out his position on a multi-party system, Yeltsin could not have looked less convincing. Here is a brief excerpt from his speech: "I have never called for a multi-party system...I clearly stated that, yes, certain people in society had begun to say that perhaps we could have an alternative party, a second party. I replied that as things stood, of course, none of the grounds and none of the ingredients were in place in order to create a second party. Since these sorts of questions are being asked, however, I have set out my opinion as regards what needs to be done, so that the mass media — within the confines of our policy of glasnost — do not think of this as a forbidden topic." (Noise in the hall).

M.S. Gorbachev: "On 11 March, in the Kuntsevo district, comrade Yeltsin said: 'The CC administration is clinging onto power so as not to lose its privileges. A multi-party system is impossible at the moment, but in theory it is essential.' Did you not say that?"

Yeltsin: "No." Voices: "Yes he did. How can he deny it? There's a transcript to prove it."[513]

---

512   RGANI. F. 2. Op.5 D.227. L.6 ob.
513   RGANI. F.2. Op.5 D.227. L.9.

It was clear to the delegates at the plenum that Yeltsin was trying to deny what was obviously true. Gorbachev had a wonderful opportunity to arrange for the disobedient Yeltsin to be excoriated in public yet again, after daring, despite the ban he had imposed, to make a bid for a return to front-line politics. But Gorbachev could not bring himself to use the compromising material that was at his disposal. The obvious reason for this was that his criticism of Yeltsin had turned into support for Yeltsin among broad swathes of the public. The plenum continued in its customary vein.

It seemed as though there was nothing left to say on the matter, but on the second day of the plenum messages began to be sent to the presidium asking for a political assessment of what Yeltsin had said. Opinions were divided in the presidium. Some said that the plenum ought to continue, others said that Yeltsin's speech should be discussed and a decision taken. In the end, however, the presidium decided not to kick up a fuss but to set up a commission to examine the matter. On the commission were V.A. Medvedev (who chaired it), G.P. Razumovsky, B.K. Pugo and V.A. Zatvornitsky.

The commission came to the unanimous conclusion that, in spite of the subjectivity of some of the things he had said, Yeltsin's comments did not, on the whole, contradict the party's political line. This conclusion was forwarded to the general secretary, but did not get as far as the plenum.[514] Medvedev explained this by saying that other events and concerns had come up and got in the way. This was indeed the case: in May the First Congress of people's deputies, which was to bring with it quite a number of surprises, began its work. It seems there was another reason as well, however. Each new condemnation of Yeltsin at party forums only served to make him more popular among the people and strengthened his halo as a fighter who had faced harassment but had refused to bow down to it.

All the attempts to discredit Yeltsin in public had the opposite effect. On 19th March 1989, Moskovskaya pravda published an open letter from the factory worker Tikhomirov, headed 'I consider it my party duty'. Its author sought to expose Yeltsin's hypocrisy: he was waging war on privileges, yet enjoyed using the services of the 4th main directorate of the Ministry of Health; he would take the tram to visit a factory, but would only get on it one stop away from the factory. A protest rally was held in front of the editorial offices that same day, and the editors were forced to publish a riposte from Yeltsin.

The election results for the Moscow region were overwhelmingly one-sided: 5,117,745 people voted for Yeltsin. This figure amounted to 89.6% of the electorate. Since the Law on elections stipulated that the heads of ministries could not be people's deputies whilst they were still in office, Yeltsin wrote a statement immediately after being elected to N. Ryzhkov, requesting that he be relieved of his duties as deputy chairman of the ministry of State construction. When he became a people's deputy, he declined to accept the privileges which were normally enjoyed by members of the CC — a dacha in Uspensk, the services of the clinic in the 4th directorate, and special rations. He switched from the ministerial car he had been using to A. Korzhakov's *Niva*.

The results of the first elections of people's deputies of the USSR which were at least partially democratic turned out to be entirely different from what the party leadership had been hoping for. The CPSU had failed to run an effective election campaign. This was all the more surprising given that it had at its disposal a sizeable administrative team, which could reach every single town and village, every industrial, academic and administrative institution, and it had the party press and significant resources. There was a lack of trust in all these things, however. The recent enthusiasm about 'updated socialism', 'the acceleration' and 'restructuring of every aspect of life in society' had died a death, leaving nothing but disappointment, vouchers for most foodstuffs, huge lines for vodka, endless talk of corruption within the party administration and of its unlimited special privileges — whether real or imagined. Articles in the press served to discredit the CPSU, and presented its history as a series of acts of aggression, crimes and deceits. The only half sensible, half tongue-in-cheek reason that could be put forward for keeping the one-party system going was the joke that "there won't be enough food for more than one party." The elections served as a serious challenge for the party, which had proclaimed itself to be "the kernel of the political system in the USSR".[514]

Complete unknowns now found themselves to be deputies, elected precisely because they had been opposed to the party's ruling class. For example, G. Burbulis, A. Sobchak, Y. Boldyrev, A. Kazannik, Y. Kraiko, S. Stankevich and others. People who were very well-known were also elected people's deputies, after receiving their mandates via a host of charities and arts organizations: the academics A.D. Sakharov and D.S. Likhachev, the poet Y. Yevtushenko and the economist G.K. Popov. Some 30 secretaries of regional committees and city committees of the CPSU, meanwhile, failed to get elected. In Leningrad, all the party leaders and Soviet leaders were voted out, along with a local military commander. In Moscow almost all the party workers suffered defeat.[515]

Two days after the elections held on 26th March 1989 there was a Politburo assembly to discuss the results. "Most of those present were in a foul mood, and there was defeat in the air," M.S. would later say of this meeting.[516] The General Secretary attempted, nevertheless, to prove that the CPSU had not lost the election, because 85% of the deputies were communists, and the

514   V. Medvedev: In Gorbachev's team. A view from the inside. M. 1993. P.89-91.
515   In the Politburo...P.474.
516   M.S. Gorbachev. His life and reforms. Vol. 1. P. 427.

party had won in areas where people could see the real change that had been brought about as a result of perestroika. A large number of accusations were levelled at the press, which — in its entirety, and with *Pravda* at the forefront — "was creating a negative attitude towards the members of the party".

A minority of Politburo members spoke out in defence of the election results: A.N. Yakovlev maintained that the elections had become a referendum in which perestroika had been defended. V.A. Medvedev deflected the allegations levelled at the press, saying that the real problem was that many party committees had let the elections drift.[517]

Preparations for the forthcoming congress of people's deputies were moving along at full pelt. Gorbachev was going through advance preparations for his election to the post of chairman of the Supreme Soviet of the USSR. This status gave him the weight he so needed in the international arena; moreover, given that a shift in power was taking place towards the congress of people's deputies, the role of chairman of the Supreme Soviet had become the key position in the system of power within the country — particularly since the man in the job was the General Secretary of the Central Committee of the CPSU.

Following negotiations with the first secretaries of the regional committees, Gorbachev was given assurances that he would have their support when standing for this position.[518] At the plenum of the CC CPSU on 22nd May 1989, Gorbachev proposed, as if it were a long-standing tradition, that those present approve candidates for extremely important state roles — candidates who were supposed to be approved by the congress. The candidates were himself, as chairman of the Supreme Soviet, combining this role with that of General Secretary; A.I. Lukyanov as deputy chairman, N.I. Ryzhkov as chairman of the Council of Ministers of the USSR, and so on. The only person who spoke out against the idea that the party's plenum should determine who would take up these important state positions was B.N. Yeltsin.[519]

A man for whom almost 90% of the electorate in Moscow had voted could not be ignored, all the more so given that rumors abounded to the effect that Yeltsin intended to stand against Gorbachev for the post of Chairman of the Presidium of the Supreme Soviet of the USSR at the Congress of people's deputies. Roughly a week before the congress was due to open, Gorbachev proposed to Yeltsin that the two men meet. Yeltsin recalled that the conversation they had was a tense and nervous affair, and that the longer it went on, the more the wall of incomprehension between them grew stronger. Gorbachev expressed an interest in what Yeltsin planned to do and asked him

---

517   In the Politburo...P.477, 478.

518   V.I. Boldin: The fall of the pedestal. P. 342-344.

519   V.I. Vorotnikov See above. P. 269-271.

what he would think of an administrative role, perhaps within the Council of Ministers. Yeltsin, however, did not want to tie himself down with any prior agreements.[520]

People opposed to the status quo were preparing for the congress as well. On the eve of the Congress an alternative system of regulations for the congress and an alternative agenda were proposed at the House of political enlightenment, where the Moscow discussion group had gathered. The proposals became something of a national treasure after articles about them were published in the magazine *Ogonyok*.[521]

The first congress of people's deputies of the USSR

The first congress of people's deputies of the USSR opened in Moscow on 25th May 1989. The congress immediately went in a different direction to the one its organizers had envisaged. The chairman of the Central electoral commission, V.P. Orlov, had not even finished his introductory remarks when, without asking permission from anyone, and before the very eyes of an astounded auditorium and a stunned country, a doctor from Riga, V.F. Tolpezhnikov — whom nobody had ever heard of before — flew up to the stage and proposed that the delegates pay their respects to those who had died during the breaking up of a demonstration in Tblisi. Hardly had the lists of participants in the congress's presidium been read out, along with the proposals as to the agenda for the day, when a man appeared on the stage who was a household name throughout the land: the academic A.D. Sakharov. He had been famous for decades as a dissident who had been exiled to Gorky, as the man who invented the hydrogen bomb, and who had the three stars awarded to him as a Hero of socialist labor taken away because of his activity as a civil rights activist. People may have known who he was, but for the majority this was the first occasion on which they had laid eyes on him or heard him speak. That fact lent added significance to what he said.

And what Sakharov said was this: "I propose that we adopt, as one of the first items on the agenda, the decree from the congress of people's deputies of the USSR. We are going through a revolution — perestroika is a revolution, and the word 'decree' is the most appropriate word to use in this instance. It is the exclusive right of the congress of people's deputies of the USSR to adopt laws of the USSR and appoint senior officials... Amendments must therefore be made to those clauses of the Constitution of the USSR which concern the rights of the Supreme Soviet of the USSR... The second question of fundamental importance which we must resolve is the issue of whether or

520   B.N. Yeltsin: See above P. 222
521   A.S. Chernyaev: See above. P. 293.

not we are able, whether or not we have the right, to elect the head of state — the chairman of the Supreme Soviet of the USSR, before having a discussion and debate on a whole range of issues which will determine the fate of our country..."

Sakharov declared that he supported Gorbachev's candidacy for this role but that this support was, in his words, "of a conditional nature". He insisted that there should be an alternative candidate in the election for chairman of the Supreme Soviet, and a compulsory discussion of the candidates' political manifestos.[522]

It was not the speech of a seasoned orator. He did not have the 'voice of a commander', or any powerfully worded phrases. What he had, however, was striking courage and a sense of responsibility which went transcended political calculations. He was addressing not only the congress, but the entire nation. The nation saw what kind of man he was, and took good note.

The nation also heard the voices of deputies from the Baltic republics. Their speeches, at first glance, concerned technical issues related to parliamentary procedures. These included the right of deputies from the republics to have issues discussed at meetings of the congress, if the proposal was supported by up to two thirds of the deputies from the republics; the immediate adoption of the regulations for the congress; and only thereafter a discussion of other matters. Several Russian deputies spoke in support of them. And when Gorbachev, who was presiding over the congress, read a note which said that "the attempts by certain deputies to sidetrack the congress into a discussion of procedural issues are a very damaging business," something became clear to those who were tracking the course of the meeting: procedural issues were an important matter, and were the things which distinguished a meeting of parliament (although people were afraid to use the word 'parliament' at first) from a party congress, where everything is agreed and decided in advance, and all the delegates have to do is vote in favor unanimously.

On the very first day of the congress, some extremely pressing and contentious national problems were identified. Deputies from Georgia called for an investigation into the events which had taken place in Tblisi, and deputies from Armenia and Azerbaijan levelled allegations at one another regarding the events in Sumgait and Karabakh; lieutenant-colonel V.I. Alksnis accused the leaders of the Latvian SSR of discrimination against the Russian-speaking population in the republic, and the deputy P.P. Falk spoke of the need to restore German autonomy (the Autonomous Soviet Socialist Republic of the Germans in the Volga Region had been destroyed during the war).

---

522   The first congress of people's deputies of the USSR. Transcript. M., 1989. Tome 1. P. 9-11.

The clear and undisputed favorite for the role of chairman of the Supreme Soviet of the USSR was Gorbachev. The critical remarks made against him concerned the issue of whether or not it was sensible to combine the roles of General Secretary and chairman of the Supreme Soviet; he was asked to explain why a dacha had been built for him in the Crimea, and he was given 'mandates' for the future. B.N. Yeltsin was put forward as a candidate for the role on two occasions: firstly by V.A. Biryukov and then by G.A. Burbulis; both men came from the Sverdlovsk region. Yeltsin refused to stand, however. A certain amount of intrigue was created during the course of the congress by the fact that A.M. Obolensky, an engineer from Apatita, put himself forward as a candidate. He was not even included on the voting slips, however. Following the vote, Gorbachev had an overall majority. There were 2123 votes in his favor, and 87 against him.

The congress was endowed with a special intensity due to the fact that all the sessions were broadcast on live television. For a period of several days, people who had been little-known prior to then, and who had been elected deputies, achieved nationwide fame — the public not only knew what they looked like but could also identify them based on the sound of their voice. Television killed off the 'sacred mystery' of power. The general public now had the ability to compare and contrast politicians, to form an assessment of them, to agree with what they said or to object to it. The broadcast of the sessions at the congress became a powerful and unprecedented catalyst for changes in the political mood.

The congress of people's deputies gave people a national platform, for the first time ever, on which they could express a variety of views and opinions. Whilst the congress was in session, the republics actually became what they had hitherto been only on paper, under the Constitution — subjects of the USSR. The problems which were actually bothering the population of each republic were openly identified. Delegates from the Baltic republics made pressing calls for an investigation into the circumstances surrounding the signing of the Molotov-Ribbentrop pact, and an assessment of the consequences of it, and for the introduction of republican cost accounting; they also proposed a draft law on economic independence for the republics. The delegations from Ukraine and Belarus had their own unique views on how the budget of the USSR ought to be allocated, taking account of the aftermath of the Chernobyl disaster. The Uzbek delegates protested about the activities of Gdlyan's investigative commission.

In the elections for the deputies who would form the Supreme Soviet of the USSR — a body of power which was constantly in operation — there was an inevitable split. The list of candidates for the Supreme Soviet, which had been prepared very carefully within the administration, did not include any of the people who had become leaders of the opposition. This caused Y.N. Afanasiev to accuse both the deputies at the congress, and M.S. Gorbachev, who was presiding over it, of forming a "Stalinist-Brezhnevite" Supreme Soviet, and to describe the delegates at the congress as "an aggressively obedient majority".[523]

Yeltsin failed to get elected, too. The RSFSR had 11 seats in the Soviet of nationalities. Yeltsin secured more than half the votes, yet ended up in 12th place. A. Kazannik, a deputy from Omsk who had been elected to the Supreme Soviet, unexpectedly asked to be withdrawn from it, on condition that his place would be taken by Yeltsin. This was an unprecedented occurrence. The regulations governing the congress made no provision at all for a candidate's withdrawal being dependent on conditions of any kind. Withdrawals could be accepted by the congress, but not if conditions were attached to them. Sobchak ramped up the general sense of confusion. The logical conclusion to be drawn from his remarks on legal practices around the world, and on the various decisions which could be taken in this particular case, was that Kazannik's withdrawal should be accepted, and that his place should be taken by whoever had received the next highest number of votes.[524] This procedure was indeed approved by the congress. Thus Yeltsin became a member of the Supreme Soviet of the USSR.

Yeltsin was at the center of journalists' attention at the congress, but he was not unduly eager to take to the stage. He only took the floor on two occasions, and when he did so he was not nearly as cool about it as A. Sakharov, A. Sobchak, G. Popov or S. Stankevich.

On the final day of the congress, G.K. Popov announced that an 'inter-regional deputy group' (IDG) had been created, which effectively became the political opposition within the congress of people's deputies. At the heart of the IDG was a cluster of deputies from Moscow. The declaration regarding the formation of the IDG was signed by 157 deputies at the congress.[525] Thereafter the number of signatories grew. During his election campaign, Yeltsin had steered clear of the democratic movement among the Moscow intelligentsia. Whilst criticising the course of perestroika, he strove not to pour out too much bile, refrained from threatening those in power, and constantly emphasized that his campaign manifesto did not go against that of the party, that he supported the strategic course the party was taking, and that the only area in which his opinion differed was on tactical issues.

The vagueness of Yeltsin's political views was commented on by both his adversaries and those who sided with him. V. Fedorov (Sakhalinsky) V.[526],

523   Same ref.. P. 223-224.
524   The first congress of people's deputies of the USSR. Transcript. M., 1989. T.
525   V. Logunov: The inter-regional deputy group: a year in opposition //A people's deputy. 1990, No.12. P.21.
526   V. Fyodorov-Sakhalinsky — in 1990 the chairman of the Sakhalinsk regional

commenting on an interview with Yeltsin published in *Rodina* on 19th October 1989, wrote: "...if one studies Yeltsin's manifesto and subsequent speeches, one does not get the impression that he has an integrated concept for the overall development of the Soviet state." "Boris Nikolaevich has demonstrated how bold his thinking is on several occasions, and has broken many taboos which we imbibed with our mother's milk for the good of democracy. And yet his political credo remains not entirely clear to this day. It is more the case that the things we hear coming out of his mouth are fragmented and not always interrelated, as opposed to the idea that he is simply passing over certain things in silenece.[527]

To the democrats on the CC CPSU, Minister Yeltsin retained his otherness, and was still a representative of the party elite — albeit a disgraced one. Let us cite two views of him which were expressed in April 1989. Firstly, that of Sergei Mitrofanov: "What exactly is it that Yeltsin is seeking to achieve in his battle with the administration? What if all he is doing is battling for a new administration, attempting to rescue whatever can still be rescued, and he is in fact not a subverter of principles, but a representative of a new generation of leaders, who have come to the realisation that they are biting the hand that feeds them?"

Secondly, Pavel Felgengauer: "The phenomenon that is Yeltsin is unprecedented in modern Russian history. A trusted party functionary is being transformed into the center of political life, not by means of behind-the-scenes intrigues within the administration but by relying on the will of the people, which has been so clearly expressed; before our very eyes he is assuming all the traits of one of the heroes of yesteryear. The liberal and radical opposition is hopelessly estranged. There is no possibility of it being able to unite around any ideological platform at all, but it can unite around a charismatic individual. Yeltsin is a figure around whom everyone can unite."[528]

Yeltsin's first speech at the IDG assembly did not go down well. He was accused of having spoken like the secretary of the regional committee. Many organizers within the IDG had doubts as to whether or not Yeltsin would be invited. For all the arguments he had had with the party nomenclature, he always stayed within the bounds of the rules of the game, as dictated by the System.

---

executive committee was invited, after the elections, to join the senior consultation and coordination council in the Presidium of the Supreme Soviet, which was then transformed into the president's council.

527   Rodina. 1990. No. 1. Quoted by: Fyodorov (Sakhalinsky) V. Yeltsin. Notes. – M.: Golos, 1995. P.14, 18-19.

528   Referendum. Journal of independent opinions, 1987-1990. Selected material. Published and edited by Lev Timofeyev. M., 1990. S. 166-167.

G. Shakhnazarov recalled a conversation he had had about Yeltsin with G. Popov. When asked what the democrats liked about Yeltsin, Popov replied: "The people like the fact that...He's bold, and he fights back against the system with more gusto than anyone else." Shakhnazarov: "His intellectual potential is not unduly excessive, though." Popov: "He doesn't really need to assert himself all that much anyway, that's for us to take care of." Shakhnazarov: "But tell me, Gavrill Kharitonovich, what will you do if he decides to go it alone, as they say?" Popov: "You know what, dear, in that case we would simply drop him by the wayside, and have done with it."[529] A. Sakharov proved to be more far-sighted — he is attributed with having said: "we all have our own interests, to which we can shift our focus — science, teaching, art. Yeltsin has nothing other than his political future. He is coming with us as far as the road takes him." As S.S. Alekseev observes, Yeltsin had been given a specific role: not that of a spiritual fellow campaigner, but that of a mighty force, a leader.[530]

However that may have been, Yeltsin was not only a member of the IDG but was also elected as one of its five co-chairmen. Also chosen as co-chairmen were Y.N. Afanasiev, V.A. Palm, G.K. Popov and A.D. Sakharov. The core provisions of the IDG platform were: that the right to own private property should be recognised, including the right to own real estate; that there should be a decentralization of power; that the republics should be independent and that they should be given greater sovereignty.[531]

Within the Supreme Soviet of the USSR, Yeltsin was elected chairman of the committee for construction and architecture, and he was therefore the only member of the IDG to become a member of the Presidium of the Supreme Soviet of the USSR. This committee, formed under the principle of having affiliates, was specially created to suit Yeltsin, at Gorbachev's suggestion. The other committees and commissions in the Supreme Soviet were supposed to be formed in order to deal with specific problems. The Committee experienced serious difficulties as it went about its work. All the executive bodies in charge of managing capital construction in the country were closed down, and as a result of the reorganizing of the Ministry of State construction of the USSR there were no more administrative functions any more. The committee found itself inundated with paperwork, and did not have enough staff or resources to deal with it.

Yeltsin now had an office situated in the Moskva hotel, where luxury hotel rooms had been set aside for the committees of the Supreme Council. As Olbik recalled, Yeltsin's office contained two large T-shaped tables, three

529   G. Shaknazarov: The price of freedom. M.: Rossika, 1993, p.157
530   S.S. Alekseyev: Gorbachev and Yeltsin: Triumph and drama // Izv. Urals state university. — Yekaterinburg, 2003. No.25. P.92.
531   RGANI. F. 89. Op. 9. D. 12. See also: Power and opposition. The Russian political process in the 20th century. M., 1995. P. 309.

chairs with green velvet upholstery, two armchairs with a similar design, a small coffee table, light-colored drapes over the doors, a gleaming parquet floor and a single, ordinary telephone. The journalist noticed a copy of the book *Gorbachev's Russia and American foreign policy* by Severin Byaler and Michael Mendenbaum, published by Progress. On a shelf were several books, including *The architecture of Soviet Georgia*, a book about Gorbachev in English, *The bulletin of the parliamentary group of the USSR*, a catalog entitled *New books from overseas* and several others. Next to his office was a fairly spacious ante-room, in which his advisors L. Sukhanov and A. Korzhakov worked.[532]

The trip to the USA on 9th-17th September 1989 and beyond

1989 was the year in which Yeltsin the international politician was born, and a significant role in this was played by his visit to the USA in September 1989. This was not his first overseas trip, but on previous occasions he had gone abroad either as part of a delegation, as had been the case in Paris in 1966, or as a representative of the Soviet party leadership, as had happened in 1986 in Hamburg.

In the USA he was representing himself, rather than Soviet civil engineers or the leaders of the CPSU — and this was a first. His new political career was taking off, more than 5 million people had voted for him in the elections for people's deputies, and now he was able to rely on that support, and was not dependent on the party's lawmakers. All this gave him confidence in himself, inner freedom and the ability to be completely relaxed. He was able to look at America without blinkers, and the impressions he was to take away from the country broke down for good the ideological stereotypes which had been hammered into him.

According to Yeltsin's first biographers, V. Soloviev and Y. Klepikova, "even before his first trip to America Yeltsin was already an inveterate Americanophile, and "learning a thing or two from the Americans" became not just a slogan but one of the building blocks of his political manifesto."[533] It is clear that this assertion, which is not supported by any evidence at all, was made with the American readership in mind. The subject of America did not come up in any of Yeltsin's numerous pre-election speeches or interviews. It would be fairer to suggest that discovered America during his first visit, and took in what he saw with naive admiration. His amazement on visiting

532   Alexander Olbik: Boris Yeltsin's Baltic vector http://bookz.ru/authors/ol_bik-aleksandr/ebn/1-ebn.html

533   V. Soloviev, Y. Klepikova: Boris Yeltsin. Political metamorphoses. M.: VAGRIUS, 1992. P.221.

an American supermarket was similar to the feelings that any Soviet citizen would have experienced in his place.

His interest in the events taking place in the USSR and throughout the world was huge, and this served as a guarantee that the American media took an interest in Yeltsin's visit. In the Western consciousness, however, the reforms taking place in the USSR were associated with Gorbachev, who, to those in the West — who were suffering from Gorbimania — was the symbol of change and the guarantor that there would be no going back. Their attitude towards the man who had entered into conflict with Gorbachev was cautious. The US broadsheets saw Yeltsin not as a leader of the opposition but as an opponent of Gorbachev. The journalists' prejudice was also related to the fact that preparations were under way at the time for a Soviet-American meeting at the highest level.

Yeltsin was accompanied on his trip to the USA by his advisor L. Sukhanov, a reporter from *Komsomolskaya Pravda*, P. Voschanov, and the people's deputy of the USSR V. Yaroshenko.[534] In actual fact this trip was organized by Yaroshenko and Voshchanov with the aim of convincing Yeltsin of the potential benefits of a market economy. Yaroshenko and Voshchanov had spent a bit of time in the USA at the beginning of 1989. With the help of the American journalist Jack Anderson they arranged for an invitation to be sent out from members of the Sentate and the House of Representatives, the Rockefeller brothers' foundation, the Ford Foundation, Oberlin college, Johns Hopkins University and the Esalen Institute. The executive director of the Esalen Institute, James Garrison, took the invitation to Moscow in person. The visit was supposed to last two weeks, but Yeltsin was only given a one-week visa, so his itinerary ended up being jam-packed.[535]

On the very next day after his arrival Yeltsin was interviewed on CBS for the program Face the Nation, and this was followed by a breakfast meeting with the millionaire Bob Schwartz, a ride on a helicopter above New York, a visit to the Metropolitan museum, a stroll in Central Park, a press conference at Shwartz's house and a meeting with the chairman of the Foreign Affairs Committee in the Senate, Claiborne Pell. The third day also began with a TV interview, this time on the program Good Morning, America!, which was broadcast to 84 countries; this was followed by a meeting with representatives of the business elite in Wall Street, a lecture at the Council for foreign relations, a live TV appearance on Macneil and Lehrer's Newshour, a lecture at the Harriman Institute at Columbia University, and a journey to Baltimore late in the evening.

---

534   V. Yaroshenko — a doctor of economic sciences, deputy director of the NGO on economics, independent candidate in the elections for people's deputy of the USSR. After Yeltsin was elected Chairman of the Supreme Soviet of the RSFSR — minister of external em. relations RSFSR. February 1992 — trade representative of Russia in France.
535   V. Yaroshenko: Yeltsin: I'll be responsible for everything. M., 1997. P.17.

In Baltimore Yeltsin gave an ill-fated lecture at Johns Hopkins University, which was later broadcast on Soviet television. After the intensity of the first few days of his trip to America, a late-night dinner in Baltimore, a bout of insomnia and a few sedatives, Yeltsin was not in good enough physical shape to speak in public. It was not possible to cancel the lecture he was due to give, however.

The next day's edition of the *Washington Post* contained an article, in the Style section, by Paul Hendricksen entitled *The drunken bear embraces capitalism*. Yeltsin's aides did not let him see the article.[536]

Yeltsin and his team then travelled from Baltimore to Washington, where he was due to meet national security attaché Brent Scowcroft. Yeltsin was extremely keen to meet the president and had asked ambassador Matlock to try to arrange a meeting, before he left Moscow. According to Sukhanov, on the way to Washington Yeltsin suddenly announced that he would not go to the meeting, since it was not a sufficiently high-level one.[537]

He was met at the side-entrance to the White House by Condoleezza Rice. There was a bit of a hitch at the doorway, however. Yeltsin placed his arms across his chest and announced: "I shall not move from this spot until I receive an assurance that I will meet the president!" Rice, speaking in Russian, tried to persuade Yeltsin to come inside, but he refused to budge. Eventually she said: "Unfortunately General Scowcroft is a very busy man, and if we are not going to go in and see him, I need to inform him of this."

Yeltsin caved in.[538] Yeltsin's insistence got things moving, though. It may be that the political far-sightedness and plain old curiosity of the American president played a role. He was interested to see what sort of a man this was, who had managed to challenge Gorbachev and was quickly picking up political clout in his own country, and yet was being careful not to show any insubordination. During the meeting between Yeltsin and Scowcroft, Bush walked into the room as if he just happened to be passing, had a conversation with Yeltsin which lasted 12 minutes, and then the vice president, Dan Quayle, came in. On the same day Yeltsin met some senators and spent one and a half hours talking to the US Secretary of State, James Baker.

Yeltsin spoke in Chicago, Dallas and Miami, met a university audience, politicians and businessmen, visited Ronald Reagan in hospital, looked around a farm and spoke at a huge number of press-conferences. "I slept for two to three hours a day, and flew from one state to the next; there were between five

---

536   V. Soloviev, Y. Klepikova: Boris Yeltsin. Political metamorphoses. M.: VAGRIUS, 1992. P. 228.

537   L.Y. Sukhanov L. See above. P.122.

538   see M. Beshlyuss, S. Talbot, Andriyanov and Chernyak

and seven meetings and speeches a day, and that went on all week without a moment's let-up," he wrote in *Against the grain*.[539] A late-evening swim off the coast of Miami could easily have had tragic consequences. It transpired in the morning that there was a warning sign hanging over the beach that read: 'No swimming — sharks'.[540]

Yeltsin was paid handsomely for his speeches — by Soviet standards, the sums he received were fabulous. He made a total of $100,000, once his expenses had been deducted. Yeltsin later wrote in *Against the grain* that he procured a million hyperdermic syringes as part of an anti-Aids campaign, and within a week the first consignment of 100,000 arrived in Moscow, at one of the pediatric hospitals.[541]

Yeltsin made an indelible impression on the American public. The auditoriums at the universities he visited were packed to the rafters. By contrast with the stiff, buttoned-up Soviet leaders, he behaved in a deliberately relaxed and informal manner, striving to highlight, in every aspect of his behavior, the fact that he was different from them. The media relished the details of his unusual behavior and his unpredictable comments. He spoke with feeling and with scant regard for what the powers that be might think. He talked about the deepening crisis in the Soviet Union, about the fact that 48 million Soviet citizens were living below the poverty line, and the fact that communism was a form of utopia. His ecstatic praise of America appeared in the newspaper under the headline "What you people consider a slum looks to us like a dream." It was the first time ever that a senior representative of the Soviet leadership, a member of the Central Committee and the Supreme Council of the USSR, had been able to take the liberty of making such a statement. With regard to the Baltic republics, Yeltsin said that the Supreme Soviet of the USSR should bring some clarity to the issue of the legality of their potential exit from the Soviet Union. And that followed a warning from the CC CPSU with regard to the Baltic republics which had been made on 26th August. In response to the question "do you, Mr. Yeltsin, consider yourself a communist?" he said: "Well... I don't know what is going to happen after I return home from America."

After his return home, the unpleasantness began. Yeltsin's enemies now had some good material for their next smear campaign. They talked about Yeltsin's astronomical expenses during his trip. On 18th September *Pravda* published an article by Vittorio Giucconi from the Italian newspaper *Reppublica*, which described in vivid detail Yeltsin's "adventures" in America and the amount of

---

539   B.N. Yeltsin: See above P.232.
540   L.Y. Sukhanov: See above P. 156.
541   B.N. Yeltsin: See above. P.222-233. According to data from L.E. Sukhanov, the American side only sent 10,000 disposable syringes. See L.E. Sukhanov See above P. 157

alcohol he had consumed. On 1st October channel one broadcast a 90-minute film about Yeltsin's trip to the USA. The highlight of the visit was his lecture at Hopkins University. The TV audiences saw that Yeltsin was having trouble keeping his balance and was speaking slowly, drawing out his words. It looked for all the world as if Yeltsin was drunk.[542]

All the attempts to discredit Yeltsin, however, had an effect that was the polar opposite of the one intended. Picket lines appeared next to the editorial offices of *Pravda*, with placards which read: 'We'll respond to every provocative article in the press with speeches at rallies!' '*Unita* and *Repubblica* have got a campaign going: they're acting up, defaming and shouting!' This campaign — take a look, folks! — is making Yegor's ears stick up!'

Declarations from party meetings and assemblies were sent to the editorial offices condemning the publications for besmirching the name of Boris Nikolaevich Yeltsin, a member of the CC and a member of the SS USSR.[543]

Giucconi's article caused such a fuss that on 21st September *Pravda* was forced to apologize to Yeltsin and acknowledge that the Italian journalist was merely describing what he had seen with his own eyes. TV viewers, meanwhile, were prepared to believe that the recording had been falsified, that the sound engineers had been unscrupulous or that the soundtrack to the video had been deliberately slowed down — but did not believe in what they could see on the screen. On 15th October, in an interview with *Komsomolskaya pravda*, Yeltsin explained that he had taken sedatives before the speech, and that he had caught a cold before travelling to America and fallen ill.

This was a clever bit of sleight-of-hand. He had caught a cold whilst going for an unplanned dip in a Moscow reservoir on a cold September evening. This mysterious event had taken place 11 days after his return from America, on 28th September. That day he had met some of his electorate, in Ramenki. Then he had set off to see some friends at his dacha in the village of Uspenskoe, outside Moscow. The driver took him as far as the area where the dachas were, then Yeltsin walked towards the dacha of the former chairman of the Ministry of State Construction, Bashilov. Since nobody witnessed the incident, let us

---

542   According to an employee of the Moscow division of the American TV channel CBS, Johnathan Sanders: "Boris Yeltsin looked a good deal more uninhibited than the majority of the Soviet political figures. He was the one who initiated efforts to 'get into the swing' of the informal American style used by this channel. One must also take account of the fact that Yeltsin, who was very tired after his flight, had taken a sleeping pill, and therefore, when you combine this with the TV studio environment, he was obviously quite excited. Was he under the influence? I wouldn't say so, no!" see: Alexander Olbik. Boris Yeltsin's Baltic vector http://bookz.ru/authors/ol_bik-aleksandr/ebn/1-ebn.html

543   For more details see: V.S. Gubarev 'The President or the Russian Watergate' MNO 'Forum of academics and experts for Soviet-American dialog', forecasts section. M., 1990. P.32-41. Author — a journalist at Pravda, a signed issue with an article by Giuconna in print.

quote what Yeltsin himself said about it: "A short distance from the building I let the driver go, as I always do, so that I could cover the last hundred meters on foot. The *Volga* drove off and I walked on a few meters, when suddenly a different car came up behind me. And...I ended up in the river. I am not going to get into my emotions at that point, and what I experienced in those few moments — that is another story altogether.

The water was terribly cold. My legs cramped up and it was a great effort to swim to the shore, although it was only a few meters away. Once I reached the shore I heaved myself onto the ground and lay there for some time, coming to. Then I got up; I was shaking because of the cold — I think it was about zero degrees. I realised I wasn't going to make it home by myself, and I wandered over to the police checkpoint."[544]

This was the checkpoint for the dachas owned by members of the government, where two policemen were on duty. They called his wife, Nina Iosifovna, who soon arrived along with her brother-in-law and Alexander Korzhakov. Yeltsin asked them not to tell anyone what had happened, yet this attempt on the life of a member of the Supreme Council could not go unnoticed. On 16th October, at an assembly of the Presidium of the Supreme Council, the minister of internal affairs, V.V. Bakatin reported that the investigation had revealed that there was nothing to substantiate Yeltsin's version of events. On the same day this information was read out at an assembly of the Supreme Soviet. V.I. Vorotnikov wrote down what Yeltsin said in his diary: "I have no objections about what the Ministry of Internal Affairs has said. There was no attack. I did not make any statements. This is a private matter."[545]

The assembly of the Supreme Soviet was broadcast on the TV, and the next day the transcription of it was published in *Izvestiya*. The incident was attracting quite a bit of publicity, and that alarmed Yeltsin. He was preparing a statement for the media.

The text of his statement read:

"On 16th October 1989, at a meeting of the Supreme Council of the USSR chaired by M. S. Gorbachev, an incident was made public which concerns my honor and my dignity. Against my own volition, the Minister from the Ministry of Internal Affairs of the USSR, comrade Bakatin, was brought in to help clear up this issue; with his combination of truths and half-truths, he had no moral right to facilitate the spreading of rumors which blacken my name in society's eyes. Furthermore, comrade Bakatin had stated on a previous occasion that no investigation, or disclosure of information, which

---

544   B.N. Yeltsin: See above P.235.
545   V.I. Vorotnikov: It was like this...Notes from the diary of a member of the Politburo of the CC CPSU. M.: 'The Council of veterans of book publishing' SI-MAR, 1995. P.309

concerned me personally was going to be undertaken. The explanation for this new political farce, played out by M. S. Gorbachev at the session of the Supreme Council and escalated by the official national media as a front-page news story, is not, of course, concern for my health and safety, or an attempt to bring the electorate into line, but a fresh attempt to undermine my health and exclude me from the political field of battle.

The creation of an Inter-regional group, which has incorporated almost 400 people's deputies of the USSR around one platform, my election as one of the leaders of its coordination councils, the independence of our position, the alternative proposals which go completely against the conservative views of those on the side of the administrative-command system, and even my private visit to the United States of America — all of this has enraged the party administration. On its orders, a whole series of provocative, deceitful, biased articles were concocted in the Soviet press, whist in the programs on the Central television and among the general public, all sorts of improbable rumors about my behavior and my private life were spread.

In connection with the aforesaid, I consider it essential to declare the following:

1. All of these things are links in the same chain — a campaign of harassment against me, and this is all being done under the guidance of comrade M.S. Gorbachev.

2. Issues concerning my personal safety and my private life concern me alone, and must, under the constitution, be protected against any intrusion whatsoever, including on the part of the party leadership.

3. In the event that this political harassment continues, I reserve the right to take appropriate steps in relation to the individuals who have attacked my honor and dignity, as a citizen and deputy.

I consider this an unacceptable and dangerous shift in the types of methods used in political struggle, towards immoral, unprincipled methods or moral and psychological destruction of an opponent. This will lead to the complete collapse of moral and ethical principles, to a breaking down of the progress towards democracy seen under perestroika, and, eventually, to a brutal, totalitarian dictatorship.

People's deputy of the USSR B.N. Yeltsin. 17.10.89 Moscow.[546]

According to Oblik, Glavlit hindered the publication of this statement. On 9th October, when an issue of the Latvian republic's newspaper *Sovetskaya*

---

546   Alexander Olbik: Boris Yeltsin's Baltic vector http://bookz.ru/authors/ol_bik-aleksandr/ebn/1-ebn.html

molodezh was being signed off for printing, the duty officer for the edition sent a message saying that there was a ban on publishing it, citing a circular from Moscow.[547] The editorial team managed to have their decision upheld — a significant bit of evidence suggesting that times were changing and that this change could not be held back.

These events were small fry, though, by comparison with the upcoming elections for the congress of people's deputies of the RSFSR. Power in the country was slowly but surely being transferred from the union itself to its constituent republics. It transpired that the fate of the Union of Soviet Socialist Republics was directly dependent on the outcome of the elections in Russia.

This was something that both Yeltsin and Gorbachev understood perfectly well. The most important storming of all was drawing near.

547　　　Alexander Olbik: Boris Yeltsin's Baltic vector　http://bookz.ru/authors/ol_bik-aleksandr/ebn/1-ebn.html

PART 3.THE KREMLIN

Chapter 6.
Chairman of the Supreme
Soviet of the RSFSR

The preparations for the Russian elections in 1990

The center of political life in the USSR was moving, with ever-increasing resolve, towards the elections for people's deputies at the Congress of people's deputies of the RSFSR. In accordance with the Law of the USSR dated 1st December 1988, the eleventh session of the Supreme Soviet of the RSFSR, 11th convocation, adopted, on 27th October 1989, the Law of the RSFSR 'On amendments and addenda to the Constitution (The Primary Law of the RSFSR in the Russian Federation'). These amendments and addenda stipulated that a Congress of people's deputies of the RSFSR must be created and that elections must be held for people's deputies of the RSFSR. The Russian law 'On the elections for people's deputies of the RSFSR' was more democratic, because (unlike the union-wide legislation) it did not give any quotas for charitable organizations, the norms for holding pre-election meetings were cancelled, and oversight of the manner in which the elections were held by the general public was permitted.

The official party ideology had 'failed to grasp' and underestimated the significance of the Russian factor. One of Gorbachev's close peers and a fellow member of the Politburo, V.A. Medvedev, wrote: "The first signs that the Russian factor had come into play could be seen approximately a year before this, or slightly earlier, in publications and statements coming from the humane intelligentsia, and first and foremost from writers who were still of a so-called Russophile persuasion. The extreme pranks undertaken by the society *Pamyat* were seen back then as odious incidents which in no way reflected the deep-rooted processes taking place in society. As national movements began to spring into life in the republics, interest in the state of affairs in Russia began to grow, although for some time nobody took this seriously. And when Valentin Rasputin, in one of his speeches, "threatened" that Russia might leave the Soviet Union, many interpreted his choice of word as a joke.

The situation changed radically, however, when the issue of the elections of people's deputies came up on the agenda, and the creation of new bodies of state power in the republics, including in the Russian Federation. The Russian factor began to assume increasingly realistic dimensions, and move towards the center of the political struggle. One after another the complex fault-lines of the specific set of problems in Russia became apparent — whether political, economic, social or environmental, which is quite natural: after all, the RSFSR, which was the nucleus of the Union, also contained within it the most important center of gravity of the nation's problems. The opposition forces probably latched onto this more quickly than the leaders of the CPSU, transforming Russia's problems into a trump card in the political game of cards."[548]

Right from the outset, the election campaign in Russia was characterized by ferocity and political edginess. It transpired that among the leaders of the CPSU were quite a number of people who advocated the creation of an independent Russian communist party — as a form of counter-weight to Gorbachev. In the end, even some of those who were on Gorbachev's side came to the conclusion that it would make sense to resurrect the Communist Party of the RSFSR.

At the 1st session of the Russian Bureau of the CC CPSU, chaired by Gorbachev, where the main issue on the agenda was the restoration of the Communist Party of the RSFSR, two more extremely important issues were examined which had a direct bearing on the elections in Russia. The second point was a discussion of the Concept for the economic sovereignty of Russia. The third was: On the course of the election campaign in the RSFSR for the elections of people's deputies to the local Soviets and the Soviets in the republics.[549]

548   V.A. Medvedev: On Gorbachev's team. A view from the inside. M., 1994, P. 135-136
549   Archives of the Kremlin and Staraya ploshchad. Documents related to the CPSU affair. Annotated reference guide to documents submitted to the Constitutional court of the Russian Federation related to the 'CPSU affair'. Novosibirsk, 1995, P.215

Thus, as it prepared for the elections, the CPSU had prepared in advance, as powerful agitatatory factors, not only the restoration of the Communist Party of the RSFSR but also the expansion of the republic's economic rights. The idea of economic sovereignty, which was later declared to be a separatist idea at the very same CC session, was conceived in Staraya ploshchad! Another move that was open to Gorbachev, which was unexpected yet, in equal measure, one that he was forced into, would be to strengthen central power in the USSR by bringing in the institute of President. Gorbachev 'voiced' this idea at the Plenum of the CC on 5th February 1990. He said that "there is a need to regroup and gather our strength in the upper echelons of power. The issue of the institute of president has been raised."[550]

The inter-regional deputy group and the Russian elections

The supporters of the Inter-regional Deputy Group, united (initially in form only, and later on paper) within the movement Democratic Russia, had become a force to be reckoned with in political life. On the evening of 21st December 1989, at an assembly of the Second Congress of people's deputies of the USSR, during a discussion of the about the status of the people's deputies and the draft law on constitutional oversight, Y.N. Afanasiev took the floor to talk about the group's political manifesto. In this statement, which was signed by 140 people's deputies, the Inter-regional Deputy Group declared itself to be the opposition to the majority in the Congress. The key provisions of the opposition's manifesto could be summarized as follows:

"We are against the governing role of the CPSU which has been decreed, i.e. the party's monopoly on power, power which has brought down untold problems on the country.

We are against direct interference by the party administration, the Politburo and the CC CPSU into state, economic and other aspects of society, which ought to fall under the exclusive competencies of the Soviets and be regulated by the law alone. ...

We are in favor of citizens' freedom of association within political organizations, and of the equal status of these organizations in the eyes of the law.

We are against the state-run economy and do not believe it will be possible to halt the breakup of the national economy with the help of administrative bans and orders alone. The attempt to postpone the transition to an authentic market economy, and to independent companies, for another few years is extremely dangerous. ...

---

550   V.I. Vorotnikov: It was like this..., P. 348

We consider it essential that the agricultural workers be allowed, with immediate effect, to select whatever forms of farming they wish, including allowing them to leave collective farms and state farms unimpeded, with their own particular share of land and property. ...

We are against the fact that the national republics are subordinate to a strong center, i.e. we are against the unitary, imperial state created by Stalin and preserved to this day. We consider it essential that a new agreement be drawn up, as soon as possible, on the Soviet Union as a free and voluntary association of sovereign republics, in accordance with the formula 'strong republics and a center created by them.' ..."[551].

Though they spoke out against the monopoly enjoyed by the CPSU, the democrats, most of whom were members of the party, did not turn down positions within the party. The task of bringing democracy to the CPSU needed to be dealt with. In the summer of 1989, the Moscow municipal party club 'Communists for perestroika' was set up, with its headquarters at the Sebastopol district committee in Moscow. On 2nd August 1989 the proposal to create a 'Democratic platform within the CPSU' was read out for the first time at a meeting of this club, and on 28th October 1989 it was announced that the 'Movement of communist-reformers for a democratic platform in the CPSU' had been created.[552]

The ideas expressed by the Inter-regional deputy group formed the basis for Yeltsin's campaign manifesto. He stood for election as a people's deputy of the RSFSR in his native Sverdlovsk, in district No. 74. The committee for the preparations for the elections was led by a teacher from the Urals Polytechnical Institute, A.N. Urmanov. His authorized representatives were Dmitry Sergeev (dep. secretary of the party committee), Gennady Kharin (a lecturer from the faculty of the history of the CPSU at UPI), Vladimir Malov, Artur Yezhov (dep. director of the planning and construction association from the Sverdlovsk house-building combine). Individuals from Yeltsin's inner circle played an active role in the election campaign — Sukhanov, Ilyushin and Korzhakov.

On 28th January 1990 Yeltsin travelled to Sverdlovsk, and on the 30th he met leaders of the major party organizations at the offices of the city committee of the CPSU.[553]

The leaders of the party's regional committee refrained from actively opposing Yeltsin — all that happened was that articles appeared in the local press about

---

551   V.B. Isakov: Chairman of the Soviet of the Republic. Parliamentary diaries 1990-1991. Yekaterinburg: IPP Urals worker, 1997. P. 97.

552   The Yeltsin era: Sketches from a political history. M.: Vargius, 2001. P.72.

553   L. Sukhanov: See above. P.242-244.

his popularity and about how he had "stabbed the party in the back". The party organizations which contained supporters of the 'Democratic platform in the CPSU' supported Yeltsin.[554]

During the course of the election campaign, Yeltsin's intellectual team took shape. It included tutors from the Urals Polytechnical Institute — two professors in the historical sciences, L. Pikhoya and G. Kharin, and a professor in the philosophical sciences A. Ilyin. Each of the candidate's speeches was analysed, and the component parts and particular phrases for his manifesto were ground out of it.

Thus, following his speech at the Urals palace of culture, a group of analysts made the following observations:

1. Be clearer on the provision about the formation of an independent Russian party with an 'administration-less' structure and show its advantages...

2. The auditorium did not accept the idea of forming Russian republics within the RSFSR: many people maintained that Yeltsin "had made a slip of the tongue, and had meant to say socio-economic territories". The phrase "the Russian republics" grated on the ear, and sounded like a made-up term.

3. It would be nice to reinforce the argumentation and evidence contained in the section about state and economic sovereignty: how can this be achieved, and what will Russia stand to gain from it; underline the need to liberate Russia from its colonial condition, particularly the Urals Region and the Siberian Region. There is probably a need, too, to identify the method by which the local, federal and union budgets will be formed — 'from bottom to top'.

4. Decrease the number of experts trained overseas (1000 people). It occurs to me that politicians ought not to confine themselves to specific instances. Life itself will dictate how many experts are going to need to be trained in the future, and where this will happen.

5. The item on the manifesto about national mobilization is contentious. Russia is a nuclear republic and in this regard is propping up the USSR, and we should probably leave in a strong message about the professional army. Those around me — did not get the point about mobilization. Reinforce the idea that there is no need to send the army off to suppress the people, particularly Russian lads being pitched against national republics.

---

554   The Yeltsin era: Sketches from a political history. M.: Vargius, 2001. P.78-79. The transcript for one of the pre-election speeches and the Q&A session can be found: Science in the Urals. 1990. 15 February.

6. Demonstrate, in a more detailed manner, how accounts formed using cash (convertible) accounts are going to be created. And most importantly — "what a specific individual will get out of this (there was some evidence which ran deep and some which did not — at various meetings we probably need to pay serious attention to this idea).

7. Talk about what people will get out of the transition by academic institutions towards self-governance. Set forth a mechanism for financing of education from school to higher education institution, and emphasize that the education and training system are a top priority in the manifesto, as an important lever with which to construct a national spirit, without which the nation will be dead (when the manifesto was unveiled, this was a weak point).

8. It would be a good idea to get rid of the repetitions.

9. It might be sensible to tone down the pressure on M.S. Gorbachev. Demonstrate the areas where you support him, and the areas where you disagree with him. Distinguish Gorbachev from Ligachev. Emphasize that Gorbachev is in some places and in some ways hostage to the conservative CC, which was formed by Ligachev. It would be better not to focus too much on Gorbachev's private life.

10. You should always keep in mind that you are already seen as a candidate for the role of President of Russia, not just as a candidate for the role of senator.

11. When asked about your visits to Japan and the USA, emphasize that you are not "selling off Russia", as some of your opponents have been claiming, but making contact with people in order to expand the framework of economic, scientific and technical cooperation, because we have greater need of it at present than they do. The center has in effect isolated Russia from the external world — it has taken everything for itself.

At the heart of your policy, and throughout your entire manifesto you must convey the idea of the Individual. What will Russia, and the ordinary Russian, stand to gain from all this. As things stand, the individual remains on the periphery of your consciousness and your policy."

The manifesto which Yeltsin took with him into the Russian elections was a significant step forward by comparison with his manifesto in 1989. Whereas his manifesto when he stood to be a people's deputy had talked in general terms about perestroika and democratization, now Yeltsin was proposing specific steps which aimed at renewing Russia.

In the political sphere it contained the following provisions:

— To adopt the Constitution of Russia by means of a referendum, thereby transforming the current economic and political system.

— Power in its entirety — to the Soviets and the people. Bring an end to the CPSU's monopoly on power. Within the multi-party system, the said communists were to form an independent Russian communist party based on an 'administration-less' structure, focused on a humane and democratic form of socialism;

The state system in Russia ought to be a presidential republic. The president was to be elected by the people. The president would cease to be a member of any parties or charities.

Russia's constitutional court was to be a guarantor that the rights and freedoms of the individual would be respected.

Yeltsin proposed that the army be reformed and put on a professional footing, that the length of compulsory military service should be drastically reduced, and brought down to 10 months; that staff numbers in the KGB should be reduced; and that the 9th Directorate, which provided security details for state and party dignitaries and representatives of companies and organizations, should be abolished.

He proposed bringing an end to discrimination against those with religious faith, ensuring freedom of conscience, and enshrining churches' right to be legal entities in law.

In the field of national and state construction he proposed that a new Union agreement be signed and that the national and state mechanism of the RSFSR be reformed, by expanding the right of the peoples of Russia to self-determination. He proposed that the constituent members of the RSFSR, after the referendum, could consist of socio-economic territories and regions capable of self-governance: Central Russia, the North, the South, the Urals Region, Siberia and the Far East Region, and that Russian citizens be afforded protection in the other republics. Adopt a law on the status of refugees.

In the economic sphere Yeltsin proposed a program featuring a managed transition to a market economy and the development of diverse forms of property ownership. Expanding on this, he called for the State Bank of the RSFSR to be separated from the government, for commercial banks to be developed, stock exchanges to be created, for it to be possible to convert the ruble, and for inflation to be curbed. Cash accounts (containing convertible money) should be created for companies by increasing the volume of consumer goods produced, and increasing the amount of produce in excess of state orders and sales of it.

Yeltsin's calls to reject the pumping of money earned in the RSFSR into the union-wide budget, and to other republics, had a familiar ring to them by now, as did his demand that laws should be adopted to strengthen the status of property from the republics which was transferred to the Union when there was a need for it.

In order to increase the role of state sovereignty in the RSFSR, there were calls to increase the role of the republic in international relations. Yeltsin proposed that the republics enter into direct negotiations with the USA, Japan, the UK and other developed countries on economic and scientific collaboration, the construction of roads and housing, supplies of food, consumer products and staff training.

The social program had a special place in the election manifesto, and it included:

- an expansion of residential construction;

- the creation of Russia-wide programs: childhood, encouraging a higher birth-rate, the fight against poverty, the regeneration of Russian culture, assistance to young families, healthcare, the environment, education;

- providing generous salaries, bursaries, benefits and pensions which would increase annually in line with inflation;

- capping inflation in respect of foodstuffs and essentials.

- Some of the popular slogans from political life in the late 1980s were also reflected in Yeltsin's campaign manifesto. Among them was:

- 'put the environment under the people's supervision';

- cancel all privileges by law, and allow all government dachas, private houses and other social infrastructure to be used by children and sections of society which are afforded less social protection.[555]

Yeltsin's manifesto, when quoted in more detail, is in some ways a manifesto for Democratic Russia — the section of the political opposition which had joined battle with the government of the union. If the opposition's demands were to be summed up, they would be as follows: increase Russia's political and economic status in the USSR, via the signing of a new Union agreement; (incidentally: there was no sign of the calls for Russia to leave the USSR!); expand the autonomy of the subjects of the RSFSR; radically reform the country's economy along market lines; improve the quality of life for a majority

---

555   V.B. Isakov: Chairman of the Soviet of the Republic. Parliamentary diaries 1990-1991. Yekaterinburg, The Urals worker, 1997. P. 107-109.

of the electorate; and promises to the effect that reform of the economy would not lead to a fall in living standards for citizens of the RSFSR. All of these provisions were combined with sharp criticism of the central authorities and the leadership of the CPSU.

The elections were going ahead in conditions that were now qualitatively different. 6705 candidates put themselves forward, in 1068 districts of Russia. In the majority of these districts voters had more than one candidate to choose from in the elections. In only 33 districts was there only one candidate on the voting slip. On average there were six candidates fighting it out for each seat.[556]

The results of the elections were as follows: the body of deputies now had an almost entirely new look. 93.9% of the deputies were elected for the first time. The delegates at the Congress were relatively young. Only 16 of the deputies were over 60. Very few women were elected — only 5.3%. Few workers were elected — only 5.6%, and only 6 state farm employees were elected. The professions with the highest representation among the deputies were: people from party organizations, soviet organizations and charities — 24.8%; employees from industrial enterprises and the construction industry

- 23.2%; the scientific and artistic intelligentsia — 19.5%; representatives of the agro-industrial complex — 12%. Law enforcement agencies (the police, the KGB, the procurator's office) accounted for 5.6% of the deputies, whilst servicemen accounted for 4.3% of the total. 86.3% of the total number of deputies were members of the CPSU.[557] 75% of the first secretaries of the regional committees (or territorial committees) of the CPSU and the chairmen of the regional (or territorial) committees were given mandates as deputies.[558] 85% of voters in Sverdlovsk voted for Yeltsin.

The elections to the RSFSR took place on 4th March, and on 12th March the Third emergency congress of people's deputies of the USSR opened, at which several fateful decisions were made: amendments were made to the Constitution, abolishing the status of the CPSU as a "guiding and organizing" force in Soviet society; and the post of President of the USSR was introduced, with M.S. Gorbachev elected to the role.

The preparations for the First congress of people's deputies of the RSFSR, which was due to open on 16th May 1990, were made at a time of worsening political crisis in the country and of increasing radicalization within society. A deep divide could be observed in the party, in which, for the first time since the 1920s, new movements and platforms had emerged. The preparations for

556   GARF. F. 10026, Op.1, D.3, L. 3-5
557   GARF. F. 10026, Op. 1, D. 3, L. 3-5, 195
558   GARF. F. 10026, Op.1, D.3, L.8

the creation of a Communist Party of the RSFSR and for the next congress of the CPSU only served to deepen the sense of discord. Rallies were held in Moscow to the sound of anti-communist slogans. During the May Day demonstration, thousands of people walked along with placards reading 'Sack the Politburo', 'Down with the CPSU', 'Down with Marxism-Leninism', and there were shouts of: 'Gorbachev — resign'; the historic Russian tricolore, a flag which had been banned after the 1917 revolution, was hung up on the columns in place of the customary red flags. The insults shouted out by the crowd about the CPSU, the Politburo and Gorbachev in person forced him to leave the stand above the mausoleum.

The threat of the collapse of the USSR was becoming an increasingly likely prospect. In the spring of 1990, the Supreme Soviets of Estonia and Latvia decided to abolish the documents drawn up in 1940 under which these republics had become part of the USSR. On 26th April 1990 the Supreme Soviet of the USSR adopted the Law 'On the delineation of powers between the USSR and the subjects of the federation', which guaranteed the autonomous republics the status of members of the federation of the USSR. This directive introduced contradictions into the relationships between the leaders of the Russian Federation and the autonomous republics in the RSFSR.

Against the grain. Adventures with a presentation

Immediately after the elections Yeltsin went off an a tour of Europe to unveil his autobiography, *Against the grain*. Publishing houses in a series of countries (Sweden, Norway, Italy, France, the UK and the USA) had invited the people's deputy Yeltsin to attend in person the presentation ceremony for his autobiography. The countries which had invited him over were to cover all his expenses themselves.[559]

In connection with this trip, a note was prepared by the Deputy head of party construction and human resources in the CC, Y. Ryzhov: "Although this trip is to take place whilst the Supreme Soviet of the USSR is in session, and the book, according to information we have received, contains a fair amount of calumny, it seems as if it might be a good idea not to impede B.N. Yeltsin as he undertakes this trip, so as not to give him cause to attract even more attention to himself."[560]

Between 4th and 10th March he visited Amsterdam, Stockholm, Oslo, Hamburg, Munich, Milan and Paris. On 27th April he attended a book signing in London, and on 28th April he flew to Spain, where he was due

---

559   RGANI. F.89. Op.11. D.26. L.4
560   RGANI. F.89. Op.11. D.26. L.1

to attend a conference in Cordoba on the subject 'A Europe without borders and the new humanism'. The conference was attended by A. Dubchek, W. Brandt, A. Mikhnik and V. Giscard-d'Estaing. Yeltsin spoke on the subject of '*Perestroika* and *glasnost* in the USSR'.[561]

Yeltsin flew from Cordoba to Barcelona in a six-seater sports monoplane chartered by the television company, and it was a flight which very nearly ended in disaster. Yeltsin's trusty adviser, L. Sukhanov, who was on board the plane with him, recalled that at one point the power suddenly went off, the devices stopped working, and they had to turn back in emergency mode. They only just managed to get the landing gear down, and the landing was extremely rough. Two hours later they flew to Barcelona in a reactive plane. But this flight didn't go smoothly either: the plane flew into thick thunder-clouds and began to shake violently. Yeltsin felt a sharp pain in his back, which became unbearable later that night, almost paralysing his leg. The doctors gave the following diagnosis: he had trapped a nerve in his hernia. On 30th April Yeltsin underwent an operation. Just a few days later, on 5th May, he went home.[562] On 7th May he attended a meeting in Priozersk (160 km from Leningrad) organized by the Leningrad organization Democratic Russia, to discuss strategy and tactics at the forthcoming congress.[563]

The Central Committee was busy preparing for the congress, too. A day before it opened, some communist deputies were invited to the CC. As S. Alekseev later recalled, the meeting did not turn out well. The deputies were openly called upon to stir up anti-Yeltsin feelings at the congress, and not to entrust him with the most senior role.[564] The CC backed the candidacy of A.V. Vlasov for the office of Chairman of the Supreme Soviet of the RSFSR.[565]

The elections for Chairman of the Supreme Soviet of the RSFSR

Yeltsin had first been spoken of as a future Chairman of the Supreme Soviet of the RSFSR immediately after the elections of people's deputies, when the head office that was to prepare the First congress was formed. The head office was located in the office of the Committee for construction and architecture, which Yeltsin had been in charge of in the Supreme Soviet of the USSR.

---

561   L. Sukhanov. See above. P. 281.
562   For more details see: L. Sukhanov. See above. P. 283-294.
563   V.B. Isakov: Chairman of the Soviet of the Republic. Parliamentary diaries. 1990-1991. Yekaterinburg, 1997. P.103-104.
564   S.S. Alekseyev: Gorbachev and Yeltsin: Triumph and drama // Izv. Urals state university. — Yekaterinburg, 2003. — N 25. — S. 93.
565   V.B. Isakov: Chairman of the Soviet of the Republic. Parliamentary diaries. 1990-1991. Yekaterinburg, 1997. P.114.

During the preparations for the congress, Yeltsin was on holiday for a while — he had gone with his wife to Kislovodsk. As S. Filatov later recalled, when Yeltsin appeared in early April 1990, in a small auditorium on Novy Arbat that held only three to four hundred people, he was greeted with stormy applause, flowers, smiles and people wishing him success.[566]

On this occasion, most of the deputies from Democratic Russia amicably supported Yeltsin and insisted that he ought to prepare seriously for his most important speech — the one in which he would set out his manifesto and answer any questions that might come up.

The preparations for the congress were continuing. S. Filatov recalls: "Boris Nikolaevich himself did not join us at our parties, or in our work at the commission, but we sensed his presence and influence throughout. I can't tell you how it came about, but we sensed him, and could often hear him giving his view on whatever issue we were discussing. Our work with Yeltsin in the future continued in much the same vein: he sort of distanced himself from the planning as regards an issue, but we always knew how he felt about it, so we always had the sense that he was by our side."[567]

The 1st Congress of people's deputies of the RSFSR began on 16th May 1990. Lively discussion and argument flared up at the congress on practically every single issue, starting with the agenda itself. The arguments about the agenda continued on the second day of the Congress, on 17th May. The main news from the second day of the congress was the process which had got underway to create parliamentary groups and factions which were to a greater or lesser extent attached to the biggest political blocs — Democratic Russia and Communists of Russia. In terms of the number of members, neither group had a clear majority of votes (each had between 400 and 450), so each side was fighting to secure votes from the neutral deputies, with furious disputes erupting as a result.

All sorts of deputy groups formed: 'Smena', the independent professional unions of the RSFSR, medical workers, groups focusing on upbringing, education and culture, foodstuffs and healthcare, deputies from the military, the groups Sever and Chernobyl, and autonomous groups.

On 18th May 1990 the congress managed to approve the temporary regulations for the Congress — this could probably be chalked up as a victory for the supporters of Democratic Russia. The agenda was to include:

- the election of a mandate commission;

- the draft temporary regulations;

---

566   S. Filatov: An open secret. M.: Vagrius publishing house, 2000. P. 40
567   S. Filatov: An open secret. M.: Vagrius publishing house, 2000. P. 41

- the socio-economic situation in the RSFSR (including a speech by A.V. Vlasov);

- the sovereignty of the RSFSR, the new Union agreement and the mechanism for power on the part of the people (a report by V.I. Vorotnikov);

- the election of a Chairman of the Supreme Soviet of the RSFSR;

- the election of a deputy Chairman of the Supreme Soviet of the RSFSR;

- the procedure for the formation of the Supreme Soviet of the RSFSR and the election of the members of the Supreme Soviet of the RSFSR;

- the amendments and addenda to the Constitution of the RSFSR and the formation of the Constitutional commission;

- the situation as regards agriculture and the growth of the agricultural-industrial complex;

- the approval of the Chairman of the Council of Ministers of the RSFSR;

- the approval of the Chairman of the Supreme Court of the RSFSR and the Main state arbiter of the RSFSR;

- the committee for people's supervision of the RSFSR;

- the development of laws of primary importance in the RSFSR and of the directives from the Supreme Soviet of the RSFSR;

- the mass media in the RSFSR;

- the status of people's deputy of the RSFSR;

- miscellaneous.[568]

A serious contender for the role of Chairman of the Supreme Soviet of the RSFSR was the candidate for membership of the Politburo, member of the Presidium of the Council of Ministers

and chairman of the Council of Ministers, A.V. Vlasov. In his address to the congress he expressed some fairly radical views, as he attempted to beat off his rivals: "Life has brought us to the unwavering conviction, achieved after much suffering: a radical solution to the problems facing the republic is only to be found in full-scale economic and political sovereignty." Vlasov called for a division of powers between the USSR and the federal subjects, so that Russia would have an exclusive right to take control of, and have at its disposal,

---

568   GARF. F.10026. F.1. D.7 L.28

all its natural resources, and all the economic, scientific and technical, and intellectual potential it had accumulated.[569]

"Our view," Vlasov said to the deputies, "is that everything that is situated on Russian soil must belong to the peoples of this country, fully and completely. (Applause). It is essential that we adopt a Law of the RSFSR, as soon as possible, and devise a mechanism for a phased transfer of companies from the union to the republics."

V.I. Vorotnikov spoke in support of the idea that Russia should maintain its sovereignty. In his opinion, the rules governing the new relations with the republics in the union should be founded on an equal exchange, mutual benefit and respect for sovereignty.[570] "I propose," Vorotnikov said, addressing the deputies, "that the Congress adopts the Declaration on the sovereignty of the Russian Federation, which would not only express principles of its own, but would also be the fundamental state document, which would determine the main areas of activity of the Supreme Soviet and the Government of Russia."[571]

The well-coordinated speeches by Vlasov and Vorotnikov were designed to seize from the more radical deputies the idea of the state sovereignty of Russia. It was their speeches at the Congress which contained all the key, fundamental provisions of state sovereignty.

Boris Yeltsin gave a speech in which he presented an alternative approach to the issue of sovereignty. His speech contained far fewer specific examples than those of Vlasov or Vorotnikov, but his criticism of the center was more cutting and more comprehensive. "The imperial policy of the central government, over many years," Yeltsin began, "has led to a lack of clarity with regard to the current position of the republics in the union, to uncertainty over their rights, duties and responsibilities. First and foremost this concerns Russia, which has suffered more damage than anyone else as a result of the administrative and command-based system, which has outlived its use but is still clinging on to life.

We must not resign ourselves to a situation in which the republic is in first place in the country in terms of labor productivity, yet comes fifteenth and last in terms of the amount spent on social needs."[572]

Yeltsin spoke of the need to ensure genuine power to the people in Russia. A key means of achieving this goal was to ensure genuine sovereignty in Russia,

---

569   GARF. F. 10026, F. 1, D. 7, L. 151
570   GARF. F. 10026, Op. 1, D. 8, L. 78
571   GARF. F. 10026, Op. 1, D. 8, L. 96
572   GARF. F. 10026, Op. 1, D. 8, L. 108

which would be equal among the equal republics in the union. He set out the principles on which Russia's sovereignty would be based:

"1. The Russian republic is a legitimate, sovereign democratic state, consisting of a voluntary association of peoples with equal rights.

2. All power in the republic belongs to the people, who exercise this power directly and through the Soviets of people's deputies.

3. The relations between Russia and the other republics in the union shall be regulated by means of separate agreements, and relations with the Union shall also be regulated by a special, seperate agreement. ...Today, it is for Russia, not the central government, to think about which functions should be transferred to the central government, and which ones it should hold onto. Is it not time to pose the question of whether Russia and the other republics in the Union really need a central government. (Applause.)

4. The acts signed into law by the Union must not contradict the new Russian Constitution or the agreement with the Union.

5. Outside the framework of the powers delegated to the Union, the republic must take charge, independently, of both domestic and foreign policy.

6. The relations between the federal subjects inside Russia are regulated on the basis of the federal agreement, under which they are guaranteed sovereignty, economic independence, autonomy, their culture, their national identity, the right to fair and equal representation in all the federal bodies.

7. Common citizenship of the republic is in effect in Russia. Nobody can be deprived of this citizenship.

8. The constitution of the republic is a guarantee of political pluralism and a multi-party system, acting within the framework of parliamentary democracy. It is not possible for any party to have a monopoly on power. The parties and the social organizations act in adherence to the special law. (Applause.)

9. The citizens of Russia and of the other republics in the union, residing within its borders, are guaranteed all their civil and political rights and their rights to property.

10. All the forms of property of Russian citizens are protected by law.

11. In the republic there is a full and unconditional division of legislative, executive and jurisdictional powers.

12. Elections to the bodies representing state power are universal, fair, direct and secret.

13. The national symbols of Russia must be reviewed, and we must look, in particular, at the idea of having a national anthem for the republic.

Economic sovereignty in Russia is only possible on condition that the idea of republican property is established, the basis of which must be formed by the land, the soil itself, the air, the forests, water and other natural resources, enterprises, the entirety of the country's manufacturing output, and the entirety of our scientific and technological potential and our intellectual potential. It is essential that we ensure these are used exclusively in Russia's interests, by means of the legislation.

The transfer of the natural resources and other resources used by the republic to the Union and the other union republics could be effected on an unremunerated basis, or at a profit to the republic, solely by the Russian parliament."[573]

Yeltsin talked about the need to have a State bank of our own, and an external economic institution of our own. As he brought his speech to an end, he emphasized that all these proposals were designed with a single objective in mind: to strengthen the USSR.

Vorotnikov, assessing his opponent's speech, wrote in his diary: "In essence, B.N. Yeltsin presented a pre-prepared version of a declaration which, on a number of its provisions, coincided with our draft program. At the same time he put forward fundamental demands of a political and economic nature, which incorporated ultimatums. He accused the Center of conducting an imperial policy for many years with regard to the union republics, including Russia. He set out the conditions for adopting a new Russian Constitution, prior to a Constitution of the USSR. He said that all power in the Russian Federation belonged to the people, who exercised it through the Soviets, and that the acts adopted by the Union of SSRs must not contradict the Russian Constitution and the Agreement with the Union."[574]

Against all expectations, M.S. Gorbachev's speech at the congress played into the hands of Yeltsin and his supporters. The desperate attempt by the President of the USSR to go against the tide of the Russian congress, and drag all the waverers over to his side, backfired badly. The more he criticised Yeltsin personally, and the more irritatedly he did so, the greater the significance Yeltsin's political manifesto took on. As the observant V.I. Vorotnikov pointed out, "at the beginning of 1990 his (Gorbachev's) authority had been severely dented, and people's attitude towards him had changed markedly by comparison with the preceding years. Yeltsin's ratings, meanwhile, had shot

---

573   GARF. F. 10026, Op. 1, D. 8, L. 109-112
574   V.I. Vorotnikov: It was like this..., P. 382

up, and therefore the criticism directed at him did not go down well."[575] The upshot of Gorbachev's speech was as follows: he was against sovereignty and against Yeltsin. Since the idea of sovereignty was supported by an overall majority of deputies at the Congress — from the communists to Democratic Russia, Yeltsin ought to have been grateful to Gorbachev, who had clearly contributed to the number of deputies supporting him.

On 24th May 1990 the deputy A.V. Deryagin took the floor of the Supreme Soviet of the RSFSR. He was the director of the All-Union R&D Institute for electro-technical materials: "Dear comrade deputies, never in my life did I think that I would be required to speak from this stand, and put forward a candidate for the role of Chairman of the Supreme Soviet of the Russian Federation. I'm sure you probably understand my feelings and the concern that grips me. (Noise in the auditorium). I wish to propose for the office of Chairman of the Supreme Soviet of the Russian Federation the candidacy of Boris Nikolaevich Yeltsin. (Applause).[576]

Originally from Kaluga, he lived and worked in Sverdlovsk for many years, and I know Boris Nikolaevich through Sverdlovsk, and also through his activity as a deputy in recent years. He is a man with an incredible capacity for work. As far as perestroika is concerned, particularly as regards democratization and glasnost, then as far as I understand it, it began in Sverdlovsk long before it began anywhere else. And we have Boris Nikolaevich Yeltsin to thank for this. <...> You can see that in spite of the difficulties we are facing, the electorate of Sverdlovsk, of the industrial Urals Region, have — even now, when there are so many other candidates standing — voted overwhelmingly for B.N. Yeltsin in the very first round. I am voicing the opinion shared by my electorate, who have been calling me non-stop since 7 o'clock this morning. Their views are absolutely unambiguous: they have been asking me to express their opinion, and, as a deputy, to support Boris Nikolaevich Yeltsin's candidacy.

I would like to draw your attention to an important point. All of us voted amicably in favor of Russia's sovereignty, or rather, of including this issue on the agenda. We had an amicable discussion on this issue. This is the version of the agenda which united all of us. And Boris Nikolaevich Yeltsin's speech on Russia's sovereignty served to convince me once again of the fact that he is the man who, in the role of Chairman of the Supreme Soviet of the RSFSR, would protect our sovereignty and the renewed Russian Constitution.

And one final thought. We have some very difficult and arduous times in store for us: the transition to a market economy. And it is not beyond the

---

575   V.I. Vorotnikov: It was like this... P. 383-384

576   GARF. F.10026. Op. 1. D. 10. L. 173

bounds of possibility — on the contrary, it will probably be the case — that both all of us here today, and our electorate, will feel the squeeze when it comes to our quality of life. The man in the role of chairman ought, therefore, to be someone who can open up his heart, whom the people genuinely have faith in, and who is capable of dealing with temporary difficulties.

Thank you very much for listening. I ask you to support this candidate and I am convinced that the First Russian Congress of people's deputies will not be making a mistake if it elects, for the role of Chairman of the Supreme Soviet of the Russian Federation, B.N. Yeltsin. Thank you for listening. (Applause).[577]

The list of candidates in the elections for Chairman of the Supreme Soviet of the RSFSR contained the following: B.N. Yeltsin, I.K. Polozkov and V.I. Morokin. The political leadership of the USSR were inclined to back the candidacy of I.K. Polozkov.[578] At the time he was first secretary of the Krasnodarsk Regional Committee of the CPSU, and was known for having made a series of speeches that were highly critical of the union Government at the Congress of people's deputies of the USSR; he was being groomed for the role of leader of the communist party of the RSFSR.

Yeltsin, as he set out his manifesto, announced: "Russia is ailing. And today, more than ever, we need a decisive, bold and — above all — forward-thinking policy, with the help of which, by acting with energy, we will be able to haul ourselves out of the crisis. What must we do in order to achieve this? By not breaking down the system straight away; by building a new structure alongside it, rejecting the party's monopoly on power, transferring power to the people and the Soviets, and shifting to a market economy — this will make the entire administrative and command system obsolete. And it will die out well and truly..."[579]

Yeltsin spoke of the need for constitutional reforms, and about the fact that the party should adopt not only a declaration but also a Law on Russia's sovereignty in the renewed Union, and prepare a draft federative agreement regulating relations within the federation. In his opinion, laws should be adopted on agricultural policy, on a Constitutional committee (or court) in Russia, on freedom of speech and of publication, and freedom of conscience. In his opinion, the courts and the entire justice system should be depoliticized and fully exempted from supervision by executive power.

The top priority in the economic sphere must be preventing the economic crisis that was on the horizon. In his opinion, it was essential to "take emergency

---

577   GARF. F.10026. Op. 1. D. 10. L. 173-176
578   V.I. Vorotnikov: It was like this... P. 384
579   GARF. F.10026. Op. 1. D. 11. L. 4

measures in order to rescue the consumer market. The collapse of it, and the inevitable social rupture which would result, would lead to the failure not only of government structures but also of socio-political structures. The key thing for us at present is the question: how are we to shift towards a market? It is my view," Yeltsin said, "that this must not be forced through, nor must it be done at the cost of a reduction in the people's quality of life."[580] Yeltsin's closing remarks were: "The fate of Russia, and the fate of each individual, depends directly on how we come together, how we win people's trust, how we stand up for our independence as a republic, constructively and as a matter of principle, taking on an additional burden from the central government. I am prepared to put into this my full responsibility, and to set about achieving this together with you. Thank you." (Lengthy, raucous applause)[581]

On 26th May the results of the vote were announced. To be elected, candidates had to secure at least 531+1 votes.

The results were as follows: Boris Nikolaevich Yeltsin: 497 for, 535 against; V.I. Morokin: 32 for, 1002 against; and I.K. Polozkov: 473 for, 559 against.

The outcome was that there were two people left on the voting slips for the second round — Yeltsin and Polozkov.

The results of the second round were as follows: Boris Nikolaevich Yeltsin — 503 for, 529 against;

I.K. Polozkov: 458 for, 574 against.

Yeltsin had secured more votes than Polozkov. Neither man had made it through, however. Since the elections had failed to provide a positive outcome, the next item on the agenda was the task of proposing new candidates.

On Sunday 27th May, an assembly of the Central Committee decided to reconsider Vlasov's candidacy for the role of Chairman of the Supreme Soviet.

On 28th May a new phase of putting forward candidates began at the Congress. After a series of withdrawals, the only names left on the list were Vlasov, Yeltsin and Tsoi.

V.A. Medvedev, the Politburo member "responsible" for the elections for the Russian Chairman of the Supreme Soviet, wrote in his memoirs: "Of course, when setting out his manifesto in his speech the next day, Polozkov came across as weaker than Yeltsin, although he answered questions fairly dexterously. The results of the vote were announced that night. None of the candidates had secured the required number of votes...

---

580   GARF. F.10026. Op. 1. D. 11. L. 10
581   GARF. F.10026. Op. 1. D. 11. L. 22

In the second round Yeltsin's share of the vote went up by 6, whilst Polozkov lost 15 votes. It was decided to put everything on hold once again, to work with the groups of deputies, find out what they thought and meet the next day, a Sunday."[582]

The elections had failed to provide a result for the second time. There was nothing for it but to start over: new candidates must be put forward. V.A. Medvedev recalled, in his memoirs: "The meeting which was held by the secretaries of the CC on the Sunday, with Vorotnikov in attendance, as well as Kapto, Babichev, Degtyarev and Shenin, came to the conclusion that Polozkov had no chance of building a lead. Even if all of the remaining 71 votes still up for grabs were added to Polozkov's total from the second round, he would still not have the required minimum of 531 votes, whilst Yeltsin only needed 28 more votes.

Polozkov undoubtedly alienated many of the waverers in the center with his conservatism. That said, Vlasov's ratings shot up noticeably after he withdrew his candidacy. It was therefore decided that the focus should be switched to Vlasov. Our opinion was reported to the General Secretary straight away. He was slightly taken aback by the proposal, but he took note of it."[583]

Vlasov was advised to make his speech as critical as possible, and not to confine himself to criticism of the leadership of the union. As V.A. Medvedev observed, "The manifesto itself didn't turn out too bad — in places it bordered on the admissible."

Let us quote Medvedev a little more: "That same evening a group of leaders of the communist deputations met in the auditorium for the Plenums of the CC, plus a few people whom they trusted. There were 450 people present. I noticed that there were also a few people from Democratic Russia in the auditorium. It was hard to stop this happening — and there was no real point in doing so anyway. Gorbachev was out of town at the time, getting ready for his visit to the USA. He turned up, however, and spoke unambiguously in support of Vlasov."[584]

On 29th May the Congress voted once again. The candidates on the voting slips were B.N. Yeltsin, A.N. Vlasov and V. Tsoi.

The results were as follows:

Vlasov — 467 for, 570 against; Yeltsin — 535 for, 502 against; Tsoi — 11 for, 10026 against.[585]

---

582   V.I. Medvedev: In the President's team...P. 137
583   Same reference. P.139
584   Same reference. P. 139-140
585   GARF. F. 10026. Op. 1. D. 14. L. 9

By just four votes, Yeltsin had "got over the line". He was duly elected Chairman of the Supreme Soviet of the RSFSR.[586] V. Isakov wrote in his parliamentary diaries: "...When the board was lit up with the results confirming his election (it was approved by an open vote) a thunderous ovation broke out and dozens of TV cameras and hundreds of pairs of eyes turned towards Yeltsin. He got to his feet, stood looking slightly at a loss for two or three seconds, and then, to the accompaniment of applause, walked up to the presidium and sat down in the chairman's seat."[587]

In his first speech as Chairman of the Supreme Soviet of the RSFSR, B.N. Yeltsin called on the delegates to form an approval commission in order to determine the candidates for key positions on the Presidium of the Supreme Soviet, for the committees and the commissions of the Supreme Soviet and for the most important positions in the Government. To this end he proposed a break lasting one and a half days in the congress, and suggested that in that time all registered groups of delegates appoint five people for the approval commission.[588]

The creation of an approvals commission made it possible to 'structure' those attending the congress into political groups and, ultimately, make it more effective. The approvals procedures had positive results. A compromise was even reached with the 'communists of Russia' faction. On 1st June deputies were elected for the Chairman of the Supreme Soviet — B.M. Isaev, who was close to the Communists of Russia faction, and S.P. Goryachev, who spoke out openly against those who supported Democratic Russia. On 5th June the first deputy was the Chairman of the Supreme Soviet, R.I. Khasbulatov, was elected. On 11th June, after arguments about the number of people in the Supreme Soviet, elections were held for the two-chamber Supreme Soviet.

The agreements drawn up by the approvals commission were also reflected in the members of those in charge of the chambers. V.B. Isakov was elected Chairman of the Council of the Republic — he was considered an outstanding representative of Democratic Russia. The man elected as his deputy was V.A. Veshnyakov, who at the time was close to the Communists of Russia faction. The Chairman of the Soviet of Nationalities was R.G. Abdulatipov, who had worked in the administration of the CC CPSU, whilst his deputy was D.A. Volkogonov, who had been involved with the Smena faction, which had adopted radical and democratic stances on a number of occasions.

---

586   V.A. Medvedev had to put in a call to the private jet of the President of the USSR and inform Gorbachev, who was on a visit to Canada and the USA, that Yeltsin had been elected Chairman of the Supreme Soviet of Russia.

587   V.B. Isakov: Chairman of the Soviet of the Republic. Parliamentary diaries. 1990-1991. Yekaterinburg, 1997. S. 125.

588   GARF. F. 10026. Op. 1. D. 14. Ll. 12-15

A complex struggle was also played out in the elections of deputies for the Chairman of the Supreme Soviet — one first deputy and three 'ordinary' ones. In accordance with a tradition which had begun back in Soviet days, a representative of one of the autonomous nationalities was elected as first deputy. The candidates put forward were R. Abdulatipov, T. Mukhamadiev and V. Shtygashev. Not a single one of them managed to secure the required number of votes. Taking advantage of the situation, the democratic wing proposed S. Shakhrai for the role. But he too was unable to achieve victory — although he very nearly did so.

In order to find a way out of the stalemate, the only option was to set up an approvals commission. Following lengthy debates, Boris Yeltsin once again proposed that his deputies should be S. Shakhrai and a new person on whom he hoped a compromise could be reached — R. Khasbulatov. When introducing the latter, he described the candidate as follows:

"I have come to the conclusion that he is precisely the man we need to take charge of the Supreme Soviet. He is an economist. He is a specialist on the transition to a market economy, which is something that is going to crop up extremely soon. He is an economist who has in-depth knowledge of issues related to the transfer of powers and regions to economic independence. He is an academic and, of course, someone with the sort of intellect for which there is a strong need at the top of the Supreme Soviet."[589]

Khasbulatov was elected after his candidacy was put forward once again, but it proved too much to ask to secure victory for Shakhrai as well. S. Filatov later recalled that Khasbulatov left a strong impression on everyone at the time thanks to his wit, his depth of thought and his ability to force himself to listen. It may be that his experience as a professor and lecturer assisted him in this regard. Right from the start, Khasbulatov would always come to Yeltsin's aid, when he was subjected to frequent attacks, either from Gorbachev, from Yanaev or from journalists representing the nomenclature.[590]

The declaration on the state sovereignty of the RSFSR. The climax of the Congress of people's deputies of the RSFSR was the approval, by an absolute majority of deputies, of the Declaration on the state sovereignty of the RSFSR on 12th June 1990. This day was made a public holiday in Russia.

The problem of ensuring Russia's economic sovereignty, as the basis of its political sovereignty, became the key problem during the election of the Chairman of the Council of Ministers of the RSFSR. On 18th June 1990 I.S. Silaev was elected to the position. Silaev was an extremely experienced manager from the aviation industry and a Hero of Socialist labor; in the past

---

589   The Yeltsin era. Sketches from a political history. M., 2001. P.85
590   S. Filatov: An open secret. M.: Vagrius publishing house, 2000. P.67

he had been the minister of machine-tool and instrumental industry in the USSR, minister of the aviation industry in the USSR, deputy Chairman of the Council of Ministers of the USSR, and chairman of the Board of the Council of Ministers of the USSR for engineering (1985-1990). His candidacy was very obviously a compromise — on the one hand, he had spoken in support of the idea of Russian sovereignty, and moreover had declared his intention to work alongside the Congress of people's deputies of the RSFSR and the Chairman of the Supreme Council; on the other hand, he was, without question, a figure who commanded authority among the communist faction at the Congress as well — he had been a member of the Central Committee since 1981.[591]

Some time earlier, on 15th June, the Congress of people's deputies had appointed N.P. Zarubin as Chief state arbiter of the RSFSR. On 16th June a Constitutional commission was formed at the Congress (its chairman was B.N. Yeltsin, his deputy was R.I. Khasbulatov, and the secretary of the commission was O. G. Rumyantsev).

On the same day the fundamental Directive 'On alterations and amendments to the Constitution — the Primary law of the RSFSR'. These amendments changed the role of the CPSU in Russia. Article 6 of the new edition of the Constitution established that political parties, youth groups and other social organizations must play a role in devising the state's policy, and in the governance of state and societal issues via their representatives, elected to the Soviets of people's deputies. Clause 7 of the Constitution stated that "all political parties...shall act within the framework of the Constitution of the USSR, the Constitution of the RSFSR and the Constitution of autonomous republics".[592] Thus the CPSU was distancing itself from the state government, and bringing itself to the same level as other parties and organizations in society.

Boris Yeltsin's victory in the elections for Chairman of the Presidium of the Supreme Soviet of the RSFSR represented a new high-point in his career.

Yeltsin had well and truly emerged from the shadowy world of the party administration. He had become an independent political figure in his own right. It should be noted that this was a first in many decades of Russian history in the 20th century.

His program was designed for future growth, for the country's future political development. It incorporated the idea of Russia's sovereignty, the need for a multi-party system and for the inevitable shift towards market relations. Even then everyone could tell: Yeltsin was going to stand for President of Russia.

---

591   Who's who in Russia and her near neighbors. Reference guide. M., 1993. P. 593-594

592   Sovetskaya Rossiya, 17 June 1990

Yeltsin and the CPSU: the start of 'departization'

On 19th June 1990 the Russian party conference got under way. On 20th June the party conference was turned into a congress for the establishment of the communist party of the RSFSR. I.K. Polozkov was elected first secretary of its Central Committee. At the very same time that the Russian party conference was announcing that the communist party of the RSFSR had been formed, the Congress of people's deputies was adopting the Directive 'On the mechanism for giving power to the people in the RSFSR', which stated that all power in the RSFSR belonged to the people, who would exercise it via the Soviets of people's deputies, and in the form of direct democracy.[593]

A watershed of sorts in the relations between the Supreme Soviet of the RSFSR and the CPSU was the statement by Boris Yeltsin at the 28th congress of the CPSU on 12th July 1990.

"In connection with my election as Chairman of the Supreme Soviet of the RSFSR and my huge responsibility before the people of Russia," Yeltsin said to the delegates, "and taking into account the transition of society to a multi-party system, it shall not be possible for me to execute the decisions of the CPSU alone. As the head of the highest body of legislative power in the republic, I must be subordinate to the will of the people and its authorized representatives. For that reason, in accordance with the obligations given to me during the election campaign, I hereby announce that I am to leave the CPSU, so that I can exert as much influence as possible on the Soviets' activity. I am willing to collaborate with all the parties and socio-political organizations in the republic."[594]

After making this statement Yeltsin walked demonstratively out of the auditorium.

Yeltsin's statement was evidence of a radically new phenomenon in Russia's post-October history — a distancing of the communist party from the senior echelons of state power and from the government in the republic.

The outcomes of the Russian congress

The main outcomes of the 1st Congress of people's deputies of the RSFSR were:

a policy aimed at restoring the institutes of statehood in Russia, and making them truly meaningful;

---

593   Sovetskaya Rossiya, 22 June 1990
594   Izvestiya, 13 July 1990

the adoption of a Declaration on Russia's state sovereignty, as a means of enhancing the republic's status in the USSR;

amendments to the existing Constitution of the RSFSR and the adoption of a decision to create a new Constitution;

the exclusion of the CPSU from the system of state governance created by the decisions of the 1st Congress;

the congress abolished the bodies for supervision of the people and state product inspectorate in the RSFSR, adopted a directive on the mechanism for giving power to the people and introduced a ban on combining party roles with state roles;

the congress reflected the burgeoning radicalism which had begun to be shown by many Russians, their desire for change and their critical appraisal of Soviet life in the past; it was established at the Congress that there would be a distribution of powers between the bodies of power in the union and the republic, operating on Russian soil.

The '500 days program'

On 14th July 1990 the following Law was adopted: 'On property in the territory of the RSFSR'. The new government had clearly adopted a reformist policy, particularly against the backdrop of the activity of the union's Council of Ministers, headed at the time by N.I. Ryzhkov. Further evidence thereof was provided by the appointment, as deputy chairman of the Russian government and chairman of the State commission on economic reform, of G. Yavlinsky, who had previously worked in the administration of the Council of Ministers of the USSR; and the appointment to the role of Minister of Finance of the young, ambitious B. Fedorov, who had experience of working not only in the union's bodies of power, but also for international financial organizations; the government undoubtedly realised there was a need for agricultural reforms. In the summer of 1990 intensive work began in Russia on the preparations for the economic reforms.

The idea of rapid reforms to the country's economy met with support from a significant proportion of the body of deputies in Russia, and in the media. The need for reform was acknowledged both by the government of the union and the republics. There had been a reduction in manufacturing output, inflation was on an upward trajectory, the deficit in the state budget was growing bigger and the country's gold and currency reserves were rapidly diminishing. There was not enough food, there were occasional riots related to the lack of tobacco or vodka, which would take hold of some of the biggest cities in the country, such as Sverdlovsk and Chelyabinsk. The first secretary of the CPSU's Leningrad regional committee, B.V. Gidaspov, openly declared at the assembly of the Politburo in the fall of 1990: "I go to work in the morning, and I look at the 'tails' (the lines for food) with a hundred or a thousand people. And I think to myself: someone among that lot might suddenly smash in a window — and before you know it a counter-revolution would break out in Leningrad. And we would not be able to save the country."[595]

It was clear to all serious economists that urgent measures were needed in order to alter economic policy, that pricing reform was needed and that the volume of state subsidies for inefficient areas of production should be cut.

During the preparations for economic reform there was a distinct coming together between the leadership of the union and the new government of Russia. In July 1990 a five-hour meeting took place between Gorbachev and Yeltsin. Gorbachev would later write in his memoirs that Yeltsin "admitted that the leadership of the Russian Federation, following the attempt to create its own Russian program for the transition to a market economy, became convinced that it would not be possible to make it reality within a single republic. Yeltsin expressed his conviction that the Supreme Soviet of Russia would approve this program, which stipulated that an economic union would be created between the republics, and also defined their relationship toward the government of the union. The joint program ought to be implemented, however — in the Russian leader's opinion — by a special committee led by the president, rather than by the government of the Union."[596]

The agreement between Yeltsin and Gorbachev was cemented by means of special agreement. Ryzhkov dated this document 27th July 1990.[597] A few days later, on 2nd August 1990, a Directive from the President of the USSR M.S. Gorbachev was released, entitled 'On the preparations for the concept of a union program for the transition to a market economy as the basis of the Union agreement'. A commission was set up, whose members were S.S. Shatalin, N. Petrakov, L.I. Abalkin, G. A. Yavlinsky, A.P. Vavilov, L.M. Grigoriev, M. M. Zadornov, V.A. Martynov, V.M. Mashchin, A.Y. Mikhailov, B.G. Fedorov, N. P. Shmelev and Y. G. Yasin. The commission was supposed to include authorised representatives of the governments of the union republics. A draft of the concept for the transition to a market economy was due to be provided by 1st September 1990.

This signified the formal rejection of the concept for economic reform which had already been proposed to the Supreme Soviet, the Ryzhkov-Abalkin concept.

---

595   Quoted from: R.G. Pikhoya: The Soviet Union: a history of power... P.608

596   M.S. Gorbachev. His life and reforms. M., Book 1. P.574

597   N.I. Ryzhkov: Ten years of major upheavals, p.431-433; M.S. Gorbachev Life and reforms. Bk. 1, p.572

It is essential to note the personal courage displayed by both Gorbachev and Yeltsin, who found it in themselves to work together following the incredibly bitter confrontation which had characterized their relationship for several years — ever since October 1987. It appeared that the rancour between the two men had now been consigned to the past. They called one another frequently and informed one another about the agreements that their respective teams had managed to thrash out.

L.A. Ponomarev, one of the leaders of the Moscow branch of Democratic Russia, and a man who was close to Yeltsin in those days, told one of this book's authors that during that period in 1990, Yeltsin had spoken with obvious satisfaction of an improvement in his relations with Gorbachev, and about their shared interest in successfully concluding the '500 days' program. Gorbachev was enthusiastic too, saying, as his adviser A. Chernyaev later recalled: "The most important phase of all is beginning. This is a decisive breakthrough towards a new phase of perestroika. ... It is for us to place it on a solid footing...". "He [M.S. Gorbachev] would always bring the conversation back to this point," A. Chernyaev wrote in his memoirs, "whatever he had just been discussing."[598]

The idea of a transition to economic reforms within all the republics in the union which had expressed the desire to stay in the USSR received backing from the leaders of these republics. The Council of the Federations and the Presidential council, at an assembly on 30-31 August 1990, gave their support to the Shatalin-Yavlinsky program, the '500 days' program.

Gorbachev talked about his successful cooperation with Yeltsin, the high hopes he had that the '500 days' program would be approved, and his desire to start implementing genuine economic reforms, to his partners in the West — Mauno Koivisto, Giulio Andreotti, George H.W. Bush, James Baker and Douglas Hurd.[599]

Gorbachev's support for the program for the transition to a market economy meant that he was guaranteed support from a substantial section of the press, and from more radical circles in the intelligentsia; it also gave him grounds for optimism that he would be able to overcome the economic crisis in the country, and created the conditions required for successful negotiations with the republics on the signing of a new Union agreement.

It was in Yeltsin's interests to form a union with Gorbachev, too. The '500 days' program had its conceptual origins in the common, coordinated economic policy which had been in place throughout the whole of the USSR. For this reason it was essential to normalize relations with the center of the union —

---

598   A.S. Chernyaev: Six years with Gorbachev. Based on diary entries. M., 1993, p.365
599   Same ref, p.366-367

in this case the President of the USSR. Russia's economy was integrated into the economy of the Union incredibly tightly. On many occasions Russia acted as the initial link in the technological chain of the manufacturing process, providing the Union with matal, wood, oil and gas, whilst the final stages of production took place in other republics in the union — Ukraine, Belarus and so on. The severing of economic ties with the union's republics and ministries was fraugt with a worsening of Russia's economic position.

The rapprochement with Gorbachev strengthened Yeltsin's political position, gave the lie to the accusation frequently levelled at him by his enemies that he was "incapable of agreeing on anything" with Gorbachev, and enabled a normalizing of his relations with the sizeable communist faction in the Congress and the Supreme Soviet of the RSFSR.

When they set to work, however, serious disagreements came to light between the two 'teams' — the team of reformers, which included members of the Russian government and a number of economists from the Academy of Sciences — S.S. Shatalin, N. Petrakov and A. Aganbegyan — and those in power in the union, as represented by the prime minister, N.N. Ryzhkov, and his deputy, the academic L.I. Abalkin.

The main opponent to the program was Ryzhkov's deputy — the academic Abalkin, who was strongly in favor of 'stabilization prior to reform'. At practically the same time that the agreement was reached between Gorbachev and Yeltsin, an attack was launched on Yeltsin's standpoint, and he and his supporters had all manner of accusations levelled at them.

The legislature in the RSFSR adopted a policy which was, in its own peculiar way, ambiguous and contradictory: on the one hand, the conceptual '500 days' program called for economic reforms to be brought in simultaneously in all the republics in the USSR; on the other hand, the objective logic by means of which the 'Declaration on the state sovereignty of Russia' came into being demanded a raising of the republic's status within the USSR, and led to the economic interests of the RSFSR being put up in opposition to the interests of the government of the union. The Supreme Soviet of the RSFSR and the Presidium of the Supreme Soviet worked intensively in the summer and fall of 1990 to enhance Russia's status as a state within the USSR, and on the creation of the legal basis for the transition toward market relations in Russia.

On 13th July 1990 the Supreme Soviet adopted the Directive 'On the State Bank of the RSFSR and on the banks within the territory of the republic', which laid the groundwork for the establishment of the Russian banking system.

On 14th July 1990 the Presidium's Directive 'On the core principles behind the conducting of external economic activity within the territory of the

RSFSR' was adopted. This directive established that "...all legal entities and individual citizens, regardless of the form of ownership, acting within the territory of the RSFSR, are entitled to undertake external economic activity and go directly onto the external market."[600] This Directive brought an end to the state's monopoly on external trade, which for many decades had been one of the distinctive features of the Soviet economic system.

A conflict began between the Russian legislation and the legislation of the union. In parallel to this genuine conflicts erupted in the field of the exercise of rights by Russia and the Union of SSRs in the management of the economy. The union bodies hurried to sign big contracts with overseas corporations, for which the party that would have to pay most, objectively speaking, would have to be Russia.

The process of corporatization and privatization of companies which were subordinate to the union and located on Russian territory began. All this caused direct harm to Russia's economic interests and sovereignty. Disagreements between the leaders of Russia and the leaders of the Union grew.

On 31st August, at an assembly of the Presidium of the Supreme Soviet of the RSFSR, Yeltsin gave a speech in which he gave an update on the course of negotiations with the leaders of the union on the economic reform. "Comrade Gorbachev, M.S., proposed that the two programs be merged," Yeltsin said. "That would be like combining amperes and kilometers. It's not possible. The two programs contain completely different principles." The conceptual difference that Yeltsin identified between the two programs was that the Shatalin-Yavlinsky group was proposing that economic policy be implemented via the sovereign republics in the USSR, "whereas the government program is once again a program enforced from above: we are dictating this to you, you are going to perform it, and that's that."[601]

In this emotional outburst by Yeltsin lies the key to understanding the conflict which sprang up around the '500 days' program. At the forefront of these disputes were not the economic aspects of it — these were only of interest toa small number of experts.[602] The overall need for a transition to market relations was something that was self-evident to most politicians at that time. One bone of contention was the future political structure of the Union: should it remain a single state, as was implied by Ryzhkov's concept,

600   GARF. F. 10026. Op.1. D. 1247.

601   Same reference. L. 8

602   It is important to note that those who spoke against several aspects of the economic concept in the 500 days program included not only the 'union' economists, (L.I. Abalkin, V.A. Medvedev and a number of others), but also the following, who were close to the leaders of the Supreme Soviet: doctor of economic sciences I.V. Nit, adviser to the Chairman of the Supreme Soviet RSFSR, and the doctor of economic sciences, and people's deputy of the RSFSR P.A. Medvedev.

or ought it to be replaced by a confederation of republics, as the '500 days' program suggested. In this regard Gorbachev's sympathies ought ultimately to have lain with Ryzhkov.

Yeltsin had declared his support for the Shatalin-Yavlinsky program decisively and unambiguously. He reiterated this on 1st September at a press-conference about the results of a month-long trip he had made around the country — in the space of 22 days he went to Kuzbass, Vorkuta, Tatariya, Bashkiriya, Sakhalin and Primorye, and spent time chatting to many local people.[603] He had seen with his own eyes that people's patience was running out.

The economic crisis led to a riot in Chelyabinsk — the civil disorder in the city lasted several days, and there was a raid on the building of the Kurchatovsky district executive committee. "Having to stand in line for hours, the endless food shortages, the search for the bare essentials and foodstuffs — all this is making people desperate and forcing them to go out onto the city's streets and squares," wrote *Sovetskaya Rossiya*'s reporter in Chelyabinsk, A. Usoltsev.[604] There were vast lines of people waiting for bread in Novgorod, the bread had run out in the bakery kiosks in Leningrad, there was no tobacco left in Sverdlovsk, and soap, washing powder and other essential items were hard to come by.[605]

On 11th September, when the Shatalin-Yavlinsky program for the transition to a market economy was adopted by the Supreme Soviet of the RSFSR, and the Supreme Soviet of the USSR began to discuss Ryzhkov's report on economic reform, units of paratroopers from the army were marched into Moscow. Yeltsin made no attempt to hide the concerns he had about this. "They are trying to convince us," he said, addressing an assembly of the Supreme Soviet of the RSFSR, "that this is a peaceful event, related to the preparations for the parade, but there are serious question marks about that."

The commander of the paratrooper force, General-Colonel V. Achalov, responded with a furious denial in *Izvestiya*, declaring that the troops had entered Moscow to prepare for the parade, and that other paratrooper units had been sent off to take part in the potato harvest. These strange and somewhat alarming military manoeuvers were taking place against the backdrop of the battle for the future of the economic and political reforms in the USSR, and were interpreted, understandably, in this context.

At a meeting of the Politburo on 13th September there were whisperings that Yeltsin, under cover of the talks being held on unified action, was preparing to topple Gorbachev. As for Gorbachev, he was effectively making a move

---

603   Sovetskaya Rossiya. 1990, 2 September
604   Sovetskaya Rossiya. 1990, 26 August
605   Sovetskaya Rossiya. 1990. 5, 6 August

for the breaking-up of the previous agreements on joint fulfilment of the 'Yavlinsky-Shatalin program'. The Supreme Soviet of the USSR took a decision which was essentially neutral, on the face of it: it asked Ryzhkov to unite his program and the Shatalin-Yavlinsky program. This was an elegant way of taking away all possibility of a discussion in advance, by the leaders of the union, on the "undiluted 500 days program". The very man who had been fundamentally against this program was being asked to "adjust it".

At 8.25 am on 21st September, at the intersection of Gorky Street and Alexander Nevsky Side-street, the driver of a VAZ 2102 Zhiguli crashed into a Volga-GAZ 3102 in which Boris Yeltsin was seated. The impact occurred on the front right-hand door, behind which Yeltsin was sitting. Both of the car's doors were smashed in, and Yeltsin suffered brain damage. He was hit on the temple and in the ribs. He suffered an injury to his spinal cord. There is a great deal that remains unclear about this incident: the American publicist I. Valenta maintains that the collision took place the very next day after a meeting between Yeltsin and a delegation whose members included S. Foyo, a man who was close to the US president George Bush and had been a member of his campaign team. At this meeting, on 20th September, Yeltsin asked S. Foyo to arrange a meeting with the US president. The next day Yeltsin was involved in a car crash, for which I. Valenta claimed the KGB was responsible.[606] Yeltsin himself felt there was nothing untoward and that this was merely a run-of-the-mill road traffic accident.[607] Set against the events of September, however, the car crash was interpreted as sending a clear message: someone wanted Yeltsin dead.

The views adopted by the leadership of Russia and the leadership of the union were becoming increasingly divergent. On 21st September, addressing an assembly of the Supreme Soviet of the USSR, the President of the USSR demanded that he be given emergency powers, including the right to introduce presidential governance in the union republics and to disband their most senior bodies of state power.

This statement was interpreted by the leaders of Russia as a direct threat and an assault on the rights of the republic, and the very next day, on 22nd September, the Presidium of the Supreme Soviet of the RSFSR adopted a Directive declaring that in light of what had happened it was not acceptable for the President of the USSR

to be granted emergency powers; and that if emergency powers were indeed granted to him, the Presidium of the Supreme Soviet of the RSFSR would take all necessary steps in order to protect the constitutional status quo.

---

606   I. Valenta: My meetings with Yeltsin in the USA and in Russia // A&F, No. 25 (818), June 1996.

607   B.N. Yeltsin: Notes by the president. M., 1994, p.45-46

That same day the Presidium confirmed who the members of the delegation from the Supreme Soviet of the RSFSR and the Council of Ministers of the RSFSR would be, so that negotiations could be commenced with the union republics.[608]

On 24th September 1990 a Law of the Union of SSRs was released, entitled 'On additional measures to stabilize economic and socio-political life', by means of which the President of the USSR was given powers he had requested for a period lasting until 31st March 1992. He was entitled to publish edicts which would have the same force as laws, "...unless the Supreme Soviet of the USSR deems it necessary to introduce other rules," and to create the bodies of power and state structures required in order to introduce the reforms.

On 24th September 1990 a Directive of the Supreme Soviet of the USSR was released 'On the measures required as a matter of urgency to stabilize the national economy and the program for a shift to a market economy', which deemed it essential that "a unified program for the transition to a market economy be prepared, on the basis of the draft program provided by the Council of Ministers of the USSR."[609]

Russian sovereignty. The economic aspect

The Supreme Soviet of the RSFSR, for its part, demonstrated a clear lack of desire to resign itself to the position adopted by the leaders of the union; instead it wanted to introduce the reforms on its own. On 9th October the Supreme Soviet of the RSFSR addressed the citizens of Russia, calling on them to support the '500 days' program. On 16th October 1990, at an assembly of the Supreme Soviet of the RSFSR, the Chairman of the Supreme Soviet of the RSFSR, Yeltsin, gave a long speech in which, in every respect, he can be said to have set out his program. "At present, the most important question of all is being decided: will we be able to make a reality the very thing for the sake of which we became deputies: will we be able to continue our work on the creative task of regenerating Russia," he said, "or will we resign ourselves to the hardships, to brutal resistance on the part of the Central government, which attempts to lay the blame for its indecision on the unfavorable political situation."

Yeltsin told the deputies it was essential that they clarify their views on this and make a choice. "All the work that the Supreme Soviet of Russia is doing is being determined by the 'Declaration on sovereignty' adopted by the Congress of people's deputies. ...As we go about our work we are remaining committed to the conviction that our actions must not cause harm to any other republics or peoples of the USSR. It is for that reason that we consider it extremely

608   GARF. F. 10026. Op. 1. D. 1261 L. 1-4
609   Sovetskaya Rossiya, 1990, 25 September

important that bilateral agreements with the republics in the union should be drawn up and signed...The system of agreements will not create an artificial unity among the republics, thrust on it from the outside, but provide a Union formed on the economic basis of each republic's interests. ...

The most significant consequence of the work we are doing is that we are creating, in an extremely short period of time, a radical set of economic reforms. It was Russia that took the initiative in drawing up these reforms. ...Yet the situation in the republic is not improving. The main reason for this," Yeltsin observed, "is the fact that our sovereignty lacks sufficient finances."

Describing the economic state of affairs in Russia, Yeltsin pointed out that in industry, 70% of industrial output went to companies subordinate to the union, as did 73% of the industrial and manufacturing reserves, and 87% of the main industrial and manufacturing funds. Russia was getting an incredibly small return from the annual exports made by Russian companies, which amounted to 40 billion dollars or more. The Russian budget was not getting a cut of the foreign-currency revenue made from supplies of the country's key exported products (oil, gas, oil-related products and so on).

Yeltsin accused the union's ministries of "open sabotage" on the question of where the boundary lay between what was owned by the union and what was owned by the republic. "The central bodies are attempting to keep control, at any cost, over material and technical resources and food, so that they can continue to have them at their disposal. The corporate interest of the civil servants is being given higher priority, it transpires, than the interests of Russia. ...It is self-evident today that the Center's efforts are being focused mainly on not allowing a strengthening of the economic basis of our sovereignty."

According to Yeltsin, the Supreme Soviet of the RSFSR, by advocating the sacking of the Union government, had made clear how it felt about his program, and given its assessment of the activities of N.I. Ryzhkov's cabinet over the previous 5 years, holding him responsible for the catastrophic state of affairs in the country's economy.

Yeltsin, after being extremely critical of Ryzhkov's actions, was far more cautious with regard to Gorbachev. "I would like to put it on record that on the fundamental issues the President and I are heading in the same direction, but are advocating different tempos of forward movement, and different methods. The differences between us are predominantly to do with tactical issues. For that reason, both of us — both Gorbachev and I — are open to dialog. Recent events have shown that when this dialog becomes a reality, this has a positive impact which is felt immediately. But it is clear that this is not to everyone's taste. ...I wish to reiterate that I am prepared for a constructive dialog, but not if it harms the interests of the peoples of Russia."

The chairman of the Supreme Soviet of the RSFSR described the situation pertaining to the '500 days' program. He reminded those present that the President of the USSR supported the creation of this program. "During the conversation we had," Yeltsin said, "the President said he would support this program alone.

It would have been realistic to start the countdown from 1st October — and we were willing to do so. But the government of the union, which was floundering, put pressure on the President, and he, in turn, changed his mind. A program was released which included amendments made by the academic A.G. Aganbegyan. It could have been accepted, after a few amendments had been made. But N.I. Ryzhkov was not happy with it. Once again pressure was put on the President. And then yet another union program is cited as the President's program, in which an attempt has been made to merge, by mechanical means, the programs of the Shatalin group and the Government. Another attempt is being made to preserve a system which has become hateful to the people: Presidential directives are being published simultaneously, before the Supreme Soviet of the USSR has made a decision on the matter, aimed essentially at implementing the program drafted by the government of N. Ryzhkov — the government which brought the country down a dead-end, and is now taking it towards chaos."

"What is to be done, then?" Yeltsin asked the Supreme Soviet. "What position is Russia to take under the circumstances?

The 'Program of the President of the USSR', which is bound to fail, is clearly going to be approved by the country's parliament. In any event it is already being implemented, to all intents and purposes. In these circumstances, the government of the republic can choose one of three possible ways forward. ...

Scenario number one. Russia announces that it is not going to take part in implementing the President's Program. The budget, property and all the structures are divided up. It implements its '500 days' program, regardless. In this case it would be necessary to introduce our own currency, introduce customs systems along all the republic's borders, organize an independent banking system and foreign trade, and divide up the army and the armaments. ...

Scenario number two. At the heart of this scenario is a genuine coalition. A new ministerial cabinet (executive structures within the union) must be formed, on an equal footing. Some of the candidates would be put forward by the President, and some would be put forward by ourselves — the advocates of radical reforms. This scenario will make it possible to alter the hopelessly outdated structure of the Union Government, and some of the ministers will become surplus to requirements. The activities of the Center will become more effective, and will be capable of effecting radical economic reform which takes account of the reality which has come about (the sovereignty of the republics, the new role of the Center and so on).

And, finally, scenario number three. If the Union Government adopts this Program, which has little chance of succeeding, today, then it will take at least another six months for it to acknowledge that it has made yet another mistake, and chosen the wrong path. We are in any case going to be putting forward economic steps for the entire Union over and over again.

...Whatever the Supreme Soviet's view of things might be, or that of the Government of the USSR, Russia will begin radical economic reforms in 1990 — and let no-one say that this is mere ambitious talk. If we go on postponing the reforms, there won't be anything left to reform — the economy will simply collapse."

In his relations with the union's central government, Yeltsin called on "every Directive and Law of the Supreme Soviet of the USSR to be ratified by the Supreme Soviet of Russia, and on each decree of the Council of Ministers of the USSR to be ratified by the Presidium of the Council of Ministers of the RSFSR."

During the period of reform, the main task in social politics ought to be, according to Yeltsin, holding off a fall in living standards among the general public. Yeltsin warned that "worst off will be the poorest sections of society — the pensioners (in spite of the increase in pensions), the disabled, large families and so on. Special assistance will be provided to those living below the poverty line. It is also essential that we devise a set of measures for the provision of real aid to them; from the targeted distribution of foodstuffs, goods and cheap medicines to direct care for these people."

The reforms would inevitably lead to unemployment and the problems associated with it.

"In other words, when it becomes clear for all to see that the latest program to be put forward is failing once again, the Russian Federation must be prepared to implement its own Program for stabilization of the economy and the transition to a market economy, perhaps not within '500 days' by then, but within however much time the people give us," Yeltsin said, in conclusion.[610]

Thus a 'third scenario' for introducing the reforms had been put on the agenda, which in practice hardly differed at all from the first one. The main thing was that it could only be implemented separately from the union's economic policy. The '500 days' reform had lost the part of its contents which was related to the 'union'.

---

610   Yeltsin, Khasbulatov: Unity, compromise, struggle. M. 1994. P. 48-51

Yeltsin's speech on 16th October 1990 proved a turning point of sorts in his entire policy.

This turning point was without doubt enforced, and did not bring him any quick benefits. Yet it became inevitable at the moment when it became clear: the central government of the union intended to ignore the Declaration on Russia's state sovereignty.

The Russian government had to decide: how was it to construct its economic and political relations within the political framework of the USSR.

Yeltsin declared, in no uncertain terms, that if the union's ministries were to ignore Russia's interests, the republic would have no choice but to strive to achieve, and implement in practice, the idea of economic sovereignty.

This threatened to destroy the unity of the economic area within the soviet union, which, by 1990, was already disintegrating in any case, and melting away like snow in the rain.

The sharp tone of Yeltsin's speech to the union's deputies made Gorbachev's position somewhat easier. He managed to secure almost unanimous backing for the union's program among the USSR's deputies.[611]

On 25th October 1990 the Supreme Soviet of the RSFSR gave a special address to the Supreme Soviet of the USSR, the Supreme Soviets of the republics in the union and the President of the USSR. "In light of the complex circumstances which have come into effect in the country, and as a result of the struggle to create realistic conditions in which to safeguard the process of stabilization of the economy and the transition to a market economy, the implementation of radical structural transformations within the system of government, and effective social protection of citizens' interests, the Supreme Soviet of the RSFSR wishes to put the following proposals to you:

In parallel to the drafting and implementation of programs for the transition to a market economy and the legislative acts safeguarding these programs, direct talks must be commenced without delay between the delegations representing the republics and the Union of SSRs, in order to resolve issues related to the division of competencies between the bodies of power and governance within the union and the ones in the republics, the division of property, the coordination of the effect of laws and other regulatory acts, the development and implementation of anti-crisis measures, and protection of civil rights.

Measures must be taken for the urgent formation, on the basis of consultations between the republics in the union and the Inter-republican economic

---

611   Sovetskaya Rossiya. 1990, 20 October

committee, a body endowed with sweeping powers, which could form the basis of a government which would be trusted by the people and by the nation.

Direct talks should be commenced between the republics in the union, with the aim of signing bilateral and multilateral agreements on economic and scientific and technical collaboration.

In this difficult period for our states and peoples, the Supreme Soviet of the RSFSR is counting on mutual understanding and a resolute will in standing up for citizens' interests."[612]

Restoring relations to the previous level, in July and August, proved too much to ask, however. The economic concepts and logic behind the economic behavior of the union and the Russian government were growing further and further apart.

The political outcome of the split in the union between Gorbachev and Yeltsin was that it became impossible for joint action to be taken by the republics and the central government of the union.

How the new Constitution of the RSFSR was not adopted

The composition of the people's deputies of the RSFSR reflected the divided political structure of Russian society. The two largest political blocs — Democratic Russia and Communists of Russia — each had roughly the same number of supporters — 400-450 votes each. A furious battle was raging between them over those deputies who remained neutral.[613]

There were fundamental differences of opinion between them as regards their objectives for Russia's future, the fate of the legacy of socialism, the conceptual differences in the way domestic policy should be run, and relations with the Union's central government. The position of Democratic Russia was strengthened by the fact that the Chairman of the Supreme Soviet of the RSFSR, Boris Yeltsin, was a supporter of this political movement. His enemies in the Supreme Soviet and at the congresses, however, were not only numerous, but were also tied to the leaders of the Union of SSRs, and the administration of the CC CPSU in the center of power and in the regions. It is no exaggeration to say that a political war of sorts was being waged on Yeltsin and Democratic Russia — one which would by turns go quiet, then become more forceful; one which was by turns kept secret, hidden behind a curtain of parliamentary procedures and consultations with the union's

---

612   The institutions of the Congress of people's deputies of the RSFSR and the Supreme Soviet of the RSFSR. M., 1990, No. 25
613   S.A. Filatov: On the road to democracy. M., 1995. S.

ministries, and then blatant, implemented by means of directives from the President of the USSR, and in noisy political arguments.

The first political conflict, which has gone practically unnoticed not only by researchers but also by the press at the time, was the conflict surrounding the draft version of the new Russian Constitution.[614]

In accordance with the decision of the Congress taken on 22nd June 1990 an order was issued from the Chairman of the Supreme Soviet of the RSFSR entitled 'On the procedure governing the activities of the Constitutional commission'. This directive created the working group of the Constitutional commission, consisting of both theoreticians and practically minded deputies. The group was required to conduct its work on a permanent basis. Its members were: R.I. Khasbulatov, O.G. Rumyantsev, V.M. Adrov, Y.A. Ambartsumov, F.S. Arslanova, S.N. Baburin, B.P. Balovnev, I.A. Bezrukov, R.I. Bignov, V.K. Varov, N.T. Vedernikov, L.B. Volkov, M.L. Zakharov, B.A. Zolotukhin, V.D. Kadyshev, V.V. Klyuvgant, S.A. Kovalev, Y.M. Kozhokin, V.P. Lukin, V.D. Mazaev, N.P. Makarkin, P.A. Medvedev, M.A. Mityukov, R.I. Pimenov, V.N. Podoprigora, Y.A. Ryzhkov, O.I. Tiunov, F.V. Tsann-Kai-Si, S.M. Shakhrai, V.L. Sheinis and F.V. Shelov-Kovedyaev. Yeltsin became the Chairman of the Constitution Commission, Khasbulatov was appointed his deputy and O.G. Rumyantsev was appointed secretary.

39 copyrighted texts were submitted to the Presidium of the Russian parliament during a contest for draft versions of the Russian Constitution, 18 of which were selected for further examination. On 21st November 1990, at an assembly of the Presidium, the secretary of the Constitution Commission, OG. Rumyantsev, announced that work on the draft Constitution had come to an end, and the draft version might be published for the purposes of discussion and subsequent adoption at the second congress.

The very next day — on 22nd November 1990 — the draft version of the new Russian Constitution was published in *Rossiskaya gazeta*, and on 24th November it appeared in *Sovetskaya Rossiya*. Before long, however, there was to be a dramatic twist in the process of the Constitution's adoption, however.

On 23rd November Boris Yeltsin addressed the Presidium. "A quick question: on the changes to the agenda of the Congress, in light of the fact that open warfare is already being waged with the draft Constitution, which has only just been unveiled to the public, and in light of the fact that...public opinion of some form or other will surely take shape, and the people must be given a chance to read it, really familiarize themselves with it and somehow either accept it or reject it. So that in this battle, which is already due to take place at the Congress, we do not lose sight of the issue of foodstuffs, and

---

614   In archive 10026 there is a very important archive from the Constitutional commission.

the question of the agricultural industry — i.e. the proposal that the issue of the new Constitution be taken off the agenda, and that we only discuss the amendments to the Constitution which have taken shape in accordance with the laws.

The draft version of the Constitution has been printed; let it now be debated and studied. We are going to conduct a great deal of work to promote it, all manner of seminars, studies and so on. And we will raise this issue at the Congress of people's deputies scheduled to take place in March.

The members of the Presidium: We ought to vote on it.

B.N. Yeltsin: Why have a vote every time? I might as well ask, who is against this idea? One person is against it.

I spoke to the working group, and we may indeed be accused of having been hasty. It has only just been published and yet straight away we're taking it off to the Congress. There might perhaps be noises off, such as "the people won't get it", "the people won't accept it" — there's no question we may hear such things. But once we have accumulated a fair amount of positive material in this time, and genuine feedback from the public, once the people are genuinely thinking about the Constitution, and we have spent three months carefully putting it together, then we will have sufficient grounds for saying "no". I get the impression you are all in agreement."[615]

The arguments put forward by Yeltsin — "it is the question which was determined at the Congress, that the matter of agriculture and food supplies would be discussed at the extraordinary 2nd congress. We are going to start off with this one. ...And people will realise this, they will see that the congress is commencing with a discussion of this extremely topical and important issue" — ought not to pull the wool over our eyes. The decision not to discuss the draft text of the new Constitution at the Congress signified a political defeat for the Chairman of the Supreme Soviet. Yeltsin chose not to risk taking this issue to the Congress, because there was a genuine threat that the document would fail to be adopted.

Yeltsin's approach is understandable. As a practical man in government, who was only just starting to master the arsenal of political government, the issue of food and agriculture was one with which he felt more at home. Providing people with food had been the number one priority in Sverdlovsk. Now he was responsible for the whole of Russia. Finding a solution to the issue of food and agriculture seemed more important. It was an issue that was closer to the hearts of the electorate, too.

---

615   GARF. F. 10026. D. 1289. L. 1-2

It was not quite so close to the heart, however, of the lawyer, professor and chairman of the Soviet of the Republic, V.B. Isakov. He objected strongly to the idea of the new constitution being accepted. V.B. Isakov had suggested to B.N. Yeltsin and the members of the Presidium of the Supreme Soviet of the RSFSR on 22nd October 1990 that they reject the idea of accepting the new Constitution.[616] In his opinion, the draft Constitution was still a bit raw, and needed further attention.

Isakov's stance corresponded, from a tactical point of view, to the demands made by the Communists of Russia faction, whose members had nothing to gain from any alterations to the Constitution.

The failure of the plans to discuss the drafts of the Constitution at the 2nd Congress of people's deputies and the subsequent approval of the Constitution in the nationwide referendum was more serious than it seemed to Yeltsin at the time. At the 2nd Congress Yeltsin and his supporters managed to secure the support of a majority of the deputies. They succeeded in making a host of key amendments to the existing Constitution. These included the law of the RSFSR dated 15th December 1990 'On the amendments and addenda to the Constitution (the Primary Law) of the RSFSR', which enshrined into law the notion that laws and other acts of the Union of SSRs, directives and other acts created by the President of the USSR adopted within the remit of the powers transferred from Russia to the Union of SSRs, were to be in effect within the territory of the RSFSR. The effects of Acts of the Union of SSRs, within the territory of the RSFSR, which infringed on the sovereign rights of the RSFSR, was curtailed by the RSFSR" (p. 76).

Following the 2nd Congress, the socio-political situation in the country became significantly more complex, and at the same time the hopes that had been entertained by Yeltsin, among others, to the effect that the draft of the new Constitution would be approved at future congresses, began to disappear.

'The Insurrection of the Deputies'

There was an out-and-out clash within the leadership of the Supreme Soviet of the RSFSR at a session convocated in connection with the events which took place in Lithuania on 13-15th January 1991, when troops were sent into Vilnius and clashed with supporters of the 'national front'. Yeltsin acted decisively on behalf of the democratic movements in Lithuania. Isakov declared that the Russian leadership had in no small degree helped to enable a worsening of the chaos, and the growth and exacerbation of the state of crisis. This was an open declaration of war on Yeltsin.

---

616   V.B. Isakov: Chairman of the Soviet of the Republic. Parliamentary diaries. 1990-1991. Yekaterinburg, 1997. S. 151-152

At the end of January, these two mutually exclusive political processes clashed with one another. The first was related to the demands made by the organization Democratic Russia that the text of the referendum on union include a second, Russian issue: the introduction of the post of President of the RSFSR. If this issue were to be supported, it would be possible to hold elections for President, which was an element of Yeltsin's political manifesto. Meanwhile, however, the Communists of Russia faction, with strong support from the government of the union, began a campaign calling for an early convocation of a 3rd, extraordinary Congress of people's deputies, where they planned to depose Yeltsin from the post of Chairman of the Supreme Soviet of the RSFSR and thereby do away with the issue of introducing the post of President of Russia.

On 15th February 270 deputies from the RSFSR who were of a pro-Communist persuasion demanded that a 3rd Congress of people's deputies be called as a matter of urgency, and that Yeltsin's report be supplied at the congress. At this early stage it was already clear that there were disagreements between the Chairman of the Supreme Soviet and most of his deputies.

Against the backdrop of a real weakening of his standing among the leadersip of the Supreme Soviet, Yeltsin took full advantage of the skill he had mastered better than anyone else in the country at the time: direct dialog with the electorate, and open public debate with his adversaries. On 19th February Yeltsin addressed the nation on live television. His 40-minute address contained sharp criticism of the union's leaders, and Gorbachev in particular, accusing them of being responsible for the tragic events in Vilnius. Yeltsin called for the President of the USSR to be removed from office.

Yeltsin's TV address enhanced his ratings in Russia but made his position in the Supreme Soviet of the RSFSR more complicated.

On 21st February all the leaders of the chambers of the Supreme Soviet, their deputies, and the deputies of the Chairman of the Supreme Soviet of the RSFSR, except for Khasbulatov, made a joint political statement at the Supreme Soviet. It was read out by S. Goryacheva on behalf of himself and also B. Isaev, R. Abdulatipov, V. Isakov, A. Veshnyakov and V. Syrovatko. The statement contained strong attacks on Yeltsin. He was accused of having an extremely ill-defined position on economic issues, and it was claimed that "a significant portion of the body of deputies" did not share his assessment of the events in the Baltic republics. "Taking full responsibility, we are hereby asserting," the deputies stressed, "that these political measures were taken without the approval of the Supreme Soviet of the RSFSR and his Presidium".

What could almost be described as the key provision in the "deputies' statement" was the assertion that "whilst rapidly losing authority and support among the body of deputies in Russia, the Chairman of the Supreme Soviet of the RSFSR attempted to fall back on a Russia-wide referendum, which was scheduled incorrectly, with numerous violations." There followed a formidable list of signatures: "The Deputy Chairman of the Supreme Soviet of the RSFSR, S. Goryacheva, the Deputy Chairman of the Supreme Soviet of the RSFSR, B. Isaev, the Chairman of the chamber of the Soviet of Nationalities in the Supreme Soviet of the RSFSR, R. Abdulatipov, the Chairman of the chamber of the Soviet of the Republic of the Supreme Soviet of the RSFSR B. Isakov, the Deputy Chairman of the chamber of the Soviet of the Republic of the Supreme Soviet of the RSFSR A Veshnyakov, the Deputy Chairman of the chamber of the Soviet of Nationalities in the Supreme Soviet of the RSFSR V. Syrovatko."[617]

At this session, 272 deputies called for an extraordinary congress to be convened. An extraordinary congress became an inevitability. The only contentious issue was when the congress would start. The communists demanded that it start on 5th March, whilst their opponents tried to have it postponed until a later date — late March or early April. The Congress was due to start on 27th March 1991.

Yeltsin's enemies in the leadership of the Supreme Soviet of the RSFSR were counting on the support of the CC CPSU, and they got it. On 28th February a joint meeting took place in the CC CPSU for communist deputy groups from the Supreme Soviets of the USSR and the RSFSR. It was led by the secretaries of the CC CPSU A.N. Girenko and V.M. Falin, and the secretary of the CC CP RSFSR A.S. Sokolov. Among the many questions asked at the meeting were questions such as this: "When will the CC CPSU finally get to grips with the mass media?", "Yeltsin has managed to unite a variety of intelligent people around him. But why is this not happening in the CC CPSU; after all, someone ought to be monitoring and reacting to the actions of the 'democrats'", and a demand that "individual people's deputies of the RSFSR" be protected.

A rally was held on 23rd February by communist supporters and servicemen in Manezh Square. The following day a rally was held by Yeltsin's supporters, attended by many thousands of people.

At a press-conference held on 5th March by Yeltsin's adversaries among the leadership of the Supreme Soviet — B.M. Goryacheva, B.M. Isaev, V.B. Isakov, R.G. Abdulatipov, V.S. Syrovatko, and A.A. Veshnyakov — there was a call for the authorities in the union to interfere in the situation related to the preparations for the congress. They called on the authorities to "protect them from terrorism".

An assembly was held between 10-17th March at the CC CPSU. M.S. Gorbachev himself spoke at the assembly. Below are the hand-written notes

---

617   Quoted from: V.B. Isakov: Chairman of the Soviet of the Republic. P. 241-242

on his speech made by Girenko. "We are reaching the end-game," Gorbachev declared. "We must win the Russian congress. We must introduce tight controls on television. More than 50% of the speeches there were a campaign on the part of the Jews. We must fill the airwaves with our points of view. We must win the referendum and the congress. A decision was taken with regard to Moscow. A rally must be prepared in Moscow for 23rd March."

The Deputy General Secretary of the CC CPSU, V.A. Ivashko, judging by those same notes, said: "This is a call to action. Preparations for the administrative measures must have been made by the time of the Russian congress. We must shield the deputies from terrorism.

This phrase — shield the deputies from terrorism — became the key phrase for those in power in the union, which opened the way to the implementation of the administrative measures.

Yeltsin's response was the speech he made on 9th March 1991 at the 'House of Cinema'. His 25-minute speech was interrupted 20 times by ovations. Yeltsin called on his supporters, saying that in response to the strengthening of the communists' revenge, "It is time to go on the attack... The time has come to create a powerful political party on the basis of Democratic Russia. We have seen the CPSU organizing itself before our eyes, and we must realise something: they are marching onwards as an organized front. ... And March, and the whole of this year, is going to play a decisive role," he said, turning to his audience: either democracy will be strangled, or we — the democrats — will not only survive, but will also be victorious this year, without question.

We are being accused of bringing about the collapse of the Union. Who was it that broke up the Union, who pushed seven republics out of it? The Democrats? The Russian parliament? The parliament's leaders? The Russian government? Seven republics were knocked out of the Union by the president and his policy. We have no need for a Union in the sort of shape it's in now. We have no need for this sort of central government — huge and full of bureaucracy. We have no need for ministries, we have no need for this huge bureaucratic machine, which has been dictating everything brutally from above for over 70 years. We must rid ourselves of it.

... Today the draft version of the Union agreement has been printed. When addressing the assembly of the Supreme Soviet of the Union once again, the President lied when he said that nine tenths of all this had already been approved. On the Russian side, the leader of the working group, Khasbulatov, did not sign...

I am in favor of the President being elected by the whole nation. I said as much before the elections as well. But I am also for a situation in which the entire structure of power is supported by the people in exactly the same way.

I.e. a situation in which all the chairmen of the Soviets are elected by the entire nation. Firstly, when the chairmen are not allowed to be voted in, the people will see right through them. Secondly, this will mean that there is strong executive and legislative power in the regions. We will know on whose behalf we are acting."[618]

That evening, Lukyanov addressed the nation on the Central TV program *Vremya* and described Yeltsin's speech as an attempt to heat up the situation in society, provoke confrontation and stir up the people against the legitimately elected bodies of power.

On 10th March a rally was held in Moscow's Manezh Square, attended by many thousands of people supporting Yeltsin and the 'defence' of the democratic rights which had been won. The rally, which was organized by the coordination council of the Democratic Russia movement, attracted a record number of participants.[619] It was led by Y.N. Afanasiev. The speakers were: G. Popov (the chairman of Moscow city council), V. Aksyuchits (the leader of RKDD), N. Travkin (the chairman of the DPR), T. Gdlyan (a deputy of the USSR), A. Malykhin, V. Kuzin, B. Denisenko and others. The speakers called for the sacking of the President of the USSR, the Supreme Soviet and the Government of the USSR, the prohibition of the CPSU and the trial it was facing.

On 15th March M.S. Gorbachev gave a TV address calling on people to vote in favor of preserving the USSR in the referendum. The next day a message was published from the Central Committee and the CCC of the Communist Party of the RSFSR to the people's of the Russian Federation, calling on them to preserve the USSR and postpone the issue of the Russian referendum.

The referendum took place on 17th March. 76% of the country's population voted to preserve the Union of SSRs. Most of the citizens of Georgia, Moldova, Latvia, Lithuania and Estonia did not take part in the vote on the future of the Union. The proposal to bring in the post of President of Russia was supported by 70.88% of the electorate.[620]

The result of the vote on the Russian issue of the referendum was a clear defeat for the 'deputies'. The main events, however, were supposed to take place at the 3rd congress of people's deputies of the RSFSR. In early March 1990 a detailed plan was drawn up by the administration of the CC CPSU for the preparations for the congress, dubbed by its creators 'Action plan 28' (the third congress of people's deputies of the RSFSR was scheduled for 28th

---

618   Yeltsin-Khasbulatov: Unity, compromise, struggle. M., 1994, p.67-69

619   RGANI. F.89. Op.22. D.59. L.5

620   See R.G. Pikhoya: The Soviet Union: a history of power. P.626-628

March 1991). 'Action plan — 28' was a scenario for a future congress, which included a prediction of the possible actions of Yeltsin's supporters, and the measures which the communists had to take in order to force Yeltsin out of the post of chairman of the Supreme Soviet of the RSFSR.

The members of the communist faction signed up to the following: "resist the microphones, by means of the procedure, the order of implementation and so on (Separate plan for 10-15 people)." The following were defined as bearing responsibility: those deputies who had to speak at the congress or lead a group of their communist peers. Below are a few excerpts from this document:

"bring up the proposal on another scheduled congress made by the chairman and his deputies. Conduct the congress strictly in accordance with the rules, prevent comments being made on speeches made by the deputies (Khasbulatov), if necessary by refusing to let Khasbulatov lead the congress. (prepare 12-15 people under a separate plan).

response from V.V. Kalashnikov

...

- insist that the Chairman give a speech, rather than a report

- insist that the 300 deputies called for an unscheduled, extraordinary congress on a single issue only — the Chairman's report. No other issues are to be looked at, and these are to be postponed until the next congress. Give reasons for postponing the issues of the union agreement and the federation.

- firmly resist the inclusion of any other issues

response from M.M. Zakharov ...

U1. The Chairman's report

- prepare questions and insist that they are answered after the speech: 45 mins. behind the microphone.

in written format and to all the questions posed (prepare a separate group —

40 people).

response from I.P. Rybkin G.V. Saenko I.M. Bratishchev B.V. Tarasov

...

1X. Discussions on the report...

- inform the speakers that every second or third speaker must engage with the challenge put forward by the Chairman. (and possibly by his deputies too)

- if, during the course of the discussions, the question of the removal of the Government is raised — support it. Fiercely criticize the Government, but do not bring up the issue ourselves, do not raise it in our speeches. Hold fast to the view that the Chairman of the Supreme Soviet should be sacked

- the resp. leaders of the territorial deputy groups, X. On the issue of recalling the Chairman

- on the basis of the proposals of the speakers at the end of the discussions, make sure that the issue of recalling the Chairman is included on the agenda before the directive is adopted. (under a separate plan, a group of 15-20 people).

response from G.V. Saenko

V.V. Kalashnikov

- ensure that norms are adopted for the recall of the Chairman by means of a simple majority vote. Have a draft directive for the congress prepared on this issue. (under a separate plan, a group of 15-20 people).

response from G.V. Saenko V.V. Kalashnikov."[621]

The result must be the sacking of B.N. Yeltsin from the post of chairman of the Supreme Soviet of the USSR, and the sacking of the government of I.S. Silaev. For this purpose there was going to be a carefully written 'score' for the actions of each of the communist deputies and official representatives. They were broken down into groups, and each group was given specific tasks.

On 20th March a meeting was held at the CC CPSU, which was led by a man who would go on to play an active role in the August coup, the Central Committee secretary O.S. Shenin. He asserted that the situation in Russia would get worse from 23rd March onwards, and said that once again tasks had been set for the 3rd congress of people's deputies of the RSFSR — demand a report from the Chairman of the Supreme Soviet of the RSFSR, Yeltsin, organize interrogation by the procurator of the USSR on the actions of the Russian government, and protect the communist deputies from possible violations of their rights by the supporters of Democratic Russia.

On 25th March a Directive of the Cabinet of Ministers of the USSR was adopted, entitled 'On the temporary cessation in the city of Moscow of rallies,

---

621   Quoted from: R.G. Pikhoya: The Soviet Union: a history of power. P.629-632

street processions and demonstrations'. This was followed by a request from 29 people's deputies of the RSFSR — communists who were demanding protection from the prime minister of the USSR, V.S. Pavlov, from the supporters of Democratic Russia. This was a step which had been prepared in advance, and which had been talked about on more than one occasion at meetings of the Central Committee.

The Prime Minister gave a TV address to the general public and announced a ban on rallies, picket lines, street processions and demonstrations. V.S. Pavlov promised to give a guarantee to the communists among the people's deputies, and committed to "protect them from outrageous pranks and open ridicule."

On 26th March a Presidential Edict of the USSR was adopted, entitled 'On the creation of a Chief directorate of the Ministry of internal affairs in the USSR for the city of Moscow and the Moscow region'. The Moscow police force were removed from a position of being subordinate to the city and Russia, and made directly subordinate to the minister of internal affairs of the USSR.

The third emergency Congress of people's deputies

After visiting Moscow on 20th March 1991, the newspaper magnate Rupert Murdoch told readers of the British newspaper *The Sunday Times* about his meeting with the president of the USSR, M.S. Gorbachev. He began his article, incidentally, by quoting something the president's wife, Raisa Maksimovna Gorbacheva, had said: "The peak of tension has reached a climactic moment. The storm is coming, and Mikhail Sergeevich is observing all this avidly."[622]

Both Mikhail Sergeevich and the Central Committee which he led were not only observing everything avidly — they were also getting ready for the approaching storm. The first stage of the preparations for the storm was, of course, the referendum. The support of a majority of the general public for the idea of preserving the USSR ought, according to those who had initiated the referendum, to weaken the position of the republican leaders and create a qualitatively new basis for the battle with national separatism. Under the circumstances, which are well documented, it was possible to consider this task satisfactorily resolved. The second stage was supposed to be the defeat of the political movement which was associated with the name and actions of Yeltsin — the chairman of the Supreme Soviet of the RSFSR. His removal from political life, and the refusal to allow him to take part in the elections

622   Quoted from: L.M. Zamyatin: Gorby and Maggie. An ambassador's notes on two famous politicians — Mikhail Gorbachev and Margaret Thatcher. M., 1995, p. 140-142

for the post of Russian president, was intended to resolve many issues: by breaking him, the union's central government was demonstrating its ability to handle the opposition in the other republics in the union. Moreover, it was now out of the question to preserve and spread the practice of concluding bilateral agreements between the republics, which the Russian government proposed and implemented — agreements which weakened the role of the union bodies. The sense of choice in the political development of the USSR, which had in many ways been determined by the confrontation between the personalities and programs of Gorbachev and Yeltsin, had been removed.

On the morning of 27th March 1991, the first day of the congress, hundreds of military lorries stood lined up in the streets of Moscow.

The auditorium chosen for the Congress — the long, narrow hall of the Kremlin Palace — was full of noise. The deputies who had travelled to the congress, most of whom were staying at the hotel Rossiya, not far from the Kremlin, had to walk through a crowd of supporters of Democratic Russia, and their adversaries from the communist party — reinforced by police lines — to get to the assembly. Troops added to this picture of emergency measures were being taken. Right from the outset, the communist deputies attempted to follow the script of 'Plan 28'. Calls were heard to "replace the audit commission", and "demand a report from the chairman of the Supreme Soviet". This act did not result in any success for the organizers. The fact that the plan was being implemented, however, began to have an effect. A stir was kicked up in the auditorium against the fact that the congress was taking place practically in conditions of an emergency situation. A significant proportion of the deputies demanded categorically that the president of the USSR send the troops out of Moscow. 220 deputies sent a message to this effect to the president of the USSR.

The deputy chairman of the Supreme Soviet of the RSFSR, R.I. Khasbulatov, was sent in for negotiations with Gorbachev. The congress did not go at all according to the plan devised by the Central Committee. On his return, Khasbulatov reported that the President "expressed his respect for the Congress but was not going to revoke his decision." These words from Gorbachev provoked a new wave of consternation among a significant proportion of the deputies. The deputies demanded that the congress be stopped, and that they look into the idea of moving it to Leningrad. Ultimately the view which prevailed was that the congress should be interrupted, the troops should be sent out of the city, and the deputies should reconvene the next day, 29th March.

That evening, 28th March, a huge demonstration was held in Moscow in spite of the ban imposed by the government of the union. It was attended by many tens of thousands of people. The demonstration passed off without any acts of provocation, although each of the people involved was mindful of the fact that the authorities might clamp down on it at any moment. But that didn't happen.

The first day of the Congress provided clear evidence that the leaders of the union had failed. Firstly, the carefully planned removal of Yeltsin from the post of chairman of the Supreme Soviet of the USSR by means of the communist bloc at the congress had not come off; secondly, the attempt to introduce a state of emergency in Moscow had in effect failed. The troops had been brought in and the legal grounds for their actions had been drawn up, but it had proved impossible to use force in the face of the powerful opposition. Thirdly, Gorbachev's 'Moscow maneuvers' sparked off an unwelcome ripple effect.

At "...the most tense moment, when an assembly of the Russian parliament had opened and the parliament demanded that the troops be taken out of the city," wrote L.M. Zamyatin in his memoirs, whilst he was ambassador in London, "an unambiguous statement was made on behalf of the United States aimed at Gorbachev. The State Department's press secretary Margaret Tutwiler read out a statement in which the US State Department called on the Soviet Union "not to impede freedom of speech or prevent the people from expressing their will." The US Administration, the statement read, is concerned by the appearance in the capital of tanks and motorized military units, and is carefully monitoring how the situation unfolds in Moscow. "I think that in the Soviet Union, they are pretty clear about what our firm beliefs are as regards the use of force."[623]

That evening Gorbachev hosted a meeting attended by several future participants in the GKChP (the State Committee for the State of Emergency): the vice-president G. Yanaev, the chairman of the KGB V. Kryuchkov and the Ministry of Internal Affairs minister B. Pugo. The troops were pulled out of Moscow the next day. The 'emergency measures' scenario was cancelled. We shall allow ourselves to express the firm belief that it was as a result of these events, in particular, that a wedge was driven once and for all between Gorbachev and his inner circle, who had reached the heights of political power in late 1990 — early 1991, when the president of the USSR had defined his policy of preserving the USSR by means of political resources. Gorbachev stopped short of using force, and did not assume personal responsibility for the possible use of force.

The men who until recently had been Gorbachev's peers proved surplus to requirements in this situation. They realised this.

---

623   L.M. Zamyatin: Gorby and Maggie. An ambassador's notes on two famous politicians — Mikhail Gorbachev and Margaret Thatcher. 1995, p.140-142

On 29 March the Congress continued its work. The Democratic part of the congress had already secured its first important victory: it had managed to seize the initiative. The attempts to abide by Plan 28 had already had the sting taken out of them. Two key speeches by the communists had turned out to be outright failures — V. Isakov's speech on political and legal issues and Y. Voronin's speech on economic policy.

The speech made at the Congress by the Afghan war veteran, colonel and Hero of the Soviet Union, the fighter pilot and member of the Russian Communist Party's Central Committee, A.S. Rutskoi, caused a genuine sensation. In a powerful speech featuring several changes in mood, he declared that the Russian communist party did not understand what was happening in the country, and that the RCP's objectives were no longer the same as those of the people. He announced that he would be leaving the 'Communists of Russia' bloc and setting up his own parliamentary group — 'Communists for democracy', which would include 95 delegates from the congress, including some of the members of the Communists of Russia bloc.[624] Essentially this signified a split in the Russian Communist Party.

The actual results of the Congress were as follows:

- a split in the Communists of Russia bloc and the departure from the group of Communists for democracy, the group led by A.V. Rutskoi;

- the adoption of a Congress Directive instructing the Supreme Soviet of the RSFSR to draft and adopt a Law on the President of the RSFSR, which was approved by the Supreme Soviet on 24 April 1991[625];

- the election campaign for the election of the President of the RSFSR officially began;

- the Congress Directive 'On the main foundations of the national and state structure of the RSFSR' (on the agreement on Federation)'[626] the strengthening of the political position of the Chairman of the Supreme Soviet of the RSFSR.

On the road to the Novo-Ogarovo accords

Yeltsin had not only held onto his post as chairman of the Supreme Soviet of the RSFSR at the Congress, but had also managed to secure additional

---

624   The unknown Rutskoi: a political portrait. M., 1994, p.25

625   The institutions of the Congress of people's deputies of the RSFSR and the Supreme Soviet of the RSFSR. 1991, No. 17

626   The institutions of the Congress of people's deputies of the RSFSR and the Supreme Soviet of the RSFSR. 1991, No. 16

powers for the Congress so that it could implement reforms. In his speech at the Congress, Yeltsin set out his political program, taking into account the changes which were occurring in the Soviet Union. Commenting on the need to prepare a new Act of Union, he observed:

"At the Union-wide and republican levels it is essential that we satisfy the following political conditions. Number one. The immediate start of dialog between all the political forces and professional associations of all the republics, on the principles of a 'round-table discussion'.

Number two. The formation of a broad democratic coalition of parties, workers' movements and various associations, including forward-thinking members of the CPSU.

Number three. The official rejection of the use of force, including military force, as an instrument of conducting a political battle.

Number four. The development of a system of direct democracy, and the implementation of decisions taken in union and republican referenda.

Number five. Genuine departization of the bodies of the procurator, justice department, KGB, army and state administration; a ban on combining party roles with senior positions in executive bodies and government, including for the President of the country.

Number six. The introduction of a system of delineation of powers as the start of the construction of a legal state. An immediate moratorium on unsanctioned lawmaking at various levels of the legislature.

Number seven. The cancellation of unconstitutional decisions made by union and republican bodies, which impinge on citizens' political, economic, social and personal rights and freedoms, and the creation of an effective system of guarantees that they will be provided.

Number eight. The creation of genuine political pluralism, and guarantees of a multi-party system.

Number nine. The creation of the right conditions for the exercise of citizens' constitutional rights to receive accurate information, and a guarantee of independence on the part of the mass media."

Yeltsin insisted that a coalition government of popular trust and national consensus be set up immediately, and that an Act of Union between sovereign states be signed very soon, as a federative, voluntary association, whose members had equal rights and which was open to new members, and on the immediate formation of new Union bodies. He spoke of the need "to effect the transition to a market economy...quickly and decisively, or else we will see not only the processes of collapse developing, but also processes of divergence. And it is not as a result of good standards of living that the republics and regions are attempting to withdraw into themselves, but because of economic instability, devastation, and social apathy, which are all related to the fact that social problems have not been solved. For this reason a rapid and determined movement towards market relations is capable — uniquely capable! — of binding together in an economic sense our regions, our republics, all of our territories into a single whole — what you and I call the RSFSR."[627]

The political consequences of the events of late March 1991 have been well documented. It became clear to Mikhail Gorbachev that he could not get by without the tried and trusted methods of the party and the administration. A compromise was called for. To the surprise of many, there followed a coming together of two men who had once seemed irreconcilable enemies — the President of the USSR and the chairman of the Supreme Soviet of the RSFSR. The Novo-Ogarevsky process, and the genuine attempts to renew the USSR, had begun. Yet another phenomenon had begun, too — a loss of faith in Gorbachev on the part of the section of the 'Soviet leadership' which planned a "decisive victory" in late March of 1991.

Against this backdrop, Gorbachev did a clever bit of maneuvering: he decided to collaborate with some of the leaders of the republics, who would stand to gain from the signing of a new agreement on Union, but who were insisting on greater sovereignty for the republics which intended to join the Union. To this end, agreements with Gorbachev and Yeltsin were required. On 16th April 1991, B.N. Yeltsin addressed a meeting of the European parliament. Regarding the future of the USSR, he declared: "I want to be frank and direct about this: the renewed Russia is in no way advocating that the Soviet Union cease to exist. On the contrary — we envisage the future of the entire nation as precisely that, a free, voluntary union — a Union of sovereign states which will be held together by a clearly-defined system of agreements with one another. They shall decide, conjointly, which functions are to be exercised on their behalf at the central level. ...The new Union must be built from the bottom up, through the efforts of the republics themselves." This clearly expressed desire to sign a new agreement on union became a platform for cooperation and for future binding agreements.

Preliminary agreements were reached, and on 23rd April, at the suburban government residence of Novo-Ogarevo, a very old estate situated 35 kilometers from Moscow, once the site of a dacha whose occupants had included Voroshilov, then Khrushchev, Chernenko, and which Gorbachev had used for one-to-one meetings with Ronald Reagan and the other leaders

---

627   Yeltsin-Khasbulatov: Unity, compromise, struggle. M., 1994, p.70-73

of the Western countries.[628] It was that the president of the USSR held meetings with the leaders of the RSFSR, Ukraine, Belarus, Uzbekistan, Kazakhstan, Azerbaijan, Kyrgyzia, Tajikistan and Turkmenia. The meeting, like so many others which featured the same set-up, was dubbed '9+1' — nine republics from the USSR plus the president of the USSR, who personified the union's central leadership.

After lengthy, complex negotiations which went on for 9 hours, a 'Joint statement on the emergency measures required to stabilize the situation in the country and overcome the crisis' was signed. This document contained a statement about the need to "sign a new agreement between the sovereign states, taking into account the result of the all-union referendum", the need for a new Constitution of the Union, and the need to re-elect the members of the Union's bodies of power once the Constitution was adopted. In addition, the statement also contained a call for anti-crisis measures to be taken conjointly, for the norms set out in the old Constitution to be adhered to until the new one was adopted, for a range of social measures to be implemented and for a rejection of strike action.[629]

This 'Joint statement' was a very strong political step by Gorbachev, since literally on the day before the April plenum he had enlisted the support of the leaders of the union's republics, and his — Gorbachev's — activity as president of the USSR had become a precondition for the signing of a new Act of Union. The 'Joint statement' had another side to it as well, though, which suggested the president of the USSR would have to make major, fundamental concessions. First and foremost, the union's republics must become, in the immediate future, "sovereign states" — the concept of the USSR is not mentioned once in the text of the document in relation to the future Union. Its political structure remained deliberately vague. Nowhere was it stated that the new Union was going to be socialist in nature. It was natural to conclude from this that those attending the meeting at Novo-Ogarevo had re-examined a series of provisions from the recent referendum on 17th March 1991 and that they reflected the position of the Russian leadership. An undoubted threat to the bodies of power in the union was posed by the provision which stated that after the adoption of the new Constitution, there must be a re-election of the members of the senior bodies of power in the USSR.

Yeltsin, who had in the meantime become one of Gorbachev's allies, had given a clear indication that he — the Chairman of the Supreme Soviet of

---

628 V. Boldin: The fall of the pedestal, p. 395-396
629 The Union could have been preserved. The White book. Documents and facts about the politician M.S. Gorbachev on the reformation and preservation of a multi-ethnic state. M., 1995, p.153-157

the RSFSR — was in favor of preserving the unity of the Union, a Union founded on radically new principles, but which should preserve the best bits of what had happened during the centuries and decades in which the peoples in the Russian Empire and the Soviet Union had shared a common history.

Chapter 7
President of the RSFSR

The presidential elections

The 3rd emergency Congress of people's deputies decided that elections for President of Russia had to be held, featuring a direct, universal vote. The 4th congress determined the date on which they were to be held. The elections were scheduled for 12th June 1991. The various political forces made ready for the election campaign. It was clear who one of the candidates was going to be: Boris Yeltsin, who was backed by the Democratic Russia movement and by the new parties which had come into being in 1990. Ranged against Yeltsin were the powerful party organizations of the CPSU and the Russian Communist Party, and a range of state structures within the union, including the KGB and the Ministry of Defence. The harmony of thought which had once existed among all these parties, however, was now a thing of the past, and the stances of the directors of these institutions differed greatly from the views of many of their employees.

On the eve of the 4th Congress, the sector for political analysis and forecasting in the Humanitarian department of the CC CPSU prepared a comprehensive analytical report entitled 'The Presidential elections in the RSFSR (objectives and tactics of the CPSU')[630].

The forecast made by the analysts from the CC CPSU was not a particularly optimistic one. "The following main objectives," the report's authors wrote, "may be identified:

1. prevent the election to the post of President of the RSFSR of B. Yeltsin and ensure that a candidate from the Communist party is elected;
2. prevent the election of B. Yeltsin, without necessarily submitting to the objective of putting forward our own candidate for the role of President;

---

630   The note was prepared by 17 May 1991, before the 4th congress of people's deputies of the RSFSR. Dated based on content. — Author.

3. after acknowledging that it would be impossible to prevent B. Yeltsin being elected to the post of President of Russia, try to make the best possible use of the election campaign for the purposes of weakening B. Yeltsin's position as President and strengthening the position of the Communist Party."[631]

The report's authors described the first scenario — the optimum one for the CPSU — as unrealistic. A number of reasons were given: in society, a certain "view about the historical guilt of the CPSU for everything that took place, and for its inability to stop the country sliding over the edge," had formed.

There was no leader in the CPSU at the time who might have sufficient authority to oppose Yeltsin, although, in the authors' opinion, possible opponents to Yeltsin in the Communist Party could have been Y. Prokofiev, the first secretary of the Moscow city committee; A. Lukyanov, the chairman of the Supreme Soviet of the USSR; V. Bakhatin, a member of the Security Council under the president of the USSR; or S. Goryacheva, a people's deputy of the RSFSR and one of the leaders of the Supreme Soviet of the RSFSR, who had led the rebellion against the Chairman of the Supreme Soviet, Boris Yeltsin, in the winter and spring of 1991. Furthermore, the CPSU was in no fit state to provide active opposition to Yeltsin and his supporters.

"The party is demoralized right now," the analysts from the CC CPSU wrote. "Confusion, passivity and apathy; a lack of understanding of what the central bodies are doing, and whether they are indeed doing anything at all — these are the characteristic signs of the state the primary organizations are currently in."[632]

The second scenario implied that it would be possible to elect to the role of president of Russia someone who had no formal dependence on the CPSU, but was supported by the party. This scenario was seen as the most realistic one. Potential independent candidates from outside the party might be N.I. Ryzhkov, the former chairman of the Council of Ministers and the man who had been considered a "victim" of Gorbachev (He was supposed to have retired, but before he could do so suffered a heart attack) and V.V. Bakatin, who had a reputation as a liberal and had been removed from the post of minister of internal affairs (although he had also been given a role in the Security Council under the president of the USSR).

The candidates who presented themselves for the role of vice-president in the circumstances were the leaders of the anti-Yeltsin opposition in the Supreme

631   R.G. Pikhoya: Moscow. The Kremlin. Power. Two histories of a single country. Russia at the dawn of the new millennium. 1985 — 2005. M., 2007. P. 285
632   R.G. Pikhoya: Moscow. The Kremlin. Power. Two histories of a single country. Russia at the dawn of the new millennium. 1985 — 2005. M., 2007. P. 286

Soviet, S. Goryacheva, S. Baburin and V. Isakov. This scenario was deemed to be more realistic. "He is making it possible," the report continued, "for the opposition powers to avoid, either wholly or substantially, playing the anti-Communist card. And it is not beyond the bounds of possibility that a communist will be put forward for the role of President, though not as a direct candidate from the Communist party. Moreover, it may be possible in this case to put forward a candidate of our own, but to focus our main efforts on making the second scenario a reality, after thinking about the issue of which organizations might put forward a candidate as an 'independent'.

The analysts found that the third scenario was practically inevitable, however: Yeltsin was going to be elected. "If this happens," they advised, "a series of effective and serious steps should be taken in a spirit of political cooperation and social consensus with the leadership of the Supreme Soviet of the RSFSR and with B. Yeltsin specifically. ... After 'resigning itself' to the election of B. Yeltsin under the terms of a mutually beneficial compromise, the Communist party shall shift its main focus to a second issue, to the contest for the election of the leaders of the local bodies of power. It is here that the communist party has the greatest opportunities and the highest chance of success." B. Yeltsin's supporters are currently putting all the resources they have — though these are not as numerous as those of the CPSU — into securing victory in the presidential elections. The Communist party, meanwhile, must do absolutely all it can to achieve victory in the local elections."

The candidates from the CPSU, or those backed by the CPSU, were given the following recommendations from the Central Committee:

1. Criticize the activities of the Union's central government, the mistakes made by the Cabinet of Ministers and so on,

2. Criticise the inaction and inconsistency shown by the President of the USSR.

3. Expose the practical action taken by the 'Democrats', using the example of the municipal Soviets of Moscow and Leningrad, the swindle involving the '140 billion', etc.

4. Criticize B.N. Yeltsin for being unpredictable and puppet-like, and emphasize his poor personal qualities."[633]

In at least two of the four areas there was evidence of a deep crisis in the CPSU and a split within it, because the Humanitarian department of the Central Committee, which until recently had been called the ideological department,

---

633   R.G. Pikhoya: Moscow. The Kremlin. Power. Two histories of a single country. Russia at the dawn of the new millennium. 1985 — 2005. M., 2007. P.287

recommended that public criticism should be directed at the 'Union's center' (which included the Central Committee, incidentally), and the president of the USSR, who was the General Secretary of the Central Committee.

On 18th May 1991 the leaders of the communist party of the RSFSR gave its official backing to the candidacy of N.I. Ryzhkov for the post of president of Russia, and stated that there was a need for the party organizations to back him in the elections.

On 20th May 1991 the Central electoral commission registered the following candidates for the presidential elections: Boris Nikolaevich Yeltsin, the chairman of the Supreme Soviet; Vadim Viktorovich Bakatin, a member of the security council of the USSR; Nikolai Ivanovich Ryzhkov, a people's deputy of the USSR; Aman-Gelda Moldagazyevich Tuleev, a people's deputy of the RSFSR; and Albert Mikhailovich Makashov, a commander from the Volga-Urals military district. A later addition to the list of candidates was Vladimir Volfovich Zhirinovsky, the chairman of the recently formed Liberal Democratic party.

In the fiercely contested election campaign, a particularly important role was played by the candidates for the role of vice president. Their popularity was intended to help those aiming for the post of president to receive as many votes as possible.

General Makashov, who had declared Russia a republic of workers and peasants, spoke out fervently against private ownership of property, and in favor of maintaining Russia's borders as they had been in 1945,[634] invited Professor A. Sergeev, a member of the Central Committee, to be his running mate.

V. Bakatin invited R. Abdulatipov to stand for vice-president. Abdulatipov was one of the leaders of the Supreme Soviet of the RSFSR, a philosopher who had formerly worked in the faculty of international relations in the Central Committee, and someone who had been critical of Yeltsin but had held on to his reputation as a 'centrist', and who was thought to have support in the regions dominated by other ethnicities.

N.I. Ryzhkov's partner was General B. Gromov, one of the most famous military men in the USSR, not least because he had commanded the 40th army in Afghanistan and brought it out of Afghanistan.

V. Zhirinovsky's running mate was A. Zavidiya, a businessman and entrepreneur with links, via his business activity, to the Directorate of

---

634   This meant, specifically, Russia's claims on the Crimea, which Khrushchev had handed over to Ukraine, and also a host of territories in Kazakhstan which had joined this republic from the RSFSR when the virgin soil was captured.

affairs of the Central Committee. In this instance a character trait for which Zhirinovsky was to become known manifested itself: he conducted the elections as if it was his own personal campaign, and A. Zavidiya was only required as a sponsor.

The situation as regards B.N. Yeltsin was somewhat more complicated. Essentially, all the candidates for president were fighting their own election campaign against him. It was also clear that a convincing win was needed in the elections, otherwise the results might be contested. It would be preferable to win outright in the first round, for there was a sense of unrest in the air among the general public. The legislation on the presidential elections, which had been adopted by the 4th congress of people's deputies of the RSFSR, was incomplete. One of the stipulations, for example, was that the president was supposed to be elected by a majority of electors registered in the lists. This would be a great deal more difficult than securing a majority among the voters taking part in the elections. It was therefore of the utmost importance that the candidates mobilized as many of their supporters as they could. The candidates for vice-president were supposed to help with this task — they were meant to help secure more votes for their candidate.

Among the candidates Yeltsin considered for the role of vice-president was G.E. Burbulis, a people's deputy of the USSR and philosopher who had come of age as a politician in Yeltsin's home city of Sverdlovsk. Burbulis managed to combine, in a remarkable way, systematic thinking, the talents of an analyst, the ability to plan strategically (he led Yeltsin's election campaigns in 1990 and 1991) and organizational ineptitude, the ability and capacity to influence the country's political development and what could best be described as 'the opposite of charisma' when interacting with people. G. Burbulis, who was too academic and overly rational for all his good qualities, would have been unable to secure any additional votes for Yeltsin.

Another potential candidate for this role was R.I. Khasbulatov, an economist and deputy chairman of the Supreme Soviet of the RSFSR, who had made his name during the stormy events at the end of 1990, and in the first half of 1991, as a loyal supporter of Yeltsin. He was one of the few representatives of the leadership of the Supreme Soviet who did not take part in the attacks on Yeltsin on the day before the 3rd congress. Yeltsin hesitated about the decision, however. He would later write in his memoirs that he was bothered by Burbulis and Khasbulatov's inability to be liked by people, their inability to bring themselves down to the level of the average voter. "I could sense how tense these two men were as they waited to hear my decision — Gennady Burbulis and Ruslan Khasbulatov," Yeltsin later wrote in his memoirs. "But neither of them suited me."[635]

---

635   B.N. Yeltsin: The president's notes. M., 2006, p.54-55

When Yeltsin chose as his running-mate colonel A.V. Rutskoy, a Hero of the Soviet Union, people's deputy of the RSFSR and the leader of the group 'Communists for democracy' — a man who had not been in his close circle prior to that — it caused a political sensation. Yeltsin wrote that the idea of putting forward A. Rutskoy for the role of vice-president was suggested to him by his speechwriters, L.G. Pikhoya and G.N. Kharine.[636]

Rutskoy's candidacy came as a surprise, but it proved extremely useful for the election campaign. A. Rutskoy enjoyed a reputation as a courageous soldier who had experienced the hardships of war (he had been wounded during the war — his plane had been shot down and he had been held prisoner by the Mujahideen); he was popular in the army and among the general public. At one stage, whilst campaigning to be elected a people's deputy, he had indulged in some fierce criticism of the leaders of Democratic Russia — the academic A. Sakharov and B. Yeltsin. He was not elected a deputy of the USSR, but successfully stood for election as a people's deputy of the RSFSR. His position had now changed. Whilst still a member of the Central Committee of the RSFSR, he spoke out at the 3rd Congress against the party leaders, taking some of the other communists with him: this meant that part of the communists' electorate would vote for him; on top of this there were certain notions about Rutskoy's honor as an officer, and the fact that his morals would not allow him to countenance any plotting against the future president.

The start of the election campaign provided evidence that Yeltsin's move had paid off. When Yeltsin brought in Rutskoy, it caused consternation among the communist party functionaries. The newspaper *Sovetskaya Rossiya*, which was the mouthpiece of the anti-Yeltsin forces, wrote that a bit of far-sighted political plotting could be perceived behind the decision. Perhaps Yeltsin needed Rutskoy as a reliable partner in this fiercely contested, uncompromising game — this was what Rutskoy had been when he broke up the parliamentary bloc of communists at the Congress and rescued Yeltsin from possibly having to resign. Or perhaps he was a Trojan horse in the ranks of the party, which had been veering to the left — designed to break it up and destroy it. And then Yeltsin would restore his own party, from these ruins — since, thus far, no serious political force had emerged capable of making a claim for power on equal terms with the communists.

The other newspapers (*Nezavisimaya gazeta*, *Rossiskaya gazeta*) wrote that Rutskoi's appointment was the right decision, politically, on all counts: as a response to Ryzhkov's appointment of general Gromov as his running-mate; as an attempt to make use of the 'Afghan effect'; and as a move designed to bring the army, the Ministry of Internal Affairs and the KGB into the

---

636   B.N. Yeltsin: The president's notes. M., 2006, p.55

ranks of Yeltsin's supporters. According to many media sources, Rutskoi was a man who could attract votes from most communists and servicemen, veterans of the Great Patriotic War and the war in Afghanistan. He would be able to become a sort of 'detonator' who would trigger the break-up of the CPSU (according to the newspaper *Rossiya*). Moreover, by bringing on board a progressive communist, Yeltsin was demonstrating his reconciliatory, constructive intent (so said *Robochaya tribuna*).

Second in terms of influence after Yeltsin and Rutskoi was the duo of Ryzhkov and Gromov. *Nezavisimaya gazeta* was extremely complimentary about this alliance — Gromov gave Ryzhov added backbone and decisiveness, and gave Ryzhkov a wider circle of voters. With this move Ryzhkov warded off the myths about his alleged indecision, and strengthened one of the main components of his manifesto — the struggle for stability and the rule of law and order in the republic. Ryzhkov's adversaries put forward theories about the fact that this was a union of the military and conservatively minded politicians (*Rossiskaya gazeta* and *Robochaya tribuna*).

Bakatin was thought of predominantly as an extension of the liberal tendencies of Gorbachev. It was noted that he preached a "philosophy of common sense", acknowledged his accountability, and was honorable; it was not in his nature to indulge in sensationalism, populism, hollow scheming, or making promises that could not be kept. (*Izvestiya*) The candidates who featured least of all in the press were the ones who were considered clear outsiders: general Mashkov, A. Tuleev and, in the first instance — Zhirinovksy. The press treated the latter with a fair degree of humor, describing him as a character from a joke and accusing him of 'Khlestakovism' (Khlestakov was a character in Gogol's play *The Government Inspector*), and rejected the idea that he would be backed by the electorate in the future.

Rabochaya tribuna went against the tide, noting Zhirinovsky's ability as an orator, his enviable ability to remain on his feet for long periods and his abundant reserves of energy. "One gets the sense that things might start to happen around this figure, who is not in politics by accident — not by any means. If Zhirinovsky were given sufficient air-time, he might take some very important percentage points away from Yeltsin. What Zhirinovsky did right was to propose shifting the goalposts and setting new priorities. He said much that was pertinent and accurate, particularly about the greatness of the state and about returning a sense of pride to the nation."[637]

The new reviews of the press confirmed that Yeltsin's election campaign had been a success. *Pravda* acknowledged that Yeltsin, by proposing Rutskoi as his running-mate, had secured the support of the best part of the Russian

---

637   Review of material from ten major newspapers in the period 20-25 May 1991 regarding the candidates for the role of president of the RSFSR

communists. *Moskovskiye novosti* gave the following prediction on this subject: choosing Yeltsin as his vice-president meant that much was predetermined in terms of the delineation of powers. Yeltsin was condemned to cooperation with the reformist wing of the communist party. Rutskoi's candidacy was a resounding success, and the duo were expected to win. *Moskovskiye novosti* felt that the reasons for the choice were:

1) a demonstration of a policy of civil harmony;

2) a guarantee of extra votes in the elections;

3) perhaps, honorable fulfilment of the terms of the '9+1' agreement.

"Yeltsin demonstrated," said experts from *Moskovskiye novosti*, "that he wasn't an anti-commmunist, that he wasn't going to do battle against the communists, and in doing so he took a valuable trump card away from his key opponents. In terms of tactics, it was an extremely clever move. Admittedly," the experts warned, "there are some doubts as to Rutskoi's role following a victory by Yeltsin in the election. Is he going to become a fellow reformer? Will he take up the role of a political middle-man between two political camps? Or is he just going to be a Trojan horse within the changeable structures of the party and the union? It was highly unlikely that the vice-president was genuinely going to be the second most important person in Russia. Was Yeltsin completely sure that he was reliable as a democrat and would behave in a predictable way? If he wasn't, there might be some serious problems in store for him.[638]

On 12th June 1991 Russia's first ever presidential elections were held. The results were as follows: B. N. Yeltsin secured 57.3% of the votes; in second place, a long way behind him, was N.I. Ryzhkov, with 16.85%, and in third (this, too, came as a complete surprise) — V.V. Zhirinovsky, with 7.81%. The press had predicted he would get around one percent of the votes, but he managed to beat rivals who were seen as experienced politicians: A.M. Tuleev, with 6.81%; A.M. Makashov, with 3.75%; and V.V. Bakatin, with 3.42%.[639] Particularly noteworthy was the defeat of Bakatin, who was seen as someone who expressed the political course steered by Gorbachev.

In 22 regions, Yeltsin received fewer than 50% of the votes: the Amur, Kaliningrad, Kemerovo, Kirov, Kostroma, Novgorod, Smolensk, Tambov, Tver, Krasnodar and Stavropol, Bashkiria, Buryatya and Kalmykia regions, to name but a few.[640]

---

638   Review of the press (ten major newspapers) in the period 27 May — 1 June 1991 regarding the candidates for the role of president of the RSFSR.
639   RGANI. F.89. Op.22. D. 81 L.5
640   RGANI. F.89. Op.22. D. 81 L.6

Yeltsin led in the big cities and industrial centers: he scored 85.06% in Sverdlovsk, 77.15% in Chelyabinsk and 71.96% in Moscow.

Most women voted for Yeltsin, too. Ryzhkov won the most votes in rural areas.

People's hopes with regard to the rehabilitation of oppressed peoples meant that Yeltsin won support in Chechnya and Ingushetia, Kabardino-Balkaria, Dagestan and Karachaevo-Cherkessia.[641]

Another aspect of the results must also be noted: by voting for Yeltsin, the electors were voting for his program and for him as a person.[642]

Of great significance in his victory was the fact that Yeltsin enjoyed complete support in the mass media.[643]

The inauguration of the new president was supposed to take place within a month of the end of the election. Nobody yet knew how to conduct this procedure — one that was expected to lay the foundations for a new tradition — in Russia. Boris Nikolaevich attached great significance to the new accoutrements of this process: it was essential that everything be thought through, right down to the smallest details, including the dimensions of the Russian flag, which from now on would be hung on the flagpole at the Kremlin, the height of the flagpole itself, and the structure of the pedestal, which would be along the same lines as the ones used by the US presidents, and which could later be taken on presidential tours.

Also requiring some thought was the issue of where to put those invited to the ceremony for the heads of the union republics. At first it was suggested that they be seated on stage, on the platform. Then this idea was rejected — the recent party-nomenclature presidiums were too fresh in everyone's memories.

Every aspect of the way the day was organized was a novelty for those who established it, but the script for it slowly but surely took shape, taking on a certain logic and legitimacy. First of all the Russian national anthem would be played, then the president would give his speech. The guest speakers were the Patriarch of Moscow and all Russia, Aleksei II, and the famous actor Oleg Basilashvili, who was known for his support of democracy and was held in high esteem by the members of parliament.

Talks were also held with M.S. Gorbachev over a possible speech. It was agreed that he would give his speech after the Patriarch. And then out of the blue, on 9th July, on the day before the inauguration ceremony, Gorbachev,

641   RGANI. F.89. Op.22. D. 81 L.7
642   RGANI. F.89. Op.22. D. 81 L.8
643   RGANI. F.89. Op.22. D. 81 L.12

after receiving a copy of the script for the day's events, sent a message via his own people to the effect that he was not going to come to the opening, but would arrive later and speak at the very end of the procedure, i.e. he would be the final speaker, after the official part had finished. Meanwhile his colleagues, and the leaders of the Supreme Soviet of the USSR, ordered a huge number of tickets — enough to fill up the whole of the box on the right wing of the Kremlin palace of congresses, which, on the day of the inauguration, were completely empty — and it is unlikely this was a coincidence — it is quite possible the thinking was that the empty rows would have a suitably demoralizing effect both on those attending the ceremony and on those watching on TV.[644] Admittedly even without that there were more than enough people who wanted to fill the empty seats.

On 10th July 1991 at Moscow's ancient Kremlin, in the Kremlin palace of congresses, specially built under Khrushchev to host congresses of the CPSU, an inauguration ceremony for the president of Russia was held for the first time in Russia's history. Everyone involved in the procedure was aware of the sheer magnitude of this event, as were the millions of people watching on television. Central to what was taking place was the theme of the succession of power throughout Russia's historical development. In the foyer of the Palace of congresses, under the coats of arms of the Soviet republics, displays of the state awards of Russia and the USSR from the 16th to the 20th centuries were unveiled, along with holy relics — the holy books of all the main faiths in the country — Orthodoxy, Islam, Buddhism, Judaism, Catholicism and Protestantism. Prior to this, the country's new national anthem was played. The anthem, which had been approved by the Supreme Soviet of Russia, was based on the tune of the Patriotic song by a contemporary of A. S. Pushkin, one of the founders of Russian classical music, M.I. Glinka.

Presiding over all this was the first deputy of the Chairman of the Supreme Soviet of the RSFSR, R.I. Khasbulatov:

"Dear people' deputies and guests of the congress! Fellow countrymen! Today a new chapter is beginning in the history of the Russian state. Here, in the historic center of the Russia state, the Kremlin, the residency of the President of the Russian Federation has been determined. *(Applause.)* At the moment when the oath is sworn, the flag will fly over it. *(Applause.)*"

Next Ruslan Imranovich began greeting the guests — the president of the country, Mikhail Sergeevich Gorbachev *(applause; Gorbachev was not present in the auditorium)*, the Chairman of the Supreme Soviet of the USSR Anatoly Ivanovich Lukyanov *(applause, not present in the auditorium)*, the prime minister Valentin Sergeevich Pavlov *(applause, not present in the auditorium)*...[645]

---

644   S. Filatov: An open secret. M.: Vagrius publishing house, 2000. P.85
645   S. Filatov: An open secret. M.: Vagrius publishing house, 2000. P.85

Once Oleg Basilashvili had delivered his speech, Boris Yeltsin made his way up to the lectern. *(Applause. Fanfares were played)*. He was extremely nervous — this could be sensed both in the tone of his voice and in the tension in the way he was standing. Placing his left hand on the Constitution and his right hand on his heart, President Boris Nikolaevich Yeltsin swore the oath of allegiance:

"Citizens of the Russian Federation!

I swear that in the exercise of my powers as President of the Russian Soviet Federal Socialist Republic, I shall abide by the Constitution of the RSFSR and the laws of the RSFSR, protect its sovereignty, respect and defend the rights and freedoms of the individual and the citizen and the rights of the peoples of the RSFSR, and perform the duties placed on me by the people in good faith."[646]

The natinal anthem of Russia was played. An image came up on the TV screens: the State flag of the RSFSR being hoisted up the flagpole above the residence of the first President of the RSFSR, Boris Nikolaevich Yeltsin, at the Kremlin.[647]

There followed a speech by the Patriarch of Moscow and all the Russias, Aleksei II. For the first time in 74 years the head of state was given a blessing by the patriarch of all the Russias.

This was followed by a speech by the President of the RSFSR, Yeltsin. Yeltsin talked about the path which Russia must now take, the path of democracy and reform. He talked about a radical renewal, at the heart of which would be a strengthening of Russia's sovereignty, genuine rights for the people, the republic, and its citizens, regardless of their ethnicity. He talked about the special place of religion in Russia.[648]

"I look towards the future with optimism, and I am ready for activity that will require a great deal of energy; I am counting on the support of the people's deputies, the Supreme Soviet, the Council of Ministers of the RSFSR, my supporters and, of course, the first vice-president of Russia, Alexander Vladimirovich Rutskoi.

The great nation of Russia is getting up off its knees. We are without question going to transform the country into a flourishing, democratic, peaceful, law-abiding and sovereign state. The work has already begun — work which will require great effort from us all. By going through all the challenges which

---

646   GARF. F.10026.Op.1. D.111. L.2
647   Same reference.
648   GARF. F.10026.Op.1. D.114. L.4

await us, and having a clear vision of what our goals are, we can be firmly convinced of one thing: Russia is undergoing a rebirth! *(All those present rise. M. Glinka's 'Glory' is performed by a choir and an orchestra. Furious applause).*[649] The President of the Russian Federation, Yeltsin, congratulated the president of the USSR, Gorbachev.[650]

All these magnificent and triumphal procedures spoke of one thing: Russia was being resurrected before people's very eyes, and taking awareness of itself as the successor and inheritor of its centuries-old history.

Yeltsin was the first head of the Russian state to whom this office had been given by the people themselves, by means of direct elections. And he strove to demonstrate this even in the tiniest details. Many remember this particular episode: after his speech, the presidents walked towards one another to shake hands. Some years later, Yeltsin went into some of the details of this in a private conversation: "Do you remember when Gorbachev congratulated me on being elected President?... I spent a long time thinking how I could arrange it so that he came up to me to shake my hand, rather than vice-versa. I weighed up my options, and after taking a few steps along the stage, came to a stop. He had no choice but to walk over to me."[651]

Thus Boris Yeltsin's election as President of the RSFSR (albeit within the Union of Soviet Socialist Republics) showed everyone who was now leader number one in the country. With characteristic stubbornness, Yeltsin demanded that his main residence be located at the Kremlin. Gorbachev was forced to give his consent. There was now something of a paradox: the heads of two states now resided at the Kremlin, so there ought to have been two flags flying above them. In order to inflame the situation even more, however, Yeltsin did not insist on the formalities. He was given an office in the less prestigious 14th building, which had been built in Soviet times. Admittedly he spent hardly any time there before year's end, working instead in the White House on Krasnopresnenskaya Embankment.

The August coup of 1991

The most eagerly anticipated political event of the summer of 1991 was supposed to have been the signing of the new Act of Union. The discussions had reached the stage in the development of the new Union, which was supposed to commence after the signing of the Act of Union. A meeting took place between Gorbachev, Yeltsin and Nazarbav on 29th July in Novo-

649   GARF. F.10026.Op.1. D.114. L.5
650   GARF. F.10026.Op.1. D.114. L.3-7
651   The Yeltsin era. Sketches from a political history. M.: Vagrius, 2001. P.122

Ogarev, to discuss these issues. The meeting was of a confidential nature. Some key agreements were reached during the course of it: vice-president Yanaev, the head of the KGB, Kryuchkov, the Minister of internal affairs, Pugo, the minister of defence, Yazov, and the head of State television and radio, Kravchenko, were all removed from the government of the new Union. At Yeltsin's suggestion it was agreed that the new prime minister of the Union would be N. A. Nazarbaev. It was also decided that Gorbachev would take up the role of president of the Union of Sovereign States. As the conversation was in full swing, Yeltsin suddenly grew anxious and said: "someone's listening in on us." His concerns proved to be well-founded. "They recorded this conversation, and it may be that this recording was the trigger for the events of August 1991," he later wrote in his memoirs.[652]

On 2nd August the President of the USSR gave a TV address in which he said that the draft of the new Act of Union was ready and that the signing of it would commence on 20th August. On 4th August he departed for a holiday in the Crimea. Awaiting him was a government dacha in Foros.

There are still some mysterious elements to the story of how the coup came about even today, which are yet to have sufficient light shed on them by the huge flow of memoirs and documentary publications.

The possibility that a state of emergency might be announced was something for which provision had been made in the legislation, as was the mechanism for declaring one. These things were set out in the law 'On the legal framework governing a state of emergency', adopted by the Supreme Soviet of the USSR in 1990. Under this law, a state of emergency could be introduced in the country by the Supreme Soviet or the president, but this must happen either at the behest or with the consent of the Presidium of the Supreme Soviet or the most senior executive body in the relevant republic.

Preparations for the possibility of announcing a state of emergency were made in March 1991, on the eve of the 3rd Congress of people's deputies of the RSFSR. After the failure of the attempt to introduce a state of emergency in April, the Security Council returned to the subject of developing the relevant documents. Gorbachev himself had spoken on many occasions of the need for "emergency measures". On 3rd August 1991, for example — the day before he left for Foros — he announced at a meeting of the Cabinet of ministers of the USSR that there was an "emergency situation" in the country and said there was a need for "emergency measures".[653]

On 13th August a long conversation took place between the Chairman of the Supreme Soviet of the USSR,

652   B.N. Yeltsin: Notes by the president. P. 56.
653   R.G. Pikhoya: Moscow. The Kremlin. Power. Two histories of a single country. Russia at the dawn of the new millennium. 1985 — 2005. M., 2007. P. 303

Lukyanov, and Gorbachev. Lukyanov informed him of Yeltsin's position on the Soviet of Federations, and the situation in the country. The next day Gorbachev called Yeltsin. Gorbachev was told that among those speaking out against the agreement were not only his "supporters"[654] in the Supreme Soviet of the USSR, but also some radicals from Democratic Russia — Y. Afanasiev, Y. Bonner and G. Starovoitova. It seemed to Gorbachev that Yeltsin was wavering, that he was beginning to have doubts. "On the whole, we ended our conversation on a good note. I was left with an after-taste, however — I could not shake off the feeling that Yeltsin was not quite giving me the full picture."[655] It is fair to assume that Lukyanov's message had got through. An extremely experienced activist in the party administration who knew Gorbachev's character inside out, he may have played on the suspicions of the president of the union, and put new impetus into provoking his distrust of Yeltsin.

On 14th August the chairman of the KGB, Kryuchkov, told an aide to his first deputy, Yegorov, that Gorbachev was suffering psychological distress and was not fit to work. It was therefore necessary to prepare documents enabling the introduction of a state of emergency. The next day, 15th August, the key documents regarding the introduction of a state of emergency were ready. On 15th or 16th August Kryuchkov ordered that B.N. Yeltsin, I.S. Silaev — the Chairman of Russia's Council of Ministers — and G. Burbulis, Russia's secretary of state, were to have their phones tapped.[656]

Negative information was sent to Gorbachev every day, with the aim of convincing him that the state of affairs in the country had worsened dramatically. It was hinted to him that there was an ulterior motive for Yeltsin's trip to Alma-Ata to meet Nazarbaev. According to the director of his administration, V. Boldin, Gorbachev was deeply annoyed when he found out about the meeting in Alma-Ata involving the leaders of a number of union republics.

On 17th August, in a secret KGB building situated on the outskirts of Moscow, a meeting was held, attended by the chairman of the KGB, Kryuchkov, prime minister Pavlov, defence minister Yazov, the director of the administration of the President of the USSR, Boldin, Central Committee secretary Shenin, Central Committee secretary Baklanov, the deputies to the minister of defence generals Varennikov and Achalov, and the deputy chairman of the KGB, general Grushko. Kryuchkov later recounted that they were all united by their disagreement with the domestic

---

654   'Allies' — the 'Union' group in the Supreme Soviet and the Congress of people's deputies of the USSR, the de facto leader of which was A.I. Lukyanov.

655   M.S. Gorbachev: Life and reforms. Vol. 2. P. 553.

656   R.G. Pikhoya: Moscow. The Kremlin. Power. Two histories of a single country. Russia at the dawn of the new millennium. 1985 — 2005. M., 2007. P. 306

and foreign economic course which had been steered by the Gorbachev administration in the last few years.[657]

On 16th August Yeltsin made an official visit to Alma-Ata — an agreement was signed between Russia and Kazakhstan. At a press conference in Alma-Ata, the President of Kazakhstan, N. Nazarbaev, announced that the signatories to the agreement on 20th August would include — in addition to the ones announced earlier — Russia, Kazakhstan, Uzbekistan, Belarus and Tajikistan. In the following stages, in September and October, Azerbaijan, Turkmenia, Kyrgyzstan and Ukraine would also add their names to the agreement.

On 18th August, a Sunday, Yeltsin's trip to Alma-Ata came to an end. Yeltsin flew back to Moscow that evening.[658]

Monday, 19th August was to be a difficult day for the whole country. The following announcement was made on the televisions and radios of Soviet citizens: the chairman of the Supreme Soviet of the USSR, A. Lukyanov, considered that the draft of the new Act of Union, which had been prepared for signing, contravened the Constitution of the USSR and the hopes of millions of Soviet citizens, expressed at the referendum on 17th March 1991. The radio and television announcers said that Gorbachev was severely ill, and that the country had a new president — Yanaev; they added that a State Committee on the Emergency Situation in the USSR had been established, whose role it was to bring order to the country, ensure that the harvest was gathered, restore the ties between the industrial enterprises and give every citizen of the USSR 15 hundreds-worth of land.

It was clear to everyone: a coup was taking place in the country, Gorbachev had been removed, just as had happened some years earlier with Khrushchev, and the GKCHP had been set up to settle scores with the Russian president, Yeltsin, and his supporters.

The center of political life was now the White House, as the building of the Supreme Soviet and the Government of the Russian Federation, situated on the Presna River, not far from the Moscow River, was known colloquially in Moscow.

On Yazov's orders the Tamanskaya Mobile Rifle Division, consisting of three mobile regiments, one tank regiment and a reconnaissance battalion, the Kantemirov tank division consisting of three tank regiments, one motorized infantry regiment and a reconnaissance battalion. At the GKCHP's disposal

657   R.G. Pikhoya: Moscow. The Kremlin. Power. Two histories of a single country. Russia at the dawn of the new millennium. 1985 — 2005. M., 2007. P. 307
658   L. Sukhanov: Three years with Yeltsin. A first adviser's diary. Riga, 1992. P.14-15

was the elite Alpha unit and B group, which was known as the Separate training center of the KGB, but which was in fact a military unit of saboteurs. The Ministry of internal affairs had at its disposal special-purpose police units (OMON) and a separate special-purpose mobile division named after Dzerzhinsky (OMSDON).

This vast array of forces was intended to demonstrate the GKCHP's determination to break the will of its enemies and force them into submission.

Meanwhile, the day before that, on 18th August — a hot Sunday — many senior Russian leaders were at a private estate outside Moscow called Arkhangelskoe, owned by Russia's Council of Ministers. President Yeltsin had just returned there from Alma-Ata. On 19th August, ten minutes after his first TV address, Yeltsin was joined by the head of his security detail, A. Korzhakov, who began allocating roles to people. Yeltsin called up anyone who was in the vicinity and might come in handy in the work that had to be done, and his wife Naina helped him. Early that morning the prime minister I. Silaev, the acting Chairman of the Supreme Soviet of Russia, R. Khasbulatov, the secretary of state G. Burbulis, and the people's deputy of Russia and lawyer S. Shakhrai had gathered at Yeltsin's house; the deputy Mayor of Moscow, Y. Luzhkov, and the mayor of Petersburg, A. Sobchak, also arrived. That morning, at Yeltsin's house, the message 'To the citizens of Russia' was written. The text was written down by hand by Khasbulatov, and composed and dictated by everyone in the vicinity — Shakhrai, Burbulis, Silaev, Poltoranin and Yaroshenko.[659] "On the night of 18th August to 19th August the country's legally elected president was removed from power. Whatever the reasons given as grounds for this removal from power, we are dealing with a right-wing, reactionary, unconstitutional coup," the message read. It also indicated that there was a now a threat that the Act of Union was goin to be torn up. The message defined the imposition of the state of emergency as a state coup, the object of which was to the restoration of communist power. It was signed by Yeltsin, Silaev and Khasbulatov. The text of the message was then faxed, directly from Yeltsin's dacha, to the editorial offices of newspapers and the information agencies; it was copied and distributed throughout the country and the world. If the members of the GKCHP had harbored hopes of reaching agreement with the Russian government, then this became impossible after this message was published.

The state of emergency had only been in place for a few hours when an event took place which was to have a significant impact on the outcome of the coup. Not long before the coup, in the summer of 1991, Yeltsin had been in Tula, where he was introduced to the Tula airborne division. The commander of this

---

659   B. Yeltsin: Notes by the President. M., 2006. P. 95

division was general Lebed. It was presented to Yeltsin by the commander of the airborne troops, the Hero of the Soviet Union general P. Grachev — the same Grachev who was later tasked by Kryuchkov and Yazov with drawing up the plans for the GKCHP, along with two KGB directors. Back then, Yeltsin had taken note of Grachev, and had asked him: "Pavel Sergeevich, say it were to happen that our legally elected individual in power in Russia were to be threatened with danger — some form of terror or plot, or if people were trying to arrest him...Can we rely on the military, can we rely on you?" He had replied: "Yes, you can."[660]

Finding himself in dire straits, Yeltsin put in a call to Grachev that morning. He reminded him that he had promised to provide assistance to the legally elected authorities in Russia. On the other end of the line, as Yeltsin later recalled, "there was a long pause." Grachev made his decision. And it was no easy one to make. If he opted to go one way, he would remain in his former role, adding to his reputation as a military general the dubious glory of a participant in a coup — and not necessarily a successful one, at that. If he went the other way, the same career path would open up for him in Russia as the one which another veteran of Afghanistan, Rutskoi — a colonel and Hero of the Soviet Union — had rapidly followed, when he became vice president of Russia. Grachev attempted to adopt a neutral position, saying no to neither side - neither his bosses in the union, nor the Russian leadership.

Grachev promised to send a reconnaissance unit to protect Yeltsin at Arkhangelskoye (a move for which there was no need, incidentally, since Russia's senior leaders had already left for the White House), then turned his attentions to defending the White House. This enabled Grachev to do his best by everyone — to Yeltsin, whom he was protecting, and to Yazov, to whom he could have spun the line that he was keeping watch over the rioters.

When interrogated at the procurator's office, after the coup had failed, Grachev said the following: "On 19.08.91 I got a call from Yeltsin, and he asked me what was going on. I explained to him that a state of emergency had been imposed and that troops were marching on Moscow. I asked him: what shall I do? He said I should mobilize a private airborne unit to guard the White House. I promised to do so. At 8 o'clock Portnov, one of the president's aides, arrived at my place and we agreed to collaborate with one another. I tasked Lebed with mobilizing a battalion to guard the White House, to lead it there in person and to report to the President of Russia. Lebed led one battalion to the White House, where he ranged the tanks in an...going right up to the building, thereby ensuring that it would be protected."[661]

---

660   B. Yeltsin: Notes by the President. M., 2006. P. 96
661   Quoted from: R. Pikhoya: Moscow. The Kremlin. Power. Two histories of a single country. Russia at the dawn of the new millennium. 1985 — 2005. M., 2007. P. 318

The commander of Alpha group, general Karpukhin, after receiving an order early on the morning of the 19th August to look after Yeltsin's dacha, and then — in a directive over the radio and television — to arrest Yeltsin and lock him up in Zavidovo, in one of the distant government residences, refused to obey the order. His explanation for this was that he had not wanted to obey this order. Yet it was no coincidence that Karpukhin took note of the fact that he had been given the order orally. This signified that if the coup were to fail, he, Karpukhin, would be held accountable for the whole thing. He had no wish to assume such responsibility. Another scenario was also possible: the special group had simply identified the cortege of government cars which was tearing away from Arkhangelskoye at break-neck speed in the direction of Moscow. The column of four cars was going so fast that the lights of the accompanying cars were smashed to bits by the tiny pebbles sprayed out from under the wheels of the cars as they hurtled onwards.

At half past eight, all was quiet at the White house. There was nothing unusual going on. The buffets were operating as normal and the kiosk owners were selling that morning's newspapers. The only bit of newsworthy information was that the policemen surrounding the building were now armed. In the assembly hall of the Supreme Soviet, the members of the government were slowly assembling; most of them were fairly old and had been in the job for many years. They quietly shared their news with one another, and it was evident that the prospect of "restoring order in the country" suited them down to the ground.[662]

At 10 am broadcasting ceased on all the TV channels in Moscow other than channel one.

The scene that could be seen taking shape from the windows of the White House was frightening. A column of armed vehicles was making its way down Kutuzovsky Prospekt and crossing the wide Kalininsky Bridge, its tank engines roaring; the line of tanks stretched into the distance as far as the eye could see. The vehicles at the front headed towards the White House and began to circle the building.

Yeltsin immediately began to wrest back the initiative, however. He invited to the White House representatives of the diplomatic corps and journalists from Russia and other countries, and at 10.30 prime minister I. Silaev went out to see them and read the text of the message 'To the citizens of Russia'. Whilst he was addressing them, Yeltsin strode quickly up to the pedestal. He began speaking as soon as the message had been read out, but did not say a great deal: he asked the diplomats and journalists to inform the global community and the citizens of our country what the Russian government thought of all

662   R. Pikhoya: Moscow. The Kremlin. Power. Two histories of a single country. Russia at the dawn of the new millennium. 1985 — 2005. M., 2007. P. 320

340

this, since, regrettably, there were no longer any other means of doing this open to them. He ended his speech by advising the diplomats to leave the White House, because the tanks had already started to surround the building. The words spoken by Yeltsin, and his confidence and incredible ability to crack jokes at such a time, meant that people could not help thinking: the GKCHP is going to come up against some serious problems.

Throughout this tragedy, Yeltsin's office was very much accessible, both day and night. He did not shut himself away at all, and was almost constantly talking to someone or other.[663] He made a decision that was the correct one: not to wait it out, but to take action. He sent messages to the people, and to the army — the directives came thick and fast. Russia must know that the President had not caved in: he was at the White House and was performing his duties.

The Russian government had absolutely nothing at their disposal at that moment, other than the law. And they managed to take full advantage of having the law at their disposal. Members of the President's administration drafted the text of directive No. 59, which the president signed at 12:10, a few minutes before his famous speech from the top of a tank in front of the White House. The directive contained the legal description of what was taking place and defined it within the norms of the Criminal code. The directive read: "In connection with the actions of the group of individuals which declared itself to be the State committee on the state of emergency, I hereby order that:

The Committee's announcement be declared unconstitutional and the actions of its organizers described as a coup d'état, which was nothing less than a crime against the state.

All the decisions taken in the name of the so-called Committee on the state of emergency be deemed unlawful and invalid within the territory of the RSFSR. Legally elected authorities are in operation within the territory of the Russian Federation, as personified by the president, the Supreme Soviet and the chairman of the Council of Ministers, all the state and local bodies of power and the government of the RSFSR.

The actions of officials implementing the decisions of the aforesaid Committee shall be punishable under the Criminal code of the RSFSR and shall be held accountable by law.

This Directive shall come into effect from the moment it is signed. The President of the RSFSR B. Yeltsin."

Immediately after the press-conference came to an end, and at practically the same time, the Presidium of the Supreme Soviet of the RSFSR gathered

---

663   O. Poptsov: A Chronicle of the age of 'Tsar Boris' Russia, the Kremlin. 1991 – 1995.P.53

together and an assembly of the Council of Ministers of the RSFSR was held. The Presidium of the Supreme Soviet expressed its support for the address 'To the citizens of Russia' made by Yeltsin, Khasbulatov and Silaev and described the creation of the GKCHP as a coup d'état. An extremely important decision was taken: to call an emergency session of the republic's most senior legislative body — the Supreme Soviet. Only two people voted against the motion — Isakov and Isaev.[664]

There was a surprising degree of unanimity at the assembly of the Soviet of Ministers of the RSFSR. In attendance was the director of the biggest professional union in Russia — Klochkov. The formation of the GKCHP was described as a coup d'etat, and the Council of Ministers also expressed its support for the address 'To the citizens of Russia' and directive No. 59, and called on the actions of the GKCHP to be responded to by means of strike action. At the very moment when the Council of Ministers was convening, the tanks were circling beneath the windows of the White House. During the assembly Silaev announced that he and B.N. Yeltsin would go and talk to the soldiers. The column of tanks had come right up to the main entrance to the building. Yeltsin and Silaev, surrounded by a handful of bodyguards, went up to the tank drivers, climbed onto an armored vehicle and read out to the soldiers, and the crowd which had begun to form outside the White House, his address and directive. At that moment, there was nothing deliberately theatrical about what he had done at all: it was simply easier to address the soldiers in the tanks from the top of a tank. "And through the window I could see a tank. It looked absurd and yet at the same time so very real... the armored vehicle was surrounded by a crowd," he would later write in his memoirs. "I stepped down towards the people, decisively. I got up on the vehicle, and stood up tall. It was perhaps at that moment that I got a clear sense that we were winning, that we could not lose."[665] This gesture went on to become famous, thanks, it would seem, to the TV crews of CNN, and, in the USSR, to the evening TV program *Vremya*, which featured this clip from the Western news reports.

Silaev returned to the assembly of the Soviet of Ministers. The assembly ended with a unanimous vote in favor of adopting the government statement. The statement not only expressed support for the president's directive and for the demand that all the state bodies in Russia abide by it strictly, but also contained a call for the governments of the other republics in the union to "join forces to protect constitutional order throughout the entire territory of the USSR."[666]

---

664   R. Pikhoya: Moscow. The Kremlin. Power. Two histories of a single country. Russia at the dawn of the new millennium. 1985 — 2005. M., 2007. P. 321
665   B. Yeltsin: Notes by the President. M., 2006. P. 107
666   R. Pikhoya: Moscow. The Kremlin. Power. Two histories of a single country. Russia

The assembly soon came to an end. The last person to speak was general-colonel K. Kobets, who led the State committee on matters of defence. He suggested that the members of the government, if they wanted to help defend the White House, should obtain a fire-arm from the security detail's armory. There weren't many weapons available. A few dozen shotguns and pistols were handed out. This was highly unlikely to make much of a difference in helping to defend the White House.

What was taking place around the White House was of a different order altogether. The directives and statements from the Russian leaders began to spread rapidly around Moscow. Fax machines, photocopiers and telephones were all put to use to help spread the word. Copies of the directives could even be seen in the metro, attached to the walls. People headed to the White House. Fences and barricades were put up around the building. Rallies were held throughout the city. Crowds of people stood in the way of the armored vehicles. They spoke to the soldiers and officers, explaining to them that the army was being dragged into a mucky affair all over again. Caroon caricatures of Yazov, Kryuchkov, Yanaev and Pugo were drawn. Civil disobedience was on the increase. It was at this point that the tank regiment of the mayor, S. Yemelyanov, defected to Yeltsin's side — it was to stay with him until the end. Six of his tanks, with their ammunition removed, were the sole military unit of the Soviet army to switch allegiance to the President of Russia.

On the morning of the 19th, the delegations arrived in the city, ahead of the signing of the Act of Union. The Act was due to be signed on 20th August. The leaders of a "host of republics" asked the leaders of the USSR to give them an explanation regarding the behavior of the GKCHP, and Yanaev and Lukyanov informed them that the democratic processes were going to continue. It was announced that the GKCHP was going to act within the framework of the Constitution of the USSR. The leaders of the republics expressed the hope that the former autonomous republics would cease to be the bargaining chips in the political struggles between the central government and the republics.

A sense of unease began to spread through the ranks of the State committee on the state of emergency. On the evening of 19th August it became clear that the GKCHP had lost its first day. The hopes it had entertained of giving its political enemies a scare and keeping up the semblance of legitimacy in the transition of power from Gorbachev to the "Soviet leaders" lay in tatters. There was a growing tide of support for the Russian president, and rejection of the GKCHP. Against this backdrop, there were growing signs of disagreement within the GKCHP. Its most imaginative members quietly jumped ship. On the morning of the 19th the leader of the administration of the president

---

at the dawn of the new millennium. 1985 — 2005. M., 2007. P. 322

of the USSR, V. Boldin, went to hospital. On the afternoon of the 19th, V. Pavlov went to hospital. They were never seen in the GKCHP again thereafter. A. Lukyanov attempted to distance himself from the GKCHP.

V. Varennikov, the commander-in-chief of the Ground Forces, sent a disgruntled letter to the GKCHP. He wrote from Kiev: "After assessing the first few days, I have reached the conclusion that most of the executive structures are behaving in an extremely indecisive and disorganized way. The law enforcement agencies have completed practically no tasks whatsoever. This has led to some very problematic outcomes. ...the eyes of an entire nation, and of all its soldiers, are currently fixed on Moscow. We all strongly urge you to take steps to destroy the groups of the adventurist B.N. Yeltsin. The building of the government of the RSFSR must be blocked up immediately, and all water supplies, electricity supplies, television and radio connections etc. must be turned off. Today the fate of the nation hinges on the solution of this problem, and therefore nothing and no-one must stop us from achieving the goal we have set ourselves. Indecision and half-measures will only prompt extremists and pseudo-democrats to take even more brutal and decisive action."[667]

On the morning of 20th August it became clear to everyone: a decisive storming of the building was approaching, and becoming almost inevitable. By evening the tension was at its highest. Everyone realised that the night to come was going to decide everything — after all, on the previous night, the night of the 19th, the men behind the coup had made no headway. O. Poptsova later recalled: "The previous night, and in the late evening of the next day, reports about the likelihood of a storming of the building was the main subject, and essentially the only subject, of all the conversations among the great mass of people who had surrounded the White House, and inside the White House itself.

It was unusually noisy in the presidential wing of the building. Burbulis's office was used as a head office. Those three nights and three days were packed full of drama, alarm, confusion and at the same time a fascinating mutual understanding between the democrats, the centrists and the semi-democrats. They were united by woe and by a sense of threat which hung heavy over their hopes. For all this diversity of opinion, everyone was pinning their hopes on living in a different Russia. What sort of Russia this would be was not yet clear — but it would be different. The atmosphere of the barricades made itself felt here as well, inside the White House: the sleeping bags, the tea in thermos flasks, an abundance of stained special ops uniforms, gas-masks piled in a heap, an unusual abundance of stubbly faces, crumpled clothing, and red eyes wracked with insomnia."[668] People continued to pour towards

667   V. Stepanov, Y. Lisov: The Kremlin plot. The prosecution's version of events. M., 1992. P. 149 — 150

668   O. Poptsov: A Chronicle of the age of 'Tsar Boris' Russia, the Kremlin. 1991 –

the White House. On this most dicey, most unpredictable of occasions, they felt obliged to show their faces here, alongside the President. Among them was Mstislav Rostropovich. He revealed that he had not told his wife he was leaving for Moscow: "I have come here," he said, "and if it is the will of God, I shall share the same fate as Russia along with you. The nation's fate is being decided here, today."[669]

The key events instigated by the supporters of the GKCHP were to take place inside the building of the General Staff, however. Gathered together in the office of the deputy minister V. Achalov were the head of the General Staff, Moiseev, the personal attaché to the President of the USSR on military affairs Marshal Akhromeev, the commander-in-chief of the land forces V. Varennikov, who had returned to Moscow from Kiev, the commander of the airborne troops P. Grachev, the head of Alpha group V. Karpukhin, the head of B group B. Beskov, the deputy minister of internal affairs B. Gromov, and the first deputy chairman of the KGB, G. Ageev — a total of about 20-25 people. A. Lebed was also among those present.

The task facing them was to achieve what had been beyond the GKCHP by means of a military-political rally: to break the resistance of the Russian leadership. A plan to storm the White House was discussed. Army units of airborne troops, under the command of A. Lebed, in conjunction with the division named after Derzhinsky, which was subordinate to the MIA, was ordered to block access to the White House, and pull away the people surrounding the building, towards the Krasnopresnenskaya embankment; a unit of the special armed police (OMON), was ordered to break through the barricades put up around the building, aided by tanks; Alpha group and B group would then follow them into the breach. Alpha group's orders were to burst into the building and arrest the Russian President, Yeltsin. Another special ops unit from the KGB — B group — was to destroy the pockets of resistance inside the building, using special resources to do so. Helicopters were to provide cover for the attack from above. Overall coordination of operation Thunder, as the plan for the storming of the White House was christened, was the job of the commander of Alpha group, general Karpukin. The storm was due to begin at 3 am on the night of 21st August.[670]

Serious obstacles arose when it came to putting the plan into action, however.

Democratic Russia had scheduled a rally in support of the Russian government to start at 12 o'clock. The entire area around the White House

1995.P.53

669   O. Poptsov: A Chronicle of the age of 'Tsar Boris' Russia, the Kremlin. 1991 – 1995.P.54

670   R. Pikhoya: Moscow. The Kremlin. Power. Two histories of a single country. Russia at the dawn of the new millennium. 1985 — 2005. M., 2007. P. 329

was filled with tens of thousands of people. There were some 200,000 people in the crowd; a huge number of Russian national flags were being waved, and the flags of Ukraine, Lithuania and Georgia could also be seen. The rally lasted roughly 5 hours. Speeches were made from the balcony of the White House, where Yeltsin stood, by the Chairman of Russia's Council of Ministers, I. Silaev, the acting Chairman of the Supreme Soviet of Russia, R. Khasbulatov, the vice president A. Rutskoi, the mayor of Moscow G. Popov, the 'father of perestroika' A. Yakovlev, the former minister of foreign affairs E. Shevardnadze and many others. The crowd went into raptures as they listened to what was being said.

Tens and hundreds of thousands of people had, to all intents and purposes, become a human shield around the White House. This seems to have been the reason why the military units planned to start the operation to storm the White House at 3 am — a time when very few of the people defending the building would be left.

On 20th August there was also a change of circumstances with regard to the defence of the building of the government and the Supreme Soviet of Russia. Thanks to the efforts of general-colonel Kobets, vice president A. Rutskoi, and the head of the office set up for the protection of the White House, colonel A. Sterligov, the rag-tag crowds of people who had come together to defend the legitimate authorities were transformed into something akin to military units. They were armed with Molotov cocktails powerful enough to bring tanks to a halt. Improvised infirmaries were set up and volunteer medics tended to the wounded.

There had been a cardinal change in the situation inside the White House, too. There were still numerous journalists inside the building. Professional servicemen and retired officers from the special forces were taking part in defending the building. Arms were now being carried — something of which there had been no sign on the first day. The interior of the building was defended by a presidential security detail led by A. Korzhakov. Protective barricades made of blocks of concrete were placed on the roof of the building, with snipers positioned behind them, ready to open fire should helicopters appear. There were units of heavily armed men in all the corridors inside the building. Steps were taken to make life very difficult for any potential attackers. The vast building of the White House, for all its outward simplicity, could be a real labyrinth on the inside for the uninitiated, and it was made all the more complicated to negotiate by the fact that lifts were switched off and had barricades put up around them. Businesslike members of the president's security detail, who were managing to keep calm expressions on their faces, attempted to restrict access to the building via the underground communications tunnels lying directly adjacent to the metro lines. Mines were planted on the steps leading down to them. A great deal of reconnaissance work was taking place. None of the people left in the building was under any illusion as regards the outcome of any storming of the building. It was self-evident that if the building was stormed, few if any of the people inside the White House would live to tell the tale.

At the same time, the political leadership of Russia continued to take steps designed to preclude the possibility of bloodshed and restore constitutional order. At 10 am a Russian delegation including A. Rutskoi, I. Silaev and R. Khasbulatov sent a message to A. Lukyanov demanding that: a meeting with the President of the USSR, M. Gorbachev, be arranged within 24 hours; an independent investigation into his state of health be carried out, with the participation of experts from the World Health Organization; that the state of emergency be brought to an end; that the troops be sent back to their former positions; and that an announcement be made to the effect that the State Committee for the State Emergency, which had been created unlawfully, be disbanded. Lukyanov tried to distance himself from the GKCHP, talked of the need to assess the situation further, and insisted that Yeltsin refrain from calling for universal strike action. Lukyanov, in essence, gave no response to these requirements.

As information began to come out about the storming of the building which was being planned, president Yeltsin issued a directive on control of the Armed Forces of the USSR within the territory of Russia. In this directive Yeltsin announced that before the activities of the constitutional bodies and institutes of state power and the Government of the Union of SSRs, he had assumed command of the Armed Forces throughout the territory of the RSFSR, as of 5 pm on 20th August 1991. Yeltsin annulled all the directives issued by Yazov and Kryuchkov from the 18th August onwards, and ordered the commander of the Forces of the Moscow military district to take their troops back to the sites where they had previously been based.

At the same time, the Russian government took steps to create a reserve seat of government in Russia. A long-time ally of Yeltsin's, the deputy prime minister of Russia O. Lobov, joined by a team of employees, secretly drove into a district in Sverdlovsk where there was a command point adapted for times of war. The minister of foreign affairs, A. Kozyrev, flew to Western Europe, after being granted authorization to represent the Russian President abroad. The minister of internal affairs of the RSFSR, V. Barannikov, asked the bosses of the senior and middle training institutions in the MIA to send out army cadets to defend the republic's legally elected authorities.[671]

The confrontation had reached huge proportions. It was becoming clear that the storming of the White House, regardless of its outcome, was going to be the precursor to civil war in the country.

---

671   R. Pikhoya: Moscow. The Kremlin. Power. Two histories of a single country. Russia at the dawn of the new millennium. 1985 — 2005. M., 2007. P. 331

The GKCHP's plans began to unravel. The first blow they suffered was the categorical refusal by officers from Alpha group (this unit consisted only of officers) to take part in the storming of the building. The professional soldiers in Alpha group demanded that their commander, Karpukhin, answer the following question: was there a written order authorizing the storming of the building? Karpukhin replied that the order had been made, but that it had been made orally. It was clear to the members of Alpha that a dangerous piece of adventurism had been planned. In spite of pressure from his commander, general Karpukhin, the officers in Alpha group categorically refused to obey the order to storm the building. Members of B group also refused to take part.

Signs of conflict emerged among the senior leaders of the GKCHP. G. Yanaev spoke openly of his concerns about the consequences of storming the building, which was surrounded by thousands of people. At an assembly of the GKCHP at 8 pm on 20th August, he declared that the rumors about a planned storming of the White House were without foundation.

Moscow's military commandant, general Kalinin, declared a curfew in the city, starting at 11pm. The purpose of this was to take away the ring of people defending the White House, thereby removing the obstacles which were hindering access to the building. Rumors circulated among those defending the building that a storm was inevitable. At 8 pm shooting broke out near the Belorussky station, and tracer fire strafed the sky above the hotel Ukraina, which stood opposite the White House on the other bank of the Moscow River. The level of unrest grew even more intense. Reports were sent into the White House from various sources stating that the storming of the building would begin between 2 am and 3 am. A direct threat had now been made against President Yeltsin. It was put to him that he should take refuge inside the American embassy, located a few hundred meters from the White House. But Yeltsin categorically rejected the idea of leaving the building. "In terms of safety, this option would of course have been the right one, one hundred percent. In terms of politics, though, it would have been one hundred percent the wrong option...It would in effect have been a form of emigration in miniature," he later wrote in his memoirs.[672]

At around midnight Yeltsin, along with the mayor of Moscow, Popov, the deputy mayor, Luzhkov, and several members of his administration and personal security detail, went down to a bunker beneath the White House. This area had been built as a place of refuge in the event of a civil war. It was now going to become the last line of defence for the president. The bunker contained several rooms, all relatively small: for the senior leadership, a large room equipped with wooden plank beds, and a relatively large hall directly adjoining the stairs. In the hall was a security team, and in the room next door

---

672   B. Yeltsin: Notes by the President. M., 2006. P. 136

Y. Luzhkov called around the directors of the construction materials plants and car manufacturing plants, demanding that they send to the White House wall panels and structures for use in construction, and that they position HGVs on potentially dangerous routes, which would make it more difficult for the tanks and armored vehicles to get close to the building.[673]

More calls were being made inside Yeltsin's office. These dramatic events had pushed Russia into the global arena. The president spoke to heads of state from around the world — announcements to this effect were made from time to time by members of his administration. Later, on 21st August, Yeltsin received a call from the US president George Bush: "My friend," said Bush, "the stakes here could not be higher. You have shown respect for the law and have stood up for the principles of democracy. I wish to congratulate you. You were the one on the front line, standing on the barricades — all we did was give you our support. You brought back Gorbachev, unharmed. You restored him to his position. You have won countless friends throughout the world. We support you, we admire your courage and what you have achieved."[674]

After the curfew was imposed, the stand-off reached new levels of tension. The White House remained barricaded, to all intents and purposes. Any breakthrough at all by the heavy machinery could signify the start of the storming of the building.

The convoy of military personnel carriers, which was conducting a patrol, was approaching the intersection of Kalininsky prospekt and the Garden Ring. The personnel carriers' path was blocked by barricades. The vehicles then turned into the tunnel which led under the Garden ring. At the exit from the tunnel, the personnel carriers once again came up against barricades. They tried to break through the barriers but people threw themselves in the way of them, trying to stop them and get inside them. Stones and pieces of equipment were hurled at the tanks. The tanks began to fire on the crowds. Three people were killed. Responsibility for their deaths lay at the feet of the GKCHP, which had sent troops into the city. The man held directly accountable for this event was marshal D. Yazov. And he it was who gave the command "Halt", thereby cancelling the planned operation. The storming of the building had not begun. By the morning of 21st August, it had become clear that the military units had begun to be pulled out of the city.

At 6 am on 21st August there was an assembly of the collegium of the Ministry of Defence, at which most of the generals spoke up for the need to bring the troops out of Moscow, and transfer the Armed Forces from being

673   R. Pikhoya: Moscow. The Kremlin. Power. Two histories of a single country. Russia at the dawn of the new millennium. 1985 — 2005. M., 2007. P. 334

674   Quoted from: The Union could have been preserved. M., 2007. P.304

on a heightened level of preparedness to do battle to the ordinary level. The military activity of the GKCHP had died out. The army had in effect refused to obey the 'Soviet government'.

An event of key significance was taking place inside the White House: the Supreme Soviet of the Russian Federation was holding a meeting. At 10 am an emergency session of the Supreme Soviet of the Russian Federation was convened. The deputies, who had gathered from all over the country, made their way into the building, clambering over the obstacles and barricades, and making their way through the rally in support of Yeltsin, which was still going on. The crowd greeted the Russian deputies jubilantly.

The Supreme Soviet of Russia gave its backing to all the directives adopted by president Yeltsin and enshrined into law those which required approval by the legislative powers. When the assembly of Russia's Supreme Soviet began to be broadcast on television, it signified the complete failure of the GKCHP.

The leaders of the GKCHP fled, heading for the government airport of Vnukovo and thence to Phoros, to see Gorbachev. They arrived in Phoros at about 4 pm. At around 8 pm the representatives of the Russian authorities arrived in Phoros. As it transpired, there was no-one for them to liberate by that time: Gorbachev was now really and truly "in control of the situation". Gorbachev, being a hospitable host, proposed that the Russian delegation stay the night at his dacha in Phoros, and that they all fly back to Moscow the next morning. Rutskoi, however, was in a hurry to carry out his orders — evacuate the President of the USSR and his family, and arrest the leaders of the GKCHP, who were also there, at the dacha.

Gorbachev expressed a desire to fly to Moscow in the same plane as Lukyanov, Kryuchkov, Yazov and the other people with them. The Russian delegation insisted resolutely, however: Gorbachev must fly to Moscow with them. At midnight, the plane carrying Gorbachev's family and the Russian emissaries flew to Moscow. In the same car was the chairman of the KGB, Kryuchkov, and this, according to Rutskoi, was supposed to serve as a guarantee that the KGB was not going to destroy the plane whilst it was in the air. In the second plane were the other participants in the GKCHP, with their entourage.

At 2 am Gorbachev landed in Moscow. There, at the airport, the Russian procurator arrested the passengers in the second plane.

After the coup. The ban on the CPSU

On 23rd August Gorbachev attended an assembly of the Supreme Soviet of the Russian Federation. It was an extremely important one. Yeltsin and the

Supreme Soviet of Russia were triumphant. Gorbachev was effectively 'the accused'. He took the floor and explained how the events of 18th-21st August had unfolded. He thanked the leadership of the RSFSR for their support. The prevailing mood at the assembly was one of extreme nervousness, at times bordering on the hysterical. The deputies were not satisfied by Gorbachev's explanations: they inundated him with questions and levelled accusations at him, and there was a great deal of noise and commotion in the hall...[675]

The President of Russia read to the President of the USSR an excerpt from the transcript of the union's Cabinet of ministers, most of whose members supported the men involved in the GKCHP and had betrayed the president of the union. There were calls from the auditorium for a ban on the CPSU, which had essentially become the ideologue behind the coup.

The leadership of the CPSU had been deeply involved in the preparations for the plot. Later, the party's senior leadership attempted, using all possible means, to distance itself from the actions of the men behind the GKCHP, but no-one was in any doubt as to who had in fact been behind the coup. This circumstance predetermined the steps taken by B.N. Yeltsin subsequently: at an assembly of the Supreme Soviet of Russia on 23rd August 1991, Yeltsin demanded that M. Gorbachev blame the CPSU. The latter, caught unawares, put up some feeble resistance. And then Yeltsin demonstratively signed the Directive calling for a cessation of the activities of the Communist Party of the RSFSR. The next day M. Gorbachev relinquished his position as General Secretary of the Central Committee of the CPSU.

It must be said that neither Yeltsin nor his inner circle were completely sure that the implementation of the Directive would run smoothly. It was hard to imagine that the party would simply give up its position without putting up a fight. A range of precautionary measures therefore needed to be taken, which at the same time would amount to psychological preparations for the destruction of the CPSU.[676]

For decades, the building of the Central Committee in Staraya ploshchad, not far from the Kremlin, had been a symbol of power and might. It had housed the offices of the general secretaries, and meetings of the Politburo had taken place inside, where all the most important decisions were taken. Essentially, it was the main hub of government in the country, and its most important center of communications. In the vast, closely guarded underground premises was an entire system for the control of defence operations. Here there was a system of secret underground transport communications with the Kremlin. Yeltsin realised that there was a need to establish control over the head office.

---

675   V.I. Vorotnikov: It was like this...M., 1995. P.442

676   The Yeltsin era. Sketches from a political history. M.2001. P.157

Formal permission to occupy the complex was granted by G. Burbulis, who was the State Secretary of the RSFSR at the time. The operation itself was led by the prefect for the Central District, A.N. Muzykantsky. The hard part would be convincing the guards not to put up resistance. But this was not called for — the guards left the building of their own accord, by means of the underground tunnels. The evacuation of large numbers of personnel took place without undue complications. But the party bosses had to be taken out through a secret metro line so as to avoid the lynch mob.[677]

All of this happened whilst the deputies in the Supreme Soviet of Russia were having their meeting with Mikhail Gorbachev. On the table next to Yeltsin was a telephone with a direct line to Staraya ploshchad. He waited impatiently for the call to come. At long last, it was reported from M. Gorbachev's ante-room that the operation had been completed, and the building was under the control of the Moscow police. After receiving this message, Yeltsin signed the Directive — the one ordering a cessation of the activities of the communist party of the RSFSR.[678]

On 6th November, the day before the anniversary of the October Revolution, under the Directive of the Russian President, all the organizational structures of the CPSU on the territory of Russia were disbanded, and its property was reverted into ownership by the state.

The Belovezha agreement

Immediately after the coup was brought to an end, unexpected problems began to arise. The joint battle by deputies of a 'democratic persuasion' from all the republics in the USSR against the dominance of the Central Committee and the union's ministries, it seemed, ought to provide guarantees of mutual understanding and cooperation between Russia and the restored Baltic states. But that didn't happen. The problems began to mount. Suddenly there were complications around the borders between the republics in the union. Disputes arose about the right to belong to the union, and about cultural achievements.

A rapidly growing problem was that of Russians living beyond Russia's borders, people who had overnight become "the non-indigenous population", "bearers of an Imperial consciousness", "occupiers", people who would have to prove their right to live in a place where they had already lived, in some cases, for several decades.

677   A.S. Chernyaev: Six years with Gorbachev. M., 1993. P. 491—492.
678   The Yeltsin era. Sketches from a political history. M.2001. P.157

The problem of creating normal relations between the republics in the Union thus became all the more important. A means of achieving this objective was the activities of the State Council of the USSR, which was presided over by the President of the USSR with the participation of the leaders of the republics in the union. The first meeting of this body took place on 11th October 1991.

Taking the floor at this meeting, Gorbachev insisted on renewing the preparations for the Agreement on a Union of Sovereign States, the signing of an economic agreement, and the preservation of united Armed Forces. The man tasked with making the preparations for the economic forum was G. Yavlinsky, who was now "in Gorbachev's team". Gorbachev's proposals stirred up a variety of responses among those present at the meeting. Yeltsin, after agreeing in principle to Yavlinsky's proposal, declared that Russia would provide the financing for the union bodies for which no provision was going to be made in the Agreement.[679]

Kravchuk's position was more complicated. The referendum which had been announced in Ukraine, and the election campaign for the post of Ukraine's first president, forced him to distance himself from the government of the union. Kravchuk therefore gave warning that he could not take part in the preparations for the Act of Union before the referendum had taken place. An important outcome of the first assembly of the State Council of the USSR was the signing, on 18th October in Moscow, of an economic agreement. As the President's press-secretary A. Grachev rightly remarked, this agreement became the latest success in the political direction which the USSR had been taking since 1985.[680]

On 28th October Yeltsin addressed the 5th congress of people's deputies of Russia and set out his political program. His report was dedicated mainly to the problems in economic policy, and went down well with most of the deputies. Moreover, the deputies supported the President's main ideas as regards the implementation of a policy of reform, and furnished him with additional powers.[681]

On 4th November the second assembly of the State Council took place. Yeltsin arrived late for it. Gorbachev began the assembly by criticising the speech made by the Russian president on 28th October. It was then announced that Russia was going to start introducing economic reforms independently. Immediately after this a series of directives were issued by the President of Russia, intended as a direct form of preparation for the introduction of the reforms. Gorbachev

---

679   A.S. Grachev: Over to you now... : A president departs. M., 1994. P. 48—51
680   Same reference. P. 64.
681   The Yeltsin era. Sketches from a political history. M., 2001. P.177

said: "We cannot allow the market to collapse…and unauthorized prices to be introduced, and so on. I must be frank about this: if we bury our heads in the sand it won't do anyone any good."[682] But Gorbachev's speech also prompted people to remember the collapse of the '500 days' program, and the fact that Gorbachev had been threatening to introduce reforms to the economy for several years, but had been unable to bring himself to take this step, which he knew would be unpopular.

When he appeared at the assembly, Yeltsin declined to put his program for Russia up for discussion by the leaders of the republics. He criticized the union's central government for trying to avoid commenting on the changes which had been taking place in the republics in the last few months, and warned that Russia would face a drastic cut in funding from the union's ministries — the amount of financing for the union's Ministry of foreign affairs was going to be reduced tenfold. At the same time Yeltsin insisted that unified control of the Armed Forces of the USSR, which was now collapsing, must be maintained. He declared that Russia would not be the first, nor the second, nor the third, nor the fourth republic in the USSR to go down the route of creating its own army.

Russia was staking an increasingly distinct claim for the role of the legal successor to the USSR. On 2nd October the secretary of state of the RSFSR, G. Burbulis, announced, at a meeting with Russian parliamentarians, that Russia was the only republic which could and should become the legal successor to the Union and all its structures.[683] This assertion was later put in writing in the so-called 'Memorandum from G. Burbulis'. The attack on the union's ownership of the territory of the RSFSR was no different from the same process which was taking place in Ukraine and in the other republics in the union. Against this was the fact that the center of the union was in Russia, and the battle for 'the Union's assets' could by no means be reduced to the declarations made by Gorbachev: if Russia was the successor to the USSR, "what did that make the other members of the union, whose offspring were they? Were they orphans?"[684] The main point was this, though: Russia was depriving the union bodies of the facilities needed for governance, and thereby taking away their *raison d'être*.

On 14th November there was a heated discussion of the draft Act of Union at an assembly of the State Soviet. An argument began about the following issue: whether it would be better to have a unified, confederative state or a confederation of unified states. Gorbachev insisted on the idea of a state that was a union, and when he failed to secure support for this he threatened

682   A.S. Grachev: Over to you now… : A president departs. M., 1994. P. 120.

683   B.N. Yeltsin: Notes by the president. M., 1994. P. 135.

684   A.S. Grachev: Over to you now… P. 105.

to walk out. His opponents — Yeltsin and Shushkevich — proposed an alternative: a confederation of states which would be able to have common armed forces. Yeltsin went farther than Shushkevich: not only would they share their armed forces: they would also have shared transport links, a common space exploration program, and a shared policy in the field of ecology.[685] Yeltsin voiced his concern: "We must make sure Ukraine does not leave us." Shushkevich expressed the hope that "they would sign up to a confederation".[686]

The confederation was seen as the last chance to preserve the unity of the political space, in place of the Soviet Union, which was rapidly collapsing. But Gorbachev was concerned about something else: the thought that a unified state would be necessary, a state that was united and had a union-based system of government. He did not acknowledge the reality of the situation: he took the liberty of saying to Yeltsin: "I am surprised, Boris Nikolaevich, by how you have let me down,"[687] by turns speaking to him as if he was a schoolboy, and then trying to persuade him to continue funding several union ministries and extend their life-span, including the Ministry of finance and the Ministry of economics.

Gorbachev's inability to see the long-term view, and to "work to get ahead" ultimately became a political factor which sped up the processes of disintegration.

Gorbachev underestimated and failed properly to understand the role played by Ukraine in the fate of the Union. A. S. Chernyaev, who knew Gorbachev well, observed that the relationship between the president of the USSR and this particular republic was too personal, and that he was clutching at straws with regard to it.[688] He did not fully appreciate the consequences which might follow the referendum on 1st December 1991. Meanwhile Gorbachev's attempts to fight all the way for a union-based state, and his refusal to accept the idea of a confederation of states, lost him a number of allies in the State Soviet of the USSR.

On 25th November another assembly of the State Soviet was held. Gorbachev proposed that those present put their initials on the draft version of the Act of Union. This proposal was rejected by Yeltsin, who said that there were certain "new aspects" to consider as regards Russia's position, which meant he was unable to put his initials on the agreement in its previous version,[689] because

---

685   A.S. Grachev: Over to you now... P. 145.
686   The Union could have been preserved. P. 246
687   A.S. Grachev: Over to you now... P. 147.
688   A. Chernyaev: Six years with Gorbachev. Based on diary entries. M., 1993, P. 494.
689   A.S. Grachev: Over to you now... P. 160.

by doing so he would be expressing support for a union state, rather than a confederation of states.[690] The document could only be initialled on the eve of the referendum in Ukraine if they said goodbye, in advance, to the idea of Ukraine being part of the future community. Without Ukraine, however, this community would in many ways lose its meaning. The referendum in Ukraine took place on 1st December. 90.32% of the population of Ukraine voted for independence. The idea of independence was one that was supported by the whole of Ukraine's population, including people living in the Crimea and in the east and south of Ukraine, where there was a large Russian population. L. Kravchuk was elected president of Ukraine.

The presidential elections were also held in Kazakhstan on the same day. Nazarbayev won 98.8% of the vote and was duly elected President of Kazakhstan.

Among the members of the USSR's 'presidents' club', only one of them had not been put in office by means of a general election. That man was the founder of the club, M. S. Gorbachev. He had been given the right to be president by the congress of people's deputies of the USSR, the political institution in whose demise he had played a role.

On 2nd December Russia officially acknowledged the results of the Ukrainian referendum.

On 5th December president Kravchuk announced that Ukraine was breaking away from of the Act of Union signed in 1922, the agreement which had established the Union of Soviet Socialist Republics. Back then, in 1922, Ukraine had been one of the founding members of the USSR. Now Ukraine was renouncing this agreement.

In these new, markedly different circumstances, the political leaders of Russia, Belarus and Ukraine acted decisively to draw closer to one another. The Presidents of Russia, Ukraine and Belarus, and the Chairman of the Supreme Soviet of Belarus, Shushkevich, met in Belarus, in an ancient nature reserve and hunting estate in the Belovezha Forest, famous for being the site of the only population of aurochs in Europe. The three 'aurochs of Belovezha', as the press immediately christened them, worked on an agreement on 7th and 8th December, which would create a Commonwealth of Independent States — and it was announced that the USSR had now ceased to exist.

The views of Gorbachev, who was categorically against the idea of a confederation, were taken into account. He was simply excluded altogether from the process of preparing the new agreement. A meeting between the Russian, Ukrainian and Belarussian delegations took place in Minsk.

---

690   The Union could have been preserved... M., 1995. P. 258.

"In Russia," Yeltsin said whilst addressing the deputy group 'Change — a new politics' on 14th December 1991, soon after the Belovezha agreement was signed, "we had, as our friends in the defence industry like to say, an official legend: an exchange of ratified certificates with Belarus. ...This was the first official basis, so to speak, on which we could act. In actual fact we introduced this. And the second official basis was the economic agreement of 1992. And we signed these Documents in Minsk, too. In other words we went there very much in an official capacity as regards this issue. At the same time, of course, we agreed to work out, with Ukraine, whether Ukraine had not yet managed to depart so far that it could not at the last minute somehow be held back, at least in some form of community or commonwealth."[691]

Yeltsin told the members of parliament that he had held preliminary talks with Nazarbayev. "I spoke to Nazarbayev before the trip to Minsk," the Russian president revealed. "He accepted what I said, but, considering that they signed the Agreement of 'the five' this year, i.e. Kazakhstan and four central Asian republics, he says that I am to consult with them and then after we will take a decision on what to do. I called him for a second time on Sunday from Minsk and read out to him the entire text of the Agreement, i.e. after it had been approved. ...I found him when he flew into Moscow, at Domodedovo... He said he approved of it in principle."[692]

Nazarbayev did not travel to Minsk, perhaps because the invitation to the meeting arrived late, when he was already en route to Alma-Ata. It is not beyond the bounds of possibility that the organizers of the meeting made a conscious decision to do this.

And yet Gorbachev's views were nonetheless examined at the meeting. On 11th December 1991, the President of Ukraine, Kravchuk, told journalists: "Yeltsin brought with him Gorbachev's text about creating the Union. Gorbachev was proposing the following: the Ukrainian side was entitled to make any amendments it wished to make, review whole paragraphs, and even draft a new version of the text, on one condition: it would be obligated to sign the agreement. Yeltsin put the text on the table and passed on Gorbachev's question: "Are you going to sign this document — whether the amendments are made to it or not?" He said he would only sign it once I had done so. Thus the fate of the agreement depended entirely on Ukraine. I replied: "No". The issue of drafting a new document was immediately raised. Experts worked on it through the night."

Kravchuk added: "It turns out that everything can be decided quickly as long as you don't run into any 'lumber' along the way, as the center calls it."[693]

691   Quoted from: R.G. Pikhoya: Moscow. The Kremlin. Power. Two histories of a single country. Russia at the dawn of the new millennium. 1985 - 2005. M., 2007. P. 367
692   Quoted from: R.G. Pikhoya: Moscow. The Kremlin. Power. Two histories of a single country. Russia at the dawn of the new millennium. 1985 - 2005. M., 2007. P. 367
693   Working newspaper. Kiev. 1991. 11 December. Quotation no.: Quoted from: R.G.

On 8th December the presidents of Russia and the Ukraine and the Chairman of the Supreme Soviet of Belarus, adopted a statement on the formation of the Commonwealth of Independent States.

B. Yeltsin, L. Kravchuk and S. Shushkevich announced: "The Union of SSRs, as a subject of international law and a geopolitical reality, has ceased to exist."

On 10th December the Belovezha agreement was ratified by the parliaments of Ukraine and Belarus.

On 12th December the Supreme Soviet of Russia ratified the agreement by an overall majority (188 for, 6 against, 7 abstentions), to much applause.

On 14th December B.N. Yeltsin met coordinators from the parliamentary bloc 'Change — a new politics'. Yeltsin told them that on 21st December, in Alma-Ata, an Agreement on membership of the CIS was to be signed by a number of states which had formerly been republics within the USSR. He emphasized: "In this regard we are being very careful to adhere to issues of equality. In other words there are no senior partners here, no older siblings — so that Russia can in no way claim any form of leadership; we are all equal."[694] He informed the deputies that ten states within the territory of the former Union were willing to sign the agreement. He said that Armenia and Moldova, two states which had declined to collaborate within the State Soviet of the USSR, intended to join the CIS.

Yeltsin reported that Russia was insisting on maintaining a common Ministry of Defence until such time as "we sign an Agreement on a Defence Union, a Defence Council and the High command of the strategic armed forces." He added that in the long-term Russia intended to maintain shared control of its strategic forces. "We agreed as follows: command of the strategic armed forces is to be unified. This covers the air force, the navy, rockets, nuclear weapons and tactical nuclear weapons, and reconnaissance. These are the five elements which will be incorporated into the strategic armed forces, which will be a single organism. This will all be unified, and will be controlled by a unified central government.

But disagreements came to light, too. Ukraine decided to take control of land forces and made a claim for part of the Black Sea Fleet. "Our take on this," said the president, addressing the deputies, "is that we should not take the army for the time being, but must be on our guard at all times."

Some of the deputies objected, claiming that nobody was in charge of the army any longer. He tried to argue that for Russia it was more important

Pikhoya Moscow. The Kremlin. Power. Two histories of a single country. Russia at the dawn of the new millennium. 1985 — 2005. M., 2007. P. 367

694   Quoted from: R.G. Pikhoya: Moscow. The Kremlin. Power. Two histories of a single country. Russia at the dawn of the new millennium. 1985 - 2005. M., 2007. P. 370

to have unified control over its strategic forces. He was firmly of the view that special agreements should be drawn up, which would, on the one hand, guarantee Russia's safety, and on the other hand make it possible to avoid spending too much on the USSR's vast military complex. "As far as the Baltic states are concerned," he said, we have agreements with each of them, the anti-aircraft missile system is still in place, because it would be too great a luxury to relocate it from the north of the Baltic states...and that's where all our heaviest, state-of-the-art anti-aircraft missiles are located, and moving them to the border with Russia would cost millions of rubles and take many years."[695]

On 21st December there was a meeting in Alma-Ata of the heads of all the republics which had been in the USSR, with the exception of the three Baltic states and Georgia (Georgia only signed up later). Eleven heads of state signed a Declaration in which they expressed their support for the Belovezha agreement. "With the establishment of the Commonwealth of Independent States," they announced, "the Union of Soviet Socialist Republics has now ceased to exist."

On 25th December 1991, Gorbachev signed a directive in which he relinquished his powers as President of the USSR, and announced that he had done so in a televised address. At 19:38 on 25th December 1991, the red flag of the USSR which hung above the Kremlin was taken down and the Russian tricolor was put up in its stead.

---

695   Quoted from: R.G. Pikhoya: Moscow. The Kremlin. Power. Two histories of a single country. Russia at the dawn of the new millennium. 1985 - 2005. M., 2007. P. 371

Chapter 8
The President during
a politico-constitutional crisis

1992. The restoration of Russian statehood begins

Following the defeat of the August coup, the situation in the Russian government developed in a complex and contradictory way. The more rights the Russian leadership was granted, the higher the bar of responsibility was raised. Russia found itself in a desperately grave position economically. At government assemblies reports were read out pretty much every week about the current state of grain imports, most of which was imported from other countries. The tasks of strategic development in Russia alternated with critical operational problems.

Let us draw attention to one important circumstance: at this stage, when an extremely deep-running economic crisis was unfolding, fraught with social upheavals, the number of people willing to shoulder the burden of responsibility and work in the government fell drastically. The apostles of market reforms in the USSR, who had trumpeted the claim that they knew precisely the right route to a bright, market-based future, took themselves off to one side with uncharacteristic modesty. Representatives of the glorious body of directors with claims to ministerial portfolios also disappeared. The decision taken by Yeltsin to take personal charge of the government during the period of reforms was thus a decision that was not taken lightly. On 28th October president Yeltsin addressed the Supreme Soviet of Russia and announced that a program of far-reaching economic transformations was to begin in Russia, which would involve a lowering of prices for most types of product, privatization and weakening of state control of economics. It was a program of 'shock therapy' — the kind of program which, as is well-documented, rarely goes unrewarded. Yeltsin the 'populist' had once again done something people were not expecting him to do. He assumed the entire weight of this responsibility.

The President's team

Russia's new governmental structure began to take shape in October, and was later enshrined into law by a directive of the President of Russia dated 6th November 1991.

Yeltsin put together the spine of his presidential team in the traditional way — he picked people whom he knew well from Sverdlovsk, the Ministry of State Construction and the Moscow city council. It was a small group of people whom he knew personally and on whom he knew he could rely. The individuals who were closest to him were G. Burbulis, Y. Petrov, V. Ilyushin and A. Tsaregorodtsev, who had all formerly been based in Sverdlovsk, and the Muscovites L. Sukhanov, M. Poltoranin and A. Korzhakov. Yeltsin would go on to change practically the entire make-up of his immediate circle on several occasions. Usually he declined to give reasons as to why he was sacking people, and he very rarely met those with whom he was parting company.[696]

Following the presidential elections of 1991, G.A. Burbulis was appointed to a role introduced especially for him — Secretary of State of the Russian Federation — and took over the leadership of the State Soviet. After that he took up the role of first deputy prime minister in the Russian Government.

In August 1991, not long before the coup, the Presidential Administration of the RSFSR was created. The man appointed director of it was Y.V. Petrov, who had replaced Yeltsin in the Sverdlovsk regional committee of the CPSU and later worked as the USSR's ambassador to Cuba.

The Director of the President's Secretariat was V.V. Ilyushin, who had been an advisor to Yeltsin for many years during his tenure as first secretary in Sverdlovsk and Moscow. L. Sukhanov, a man with whom Yeltsin had worked when he was in the Ministry of State Construction, was appointed an advisor to the President.

A group of referents, whose job was to prepare the President's speeches and carry out analytical work, was composed of staff from the Urals polytechnical institute, G. Kharine, L. Pikhoya and A. Ilyin. Later, in 1992, they were joined by two historians from Moscow, V. Kadatsky and K. Nikiforov.

A. Korzhakov was appointed director of the president's Security service.

Thus there was now a group of people around Yeltsin who could hardly be described as people who shared his views. G. Burbulis had a reputation as a radical democrat and a proponent of radical tearing down of the political, economic and personnel structures. Y. Petrov was seen as a conservative.

---

696   The Yeltsin era..P. 202

V. Ilyushin set forth his views extremely cautiously and remained a mysterious figure to many, as a result of which neither the democrats nor the conservatives thought of him as entirely one of their own.[697] This decision to combine people with differing views spoke of Yeltsin's wish to balance the opposing extremes within his team, and be protected against any possible shifts in opinion. He tried to abide by this same principle in the future, as well.

Two cabinets began to take shape in Russia. First and foremost there was the government one. The head of the government was President Yeltsin. The man appointed first deputy to the head of the government was the secretary of state of the Russian Federation G.A. Burbulis. The deputy chairmen of the government were Y. T. Gaidar, who was responsible for economic policy, and A.N. Shokhin, who was responsible for social policy. For the first time ever there was now a 'team' of people in government, a group of young, extremely well-educated and ambitious specialists, whose 'academic' training had been markedly better than their practical experience of being in office.

In December 1991, Yeltsin, when asked by a member of the Supreme Soviet why people with little or no experience had joined the government, replied: "The choice I faced, of course, was this: either haul in all the older people from the same cadres as before, who would be moved from one cage to another. The Politburo has such a wealth of experience that everything was clear to us. ...We would have to sacrifice something — either youth or experience. A combination of ideologies of that kind would never work, naturally."[698]

In order to implement the reforms, the President requested powers from the congress, during the first, most difficult stage, to publish, over the course of a year, directives on issues related to the banks, the stock exchange, the currency markets, investment and a host of other activities. If the directive was found to contradict the existing legislation, the Supreme Soviet had the right to annul it within 7 days. If this did not happen, the directive would come into effect as law. In order to bring in the reforms, radical changes were made to the structure of government in the regions and in the cabinet itself. The president was given the right to appoint the heads of local administrations. The number of ministries was reduced. The old branch-based systems of government were deliberately ignored. Totally new government bodies were introduced — the State Committee of the RSFSR for anti-trust policy and support for the new economic structures, and the State committee of the RSFSR for management of state property.[699] Associated ministries also came into being — ministries for industry, economics and finance, transport, trade and material resources.

697   The Yeltsin era..P. 202

698   Quoted from: R. Pikhoya G.: The Soviet Union: a history of power... P. 700.

699   Collected directives and orders of the president of the Russian Federation. October — December 1991. P. 63-67.

The forthcoming reforms were founded on the application of methods of macro-economic stabilization. The most important part of this in the first stage of the reforms was the task of establishing the appropriate relationship between supply and demand. This was to be achieved by means of:

- a transition to the application of free (market) prices and rates, formulated under the influence of supply and demand;

- cancellation of the restrictions on salaries and on the increase in resources put into consumption;

- giving permission to all companies, regardless of their form of ownership, to engage in foreign trade without having to go through special registration.

There were also plans to privatize state property, and it was hoped that foreign investors could be persuaded to get involved in privatization in Russia.

A significant component of the reforms which had been begun was the circumstance that president Yeltsin, as the head of the government, enjoyed the support of most of the deputies in the Supreme Soviet, and had quite a high level of support from the country's citizens.

Specific government structures were also created within the administration of the President of Russia. An institute of state attachés to the RSFSR was also introduced. Formally these had no right to get involved in the activities of the executive bodies, or issue decisions and orders which had to be performed by the executive bodies. They were entitled, however, to attend meetings of the government and make proposals to the president.[700] Among the attachés was K. Kobets, N. Malyshev, Y. Skokov, S. Stankevich, A. Granberg, S. Shakhrai and A. Yablokov. In their daily activity, the state attachés were attached to the state secretary of the RSFSR and the first deputy of the chairman of the government G. Burblis, although this convention was not enshrined in any regulatory acts.

Thus G. Burbulis became a political figure who incorporated a range of the functions of both the government and the president's administration.

The question arises: what sort of duties did the man formally considered the 'second most important person' in the state have — the vice president A. Rutskoi? It was clear that by comparison with his peer G. Burbulis they were not particularly sizeable. In the directive 'On the organization of the work of the government during the economic reforms', issued on 6th November 1991, the vice-president was only given a few short lines: he was entitled to

---

700   Same ref. P. 244.

take part in the work of the collegium of the government, and at the same time "the vice-president of the RSFSR shall introduce collaboration between the Government of the RSFSR and the governmental structures under the President of the RSFSR, shall perform other organization and control functions at the behest of the President of the RSFSR within the framework of the powers given to the President of the RSFSR."[701]

Compared to those of the vice-president, the rights of the first deputy chairman of the government and the Secretary of State of the RSFSR were simply not on the same level. G. Burbulis was granted the right to appoint deputy ministers, organize the work of the deputy chairmen of the government, issue compulsory orders and so on.

Rutskoi was slowly but surely forced to the sidelines of political life. Understandably, he was not entirely happy with this arrangement. In late November and early December 1991 Rutskoi visited Western Siberia. In Novosibirsk and Barnaul he came out with a shower of harsh criticism of the concept behind the forthcoming economic reforms and of his peers in the Russian government. He criticized the president over the fact that the government contained "a surplus of theoreticians and a shortage of specialists and practicians", and said that he did not trust these "young boys in their pink short trousers" and that he "had no wish to be the president's Chinese idiot."[702] What Rutskoi lost sight of was the fact that everything he said was going straight into the papers. A huge row erupted.

The third center of political interests was in the Supreme Soviet. R. Khasbulatov chose to go down the route of independent political activity at a relatively late stage. He strove for the post of Chairman of the Supreme Soviet — one that seemed so close yet proved very difficult to attain. The process of electing a deputy Chairman of the Supreme Soviet to the post of chairman dragged on from July to the end of October 1991. It wasn't until 28th October that, with the support of the factions 'Communists for democracy', 'Democratic Russia', 'Working union' and 'Unaffiliated' that he was elected to this post. For a long while he was overshadowed by his predecessor, Boris Nikolaevich Yeltsin. The Supreme Soviet amicably gave its backing to all the radical proposals, entrusted the president with additional powers so that he could introduce economic reforms, and provided legislative approval for the restoration of the historic tricolor as the state flag. It was hard to comprehend that the Supreme Soviet might become a potential opponent to the office of president. But sure enough that was what later happened, in 1992-1993.

---

701   Collected directives and orders of the president of the Russian Federation. October — December 1991 P. 24, 26.

702   R.G. Pikhoya: Moscow. The Kremlin. Power. Two histories of a single country. Russia at the dawn of the new millennium. 1985 — 2005.

The 'incubation' period of radical economic reforms was under way, a period which was at times difficult and painstaking, and in which there were a lot of mistakes but also a lot of breakthroughs. The reforms began on the very first days of the New Year, 1992.

The nature of power in the country had changed. On 25th December the Supreme Soviet changed the name of the country: the Russian Soviet Federative Socialist Republic — the RSFSR — was now known as the Russian Federation, or Russia. The country's name had thus lost two descriptive adjectives — socialist and soviet. Whilst the loss of the former more or less made sense, the loss of the latter gave pause for thought. The deputies had, in the heat of the moment, deleted from the name of the state the description of the form of political power in effect in the country — Soviet!

The addresses of the senior executive bodies had also changed. On 13th January 1992 the president's administration was relocated to the Kremlin, and President Yeltsin was also installed there. The government was moved to the complex of buildings which was formerly used by the Central Committee on Staraya ploshchad. The White House — the building of the former Council of Ministers and the Supreme Soviet of the RSFSR on the Krasnopresnenskaya embankment — became the site of the legislature: the congress and the Supreme Soviet.

This change of address took on a symbolic significance. The fact that the President of Russia was now based in the Kremlin was seen as the restoration of a historic tradition. Yet to B.N. Yeltsin's fervent supporters, his departure from the White House, which had been sanctified by the events of August 1991 and symbolized the burgeoning Russian democracy, came as an unpleasant surprise and a sign that the role of traditional Russian bureaucracy was gaining strength.

The whole country was on tenterhooks ahead of the "drop in prices" which was due to start in January 1992.

B. N. Yeltsin had become more than just President of Russia. He was in effect the leader of the country, and he had mass popular support. He had managed to do something incredible: bring down the almighty CPSU, and hold his own in a brutal conflict with the KGB and the Ministry of Defence in August 1991. People trusted him. He gave them hope. The hardest part was still to come. The reforms. They would be bound to bring difficulties and upset people.

This would surely wreak havoc on his popularity. Yeltsin was aware of, and understood, the cost of the decisions he was to take in the future. For that reason he made a decision which was dangerous for himself but essential for the country: he took personal control of the Government and assumed the entire burden of responsibility. Yeltsin had ceased to be a populist.

On 2nd January 1992 free pricing was introduced in the country. Against the backdrop of a rapid rise in inflation, the nominal value of salaries went up by a factor of eleven and a half between January 1992 and December 1992. In real terms, however, 1992 saw a reduction in salaries compared to the end of 1991 by a factor of more than two, and the average salary at the end of the year was approximately 40% of the average salary in 1991.[703]

Is a new constitution needed?

In October 1991 Yeltsin announced, at the 5th Congress of people's deputies of Russia, that there was a need to start introducing radical economic reform. To this end he asked the Congress to grant him the right to issue directives which would then become laws unless the Supreme Soviet contested them within a period of one week. The congress granted these powers to the president for a year — until December 1992. For a year, the executive encroached (with the consent of the congress of people's deputies, incidentally) on the competences of the legislature.

Sharp criticism of the activities of the government, which had prepared and begun to introduce the reforms, began to be heard at the end of 1991. In early 1992, however, the Chairman of the Supreme Soviet, R. I. Khasbulatov, deciding not to miss out on this opportunity to 'put the government to rights', made a decisive move to distance himself from the criticism of the President. "If I ever felt the temptation to criticize the President, I would be better off leaving parliament," he declared early in 1992.[704] At the same time, Khasbulatov called for a new Constitution to be adopted.

The text of the Constitution, as it existed at the time, was often the legal basis for existing political conflicts. Between 1989 and 1992, amending the Constitution was a straightforward, run-of-the-mill affair, since the Constitution could be amended by decision of the congress of people's deputies. In 1989, 25 amendments were made to the Constitution of the RSFSR. Between May 1990 and December 1992, the congress of people's deputies of the RSFSR passed 8 laws on amendments and addenda to the Primary Law, making over 300 corrections.[705]

---

703   Prices in Russia: a statistical digest. M., 1996. P. 124.
704   Yeltsin — Khasbulatov. Unity, compromise, struggle. M., 1994. P. 120.
705   See: R. Pikhoya. G.: The constitutional and political crisis in Russia in 1993: a chronicle of events and a historian's comments. 2002. No. 4 — P. 64.

On 27th October 1989, the eleventh assembly of the Supreme Soviet of the RSFSR, 11th convocation, passed the law of the RSFSR 'On amendments and addenda to the Constitution (the Primary Law) of the RSFSR', under which the unified system of representative bodies of state power in the RSFSR were the Soviets of people's deputies — the Congress of people's deputies of the RSFSR and the Supreme Soviet of the RSFSR, the Congresses of people's deputies and the Supreme Soviets of the autonomous republics and the local Soviets of people's deputies.[706]

The task of preparing a new Russian Constitution was put on the agenda at the 1st Congress of people's deputies of the RSFSR in 1990. By this time it had become clear that it would be impossible to get by without making radical revisions to the old Constitution of the RSFSR from 1978, without replacing it. In order to prepare a new Russian Constitution, a Constitutional Commission was set up, by means of a directive from the 1st Congress of people's deputies of the RSFSR dated 16th July 1990. Boris Yeltsin was elected Chairman of the Constitutional Commission; at the time he was the Chairman of the Supreme Soviet of the RSFSR. Within the commission, a working group was set up under R. Khasbulatov,[707] the deputy Chairman of the Supreme Soviet, which, in the summer of 1990, set to work drafting the new Russian Constitution.

In November 1991 a corrected draft of the new Constitution was, by decision of the Constitutional commission and the Soviet of the Republic of the Supreme Soviet of the Russian Federation, presented by President Boris Yeltsin to the 5th congress of people's deputies of the Russian Federation and duly recognised by the Congress.[708]

On 6th April 1992 the 6th Congress of people's deputies of the RSFSR opened. The day before the Congress opened, on 19th March 1992, the deputy Chairman of the Supreme Soviet, S. Filatov, told *Rossiskaya gazeta* that "the most important issue as regards the competencies of the 6th Congress is to pass this Constitution", and everything else can be decided by the Supreme Soviet.

The 6th Congress of people's deputies

At the 6th Congress of people's deputies, however, in April 1992, the main subject of discussion was not the Constitution, but how people felt about the government. Although the program of radical reforms had been unveiled

---

706   GARF. F. 10026. Op.1. L. 1.
707   GARF. F.10026. Op. 3. D. 170. L. 9.
708   GARF. F. 10026. Op.1. D.323. L. 4.

by Boris Yeltsin, everyone knew that it had in fact been written by leading ministers from the Russian government: Y. Gaidar, A. Shokhin, A. Chubais and others. Four months had now passed since the radical reforms were introduced, and prices had shot up; it had now become politically advantageous to criticise Gaidar. Some of the deputies flung passionate accusations against the 'monetarists', who had bankrupted Russia, sold her out and destroyed her...

The Chairman of the Supreme Soviet, R. I. Khasbulatov, said openly that the Supreme Soviet "had in a certain sense taken charge of a movement which was opposed to the economic reforms." A peculiar feature of the political debate at this stage was the fact that the main object of criticism was the government and its deputy prime ministers — Y. T. Gaidar, G. A. Burbulis and M. N. Poltoranin. Among the government's most stubborn critics was the vice-president A. V. Rutskoi. It was he, however, along with the Chairman of the Supreme Soviet, R. I. Khasbulatov, that brought the president himself "out from under the criticism". For his part, Boris Yeltsin made a decisive move at the Congress to defend the "government of reforms".

A decisive role in terms of the government being able to maintain its chosen course was the support it had from Boris Yeltsin. In his address to the Congress on 7th April (Yeltsin had wanted Yegor Gaidar, the government's first vice-premier, to present the report, but the Congress demanded that Yeltsin do so), the President acknowledged that not everything was rosy, and that of particular concern was the interruption to the program of social protection for the population and funding for subsidized areas, and that healthcare was in critical condition. The President was nonetheless convinced that he and the government had chosen the right path toward economic reform. "It is my deeply held conviction that the correct decisions were made, both at the 5th Congress of people's deputies and after it — including the decisions on the additional powers and on the head of the government. <...> In the space of three months the government demonstrated that it is able to do its job, that it is capable, without panicking, of methodically going ahead with its chosen course, and absorbing the blows of fierce criticism — criticism which was not always justified," Yeltsin said in his address.[709]

The next day, following Yeltsin's address to the Congress, the newspaper *Moskovsky Komsomolets* wrote: "after hearing B. Yeltsin's speech, the deputies have not been expressing much disagreement over the future course of the economic reforms. In essence, this dispute is of a much more deep-lying significance: the question of power arises. Immediately adjacent to this issue is that of a future cause of conflict — the new Constitution. Yeltsin and

---

709   The sixth congress of people's deputies of the Russian Federation. Transcript report. M., 1992 Vol.1-P.120-121.

the bloc of democratic parties are in favor of a presidential republic. The president must stay in the post of premier in order to free the government from the influence of parliament, which can be replaced. In their view, it is not currently possible for the republic to pull itself together without a strong executive.

It is easy to understand how the lawmakers are thinking, too: they think of their assemblies as being responsible to an equal extent for the success of the reforms, and therefore want to control everything, right down to the last detail."[710]

This clash of opinions about the nature of state power in Russia, and about what form the country's new Constitution ought to take, took place against a backdrop of furious rows in the country about the course of the economic reforms.

It has to be said that Boris Yeltsin's support for Gaidar's reforms cost him a significant share of his political authority — after all, the unpopular government was generally thought of as the Yeltsin-Gaidar government. Yeltsin, who had grown used to being popular, found himself in a dificult situation not just politically but also psychologically, and he sensed this at the 6th Congress of people's deputies in Russia. At this Congress B. Yeltsin came up against a brutal abruption of his policy, and the number of accusations made against him from the floor of the Congress seemed endless. Yeltsin was even accused of having undermined the birth rate in the country, such that Russia had a demographic catastrophe lying in store for it.

Right at the start of the 6th Congress of people's deputies, the opposition decided to deal a decisive blow to Gaidar and the course he was steering. At the Congress, a draft directive was passed on the activities of the government, which included the clause: "Declare the course of the economic reforms unsatisfactory." It was proposed that the President present to the Supreme Soviet, within a month, a draft law on the government and a new candidate for leader of it. In response to this, members of the government, led by Gaidar, served notice that they were collectively resigning, accusing the legislature of "irresponsible populism". Nobody had seen this coming — not even Yeltsin.[711] And the Congress took a step back — it voted in favor of the 'Declaration of support for economic reform in the Russian Federation'.

The notice served by Gaidar and his ministers was not accepted.

Despite the circumstances, the President managed to save his political course by resorting to certain concessions to the legislators. "Thus, if we were to

---

710   Moskovsky komsomolets. 1992. 9 April.
711   B. Yeltsin: Notes by the President. M., 2006. P. 288

use military terminology," wrote Y. Gaidar, "it could be said that in May —
August 1991 the government retreated under an onslaught from advancing
forces, fighting a rear-guard action and attempting, as far as was possible, to
hold onto some of the most important areas, and in some areas it continued
to go on the offensive."[712] Yeltsin later wrote in his memoirs that he had not
felt disappointed in Gaidar, "and I was certain that if his team were allowed to
keep working for another year, the economy would kick on, normal processes
would commence in industry, and we would start seeing the investment from
the West which all our governments dreamed about."[713]

Despite these disagreements, the Supreme Soviet was not yet ready, at the 6th
Congress of people's deputies, for direct confrontation with the president, and
the main blow was suffered by the government. The president also continued
looking for paths toward consensus and compromise. Addressing the Congress
on 10th April 1992, Boris Yeltsin said: "Personally, of course, I did not and
do not wish, nor do I intend, to get into a confrontation with the Congress,
especially given that both the Congress, and you, as deputies, were elected
by all the people, and I was elected by all the people, and therefore we must
find solutions which can be implemented together with consensus, without,
of course, absolving ourselves of responsibility for the statements which were
made before the elections for President of the Russian Federation."[714]

The federal agreement

An extremely important event which took place at the 6th Congress was the
ratifying, on 10th April 1992, of a Federative agreement, signed several days
earlier on 31st March. The federative agreement was designed, according to
President Yeltsin, to "remove the threat of collapse which is hanging over our
Motherland."[715] He restored order to relations between the central government,
the republics and the Russian regions, and laid down the foundations of
Russian federalism. The Congress gave the Federative agreement with the
status of an integral part of the Russian Constitution. The approval of the
Federative agreement — an extremely important document which ensured
that Russian unity was safeguarded throughout the difficult 1990s — was
probably the last joint act by the Congress and the Supreme Congress, on the
one hand, and the president, on the other hand. This document was supposed
to become, in the president's words, a component part of the future Russian
Constitution.

---

712   Y. Gaidar: Days of defeats and victories. — M., 1996. — S. 203.
713   B.N. Yeltsin: The Presidential marathon. — M., 2000.
714   The sixth congress of people's deputies of the Russian Federation. Transcript. Vol.
2-M., 1992. — P. 17
715   Quoted from: R.G. Pikhoya: Moscow. The Kremlin. Power. Two histories of a single
country. Russia at the dawn of the new millennium. 1985 - 2005. M., 2007. P. 414

In his speech on the outcome of the 6th Congress of people's deputies on 21st April 1992, Yeltsin said that the most important outcome of the 6th Congress was the fact that it had safeguarded the strategic course of radical reforms, but at the same time the Congress had not been wholly satisfactory, since a series of extremely important issues had been left unresolved.[716]

"Solutions have yet to be found for problems which are rendering the coming into being of Russian statehood more complicated. We may very soon come up against some extremely difficult problems in terms of the relations between our state institutions. The main reason for this is the continuing constitutional crisis, which is becoming increasingly chronic. The current Primary Law is hopelessly behind the times. It has not proved possible to address this problem by means of amendments. It is probably clear to all of us by now that the idea of updating the Constitution by means of partial amendments has long since outgrown its usefulness."[717]

The president said that the absence of clearly defined and stable division of powers between the institutions of the legislature and the executive was provoking a struggle for dominance and creating artificial competition between them. And this was undermining the principle of the division of powers and making it more difficult for them to cooperate.

The battle between the two centers of power, the Supreme Soviet and the President, was on a matter of principle: it was about a collision between two different conceptions of political reform, two different methods of organizing power, and two different methods of implementing the reforms.

The opposition

In May 1992 the newspaper *Izvestiya*, citing "authoritative sources" reported that President Yeltsin had decided to call for a referendum. On 14th May, at a Congress of the Russian movement for democratic reform, a number of speakers accused the Soviets of slowing down the path to reform, and said that the battle must be taken to the Soviets and the duopoly on power to which they had given rise. G. K. Popov, during his speech at this Congress, claimed that President Yeltsin shared this view of the Soviets.[718]

The president was a little more cautious, however: he did not wish to act "based on hints"; he demonstrated a determination to "keep out of the fray"

---

716   The sixth Congress of people's deputies. Transcript. Vol.5. — M., 1992. — P.431
717   The sixth Congress of people's deputies. Transcript. Vol.5. — M., 1992. — P.431
718   R.G. Pikhoya: Moscow. The Kremlin. Power. Two histories of a single country. Russia at the dawn of the new millennium. 1985 — 2005. M., 2007. P. 415

— or at least, he did not hasten to take any measures. What made Yeltsin's position difficult was that on this occasion he had "his own men" ranged against him. The very same Congress and Supreme Soviet which he had taken charge of in 1990-1991 — deputies, many of whom had been alongside him during those difficult days in August 1991. On the eve of the Congress of people's deputies, Yeltsin declared: "Russia needs a breather following this utterly fruitless political confrontation. We need a political truce during this stabilization period, which ought to take between a year and eighteen months.

...It is essential that we have clear delineation of their functions, powers and responsibility for the consequences of the decisions they take." The president announced that "he would not agree to any replacement of the constitutional bodies of power whatsoever."[719]

The balance of power in the Supreme Soviet had changed, too. Many active supporters of the president had left it and joined the ranks of the president's structures of power. The leadership of the Supreme Soviet had also changed. The following deputies to Khasbulatov, and supporters of the president, had left one after another: S.A. Filatov, V.F. Shumeiko and Y. Yarov. They were replaced by supporters of the communist party, Y. Voronin and V. Syrovatko.

An open and radical opposition to the president began to take shape within the Supreme Soviet, which not only began to adopt "parliamentary" methods of doing battle, but also began to call for direct defiance of the authorities. The leaders of the Associated Opposition were the deputies S. Baburin, N. Pavlov, V. Isakov, generals A. Makashov and A. Sterligov, and the leader of the Russian communists G. Zyuganov.

The Associated Opposition called for: the sacking of the Yeltsin-Gaidar government;

a refusal to grant more powers to the president and to allow any interference whatsoever in the economy;

the formation of a government of the people's trust, which would be given emergency powers so that it could get the national economy through the crisis.[720]

The leaders of the associated opposition announced at the end of June 1992: "The Yeltsin regime, in its current form, has only months to live — perhaps even weeks.

In an attempt to save itself, it is beginning to change the décor and bring new politicians, presented as squeaky clean, to the fore... B. Yeltsin is not

719   Yeltsin — Khasbulatov. Unity, compromise, struggle. P. 199.
720   R.G. Pikhoya: Moscow. The Kremlin. Power. Two histories of a single country. Russia at the dawn of the new millennium. 1985 — 2005. M., 2007. P. 416

even able to have recourse to emergency measures, since in effect he lacks the support of the army and the law enforcement agencies... It is possible we may see a dictator-like coup, the disbandment of the congress and the arrest of the leaders of the patriotic movement. But this will only serve to extend for a short time the death throes of the regime, which have already begun."[721] They demanded that an emergency congress be called, at which they intended to sack the government and impeach the president.

The actions of the associated opposition became increasingly radical. In June 1992 they began to picket the state television broadcaster in Ostankino: a protest village was set up around the TV center, where the tone was set by people who were openly and firmly opposed to the president. On 24th October 1992 the first ever congress of the Front for national rescue (FNR) took place. The FNR had become the opposition's main weapon.

The pressure on the President from the opposition intensified: his opponents wanted the entire team of reformers to be replaced. Yeltsin conducted a 'symbolic' re-shuffle of his team. In July 1992, Victor Geraschenko, who had previously been the director of the State Bank of the USSR, was confirmed as the chairman of the Central bank of Russia. Gerashchenko, a competent manager, was pretty sceptical about liberal ideas and made no secret of it. Yeltsin later admitted that this appointment had been a mistake.

P. Aven was removed from the Government — he had been the minister for foreign trade connections, and one of the men closest to Y. Gaidar. Yeltsin brought into the Government several people whom he described as "strong managers" — V. Chernomyrdin, V. Shumeiko and G. Khizha.

Though the reformers interpreted this as a catastrophe and the press predicted it would mean an end to the reforms, most of the people who had joined the Government soon got used to the new economic tools at their disposal and found their feet in Gaidar's team.

In June 1992, Yeltsin, who was now head of the Government, proposed this role to Gaidar. Realising, however, that the Supreme Soviet would not support his candidacy for the post of prime minister, he appointed him the "acting" premier.

The Secretary of State G. Burbulis, in the general public's eyes, personified the ideology of the political reforms. The opposition considered him their sworn enemy and demanded that he be sacked. On the eve of the 7th congress of people's deputies, in order partially to satisfy the demands of the opposition, Yeltsin signed a Directive on the removal of G. Burbulis from the position of Secretary of State, under the President. The position of Secretary of State itself was abolished.

---

721   Same ref.

Also sacked was the minister for print and information M. Poltoranin.

On the eve of the 7th Congress of people's deputies, the leaders of the Supreme Soviet attempted in advance to consolidate their positions in the country's regions. On 2nd November an assembly of the Novosibirsk regional Soviet agreed to the recommendation made by the 7th Congress to cancel the additional powers granted to the President of the Russian Federation.

Political conflict at the 7th congress of people's deputies of the Russian Federation

On 1st December 1992, when the additional powers granted to the President and given to him by the 5th Congress, had expired, the 7th Congress of people's deputies of Russia set to work. Now the President was "within the sights" of the law-makers.

At the 7th Congress, in December 1992, there was a need to decide the issue of the leadership of the Russian government, for which the President was supposed to propose a candidate. It was a fiercely contested battle, and the President, in addition to his work at the assemblies, held meetings and chatted to representatives of the various blocs, individual deputies and heads of administrations. "A massive amount of effort was put into the seventh Congress. And all with one objective in mind — to convince people," Yeltsin later wrote.[722]

On the eve of the Congress, the democratic branch of the group of deputies and the President made a series of proposals regarding cooperation between the executive and the legislative.[723]

A week before the start of the 7th Congress, parliament examined a program of urgent measures designed to pull the country's economy out of the crisis. It was here that an irreconcilable battle broke out on the first issue on the agenda for the Congress: the opposing sides worked on their tactics and dealt one another blows of varying severity.

By the time of the Congress, the major parliamentary blocs had taken shape: Russian unity (roughly 40% of the votes from the deputies), Creative forces (roughly 20%), Democratic center (25%) and Coalition of reforms (15%).[724]

Two of the most extreme deputy blocs, which were most directly opposed to one another, were Russian unity and Coalition for reform. The former refused

---

722   B. Yeltsin: Notes by the President. — M., 1994- P.289.
723   A. Filatov: An open secret. M., 2000. P. 205
724   See: Rossiskaya gazeta. 1992. 1 December

to take part in any compromise, and made the same demands again and again: that the government should be sacked, the President impeached and the reforms put under the control of the state. This group's biggest opponent was the Coalition for reform. At an assembly of the coalition, one of its coordinators, V. Volkov, declared: "We shall triumph, whatever happens."[725] In order to achieve this they would need to block the amendments to the Constitution which had been prepared by the opposition.

But these extreme forces depended first and foremost on the actions of the deputies in two other blocs: Creative forces and Democratic center, who, in their words, were "constructively opposed" to the president. Yet whereas Change — a new politics and Creative forces had rejected the government's course of reform at the 6th Congress, the four blocs in the Democratic center faction talked about the need for change in the cabinet and adjustments to the course of reforms.

There were around two hundred deputies who were not part of either faction, and in regard to whom it was impossible to guess which button they would press — 'for' or 'against'. The decision they made could be influenced by the speech delivered by the President, whose measures had latterly met with a variety of responses on the part of the deputies. "Much will depend on a large and fairly amorphous group of deputies — some people refer to this group as a 'bog', whilst others are kinder and describe them as 'ditherers'. Which side are they going to fall down on?" — the newspaper *Sovetskaya Rossiya* asked.[726]

The President added more fuel to the fire at the Congress by returning to the parliament the law about the government which it had refused to sign, declaring as he did so that he would announce the name of the prime minister once the law had been reworked.

The opening of the 7th Congress took place in a calm, workmanlike atmosphere. In his introductory speech Khasbulatov observed that "anything that is new is bound to come up against contrary views and temporary complications before it is accepted, particularly when political and economic transformations are being made which are comparable in magnitude to the changes in geological eras."[727] He outlined the key problems which society and the Congress were facing. On the whole, the start of the Congress passed off fairly peacefully.

The agenda for the 7th Congress of people's deputies of the Russian Federation included the following issues:

---

725   Same reference.
726   Sovetskaya Rossiya. 1992. 1 December.
727   The Seventh Congress of people's deputies of the Russian Federation. Transcript. Vol. 1. — M ., 1993 . — P . 5.

the course of the economic reforms in the Russian Federation.

a draft law of the Russian Federation on the introduction of amendments and addenda to the Constitution (Primary law) of the Russian Federation.

The Chairman of the Council of Ministers of the Russian Federation.

Information about work on the draft of the new Constitution of the Russian Federation.

The reshuffle (and rotation) of some of the members of the Supreme Soviet of the Russian Federation. The election of the deputy Chairman of the Supreme Soviet of the Russian Federation.

The election of the judges in the Constitutional court of the Russian Federation. The state of the legal system and the battle against crime and corruption.

The state of affairs in the Armed Forces and in military policy.

The law of the Russian Federation 'On the formation of the Ingush republic within the Russian Federation'.

Following the adoption of the agenda for the 7th Congress, the Chairman of the Supreme Soviet announced that there would be a break lasting 30 minutes.

After the break, the President walked up to the tribune on the floor of the congress. He began his speech with a call for unity: "I would particularly like to note that throughout all the time it has been working, the Congress has not made a single decision which would create a threat of civil war in the country. I hope that this will continue in the future, and that the deputies will not step over this line under any circumstances."

At this point the President also expressed his displeasure at the activities of some of the deputies: "At times things are all too comfortable and cosy for these people — people for whom demagoguery, intrigue, cheap political effects and their own career are dearer than the interests of the state's citizens."[728]

In his opinion, the lack of "mutual understanding and constructive cooperation" between the Supreme Soviet and the government are slowing the pace of reform dramatically. The country needed "some time to catch its breath — at least a year to eighteen months", when "the priority must, at last,

---

728   The Seventh Congress of people's deputies of the Russian Federation. Speeches. — M., 1993,- P. 5.

be achieving normal conditions for creative work." The president proposed that the deputies decide whether or not to introduce a "stabilization period".[729]

"Today calls are being made for the sacking of the government, the disbandment of the Congress, a 'shake-up' of the Supreme Soviet and so on. Let me tell you my position. To begin the stabilization period by destroying any of the senior institutions of power would be simply absurd. This would only serve to add more tension to the situation and exacerbate the confrontation. Today, we must not destroy but strengthen the existing balance of power. A moratorium is required on any actions which might have a destabilizing effect on the institutions of the state during this period."[730]

Yeltsin proposed that the Congress pass emergency measures designed to solve the most critical issues in state life, without which it would simply not be possible to complete the tasks required in order to achieve stabilization. Which measures are to be taken? During the period of stabilization, the Congress of people's deputies must focus exclusively on making amendments and addenda to the Constitution of the Russian Federation. The passing of all other legislative acts shall be the business of the Supreme Soviet, operating on a professional basis. All of the executive and administrative activity at the federal level shall be the responsibility of the government, which shall report to the Congress and the President. The decisions of the government of the Supreme Soviet may be contested either in the Constitutional court or by the President.

The President shall assume and bear responsibility for the most important decisions in the field of economics, within the framework of the competencies of executive power.

If the preceding proposals are adopted, the President shall decline to extend the additional powers in the field of the legislative regulation of the economic reforms. The law on the government must be postponed until the new Constitution is passed into law. During the stabilization period, the government shall be formed in the procedure stipulated by the Constitution, in accordance with which the chairman of the government, as presented by the President, would be approved by the Congress, and the members of the government, as presented by the prime minister, would be approved by the President.

When legislative issues about Russia's federal structure were reviewed, the decision of the Soviet of Nationalities would be the top priority. The president announced that there was a need to found a State committee for the affairs

---

729   See: The Seventh Congress of people's deputies of the Russian Federation. Speeches.
— M,, 1993. P. 5.
730   Same ref.

of the Federation and its territories. "The task facing us," Yeltsin said, "is to create a state which is qualitatively different in terms of its nature, with the principle of consensus at its heart."[731]

The President's speech did not go down well with the deputies: "there was a hostile murmuring in the auditorium, you could physically sense the hostility hanging in the air."[732] During Yeltsin's speech, lukewarm applause could be heard on just a handful of occasions, from the benches where the democratic blocs were sitting, whereas the speech by R. Khasbulatov, which followed it, was cheered and interrupted on numerous occasions as deputies applauded it enthusiastically.

Khasbulatov, in his report, identified the lines of divergence between the deputies and the president's team: one side was in favor of a market economy oriented towards the people, the other was in favor of a complete private capitalization. "Within which market area has the legislative process been developing throughout this entire period? The answer is clear and unambiguous: within the context of a socially-oriented market, whereas the government's policy reposes on the paradigm of a completely different model. This is the biggest difference between the two sides of all."[733]

Thus the different views had been identified at the Congress.

The President's proposal about the stabilization period was clearly not to the liking of the speaker, but he did not reject the proposal on cooperation: "Of course, a very serious transition period — one could describe it as a stabilization period — is needed. <...>But it is unlikely that it would be right, even in this period, to allow a departure from the Constitution and the laws."

Next to speak was the Chairman of the Constitutional court, V. Zorkin, who criticized the growing conflict between the authorities.

The next day, 2nd December, the acting Chairman of the government, Y. Gaidar, spoke to the deputies. At the start of his speech he observed that the government was aware what a huge burden of responsibility lay on his shoulders. And it had been the fear of this responsibility that had used up the energy of the union's last governments, and ultimately led to the collapse of the Union. As for the current government, it had taken the most important step of all — it had got the ball rolling, and set the market mechanism in motion. Gaidar went on to talk about his disagreements with the Supreme Soviet.

---

731   The Seventh Congress of people's deputies of the Russian Federation. Speeches. 1 December 1992 — M., 1993.-S. 16

732   The Yeltsin era. Sketches from a political history. — M., 2001. — S. 246.

733   The Seventh Congress of people's deputies of the Russian Federation. Speeches. — M., 1993.-S.24.

"It is quite natural that, firstly, there have been disagreements in connection with the approval of the budget for 1992. The Supreme Soviet is accepting and recording in the budget additional costs of 1300 billion roubles. What is this: a socially oriented policy and a market economy? The result has been a dramatic increase in the budget-related problems in practically all the regions, a crisis in the regional budgets, a dramatic increase in expenses from the federal budget and the circumstances related to it, a dramatic increase in the amount of money in circulation between July and August and an acceleration of inflation starting in the second half of August. If that is a socially oriented market economy, forgive me, but Ludwig Erhard would be turning in his grave."[734]

The president hoped that with this speech Gaidar would succeed in changing the mood at the Congress, where hostility was in the air. Yet the prime minister's "excessively smart" speech only added to the deputies' irritation.

On the second day of the Congress there was a confidential meeting between Boris Yeltsin and the heads of the Russian regions. The president secured the support of the regional leaders for his backing of the candidacy of Y. Gaidar for the post of prime minister. The mayor of Moscow, Y. Luzhkov, who was present at the meeting, warmly supported the candidacy of Gaidar, observing that "Russia will not withstand it if we try to grow yet another premier." If Gaidar did not make it, some of the heads of the republics were inclined to vote for Y. Skokov.

Everyone expected that at the 7th Congress the draft of the new Constitution was going to be discussed, but this did not happen. Yet again, for the umpteenth time, a discussion began regarding the amendments to the old, existing Constitution. This process of tearing down the Constitution could not go on forever — neither from a legal perspective nor a political one. The rise in the number of amendments began to become endless: they contradicted one another, and this could have led to legislative anarchy.

By violating the principle of the distribution of powers, the Supreme Soviet demanded that all the main political and economic actions be concluded under his control. The Congress got the President involved in a discussion which could only work against him: they asked him about the amendments to the constitution which would give the Supreme Soviet the right to form and disband governments. When Yeltsin objected, saying that the government would be weak if that were the case, the deputies refused to accept what he said. Under these amendments, the government was subordinate not only to the President but also to the Congress and the Supreme Soviet — and in the

734   The Seventh Congress of people's deputies of the Russian Federation: Speeches. — M., 1993.-P.30.

relevant line, the President was in third position in the list. In addition to the prime minister being appointed by the Congress, there was also a clause stating that all of his deputies, the ministers responsible for the armed forces and other key ministers were to be appointed only with the approval of the Supreme Soviet.

The president conceded: "I'm not against the idea of ministers for certain key posts being approved by the Supreme Soviet." Under these same amendments, it was in the remit of the Supreme Soviet to form, or indeed close down, all the ministries and institutions, based on representations by the President. And, lastly, it was stipulated that all the members of the government, all the ministers and directors of executive bodies of the subjects of the Federation have their mandates taken away.

The Congress rejected the majority of the amendments proposed by the President. The policy of the government, and, by extension, of Yeltsin himself, was declared "not to be in line with the interests of the majority of citizens."

The first "breakthrough" took place on 3rd December, in the evening. The following issue was discussed: how should the vote on amendments to the Constitution, which would make it lawful for the Supreme Soviet to adopt the status of a Council of Ministers, take place: openly or by secret ballot? The parliamentarians called for a secret ballot, and Yeltsin's enemies were in favor of maintaining their anonymity. The pro-presidential deputies, G. Yakunin, A. Shabad, Y. Sergeev and V. Varov insisted that the names of the deputies and how they voted should be revealed. A fight broke out. For the first time, Khasbulatov lost control of the deputies. The throng of deputies grew larger.[735]

Photo journalists and TV camera crews recorded the action. Once the brawl had come to an end, Khasbulatov announced a break. After these stormy scenes, the deputies nonetheless voted, and decided that the vote would be held in secret. Since the ballot boxes and voting cubicles were not ready by the time of the evening session, the vote was postponed until the next day.

The voting slips approved by the Congress featured seven texts about the Constitution: they touched on the powers of the President, the Supreme Soviet, the government, the national emblem, the land itself and so on. Whilst the voting slips were being prepared, the Secretary of the Constitutional Commission, O. Rumyantsev, spoke to the deputies. He reported that for the most part, the directives of the 6th Congress of people's deputies had been implemented. Working on the draft of the Constitution were institutions, federal subjects and prominent lawyers. In that time some six thousand

---

735   See: Moskovsky komsomolets. 4 December 1992. No.237

amendments were made, of which 650 came from subjects which had the right to legitimate initiatives. The constitutional commission proposed the following mechanism for safeguarding the constitutional structure, which needed support from the whole Congress — under this mechanism, the Constitution was effectively divided in two. The bases of the constitutional structure were to be determined by means of a nationwide referendum.

The Commission is proposing, as Rumyantsev observed, that the bases of the constitutional structure receive broad approval by 1st March 1993, from all the republics and regions and all the interested parties, and that a round table discussion then be held. It was proposed that the project be put to a referendum only after this.[736] The speech by O. Rumyantsev made it clear that the commission saw constitutional reform as a fairly lengthy process which was directly dependent on the Congress of people's deputies.

For several days the Congress examined the numerous amendments to the Constitution. On the eighth day of the Congress the following row broke out. It was proposed that an amendment be made to clause 121 (6), which stated that the President was not entitled to dissolve the parliament or the other legally elected bodies of power. The proposed amendment was to insert a clause saying that if the President were to do so, his powers would immediately be curtailed.

The deputies passed the amendment (the quorum for the decision consisted of 692 people; of these, 648 voted 'for' and 183 voted 'against'). Next to speak was the deputy O. Plotnikov (from Change — a New politics), who requested that they revisit this issue at a later time. "I entreat the Congress in the strongest possible terms to revisit this issue at a later time. Why, you may ask? Because the clause of the draft law in question is designed to regulate those cases when the Congress or the Constitutional court find themselves not in a fit state to effect a return to the normal state structure, a return to the principles of law and order."[737]

If the President violates the legislation, if he disbands the Congress, the Supreme Soviet or the Constitutional court, the mechanics of the procedure for impeaching the President will not function. If this amendment is passed, then in such cases the President's powers would immediately come to an end."

The deputies decided to return to the issue and re-examine it at a later time. V. Shumeiko spoke against the amendment: "After the passionate speech made by deputy Plotnikov, listen to what is written down in the current version of

---

736   The Seventh Congress of people's deputies of the Russian Federation. Transcript. Tome 1. — M., 1993. — P.372.
737   The Seventh Congress of people's deputies of the Russian Federation. Transcript. Transcript report.

the Constitution: "The powers of the President of the Russian Federation cannot be used to alter the national and state government..." and so on. I repeat: "shall not". And if we were to add: "Else they shall come to an end", then it sounds like complete nonsense. The president said so many times that he has no intention of dissolving the Congress, or doing anything of the sort. And these words are completely superfluous here."[738]

R. Khasbulatov supported what Shumeiko said: "Please don't have a go at me for this, but I agree with Shumeiko when he says that our President does not intend to do any of this."[739]

On 8th December there was a meeting between Boris Yeltsin and the coordinators of the parliamentary blocs. After an exchange of views between the sides, a compromise was reached: the President, as a legislative initiative, would propose that the Congress include in the Constitution a clause about the consent of the Supreme Soviet being compulsory when appointing or sacking the minister of internal affairs or ministers in charge of security and defence.

An hour later, B. Yeltsin announced his candidate for prime minister — Y. Gaidar, whom he described in his short speech as "simply an intelligent man."[740] In all likelihood, the President wished, by means of this "compromise", to elicit a response from the deputies — so that they voted for Gaidar.

On 9th December, after Gaidar had delivered a speech as a candidate for the role of prime minister, there was a discussion about his candidacy. Speeches were made by Gaidar's supporters and enemies alike. In order to be elected premier, Gaidar needed to secure at least 521 votes; the vote, held at the end of the day, produced the following results: for — 467 deputies; against — 486. Thus the Congress voted down Gaidar's candidacy.

It must be noted that there were those in the opposition who believed that Khasbulatov was Yeltsin's chief supporter, and that he was deliberately pretending to be a member of the opposition. The deputies Baburin and Astafiev were among those who subscribed to this view. Many deputies were not content with the work done by R. Khasbulatov, and felt that he was drowning out important issues in parliament or, on the contrary, "forcing through" criminal ones; and that he was now thought of as a loyal ally by the President.

At the 7th Congress the situation changed somewhat. "At this Congress the illusions regarding a conspiracy between Yeltsin and Khasbulatov have

738   The Seventh Congress of people's deputies of the Russian Federation. Transcript. Vol. 2.-M., 1993. — P. 196.
739   Same reference.
740   Moskovsky komsomolets. 1992. 9 December

melted away. And not because the speaker's speech had more to it, was more expressive, or was better suited to the mood of the opposition and the demands of the age. In this particular instance, he revealed himself to be more of an academic and market expert than a politician."[741]

Sure enough, Khasbulatov's authority among the deputies was not completely unquestioned. The circumstances and realities of political life, the opposition's lack of a single leader — that was what forced the deputies to unite around Khasbulatov.

As for the President, the esteem in which he was held by the democrats began to wane as the Congress went on. The Democratic press responded negatively to the President's wavering. "By all accounts, the combustible Yeltsin is behaving excessively peacefully, passively and even vapidly at the 7th Congress. Where has his unpredictability gone? People had expected a different sort of man altogether: bold moves, uncompromising ultimatums, declarations about dissolving the deputy forum, with which everyone is fed up, direct communication with the people, even a bit of Khrushchev-esque bashing of his shoe on the despatch box — anything and everything seemed possible. The tranquility shown by Yeltsin was something nobody had predicted."[742]

Nezavisimaya gazeta wrote: "The week of the Congress has brought fresh revelations. It transpired that the President could be forced to become resigned not only to pressure, but also to having his opinion ignored. And this ignoring of his opinion has gone unpunished."

The newspapers Pravda and Sovetskaya Rossiya were full of malicious attacks against Gaidar and the democrats.

Yeltsin's patience did not crack until the tenth day of the Congress. "Once I had had a chance to think through what had happened, I realised something: this was a case of collective madness. A body such as that cannot govern a country. There would be the whiff of a revolution about such a scenario. And the most dominant aspect of this smell is the stench of blood."[743]

It was a time of dramatic emotions for the President, as can be seen in his memoirs: "I came home to the dacha from the Congress in a completely trance-like state. It was probably the first time I had felt that way in five years, since 1987 …"[744]

---

741   A. Greshnevikov: The parliament under fire. — Rybinsk. 1994.-P. 15.
742   Moskovsky komsomolets. 1992. 10 December
743   B. Yeltsin: Notes by the President. — M., 2006. — S. 328.
744   B. Yeltsin: Notes by the President. — M. 2006 — P.330

"That evening, on 9th December, after the latest assembly, I arrived back at the dacha fairly early in the evening. I caught the gaze of my wife and children. I tore out to the banya. I locked myself in. I lay down on my back. I closed my eyes. And I'll be honest about it — all kinds of thoughts crossed my mind. I was in a bad way...A very bad way."[745]

Yeltsin was rescued from this condition by the head of his Security staff, Korzhakov, who broke down the door to the banya and persuaded him to come back inside the house.

The Congress and the President had reached an impasse from which there was only one way out — though it would not be a straightforward one. A referendum. By consulting all of the country's citizens, it would be possible to get an answer to the question: who did the people trust — the Congress or the President. The will of the people could serve as the grounds for adopting a new Constitution.

The President's team had considered the idea of holding a referendum before, but on a different question: should the Congress be disbanded or not. In this case, the question was being phrased in an altogether different way.

Yeltsin asked to be put through to his aide Ilyushin. Later that night Shakhrai and the President's speech-writers got involved in the job as well. By morning they had drafted the text of his speech.

'An address to the citizens of Russia'

On the morning of 10th December 1992, the President took the floor at the Congress and read out 'An address to the citizens of Russia'. Yeltsin accused the Congress of disrupting the course of reforms and attempting to give the Supreme Soviet all sorts of rights and powers, but no responsibility.

"Yeltsin, B.N. Citizens of Russia! People's deputies!

The way events have unfolded at the 7th Congress of people's deputies leaves me with no choice but to address the people directly.

The reforms which have been under way in Russia for the last year are under threat. A powerful attack has been made at the Congress on the course introduced by the President and the government, on the genuine changes which have warded off an economic catastrophe in this country in the last few months. They decided to have another go at doing what they failed to do in August 1991, and to effect a coup d'état by stealth. (A commotion in the auditorium.)

---

745   B. Yeltsin: Notes by the President. — M. 2006. — P.331

The presiding officer. I ask you to hear the President out. *Yeltsin, B.N.* The plan of action has already been decided on. It is as follows.

Number one. Create unbearable conditions for the government and the President here, at the 7th Congress, so as to leave them practically demoralized.

Number two. Make amendments to the Constitution, at any cost, that will bestow on the Supreme Soviet — now a bastion of conservative, reactionary forces — vast powers and rights, but protect it from any responsibility whatsoever, as before.

Number three. Block the reforms. Destroy all the positive processes which are under way and make it impossible to stabilize the situation.

And, finally, number four. To hold the 8th Congress of people's deputies in April 1993. To take the law into its own hands as regards the government, the President, the reforms and democracy, thereby doing a U-turn to the past."[746]

Yeltsin emphasized that he was not calling for the Congress to be disbanded, but was asking the citizens to decide which course they supported: the President's course of reform or the course chosen by the Congress? The President was proposing that a referendum be held, in order to bring to an end the duopoly on power in the country. "I can only see one way out of the extremely deep crisis of power in the country: a nationwide referendum. I am not calling for the Congress to be dissolved, but asking the citizens of Russia to decide whose side you are on."[747]

Yeltsin's speech was broadcast live and was effectively directed over the heads of the deputies, at the citizens of Russia. The President's address came as a complete surprise to the Congress and to the speaker. The preparations for the live broadcast of the Congress directly from the auditorium had been made in conditions of the strictest secrecy. Thanks to the solidarity amongst the TV crews working in the auditorium, the broadcast was kept secret right up until the cameras were switched on.[748]

Khasbulatov announced that he was stepping down and, giving the floor to Y. Yarov, left the auditorium, only to come back in a short time later. The President called on his supporters to leave the auditorium and gather in the Palace of Facets. By so doing, Yeltsin intended to break up the Congress — to divide it into two parts, neither of which would have a quorum, and

---

746   The Seventh Congress of people's deputies of the Russian Federation. Transcript. Vol. 1.-M., 1993.-P. 127
747   Same reference.
748   The Yeltsin era. Sketches from a political history. — M., 2001. — P. 250

consequently neither of which would have any powers. In order for this plan to be a success, however, serious preliminary work was required on the part of the deputies, but they had not been told about this in advance, and were hesitating: only a small minority walked out.

The president's press-secretary, V. Kostikov, recalled: "The thing is (and this was a clear oversight on the part of the President's team at the time), even the deputies who were loyal to Yeltsin had not been told in advance about this move. They simply didn't understand what was going on, and were unable to make sense of it quickly."[749]

The quorum was not broken up, the Congress remained legitimate and it continued its work. Confusion reigned in the auditorium. The president looked bewildered.

The deputies called the Chairman of the Supreme Soviet, R. Khasbulatov, back into the auditorium. He said that, for him, "the speech made by the President today (as you probably noticed) came as a complete surprise to me, particularly given that yesterday evening I called the President, informed him of the decisions we had taken, and also told him that we intended to pass a law about the government today, and that if he wished to have Gaidar confirmed as the stand-in, the Congress would not get in his way. He said he was satisfied by these decisions. We reached an agreement on cooperation in the future. I did not sense any negativity in relation to either myself or the Congress. The conversation ended on fairly amicable terms. Unfortunately, however, this is not the first occasion on which we have reached an agreement, only for something completely different to take place the next day."[750]

At the end of his speech Khasbulatov called on the Congress to continue its work and quickly to conclude the preparations for its address to the Russian people.

One after another, the ministers of security, defence and internal affairs walked into the hall. The Congress was addressed by the following, one after another: the General procurator, V. Stepankov, the vice-president, A. Rutskoi, the minister of security, V. Barranikov, the minister of internal affairs, V. Yerin, and the minister of defence, P. Grachev. They all announced that they would abide by the Constitution and the laws of the land.

Their appearance, and the speeches they delivered, left most of those present at the Congress convinced of something: the impression had been created that the President had no real power, no genuine support, behind him.

---

749   V. Kostikov: A love-story with the President. — M., 1997.-P150
750   See: The Seventh Congress of people's deputies of the Russian Federation. Transcript. Vol.3 — M. 1993-P. 157

According to Rutskoi, just 15 minutes before his address he was trying to convince the President to refrain from calling for a referendum. "Society might not withstand the excessive tension," he explained. That same day, Rutskoi made his choice. He would stay with the Congress. "As vice-president," he announced, "I wish to make one thing absolutely clear: for me, the highest authority is the Constitution, the law, the Congress, the Russian people."[751] The Congress continued its work and passed new amendments to the Constitution.

That same day, the Congress drafted an 'Address from the 7th Congress of people's deputies of the Russian Federation to the Russian people'. In this address, the Congress accused the President of trying to "destroy the constitutional balance between the executive and the legislature, and disrupt the work of the highest body of legislative power." The President's statement, "which had been inspired by his immediate circle, was designed to destabilize the political and socio-economic situation in the country." The Congress called on everyone not to submit to the acts of provocation, not to allow a confrontation in society and actively to collaborate with the president of the RF and the Congress of people's deputies of the Russian Federation.[752]

Yeltsin, meanwhile, went to visit the automobile manufacturing plant, AZLK, in an attempt to receive backing from the plant's employees. It was a move which was strongly reminiscent of the practices of Soviet times: the idea of "consulting the working class" when things got difficult. Yeltsin did not receive the backing he desired. The plant's employees greeted him with silence: there were no shouts of encouragement, no placards containing words of support; just a lukewarm round of applause. This was not what he was used to at all. He loved speaking in public, and was good at it. People who were close to him recall that though he was restrained and taciturn with his advisers, he would come into his own whenever he spoke in public. His final remark, "I believe in your support," was not greeted with any particular enthusiasm. Yeltsin realised something: his plan had backfired.[753]

People were clearly fed up with the dispute between the authorities, and with how it had dragged on for so long; and they could not be bothered to spend too much time working out who was right and who was wrong. As far as they were concerned, both Yeltsin and Khasbulatov represented the new regime, under which life had got a good deal more difficult.

The situation at the Congress grew more tense with each day that passed; the chairman of the Constitutional court, V. Zorkin, undertook to resolve it. In

---

751   The unknown Rutskoi. — M., 1994. P.36

752   The Seventh Congress of people's deputies of the Russian Federation (Speeches, addresses, directives) 10 December 1992. — M., 1993

753   V. Kostikov: A love-story with the President. — M., 1997.-P150

his address to the Congress, he called for negotiations between the executive and the legislature, and although many thought his interfering inappropriate, both sides were glad that an unexpected arbiter had now emerged. As a result of the negotiations, the equation with regard to a potential agreement began to take shape. The main points of it were as follows:

the Congress would annul those of the amendments to the Russian Constitution which were deemed most unacceptable.

An officially scheduled referendum would be held on the issue of confidence in the president and the Congress, which would decide the matter of the duopoly on power and open the path to mid-term elections.

After analysing the proposals put forward by the political blocs, the President would present several candidates for the role of prime minister to the Congress, and, after a vote in which the candidates would be ranked in order of preference, the three candidates with the most support would be elected. After this, the President would present one of these candidates to the Congress for approval.

In the circumstances, this was the compromise that was most likely to work. The President would save face, would not be saying no to a referendum, and would be given breathing space in his choice of prime minister.

On 12th December 1992 the Congress passed the directive 'On the stabilization of the constitutional structure of the Russian Federation'.[754] The first clause in the directive read: "Schedule for 11th April 1993 a nationwide referendum in Russia on the core provisions of the new Constitution (Primary Law) of the Russian Federation." The text of the draft Constitution which was to be put to a referendum had to be confirmed by the Supreme Soviet, with the consent of the President and the Constitutional court. In the event that no agreement was reached on individual phrases, alternative versions could be put forward for a vote. The federative agreement was subject to inclusion in the new Constitution. It was proposed that a draft of the core provisions be sent to the federal subjects and published by 31st March 1993.

A moratorium was introduced on any amendments which would impinge significantly on the President's powers, until such time as a referendum was held on the core provisions of the new Constitution. It was stipulated that the Supreme Soviet must not undertake reviews of the amendments to the Constitution or the laws of the Russian Federation, presented in the form of legislative initiatives which violate the established balance between the legislature, the executive and the courts. Prior to the new Constitution being passed into law, none of the vacancies in the Constitutional court were to be filled in.[755]

---

754   GARF. F.10026. Op.1, D.1582, L.186

755   See: N.V. Varlamova: The Constitutional process in Russia (1990 – 1993) – M., 1998 – P.31

This directive restored the equilibrium between the various powers, and although this was not peace, it was a ceasefire that was essential at that particular time. The only issue left unresolved was who was going to stand as prime minister. The President had set out his understanding of the "stabilization period" in his address at the opening of the 7th Congress — it consisted of the following: the Congress of people's deputies was to concentrate exclusively on making amendments and addenda to the Constitution of the Russian Federation. The Supreme Soviet, operating on a professional basis, was in charge of passing other kinds of legislative acts. All executive and administrative activity at the federal level was to be undertaken by the government, which was to report to the Congress and the President. The President assumed responsibility for all the most important decisions in the field of economics which fell within the remit of the executive.

Y.T. Gaidar resigns. V.S. Chernomyrdin appointed Chairman of the Council of Ministers

The deputies put forward 18 candidates for the role of prime minister, and Yeltsin put five of these individuals forward to be voted on by the deputies in order of preference.[756] The President rejected a host of candidates whom he deemed unacceptable. The initial voting slip featured the following: the secretary of the Security Council, Y. Skokov, the first vice-premier, V. Shumeiko, the vice-premier, V. Chernomyrdin, the director of VAZ from Tolyatti, V. Kadannikov, and Y. Gaidar.

Yeltsin fought to have Gaidar appointed right to the end. Even after the results of the vote at the Congress had been made known, and Gaidar's fate was virtually decided, Yeltsin tried to do something about it. At a closed session of the Soviet of the heads of the republics held at the President hotel on the morning of 14th December, B. Yeltsin said to the heads of the republics: "If Gaidar gets a decent rating, I shall propose him as a candidate. If he doesn't make it through, I'll propose him in any case as a stand-in."

It seems likely that Yeltsin's hand was forced by the decisiveness with which Gaidar had taken charge of the changes to the country's economy. Decisiveness was the characteristic trait of the course chosen by Y. Gaidar "during the transition from the conversations with Gorbachev to specific practical steps."[757]

The winner of the vote held at the Congress was Y. Skokov, who secured 638 votes; in second place was Chernomyrdin, with 621 votes. Gaidar was 200

---

756   The Yeltsin era. Sketches from a political history. — M., 2001. — P. 253
757   Rossiskaya gazeta. 1993. 9 April

votes behind, and it made no sense for the Congress to put him forward even for the role of stand-in to the premier. In spite of the fact that most of the deputies at the Congress voted for Y. Skokov, B. Yeltsin backed the candidacy of Chernomyrdin. Gaidar objected to Skokov in no uncertain terms — he felt that his views were not completely in line with the course of reforms. "And, to be honest, I wasn't convinced that in critical situations he would be firmly on the side of the President, and would not start wheeling and dealing. I said all this to Boris Yeltsin," Gaidar later wrote.[758]

Viktor Stepanovich Chernomyrdin had formerly held the role of minister of the USSR's gas industry; after the gas concern Gazprom was established within the ministry, he became its director. He joined Gaidar's government in May 1992, where he focused on the fuel and energy complex. When he put V. Chernomyrdin forward as a candidate, Yeltsin was conscious of the fact that the latter had worked with Gaidar before, and had therefore been initiated into the ideas of the reforms, whether he had wanted to be or not.

The Congress voted for V. Chernomyrdin (835 in favor, 31 against) because it saw him as the kind of strong manager typically required by the Soviet economy. The deputies took inspiration from Chernomyrdin's thank you speech, in which he promised to work with the Congress and justify the faith they had shown in him, build a market economy which had none of the elements of a bazaar, and introduce reforms without impoverishing the people.

The democrats viewed the replacement of Gaidar with Chernomyrdin with caution; they were not sure what to make of Chernomyrdin's remarks to the effect that he would exercise the will of the Congress. The mass media in Russia characterised Chernomyrdin's election almost as something that signalled the failure of the reforms.

Yet the democrats' doom-laden concerns as regards Chernomyrdin proved to be unfounded. On 14th December the 7th Congress of people's deputies of the Russian Federation came to an end. In his closing speech on the outcome of the Congress, R. Khasbulatov said: "An in-depth analysis of the results of this Congress is still to come. But already it is fair to say that right here at this Congress, the Congress has genuinely confirmed its status as the highest body of state power, and as a constructive and creative force."

After the 7th Congress there was a split in the leadership of the Supreme Soviet. The first deputy of the Chairman of the Supreme Soviet, S. Filatov, who had refused to approve the speaker in his position in the past, after expressing his support for the idea of a referendum, split with R. Khasbulatov decisively, once and for all. Filatov wrote that when the 7th Congress was

---

758   Y. Gaidar: Days of defeats and victories. — M., 1996. — P.234

drawing to an end, Khasbulatov, in a one-to-one meeting with him, suggested that he hand in his notice and leave, before he had to be forced out.[759] Filatov declined the offer. Thereafter the row between the Chairman of the Supreme Soviet and his deputy began to escalate.

In January 1993, S. Filatov left the Supreme Soviet and replaced Y. Petrov at the head of the President's Administration.

After the 7th Congress a strange equilibrium was established between the executive bodies. Following the appointment of Y. Gaidar in May 1992 as stand-in for the premier, a duopoly was effectively created: the executive and the legislature began to act on their own behalf, without paying attention to one another. The Chairman of the Supreme Soviet, R. Khasbulatov, began to be more and more influential. It seems as though the Chairman of the Supreme Soviet thought of himself as being just one step below the President in the political hierarchy, and a situation arose in which it was as if there were two heads of state. S. Alekseyev, a member of the Russian Academy of Sciences, highlighted the fact that the problem was not the Congress, nor Khasbulatov's political or moral shortcomings, but the perverse nature of the system of Soviets. "Today's Soviets are from a state which no longer exists," and until such time as this system was overcome, peace would not be possible in the country. The President's historic mission was to guide Russia from the communist system of Soviets to the path of European parliamentarianism, which had withstood the test of time.[760]

It is abundantly obvious that at the heart of the confrontation between the two sides was the inability to reach a consensus with regard to the procedures required for interaction between the executive bodies. Each new compromise was an attempt to divide up the fields of responsibility, and this meant that the various political institutions belonging to the various branches of power, were deprived of a general sense of a shared reality. With no clearly defined procedures in place to regulate the interaction between the bodies of power, each of the parties strove to shift the scales in their favor.

The dispute over the referendum on adopting the Constitution: the President and the Congress

Once the 7th Congress of people's deputies had come to an end, the structure of the political problems in the country had been altered. The 'acting premier' Y. Gaidar, who had annoyed the parliament, departed, and when Chernomyrdin was elected prime minister the matter of economic reforms took a back seat.

---

759   S. Filatov: An open secret. – M., 2000.-P. 212

760   Quoted from: The Yeltsin era. Sketches from a political history. — M., 2001. — P. 312

The main issue which began to be the biggest focus of problems in Russian politics was the new Constitution. It became clear fairly soon that the agreement between the bodies of power which had been reached at the 7th Congress was essentially a victory for the President.[761] Having agreed to the elections for premier, all he was doing was something that he was already obligated to do under the Constitution; the parliament was in an awkward situation, having lost a host of its constitutional rights. The Supreme Soviet of the Russian Federation passed a directive on 14th January 1993 entitled 'On measures intended to safeguard the holding of an all-Russian referendum on 11th April 1993', which, in accordance with a directive of the Congress of people's deputies passed on 12th December 1992, 'On the stabilization of the constitutional structure of the Russian Federation' and on the basis of the law on the referendum, a referendum in the entire territory of the Russian Federation was called on 11th April 1993.[762]

On 26th January 1993, the Central Electoral Commission for the All-Russian Referendum passed a directive on the formation of the districts affected by the referendum. The total number of districts was 89.

The honeymoon period following the Congress did not last long: immediately after the new year and Christmas holidays came to an end, feverish consultations began on issues related to the all-Russian referendum on 11th April 1993.

In early 1993 the referendum took on a key significance in Russian society, becoming the issue which determined the battle lines between the political forces. President B. Yeltsin calculated that a referendum would reaffirm, once and for all, the principle of the division of powers. After considering the matter briefly, the Chairman of the Supreme Soviet of the Russian Federation, R. Khasbulatov, disassociated himself from the idea of a referendum, declaring that a plebiscite would lead to the collapse of Russia.

On 5th February 1993 a 'Roundtable' began to operate, assembled by decision of the 7th Congress of people's deputies of the Russian Federation. This 'Roundtable' included representatives of the legislature and the executive, representatives of various political forces, the academic community and business and entrepreneurial circles. It was opened by the Chairman of the Supreme Soviet, R. Khasbulatov, the Chairman of the Council of Ministers, V. Chernomyrdin, and the vice-president A. Rutskoi. It was noted unanimously that the 'Roundtable' was a route to achieving civil consent against the backdrop of the socio-political and economic crisis in the state.[763]

---

761   See: N.K. Biryukov, V.V. Sergeyev: The making of the institutions of representative power in modern Russia. — M., 2004. — S. 401.
762   See: News from the Congress of people's deputies of the Russian Federation and the Supreme Soviet of the Russian Federation. — M., 1993. No. 4
763   See: Rossiskaya gazeta. 17 February 1993. 17 February.

At a sitting of the 'Roundtable' reflecting the opinion of those who supported the referendum, the Chairman of the government's first deputy, V. Shumeiko, emphasized that the executive was preparing for it with full awareness of how much was at stake.

An opposing view was put forward by the deputy Chairman of the Supreme Soviet, N. Ryabov. After expressing his support for the idea that there was a schism within society, he called on those present at the round-table not to exacerbate this schism but to take measures which would improve the situation.

To a greater or lesser extent, those present at the round-table formed the view that it would not be sensible to hold the referendum scheduled for 11th April. One of the issues which proved difficult was the search for a constitutional solution on how to legalize the postponement of the referendum by decision of the deputies. Some proposed that the whole issue be decided by means of a survey, whilst others advocated convening the deputies for a day to decide whether or not a plebiscite should be held.

It is important to note that what was being suggested was that the Congress's decision be annulled. The Roundtable convened by decision of the 7th Congress was annulling its own decision!

Ultimately, those attending the Roundtable decided on the core ideas of the possible agreement on the constitution. Its main objective was identified by those present, unanimously: to declare 1993 a year of national consensus and achieve stability.

The first step towards this might be a year-long ban on all political rallies within the country.[764]

In early 1993 the conflict between the legislature and the executive began to worsen with renewed vigor. The subject of the passing of the new Constitution gradually began to disappear from the speeches made by the leaders of the Congress. And one can understand this: why pass into law a new constitution if the old one can be dressed up to suit the spirit of the times. The deputies found themselves in an awkward situation: adopting a new Constitution would mean going to the polls. The majority of the deputies, however, failed to secure any support from the electorate. Since their chances of being re-elected to the new parliament were minimal, the deputies dragged out the issue of adopting the constitution until the parliament's powers expired. There were enough deputies who doubted they would be re-elected to block the adoption of the new Constitution.

---

764   See: Rossiskaya gazeta. 1993. 17 February.

Yeltsin's declarations to the effect that he had not approved the Constitution with its current amendments was interpreted by supporters of the Supreme Soviet as "unconstitutional". The only realistic resource still open to the President was the relatively high level of support he enjoyed among the general population. This was why Yeltsin insisted on a referendum. This was why the Congress of people's deputies and the Supreme Soviet were against the referendum.

A ferocious conflict broke out on the subject of the referendum. The results of the referendum would determine what sort of nation Russia was going to be — a presidential republic or a parliamentary one; and whether or not the Soviets would maintain their power in the country. The Supreme Soviet opposed the holding of the referendum, backing up its stance by saying that it would polarize Russian society and increase the risk of a civil war. According to the deputy V. Isakov, a referendum was not what the President needed: what he needed was "a political campaign which will make it possible to stoke up political passions, clash a few heads together among political adversaries, distract people from the catastrophic collapse in the economy and complete the unconstitutional seizure of power which he had begun."[765] As for the president, he insisted on a referendum, aware that it was not just the fate of the reforms and the political structure that was at stake, but his own fate as well. The prevailing mood among the deputies was extremely aggressive, and any miscalculation or political failure might lead to impeachment.

In the media outlets controlled by the Supreme Soviet, a campaign was rolled out to discredit the idea of the referendum, and it was suggested that a referendum would lead to a destabilizing of society. Then Yeltsin, for the first time since the presidential press-service was set up, asked for the information programs on Russian TV to be monitored. The results were not very comforting for the President. Editions of the news program *Vesti* reported on the activities of the opposition, and the regular program *Parlamentsky vestnik*, which was broadcast in the prime-time 7pm slot, also featured leaders of the opposition. Russian television devoted 15-20 minutes to the work of the Supreme Soviet every day. On the day when the monitoring was held, the President was not referred to once in the news reports. Yeltsin was so demoralized that he demanded that a meeting be held with the directors of radio and television channels.[766]

After S. Filatov — a man with good personal relations with the Patriarch of Moscow and All the Russias, Aleksei II — joined the President's Administration, more or less regular meetings between the President and the

---

765   See: V. Isakov. The coup d'état. Parliamentary diaries. 1992-1993. — Yekaterinburg, 1997.-P.294.

766   The Yeltsin era. Sketches from a political history. — M., 2001. — P.264

head of the Russian Orthodox Church were held, and he continued to enjoy his meetings with him right up until the final days of his presidency. At the same time, it must be said that to Yeltsin, a man brought up as an atheist, the Patriarch was the embodiment of Russia's culture and traditions, rather than a spiritual pastor.

In order to resolve the issue of whether or not to hold a referendum, Yeltsin consulted the Patriarch and asked him to support the idea of the referendum. On 6th February 1993 there was a meeting between the President and Aleksei II, following which the Patriarch announced that "at difficult moments in history, consulting the people has proved useful and desirable."[767]

Yeltsin received unexpected support from the famous ex-pat writer living in the USA, A.I. Solzhenitsyn, who wrote a letter to the then ambassador for Russia in the USA, V. Lukin. The letter was published in the newspaper *Komsomolskaya pravda* and was given a lot of publicity: "The Russian Federation, with its sheer size and diversity, cannot exist without a strong presidency, one that is no weaker than the presidency in the United States. It took centuries for the current model of parliamentary statehood in the West to be perfected. In this country it is currently a long way off."[768] Solzhenitsyn's support for the idea of a presidential republic became a significant moral support for Yeltsin.

The impeachment that never happened

The leaders of the Supreme Soviet strengthened their positions. They were now convinced that the actions of the Supreme Soviet, led by Khasbulatov, would once again receive backing from the Constitutional Court. An irony of constitutional jurisprudence was the fact that the "tool for measuring it" — the Constitution — proved to be too big to measure, or rather, precisely the size required at the time by the Congress and the Supreme Soviet. The president objected and tried to protest. "I have not sworn in the Constitution with its current amendments," Yeltsin declared on 2nd March 1993; however, these statements were interpreted as "unconstitutional".

Rutskoi's role as an opponent of the President — if not an out-and-out enemy — had been defined. The beleaguered and demoralized security services were not unduly hasty to show their loyalty to the President, either. The only real resource left open to the President was the relatively high level of support he enjoyed among the population at large. This was precisely why the President insisted on holding a referendum. And it was precisely why the Congress and

---

767   Same reference. — P.270
768   Komsomolskaya pravda. 1993. 10 March

the Supreme Soviet were against the idea of a referendum. A joke did the rounds among the President's entourage to the effect that the only security service Yeltsin now had was his press-secretary, V.V. Kostikov, who had defended the President's position rabidly and poisonously in countless spats with the leaders of the Supreme Soviet.

Following Khasbulatov's announcement in Novosibirsk, Yeltsin's press-secretary, V.V. Kostikov, accused the Chairman of the Supreme Soviet of having, "whenever it suited its interests...deliberately, and increasingly provocatively, tried to enter into a personal confrontation with the President, behavior which was in no way in accordance with his degree of legitimacy compared to that of the nationally elected President, nor with the political ratings of the chairman of the Supreme Soviet in society. One gets the impression," Kostikov went on, "that by 'denying' the President at every step, R. I. Khasbulatov is attempting to increase his own value in the eyes of the most conservative forces of all. In the political game being played by the speaker, Russia's interests and the causes of stability and national unity are increasingly being put on the back burner, giving way to the egotistical interests of the struggle for personal power."[769]

Khasbulatov, when his turn to speak came, succeeded in bringing the directors of the local Soviets over to his side. The day before the 8th Congress opened, on 6th March 1993, a statement was published by the 73 leaders of the Soviets of the Federal Subjects, in which they effectively accused the President of attempting to violate the Constitution. Addressing the deputies at the Congress, they announced:

"The economic and social situation in Russia is continuing to grow worse, finances are in a mess, the country has been swamped by crime, and impoverishment and mass discontent are on the rise among the general public."

The directors of the Soviets threatened "immediately to use all possible legal methods to thwart any attempts to violate the Constitution of the Russian Federation, regardless of the source of them", and warned "about the constitutional liability of senior officials for acting in breach of the Constitution, the laws of the Russian Federation, and, equally, any actions provoking such breaches," adding that "if a referendum is called at the initiative of whomsoever it may be, but does not take place due to citizens failing to turn up to vote..., those who initiated the referendum must resign."[770]

This last comment had a special significance. The local authorities were capable of exerting genuine influence on the elections, and could potentially

---

769   Yeltsin-Khasbulatov: Unity, compromise, struggle. M., 1994. P.271-274

770   V Isakov: The State coup. Parliamentary diaries. 1992-1993. Yekaterinburg, 1997. P. 266-267

either restrict the number of people turning up to vote or enable an increase in that number. To all intents and purposes, this threat — the threat of having to resign if there was a poor turn-out in the referendum — was aimed at the President, who had insisted on holding one, and not at anyone else.

On the eve of the Congress, on 7th March 1993, the President sent four questions to the Supreme Soviet which were to be put to the public in the referendum:

"1. Do you agree that the Russian Federation should be a Presidential republic?

2. Do you agree that the highest legislative body in the Russian Federation should be a parliament with two houses?

3. Do you agree that the new Constitution of the Russian Federation should be adopted by a Constitutional assembly, representing the multi-ethnic population of the Russian Federation?

4. Do you agree that every citizen of the Russian Federation is entitled to own, use and dispose of land, in the capacity of a land-owner?"

The 8th Congress, which had opened on 10th March 1993, completely ignored the President's proposal. The agenda for the Congress contained some different questions altogether:

"1. On the directive of the Congress of people's deputies of the Russian Federation dated 12th December 1992, "On the stabilization of the constitutional structure of the Russian Federation".

2. On the observance of the Constitution (Primary Law) of the Russian Federation by the senior bodies of state power and by officials.

The report from the Council of Ministers of the Government of the Russian Federation and the Central Bank of Russia on the course of the economic reforms".[771]

The Congress followed the direction prescribed by Khasbulatov. The speaker — N.G. Ryabov, the deputy chairman of the Supreme Soviet, announced that the agreements reached at the 7th Congress in December 1992 were a mistake; that the concessions made to the President amounted to a breach of the Constitution, that no referendum was needed, and that referenda are never held in any case in federative states (!).

---

771   The Yeltsin era. Sketches from political history. M., 2001. P. 277

The deputies passed the Supreme Soviet's proposals. What took place at the Congress was essentially a constitutional coup d'etat: the amendments which had been prepared back at the 7th Congress were included in the Constitution. Under these amendments, the Government had to be subordinate to the Congress and the Supreme Soviet. The legislature, as embodied by the Soviets

The primary task of the anti-Yeltsin opposition consisted in not allowing a referendum to take place and annulling the directive issued in December on the agreement reached at the 7th Congress. After all, this would remove the restrictions on the use of the amendments to the Constitution, which reduced the President's powers significantly. In order to achieve this strategic goal, a second issue had been proposed to the Congress, as a distraction from the main issue. The formal basis for this was the missive from the Constitutional Court of the Russian Federation to the Supreme Soviet "On the current situation as regards the lawfulness of the constitution in the Russian Federation", which was received a few days before the Congress. The third question (at this stage Chernomyrdin's Government had been in power for less than three months) enabled a wedge to be driven between Yeltsin and the prime minister.[772]

The President's attempts to alter the agenda for the Congress, and resume the discussion of the agenda, failed. The President's amendments to the draft directive on stabilizing the situation regarding the constitution were not accepted. On 13th March 1993 the 8th Congress drew to a close. On the final day, the deputies introduced a ban on the holding of referenda on the issue of confidence in the President and the Congress. The decision to put the 20 billion roubles previously earmarked for covering the cost of a referendum towards social protection and housing for the military had the ring of mickey-taking to it. The old agreements, reached in December 1992 by Khasbulatov and Yeltsin, with the involvement of the chairman of the Constitutional court, Zorkin, were contravened. The amendments to the Constitution, which made the Government subordinate to the Congress and the Supreme Soviet, came into force, and it was now prohibited to hold a referendum. Khasbulatov had played Yeltsin and deceived him, pure and simple.

Objectively speaking, Zorkin could be seen as having been complicit in this deception, along with Khasbulatov. It could not have happened any other way. If the Congress had the right to alter the Constitution several times a year, then the chairman of the Constitutional Court would be required to go into the open water of the Supreme Soviet.

An extremely important political outcome of this Congress, which had taken place so suddenly, was the fact that all the branches of power in Russia were now genuinely subordinate to the Congress and the Supreme Soviet.

---

772   The Yeltsin era. Sketches from political history. M., 2001. P. 294

A peculiarly Russian political phenomenon was the fact that the crisis had assumed a character that was not really constitutional, since there was no stable text to the Constitution, and, consequently, there could be no constitutionally organized political process. The crisis was transformed into a structural and political one.

The hallmarks of this were the attempts by the warring political factions to find 'a small island of legitimacy'. The fact of the elections was not, in itself, a serious argument: both the President and the deputies had been elected and were equal in terms of their rights, although the President's side sought to emphasize, in all kinds of ways, the fact that the Presidential elections had been a nationwide event.

In their quest for legitimacy, the Supreme Soviet and the Congress had recourse to the Constitution. Formally, this argument was almost flawless. The Congress had on its side the law, customs, and precedent, as had been demonstrated so vividly during the events of August 1991, when the coup was suppressed to the sound of slogans about restoring the constitutional standards trampled on by those who had instigated the coup.

The President appealed to the will of the peoples of Russia, as his strongest argument. A referendum would be the tool by means of which the will of the people would be established. It was for the referendum to answer the question: should Russia become a Presidential republic? Should the Soviet system be preserved? It was for a referendum, in the President's opinion, for the new Constitution to be adopted, by the whole nation. Given that the Supreme Soviet had in effect declined to collaborate with the President when it came to preparing the new Constitution[773], this job had to be done by the Constitutional assembly, which had been convened at the President's initiative.

It was also clear that each of the two sides, whilst standing up for their legitimacy, was seeking to reject the legality of the other side — with a greater or lesser degree of convincingness. Both of the parties bitterly rejected the idea of reaching a compromise, and the amount of room available for compromise was rapidly growing smaller.

I would like to note one other characteristically Russian aspect of this conflict: it was, essentially, an extra-party argument — or, to be precise, a supra-party argument. This form of marginalization of the political process affected both the subjects of the political process, and the forms it was allowed to take. The political parties played a demonstrably subordinate role in this conflict. The split between the politically active layers of Russian society followed the same

---

773   The historical irony was that the President, of all people, was the chairman of the Constitutional commission.

lines as the attitudes towards the President and the Supreme Soviet. Each of these forces had its own supporters.

On 20th March Yeltsin gave a televised address to the Russian people on two TV channels. He said: "The 8th Congress was, in essence, a dress rehearsal for the vengeance meted out by the former party nomenclature. Simply put, they want to deceive the people. We are hearing lies in the continuous slander regarding the accuracy of the Constitution: with each Congress that takes place it is ripped up and rehashed to suit people's own interests; time and again attacks are made against the very basis of the constitutional structure for popular power. ...The public have had their right to determine their own fate arrogantly rejected. ...A tragic result of the Congress was that there was a weakening of executive power, a weakening of Russia, and division of powers, as the principle of the Constitution has effectively been destroyed. The final barriers on the road towards universal power on the part of the Congress, the Soviets and parliament have been removed. Both the Congress and the Supreme Soviet declare all the decisions they make lawful and constitutional; there is no-one to stop them and no-one to prevent them doing whatever they please.

In this critical situation, the Constitutional court has still not adopted a moral position. Retribution against the principles of the constitutional system is taking place before its very eyes, and has not yet come up against any resistance."

The President announced that "the 8th Congress enabled the leaders of the Supreme Soviet in effect to release a flier for an unconstitutional coup." In these circumstances, he said, "The President has no choice but to accept responsibility for the fate of the country." Yeltsin announced that he had "signed an Edict on a special method of governance until the crisis of power was overcome. Under the Edict, a vote of no confidence in the President and the vice-president of the Russian Federation has been scheduled to take place on 25th April 1993. Special edicts and orders are going to be made on a whole range of issues regarding the organization of this vote. I resorted to this measure because I was elected not by the Congress, not by the Supreme Soviet, but by the people — and it is for the people to decide - whether or not I am to continue exercising my obligations, and who ought to be governing the country: the President and vice-president, or the Congress of people's deputies.[774]

The television had barely had time to broadcast the video of the President's address when it was announced that there was going to be an interruption to the scheduled program. On TV screens throughout the country, the chairman of the Constitutional court, Zorkin, the first vice-speaker of the Supreme

---

774   See: Yeltsin-Khasbulatov: Unity, compromise, struggle. M., 1994. P. 306-309

Soviet, Voronin[775], the general prosecutor, Stepankov, and the vice-president, Rutskoi, suddenly appeared. They launched into a public condemnation of the President's statement and Order, and accused him of carrying out a coup d'état.[776]

The very next day, on 21st March 1993, the Presidium of the Supreme Soviet ordered that an assembly of the Supreme Soviet be called, adopted an Address "To the citizens of the Russian Federation" and sent it to the subject entities of the Federation. That same day the Supreme Soviet convened and declared the President's Address to the citizens of Russia as an attack on the constitutional bases of Russian statehood, and ordered that the matter be taken to the Constitutional court, under article 74 of the Law of the Russian Federation "On the Constitutional Court of the RSFSR", with a request that the court determine whether or not the actions of the President in connection with his Address on the 20th March 1993 were constitutional, and also to the General prosecutor for Russia, with a request for an investigation into whether or not any of the officials involved in preparing the Address by the President of the Russian Federation could be held liable.

Khasbulatov, in a mocking attempt to provoke the President, decried the special procedure for governance of the country, announced by the President, to be an OPUS and declared that "the worst possible scenario has come about: the President, prompted by his own immediate circle, elected a path of direct, coarse and brutal confrontation, of rupture with the representative and judicial branches of power, a path of extreme measures which is taking him out of the sphere of constitutional rights."[777]

At the same time it was decided that the 9th Congress of people's deputies should be convened, as an extraordinary assembly.

The Constitutional court did not take very long to reach a verdict: by 22nd March 1993 it had examined the President's Address to the citizens of Russia dated 20th March 1993 and deemed it to be unconstitutional in many respects.[778]

---

775   Khasbulatov was not in Moscow at this time. He was in Alma-Ata, and flew to Moscow on the night of 20 March. — See: R.I. Khasbulatov: A great Russian tragedy. M., 1994. Tome 1. P. 101-102

776   The stance adopted by Rutskoi and Voronin was logical and understandable. They had given a political appraisal of their own. The position of Zorkin and Stepankov was strange and, to a lesser extent, unprofessional. As lawyers, it befell them to give a legal assessment, for which, as a bare minimum, the official written text of the President's address was required.

777   R.I. Khasbulatov: A great Russian tragedy. M., 1994. Tome 1. P. 102-103

778   The slyness of the president's team was the fact that the President's Directive, which had only been published on 24 March 1993. A number of points addressed by the Constitutional court were simply missing (or had been deliberately removed) from the final text of the Directive.

The 9th Congress opened its doors on 26th March 1993. Its main objective was to force the resignation (impeachment) of the President on the basis of the accusation that he had committed a coup d'état. The key protagonist in terms of announcing the accusations and launching the impeachment procedure was the chairman of the Constitutional court. Zorkin, in an address to the Congress, began to defend the Constitutional court's decision to make the accusations against the President. Zorkin emphasized that the Constitutional court had delivered its verdict, and that the issue of exempting the President of liability for going against the Constitution should be decided by the Congress alone.[779]

Yeltsin's attempts to make partial concessions, and make amendments to the identity of those in Government, and to socio-economic policy, whilst preserving the main demand — the call for a referendum — only served to infuriate those deputies inclined to side with the opposition, and were taken by them to be a sign of weakness on the part of the President. The deputies hurried to get their own back on Yeltsin for the shock experienced by those on the left after the suppression of the coup in August 1991. Y.M. Slobodkin, a member of the CP RF, declared that "pacification of Boris Nikolaevich Yeltsin has been the main theme of more than one Congress already now. But...the current President cannot be pacified, because he won't calm down until he has established a personal dictatorship or climbed onto a tank again." His words were echoed by A.M. Tuleyev, a member of the Political Council of the Front for the rescue of the nation: "After the so-called August coup, the deputies bestowed emergency powers on Yeltsin on four occasions at the Congresses and at assemblies of the Supreme Soviet, and super powers too... So why had the President decided he needed a dictatorship? So that, paying no heed to the discontent among the general public, and paying no heed to the fall in living standards, the collapse of the economy, and the unprecedented orgy of crime and violence sweeping through the country, he could continue his incorrect economic policy at the expense of impoverishing the bulk of the population. ..." Tuleev proposed that the President should be removed from his position, by means of a secret vote.

In order to force the President out of office, at least 3/4 of the deputies at the Congress had to vote in favor of making him resign. Khasbulatov, meanwhile, in effect provoked a discussion of the the deputies' confidence in Khasbulatov himself. In order to force the Chairman of the Supreme Soviet out of office, 1/2 the deputies had to vote in favor of doing so, plus 1 additional vote. Disadvantageous though this sort of distribution of powers appeared from the outside — a 'sacrifice' of sorts of Khasbulatov, there was a very astute political calculation behind it. Khasbulatov had seen enough evidence back in December 1992 to be sure that he had the backing of the majority of the

---

779   R.I. Khasbulatov: A great Russian tragedy. M., 1994. Volume 1. P. 109

deputies. In turn, he now had an eye-catching opportunity to compare the levels of support enjoyed by the Chairman of the Supreme Soviet and the President, among the deputies.[780] A kind of euphoria overcame the deputies at the Congress: they became convinced that victory would inevitably be theirs, and confident of their ability to control everyone for good.

An unexpected stumbling block emerged when the people's deputy A. Baronenko, a history teacher from Chelyabinsk, demanded that the people's deputies remove Y.M. Luzhkov from his position as mayor of Moscow. Luzhkov then took the floor of the Congress and, under the gaze of the TV cameras, became, for a few minutes, less the boss, as he had claimed he was in the past, than a political figure of Russia-wide scale. Interrupting the deputies, he announced, looking sure of his own strength and with unconcealed acrimony, that "you (the deputies — author's note) won't get anything of what you want. The mayor is elected by the people of Moscow, and the people of Moscow are entitled to do this, but the Congress, forgive me, is not."

The culmination of the Congress, however, included the planning and holding of a secret vote on the issue of removing the President from office and on confidence in the Chairman of the Supreme Soviet, late in the evening of 28th March 1993. The television broadcast the discussion taking place at the Congress and the offices being prepared for the vote, and everyone was on tenterhooks as they awaited the outcome of the vote...Scenes akin to the preparations for a public execution were being played out before the eyes of the entire country.

The President, who had no intention of becoming a 'lamb to the slaughter', and who was unsure whether or not this procedure would have a favorable outcome, was prepared to resort to extreme measures. The head of his security service, A.V. Korzhakov, later wrote in his memoirs that the measures he had in mind (disbanding the Congress by force, or arresting and detaining the deputies) were prepared and ready to be rolled out. A TV studio was set up inside the Kremlin, from which Yeltsin would be able to announce that the Congress was going to be disbanded and a referendum held.

Then, in March, it all kicked off...When the results of the vote were announced, it transpired that 617 deputies had voted against Yeltsin and in favor of removing him from power. Yeltsin's opponents had fallen around 30 votes short. Yeltsin was still President.

---

780   For a detailed analysis of the political struggle at the 9th Congress and the 'behind-the-scenes battle' around the Congress as set out by R.I. Khasbulatov, see: R.I. Khasbulatov A great Russian tragedy. M., 1994. Volume 1. P. 106-120; for his political opponents, among the President's advisers, see: The Yeltsin era. Sketches from a political history. M., 2001. P.304-310

268 deputies had voted against Khasbulatov. Khasbulatov stayed in office as Chairman of the Supreme Soviet.

Demonstrations in support of the President were held in Moscow.

The 9th Congress continued with the rest of its business. The Congress announced that a nationwide referendum on four questions would be held throughout the whole of Russian territory, on 25th April. After arguing over the matter at length, the deputies approved the following questions:

1. Do you have confidence in the President of the Russian Federation, B.N. Yeltsin?

2. Do you approve of the socio-economic policy implemented by the President of the Russian Federation and the Government of the Russian Federation since 1992?

3. Do you feel it is necessary to hold mid-term elections for President of the Russian Federation?

4. Do you feel it is necessary to hold mid-term elections for the people's deputies of the Russian Federation?

The thinking behind this was that the general public would under no circumstances express support for the socio-economic path of reform which had led to an obvious drop in living standards for the majority of the population. The second 'ticking time-bomb' was the fact that no provision was made for mid-term elections in the Constitution. This meant the opportunity had arisen for a political manoeuvre which had already been tested on several occasions. If a majority of the population had voted for mid-term elections of deputies, this opinion could simply be ignored as unconstitutional. If a majority voted in favor of mid-term elections for President, this could have been seen as an expression of the people's will. The arbiter remained, as ever, the Congress and the Constitutional court.

The outcome of the referendum on 25th April was that a referendum took place. The results of it came as a surprise to everyone. 69 million people took part in the vote, or 64.2% of all those who were entitled to vote. The support expressed for the President, and on top of that the approval shown for his chosen socio-economic course, caused a political sensation!

The results of the referendum were that 58.7% of the general public had confidence in the President, 39.2% did not;

53% of the population approved of the socio-economic policy of the President and the government, whilst 44.6% did not approve of it;

31.7% felt there was a need for mid-term Presidential elections;

43.1% of those who voted in the referendum felt there was a need for mid-term elections for people's deputies.

The President had been victorious, since, under the resolution adopted, he had secured the support of more than half of those polled.

Barely had the results of this referendum been published when arguments immediately began as to how the results of it should be interpreted. The President and his aides described it as an unconditional victory for him, and as evidence that the country's citizens supported the course chosen by the President. The Supreme Soviet had "stepped back to a position it had prepared earlier" and begun to demonstrate that although there was support for the President and his policy, this support came from those who had voted, and not from all those who were entitled to vote in the elections. It was a case of fraud. Even the Constitutional court decided, on 21st April 1993, that the first and last questions in the referendum ought to be voted on by a simple majority, i.e. among those who had voted. V.B. Isakov, who had become a stubborn and consistent enemy of the President, calculated that just 37.7% of the electorate had in fact voted 'for' the President.[781]

The leaders of the Supreme Soviet concluded that the President had not received a 'constitutional majority' at the referendum, and that any changes to the constitution could only be made via the Congress.

For the time being, the opposition decided to use non-parliamentary means of doing battle. A rally held on 1st May 1993 drew huge crowds chanting slogans aimed at the president. As red banners were waved over the heads of the crowd, some of the participants got into fierce fighting with the police. The fighting was provoked by the organizers of the rally, who had directed people along Lenininsky prospekt instead of towards the square in Krymsky val, next to the Home of artists, to the site cordoned off for the rally. There were brutal clashes with the police in Gagarin Square. Many people were wounded, and there were police vans in abundance.

In the evening the White House was surrounded by supporters of parliament, armed with sticks and makeshift shields. The building was surrounded by Urals vans owned by the army or the police, their cabins empty and their tyres punctured. I.V. Konstantinov, a member of the Supreme Soviet and chairman of the executive committee of the Front for the rescue of the nation, called directly on his supporters to wage war on the authorities by means of street clashes. "The situation has reached a point where violent methods of

---

781   V. Isakov: The coup d'état. Parliamentary diaries. 1992-1993. Yekaterinburg, 1997. P. 329

resolving it are now simply unavoidable." "Bodies representing the authorities will come out to protect the friendships between the implacable opposition and the mobilized general public. They are going to come out not because they have a powerful love of the Congress or of Khasbulatov; it is simply that at this moment in time the White House is going to be at the center of the battle against the Yeltsin regime."[782]

Looked at objectively, the events of 1st May 1993 were a dress rehearsal for the use of forceful action: for the Supreme Soviet — as a means of using their own supporters as a tool for exerting non-parliamentary pressure on the authorities, and for the authorities — of the need to bring in the police and the security structures in order to suppress their political adversaries.

A constitutional assembly: preparing the presidential version of the Constitution

On 29th April 1993, Boris Yeltsin addressed an assembly of the heads of the republics within the Russian Federation, the heads of the administrative territories, regions, autonomous areas, and the cities of Moscow and St Petersburg. At this assembly, the President proposed that an approved draft of the Constitution of the Russian Federation be drafted by late May or early June and that a Constitutional assembly be convened in order to examine this draft.[783]

On the same day, the Supreme Soviet made short work of passing a directive 'On the finalization of work on the draft Constitution of the Russian Federation', in which he proposed that the Constitutional Commission and the parliamentary houses finish, by 20th May 1993, drafting and securing the President's approval for the core provisions of the new Constitution of the Russian Federation, and send them for approval by the subjects of the Russian Federation. The draft in question was the one being prepared by the Constitution Commission.

The fact that the chairman of the Constitution Commission was also Boris Yeltsin complicated matters somewhat. The representative bodies of power in the subjects were supposed to examine the text of the core provisions at the sessions and send their criticisms and proposals to the Constitution Commission by 10th June. On 25th May parliament was to discuss the text of the core provisions of the new Constitution, with representatives of the

---

782   I. Konstantinov: The public will respond to violence with violence //A popular truth. 1993. No. 19 I wish to note: either there was a specific political prediction behind these words, or the planning for the upcoming conflict had already began. The latter scenario is more likely.
783   See: S.A. Avakyan: The Russian Constitution: nature, evolution, modernity. — M., 1997. — P.113.

bodies of state power from the subjects of the RF invited to attend, along with legal experts and academics. The Supreme Soviet was tasked with examining the text put forward by the Constitution commission, one clause at a time, by 10th October 1993. The Congress of people's deputies of the Russian Federation was due to be convened on 17th November "to review and adopt the new Constitution of the Russian Federation."[784]

The President had clearly decided to go at a pace of his own, however, and on 30th April he published his version of the Constitution in the newspaper *Izvestiya*.[785] It was clear that it would not be possible to prepare the text of the Constitution within just a week of the referendum. Consequently, in parallel to the work being done on organizing the referendum, work was also taking place on the text of the Constitution.

Once it was published, the text caused a sensation throughout the country. Swords were drawn between the President's supporters and those siding with the opposition. The pro-Presidential newspapers — *Izvestiya, Rossiskiye vesti, Kuranty* — saw the text as a panacea which would cure all the country's ills. The other papers — *Rossiskaya gazeta, Nezavisimaya gazeta, Sovetskaya Rossiya, Pravda* — interpreted it as the kind of Constitution a monarch would introduce.

President Yeltsin justified his initiative of releasing his own draft of the Constitution by citing the decree of 12th May 1993 'On measures designed to conclude the preparations for a new Constitution of the Russian Federation'. The constitutional crisis could only be overcome, and democratic reforms introduced, if a new Constitution was adopted as soon as possible. The President ordered that a Constitutional assembly be convened on 5th June 1993 in order to finish preparing the draft Russian Constitution.

On the same day, by Presidential decree, the members of the working commission of the Constitutional committee for the completion of the draft Constitution were named — the committee contained 42 people and was chaired by Yeltsin himself.

A whole series of questions arose in connection with the convening of the Constitutional committee. What kind of role would the committee play? Might the Constitutional committee not be being secretly prepared for the role of a future Constitutional assembly?

It was obvious that by now, the President and the Congress had clearly set out their approaches as regards how the new Constitution would be adopted. The President wanted it to be adopted via a committee and a referendum (so that

---

784   See: S.A. Avakyan: The Russian Constitution: nature, evolution, modernity. — M.,1997. — P.113

785   Izvestiya. 1993, 8 May

it was based on a direct expression of the will of the people). The Congress wanted the old Constitution to be preserved but amended.

Thus two different visions, two different concepts of how the Constitution was to be rendered legitimate came into collision.

Addressing an assembly of leaders of the Soviets from the republics, the territories and the regions on 12th May 1993, the Chairman of the Supreme Soviet, R. Khasbulatov, once again repeated his theory that a referendum would render the situation in the country more complicated, and that it was not possible, "without losing all sense of reason," to talk of a victory by one side or the other.[786] Khasbulatov dismissed the idea that it was impossible for the new Primary Law to be passed by the Congress of people's deputies as a myth, yet for the first time there was a suggestion, in what he said, that there was a genuine risk that the Congress might not adopt the Constitution, but that if this were the case, in the speaker's opinion, the Supreme Soviet could do so if it were reconvened. Given that there was no suggestion that mid-term elections of people's deputies were going to be held, it can be supposed that Khasbulatov felt the adoption of the new Constitution could be postponed until the elections in 1995.

By this time the deputy Chairman of the Supreme Soviet, N. Ryabov, had changed his stance and defected from the supporters of the Supreme Soviet to the supporters of the President. At a press conference on 18th May 1993, N. Ryabov said that the parliament, the President and the subjects of the Federation must now be consolidated, so that both the political crisis and the constitutional crisis could be overcome. According to the deputy Chairman of the Supreme Soviet, N. Ryabov, continuing the confrontation with the President — and, by definition, with the majority of the general public, who had expressed their support for him, would be crazy, and might lead to parliament being turned into a fiction.[787] Ryabov supported the idea of a Constitutional committee.

This was how *Rossiskye vesti* commented on the state of affairs within the Supreme Soviet: "The parliamentary leadership is currently closer than ever to reaching a compromise. There is only one thing standing between the President and the Presidium of the Supreme Soviet — Ruslan Khasbulatov. All his deputies, and the speakers of both chambers, have effectively united against him under the guise of the Supreme Soviet taking part in the work done by the Constitutional committee convened by the President.

The idea of a Founding committee had lost all its supporters. The reason for this was that any attempt by Moscow-based politicians to convene a forum

---

786   See: Rossiskiye vesti. 1993. 13 May.
787   See: Rossiskiye vesti. 1993. 19 May.

that would be more representative than the Congress of people's deputies, came up against gentle yet decisive resistance by most of the subjects of the Federation, after all, for the subjects of the Congress this was a 'roundtable' for big bosses and senior figures from the regions.[788]

A founding assembly would only serve to drag out the period of confrontation with the legislature even more. It was obvious that the Congress of people's deputies and the Supreme Soviet would not be happy with this method of adopting the Constitution. Lastly, two election campaigns in a row — the one for the Foundation committee and the one for the new parliament — might simply never have taken place. In order to minimize the inevitable political damage that would follow, the Foundation committee was replaced by the Constitution committee.

On 20th May 1993 a new directive by President Yeltsin was adopted 'On the convening of a Constitutional committee and the finalization of preparations for a draft Constitution of the Russian Federation', which clarified a series of provisions from the previous law concerning the Constitutional assembly. It was established that the Constitutional committee would contain representatives of:

- the federal bodies of power in the Russian Federation; the bodies of state power from the subjects of the Russian Federation; local autonomous bodies;

- political parties, professional unions, charities for young people and other charities, and movements within religious faiths with mass followings;

- manufacturers of goods and entrepreneurs.

The group of representatives of the federal bodies of state power was comprised of people's deputies: there were members of the Constitution commission, representatives of each bloc and an additional 50 representatives of the President and the government.

The group of representatives of the bodies of state power from the subjects of the Russian Federation was formed by means of the selection of one person from representative and executive power from each subject of the federation.

Representatives of local autonomies, political parties and movements, professional unions, manufacturers of goods and entrepreneurs, religious faiths and the Academy of sciences were given an allocation of 250 seats at the meeting.

---

788   See: Rossiskiye vesti. 1993.20 May

Under the directive, representatives of the Constitutional Court of the RF, the Supreme Soviet of the RF, the Supreme Court of Arbitration of the RF, and representatives of the General Procurator of the RF could all take part in the work done by the Constitution commission.

On 26th May 1993, a meeting was held in Moscow's President hotel for the heads of the republics in the Russian Federation, which was also attended by the leaders of regional associations.[789] The President's press-secretary V. Kostikov announced that the purpose of the meeting was to explain, to the heads of Russia's republics, the aims and objectives of the constitutional process in Russia. As it transpired, this event was to be the last occasion of any major significance on which Yeltsin consulted the heads of the republics and the subjects of the Federation before the Constitution committee opened on 5th June. This meant that it was possible, on the one hand, for the President to set out his point of view on the text he had presented, and show the heads of the republics how their interests had been taken into consideration in the new Constitution, and how the Federal Agreement was to be integrated into the new Constitution. On the other hand, it also gave him an opportunity to get a feel for and understand what the prevailing mood was in the subjects of the federation and among the heads of the republics.

In a directive dated 3rd July 1993, 'On the participation of an official representative of the Supreme Soviet of the Russian Federation in the work of the Constitution committee', the Supreme Soviet elected the Chairman of the Supreme Soviet, Ruslan Khasbulatov, as its official representative.[790]

The constitution committee opened on 5th June 1993. Of the 762 names on the list of participants, 692 arrived that morning. President Boris Yeltsin addressed those present. In his speech, the President observed that the adoption of a Constitution would be the final stage in the process of establishing a genuine democratic republic in Russia. In Yeltsin's opinion, the power structure in Russia remained essentially unchanged, and was the same as ever: it had merely had important, though one-off elements, added to it. And ultimately it became clear "that the Soviet version of power is not something that can be reformed. Soviets and democracy are ideas that are not compatible with one another."[791] As the President saw it, this was why there was a need to convene a Constitution committee — because the existing institutes of power could not be used to complete work on the draft of the Constitution: "Representative power, which we have left in

---

789   See: Rossiskiye vesti. 1993. 27 May.
790   See: News from the Congress of people's deputies of the Russian Federation and the Supreme Soviet of the Russian Federation. — 1993. No. 24 Art. 866
791   See: The Constitutional Assembly. Transcripts, material, documents. 29 April - 10 November 1993 Vol. 2. — M.,1995. — P.6

Soviet mode, is not capable of finding the consensus for which there is such a strong need today. Without it, it cannot propose a Constitution which would bring stability to society and provide dynamic forward motion."[792]

In the second part of his speech, Yeltsin talked about the attributes of his version of the Constitution: "It was drafted by a group containing some of the country's top lawyers. They were tasked with bringing together all the best bits from the most well-known constitutional texts of recent times. I feel that we have created a text which is fairly succinct, intelligible and flexible, which has a common concept at its heart.[793]

The President proposed the following procedure for adopting the new Constitution:

- The text of the draft version would be approved during the course of the Constitution committee.

- The authorized representatives of the subjects of the RF would put their initials on the text.

- The subjects of the RF would propose that the Congress of people's deputies confirm the approved version of the Constitution in its entirety.

"If the representative powers reject our proposals, we will have to examine other possibilities. This is exactly the issue you need to think about — you must establish your stance, and strengthen, with your solutions, the President's readiness to introduce political reforms in a thorough manner," Yeltsin emphasized.[794]

The rest of the speech was very much in the same vein. As he saw it, "it was not different branches of power that were in conflict, but, in essence, two independent political systems."

The pace the President had chosen for introducing the new Constitution was hardly realistic. The process of securing approval for the text from the subjects of the Federation was never going to be straightforward — and indeed it was not straightforward, as subsequent events showed. The text of the draft constitution clearly restricted the powers of the subjects of the Federation, who naturally could not agree to them. The Congress's stance was already clear.

---

792   See: The Constitutional Assembly. Transcripts, material, documents. 29 April - 10 November 1993 Vol. 2. — M.,1995. — P.7.

793   See: The Constitutional Assembly. Transcripts, material, documents. 29 April - 10 November 1993 Vol. 2. — M.,1995. — P.10.

794   Same reference. P.14.

Following the President's speech, Viktor Chernomyrdin, who was presiding over the assembly, gave the floor to A. Alekseyev. Ruslan Khasbulatov walked up to the lectern at the same time as him, however, and demanded to be allowed to speak. Since most of those in attendance harbored hostile feelings toward the Supreme Soviet and Khasbulatov personally, howls of discontent could be heard in the hall as people demanded that he be prevented from taking the floor. The presiding officer allowed him to speak, but the President's supporters began a slow hand-clap whilst the parliament's speaker was talking. In the end, the Chairman of the Supreme Soviet, most of the leaders of the Soviets, territories and regions, the General Procurator, the judges from the Constitutional court and many deputies walked out of the Constitution committee.[795]

There was another moment of confusion at the assembly, as well. During Boris Yeltsin's speech, a fervent adversary of his, Y. Slobodkin, stormed up to the lectern and began shouting and screaming. In the end, Slobodkin, a deputy who had written one of the alternative versions of the Constitution, was simply taken out of the auditorium by security guards.

The first few days of the Constitution committee provided confirmation that the most discussed issues would be the ones which concerned the powers of the federal authorities, particularly the President and the parliament, the relations between the central government and the subjects of the Federation, and also relations between the subjects of the Russian Federation themselves: the republics, on the one hand, and the territories and regions on the other hand, and the procedure for adopting the Constitution.

Boris Yeltsin continued actively consulting with those present at the Constitution committee. The President conducted negotiations with the heads of the republics, met members of the Presidium of the Supreme Soviet, and sent a message to the people's deputies, heads of committees and commissions asking them to take part in the ongoing work of the Constitution committee.[796] Yeltsin's active, front-foot style of politics in this period was timely, given that there was a fairly deep split in the ranks of the deputies, and that all was not well among the leadership of the Supreme Soviet. There was no mutual understanding between the subjects of the Federation, either. Many of the representatives and deputies who had left the Constitution committee on the Saturday were at the Kremlin the next Monday.

On 9th June the Supreme Soviet adopted a special directive 'On the participation of the Supreme Soviet of the Russian Federation' in the Constitution

---

795   See: V. Isakov: The coup d'état. Parliamentary diaries. 1992-1993. — Yekaterinburg, 1997.— P.360.

796   See: Rossiskiye vesti 1993. 10 June.

committee, convened by the President of the Russian Federation[797], in which Ruslan Khasbulatov was delegated the task of working within the Constitution committee as an official representative of the Supreme Soviet of the RF. The Supreme Soviet determined that its official representative was to be guided, in his work, by the following principles:

- develop a unified text for a new Constitution on the basis of the draft compiled by the Constitution commission, the draft provided by the President of the RF, and the other draft versions;

- reject the theory put forward by the President of the Russian Federation: "The Soviets and democracy are not compatible with one another", which had been posited in the speech made on 5th June 1993;

- the verdicts of the Constitutional court were to be considered as recommendations;

- the constitutional procedures for adopting a new Constitution were to be established by the Supreme Soviet and the Congress of people's deputies of the Russian Federation.[798]

This last point contained the key to understanding the position of the Supreme Soviet of the RF: the Congress would adopt the Constitution, but the President's plans were unconstitutional. Boris Yeltsin was unable to agree to such terms entirely — after all, this was fundamentally a procedure for adopting the Constitution and a type of state. Society nonetheless hoped for a reconciliation of the parties and did not want a deepening of the confrontation. The President was therefore unable to ignore the existing state of affairs and stick to the tough stance he had set out in his speech on 5th June. The following day, on 10th June, whilst addressing the Constitution committee, the President disavowed the theory that the Soviets were the antithesis of democracy: "I'm not in favor of any revolutionary action being taken as regards the Soviets...

The main thing I wanted to say was this: the Soviets, as a tool of the former structures of the CPSU, as a single corporation, the way their creators intended them, combined in their activities, and still combine, both law-making, and supervision, and executive-administrative functions. This is the source of their constant striving to replace the executive organs of power; this is the source of the fact that they do not accept the principle of the distribution of powers."[799]

---

797   See: News from the Congress of people's deputies of the Russian Federation and the Supreme Soviet of the Russian Federation. — M., 1993. No. 25 Art. 913

798   Same ref.

799   The Constitutional Assembly. Transcripts, material, documents. 29 April — 10 November 1993 Vol. 5. — M.,1995. — P.367.

At the start of the plenary assembly Yeltsin summed up the results of the work that had been done. In his opinion, a normal process was taking place: both draft versions were being reviewed, and the text of a new Constitution of the RF was being drafted on the basis of them. A speech was due to be made at the assembly by the Chairman of the Supreme Soviet Ruslan Khasbulatov, but the President reported that the leader of the parliament was unwell and unable to attend. During the plenary assembly, the deputy Chairman of the Supreme Soviet, N. Ryabov, took the floor. In his speech he highlighted the preliminary results of the work carried out by the break-out groups, and focused mainly on the structure of a federal state.[2]

There were brief reports by group leaders V. Chernomyrdin, S. Shakhrai, V. Yarov, A. Sobchak and V. Shumeiko. The general consensus was that a creative, joint effort was taking place on two projects, but it was quite possible that the separate groups didn't have enough time to review all of them on the days set aside for them. S. Shakhrai proposed that the Constitution committee should not be closed on 16th June, as planned, but that a break should be announced and that it should be maintained in future as a 'round-table discussion' of sorts."[800]

Giving his concluding remarks on the plenary assembly, Yeltsin agreed that the Constitution committee should not be brought to a close on 16th June and said that it should be given the opportunity to continue its work. The President also proposed that two inter-section working groups be set up, which would work on drafting the law on elections and the mechanism for adopting a new Constitution. With a directive dated 16th June 1993, 'On the organization of the continuing work of the Constitution committee', Yeltsin decided that the Constitution committee would continue its work between 17th and 25th June 1993. The Constitution committee in fact continued its work in early July as well.

Thereafter, the draft Constitution initiated by the President and approved by the Constitution committee was sent to the subjects of the Russian Federation. The President's plan was for it to be discussed or approved by late August or early September, but that didn't happen. Most of the representative bodies were guided by the Supreme Soviet and the Congress of people's deputies, but in spite of this they nonetheless wanted a single, approved draft, and for that reason refrained from clearly expressing support for one or other of the parties. The Constitution currently in force allowed for the Constitution to be adopted, and for a referendum to be called in order for the Congress of people's deputies to adopt the Constitution. For this reason, the representative bodies of many subjects of the RF did not deem it acceptable to ignore the Congress — the policy

---

800   Rossiskaya gazeta. 1993. 11 June.

chosen by the President. The President's version of the Constitution could only be adopted in spite of the Supreme Soviet and the Congress, and the parliamentary version could only be adopted in spite of the President. As far as any potential compromise was concerned, both sides had burned their bridges. The constitutional crisis had assumed all the elements of a struggle for power, a struggle for mutual destruction.

The final statement made by Ruslan Khasbulatov, at a press-conference held on 18th August 1993, is significant: "The authority of parliament today," Khasbulatov said, "is in no way less than that of the President."[801] And the point was not that parliament's authority had increased; Khasbulatov was right in another sense: the authority of the President was on the decline, and had to all intents and purposes drawn level with that of parliament.

In parallel to these events Russia was hit by a corruption scandal. In the course of the five months leading up to October 1993, the whole of Russia was shaken by the so-called 'battle of the dirt'. On the TV screens and in the newspapers, at press-conferences in the capital and inside the parliament building, Yeltsin's enemies and supporters levelled fierce accusations of disgraceful corruption at one another. The man who initiated the scandal for the vice-president A. Rutskoi, who announced that there was corruption in the upper echelons of power and said that he had 11 suitcases of compromising material. For ninety minutes, A. Rutskoi, standing at the lectern, accused vice-premiers, ministers and members of the President's inner circle of corruption, and accused Yeltsin of having connived with them.

On 24th June N. Makarov, the first deputy of the General Procurator of the RF, spoke to the deputies at an assembly of the Supreme Soviet. Makarov was the leader of a special commission set up to investigate material related to corruption on the part of those in authority. He informed the members of parliament about how the investigation of the facts set out in the vice-president A. Rutskoi's speech was going. Serious breaches of the law had been uncovered in the privatization of certain companies, and in the issuing of export licenses for gold, precious metals and energy carriers. As he drew his speech to a close, N. Makarov proposed that the parliament recommend, to the Russian President, that he remove V. Shumeiko and V. Poltoranin from office so that an investigation could be carried out.[802] By a special decree dated 24th June, the Supreme Soviet rejected the idea of cooperating with the Constitution committee due to the accusations of corruption made by some of its members.

---

801   O. Poptsov: A Chronicle of the age of 'Tsar Boris' Russia, the Kremlin 1991-1995. — M., 1995. — P.306.
802   See: Rossiskaya gazeta. 1993. 25 July.

July was noteworthy because of two other important events, as well. On 26th July 1993 the Central bank of the Russian Federation ceased circulation, throughout the entire territory of Russia, of official state tickets of the USSR, a banknote of the Russian bank between 1961 and 1992. The citizens of Russia had two weeks in which to exchange banknotes worth 35,000 roubles or less, and any savings in excess of this sum would be frozen for a period of 6 months.[803]

The Chairman of the Supreme Soviet, R. Khasbulatov, announced that the measure taken by the Central bank and the government had not been approved by the Supreme Soviet, and that freezing people's savings for 6 months was, in his opinion, a form of stealing and an infringement of their human rights.

The second event was the President's directive on the removal from office of the Russian Federation's minister of security, V. Barannikov. The Supreme Soviet declared that the directive regarding the dismissal of Barannikov carried no legal weight, since, under the law, in accordance with article 1218 of the Constitution, the President could only sack the minister of security at the instigation of the Supreme Soviet.

Thus the Constitution committee convened in June 1993 became an 'intermediary' stage in the constitutional process, an attempt to add legitimacy to the president's project. The question of the means by which the Constitution would be adopted formally remained open, although the executive had already opted decisively in favor of a referendum.

Directive 1400. The attempt to overcome the politico-constitutional crisis by force

In August 1993 Boris Yeltsin cut short a holiday in Valdai and returned to Moscow. On 12th August the President called together the Soviets of the heads of the republics in Petrozavodsk. The assembly of the Soviet was attended by the deputy Chairman of the Supreme Soviet, N. Ryabov, the vice-premier of Russia, S. Shakhrai, the heads of all the regions in the Russian Federation other than Chechnya, and the leaders of the inter-regional associations.[804] There were two items on the agenda for the meeting: the issue of the mechanism for implementing the Federal agreement and that of the subsequent steps regarding discussion and passing into law of the Constitution of the RF. President Yeltsin, in a speech marking the opening of the assembly of the Soviets of the heads of republics in the Russian Federation, proposed

---

803   See: Rossiskaya gazeta. 1993. 27 July.
804   See: Rossiskaya gazeta. 1993. 14 August.

that a new body be created: the Soviet of the Federation. It was to contain two people from the 88 subjects of the Federation — a total of 176 people. "In a Soviet of the Federation we would be able to decide many issues in a legitimate way. And no-one would then be able to rebuke us by saying that we were merely preparing an assembly of some sort. This is no assembly — it's an organ of power," he said.[805] The President also paused to discuss the issue of the work taking place on the Constitution. He emphasized that its adoption, and the implementation of the Federative agreement, were inextricably bound up with one another. The draft version of the Primary Law, once drawn up and approved by the Constitution committee, would now have to be approved by the representative bodies of power and those in charge of the executive in all the subjects of the Federation. "I am not ruling out the idea of adopting a Constitutional law during the transition period. With the help of such a law we might be able to hold new elections and thereby resolve the current duopoly on power, before it paralyzes the entire country," the President said.[806]

During the discussion of the speeches made by Yeltsin and Shakhrai another proposal came to light: holding a joint assembly of the Constitution committee and the Constitution commission in September. The President, who had not approved of this idea in the past, now supported the proposal made by the heads of the republics, with one condition: the subjects of the Federation must send their criticisms of the draft Constitution to Moscow by 15th September, or else they would not be taken into consideration.

There was also a meeting in Petrozavodsk between the President and representatives of Russia's state TV and radio companies and directors from the media. The President announced that he was going to toughen his stance with regard to the Supreme Soviet and the start of the political attacks in the autumn. "The decisive political battle in Russia will begin in September, and we must use August to do our planning," Yeltsin announced. "September is going to be packed full of battles: we face the task of resolving an issue of fundamental importance — the issue of power, i.e. that of the Constitution and the elections."[807]

The President's words about a hotly contested September and the planning that would take place in August, uttered in response to a question from a journalist, were homed in on by all the publications and quoted on the radio and the TV. No-one was inclined to interpret them as improvisation on the part of the President, or as evidence of his fondness for figurative expressions.

---

805   Same reference.
806   See: Rossiskaya gazeta. 1993. 14 August.
807   Quotation no.: R.G. Pikhoya: Moscow. The Kremlin. Power. 1985 — 2005. M., 2007
P. 439

When the President made an inspection visit to areas where military units were stationed, it was immediately seen as a step towards preparing for a state of emergency.

The President held a meeting in Petrozavodsk in order to try and gauge opinion among the leaders of the republics, and clarify whether or not they supported his decisive actions. Although the official purpose of the meeting was to discuss the "mechanism for implementation for the Federative agreement", those present realized that in light of the tense stand-off between the executive and the legislature, it would make no sense for there to be a division of powers and of spheres of influence between the central government and the republics, and everything would depend on how the President's 'autumn attack' panned out.[808]

The speeches by the leaders of the republics were restrained: they were biding their time, and wanted to sit on the fence in what was essentially a "Muscovite dispute". Another factor which influenced the situation was the fact that a host of leaders of the republics (M. Rakhimov, M. Magomedov, V. Stepanov, Y. Spiridonov, A. Galazov) were yet to assume the status of republican presidents and, whilst they were in the roles of chairman of the Supreme Soviets, did not want to ruin relations with the aforementioned Supreme Soviet of the RF or with R. Khasbulatov.

The meeting in Petrozavodsk showed Boris Yeltsin that the best he could hope for was that the republican leaders would be neutral, and that in the forthcoming battles he would have to rely on his political resources.

On 1st September the President, taking advantage of the corruption scandal triggered by Rutskoi, and of the similar accusations made against Rutskoi himself, temporarily removed from office the first vice-premier, V. Shumeiko, and the vice-president, A. Rutskoi. The directive stated that "The current circumstances, which have arisen as a result of the mutual accusations of corruption and the legal claims made by officials in the system of the executive against one another, are seriously undermining the authority of state power in the Russian Federation," and therefore, in connection with the investigation which is taking place and the lack of any orders for the vice-president, A. Rutskoi and the first vice-premier V. Shumeiko have temporarily been removed from office.[809]

The Chairman of the Supreme Soviet of the RF, Ruslan Khasbulatov, declared the directive illegal, since under the Constitution of the RF, the Supreme Soviet and the Congress of people's deputies alone had the right to remove the President or the vice-president from office, if they were found to

---

808   See: The Yeltsin era. Sketches from a political history. — M., 2001. — P.348-349.

809   See: Rossiskaya gazeta. 1993. 2 September.

have committed any of the violations of the law stipulated by articles of the Constitution of the RF, and prepared a draft directive on the appeal to the Constitutional court to check the constitutional legality of the President's directive.[810]

In response, the newspaper *Rossiskiye vesti* published a letter from Boris Yeltsin to the Supreme Soviet, in which he wrote that "the form chosen for the directive is based on the President's right to rely, in his decisions, on the totality of the regulations and principles of the constitutional legislation currently in force. The directive does not contain anything that directly contradicts the existing Constitution or the existing legislation."[811]

On 30th August a meeting took place between S. Filatov and the secretary of the Constitution commission, O. Rumyantsev, after which a draft directive was released at an assembly of the Supreme Soviet on 3rd September, in which R. Khasbulatov was ordered to hold consultations with the President on how to promote the constitutional reforms. It was put to the President that he could also consult a delegation from the Supreme Soviet.

On Monday, 6th September, Y. Baturin reported on the situation to the President and recommended that he agree to a consultation on the procedure and completion deadline for work on the new Constitution and acceptance of it, on a joint assembly of the Constitution committee and the Constitutional commission, and on the elections. The next day Yeltsin read the note and wrote in the corner of it: "Renegotiate."[812] It seems he had serious doubts as to whether or not it was worth getting embroiled in an all-out war with the Supreme Soviet.

Under the circumstances in effect at the time, considerable effort was required in order to restore good relations between the President and the Supreme Soviet. By that time the President was completely sure in his own mind: as long as Ruslan Khasbulatov was at the helm of the Supreme Soviet, collaboration with parliament was unthinkable for the President. Characterizing the relationship between President Boris Yeltsin and the chairman of the Supreme Soviet, R. Khasbulatov, O. Poptsov wrote in his book: "Relations between them (Khasbulatov and Yeltsin) had reached a dead end — and that's putting it lightly. When you're in a dead end, it's possible to turn back and start again from the beginning. What made this conflict different from any others was the principle: anyone who sticks stubbornly to their own course of behavior interprets the behavior of someone else as unavoidably hostile. The defining factor for Khasbulatov was the fact of the private "one on one" meetings with

---

810   GARF. F. 10026. Op. 2. D 35. L. 5
811   The President — to parliament: the Directive will put an end to the political skirmish and restore the authority of the government.// Rossiskiye vesti. 1993. No. 171
812   See: The Yeltsin era. Sketches from a political history. — M., 2001. — S. 352.

the President — he wasn't satisfied by any other type of contact. These tête-à-tête meetings put the Chairman of the Supreme Soviet on the same level as the President in the public imagination."[813]

The President wrote in his memoirs that in early September 1993 he asked his first adviser V.V. Ilyushin to start preparing a directive on the implementation of Constitutional reforms and the dissolution of the Supreme Soviet and the Congress of people's deputies.[814] The draft directive on the dissolution of the Supreme Soviet was first discussed on 12th September at the estate of Staro-Ogarevo outside Moscow. The head of the President's security service, A. Korzhakov, recalls: "Boris Nikolaevich had invited Kozyrev, Grachev, Yerin, Chernomyrdin and Golushko there. Neither Barsukov nor I went to the meeting, but we sat in the room next door, ready to walk in and give Yeltsin our support at a moment's notice. The directive received approval from everyone concerned. The only bone of contention was over the date on which parliament was to be disbanded. They wanted it to happen on 19th September, but after giving the matter some thought, decided to do it one day earlier, on the 18th."[815]

Chernomyrdin was not present at this meeting — he was on a business trip at the time. Yeltsin told the premier minister Chernomyrdin and the head of the President's Administration, Filatov, about his plans the next day, on 13th September. All of the planning took place under conditions of the utmost secrecy. The President's entourage insisted on postponing the announcement of the directive to a later date, so that more detailed preparations could be made, and the President confirmed the new date — 21st September.

On 14th September Boris Yeltsin chaired an assembly of the President's Council. The President invited to the Council meeting in the Great Kremlin palace representatives of the political parties and movements, people's deputies and prominent academics. In his speech at the opening of the meeting, Boris Yeltsin congratulated the members of the President's Council with the start of the new political year, although there had hardly been much of a break to speak of, he added. Very shortly, in September or October, the President said, there was a need to bring a stop to the course of these negative events and, first and foremost, get rid of the destructive impact of the duopoly in Russia. There was a need to get out of this situation, everyone had had enough of it, and what was needed was a peaceful, civilized path to overcoming the duopoly, the President emphasized. This was a vitally important condition for a return to good economic health, a strengthening of the rule of law and even the moral regeneration of the country.[816]

---

813   O. Poptsov: A Chronicle of the age of 'Tsar Boris' Russia, the Kremlin 1991-1995. — M., 1995. — P.335.

814   See: B.N. Yeltsin: Notes by the President. — M., 2006. — P. 393-394.

815   A. Korzhakov: Boris Yeltsin: from dawn till dusk. — M., 1997.

816   See: Rossiskiye vesti. 1993. 15 September.

On 15th September the President chaired a meeting of the Security Council, citing the conflict in Osetino-Ingushetia as the official reason. It was a confidential meeting, and the President requested that no transcript be recorded.[817] Immediately after the meeting, the President invited Chernomyrdin, Grachev, Yerin and Golushko into his office.[818] He probably did so in order to discuss the forthcoming directive on the disbandment of the Supreme Soviet.

At the same time, on 15th September 1993, a working group from the Constitutional Commission brought its work to an end. The members of the Constitutional Commission's Working group prepared a document in which they acknowledged the need to create a single, approved document on the basis of the two texts, taking into account the proposals and criticisms which had come in. The job of doing this befell a working group consisting of members of the Constitutional commission and the Constitutional committee, which was supposed to set to work on the approval of the phrasing in the two texts on 16th September.

On 16th September there was a working meeting for the members of the Government, attended by people's deputies from Russia. The main topic of conversation was the economic situation in the country and the agenda for the council of ministers as regards stabilizing the economy. The executive and the legislature must work together, the prime minister Viktor Chernomyrdin said to everyone, as he opened the meeting. He placed particular emphasis on the state of the Russian economy, pointing out that the "cancerous tumor" of a duopoly was having an effect on the complex economic situation. As he explained the government's position on specific issues, Chernomyrdin focused particularly on the "shocking damage" which was being done to the country's economy by the stand-off between the two branches of the executive — the resistance which the government was coming up against on an almost daily basis in parliament. The prime minister called on the people's deputies to engage in constructive cooperation, expressed the government's willingness to accept any effective proposal from the people's deputies, and to work together. The deputies told him that they wished to meet up more often, particularly with those of their number who did not work within the Supreme Soviet.[819]

That same day, President B. Yeltsin paid a visit to the Dzerzhinsky army unit, and whilst speaking to journalists there he said that in his opinion the elections to the new federal parliament would take place that autumn.

---

817   See: B.N. Yeltsin: Notes by the President. — M., 2006. — P. 401

818   See: The Yeltsin era. Sketches from a political history. — M., 2001. — P.355.

819   See: Rossiskiye vesti. 1993. 17 September.

On Friday, 17th September, the President chaired a final assembly of the Security Council, at which the final details were due to be discussed. All of a sudden, to Yeltsin's surprise, the ministers responsible for security began, one after another, to suggest postponing the address to the general public scheduled to take place on Sunday, and, accordingly, to bring into force the directive on the dissolution of parliament.[820]

The main reasons for this were mentioned. A meeting of the heads of state from the CIS was due to take place in Moscow on 24th September. Due to the coming into force of the directive it might have to be cancelled: the leaders of the republics would refuse to come to Moscow and this would deal a heavy blow to the president's authority. And the second point to note: information had clearly been leaked somehow: Khasbulatov and Rutskoi had been told that a directive had been prepared on the dissolution of parliament and that an announcement about its entry into force was going to be made on Sunday. The plan involving the taking of the White House on the Sunday, when it would be empty and not operational, and when none of the deputies or staff would be there, now had to be changed. On Sunday Khasbulatov would take his own supporters there, and the White House would be transformed into a center of resistance. There was no option but to put them in a stupid position: they had gathered together to offer resistance and take up the fight, but there was nothing to resist and nothing to fight against.[821]

At the same meeting it was announced that 19th September was not the ideal date for announcements of this nature — it would be too likely to remind people of 19th August. It would be better to postpone it until the 26th. Yeltsin agreed to postpone it — not by a week but by two days: he would address the nation on TV on 21st September.

The President's televised address to the nation was scheduled to take place at five pm on 21st September. The TV crew which arrived at the Kremlin had no idea what it was going to be filming. As Yeltsin read the text of his address, the expressions on their faces began to grow longer.[822] After the recording, the President's press-secretary suggested that he move into a room without any telephones and while away the time in there until 8 pm over some tea and sandwiches. The journalists made no objection.

After the recording, at around seven in the evening, Yeltsin called for a car and drove home, where he watched the address on the TV.

At 8pm on 21st September 1993, the 'Address to the citizens of Russia' was broadcast, and Directive No. 1400 'On the stage-by-stage constitutional

---

820   See: B.N. Yeltsin: Notes by the President. — M., 2006. — P. 401

821   Same reference.

822   See: The Yeltsin era. Sketches from a political history. — M., 2001. — P.357

reforms in the Russian Federation'. The directive stated that "the political situation has grown more complicated, and represents a threat to the country's social security and security as a state." "In these circumstances," it went on, "the only method which is line with the principle of power by the people of bringing an end to the stand-off between the Congress and the Supreme Soviet, on the one hand, and the President and the government, on the other, and of overcoming the paralysis in which state power finds itself gripped, is to hold elections for a new parliament of the Russian Federation."

The President ordered that the legislative, administrative and supervisory functions of the congress of people's deputies and the Supreme Soviet should be frozen. Before the new bicameral parliament — the Federal Assembly of the RF — began its work and assumed the relevant powers, it was to be guided in its activities by edicts from the President and directives from the RF government.

The Constitution of the RF, and the legislation of the RF and of its subjects, the directive stated, would continue to operate, within the scope of the directive. Temporarily, before the Constitution of the RF was adopted along with the law on the elections for the Federal Assembly of the RF and the holding of new elections on this basis, the President brought into effect guidelines 'On the federal bodies of power during the transition period', prepared on the basis of the draft Constitution approved by the Constitution council on 12th July 1993. The new parliament was now the Federal Assembly, which consisted of the State Duma, whose members were elected by the people, and the Federation Council, comprised of the leaders of the legislature and the executive from the subjects of the Russian Federation. With this directive the President also approved the guidelines on the elections to the State Duma, which he scheduled for 11-12 December 1993. The Federal Assembly was to consider the issue of elections for President of the Russian Federation. The President suggested to the Constitutional Court of the RF, in the directive, that it ought not to convene an assembly before the Federal Assembly of the RF began its work.[823]

The Constitutional Court did not agree to this 'recommendation', and at the assembly, which was held practically immediately after the President's speech, late in the evening on 21st September 1993, came to the conclusion that Directive No. 1400 and the 'President's address to the citizens of Russia' of 21st September 1993 contravened many of the articles of the RF Constitution and provided grounds for deposing the President or putting into effect other special mechanisms for holding him to account under articles 121.10 or 121.6 of the RF Constitution.

---

823   See: Rossiskaya gazeta. 1993. 23 September.

Most of the people's deputies of the RF refused to submit to the directive, as well. An emergency session of the Supreme Soviet of the RF, which began at the stroke of midnight, decreed that, on the basis of article 121.6 of the Constitution, President B.N. Yeltsin's powers should be deemed to have come to an end from the moment Directive No. 1400 was signed.[824] Vice-president Rutskoi was appointed Acting President and made to swear the oath of allegiance under article 121-11 of the Constitution. Immediately after swearing the oath he sat down on the chair reserved for the president. A. Rutskoi signed a directive of his own, Directive No. 1, under which he assumed full responsibility and annulled Yeltsin's directive No. 1400[825].

The 10th Emergency congress of people's deputies

When the session of the Supreme Soviet came to an end, the decision was taken to convene, with immediate effect, the 10th Emergency Congress of People's Deputies, with the following agenda: 'On the political situation in the Russian Federation which has come about as a result of the unconstitutional coup carried out by Yeltsin'.[826] The Congress got started at 10pm on 23rd September. The first issue it considered was: 'On the political situation in the country in connection with the state coup carried out by President Yeltsin'. Khasbulatov spoke on this subject for half an hour, and then there was a 15-minute speech in much the same vein made by Rutskoi. Both speakers continued the criticism of the "anti-the public" and "anti-national" course chosen by Yeltsin and Chernomyrdin, and set out the grounds for an alternative course to the Supreme Soviet and the congress of people's deputies.[827]

On 24th September 1993 the Moscow branch of the Russian Public Opinion Research Center (VCIOM) conducted an quickfire survey of 1245 residents of the city. According to the data collected in the survey, 41% of Muscovites felt that in the conflict situation which had arisen in the country, "the law was on Yeltsin's side"; 18% felt it was on the Supreme Soviet's side; and 28% felt that both sides had acted unlawfully.[828]

Of the 87 subjects of the Federation, at 1pm on 22nd September, 21 supported the decision of the Supreme Soviet of the RF[829]; at 7.00 on 23rd September 53 Soviets of people's deputies did not support Yeltsin's directive.

824   GARF. F. 10026. Op. 2. D. 36. L.1
825   See: I. Ivanov: Anathema: A chronicle of a coup d'état. Notes of a spy. — St. P.,1995. — S. 26.
826   See: R.I. Khasbulatov, I.: The Great Russian Tragedy. Vol.1 — M., 1994. — P. 208.
827   See: B.D. Babaev: The 'White House' under fire. Eye-witness accounts. — P.31.
828   F. GARF 10026. Op.2. D.66. L.33
829   GARF. F. 10026. Op. 2. D. 56. L. 3.

Among all the heads of administration from the regions and territories, the only ones that supported the Supreme Soviet were the heads of the Belgorod and Bryansk regions (V. Berestovaya and Y. Lodkin), and the Amur and Novosibirsk regions (A. Surat and V. Mukha). Surat and Mukha were the only heads of administration who declared that the RF Constitution was in effect in their regions, and that anyone who acted in contravention of it would be held criminally responsible.[830]

Genuine power, however, remained fully in the hands of B.N. Yeltsin: the police, the army, the domestic forces, the security services and so on were all at his disposal. He simply shrugged off the decisions of the Supreme Soviet and the congress of people's deputies, and described the conferring on A.V. Rutskoi of the powers of the President, in his directive of 22nd September, as an "assumption" of the President's powers by A. Rutskoi, and dubbed this "illegal" and "invalid".[831] When the deputies refused to leave the House of Soviets, the building was surrounded by policemen and soldiers, a dense line of defences and vehicles, and then lines of barb wire too. The power supply and water supply were both cut off. There was no decent food available inside.

During this period, many Soviets of people's deputies and leaders of the subjects of the Federation, and charitable associations, came up with an initiative calling for negotiations to commence at once. By 25-26th September the core subject areas of any potential negotiations had been drawn up.

The Chairman of the Constitutional Court, V. Zorkin, proposed a mediation initiative. The essence of his proposal was the so-called "zero option". In other words, all of Yeltsin's directives since 8pm on 21st September would be annulled; and then, by the end of 1993, elections would be held simultaneously for both the Supreme Soviet of Russia and for President of the RF; the powers of the legislature would be conferred on the Soviet of the Federation before the newly elected parliament began its work.

Yeltsin made no objection to this "zero option", but on the condition that the said elections would take place after an interval of six months — otherwise there would be a "power vacuum" during the transition period. Rutskoi supported the proposal made by the Chairman of the Constitutional Court, but these terms did not suit Khasbulatov. "There are two ways out open to us: either we hold simultaneous re-elections of the parliament and the President, or we are simply physically removed from office, which is what the people around Yeltsin are trying to achieve," he said to his deputy Y. Voronin.[832]

---

830   See: A. Rutskoi: A bloody autumn. — S. 55.

831   See: S.A. Avakyan: The Russian Constitution: nature, evolution, modernity. — M.,1997. P. 128

832   See: Y. Voronin M.: Hobbling Russia. — M., 2003. — P. 477.

The leaders of a host of parties and unions joined the search for a compromise on 25-27th September. Modified versions of the "zero option" emerged: prior to the simultaneous elections of a President and a new parliament, the powers of the executive could be conferred on the government. V. Lipitsky spoke in favor of this proposal on behalf of the parties and unions. But this scenario provoked strong objections as well. Particularly vehement in his objections was Rutskoi — after all V. Lipitsky, like Rutskoi, was the co-chairman of the party A Free Russia, and, according to the acting President, "a stance of agreement and acceptance of defeat on the part of one co-chairman cast a shadow over the whole party."[833]

Concerned about the situation in the country, Patriarch Aleksei II decided to cut short his visit to the USA, and returned to Moscow. Things were hotting up, and many now saw the Patriarch as the only person who might be a potential go-between and peacemaker. On 29th September the Patriarch of Moscow and All the Russias sent a message to the Supreme Soviet in which he wrote of the need for political dialog. On 30th September he held a meeting with Boris Yeltsin. Both parties to the conflict confirmed that they were prepared to begin talks. The President appointed the head of his Administration, S. Filatov, the first vice-premier, O. Soskovets, and the mayor of Moscow, Y. Luzhkov, as his representatives in the talks.

At 2.30 am on the 1st October, Protocol No. 1 was finally approved and signed: it confirmed that, "in the interests of taking the sting out of the current stand-off, the parties have agreed to take the following measures:

1. In order to ensure that arms located at the House of Soviets are secured, collected and stockpiled, these arms are to be collected and stockpiled at the House of Soviets and taken under the control of joint supervision groups, comprised of staff from the Main Directorate of Internal Affairs (GUVD) for Moscow; and the security detail of the House of Soviets. To this end, there will be an immediate switching on of the power supply, the heating supply and also the requisite number of: telephones for rapid communication in the city. At the same time, the approved measures will be taken to reduce the potential power and resources available to the outside security detail at the House of Soviets.

2. Once the first stage has been implemented, the sides will begin removing all armed resistance; this will involve the simultaneous withdrawal from the House of Soviets of all the armed units and the removal of the outdoor GUVD team. At the same time, issues related to the withdrawal of non-standard arms from the House of Soviets were being decided once and for all. The tasks in the second stage are to be performed with consent and in conformity with all legal and political guarantees."

---

833   Same reference. P.479

As Filatov recalled, the parties to the negotiations, both of which were equally satisfied, "congratulated one another on this small but very important victory."[834]

In the morning the telephones, lights and water supply at the 'White House' were turned on, the siege around the building was weakened, and the information agencies announced that the troops from the Ministry of Internal Affairs would soon be taken out of Moscow.

But that was not the point! Protocol No. 1 in fact signified more than was written down in those two points. It is worth noting that by this time Sokolov and Abdulatipov had already shown themselves to be in favor of resolving the conflict by means of the proposals made by the regional leaders. Whereas the arms at the 'White House' had been taken under control, the conflict situation had been defused, with the siege lifted and the armed resistance now a thing of the past, the conflict now proceeded to develop in an unpredictable direction: in the manner expected based on the demands made by the subjects of the Federation. In these circumstances, the "third force" — the soldiers who sided with A. Rutskoi, V. Achalov (the defence minister appointed by the 10th congress), and general-colonel Makashov — became simply surplus to requirements. That was the first point to note. The second was that this turn of events did not suit Khasbulatov or Rutskoi. Against this form of political backdrop, their future positions looked somewhat problematic.

The 'Military defence council of the House of Soviets' assessed 'Protocol No. 1' in the following manner:

"1. The commission comprised of V.S. Sokolov and R. G. Abdulatipov went beyond the remit of the powers conferred on it by the 10th emergency Congress of people's deputies of the RF as regards the signing on 1.10.93 of protocol N 1...without first securing the consent of the Congress.

2. The signing of protocol № 1 was not done lawfully, since no terms for its entry into force within the constitutional field, in accordance with the decision of the 10th Congress of people's deputies, were drawn up in advance.

3. In order to ensure its entry into force in the constitutional field, the following steps must be taken:

a) the aforementioned protocol N 1 must be denounced by 8.00 on 01.10.93;

b) the leadership of the Supreme Soviet of the RF must, by 10.00 on 01.10.93, hold a press-conference on the mistaken position adopted by the

---

834   S.A. Filatov: An open secret. M., 2000. P. 292

delegation from the Congress on the talks with the Government of V.S. Chernomyrdin;

c) the Congress must appoint a commission for devising the tactics and strategy for conducting negotiations with the Government of V.S. Chernomyrdin at the morning meeting on 01.10.93.

The condition for the start of negotiations is that the following demands must be met, without fail:

- a broad spectrum of opportunities must be made available to set out the position of the Congress of people's deputies of the RF in the mass media;

- all the supply systems to the House of Soviets must be switched on;

- newspapers which were shut down illegally, and the television programs corresponding to them, must be restored;

- the armed siege of the building must be lifted at the near and far approaches;

- the ministers appointed by the Congress must take up office.

The question of the non-standard weapons located at the House of Soviets of Russia was posed in an unauthorized way, since all the weapons that are held are standard issue and belong to the Security Department of the Supreme Soviet of the RF."

The decision of the Military Soviet was signed by the ministers of defence, security and internal affairs, Barannikov, Achalov and Dunaev.

In essence, it was a call to continue and intensify the conflict. The military soviet dictated its will to the leaders of the Supreme Soviet. It left no room open for compromise whatsoever.

In the circumstances, negotiations had lost all meaning. The program proposed by Khasbulatov and Rutskoi, under pressure from the soldiers who supported V. Achalov and V. Makashov, signified, on the one hand, a refusal to recognize the authority of President Yeltsin and the Government, and, on the other hand, a complete and demonstrative split breaking away from the proposals made by the regions, which had demanded a return to the "zero option" — the circumstances in effect prior to 21st September, and the planning and holding of elections supervised by the Soviet of the Federation, rather than the Supreme Soviet.

Objectively speaking, the proposal made by Khasbulatov and Rutskoi was an act of provocation aimed at intensifying the conflict, and making him resort to the use of force and indulge in adventurism.

At a meeting of those taking part in the talks in the Svyato-Danilov monastery, in the presence of the patriarch, Voronin announced that 'Protocol No. 1' had been disavowed, that the problem of weapons was merely a specific example of the general problem of the unconstitutional actions of the "former President", and that there were no extra arms in the 'White House' which had not been accounted for, since "all our arms are standard issue, and Rutskoi, since he is president, is entitled to organize them as he sees fit and issue any arms whatsoever"[835] The talks came to an end. The conflict had entered a dangerous and uncontrollable new phase.

On 2nd October, a Saturday, a public celebration was organized in the center of Moscow for its most famous street — the Arbat. President Yeltsin was present at the festivities. Then, when he appeared on the Old Arbat, at the end of the street which led into the Boulevard Ring, some other 'performers' appeared at the opposite end.

They began building barricades, set fire to some protective car covers which they had picked up somewhere, and shattered the metal structures on the artists' stage. Brutal clashes with the police began. Metal bars were used against the police, and petrol bombs were hurled at them. A fire-extinguisher of sorts was made using a gas welding device, and this was used against the police. In response the police used truncheons, plastic bullets and live rounds. During the disorder, the Garden Ring was closed for several hours outside the Ministry of Foreign Affairs. There were large numbers of wounded on both sides. There were also fatalities.

The opposition had thought through their actions fairly well. The television broadcast to the whole country the images of the President in Old Arbat, and in the background viewers could see clouds of black smoke, barricades, people covered in blood...It served as an advertisement for the opposition, and advertising can be effective. This particular advertisement testified to the following: the opposition was winning out in its open confrontations with those in power, who were in disarray and had not anticipated as much from their adversaries.

No statements were forthcoming from the President that evening. It seemed as if the turn taken by events had come as a surprise to him: he had been caught unawares and was at a loss what to do.

---

835   S.A. Filatov: An open secret. M., 2000. P. 301

The next day, on 3rd October, the conflict assumed an avalanche-like character. An opposition rally was due to take place during the daytime in October Square. Tens of thousands of people had gathered there to take part in it. They were led by I.V. Konstantinov, the chairman of the executive committee of the Front for the rescue of the nation. At 2pm the crowd set off along Krymsky bridge towards the Garden Ring. Along the way it took down the police barriers on the Krymsky bridge, and threw rocks and lumps of tarmac at it, and took the shields and rubber truncheons off the policemen — in a word, anything they could lay their hands on. The crowd, which contained many thousands of people, broke through the fencing on Zubovskaya Square, knocked over all the barriers on Smolenskaya and proceeded along New Arbat. Bigger trophies were now in their sights, such as guns and military trucks.

By half past three the crowd was outside the buildings of the White House and the Moscow mayor's office. In a matter of minutes the barb wire fences had been removed, and the crowd pressed on towards the mayor's office. From there, the police who were protecting the building could be heard firing shots. The capture of the high-rise mayoralty building was pulled off incredibly quickly. The crowd smashed through its glass doors in cars and tore into the building. The guards, of whom there were not very many, were disarmed and taken prisoner. One of those directly involved in the storming of the building was the 'minister of defence', Achalov.

The Mir hotel, which stood next to the mayoralty, was the next place to be stormed. This had been used as the headquarters of the Ministry of Internal Affairs for the siege of the 'White house'. The crowd seized documents, weapons and vehicles.

The mood in the Supreme Soviet was one of euphoria, gradually turning into hysteria. From the balcony "of the White house, Rutskoi and Makashov gave speeches, cursing 'all these mayors, peers and ****'." Khasbulatov called on "our outstanding warriors to bring here their troops and tanks, in order to storm the Kremlin and seize the former usurper, the criminal, Yeltsin." When Rutskoi made this call to arms, columns of captured trucks and buses were lined up outside the 'White house', in which, under red flags, hundreds of people, armed with whatever had happened to be close at hand, under the command of the deputy general-colonel Makashov, moved forward to liberate the Empire of lies, as they had christened the Ostankino TV tower. At 5pm 15 cars and buses filled with armed people set off for Ostankino. The extremists Ampilov, Urazhtsev and Konstantinov headed in the same direction. Approximately 10,000 people formed a column and marched on the TV center.

All these events took place in the center of a city of ten million, a nation's capital. It seemed as if, for that two to three hour period, any semblance of power or authority had simply vanished and disintegrated. On this bright, sunny Sunday, a fantastically wild scene was being played out.

At 6 pm the Congress was convened once again in the auditorium of the Supreme Soviet. Khasbulatov, demonstrating confidence in his victory, said to the deputies and journalists: "At long last there are signs of a breakthrough in the situation which has gone on for 12 days... The events have shown us that people instinctively reject tyranny...

The subjects of the federation must now convene in the Constitutional Court, I have invited them here... Troops are coming this way right now. I am not aware who gave them the order to do so. But I have no doubt that these troops will not open fire on the defenders of democracy... I believe that the Kremlin must be taken today. 'Ostankino' has been taken. The mayoralty has been taken. Krasnov (the chairman of the Krasnopresnensky Soviet — R.P.) has been appointed director of the administration of Moscow. ... The decision must be made now, so that we can have an action plan in place for tonight and through to the morning — until a decisive victory is achieved... We shall honor the memory of those who died in a just cause..."[836]

In the circumstances, when there was a clear power vacuuum, the storming of Ostankino signified an expansion of the civil war which had begun to the whole of Russia.

The opposition suffered two heavy defeats at Ostankino. The first had to do with the propaganda battle, the ideological battle. The attack on Ostankino turned the TV journalists, in a matter of minutes, into irreconcilable, uncompromising enemies of the Supreme Soviet and its supporters. There was no more wavering now. An outburst of genuine, powerful hatred was directed at the Supreme Soviet and its supporters, who thenceforth began to be known as coup organizers.

The second defeat was a military one. Makashov's attempt to storm the TV center with threats — "We won't open fire first. If any idiots turn up who decide to shoot, we'll make sure of one thing: they'll be packed off to Israel"[837] — did not frighten them. The crowd tried to emulate the success it had had at the mayoralty. A huge truck began smashing through the glass wall on the ground floor. At the mayoralty, the MIA had been in charge of attempts to defend the building. As for the TV center, it was guarded by a special forces unit from the Dzerzhinsky unit, and armored tanks were ranged outside the building. They responded to the attack by firing on the crowds. The first shot was aimed at a young lad in the crowd who was getting ready to fire a grenade-thrower at the TV center. In the exchange of fire

---

836   V. Kutsyll: Notes from the White House. 21 September — 4 October. M., 1993 P. 117
837   I. Ivanov: Anathema. A chronicle of a coup d'état. Notes of a spy. Spb., 1995. P.244-245

that followed, many of the people who had come to "liberate Ostankino" were killed.

The journalist Veronika Kutsyllo, who was at the Supreme Soviet that day, wrote: "All is quiet at the White house. Something is different in the air in the corridors. People are walking around slowly, and talking in half-whispers. The leadership has begun to lurk about. Everything is heavy with dread expectation. A couple of hours ago the buses began coming back from Ostankino. Some of the people are wounded. The ones who were killed were not brought back. The people who have come back from there look shaken and oppressed. They are milling about in the White House, adding a sense of hopelessness and, to a certain extent, a despairing decisiveness."[838]

The storming of the mayoralty, the Mir hotel, the attempts to storm Ostankino and the storming of the ITAR-TASS building, the Krasnopresnensk Department of Internal Affairs and the Timiryazevsky telephone hub, and to block off access to the Ministry of Defence put the President in a position in which he had no choice but to resort to the use of force.

That night, the President met the head of the Ministry of Defence. In response to the direct question: would his orders be obeyed? Grachev evaded answering, trying to sit it out, cited his colleagues' opinions and asked for a written order. But he was unable to sit it out. Chernomyrdin, who was at the meeting, set out his opinion on the matter succinctly and in no uncertain terms, and the President said that a written order would indeed follow.[839]

At 5 am on 4th October the President's Edict 'On urgent measures to establish a state of emergency in the city of Moscow' was signed; under this edict, Yerin, the minister of foreign affairs, Golushko, the minister of security, and Grachev, the defence minister, were ordered, by 10 am on 4th October, 1993, to "set up a combined operational headquarters for the management of the armed formations and other forces whose purpose is to establish a state of emergency in Moscow."

The commander of the district in which the state of emergency was in effect in Moscow was supposed to "immediately take measures to liberate, and remove anything impeding access to, the facilities taken by criminal elements in the city of Moscow, disarm the groups which have illegally procured weapons and confiscate their weapons."

Troops were sent into Moscow. At 6.45 am shots were fired at the 'White House', initially from a light armored vehicle, and then five tanks from the Kantemirov division lined up in front of the building of the Supreme Soviet,

---

838   V. Kutsyll: Notes from the White House. 21 September — 4 October. M., 1993 P. 120

839   B.N. Yeltsin: Notes by the President. M., 1994. P. 385-386

on Kutuzovsky Prospekt. Volley after volley was fired at the windows of the building's upper floors, and a fire broke out. The scene, with all its frightening details and improbably clear definition, with shells landing on the white marble building against the backdrop of a bright blue sky, and black and red smoke streaming from the windows, was broadcast to the whole world on CNN.

At around four pm members of the special ops unit Alpha burst into the building and demanded that those present cease their resistance. The shooting stopped. At half past four, the 'squatters' inside the building — of whom there were more than 1500 — began to walk out. Some of the active members of the Supreme Soviet, led by Khasbulatov and Rutskoi, were arrested straight away. The shooting went on for several more days in Moscow.

According to the Procurator-General, 148 people died. The opposition claimed that the number of killed and wounded was far higher, with the figure of one and a half thousand fatalities mentioned.

The Civil war which had begun around a specific building, the 'White house', had been brought to an end. It was brought to an end in brutal fashion. Yet the fact remained that the civil war did not spread to the rest of the country.

The Constitution is passed into law

Under a Directive dated 7 October 1993 'On the legal regulation during the period of phased constitutional reform in the Russian Federation', the President assumed, in the period before the Federal Assembly set to work, all powers with regard to regulating matters related to finances, the budget, property and others, which had once belonged to the congress and the Supreme Soviet of the RF.

Under a different directive dated 7 October, 'On the Constitutional court of the Russian Federation'[840] the President accused the Constitutional court of having "on two occasions, in the course of 1993, brought the country to the brink of civil war, through its hasty actions and decisions." When the threat of civil war became real, however, the Constitutional court did nothing." Thereafter, it alleged that the Constitutional court, by taking a unilateral decision in relation to Directive No.1400, without giving an immediate assessment of the unconstitutional, violent actions of the extremist forces, and without looking into the issue of the constitutional acts of the former Supreme Soviet, the Congress of people's deputies, after its powers came to

---

840   See: Rossiskaya gazeta. 1993. 9 October.

an end, played what was essentially a negative, aiding and abetting role in the tragic series of events on 3-4 October 1993 in Moscow.[841]

In theory, the Constitutional court and its Chairman acted, on the whole, within the framework of what was permitted to this body. Under the law as it stood at the time, the Constitutional court issued assessments not to any old 'extremist forces' whose precise nature was unknown, but to the acts of agencies and the actions of senior state dignitaries. Given that the Constitutional court had declared Directive No.1400 and the President's actions as contravening the Constitution, it followed from this that the activity of the Supreme Soviet and the Congress of people's deputies, in accordance with their powers, were lawful under the constitution. The threat of abolition hung over the Constitutional court. The Chairman of the Constitutional court, V. Zorkin, tendered his resignation, and the work of the Constitutional court itself was put on hold.

Moreover, the President released a series of directives regarding the cessation of the activities of the representative bodies of power in the subjects of the RF and the representative bodies of local self-government. The activity of the Soviets of people's deputies was brought to an end throughout the country — in villages and small towns, districts, cities, regions, territories and so on.

After securing victory, B. Yeltsin did everything he could to make sure his version of the Constitution was adopted. Since it would be risky to hold elections for the deputies, and then wait for them to pass the Constitution into law (after all, the same old members of the opposition might hold on to their seats in parliament), it became clear to Yeltsin that the Constitution must be put to a referendum. This would look like a democratic move. Work on the draft Constitution resumed. The Constitutional assembly resumed its work as well. The draft written by the Constitutional assembly was taken as the foundation. It must be noted, however, that it was no longer relevant to the situation that had arisen in Russia after the October coup. It had been compromised and was now only half-fit for purpose, due to the attempts to accommodate the views of the president, the congress and regional leaders. Serious corrections were therefore made to it in the concluding stage of work on it.

Under the directive dated 15 October 1993 'On the holding of a plebiscite on the draft Constitution of the Russian Federation', a vote on the draft constitution was scheduled for the same day, 12 December, when the elections for deputies in the federal parliament were due to take place.[842] On the voting

---

841   See: Rossiskaya gazeta. 1993. 9 October.
842   See: Rossiskaya gazeta. 1993. 19 October.

slips, the question was phrased as follows: "Do you accept the Constitution of the Russian Federation?" — yes or no.

The provision on a plebiscite regarding the draft Constitution of the RF was approved on 12 December 1993.

It was established that if the Constitution was adopted, it would come into force from the moment the results of the plebiscite were announced. Many of the constitutional bases of the new organization of power had already been introduced through acts passed by the President. Under the provision dated 21 September 1993 on the federal bodies of power, during the transition period, the legislative and representative body of the RF would be the Federal assembly, consisting of two chambers: the State Duma and the Federation Council.

The draft Constitution, which was put to a plebiscite, was ready at the beginning of November 1993. The draft was published on 10 November 1993.

In the referendum, the Constitution received the majority vote required. 58,187,755 people took part in the vote, out of a total of 107 million registered voters (i.e. 54.8%). This meant that 49 million people did not bother to vote at all. The number of people who voted in favor of adopting the Russian Constitution was 32,927,630 (58.4%), whilst 23,431,333 people voted against (41.6%)[843]. The outcome of the vote reflected the state of Russian society in the early '90s, and its legal consciousness.

The Russian Constitution officially came into force on 25 December 1993. Under a directive dated 19 September 1994, the President declared 12 December 1993 to be a public holiday — the Day of the Constitution of the Russian Federation.

It so happened that the man who initiated the autumn stand-off was B. Yeltsin. Somehow or other, though, both branches of power were convinced that the President would make the first move.

The opposition, by all accounts, secretly wanted the same thing that B.N. Yeltsin was striving to achieve: that he would be the one to get things going. According to the President's adversaries, however, if he were to do so he would be sealing his fate, and he would be destined to suffer political defeat. The supporters of the Supreme Soviet were hoping to secure active backing from the fairly sizeable sections of the population who felt unhappy and let down by the reforms.

---

843   See: Advocate. 2003. No.12

As for the president's side, it was guided by its awareness of the legal dead-end down which the country was headed. The Constitutional crisis had brought the country down a dead-end road, towards the bloody quagmire of civil war. The President consciously resorted to breaking the law which had operated under the Constitution of 1978, with its endless amendments, so as to set up a fundamentally new kind of constitutional basis in the country. Essentially, it was a revolution, which led to the eradication of the Soviet system in the country and to the emergence of a constitution founded on the principle of the division of powers.

The drama which took place in October 1993 deepened the split in society. This manifested itself particularly vividly in the dramatic delimitation within the intelligentsia. A large group of its most prominent representatives, famous and respected throughout the country — including V. Astafiev, B. Akhmadulina, G. Baklanov, V. Bykov, B. Vasiliev, Y. Ngaibin, B. Okudzhava and R. Rozhdestvensky — assessing the situation which had arisen, demanded that the activities of the bodies of Soviet power be brought to a halt.[844]

Another equally famous and respected group of representatives of the creative intelligentsia, including Y. Bondarev, V. Belov, V. Rasputin, A. Shilov, T. Doronina, S. Govorukhin, S. Bondarchuk and G. Sviridov, called on Yeltsin and Khasbulatov to turn "one page back in the book of Russian woe", and make sure the highest law in the land immediately came into force once again.[845]

---

844   See: Power and opposition. The Russian political process in the 20th century. — M., 1995.-P. 353-354.
845   See: Power and opposition. The Russian political process in the 20th century. — M., 1995.-P. 354.

Chapter 9
Between battles: 1994-1995

In the eye of the storm

After the political storms of 1993, a calm set in. Yeltsin felt that now that the Constitution had been adopted, everything ought to change. His aides recall that the President saw the new year, 1994, as the turning over of a new leaf. "He held out serious hopes that life would be different now, without such brutal conflicts, and was counting on constructive cooperation with the new body of deputies."[846] Given the make-up of the State Duma, this was an illusory hope, and spoke only of how tired Yeltsin was.

By nature he was a sportsman above all else, in politics as in everything else. He was particularly good over short distances: he needed a quick result, and was capable of giving everything to try and achieve one. If no result was forthcoming, as had happened during his time as first secretary of the Moscow city executive committee, disillusionment and a downturn would follow, which usually led to physical malaise. But victory would drain his energy, too, and he needed a break — but in politics one must not let the pace drop for a moment: hard-won victories achieved after tense battles must be backed up.

From the end of 1993 onwards, the President's activities fell dramatically, which provided evidence of how tired he was, of his health problems and, perhaps, of being overburdened psychologically. He realized that the Supreme Soviet's victory over the opposition had been a Phyrric victory, that the economic situation was serious and that the people were tired. Exhausting, painstaking work was required on a daily basis, and he was not ready for it. Advisers who worked with the president at this time make no secret of the fact that Yeltsin was enduring a protracted period of crisis.[847] The reasons for this were wrapped up in the peculiarities of his psychological profile. As S.A.

---

846   The Yeltsin era. Sketches from a political history. M.:VAGRIUS, 2001. P.402.
847   The Yeltsin era. P.505.

Filatov wrote, "Yeltsin is not the kind of politician needed in times of stability and tranquillity. He's good, active and healthy, at times when the situation gets tense, when there is an onslaught of things to deal with. One gets the impression that he simply has to be at loggerheads with someone or other at at any given moment."[848]

The president's action plan for 1994 was not ready until late April, and in May it was still being adjusted unenthusiastically. The number of events he attended was constantly on the decline. Yeltsin was often absent.[849] The political hush which had descended would prove to be deceptive. In the stillness and hush of the offices in the Kremlin and the Duma, far-reaching action plans were discussed, and processes were taking place under the surface which might at any time interrupt this relative stability.

On 16th February 1994 the State Duma adopted a directive 'On the approval of the members of the commission to investigate the events of 21st September — 4th October 1993'. It included some of the President's enemies, and it was clear that the results of the investigation were not going to go in his favor. Another such event was the directive from the State Duma 'On the announcement of a political and economic amnesty', passed on 23rd February 1994. Under this directive, the members of the GKCHP and the people who had defended the White House in October 1993 were set free. On the third day, 26th February, R. Khasbulatov, A. Makashov and A. Rutskoi left prison, followed by some more of Yeltsin's enemies.

It was a direct challenge to the President, and Yeltsin was livid. He tried all he could to halt the implementation of the directive on the amnesty. However, in spite of Yeltsin's order and the pressure exerted by the President's Administration, the Procurator-General A.I. Kazannik, refused to resist the amnesty and tendered his resignation.[850] As he put it, over the course of fewer than five months of working as the Procurator-General, he had become convinced that "not only had Yeltsin tried to interfere in the procurator's activities, but so had his aides and advisers, including even civil servants, who believed they had the right to call me."[851]

Yeltsin was in a very decisive mood and ordered that the minister of foreign affairs, V.F. Yerin, immediately arrest those who had been released under the terms of the amnesty. The acting Procurator-General was summoned as a matter of urgency, so as to give his official consent to the president's

---

848   S.A. Filatov: An open secret. M.: 'VAGRIUS', 2000. P.429.

849   The Yeltsin era. P. 511.

850   A.I. Kazannik was appointed General Procurator of the RF by the directive of the President dated 5 October 1994 instead of V.G. Stepankov, with whom he had worked in the Supreme Soviet.

851   Nezavisimaya gazeta 12 April 1994.

order.[852] Once he had cooled down a little, however, Yeltsin agreed to a compromise. The Procurator-General could be fired, but the elected Duma was something he would have to live with. All the more so given that the Duma had decided to eradicate the commission set up to look into the events of October. On this issue, the President's interests and those of the deputies coincided. Whatever the results of the investigation might be, the only thing they would achieve would be to destroy the fragile peace which had been established in the higher elechons of power and bring in a new wave of resistance in society.

In his Message to the Federal Assembly, which the President read out on 24th February 1994, Yeltsin called for consensus in society and constructive cooperation between the various political forces. The stress was placed on the initial measures in the field of construction of the state. This was indeed the name given to the Message — 'On the strengthening of the Russian state'. It set the objective of "making Russia a flourishing country, in which there are people who are able to live freely, ..., in which power is based on the law and does not oppress the citizen; a country with an effective economy...".

In order to determine the country's strategy for growth and prepare for the President's annual message, a large group of experts and advisers was brought in. The instructions given to them by the President were not very specific at all. Yeltsin had suffered a bout of flu, was not feeling very well and confined himself to some comments of a very general nature; he did not make any amendments to the text at all.[853]

The President's team

The President's team tried to overcome the president's vagueness, and to compensate for it in part with its own activity. Yeltsin was always looking out for people with fresh ideas, and a group of representatives of the intelligentsia with democratic leanings gradually took shape around him. According to the account by V.N. Shevchenko, "by 1992 B.N. Yeltsin managed to assemble his team, the members of which remained almost unchanged right through until the elections in 1996. The basis of this team was formed by the president's aides, who formed an administration that was a body, able to plan future activity and prepare drafts for decisions sent to it to be signed, monitor the implementation of them, and also carry out all ongoing work regarding the performance of the president's constitutional powers."[854]

---

852   For more details see: V.V. Kostikov: A love-story with the president. Notes by the press-secretary. M.: 'VAGRIUS'. 1997. P.288-294.

853   V.V. Kostikov: A love-story with the president. Notes by the press-secretary. M.: 'VAGRIUS', 1997. P.286.

854   V.N. Shevchenko: Day-to-day life at the Kremlin under the Presidents. M.:

In addition to L. Sukhanov, V. Ilyushin, A. Korabelshchikov, D. Rurikov, L. Pikhoya and V. Semenchenko, who had been there ever since Yeltsin was elected President, the team now had some new members: Y. Baturin, G. Satarov, A. Lifshits, M. Krasnov, Y. Shaposhnikov and B. Kuzyk.

Yeltsin's immediate circle was being joined by a growing number of people who wanted to serve the idea of democracy, and not just the president himself. As the President's press-secretary, V.V. Kostikov, wrote, "for me and many of my friends, 'doing battle' for Yeltsin meant doing battle for democracy... It meant showing support for his democratic skills, which he had acquired whilst working for the Inter-regional deputy group. It meant fending off his old party habits, which were so much stronger than his newly acquired ones. ... In my work as press-secretary this was a kind of overarching task of mine."[855]

In 1993, after S.A. Filatov took charge of the President's administration,[856] its powers were expanded. It was responsible for issues of national security, communications with parliament, legal issues, military and technical cooperation and economics. The President's council was formed, as a continually operating consultative body; its members were D. Volkogonov, Y.T. Gaidar, S. Kovalev, Y. Luzhkov, A. Sobchak, A. Yemelyanov, S. Karaganov, A. Migranyan and others.

In April 1994 the information and analytical activity of the president's administration underwent a reorganization. Instead of having two analytical centers, one for general policy and one for socio-economic policy, an Analytical center was set up under the President of the Russian Federation (in April 1995 it was rechristened the Analytical directorate of the President of the RF) and a consultative-assembly body, the Expert and analytical council, chaired by the director of the administration S.A. Filatov. This body invited academics and experts who were famous for being pro-democracy to take part: Y.G. Yasin, D.A. Volkogonov, A.D. Dneprov, M. Urnov, A.N. Yakovlev, A.A. Pain, A.Y. Lifshits, Y.A. Levada, O.R. Latsis and others.

The president's council played a purely formal role, and did not meet regularly. But the President's expert and analytical department met almost every week, discussing strategic issues in foreign and domestic policy. That said, the ideas they came up with proved not to be greatly in demand by the President, and at times his aides found it difficult even to secure a meeting with the president on official matters. Relations inside the president's team were far from easy.

The young guard, 2005. P.161.

855   V.V. Kostikov: A love-story with the president. Notes by the press-secretary. M.: 'VAGRIUS', 1997. P.44.

856   S.A. The man Filatov replaced in this role was Y.V. Petrov, who had worked with Yeltsin in the Sverdlovsk regional committee

There was a good deal of rivalry over who could get closest to the 'boss' and for influence on him between A. Korzhakov's group and the group of aides. The following revealing story provides evidence of the nature of the relationships within his inner circle: "...all the president's aides took it as a given that we were being eavesdropped on, and, if we needed to say something to one another that wasn't intended for the 'big ears' of the Kremlin, we would simply give one another recorded messages which we would later destroy."[857]

In September 1995, in protest about the dangerous increase in influence of the president's Security Service, S.A. Filatov sent Yeltsin a short message written in an unusually terse tone. He wrote that following the events of October 1993 "The President's Security Service had become particularly active, increasing its influence on staff distribution and the preparation of analytical material, and by extension, on the expression of its particular view of the core areas of domestic and foreign policy...In this we can see without question the emergence of yet another center of political influence on state policy and human resources policy, for which no allowance was made either in the Constitution or by the law."[858] The director of the Administration felt that such a turn of events would be dangerous for a democratic state and would radically change the face of president B.N. Yeltsin. No reaction followed from the president, however — besides the fact that Filatov was soon forced to leave office.

The stable work of the president's team was hindered by the constant shake-ups among the senior management staff at the Kremlin. "On the issue of staff, relations toward staff, and the high staff turnover, the situation was unfortunately reminiscent of Yeltsin's time at the Moscow City Committee of the CPSU: then at the plenum he suffered a barrage of abuse for the chaos among the staff," wrote S.A. Filatov. "Clearly, in his character there was a constant need of some sort, some form of longing to replace people, some magic faith in the idea that everything would immediately change for the better...And on top of that — a panicked fear that someone might come a little too close to him."[859]

This sort of episode provides a clear example of Yeltsin's style of working. Following A. Kazannik's retirement, Korzhakov proposed A. Ilyushenko for the role of procurator-general, who had worked in the president's Administration as the head of the supervisory department. In the stand-off within the administration Ilyushenko was on Korzhakov's side, and from the point of view of the president's aides he was therefore a poor choice

857   V.V. Kostikov: A love-story with the president. Notes by the press-secretary. M.: 'VAGRIUS', 1997. P.11.

858   S.A. Filatov: An open secret. M.: 'VAGRIUS', 2000. P 242.

859   S.A. Filatov: An open secret. M., 2000. P.241

of candidate. Also opposed to Ilyushenko's appointment was S.A. Filatov. He was the man to whom the president gave the task of presenting the new candidate to the Federation Council. Yeltsin was told that Filatov's appearance at the Federation Council had dramatically cut the likelihood of Ilyushenko being approved as the candidate, and it was proposed that the task of presenting him be given to Chernomyrdin, whose speech would elicit a more favorable response. But Filatov was sent to do the job. One of the possible explanations was that the president was not overly keen on the idea of approving Ilyushenko, and in so doing strengthening Korzhakov's position.[860]

Another scenario is also quite likely: Yeltsin was demonstrating his power. It was the President who made the decisions, and they had to be implemented, whether you agreed with him or not.

For informal interaction and leisure there was a so-called 'President's club'. In addition to Yeltsin, who was considered the chairman, there was also M. Barsukov, P. Grachev, V. Yerin, V. Ilyushin, A. Kozyrev, Sh. Tarpishchev, V. Chernomyrdin, V. Shumeiko and V. Yumashev, B. Berezovsky, P. Borodin, Y. Luzhkov, O. Soskovets, G. Khazanov and I. Rybkin.[861]

The difficult road toward consent and cooperation

Meanwhile an independent expert group, at the Administration's behest, analysed the official data from the Central electoral commission and a host of regional ones, on the elections for the State Duma. The conclusions presented in late March 1994 provided cold comfort: the experts had unearthed a mass of falsified results, both in specific electoral districts and in the regional commissions. The 'clean' results, once the falsifications had been removed, were markedly different from the official ones:

49 million people had taken part in the vote, out of a total electorate of 106.2 million — in other words, 46.1%. The official data had put this figure at 58.2 million, or 54.8%.

Russia's Choice had received 10.34 million votes (the official figure was 8.34 million), the LDPR had secured 6.32 million votes (12.32 million officially), the CPRF — 4.90 million (officially 6.67 million),

Yabloko — 4.02 million (officially 4.22 million), Women of Russia — 3.37 million (officially 4.37 million), the PRES — 3.12 million (officially 3.62 million),

---

860   The Yeltsin era. P.408.
861   The Yeltsin era. P.528.

the DPR — 2.93 million (officially 4.97 million), the APR — 2.55 million (officially 4.29 million),

None of the above — 2.36 million (officially 2.27 million), the RDDR — 2.19 million (officially 2.19 million).

The directors of the expert group, A.A. Sobyanin and V.G. Dobrovolsky felt that the President ought to act. It was proposed that a large-scale campaign be commenced, at the very highest level, to review the results of the election, and logic dictated that this would mean the dissolution of the recently elected Duma. There was no support for this idea in the Administration for one simple reason: the method used in the recount looked fairly dubious, hence the results of the recount were unconvincing. One can imagine what sort of political tremors would be caused if there was a review of the election results. When the material from the inspection leaked out into the press,[862] the news sent such powerful shockwaves through society that the Administration was forced to defend itself against experts' opinions.

It was clear that it would not do to resort to confrontational methods: the President must cooperate with the various political forces, and learn to live with the State Duma, however opposed to him it might be. In order to take political decisions and carry out law-making work, a mechanism for approvals procedures was required. On 10th March consultations began on the preparation of a memorandum on civil peace in Russia. Meetings between representatives of the President, the State Duma, the Federation Council and the government began to take place on a regular basis.

In the current climate, the absence of the President from his place of work threatened to exacerbate the political situation. On 14th March Yeltsin unexpectedly set off to Sochi for a holiday. The fact that his departure was unplanned and that he had set off in bad weather led to all sorts of rumors and speculation. On 16th March an anonymous document was published in a number of Moscow newspapers, under the heading Theory No. 1, followed a few days later by a Theory No. 2, which featured a few clarifications. The anonymous authors predicted a state coup, which they said had been prepared by a certain "group of statesmen in senior positions", in a plot with the security ministers P. Grachev, V. Yerin and S. Stepashin. The scenario put forward was similar to that of the coup which was attempted in August 1991: citing a deterioration in his health and his physical inability to govern the country, the president would be removed from office, and his powers would be transferred to V. Chernomyrdin.

The Federal Counter-espionage Service chose not to take these publications seriously, seeing them as contentious fabrications.[863]

---

862   See: V. Vyzhutovich. 'The Central electoral committee is turning into a political institution'//Izvestiya 4 May 1994
863   For comments see Izvestiya 25 March 1994, Kommersant daily 23 March.

There was no investigation and the identities of the people who had written the article were never found out. Yeltsin was extremely slow to react to the rumors. It was not until 25th March that he agreed to be interviewed over the telephone by the editor-in-chief of *Izvestiya*, and two days later he cut short his holiday and went back to Moscow. The reason for this may have been bound up in the fact that, whilst he was on holiday, he did not receive full information about what was taking place. His aides later wrote that it was not customary to bother him whilst he was on holiday. Moreover, this long silence could be explained by the fact that he "was fairly good at sensing when something was pure invention, and when there really was something afoot, and he was guided by this rule: never react to the countless rumors about his health.[864]

The rumors about possible scenarios involving a coup d'état, and the danger that they might become a reality, prompted work to be done on an Agreement on community consensus. On 28th April it was signed by senior federal organs of state power, the subjects of the Russian Federation, the political parties and social movements. The only group to refuse to sign up to the Agreement on community consensus was the Communist Party of the RF, whilst the Liberal Democratic Party of Russia later withdrew from it. The President treated the Agreement very seriously, and was counting on reducing the tension in the stand-off currently taking place in society. The Agreement did not lead to any significant results at all, however, in part due to the fact that the period set out in it — 2 years — coincided with the two election campaigns.

At the President's suggestion, an Associated Constitutional Commission was set up, under his leadership, with the participation of representatives of the chambers and senior judges, and an associated working group consisting of representatives of all the branches of power, so that law-making work could be coordinated. Achieving consensus and full cooperation proved impossible, however.

At a practical level, support for stability at the apex of politics demanded that a complex system of 'checks and balances' be set up. In December 1993 the President wrote to his aides: "We require, in the context of the presidential apparatus, a structure strong enough to act as a counterweight to the Government. If nothing else, because there was no sense in expecting any help from the Duma. A clearly defined agreement was required between the President and the chairman of the Government with regard to this structure. They were working on one and the same issue. There was no need for jealousy. There should be access to all areas, and everything should be submitted for analysis. This was not oversight, but rather new functions for the president under the new Constitution."[865]

---

864   The Yeltsin era P.508.
865   Quotation no.: The Yeltsin era. P.425.

Yeltsin brought in as a special rule weekly one-to-one meetings with the prime minister. As his aides remarked, "he controlled the Government not because he wanted to (on the contrary, at times he felt oppressed by the responsibility), but because he considered it his duty to do so. Since there were no detailed regulations, he did his work as best he could."[866] The importance of these meetings was determined by the fact that the tasks passed on by word of mouth, which the prime minister received during these meetings, were carried out to the letter — and the same could not be said of the directives or even written instructions from the President.

A typical example of the relations between the executive and the President's orders was given by the President's aides. In 1994, in his first State of the Nation address to the Federal Assembly, the President tasked the Ministry of Justice with composing a draft Civil code, a document which was supposed to regulate the procedures for governance, and the civil servants' accountability before their citizens. The Ministry of Justice did not report on the performance of these instructions until 1997. In the event, however, a different code altogether was prepared — a code on violations of civil law.[867]

The President regularly held meetings with security agents, governors, ministries, bankers and representatives of political parties. These meetings were important to the President, and, according to feedback from his aides, he was never unprepared for them. He studied people carefully and sought back-up among the staff. He often went against the grain, and loved to take snap decisions, on the spot, without consulting anyone; he was prone to scolding people unexpectedly in connection with unrelated matters. He believed that in order to understand a person, one had to put them under pressure. If they began to show signs of regretting their past actions, he would cross them off the staff list. "He didn't like people who could be easily 'broken', and who changed their position on things at a moment's notice."[868]

There were strong tendencies within the government administration to try and get out from under the President's sway. As S.A. Filatov remarked, the presidential directives submitted for approval by the government were often delayed, and in the meantime government edicts would be published. The President was forced on several occasions to talk tough on this, both with the head of the government administration and with the Prime Minister. The Government had pulled the duvet over to its side as regards the drafting and acceptance of potential programs. Between January and May 1994, 27 programs were adopted by the government and 6 by the President, whose job it was, under the Constitution, to determine the main areas in which the state

---

866   The Yeltsin era. P.424.
867   The Yeltsin era. P.391.
868   The Yeltsin era. P.435.

would develop. Not until the summer of 1994 was a directive published which established the mechanism for presidential control over the government's most important decisions.

The relations between the President and the various groups in the political elite were founded predominantly on compromise. Due to the danger of exacerbating relations with the regions, Yeltsin would often give the governors *carte blanche*, in exchange for loyalty or neutrality from the regional authorities. He frequently upheld requests for additional resources to be allocated from the budget, a fact which irritated reformers in the government. Reluctant to get into arguments with the leaders in the regions, the president put the reforms in the hands of the local autonomies. The law 'On the general principles of organizing local autonomy' was not signed until late summer in 1995.

Relations with the Duma were founded on principles of an exchange. The fact that the president did not have majority support meant that the executive was forced to sell his decisions by handing out exemptions to the commercial structures which were behind many deputy blocs. The longer this went on, the more expensive the deputies' services became. In late 1993 the president signed into law tax-breaks and exemptions on customs payments for veterans' organizations from the Afghanistan war, the disabled and athletes. Under cover of these organizations there were in fact major commercial corporations, which were able to earn huge profits through customs-free imports.

The economic reforms in theory and in practice

In his speeches, the President did not rule out the idea of extending the economic reforms, but the number of genuine opportunities to introduce a tough policy designed to achieve financial stability was falling. In the first few days of January 1994 the prime minister V. Chernomyrdin announced his economic decisions, related to the fresh increase in budget expenses and the risk of inflation. The retirement of Y.T. Gaidar, to whom the President offered the role of deputy prime minister in Chernomyrdin's government, was a significant event. In a letter addressed to the President, Gaidar wrote that he was declining this offer because "lately decisions have been taken more and more often which I have not been involved in helping to prepare, and with which I have expressed my categorical disagreement."[869]

A few days after Gaidar's retirement, similar announcements were made by the deputy prime minister and finance minister, B. Fedorov, and the minister of social security, A. Pamfilova. This came as a nasty surprise

---

869   Y.T. Gaidar: Days of defeats and victories. P.501.

to the President. A very telling cartoon was published in *Izvestiya*: Chernomyrdin has climbed onto Yeltsin's shoulders and is trying to cover his eyes, and the President is simply walking round and round in a circle, repeating over and over: "We won't be diverted off the road to reform."[870]

In July 1994 the second, monetary phase of privatization began. The essence of it was an attempt to attract funds in order to finance industry. In the new stage of privatization, the money paid in order to acquire companies had to be invested in a genuine sector of the economy. This task went unfulfilled, however. Due to the chronic lack of funds in the budget, the state began to use monetary privatization in order to attract funding to meet the needs of the budget.

The sale of the biggest industries or mining companies was conducted in part on a 'case by case' basis, so that money could be found for the budget as a matter of urgency, in order that pensions could be paid and problems related to the exchequer resolved. Companies were sold at an extremely low price.

Since privatization was carried out based on orders, the President had to be involved in it as an arbiter. In addition, as the President's aides noted, he was inconsistent in his attitude toward economic issues, and would fluctuate between intense interest and apparent indifference.[871]

The dramatic fall in the value of the ruble on 11th October 1994 caught the President unawares. As he signed into law edicts on the allocation of extra funding to the regions, and the provision of tax breaks to various organizations, he resolved political tasks, without giving too much thought to the economic consequences. In the administrative struggle for influence over the President, the Security service was winning: it had convinced him that absolutely everything was within his remit, including direct interference in the distribution of the budget.

'Black Tuesday' was an inevitable consequence of the budget deficit, which had established the evil practice of resolving problems with the budget with the help of loans from the Central Bank. The excessive amount of rubles in circulation led to a collapse in the value of the ruble. Yeltsin was extremely angry. He ordered that a commission be set up under O. Lobov. This was followed by sackings: the chairman of the Central bank, V. Gerashchenko, his deputy S. Dubinin and the deputy chairman of the government, A. Shokhin, were all forced out. A. Chubais was appointed the first deputy prime minister responsible for economics. In March 1995 the battle against

---

870 V.V. Kostikov: A love-story with the president. Notes by the press-secretary. M.: 'VAGRIUS'. 1997. P.283.

871 The Yeltsin era. P.422.

tax breaks began. This did not come easily for the President, since he did not like to alter his decisions. Moreover, he had to withstand pressure from his sports and strength training team.

Yeltsin began taking a serious interest in the problems of the currency market, and gained quite a strong understanding of them. At a meeting of the heads of the government and the Central Bank on 5th July 1995, when the issue of introducing a currency corridor for an experimental 3 month period was brought up, the President displayed such thorough knowledge of the details of currency policy that those in attendance were astonished.[872]

In 1995 Russia went into a depression. This phase, which came after the crisis, was characterized by a strengthening of state control over finances, and a rejection by the Central Bank of Russia of the idea of financing the deficit in the state budget by means of tax exemption loans. During this phase, which was to last until the summer of 1998, the government managed to keep the exchange rate between the ruble and the dollar fairly stable. High inflation was kept down. This was achieved by means of tough control over the total amount of money in circulation. An unwanted by-product of these measures was a delay lasting many months in the payment of salaries to civil servants and pensions to pensioners, and a funding shortfall in government costs.

In order to ensure that money came into the exchequer, a mechanism of guarantee auctions was devised (the man behind the idea was the president of ONEKSIM bank, V. Potanin). On 31st August 1995 the President met a representative delegation of bankers from Moscow and the provinces, which included V. Gusinsky (Most), Y. Dubenetsky (Promstroibank), N. Raevskaya (Avtobank), S. Rodionov (Imperial), G. Tosunyan (Technobank), M. Khodorkovsky (Menatep), V. Khokhlov (Tokobank), S. Yegorov (ARB), A. Kozyreva (Tveruniversalbank), Y. Koluga (Sibtorgbank) and V. Popkov (Uralvneshtorgbank). On the same day, a directive was signed on the auctions, giving the government the right to conclude bank loan agreements. As a result, significant state-owned packages of shares in major industrial companies were held by the banks as guarantees; in 1997, after the state failed to pay back the loans, they bought them back from themselves at repeat auctions.[873]

How could the 'Yeltsin of old' be resurrected?

The redistribution of property which had once been seen as belonging to the people effectively did not affect those who represented the people. Public opinion was dramatically polarized. People were eking out a living as best they could — they were getting involved in retail, looking for additional sources

872   The Yeltsin era. P.444.
873   http://rustrana.ru/print.php?nid=9651

of income, and growing their own food on small plots of land next to their out-of-town dachas. There was a growing sense of chaos: companies might go months without paying salaries, the communal services were performing badly, and there was a surge in crime rates. The police failed to protect the public from criminals, and often aided and abetted their actions. Numerous 'investment funds' and private banks were set up, promising fabulous interest rates; yet these turned out to be Ponzi schemes, and began to burst like soap bubbles in 1994. The powers that be failed to protect the public against such things, and the President was the embodiment of state power. People's confidence in him began to fall. According to data from March 1994, only 19% of the general public believed that the President would be able to cope with his responsibilities.[874] When Yeltsin came to power, he had talked about what really concerned people — social justice and the privileges enjoyed by the nomenclature. His speeches had elicited an emotional response and had cemented his popularity. When he became President, people expected him to back up his words with actions. But no such thing occurred.

Yeltsin had lost the support of the pro-democracy camp. The democrats were still hoping, as Y. Gaidar put it, "to restore Yeltsin to the Yeltsin of old". In August 1994 *Izvestiya* published a letter from representatives of the intelligentsia, calling on B.N. Yeltsin, Y.T. Gaidar and G.A. Yavlinsky to take steps to approve the actions of democratic centers — Russia's Democratic Choice, Yabloko, Democratic Russia and other organizations.[875] The president's press service prepared a press review and an annotated letter containing the press-secretary's CV: "The current state of the pro-democracy camp makes it extremely doubtful that the president made the right choice when he appointed an outside observer to oversee the establishment of democratic parties and movements. It seemed as if his tactics of waiting for the democrats to unite, with the president giving them a helping hand only after this had happened, and relying on them, had not been justified. It may be that during this phase — the struggle for consensus within society — such tactics were essential. Today, however, it seemed as though the time had come to put things right in the relations between the President and the democrats...the President must announce a political initiative involving the consolidation of democratic forces. This had to be done in a forceful, eye-catching way, in the spirit of the "true Yeltsin".[876]

In a private letter sent to Yeltsin in late August, V. Kostikov wrote about the growing criticism of the President in the press: "...The idea is beginning to take hold that what is taking place is an imitation of politics, and that in actual fact the president is reacting too late to the ebb and flow of events and occurrences. His trips around the country, many of which do not have much

---

874   Material from the RF President's expert-analytical council
875   Izvestiya 30 August 1994
876   The Yeltsin era P.514.

serious content and are soon forgotten, are being described as an imitation of politics... The unsatisfactory nature of political planning on domestic affairs, in the press's opinion, is being compensated for more and more often by a shift of focus onto foreign policy. There have been far too many foreign trips...Society is beginning to examine with a critical eye the excesses of the ritual aspects of the foreign policy side of the "phenomenon of the people's president"...".[877] This did not elicit a response. Instead of the "real" Yeltsin, the Yeltsin "of old", people were increasingly seeing him as a tired, sick man who was succumbing to an age-old Russian ailment.

Many people were shocked by the President's inappropriate behavior during some cultural events in Berlin, held to mark the withdrawal of the last Russian troops from the reunified Germany. Yeltsin usually prepared very thoroughly for his foreign visits, familiarized himself with every last detail of the itinerary, studied the characters of his negotiating partners, and had his staff rewrite the text of his speeches multiple times. The preparations for his trip to Germany were no exception.

This was a one-off event which resonated throughout the world; it was a painful time for many people in Russia, where it was seen as a surrendering of Russia's position. Experts had been consulted and speech-writers had worked carefully on Yeltsin's speeches. Yeltsin was anxious and had a sleepless night on the eve of the ceremony; to help the time go faster he asked P. Grachev and A. Korzhakov to come and see him in his hotel room. When he addressed the crowds the next day at the ceremony, for some reason he chose not to read out his pre-prepared speech, but instead began to speak off the cuff, and made some gaffes, saying that "in the war between Russia and Germany there were no victors, nor losers." After the official breakfast, during which alcohol was served, the President threw off the formalities of protocol and began conducting the orchestra.

The man in charge of presidential protocol, V. Shevchenko, recalled: "When that unforeseen situation occurred in Germany, I rushed in to stop the president. And his security detail reacted to what was happening as well. But all the other members of our delegation were clapping and giving the thumbs up. That only encouraged him, of course. Boris Nikolaevich was an emotional man. And at that moment there were people calling out to him from all sides."[878]

This episode was shown in all the TV news bulletins. The reaction in the Russian media was extremely strong. The newspapers wrote of the "sense of dismay and shame" which had gripped the Russian people. The day after the

---

877   V.V. Kostikov: A love-story with the president. Notes by the press-secretary. M.: 'VAGRIUS', 1997. P.314-315.

878   V.N. Shevchenko: Day-to-day life at the Kremlin under the Presidents. M.: The young guard, 2005. P.217.

President's return to Moscow, a review of the Russian press coverage of his visit to Germany was lying on his desk. His press-secretary, V.V. Kostikov, had added a note: "...the live TV broadcast of the ceremony in Germany, and the television programs which followed it, revealed a whole host of external aspects related to the President's behavior in public.

A huge number of telephone calls have been made to the President's press service demanding an explanation for the President's "behavior". People are saying that the President's behavior, in a number of episodes during the withdrawal (of troops) "fell short of the mark". Many of the citizens who called the press service are angry and are saying, in no uncertain terms, that... to them this came as an insulting shock and a humiliation for Russia."[879]

After receiving the press review, the President arrived at the Kremlin looking extremely gloomy, and refrained from shaking Kostikov's hand, as he usually did. Yeltsin's aides discussed the possibility of collectively resigning, but the idea was rejected due to the categoric refusal of Filatov, who felt this would only make things worse.[880] They decided instead to send a collective letter to the President. It was signed by both the 'security men' and the 'democrats' — V. Ilyushin, V. Kostikov, L. Pikhoya, D. Ryurikov, A. Korzhakov, M. Barsukov and V. Shevchenko.[881]

They wrote about all the things that were troubling them: the President's reduced activity, the fact that he was so withdrawn, the fact that he had lost contact with the world of politics, with society, journalists, TV audiences and the newspaper readership. They wrote openly and directly about the "well-known Russian abuse in everyday life", about his calmness, arrogance, lack of patience, capriciousness, and at times offensive behavior with regard to people. These criticisms could not fail to touch a nerve.

At the same time, the letter was shot through with a deep respect for the President, and the hope that it would be possible to rectify his style and method of working. His aides wrote of the need to re-examine the president's attitude to his own health and bad habits, restore stability to his working regime and make his work schedule more complete once again, and ensure that he took part personally and on a constant basis in political planning, renew all forms of political contact and consultations, meet those who helped shape public opinion, intellectuals and independent analysts, restore contact with the public via the TV and radio, rid himself of "Tsar-like" habits and not allow himself to get bogged down in them, and spend more time at the theater, concerts, exhibitions and sporting events.[882]

---

879   Quoted from: The Yeltsin era. P.517-518.
880   The Yeltsin era. P.518.
881   See: Izvestiya 27 September 1994 V. Kononenko: 'The split within the President's team is increasing the opposition's chances'.
882   For the full text of the letter see: The Yeltsin era. P.521-523

In effect they were asking for a return to the "Yeltsin of old", the political leader for whom millions of Russian citizens had voted in 1990, thereby determining his fate and putting the future of the country in his hands. But the President did not appreciate this: he saw the writing of the letter as an act of treachery in itself. L.G. Pikhoya recalled that whenever he received a call from one of the signatories to the letter, he refused to speak to them. It was not until six months later, when Pikhoya called to wish the President a happy birthday on 1st February 1995, that he agreed to take the call. Without waiting for her to finish her message of congratulation, however, he asked: "Why did you sign that letter? What for? It was such a huge blow to me. It hurt me so much." He was unable to overcome his sense of hurt and injury, and hear the voice of reason. Nothing had changed.

The state of the president's health and his abuse of alcohol had become the number one problem in Russian politics. According to S.A. Filatov, the president became more "suggestible" and "easy to manage" when he was in that state.[883] During a visit to Kazakhstan in February 1995, the president was not feeling well, as is clear from the TV images: his speech was incoherent and he had to be held up. He managed to take revenge a few months later during a trip to Lipetsk, where Yeltsin looked much better. He walked around the city for almost four hours and spoke to the public, making optimistic promises about how quickly his health was going to improve. By now people were extremely sceptical about any promises made by Yeltsin, however.

In July 1995, Yeltsin once again disappeared from political life, for a short while. He was taken to hospital after suffering a first heart attack — a fact which his entourage managed to keep under wraps at the time. Under articles 92 and 93 of the Constitution, in the event that the President was unable to perform his obligations, they would temporarily be conferred on the prime minister, who was the second most senior figure in the state. This did not happen, however. On 17th July 1995, Oleg Moroz, a journalist from *Literaturnaya gazeta*, wrote about his anxieties in the immediate aftermath of these events: "...The president's entourage of civil servants, and, perhaps, the president himself, are concerned less about his life than about power. Report after report has come out [from the president's press service] repeating the same thing, with a maniacal insistence: the president is fit to perform his obligations under the constitution, is signing urgent documents, and is in an assiduous mood..."[884] (From his hospital bed Yeltsin scheduled new parliamentary elections for 17th December 1995. These would be an important test of strength for him ahead of the race for the presidency in June 1996).

883   S. Filatov: An open secret. M., 2000. P.80
884   Quotation no.: O. Moroz: 1996: How Zyuganov didn't become president. M., 2006. P.19.

In September 1995, when the Russian delegation stopped off in Shannon on its way back home from the USA, an unpleasant incident occurred. The President was unable to leave the plane in order to take part in the talks which he was due to have with the prime minister of Ireland. Afterwards, in response to questions from journalists, he explained this away by saying that he had fallen asleep on board the plane and that his security staff were not allowed to wake him up. His explanation sounded daft. As Yeltsin's aides later wrote, there were two main reasons for the scandal. The first was the fact that far too much had been packed into the itinerary for the trip. It had begun in New York, where Yeltsin had addressed a UN assembly, and this was followed by an official visit to the USA, talks with Bill Clinton in Washington, then a flight to Seattle; Yeltsin was initially supposed to return to Moscow via Petropavlovsk-Kamchatsky. The idea of stopping off in Ireland came up at the last minute, at Kozyrev's initiative. The President, who loved to demonstrate his incredible powers of endurance and combine multiple visits, agreed to the idea. He therefore had to fly home across the Atlantic. The second reason was bound up in the banquets, where excess was the order of the day.[885]

In October 1995, after some rest and recuperation in Sochi, Yeltsin visited the USA for the celebrations marking the 50th anniversary of the UN, where he spoke to the heads of state of some of the world's leading powers. On his return to Moscow on 26th October 1995, however, he was taken to hospital, after being diagnosed with acute ischaemic heart disease. There was no information available about the President's real state of health, something which was reminiscent of Soviet days. "A mechanism had begun to take shape for creating an imitation of the presidency. The propaganda machine kicked in...From time to time, politicians who visited Yeltsin would report that the President would soon be playing tennis again," L.Shevtsov wrote.[886] It was not until December 1995 that Yeltsin noticed an improvement and was transferred to a sanatorium; he remained there throughout the parliamentary elections and was unable to leave until New Year's Eve.

By the end of 1995, the foreign press were reporting that according to the CIA, Yeltsin needed a serious heart operation (this was dismissed as an attempt at provocation by Yeltsin's entourage), and that Russia was being run from behind the scenes on behalf of a leader unfit for office — a situation which was extremely dangerous and was putting the country on the brink of a new catastrophe.

---

885   The Yeltsin era P.477-478.
886   L. Shevtsova: Boris Yeltsin's regime M., 1999. P.227-228.

The challenge of Chechnya

The Chechen war, which began in December 1994, was a serious challenge for President Yeltsin. It dealt a tangible blow to the tasks of bringing political and economic stability, led to a dramatic polarization of political opinion and a drop in people's trust in the authorities, and also caused immeasurable damage to the Russian economy, at the expense of economic reforms, the solution of social problems, investment projects, measures designed to tackle inflation and so on and so forth.

The Chechen war was the result, on the one hand, of historical events and more recent events in the region's political history (the deep involvement of Chechnya in the events of the Caucasian War in the 19th century, the rejection of the policy of collectivization, and then the exile of Chechens branded "enablers of the fascists" to Kazakhstan); and also of serious miscalculations in national and state policy by the new Russian leadership. When the Soviet army general Dzhokar Dudaev took charge of the National Congress of the Chechen People (NCCP) in 1991, the Russian leadership saw him as "the Chechen Yeltsin". A Commission from the Supreme Soviet of the RSFSR, sent to the republic at the behest of Yeltsin and Khasbulatov following the attempted coup of August 1991, concluded that "the demands made by the democratic forces are justified, and any delay in meeting them might lead to a civil or international war in the region."

On 5th September 1991 Yeltsin addressed the people of Chechnya, calling on them "to resist the temptation to resort to ill-thought-through action and irremediable acts, which could trample over the centuries-old cultural traditions of the peoples living in the mountains of the Caucasus..., to use the mechanism of civilized talks between the representatives of the various movements within society and the republic's legally elected leaders..."[887] His call went unheeded, however. Under cover of democratic slogans, what proceeded to take place in the republic was effectively an armed seizing of power.

On 19th October 1991 the President made a second appeal, in which he proposed that all of the buildings which had been seized, and which belonged to the state bodies or to community organizations, be liberated, that arms be laid down, that the armed divisions which had been unlawfully created be disbanded and that elections and a referendum be held. This missive bore no results whatsoever. On 27th October elections were held in Chechnya for the executive committee of the National Congress of the Chechen People, the president and the parliament, which were deemed to be unlawful by Moscow. On 7th November 1991, under a directive from President Yeltsin, a state of

---

887   Quoted from: The Yeltsin era. P.584.

emergency was introduced in Chechen-Ingushetia. No action followed this move, however.

The Soviet Union was in the process of collapsing, the union's assets were being divided up and the union's government bodies were being brought under Russian jurisdiction, and the financial crisis was worsening: the Russian leadership had far more pressing concerns than little Chechnya and the unrest there. Then the economic reforms began and the political crisis unfolded. In the meantime, Dudaev had strengthened his regime, declared his independence from Moscow, refused to pay taxes into the central exchequer, refused to take part in the Russian elections, and was preparing to bring in his own currency. The situation was rendered more complex by the fact that when the Russian army was pulled out of Chechnya at the end of 1991 and the beginning of 1992, a huge amount of weaponry and ammunition was left in the republic, which Dudaev promptly seized.

Chechnya had been turned into a hotbed of criminality. Mafia-style gangsters based in Chechnya got involved in producing fake currency, narcotics, kidnapping people for ransom and train robberies.

After the Constitution was adopted in 1993, various methods of solving the Chechen problem were considered, from a softly-softly approach, such as holding talks and organizing meetings between presidents Yeltsin and Dudaev, to more extreme measures, such as building a wall akin to the Berlin Wall around Chechnya.

In the summer of 1994 the Kremlin took the decision to take advantage of the discontent felt by the Chechens due to the financial hardships they faced, and the fact that the anti-Dudaev opposition had grown stronger, and to help put forces loyal to Moscow in power in Chechnya. Armed units of Chechens, led by the field commanders R. Labazanov and B. Gantemirov, who had fallen out with Dudaev, were reinforced with Russian military vehicles and servicemen who had been secretly recruited by the special forces. These units were counting on securing a rapid victory, and tanks driven by reservists were sent into the capital of Chechnya as a form of scare tactics. However, the assault on Grozny on 26th November 1994, ended in victory for Dudaev and fatalities among the Russian servicemen, and news of this sent shockwaves through Russia and the wider world.

From 27th November onwards, the situation in Chechnya was on the President's agenda on a daily basis. On 29th November Yeltsin gave a speech to those taking part in the armed conflict in Chechnya and called on them to cease fire within 48 hours, lay down their arms, disband their armed units, and release all the citizens whom they had taken prisoner and were detaining by force. (some 70 Russian servicemen had been taken prisoner[888]). It was an

888   Filatov: An open secret P. 254

ultimatum. His speech contained the following passage: "If this demand is not met by the deadline established, throughout the territory of the Chechen republic, all the powers and resources at the state's disposal are going to be put into stopping the bloodshed, and safeguarding the lives, rights and freedoms of the citizens of Russia, and restoring the rule of the constitution, law and order and peace in the Chechen Republic."[889]

On the same day, the Security Council, chaired by Yeltsin, decided to create a Group to take charge of action related to disarming and eradicating the armed units in Chechnya, under the guidance of the defence minister P. Grachev.[890]

Yeltsin wrote about this meeting of the Security Council in his memoirs: "I had information sheets lying on my desk (there were dozens of information sheets like that at the time, prepared by various institutions), setting out the reasons why we needed to begin an operation. There were also other analytical materials to the effect that there must be no meddling in Chechnya's affairs. I set out the arguments on both sides and said: who is 'for' and who's 'against'? What awaits us? And the generally held view was this: we cannot sit by and watch as a chunk of Russia is broken off, it would be the start of the collapse of the country. One of the people who had been a staunch believer in the idea that the military operation should be 'lightning-quick' was Pavel Sergeevich Grachev, the Russian defence minister between 1992 and 1996."[891]

It is worth noting, first of all, that according to Yeltsin, the issue under discussion was whether or not to begin a military operation, and not how to bring the situation in Chechnya under control. In other words, there were in effect no other alternative ways of solving the problem. Secondly, Yeltsin stressed that there was strong faith in the idea that a military operation could achieve quick success: the prospect of it being turned into a long drawn-out, bloody war was not even considered. It was supposed that once Dudaev's army had been disarmed, the federal troops would play the role of peacekeepers in the civil war in Chechnya. The third point to make is that P. Grachev calls Yeltsin's version of events into question. In an interview he gave to the newspaper *Trud*, he said that he spoken out against the idea of sending in

---

889   Quoted from The Yeltsin era. P.597.

890   In addition to Yeltsin, the other members of the Security Council at the time were: the defence minister P.S. Grachev, the minister of internal affairs V.F. Yerin, the minister of justice Y.Kh.Kalmykov, the minister of foreign affairs A.V.Kozyrev, the secretary of the Council O.I.Lobov, the director of the Federal border service A.I. Nikolaev, the director of the Foreign intelligence service Y.M. Primakov, the chairman of the State Duma of the RF, I.P. Rybkin, the director of the Federal Counter-espionage Service S.V. Stepashin, the deputy prime minister S.M. Shakhrai, the minister for emergency situations S.K. Shoigu and the chairman of the Federation Council of the Federal Assembly V.F. Shumeiko. Soon after this Y.Kh. Kalmykov left his post as justice minister. He had been against the use of force in solving the Chechen crisis.

891   B. Yeltsin: The presidential marathon. S.

troops, particularly in December, but had received no support. As he saw it, no troops should be sent in until the spring, and in the meantime Chechnya should be put under pressure financially.[892]

The President was clearly leaning towards what seemed to him to be the simplest and quickest method of solving the problem. This method was insisted upon by a man who was considered to have thorough knowledge of the North Caucasus — N.D. Yegorov — the former head of the Krasnodar Region, who at the time was minister for ethnicities and regional policy; Yegorov set out a convincing argument that he understood the situation in Chechnya, and was sure that the troops were hardly going to be met with bunches of flowers if they were sent in.

It was no coincidence that the head of the Administration, S. Filatov, and an advisor on national security, Y. Baturin, were not privy to the discussions on the Chechen issue: these men had insisted on adopting a complex approach to the problem which took into account all its internal political aspects, international aspects and possible consequences.

No minutes were kept at the Security Council meeting, and its decision was kept secret, as was the president's directive, signed the next day, 30th November, 'On measures designed to restore the legal force of the constitution and law and order in the territory of the Chechen Republic'. The Directive stipulated that measures to establish a state of emergency be taken in Chechnya, and conferred special powers — including powers for which there was no provision under the Constitution and laws of the Russian Federation — on the group of leaders in charge of actions to disarm and eradicate the armed units. In another presidential directive, dated 1st December 1994, 'On certain measures to strengthen law and order in the North Caucasus' there was a promise of an amnesty for anyone who had taken part in serious crimes but voluntarily surrendered their weapons by 15th December 1994.[893]

The military machine had been put into operation. There was a build up of military units from the Russian army on the Chechen border. On 2nd December 1994 air strikes on the republic began. The November ultimatum on the surrendering of weapons and the promise of an amnesty, as well as the attempts to make direct contact with Dudaev and arrange talks, only served to delay the start of the operation, and were unable to prevent it. The basis for the launch of the operation was the president's directive dated 9th December 'On measures to curtail the activities of the illegal armed units on the territory of the Republic of Chechnya and in the area of the Ossetino-Ingush conflict', in which the RF government was ordered "to use all the resources at the

---

892   Trud 15 March 2001
893   'Collected legislation of the RF', 1994, N 32, art. 3334

state's disposal to provide state security, the rule of law, citizens' rights and freedoms, the guardians of public order, the fight against crime, and the disarming of all illegal armed units."

On 11th December federal troops entered Chechnya. On the same day the President signed Directive No. 2169 'On measures to ensure the rule of law, law and order and public security on the territory of the Republic of Chechnya', which annulled the directive dated 30th November. Under this directive, the group in charge of actions designed to disarm and eradicate the armed units was now supposed to act outside the framework of the state of emergency for an indeterminate period.

That same day Yeltsin gave a brief address to the citizens of Russia, in which he explained the objective for which federal troops were being led into the Republic of Chechnya: "Our goal is to find a political solution for the problems faced by one of the subjects of the Russian Federation — the Republic of Chechnya, and to protect its citizens from armed extremism. Now, however, the peace negotiations and the ability of the Chechen people to express their will freely is being hindered by the looming danger of a full-scale civil war in the Republic of Chechnya. Talks have been scheduled to take place between representatives of the Russian side and the Chechen side on 12th December. We must not allow them to be interrupted."

On 15th December Yeltsin, in an address to the residents of Chechnya, once again extended the deadline for voluntary surrendering of weapons and ending resistance to federal forces by 48 hours.[894] The Kremlin was still holding out hope that it would be possible to solve the problem without too much bloodshed, by making use of the anti-Dudaev opposition. On 16th December Yeltsin received a letter from Y. Mamodaev containing a program for regulating the situation in Chechnya. The letter also contained open attacks on the Russian president. Mamodaev wrote: "It is clear today that the Dudaev regime, which was against the people, and which had lost all popular support, has suddenly received popular support. And this happens every time you try to intervene personally in the "Chechen issue" — believe you me, it's no accident...". Yeltsin, who was usually so quick to take offence, managed to overcome his emotions on this occasion, and drew up a resolution: "I ask O.N. Soskovets, O.I. Lobov, N.D. Yegorov and S.M. Shakhrai, as a matter of urgency, to review the proposals made by Y. Mamodaev. They are to check the extent to which they correspond to the circumstances that have arisen."[895]

On 17th December Yeltsin sent Dudaev a telegram in which it was suggested that he come to Mozdok, to meet an authorized representative of the RF

---

894   The Yeltsin era. P.612
895   The Yeltsin era. P.612-613.

president in Chechnya, and the minister for matters of ethnicity and regional politics, N.D. Yegorova and the director of the FSB S.V. Stepashin, and sign a document on the surrendering of weapons and a ceasefire.

But events unfolded altogether differently from the manner envisaged in the President's directives and speeches. The talks came to an end, Dudaev did not come to Mozdok, and his troops had no intention of surrendering their weapons. On the contrary, when federal troops were sent into the republic they were met with extremely fierce resistance. The military operation by the federal forces was turning into a long drawn-out war.

As the military operations in Chechnya were in full swing, Yeltsin was in hospital awaiting an operation on the bridge of his nose. He was still issuing orders over the telephone. One particular thing that he did, on 18th December, when the deadline set in the ultimatum on the ending of resistance and the surrendering of weapons was about to pass, was to call P. Grachev.[896] But his disappearance from the Kremlin looked more like flight than anything else. It seems highly unlikely that an adjustment to the bridge of his nose required urgent surgical attention. According to the President's aides, after he left hospital on 20th December Yeltsin decided not to go to the Kremlin, but instead went to his residence outside the city, where some working meetings were arranged. It was impossible to secure a meeting with the President at this time: personal access to him was closed off, and the only things that reached him were documents which he had ordered himself. Normal working relations between the president and his advisors did not resume until February-March 1995.[897]

G. Satarov, one of Yeltsin's aides, wrote on 24th December 1994, in a note addressed to the President: "Ever since the 10th December I have been becoming more and more sure of something: the sending in of troops was an ill-planned and poorly thought-through bit of improvisation, without any proper planning to speak of and with an absolutely hopeless way of implementing any sensible objectives;" there had been no coordination between Moscow and the Caucasus, between the politicians and the soldiers, between the government and the presidential structures. There was no effective technology of power.[898]

Yeltsin's words about the situation in Chechnya attested to the fact that at the end of December the President still had a poor understanding of what was going on there. On 26th December, at a Security Council meeting, he thanked the government and the migration services, and expressed his

---

896   The Yeltsin era. P.615.
897   Same reference. P. 635.
898   Same reference. P.637.

satisfaction with the actions of the Russian military and border guards in the Republic of Chechnya and his confidence that the situation in Chechnya would soon go back to normal.[899]

It seemed as if he was trying to reassure himself more than anyone else. The failure of the New Year storming of Grozny forced him to confront the truth. Between 1st and 3rd January the President refused to see anyone; on his orders, the only documents that were sent to him were Y. Baturin's reports. On 4th January Yeltsin hosted a meeting about Chechnya with officers, at the Kremlin. He asked them tough questions about the way the military operation was being run, and the responses he got were not particularly clear. In his memoirs Yeltsin adopted a sharp tone when writing about the first few months of the Chechen war: "The army was catastrophically underprepared. The actions taken by the security ministries were completely out of kilter. There was a great deal of obstruction, a lack of understanding of our actions on the part of journalists, and a brutal reaction in public opinion."[900]

Following some fierce fighting, however, the federal troops managed to take Grozny, and the war in Chechnya dragged on. The Chechen resistance was pushed back into the mountains and resorted to using guerilla tactics. The military actions began to go beyond the borders of the republic, when the Chechen fighters began resorting to terrorist acts involving the kidnapping of hostages. The population of the regions in the vicinity were now under threat.

The Chechen war had been unpopular in society right from the beginning. In January 1995, 54% of those surveyed said they wanted it to be brought to an end, whilst only 27% supported these measures (the rest were not sure)[901]. Yeltsin's authority, which was low enough as it was, was falling. "By sending troops into Chechnya, Yeltsin effectively committed political suicide. He put the final nail in the coffin for the Yeltsin for whom the country had voted on 12th June 1991," the journalist O. Moroz wrote at the time.[902]

The President's behavior in cases of emergency made a negative impression: for example, when terrorists kidnapped large groups of hostages, as happened in June 1995 in Budennovsk in the Stavropolsky Region, where approximately 120 Chechen insurgents led by S. Basaev stormed a hospital and took over 1000 patients and hospital staff hostage. The terrorists demanded that Russia withdraw its troops from Chechnya and recognise Chechnya's independence, as the price of the hostages' freedom. At that point Yeltsin, after ordering that a special operation be carried out to destroy the insurgents, boarded a plane to Canada to attend a meeting of the G7. The storming of the hospital led

899   Same reference. P.621.
900   B. Yeltsin: The Presidential marathon. S.
901   L. Shevtsova: Boris Yeltsin's regime M., 1999. P.184.
902   O. Moroz: 1996: How Zyuganov didn't become president. M., 2006. P.120.

to large numbers of victims and was brought to an end. A message was sent through from the Department of government information saying that the order to storm the building had not arrived. Yeltsin confirmed from Halifax that the decision had been taken by him and by the minister of internal affairs, Yerin.[903] In an attempt to rescue the hostages, V.S. Chernomyrdin entered into talks with Basaev, promising an end to military operations in Chechnya and the start of peace talks. In return for sparing the lives of the hostages, Basaev was allowed to leave for Chechnya, along with the rest of his men.

The President's ratings fell lower still in January 1996, after the failed storming by federal troops of the Dagestani village of Pervomaiskoye, which had been occupied by a brigade of Chechen insurgents under the command of Salman Raduev. In a televised speech, Yeltsin promised Russians that the operation would be a "high-precision" one, and that the hostages would remain alive. He then proceeded to give a vivid description of the special forces' brilliant preparations for the operation, repeating a report someone had made long ago, and even disclosed that 38 snipers had their sights trained on the insurgents. Practically nothing that the President said at the time corresponded to the reality of the situation, and when events had reached their most climactic moment he had flown off to attend the funeral of the French leader F. Mitterand. The federal forces carried out a standard military operation involving the use of artillery and air power. A large number of innocent civilians were killed, and Raduev managed to break through the lines surrounding him with a group of brothers-in-arms and hostages. This resulted in a wave of unrest in Dagestan.

At the end of June 1995 the talks promised by Chernomyrdin with Dudaev's representatives began, overseen by the Organization for Security and Co-operation in Europe. On the night of 29th July, an Agreement was signed on the peaceful restoration of the situation in the Chechen republic as regards military issues; political and economic issues were postponed to a later date. The issue of Chechnya's status remained open. Within the framework of the military agreement, Russia withdrew most of her troops from Chechnya, whilst Dudaev disarmed his forces, leaving only self-defence brigades in populated areas. It soon transpired, however, that Dudaev had taken advantage of this lull in the fighting to relocate his forces, many of which had been chased into the mountains by the time the peace talks began, or were surrounded by federal troops.

Would new elections be held?

Even among his closest advisers, Yeltsin never brought up the subject of the next presidential elections. All they could do was guess at what his intentions might be, based on subtleties and indirect clues. Nonetheless, by 1994 there

---

903   The Yeltsin era. p.674.

was a growing feeling that Yeltsin had already decided, in his own mind, to bid for a second term in office.[904] The president's aides, who had a good understanding of how his mind worked, knew that he would never leave the Kremlin unless forced to do so by strictly personal circumstances.

On 29th March 1994 some reports were published in *Izvestiya* which stated that the President intended "to take part in the elections as a voter only." Yeltsin took a strong disliking to this turn of phrase: he called his press-secretary and began complaining that lies were once again being told about him, and suggested that this theory should be carefully disavowed, by means of a hint of some sort. By means of a hint. 3 days later an editorial was published in *Izvestiya* under the headline 'Yeltsin may stand for president in the elections in 1996'. It read: "The analysts who are predicting that Yeltsin will leave the political arena in 1996 are basing this idea on the party-based structure of present-day Russian society. In doing so, they are ignoring the most important factor of all: the general public, the electorate. Can we rule out the idea that large groups of Russians would be keen to initiate putting Yeltsin forward as a candidate for a new term as president? If this were to happen, Yeltsin would of course have a decision to make. And that decision would depend on his own personal desires, on the concept of a debt, on political responsibility..." [905]

The subject of the forthcoming elections was ever-present in the work of the President's Expert-analytical council from the spring of 1994 onwards. The main talking points were how to expand the president's support base in society, and how to improve his image. The problem was that the experts' findings and recommendations were simply not required by the president himself.

Since the President's ratings were continuing their relentless fall (it was reported at a meeting of the Expert-analytical council on 24th May 1994 that two thirds of voters were against the idea of Yeltsin standing for a new term), the idea of postponing the elections arose. The idea of postponing the elections for the State Duma and the President was advocated by the chairman of the Federation Council, V. Shumeiko, in a conversation with journalists on 21st June 1994. Shumeiko justified the idea by saying that if the elections were held too soon, the deputies would be more concerned about the elections than about drafting new laws. According to S. Shakhrai, who also advocated this idea, postponing the elections would help create stability in society. The simultaneous speeches by these two politicians, who were both supporters of Yeltsin, left the public in no doubt that this idea had been approved by the President. The idea of postponing the elections was supported by G. Burbulis,

---

904 The Yeltsin era. P.529.
905 Quoted from: The Yeltsin era. P. 526.

who proposed extending the President's term in office until 1998 (the "plus 2" scenario), with the proviso that Yeltsin would not stand for re-election.

As for Yeltsin himself, he gave a brief but indeterminate answer when asked about the idea of postponing the elections. In response to a question on the subject from I. Khakamada, he said: "The elections of 1996 should not be moved anywhere." [906] These words may have cloaked either a desire not to discuss the issue, or the conviction that the elections must take place when they were due to take place. As for Rybkin, he made his thoughts on the matter as clear as mud: "...I believe the people are tired of the electoral marathon — we are constantly holding election after election. Before we talk about extending the deputies' mandates, though, we ought to earn people's trust by passing laws which might improve everyone's lives at least a little bit..."[907]

S. Filatov persuaded the President to distance himself from the idea of postponing the elections. On 27th June, after a conversation with the head of his Administration, Yeltsin asked his press-secretary to announce that he did not support Shumeiko's idea. The people close to the president, though, were adept at picking up on the slightest change in his mood. Since Yeltsin's tone lacked its usual conviction, the press-secretary decided to play for time, and to put her own spin on the matter.[908]

Meanwhile the Expert-analytical council worked on a strategy for the upcoming elections, with the help of the President's Administration. The lack of a strong party of power with any genuine consolidated support among the people dictated a strategy of "The President is the father of the nation". The creation of the image of the "father of the nation" demanded effort, first and foremost, from the President himself. An analysis of the prevailing trends in society showed that the negative perception of Yeltsin was prevailing: "he's old", "he's sick", "he makes promises but doesn't keep them", "he doesn't monitor whether or not laws and directives are implemented", "he has bad habits". In an analytical note from a member of the expert-analytical council, L. Gozman, it was noted that the political demobilization of those who had supported Yeltsin in the previous elections was related to changes in the President's identity and behavior. His remaining support was based on the idea that he was "the lesser of two evils". The experts proposed establishing an image of him as a "lion roused from his slumbers".[909] When the President came down with another illness, however, all these efforts came to nothing.

---

906   These words are quoted by the Chairman of the State Duma I. Rybkin, in response to a similar question. See: I.P. Rybkin Russia is acquiring consensus. – M.: The International humanitarian foundation 'Knowledge', the International foundation 'Consensus', 1997. P.110.

907   Same ref.

908   The Yeltsin era. P.528.

909   The Yeltsin era. P.547.

The war in Chechnya dealt a serious blow to the authority of the man at the top. In response to the unsuccessful actions of the federal troops during the storming of the hospital in Budennovsk by Chechen insurgents in the summer of 1995, the communists tried to begin impeachment procedures against the president. The State Duma initiated a review in the Constitutional court of whether or not the commencement of military actions in Chechnya was lawful; if it was found to be unlawful, this could form the basis of an impeachment. The Constitutional court found that Yeltsin's actions were lawful, however. Admittedly, soon after this five members of the court expressed their own personal views, which indicated that most of the president's directives as regards Chechnya did not, in fact, comply with the requirements of the Constitution.

The proposal regarding the creation of a special impeachment commission did not secure the required number of votes. At the same time, the Duma passed a no confidence resolution in the government. In the end the parties reached a compromise: in exchange for leaving Chernomyrdin in his post, Yeltsin agreed to the State Duma's demand regarding the sacking of the "security" ministers responsible for the shameful events in Budennovsk — Stepashin (from the FSB) and Yerin (from the MIA). Stepashin's place was taken by M. Barsukov, a former commandant in the Kremlin and one of Korzhakov's peers, and A. Kulikov, the former commander of the domestic forces, took charge of the MIA.

The parliamentary elections of 1995

Preparations were being made meanwhile for the parliamentary elections of 1995. At Shakhrai's suggestion, it was decided that two major electoral movements should be formed, which would compete against one another externally but be internally compatible. As Shakhrai wrote in a diary entry towards the end of March 1995, the "two leg" strategy made it possible to assemble, in the new Duma, a reliable parliamentary majority for the president and the government, and meant that the extreme left and the extreme right could be squeezed onto the fringes of the political process. In the elections of 1996, two major electoral movements became a powerful support for the Russian President, and in the long-term would go on to form the basis of the two-party system.[910] It was expected that the left-centrist bloc would be led by the speaker of the State Duma, I. Rybkin, and that the right-of-center bloc would be led by V. Chernomyrdin.

Yeltsin made a conscious decision to distance himself from the political struggle in the parliamentary elections. At a press-conference held on 8th

---

910   Quoted from: The Yeltsin era. P.536.

September, he announced: "I might, of course, be asked what my own personal sympathies are, what the president's personal attitude towards these elections is, and what his involvement in the elections for the State Duma will be. First of all, I am not going to be involved in the elections politically at all. As President, I am the guarantee that the Constitution is going to be upheld as regards the elections to the State Duma, so that they are held in such a way that all the movements, parties and voters have equal rights....".[911]

An unprecedented number of parties and associations took part in the election campaign — 43, of which there were 6 leaders: the CPRF, the LDPR, the agrarians, Yabloko, Our home is Russia and the Congress of Russian communities. The attempt to create a left-of-center bloc as a counterweight to the communists had fallen through, and the CPRF were among the leaders.

The pro-presidential party Our home is Russia, which was led by V. Chernomyrdin, was on very shaky ground, thanks in large part to the unpopular measures taken by the government. A wave of discontent was caused by the concept for pension reform, published in the autumn of 1995, and the announcement about a forthcoming referendum on the question of land. The lack of support for Our home is Russia on the part of the President left the regional leaders confused. All the more so given that a distinct cooling of relations between Yeltsin and Chernomyrdin could be observed following the events in Buddenovsk. During the incident, the prime minister had assumed responsibility, in the president's absence, for holding talks with the terrorists, and had in effect saved the hostages' lives. And Yeltsin was envious of him. His demonstrative neutrality during the parliamentary election campaign signified that he did not want to enable any strengthening of a potential rival in the forthcoming race for the presidency. On the other hand, the unspoken rivalry between the president and the prime minister undermined the Kremlin's stance as a whole.

A symptom of the weakness of the "party of power" was the election of A. Rossel, in August 1995, as governor of the Sverdlovsk Region. Two years earlier, Rossel had been sacked by Yeltsin due to an attempt to proclaim an Urals Republic. In the elections, Rossel had defeated the leader of the Sverdlovsk branch of Our home is Russia, A. Strakhov, who was also in charge of the local administration.

The Expert-analytical council looked into the possibility of holding a Congress of democratic forces, at which the president would make a speech advocating the idea of merging all the democratic forces, as a counterweight to the opposition. Yeltsin agreed, but yet again his health let him down. Towards the end of October 1995 the President was taken to hospital for urgent treatment, with a diagnosis of acute ischaemic heart disease. He remained

---

911   Quoted from: The Yeltsin era. P.541.

in hospital until the end of the year. Observing the political situation from his hospital ward and then from a sanatorium, on the eve of the elections for the State Duma, he was living under an illusion. When V.V. Ilyushin and G.A. Satarov came to visit him at the Barvikha sanatorium three days before the election, to tell him the final prediction for the election results, prepared by the Administration's Analytical department, the president crossed out their figures and wrote his own in. As it turned out, he had made a serious miscalculation. The election results turned out to be even worse than the analysts had predicted.

Following the election on 17th December 1995, 4 parties gained seats in parliament. The CPRF won a landslide victory, securing support from 22.3% of the electorate, or almost 15.5 million people. To summarize the distribution of votes received by the party lists and the districts with a single candidate, the communists received 157 seats in the new Duma (34.9%), and 177 seats when one added to this their allies, the agrarians. Behind them, with three times fewer votes, were Our home is Russia, with 55 candidates elected; the LDPR, with 51 candidates, and Yabloko, which won 45 seats. General A. Lebed was elected to the State Duma in one of the single-candidate districts, for the first time.

The elections for parliament reflected the shift towards the left among the electorate. The number of people voting for the LDPR had halved by comparison with 1993. The Communists, by contrast, had more than doubled the number of people who supported him (in the 1993 election they had secured only 6.7 million votes). The share of the vote secured by Our home is Russia — the only party of power which had won seats in the new parliament via the party lists — were interpreted by the Kremlin as a defeat.

Chapter 10
The presidential elections of 1996

The candidates put themselves forward

1996 was a year that featured a serious test of strength for the model for statehood defined by the Constitution in 1993, and also for President Yeltsin. The Communist opposition, which in December 1995 had secured 22.3% of the vote in the elections for the State Duma, was preparing to get its revenge in the presidential elections scheduled to take place in June. An increase in the communists' popularity could also be seen in some of the other former socialist countries, whose people had suffered a sharp fall in living standards. In Lithuania, Poland and Moldova, however, where the representatives of the communist party had won both the parliamentary and presidential elections, all the talk was about making adjustments to the course of reforms, rather than returning to the socialist past. The situation in Russia was of a different nature: here, the arrival of the communists in power threatened new tremors in society, related to the division of property, and an attempt to restore a Soviet type of Statehood.

The CPRF had managed to unite in its election coalition organizations such as Working Russia (V.I. Anpilov), The State (A.V. Rutskoi), The Agrarian Party (M.I. Lapshin) and The Russian National Union (S.N. Baburin), and to put forward a single candidate to represent them. The man chosen was the leader of the CPRF, G.A. Zyuganov. A survey of public opinion carried out at the beginning of 1996 revealed that he was considered the most likely winner of the upcoming presidential elections.

Zyuganov's popularity had increased off the back of disappointment in the "democratization"[912] of power. The establishment of constitutional order in

---

912   It was in this period that the term 'democratic' began to be used in an offensive, pejorative manner. In the usage of the word, there was an implied criticism of the Government and the President from the communists' camp, Zhirinovsky's Liberal Democrats, the supporters of Yavlinsky and activists from the abolished Supreme Soviet who had moved over to the opposition.

Chechnya by force, which had begun in December 1994, resulted in a bloody, long-drawn-out war. The growing financial crisis, low levels of tax collection and shortage of money in circulation led to delays in the payment of salaries, pensions and social benefits. It would be impossible to overcome the crisis in the budget whilst over 40% of businesses in the country were running at a loss. (As of 1st July 1996, 41.3% of companies were running at a loss)[913].

In December 1995, in response to a survey which asked "Who would you vote for if the election was held today?" 5% of those questioned said B. Yeltsin, whereas 13% said G. Zyuganov, 10% said A. Lebed, 9% said G. Yavlinsky and 7% said V. Chernomyrdin.[914] Many people were convinced that given the circumstances, Yeltsin would not stand for a second term, and that if he did stand, he was bound to be defeated.

What were the communists proposing by way of getting out of the crisis? Zyuganov had run on a platform in which the strategic objective was phrased in a fairly round-about way, so as not to put off any potential allies: "This is not a road back to the past, as those who are currently governing Russia would have you believe. This is Russia's path towards self-discovery, a path towards spirituality, abundance, sufficiency and dignity. This is precisely the path which has been taken by the countries which currently set the standard for the rest of the world. These states live in accordance with a simple rule: the wealth of their citizens above all else."[915] In a speech at the World Economic Forum in Davos in February 1996, Zyuganov tried to persuade the Western elite that, as the most likely candidate for president, he shared Western values; he advocated a multifaceted economy and political pluralism, and emphasized that there were huge differences between the CPRF and the CPSU in terms of both agenda and tactics. These assertions contradicted the official party line, however. The CPRF's manifesto, which was adopted in January 1995, talked of the need to return to the people, and take under control of the state, assets which had been seized against the public interest. On the last day of the forum, A.B. Chubais held a press-conference at which he scolded Zyuganov for telling the "classic communist lie". Chubais had read the Communist party's manifestos, and demonstrated that there were two Zyuganovs, one for foreigners, the other for domestic consumption, and that if he won the election there would be "great bloodshed" in Russia, and big business would be forced to leave Russia.[916]

Russian businessmen agreed, in Davos, to support Yeltsin in the presidential election.[917]

---

913   http://www.council.gov.ru/inf_sl/bulletin/item/179/index.html
914   A. Oslon: How the Analytical group made polls a fact of life in 1996 //Social reality. 2006. No.6.
915   Pravda. 1996. 1 July
916   Nezavisimaya gazeta. 1996. 6 February.
917   For more details see: D. Hoffman: The oligarchs. Wealth and power in the new

Thus the presidential election would decide not only the matter of who would hold the most senior position in the Russian Federation, but would also determine the fate of the country. The outcome of the elections depended in many ways on the ability of the ruling elite to unite behind a single candidate. At the start of 1996 President Yeltsin's ratings were hovering between 4 and 8%. In addition to the long-term reasons for his low popularity in society — his obvious health problems, the delays in the payment of salaries and pensions, the increasing crime rates — the president's rating was also affected by the unsuccessful hostage rescue operation in the Dagestani village of Pervomaiskoye.

The decision to stand in the election was not an easy one for Yeltsin to take. At the end of 1995 he suffered a heart attack. As he later confessed in his memoirs, he was utterly exhausted, felt a sense of almost complete political isolation, and, ultimately, a significant factor was his wife's opinion — she was against the idea.[918] What on earth was it that prompted Yeltsin engage in a gruelling "presidential marathon"? Yeltsin himself said that it was a form of epiphany: he had suddenly spotted the danger that a "semi-martial team of post-Soviet generals" might come to power: "the head of the security service, Alexander Korzhakov, and the director of the FSB, Mikhail Barsukov, whom the first deputy prime minister, Oleg Soskovets, covered with his almighty body."[919] This danger did indeed exist, but the more likely scenario is that Yeltsin acknowledged it whilst he was writing his memoirs, and not at the time the decision was made. His memoirs also refer to the danger that the communists might come to power.

It is generally thought that a decisive factor in Yeltsin's decision was the fact that he hated losing. And to him, not standing in the election would be exactly that — a defeat, and one that would have unpredictable consequences. Yes, his strength was on the wane, but he still had enough willpower to offer resistance and to be confident of victory. His inaccurate assessment of the situation also played a role. Still fresh in the memory were the crowds of many thousands, shouting out "Yeltsin is Russia!", the election in 1991, which he had won in spite of resistance by the powerful party machine, and his defeat of the opposition in 1993. He believed that the people would support him this time, too.

Yeltsin was in no hurry to make a public announcement regarding his wish to stand in the election. Among his inner circle, however, he made no secret of it. Immediately after the new year festivities, on 4th January, the head of the

---

Russia. Translated from the English by M. Astrel, 2010.

918   B.N. Yeltsin: The Presidential marathon. Thoughts, reminiscences, impressions... M: Publishing house AST, 2006. P.23

919   B.N. Yeltsin: See above P.24

president's administration, S. Filatov, found out to his surprise that he had been sacked and given a new role in the president's Election HQ. Yeltsin's words lived long in Filatov's memory: "We fucked up the elections for the State Duma — it's a communist stronghold now...I didn't want to stand in the election, I thought about it long and hard, hesitating, but in the end circumstances dictated that I took the decision to stand for a second term as president." Filatov wrote that this was the first time he had heard a coarse swear-word pass the president's lips: "It was unexpectedly and unpleasantly grating on the ear, because Boris Nikolaevich had never used language like that before and never tolerated other people speaking like that in his presence."[920]

Filatov was replaced by N.D. Yegorov[921], who used to be an advisor to the President. The dismissal of Filatov, who was known for his pro-democracy views, was seen by many as symbolic. All the more so given that Yeltsin soon afterwards made certain changes in the government which spoke of an adjustment to the chosen course in both foreign and domestic policy. Rather than appointing A.V. Kozyrev, who embodied the pro-Western trend in Russian foreign policy, the president appointed as foreign minister Y.M. Primakov, who had shown himself to be a true professional in the field of international relations ever since Soviet days. Yeltsin, as it turned out, had chosen well, and Primakov received backing from the main political forces.

The final member of the Gaidar team in Chernomyrdin's government, A.B. Chubais, was relieved of his responsibilities as first deputy chairman, and replaced in the role by an "administrator", the CEO and president of AVTOVAZ, V.V. Kadannikov. Yeltsin subjected Chubais to public criticism, blaming him for Our home is Russia's failure in the parliamentary elections in 1995 and for the mass delays in the payment of salaries and pensions in the country. The satirical TV program *Puppets* portrayed the president uttering a phrase which caught hold in the popular imagination: "Blame Chubais."

In January 1996 Y.T. Gaidar, S.A. Kovalev, O.R. Latsis and S.S. Alekseev left the President's council; none of them had agreed with the decision to sack Chubais or with the accusations about mistakes, which he had not in fact made, in connection with the failure by the pro-Kremlin party Our home is Russia in the elections. The democratic camp was being broken up (it had never been united, incidentally). As S.A. Filatov wrote, "there was quite a broad spectrum of opinions among the democrats: from A. Chubais ("Yeltsin is needed as a guarantor that the reforms will continue") and V. Nikonov ("the election of Yeltsin is the lesser of two evils") to Y. Gaidar ("Yeltsin standing would be the best possible gift to the communists")"[922]. The option

---

920   S. Filatov: An open secret. M.: 'VAGRIUS' publishing house, 2000. P.373.

921   He spent just six months in this job and was fired on the eve of the election — 15 July 1996.

922   S. Filatov: An open secret. M.: 'VAGRIUS' publishing house, 2000. P.378.

of postponing the elections was also considered. On 13th January an article by M. Zakharov headed 'We don't need any fateful elections' was published in *Izvestiya*. It read: «A national referendum on extending the president's powers to the year two thousand, or any other form of rendering his activity legitimate, including direct rule by the president for the four transition years, could bring our long-suffering nation towards the age of stability which can already be glimpsed on the horizon."[923] It was obvious that the author was expressing something that was not just his own personal view.

Postponing the elections, however, was not something for which provision was made under the Constitution and the existing legislation. The president could not countenance infringing the rules of his own constitution just two years after it was adopted. The events of 1993 were still too fresh in the memory.

On 17th January it was announced that a Russian Head Office for the elections of the President of Russia would be set up, led by the first deputy prime minister, O. Soskovets. Soskovets was seen as Korzhakov's man, and, according to the memoirs of Yeltsin himself, the main candidate for the role of prime minister in place of Chernomyrdin. The job of interacting with the intelligentsia and the general public was given to S.A. Filatov, who was appointed deputy director of the head office. The staff of the head office were something of a motley crew: its other members were B.A. Berezovsky, T.B. Dyachenko, M.A. Zakharov, V.N. Ignatenko, V.G. Kinilev, A.I. Korabelschikov, V.A. Petrenko, V.I. Resin, S.A. Tarpishchev and others. In all, some 43 people.

A campaign began to collect signatures for Yeltsin's candidacy and to prepare public opinion for it. The president began signing orders one after another regarding the allocation of funds from the budget for social needs. On 22nd January came the directive "On measures to ensure prompt payment of salaries by means of the budgets at all levels, pensions and other social welfare payments", and on 25th January there were directives regarding compensation payments to pensioners and a 20% increase in the bursaries given to students and graduates. On 2nd February an agreement was reached regarding the payment of debts on salaries, tax breaks and subsidies for the coal industry, and this enabled the miners' strike to be curtailed.

A big bone of contention was the payment by the IMF, in late February 1996, of a 10 billion dollar loan to Russia. The West was thereby making it abundantly clear on which side its sympathies lay.

---

923   Quotation taken from: From Yeltsin to…Yeltsin: the race for the presidency in '96. M.: TERRA, 1997. P.28.

In order to secure backing from the regional elites, Yeltsin decided to expand the regions' powers. On 12th January 1996 an agreement to this effect was signed in the Sverdlovsk Region. At the same time, the Kaliningrad Region secured greater independence from Moscow. A total of 10 agreements regarding the distribution of powers between the central government and the regions were signed during the preparations for the elections.

Meetings were held with senior generals and directors from the security services, and members of elite units were given awards — the Tamansk and Kantemirovsk units, as well as the 27th special forces brigade, which had played a decisive role in the events which took place around the White House in October 1993.

As Yeltsin began actively preparing for the elections, the democratic community continued to discuss the matter of whether or not it ought to support him. The possibility of putting forward V.S. Chernomyrdin as a potential alternative was considered. In a 2006 interview, V. Nikonov, who had been a member of the electoral campaign office during the presidential campaign, said that "no surveys or studies had given Chernomyrdin the right to sit in the chair. Moreover, victory was only possible if it was the result of a complete consolidation of the elites, and Yeltsin alone could provide this. The prime minister would certainly not be able to do it, as Chernomyrdin had demonstrated, incidentally, in the elections, as the leader of the party Our home is Russia: he was not able to bring the elites together. The president, on the other hand, could do this: he was capable of bringing together the elites, who were frightened by the idea that the communists might gain power."[924]

The famous political strategist made these comments in connection with the 'anniversary' of the presidential elections, some ten years on from them. If one looks at the newspapers published in January-February 1996, it is easy to see that Chernomyrdin's candidacy was seriously considered — if not as an alternative to Yeltsin, then as an understudy. This view was espoused, for example, in *Izvestiya*.[925] It was reported that groups promoting Chernomyrdin were being set up in St Petersburg, Orenburg and other cities. Chernomyrdin distanced himself from these suggestions, however, and on 3rd February he unexpectedly left for a two-week vacation. It was suggested that his vacation was the result of a conversation which had taken place between the president and the prime minister, during which the prime minister had been advised to leave Moscow for a while, so as not to bother the democrats by being around.

"In the face of the Bolshevik threat", the democratic intelligentsia had begun to lean towards Yeltsin. A letter sent by members of the President's council, and published in *Izvestiya*, stated that Yeltsin would stay on as a vitally

---

924   Moskovskiye novosti. 6 July 2006
925   See: Izvestiya 30 January 1996

important support for democracy in Russia and the guarantor of Russia's Constitution; that it was necessary "conjointly and constructively to work with the president, regardless of any disagreements people might have — even sizeable ones — with him or with one another." The letter was signed by various writers and academics who were well-known in Russia: D.A. Granin, A.M. Yemelyanov, M.A. Zakharov, S.A. Karaganov, A.M. Migranyan, E.A. Pain, L.V. Smirnyagin, M.O. Chudakova and others.[926]

After a fruitless search for an alternative figure, Gaidar's party also declared its support for Yeltsin. A considerable role was played by the particular circumstance that Yeltsin managed to regain his mobility at a critical juncture. Gaidar later recalled of his meeting with the president on 29th February: "During the conversation I unexpectedly caught myself thinking that the man I saw before me was in no sense the same Yeltsin who, literally one month earlier, had been saying something vague on my TV screen about thirty-eight snipers and a reinforced area in Pervomaiskoye. He was speaking clearly, self-assuredly and with energy, and was able to pick up on his interlocutor's train of thought in mid-flow. One got the feeling that the last five years had never happened, and we were back in October 1991 all over again... After the conversation, the hope emerged, for the first time in recent months, that now, perhaps, at a key moment for Russia, Yeltsin would be able to undergo a dramatic change, regain that energy of old and restore contact with the electorate...In March 1996 the public suddenly saw before them a completely different president, one they had long since forgotten: the 1991 model of Yeltsin, with his unique ability to talk to people, and win people's sympathy with his energy and insistence."[927]

On 15th February Yeltsin announced his decision to stand for a second term. He made the announcement in his native city of Yekaterinburg. Right from the outset his election campaign was founded on the idea of "consolidating the forces for good in society" in order to prevent any possible setbacks. Starting with his first speech as a candidate, he never tired of talking about the danger of the communists exacting revenge, and constantly underlined the fact that, by making their choice of president, the people were deciding Russia's fate.

A total of 78 candidates stood for president, and 11 of them were included on the voting slip on 16th June 1996.[928] A fundamentally new procedure for financing election campaigns, by comparison with the one in place in 1991, was adopted. Events related to the preparation and holding of the elections were financed using resources from the federal budget. In order to finance canvassing, the candidates for president compiled their own election funds,

926   Izvestiya 7 February 1996
927   Y.T. Gaidar: Days of defeats and victories. P.549-550.
928   The elections in the Russian Federation. M.: 'VALTI', 1998. P.95.

which, in addition to money from the state budget, also received money from legal entities and individuals, the candidates' own resources, and funding from electoral associations. The Federal Law on the elections for President established limits on the elections funds and the maximum contributions that could be made.

The March crisis

The election campaign, which had begun to gather momentum, almost came to an end in the middle of March 1996, when the State Duma cancelled the decision of the Supreme Soviet of the RSFSR of 12th December 1991 which denounced the Agreement on the formation of the USSR. The directive from the Duma was clearly populist in tone, and satisfied the nostalgia felt by the majority of people over the break-up of the USSR. The legislators, however, did not allow for the inevitable legal and political consequences of their decision. After all, the Soviet republics which had signed the agreement in 1922 no longer existed, and the new states which had come into being in the post-Soviet expanse had no wish to give up their newly acquired independence. It is likely that the communist bloc in the State Duma, which was behind this directive, had a conscious desire to get into a confrontation with the president during the election campaign.

Yeltsin's response was indeed extremely strong. On 14th March, on the eve of the Duma vote, the President announced in a TV interview, in threatening tones, that if the Belovezha agreements were disavowed he would "take extreme measures", since he would see it as a threat to Russia's constitutional system. The Duma, however, paid no heed to his warnings and voted in favor of restoring the USSR.

When he recalled these events in later years, he wrote: "Why try to hide it: I was always inclined towards the most straightforward solutions. I have always thought that it is easier to cut up a Gordian knot than to spend years trying to untie it. At a certain point, as I weighed up two different strategies put to me by teams with different mentalities and approaches, I sensed something: I must not wait until the results of the elections in June...I had to act now! ...A series of directives were drafted: there was one on the banning of the communist party, one on the break-up of the Duma, and one on postponing the presidential elections to a later date. Behind all these statements lay the following verdict: within the framework of the current Constitution, I had failed to cope with the crisis."[929]

---

929   B.N. Yeltsin: See above P.31-32.

As the minister of internal affairs, A. Kulikov, recalled in his memoirs, on 17th March he was invited to Yeltsin's office and ordered to calculate how much money and effort would be needed to implement a decision by the president to disband the State Duma, ban the CPRF and postpone the elections. As a military man, he had to obey his orders, and he gave the appropriate order to his ministry.

That same day, Yeltsin ordered that a directive to this effect be drafted, and an address to the people prepared. Instead of doing so, however, his aides drew up a document entitled 'Opposing conclusions and alternatives', in which they attempted to dissuade Yeltsin from going ahead with his plan. The president's aides V. Ilyushin, G. Satarov, M. Krasnov, Y. Baturin and the deputy of the State Duma S. Shakhrai managed to persuade Yeltsin to refrain from opting to use force. They quite justifiably felt that an unsuitable response to the Duma's decision could lead to social upheaval, and suggested that the president consult the Federation Council and the Constitutional court.[930]

The military machine, which was already kicking into action, was, by some miracle, brought to a juddering halt. By evening on the 17th March, under the pretext of the evacuation bell ringing, the State Duma had been occupied by special armed police (OMON) and GUO (chief defence division) units.[931] The next morning, however, the deputies were allowed to enter the building.

Recalling these events, Yeltsin wrote that Kulikov and Chernomyrdin had spoken out against his plans, but that the majority of those present at the meeting supported the idea of postponing the elections. A decisive role in making him change his mind was played by a conversation he had with A. Chubais: "...We talked for about an hour. I was making objections. I raised my voice. I was practically shouting, which is something I never do. And yet I ended up backing down on a decision which had almost been taken."[932]

The subject of cancelling or postponing the elections was brought up in the press and in speeches made in public for a few more days, but in the end the scenario involving the use of force was prevented. The directive of the State Duma dated 15th March, after a discussion in the Federation Council, was sent back to the lower chamber, where it was not returned to again. The March crisis revealed the fragile nature of Russian democracy, and showed how easy it was to make the president tend towards solutions involving the use of force — solutions which might have far-reaching consequences.

---

930   For more details see: The Yeltsin era. Sketches from a political history. M.: VAGRIUS, 2001. P.558-563.
931   O. Moroz: 1996: How Zyuganov didn't become president. – M.: OJSC Raduga publishing house, 2006. p.181.
932   B.N. Yeltsin: See above P. 33.

Soon after these events, Soskovets' election campaign office was closed down. The motive for this was the information that had leaked through into the press to the effect that at some companies, staff had only been given their salaries after they had agreed to add their signature to the petition calling for Yeltsin to run for election. One can understand why such 'agitating' on behalf of the president could only have the opposite effect to the one desired. Yeltsin's team of advisers had prepared an analytical note for the president as early as in January 1996, which stated: "It will not be possible to secure enough votes without the democratic electorate, whom it will not be possible to attract without the help of the democratic press and the elite. We must not count solely on securing the votes of the communists and the patriots. We can't win the election solely with the help of the ministers and the heads of administration, by pulling the administrative levers; the campaign by Our home is Russia provided ample evidence of this."[933]

Counting on the administrative resource, Soskovets' campaign office did not give much credence to the opinion polls, and believed that everything would fall into place when election day came. Dutiful consultants from head office tried to convince Yeltsin that people loved him, but were too shy to admit it. Experts from the Administration's analytical department held a different view. On 14th March the expert-analytical group sent a letter to the president in which they said that the only way to rescue the election campaign was by immediately removing Soskovets from his position as director of the head office.

Eventually the president agreed to the proposal to change the whole management structure of the election campaign. On 19th March there was a meeting organized by A. Chubais, at which Yeltsin met the leaders of the biggest banks and media groups: V. Gusinsky, M. Khodorkovsky, V. Potanin, B. Berezovsky, M. Fridman and others.[934] That same day, a Council for the election campaign was set up, chaired by Yeltsin himself and containing the following members: V. Ilyushin (the deputy chairman), V. Chernomyrdin, Y. Yarov, S. Filatov, A. Chubais, I. Malashenko, N. Yegorov, Y. Luzhkov, O. Soskovets, M. Barsukov, A. Korzhakov and T. Dyachenko. The main center for political decision-making was the analytical group set up by Chubais, consisting of A. Chubais, G. Satarov, B. Berezovsky, S. Shakhrai, T. Dyachenko, I. Malashenko, N. Gonchar, V. Shakhnovsky, A. Oslon, V. Nikonov and S. Zverev.[935]

As A. Oslon, one of the members of the Analytical group, put it, the group comprised "pragmatists whose sole focus was to solve the task which had been set, and who, thanks to the *carte-blanche* which they had been given, were

---

933   Quoted from: The Yeltsin era. P.549
934   For more details see: B.N. Yeltsin: The Presidential marathon. P.29-30. For the interview with Chubais see Kommersant and Trud 26.03.96
935   The Yeltsin era. P.556-557.

now able to carry out this task without having to check any kind of formal agreement with any of the appeals institutions whatsoever. The decisions suggested were reported even to the candidate as having already been taken, and awaiting implementation. This happened both at the general meetings (particularly in the early days, when there was a need to "synchronize watches" and "reach an agreement on the shore"), and via T. Dyachenko, Yeltsin's daughter and an active member of the Analytical group. The presence of a 'bridge' such as this soon led to the candidate understanding and accepting the initial ideas of the campaign: he believed in them and felt a powerful, reckless urge to make them a reality."[936]

As a new figure in the president's inner circle, it seemed to Oslon as though those involved in the campaign were working together like an exceptionally well-oiled machine: "For all the diverse types of motivation that people had — both in the Analytical group, and among those who were working around it (and this included hundreds of people from all walks of life), in that particular situation, in the spring of 1996, there was a common wish to be as pro-active as possible in the effort to get Yeltsin re-elected."[937] Kremlin veterans could see, however, that as the campaign marathon went on, the old disagreements within the president's team only intensified.

As S. Filatov recalled, clashes were constantly taking place between Korzhakov and Malashenko, who worked with the mass media.[938] Korzhakov, whom Yeltsin referred to in his memoirs as the informal leader of his inner circle, using his position, was forever turning the president against the other members of the team. Filatov, he recounted, did not always find it easy to see eye to eye with T. Dyachenko.[939]

The problem of sorting out the Chechen crisis

In the battle for the electorate's votes, the incumbent president found himself in a far more complex situation than his rivals. Not only was he required to make promises: he also had to keep them. And the most pressing and complex problem of all, in this regard, was ending the war in Chechnya. The inability of the federal powers to end the bloodshed, and bring an end to a war which had in effect gone beyond the borders of the Republic of Chechnya and moved into neighboring Dagestan, caused discontent in society. If the war continued it would mean that separatist terrorist groups would be able

---

936   A Oslon: How the Analytical group made opinion polls a fact of life in 1996 //Social reality. 2006. No.6.
937   A. Oslon: See above.
938   S.A. Filatov: An open secret. P.399.
939   S.A. Filatov: See above P.394.

to disrupt the elections, or affect the outcome. The Chechen problem was significant in a way that went beyond the immediate tasks of the election campaign, of course. Setting aside the international aspect of the issue, let us note the importance of ending the war and restoring the status of the Republic of Chechnya as part of the Russian Federation from the point of view of strengthening Russian statehood.

In February 1996, in order to draw up a peace plan for the situation in Chechnya, a government commission was set up, along with a working group within the President's Administration, led by E.A. Pain (the deputy head of the Administration's analytical center). The fact that there were now two groups involved in solving the same problem suggested there was an unspoken rivalry between the Government and the Administration, and also between Chernomyrdin and Yeltsin — all the more so if one considered that the prime minister could be considered as a candidate for president. By this time, however, Chernomyrdin had said on several occasions, and in no uncertain terms, that he did not intend to take part in the presidential elections. It is more likely that this 'brainstorming' technique involving two parallel groups was needed in order to find the optimum solution. At the end of February the proposals were ready, and in early March Yeltsin met the groups' leaders, as well as N. Yegorov and D. Zavgaev, to discuss them in depth.

The program for resolving the Chechen crisis was presented to the citizens of Russia by Yeltsin on 31st March in a televised address. The plan was to cease military operations at midnight on 31st March in the territory of the rebel republic, and begin a gradual withdrawal of federal troops from the peaceful areas of Chechnya. The second point in the program put forward by the president was the holding of free democratic parliamentary elections in the republic of Chechnya, and the restoration of the bodies of executive power, which, as they grew stronger, would have sufficient responsibility and powers passed to them in order to bring the situation under control once and for all. Any agreement on the issue of the Chechen republic's status was postponed until normal circumstances were fully restored.

The program could be seen in many ways as a compromise. The State Duma was being invited to declare an amnesty for those involved in armed conflict in Chechnya, with the exception of those who had committed crimes. Yeltsin expressed his willingness to engage in talks with Dudaev's side, admittedly via middle-men.

The process of finding a peaceful solution began with the signing of a trilateral peace agreement between representatives of the federal forces, representatives of the government of Doku Zavgaev and the local administration: the military undertook not to fire on populated areas, and to begin removing mines, and the local people undertook not to let the insurgents through. The separatists refused to recognise these treaties, however — and this was to have tragic consequences. On 15th April the first stage of the troop withdrawal began, and literally on the very next day a column of federal troops was ambushed and almost completely wiped out on a mountain road between the villages of Dachu-Borza and Yarysh-Marda, with which a peace treaty had been signed. On 19th April RIA Novosti reported that 92 soldiers had been killed, 56 had been wounded and 21 armored vehicles had been destroyed. Only 12 people survived the ambush.[940]

Following the death of the president of the Chechen republic, Ichkeri Dzhokhar Dudaev, the situation became more complex. On 23rd April a statement from Ichkeri's government was broadcast on ITAR TASS to the effect that due to the death of Dudaev, it was rejecting the peace plan proposed by Yeltsin.

One month later, however, on 27th March, talks were held at the president's Kremlin residence between Yeltsin and Dudaev's successor, Zelimkhan Yandarbiev. The document that was signed as a result of this meeting stipulated the following:

1. A complete end to military action in Chechnya at midnight on 1st July.

2. The release, within 2 weeks, of all those who had been forcefully detained.

3. Talks between special commissions, with the purpose of devising specific mechanisms.

The next day, on 28th May, Yeltsin flew to Chechnya — a move no-one had foreseen. The preparations for the trip had been kept top secret. Yandarbiev and the members of his delegation found out about Yeltsin's visit from the TV news reports. They spent the day in the residence outside Moscow, essentially as hostages.

This was the most eye-catching and the most dangerous of the 30 trips around the country made by Yeltsin during the election campaign. On the front of an armored personnel carrier he signed a directive on a complete transition of the military onto a system of conscription starting in 2000.[941] During his trip he ordered that conscripts who had served 18 months, including six months in trouble-spots, be demobbed ahead of time.

The agreements reached at the Kremlin were backed up by the protocols signed in Nazran on 10th June regarding an end to all military action, the withdrawal

---

940   O. Moroz: 1996: How Zyuganov didn't become president. – M.: OJSC 'Raduga' publishing house, 2006, p.264.
941   On this subject Y. Baturin, an adviser on national security, sent Yeltsin a report in which he said it was impossible to cross over to a contractual system. See: The Yeltsin era P.462.

of federal troops and the release of prisoners. On 25th June Yeltsin signed Directive No. 985 on the gradual withdrawal of troops from Chechnya by 1st September. The 205th mobile brigade (8000 people) and the 101st brigade of internal troops (4000) remained in Chechnya on a permanent basis.

The election campaign

The election campaign, meanwhile, was gaining momentum. This could be seen in the socially-oriented nature of the president's directives. In addition to wiping out the debt due on salaries and increasing social welfare payments, a directive was passed entitled 'On the exercise of citizens' constitutional rights to land', in which the government was ordered to take to the Duma a law on the free transfer to citizens of plots of land which could be used to grow food, for gardening purposes, or for the construction of residential property or a dacha.[942] In another directive the president initiated the development of the Federal targeted program 'A house of one's own'.[943]

In order to wrest the initiative from the opposition blocs in the State Duma, who were playing with nostalgia for the Union, the president's side took steps to strengthen the CIS. On 29th March 1996 Yeltsin signed a four-way agreement with the presidents of Belarus, Kazakhstan and Kyrgizia on a deepening of integration in the economic and humanitarian fields.[944] Three days later, on 2nd April, an Agreement was signed on the creation of the Commonwealth of Belarus and Russia.[945]

In April a congress of the President's supporters was convened; it was prepared by the Russian national movement for support by the public of B. Yeltsin in the elections for President of the Russian Federation (ODOP).[946] Addressing the congress, Yeltsin set out the ten core areas of his presidential program: the fight against poverty; protecting the family, motherhood and children; developing culture, education and science; the fight against crime and corruption; the introduction of legal and military reforms, and others.

Social surveys revealed that the president's actions in the battle for votes were having a noticeable effect. (See table 1.).

---

942 http://www.innovbusiness.ru/pravo/DocumShow_DocumID_57804.html
943 http://www.tehlit.ru/1lib_norma_doc/1/1692/
944 http://www.evrazes.com/print/docs/34
945 http://www.sngcom.ru/belarus/legislation/commonwealth A year later the Union of Russia and Belarus was founded, on the basis of the Commonwealth.
946 The Russia-wide movement for social support for B. Yeltsin in the elections for President of the Russian Federation. Material on the congress on 6th April 1996, M., 1996.

Table 1. The impact on the electorate of political events in March–April 1996 (%)[947]

Political events and measures	Worked in B.N. Yeltsin's favor	Worked in G.A. Zyuganov's favor
The Duma's Directive on of the Belovezha agreements	15.0	20.6
The Program for dealing with the crisis in Chechnya, announced by Yeltsin	25.3	8.9
The four-way agreement on the deepening of integration between Russia, Belarus, Kazakhstan and Kyrgizia	26.4	7.6
The formation of the Commonwealth of Russia and Belarus	28.5	7.3
The Edict from the President of the RF on the exercise of the constitutional rights of citizens to land	26.8	8.1
The Edict of the president of the RF on the development of the federal targeted program 'A house of one's own'	30.4	3.5
Events organized by the central government regarding the payment of debts on salaries	37.7	5.4

New political technologies played a huge role in the election campaign. Nobody sought to hide this. Immediately after the second round of the elections, *Nezavisimaya gazeta* published an article by L. Ionin entitled 'The Technology of Success', with the sub-heading 'Elections cannot be won nowadays without political analysts and consultants'. The article's author wrote that "it was the gigantic efforts and amounts of money spent on running the campaign, from an intellectual and technological point of view, that Boris Yeltsin owed his victory. This was the first such incident in the history of Russian politics."[948]

The election campaign was founded on the idea of restoring the "Yeltsin of old". The idea was that the President would be seen by the electorate as

---

947   M.K. Gorshkov: Russian society in a state of transformatin (sociological analysis). – M.: 'The Russian political encyclopaedia' (ROSSPAN), 2000. p.147.
948   Nezavisimaya gazeta. 1996. 5 July.

the man they had known in 1990-91: as an energetic, decisive leader, who understood people's desperation, and who was able to talk to them in a language they understood. The president's Directives were prepared on the basis of an analysis of questionnaires, and were designed to have the greatest possible effect on the electorate for a variety of social groups. From early April onwards, B. Yeltsin began to speak in straightforward, non-governmental language about the problems faced by women, pensioners and children, about mass impoverishment and so on, with a genuine expression of empathy.

Moskovsky komsomolets published an in-depth report on the launch of an advertising campaign in which the key slogans were 'Vote with your heart!' and 'I believe! I feel love! I feel hope!' The main purpose of it was to draw over to Yeltsin's side the 30% of the electorate who were yet to decide whose side they were on — the communists or the democrats. In a series of video clips entitled 'I believe. I feel love. I feel hope', ordinary people going about their business were shown expressing their support for Yeltsin. Five film crews had set off around the country to look for characters to talk to for these clips. The short movies that they filmed were shown to focus-groups, and then fine-tuned based on the audience's comments and broadcast on the TV. An extremely diverse range of randomly selected people in a natural setting were shown talking about the elections and about the candidate in their own words. They did not praise the candidate or urge people to vote for him, but simply espoused the view that "you don't change the horses in mid-journey".[949]

In order to get the section of the public which traditionally played a passive role in the elections — young people — to the polling stations, the election campaign by the US president Bill Clinton in 1992 (the 'Choose or lose' campaign) was adapted to suit the conditions pertaining in Russia.[950] Television was selected as the main resource in terms of influencing young people, and the main cast members were stars from the music industry, rock and the movies.[951] The campaigning on behalf of Yeltsin was not done in a direct way. The 'Vote or lose' campaign was founded on visual images which symbolized the dark Soviet past, on the one hand, and a bright future on the other. Campaign meetings attended by young people, even ones such as the forum for democratic youth, which was held at the Higher Komsomol School on 2nd June, were conducted in the spirit of a party for young people. Baseball

---

949   Moskovsky komsomolets. 1996. 31 July.
950   The election campaign was run entirely by Russian political scientists. The Analytical group neither used nor inspected the material or advice submitted by the American consultants working in Moscow. The story about how the Americans 'engineered' Yeltsin's victory, as portrayed by the film Project 'Yeltsin', is not an accurate account of what actually happened. For more details see: A. Oslon: How the Analytical group made polls a fact of life in 1996 // Social reality. 2006. No.6.
951   For more details see: S. Lisovsky, V. Yevstafiev: Electoral technologies: history, theory, practice. M., 2000.

caps, T-shirts, placards with campaign slogans and CDs were handed out in the foyer, and in the auditorium a group of 'fans' responded to speeches with howls of approval, chanting "Yel-tsin, Yel-tsin!"[952]

The campaign on behalf of the incumbent president included a demonizing of his main rival — G. A. Zyuganov. According to G. Pavlovsky, the director of the Foundation for effective policy, which, under a contract signed with Yeltsin's head office, carried out "counter-propaganda work in the regional media": "No-one had any scruples about the launch of an open 'smear campaign'. A civil war was going on in the field of information (...). The electorate were fed the following ideas: the communists want to take something away from you: your apartment, your land, the 500 dollars sewn into your stocking."[953] The main psychological reasoning behind the campaign was to contrast the idea of "freedom and democracy under Yeltsin" with that of "famine, civil war and labor camps under Zyuganov". Using this method, the campaigners made people believe that there was no alternative to Yeltsin.

An important role was played by Yeltsin's trips around the country and his meetings with voters. After Chubais set up an analytical group, there was a dramatic change to the way these trips were conducted. Yeltsin recalled that Igor Malashenko had carried out an experiment, by placing photographs of two election campaigns in front of him: "In the first photograph, which was an up-to-date one, taken in 1996, there was a group of leaders and a crowd of frightened people awaiting them behind a "sanitary cordon" (I think it was taken in Krasnodar). The second photo, an old one from 1991, showed a huge mass of people with lively expressions on their faces and shining eyes. I spotted the happy look on the face of a woman, who was stretching out her hand to me, to a different Yeltsin, and almost cried out with pain. This had a powerful effect on me. After all, this had happened just five years ago! I remembered the feelings I had got when I met people, and everything suddenly fell into place."[954]

In all the cities Yeltsin visited (and he must have been to at least fifteen in the space of two and a half months), questionnaires were sent out before and after his visit, so as to get a sense of how effective these trips were and what mistakes had been made. After the president's first trip to the south of the country, the questionnaires revealed that it had damaged and negatively affected people's attitude toward Yeltsin. Roads had been closed in the city, the large team of security guards had been rough with people as they sought to keep them away from the head of state, and there was a very official feel

---

952   Kommersant. 1996. 4 June.

953   Quoted by: V. Avchenko: The theory and practice of political manipulation in modern Russia.

954   //http://psyfactor.org/polman6.htm //http://psyfactor.org/polman6.htm

to the visit. This format for visits was immediately scrapped, and a whole creative unit was set up to plan visits and even come up with dramatic scripts for more "lively" events and interaction with people. Yeltsin got into the spirit of it, coming up with unexpected ideas in his own right and getting genuine pleasure out of doing so. A TV audience of millions could see his inner drive, but this was not something that the Analytical group had programmed in him, of course — it was merely that the group had managed to activate in Yeltsin resources which had hitherto lain hidden beneath the surface, and these resources also began to further the campaign's main objective — "to evoke surprised approval among voters."[955]

The tense rhythm of the race for the presidency was something that Yeltsin found it hard to keep up with, and this inevitably caused concern among his inner circle. One of his advisers told V. Ilyushin: "The event held on 15th April (N.N. Semenov's anniversary) left me in no doubt that the President's schedule ought perhaps to be revised (both in terms of the number of events and the content of these events) by 16th June. The boss's speeches were lacking in vigor (perhaps because he had picked up a sore throat the day before), and he stuck strictly to the text. In short, he was lacking the inspiration which had become customary in recent weeks. One got the sense he was terribly tired...".[956]

The president's doctors raised the alarm. In the spring a letter was sent to A. Korzhakov, signed by ten doctors, in which they stated openly that "in the last two weeks negative changes have been observed in the health of the President of the Russian Federation, Boris Nikolaevich Yeltsin. All of these changes are directly related to the dramatic increase in the burden placed on him, both physically and emotionally. A significant role has been played by the frequent changes in climate and time zone, when he covers large distances by plane. The amount of sleep he gets has been cut to the bare minimum — about 3-4 hours a week. This sort of working regime presents a real threat to the life and health of the president."[957] In effect, the president's life was at stake, and Yeltsin understood this. To step back now, however, would mean losing — and he could not allow himself to do that.

Would the election take place?

Yeltsin's ratings had gone up, but there was no real confidence in the idea that he would win the election. Some businessmen from a group of Yeltsin

---

955   A Oslon: How the Analytical group made opinion polls a fact of life in 1996 //Social reality. 2006. No.6.

956   Quotation taken from: The Yeltsin era. P. 571.

957   B.N. Yeltsin: The Presidential marathon. P.49.

supporters made another attempt to get the election postponed. On 27th April an open letter to the candidates was published in Russia's newspapers entitled 'Let's back out of this dead-end!', signed by the president of LogoVAZ, B. Berezovsky, the chairman of the board of the Siberian oil company, Viktor Gorodilov, the chairman of the board of directors of the Most group, V. Gusinsky, the president of the Yakovlev Commercial Bank, Alexander Dundukov, the president of the Inter-state joint-stock company Vympel, Nikolai Mikhailov, the president of the oil company Yukos, Sergei Muravlenko, the president of Rosprom, L. Nevzliny, the CEO of AvtoVAZ, Aleksei Nikolaev, the chairman of the board of the bank Vozrozhdenie, Dmitry Orlov, the president of ONEKSIMbank, V. Potanin, the president of Capital savings bank, A. Smolensky, the chairman of the board of directors of the Alpha-group consortium, M. Fridman, and the chairman of the board of directors of the Menatep bank, M. Khodorkovsky.

The letter from this group of 13 contained the following passage: "At this time of great responsibility, we, Russia's entrepreneurs, propose to the nation's intellectuals, military, representatives of the executive and the legislature, law enforcement agencies and mass media — to all those in whose hands real power is concentrated and on whom the fate of Russia depends, to join forces in the search for a political compromise capable of preventing intense conflicts which would threaten the core interests of Russia and its very statehood..."[958]

Citing their fears that Zyuganov might win the election, the entrepreneurs proposed that the elections be postponed. As M. Khodorkovsky later wrote, "the idea behind the letter was very simple, and, above all, we believed in it. Boris Yeltsin must remain President of Russia — as a guarantor of civil liberties and human rights. The leader of the CPRF, on the other hand, should be made prime minister — with expanded powers, of course...A shift towards the left is required in order to reconcile freedom and justice, the few who have been victorious with the many who feel that they have lost out amid the universal liberalization of society.[959] The terms of a compromise agreement were discussed at a meeting between the entrepreneurs and the leader of the CPRF. Zyuganov saw as a potential compromise the restriction of the president's powers and the conferral on the State Duma of the right to form a government.

Korzhakov once again spoke out in favor of postponing the election, saying in an interview with the British newspaper *The Observer* that the presidential elections should be postponed so as to avoid the unrest that was bound to follow, whatever the result.[960]

958   http://www.politika.su/raznoe/pismo13.html
959   M. Khodorkovsky: Left-turn // Vedomosti 01.08.2005 http://lib.rus.ec/b/132588/read#t1
960   Excerpts from the interview were published in the newspaper Sevodnya. 1996. 6

The press engaged in scaremongering, too. On 8th June an anonymous analytical report was printed in *Nezavisimaya gazeta* which said that the communists intended to exacerbate the political situation dramatically if the first round of voting did not go their way. The article quoted material from a closed session of the CC CPRF, which had taken place on 18th May: "The relatively democratic period of the CPRF's struggle for power has come to an end...On the agenda now is the issue of effecting a transition to a new strategy and tactics, which have at their heart active, mass action and non-parliamentary methods of fighting against the anti-popular regime." It was reported that the hard-liners within the CPRF now had greater influence. The article's author noted that the CPRF's internal documents led one to believe that the party was planning to refuse to recognise the results of the expression of the people's will, in the event that it lost the election. This was precisely the purpose served by a provocative propaganda campaign by the CPRF about the allegedly inevitable falsification of the election results by the Central Electoral Commission at the behest of the authorities...The scenarios for "seizing power" devised by the CPRF stipulated some extremely speculative action which might drag the country into a civil war and put it on the brink of a national catastrophe." "The political and military alliance between radical communists and nationalist patriots has already reared its head, in the bloody events of October 1993...These people have already demonstrated that they are prepared to do anything and that they have learnt nothing from the past. They are currently making their preparations, but with far more energy this time, for a fresh attempt at armed rebellion."[961]

No-one who might have been planning a rebellion was arrested. And thus there must have been no evidence that a rebellion was being planned. It was clear that the people behind this article wanted the election to be cancelled.

'A box for photocopier paper' and the cost of victory

The key thing about the presidential election in 1996 was the fact that they actually took place, and that the nation managed to avoid social and political upheaval. The first round, which took place on 16th June, gave Yeltsin 35.28% of the vote and Zyuganov 32.03%. In third place was general A. Lebed, with 14.52%. Work had begun on the preparations for the second round. Their outcome would depend on the voters who had not backed either of the two favorites in the first round: who would they vote for this time? In order to attract Lebed's voters to his side, two days after the first round the

---

May. Quotation taken from: From Yeltsin to...Yeltsin: the race for the presidency in '96. M.: TERRA, 1997. P.279

961   Nezavisimaya gazeta. 1996. 8 June.

president appointed Lebed secretary of the Security Council and an adviser to the president on national security. At the same time, the defence minister P. Grachev was sacked. Yeltsin began talking about the general as a potential successor in the next elections in 2000.

There was a threat, however, that the second round of voting might not take place. On 19th June, on the orders of M. Barsukov and A. Korzhakov, S. Lisovsky and A. Yevstafiev, who had been members of A. Chubais's team, were arrested. In a box for photocopier paper which Lisovsky was holding there were 500,000 US dollars. As the president's advisers and active participants in the election campaign noted, "the disparity between the requirements of the Law on the elections, which set a cap on campaign costs, and the actual costs always led to a situation in which campaign costs were calculated on a cash-in-hand basis. This was a practice that everyone engaged in, and this was why neither of the opposing sides ever accused one another of it." [962]

Korzhakov's aim was to compromise A. Chubais and to have him removed as head of Yeltsin's election campaign on the eve of the second round. The battle between the two groups within the president's team ended in Korzhakov, Barsukov and Soskovets being forced out. On 25th June Presidential Directive No. 986 on the relieving of 7 generals from their positions was signed.

The next day, on 26th June, there was a sharp decline in Yeltsin's health, and during the second round of the elections, which was held on 3rd July, he was at a health spa.[963] This was a state secret, however. In the second round Yeltsin secured a landslide victory: he secured 53.83% of the vote (40,203,948 people), whilst Zyuganov managed to get 40.3% (30,102,288 people).[964] The turnout was 68.89%. These results were similar to the ones predicted by sociologists from the Russian Public Opinion Research Center (VCIOM).

Despite his victory in the election, the grand ceremony marking his return to the role of President for a second term, which took place on 9th August 1996, was by no means a triumph for Yeltsin. He did not feel well and struggled to make it through the inauguration ceremony, which was reduced to the shortest possible format. On top of this, it turned out that all the efforts to establish peace in Chechnya had come to nothing. On 6th August Grozny was stormed by units of Chechen insurgents, and many people were killed. The day after the inauguration, a period of mourning was declared in the country.

In August the main powers as regards achieving peace in Chechnya were conferred on the Security Council and its secretary, general Lebed.

---

962   The Yeltsin era. Sketches from a political history. M.: 'VAGRIUS' publishing house, 2001. P.572.

963   For more details see: B. Yeltsin: See above. P.44-48.

964   The elections in the Russian Federation. M.: 'VALTI', 1998. P.104.

The State Commission for dealing with the crisis in Chechnya, headed by Chernomyrdin, was disbanded. On 22nd August Lebed and Maskhadov signed an 'Agreement on urgent measures to bring about a ceasefire and end military operations in the city of Grozny and in the territory of the Chechen Republic'. On 31st August two documents were signed in Khasavyurt (in Dagestan) which put an end to the first Chechen war: a 'Joint statement' and 'The principles behind the determining of the bases for relations between the Russian Federation and the Republic of Chechnya'. Lebed signed these documents on President Yeltsin's orders, and A. Maskhadov signed them on the orders of the president of the Republic of Ichkeria, Z. Yandarbiev. Chechnya remained a part of the Russian Federation, with its status still to be determined. It was stipulated that an agreement on the principles of relations between the Russian Federation and Chechnya must be reached by 31st December 2001. There were plans to form an Associated Commission composed of representatives of state power in Russian and Chechnya by 1st October, which could monitor the implementation of Directive No. 985, ensure the people were provided with food and medicine and prepare programs for the restoration of the republic.

On 23rd November, Presidential Directive No. 1590 was signed, on the withdrawal of the last Russian military units from Chechnya (the 205th army brigade and the 101st brigade of internal forces). On 12th May 1997 Yeltsin and Maskhadov signed an 'Agreement on peace and the principles governing relations between the Russian Federation and the Chechen Republic of Ichkeria'. As it soon transpired, the problem of Chechnya had not been solved — it had merely been postponed.

Chapter 11
"The patriarch in his twilight years."
The President's second term

B.N. Yeltsin's second term as president was markedly different from his first term. Whereas in the first few years of Yeltsin's time as President he had been a busy, active figure, after his election victory in 1996 Yeltsin was forced to spend a substantial chunk of his time outside the Kremlin, "working with documents" in his out-of-town residence. The president's health begame a serious factor in the political life of the country. The political system created in December 1993 featured no effective insurance mechanisms, and on the occasions when Yeltsin was absent for long periods, the Kremlin was left in a permanent state of paralysis of power.

Against this backdrop the role of the President's Administration and the Government in governing the country increased. A serious problem for the President and the Government was the absence of any constant support whatsoever in the State Duma. The majority in the Duma was held by supporters of the communist party and their allies. There was no political party with any real influence behind Yeltsin at all. The attempts to create a pro-president, pro-government party called Our home is Russia, led by the Chairman of the Government V.S. Chernomyrdin, proved ineffective. Any "party of power" recruiting its members mainly from among the civil servants and those near to them would serve as a symbol of power — the head of state — until it could standly firmly on its own two feet, and had a political future ahead of it. If its leader had a future, that meant the 'party of power' had a future. If not, then such a party would quietly begin to fall apart. The party Our home is Russia was no exception.

After the elections: illness and changes to the team

The election campaign, as the doctors had warned, proved too much for a man who had already suffered more than one heart attack. All the more so given that Yeltsin put everything into the struggle for the president's seat. Ever since he was a boy it had been his wont not to look after his health, and to overestimate his strength. He would run away from hospitals before he had been properly cured, swim in ice-cold water and drink too much alcohol. As the years went by these problems multiplied, and age played its part as well. After the election Yeltsin was advised that he needed to have heart surgery "judging by his vital signs", medical jargon which meant that the operation simply had to happen. The operation was put off, however, due to a worsening of his condition. Yeltsin spent practically no time at all at the Kremlin, and this had to be explained to the people somehow. The heart attacks which the president had suffered remained a state secret, but his appearances on TV during the election and at the inauguration ceremony, and occasionally in the TV news, were far more telling than any medical reports. On hearing the reports that the president was "working with documents", it was not hard to speculate that Yeltsin was unwell, and that if he was indeed working at all, he was working at home.

At the same time, the President did not intend to let go of the reins of power for a moment. He made an announcement about the impending operation in a televised address. During the period when the president was under anaesthetic, his powers had to be conferred on the prime minister, and that troubled him. Two directives were drafted and signed on the transfer of the president's powers from Yeltsin to Chernomyrdin and back again. The operation on 5th November was a success, and the moment the effect of the anaesthetic wore off, Yeltsin declared that the directive on the return to him of his powers as president had now taken effect. He had relinquished his duties as president for less than a day — 23 hours.

Just six weeks later, on 23rd December, he went back to work at the Kremlin. "Judging by his outer appearance and what he has said to journalists," wrote a reporter from *Nezavisimaya gazeta*, "the president is in good health, ready to do battle and prepared for some energetic work."[965] In his first address to the people the President hastened to demonstrate that he was in control of the situation and that he would be asking tough questions of his negligent civil servants. He demanded that the government resolve the issue of the debt owed on pensions and salaries, and then made a solemn promise that the year ahead [1997] was going to be better for Russia. Soon after the New Year, however, the President once again found himself in hospital suffering complications. The reason was the same as before — failing to stick to his dietary regime. His illness dragged on for more than six months in total, until March 1977.

The president's lengthy absence, and the reports and rumors about his illness, sparked off a situation of extreme uncertainty in the country. The role of

---

965   Nezavisimaya gazeta. 1996. 24 December.

the President's Administration became dramatically more important: it was responsible for preparing presidential directives and handled the president's contact with the world beyond the walls of the hospitals and health spas.

The component parts, structure and nature of the Administration's work had changed after A. Chubais took charge of it on 16th July 1996. Y. Yarov, who had been put in charge of the electoral campaign office, was appointed his first deputy, with M. Boiko and Y. Savostyanov as his deputies. The role of press-secretary was bestowed on S. Yastrzhembsky, brought in to replace S. Medvedev. A. Kudrin took charge of the Adminstration's Supervisory department. As V.N. Shevchenko later wrote, "the Administration now included the people who had taken part in the campaign for the presidency and worked actively in the campaign office. In other words it could be said that a Western-style system was used, with an entire presidential team coming to power. The structure of the administration was reconfigured. In the past, the main focus had been on the group of advisers who worked directly for the president. Chubais proposed a complete rejection of the institution of advisers. The President's council also ceased to operate. The entire central government was focused on the head of the administration and his deputies, who were responsible for specific areas."[966]

The service provided by advisers was abolished — their functions were narrowed and their status was lowered; the analytical services were eradicated, and in their place sub-departments were set up in order to solve promotional and advertising tasks. The Administration's day-to-day political work began effectively to be replaced by technological approaches which had been tried and tested during the election campaign. Instead of a president's council, there was now a small group operating which was engaged in upholding a positive image of the President. This group included T. Dyachenko, V. Yumashev, M. Boiko, S. Yastrzhembsky, A. Oslon, G. Pavlovsky and others.

According to Y.M. Primakov, the President's Administration "became pretty much the most important body of power, determining strategy, tactics, appointments to literally all roles of any importance whatsoever, interfering in the affairs of the government, the parliament and the regions. This unusual phenomenon could be explained in part by the fact that the president was not, regrettably, on top 'form' due to his ill health. The existence of such a central government, however — one that was mighty and at the same time not responsible for anything specific — was extremely advantageous, and was supported in everything it did by separate groups of oligarchs, who made sure their people were given senior roles within the administration." [967]

---

966   V.N. Shevchenko: Day-to-day life at the Kremlin under the Presidents. M.: The young guard, 2005. P.162.
967   Y. Primakov: Eight months plus...M: 'Thought', 2001. P.88.

The other center of power was Chernomyrdin's government, in which there was a re-shuffle after the Presidential election. As a thank you for his help during the election campaign, Yeltsin gave his long-time first adviser, V.V. Ilyushin, a position in the government. Ilyushin was made deputy prime minister and put in charge of social issues. The transfer of Ilyushin to the government was also related to the reorganization of the Administration, and Chubais's desire to get rid of an influential adviser who had worked with Yeltsin for many years. The post of deputy prime minister responsible for economic matters was given to the chairman of ONEKSIM bank, V.O. Potanin, one of the oligarchs who had supported Yeltsin in the election. A.Y. Lifshits was appointed an adviser to the president on economic issues. Several key changes within the government had been made by Yeltsin literally on the eve of the election, and he had no intention of changing his mind. These had included the sacking of O.N. Soskovets from the role of First deputy Chairman of the Government, the dismissal of the minister of defence P.S. Grachev and the appointment of I.Y. Rodionov in his place.

The new government faced a difficult task. The election campaign in 1996 had emptied out the coffers in the exchequer. The government managed to pay off the debts owed on pensions and salaries, but this only served to exacerbate the budget deficit. On the eve of the election, a huge number of copies of president Yeltsin's manifesto for 1996-2000 had been printed,[968] on the basis of which the government's program for the medium-term was adopted. Its contents boiled down to the need to switch to economic growth and a structural reshaping of the economy. There was talk of the active role that the state must play in bringing about institutional change and supporting the reprocessing industries, particularly in high-tech manufacturing. The need to reduce the budget deficit was declared.

All these things remained no more than good intentions. The government's program of measures — like that of the president, incidentally — remained unimplemented. There were several reasons for this. Serious miscalculations had been made in the contents of the program itself. It is worth noting that it was supposed to take effect even before the old one, which had been a complete failure, was due to end. Although the new program painted a fairly objective picture of the state of the economy, the conclusions it drew were unjustifiably optimistic. The program was based on the supposition that the Russian economy had already become predominantly a market economy. The calculation was that the economy would continue to follow a path of "self-development" in this direction, and that the government had assumed responsibility merely for "announcing the conditions required" for this, rather than actually creating them.

---

968   See: B.N. Yeltsin: Russia: the individual, the family, society, the state. An action plan for 1996-2000. M., 1996.

No properly functioning mechanism had been put into effect in the country for implementing the programs and decisions taken by the executive. Laws were passed to which the bodies of state government themselves failed to adhere. The tax system was not working.

According to the tax inspectorate, in 1996 there were 2.6 million companies and organizations in the country, of which only 1.7 million were genuinely doing business. As of 1st July 1996, 41.3% of the companies which were doing business were making a loss.[969] Those who were working with profits attempted, by resorting to all sorts of truths and fictions, to reduce the amount of tax they paid into the budget. During the election campaign the President was generous in handing out all kinds of tax breaks. In January 1996, for example, a directive was signed 'On providing companies and organizations with more time to pay off tax debts, penalties and fines for breaches of the tax legislation passed into law prior to 1st January 1996.' It transpired that those with the biggest debts to the budget were practically all the oil-producing and oil-refining companies in the country. It was by these companies, in April 1996, that a new type of financial abuse was discovered, at the expense of budgetary tax remissions (BTRs). All of these companies (and they were the main tax-payers into the budget) had settled their account with the budget in 1996 not by means of cash, but by means of supplies of oil and oil-related products to meet the needs of the security structures (the army, the MIA etc.) and agriculture. This method of calculating tax payments created the opportunity for significant abuses.

The economic situation was rendered more complex by the internecine warfare taking place between the various groups of oligarchs and with the authorities. Russian capital had invested in a victory for Yeltsin and was now looking to receive dividends from the state in the form of senior roles in government and property.

Given the collapse in manufacturing and the crisis in the budget, the increase in the debt owed by the state, and in the cost of servicing it, became unmanageable.

The political battalions without their 'boss'

A tense struggle was taking place behind the scenes among the political elite, echoes of which made their way into the press in the form of scandals and resignations. General A.I. Lebed, whom Yeltsin had been appointed secretary of the Security Council in exchange for his support in the second round of the presidential election, began to play an increasingly active role. Lebed took

---

969   Administration of the FC of the Federal assembly of the RF Information and Analytical department. Analytical gazette No. 20 (44) November 1996 (hereinafter Analytical gazette) http://www.council.gov.ru/inf_sl/bulletin/1996/index.html

charge of the commission for senior military positions, senior ranks in the military and senior special ranks, i.e. he was handed an important lever in terms of ensuring support for the president among military personnel. The popularity of this decisive general, against the backdrop of a sick president, shot up. Though he had only secured a little over 14% of the vote in the presidential election, by the fall his approval rating was nearing 30%. When speaking to the press, he did not shy away from saying that other people were running the country on behalf of the president, who was sick. In one of these interviews he advised Yeltsin to hand over power to his prime minister, Chernomyrdin, until his illness had passed, as provided for under the Constitution: "Otherwise it sets a dangerous precedent, when a country can be governed by someone else on the president's behalf. I don't like that. I would rather deal with someone who was my boss — even if he were just a temporary one."[970]

Lebed began to get involved in several foreign policy issues, and visited the headquarters of NATO and the Western European alliance. He took part in the campaign to elect the former head of the Security Service, A. Korzhakov, for a recently vacated seat in the State Duma. His speech in support of the former head of the president's security service cannot fail to have pleased Yeltsin. One of the actions taken by Lebed which tested the President's patience to breaking point was a speech he made on 15th October at the military council of the airborne forces against the reassignment of sections of the airborne forces to the commanders of the military districts. Lebed declared that the directive from the Ministry of defence of the RF, I.S. Rodionov, about this reassignment "bordered on the criminal" and must not be obeyed. Lebed's speech at the council was greeted with a standing ovation and shouts of "Glory to the army! Glory to Russia!"

The following day, the minister of internal affairs, A. Kulikov, accused A. Lebed of striving to seize power by force. According to Kulikov, Lebed had sent a proposal to the security ministries for discussion back in August that they create a 'Russian legion' consisting of 50,000 people that was directly subordinate to the secretary of the Security Council. This 'Legion' was supposed to take action to "identify the location of political and military confrontations, and eradicate the leaders of political, separatist and other organizations, whose activities were going to pose a threat to national security". According to Kulikov, these plans met resistance on the part of the Minister of defence, Rodionov, and Kulikov himself. Among the allegations made against Lebed was the assertion that "the Chechens promised to give Lebed one and a half thousand insurgents to help him seize power in Moscow."[971]

970   Moskovsky komsomolets 1996. 28 September.
971   Nezavisimaya gazeta. 1996. 17 October

To leave such an unpredictable character in the Kremlin, particularly on the eve of an operation on the president, would have been dangerous. On 3rd October Yeltsin signed a directive which removed from Lebed his levers of influence on the military. Leadership of the commission on senior military ranks and titles was conferred on the secretary of the Defence Council, Y. Baturin. On 17th October Lebed was fired from his role as secretary of the Security Council. Yeltsin read out the directive on the removal of Lebed from office live on air. Yeltsin later wrote in his memoirs that there had been serious discussions in the Administration of the possibility that Lebed might seize power, by sending troops into Moscow, storming the buildings of the defence ministries and so on[972] — but these allegations were never actually levelled at Lebed. There was no evidence. The President justified his decision by saying that Lebed had not yet learnt to work with the other leaders without starting arguments, was getting involved in a "race for office" four years before the elections, and was also taking part in the campaign by the retired general Korzhakov for a seat in the Duma. Interestingly, as he recalled all the general's various bits of "artistry", Yeltsin commented: "...as strange as it may seem, Alexander Ivanovich reminded me in some ways of myself. Only he was like a caricature of me. As if I were peering into a dirty mirror."[973]

The new secretary of the Security Council was the former speaker of the State Duma I. Rybkin, and B. Berezovsky was appointed one of his deputies. Berezovsky had helped to finance Yeltsin's campaign for re-election. One of the richest men in the country, and an adroit and influential behind-the-scenes politician, he emerged from the shadows and, for the first time, took up a senior post within government. In the Security Council he began to take responsibility for the restoration of Chechnya, an area to which huge sums of money from the budget had been directed. (The well-known Russian proverb about the goat let out into the front garden comes to mind!)

The local elections in the fall of 1996 were an important event. During these elections, the heads of bodies in the executive and the legislature were not appointed by the Kremlin but elected by the local people, for the first time. By year-end a total of 47 heads of administration (governors) had to be elected, in subjects governed by people appointed by the president. In the same time-frame 3 heads of republics faced a vote to try to stay in power. The system of elections was established in a different way in each region.

An intense battle began for the governorships, in which the main players were political coalitions which had formed during the campaigning for the presidency. On the basis of the bloc which had backed Zyuganov in the election on 16th June the Popular-patriotic alliance of Russia (NPSR) was

---

972   B.N. Yeltsin: The Presidential marathon. P.75.
973   B.N. Yeltsin: The Presidential marathon P.77.

created, with G. Zyuganov as its leader. On the basis of the ODOPP — the Russian Movement for Social Support for the President — which had been Yeltsin's bloc in the presidential elections in '96, the Russian Coordination Council (OKS) was set up, with S. Filatov as its leader.

OKS gave its support first and foremost to the existing governors, with whom the Kremlin had already begun working effectively. With the president unwell, however, and given the general sense of uncertainty, the possibility of influencing the situation in the regions was extremely small. In October, OKS almost disintegrated, and in mid-November decided to back two candidates at the same time, in three different regions (the Ryazan, Volgograd and Ivanovskaya Regions). At first the NPSR put forward its own lists of candidates, but before long it changed its focus and gave the initiative to the regions. Following the regional elections in 1996, 22 of the 49 leaders who stood for re-election were given a mandate to take up office again.[974] These results reflected the prevailing mood in the country: the weakening of central government and a fall in the incumbent president's authority.

That said, a fairly positive spin was put on the results within the President's Administration. The Kremlin viewed anyone who was not a member of an opposition party as acceptable, and certain communists were even included. On 25th December the Administration's 'black list' contained 8 surnames, including the former vice-president A.V. Rutskoi, who had been an implacable enemy of Yeltsin's during the crisis of 1993 and had been elected head of the Administration of the Kursk Region. By the fall of 1997 there was not a single head of a region left who had been appointed by the Central government. This had serious political consequences. All the heads of the regions had acquired legitimacy and become full-scale directors in their own right, who were not dependent on the human resources policy of the Central government. The regional bodies of power were given their own independent legal status. For the Central government this made governing the regions much more complicated.

The situation worsened in early 1997, when the president was once again taken to hospital to be treated for pneumonia. On 17th January the opposition blocs in the State Duma added to the agenda the question of whether the president should step down for reasons of ill health. This caused a new wave of anxious expectation. The Constitution did not prescribe with any clarity the circumstances in which the president could be considered incapacitated. Taking advantage of this fact, the communists in the Duma attempted to pass a law on a medical commission, whose job it would be to decide on the state of the president's health. The proposal was not accepted, however.

---

974   http://www.politika.su/vybory/rre96t.html. See also: The elections for the heads of executive power in the subjects of the Russian Federation. 1995-1997. Electoral statistics. — M., Central electoral commission of the RF, The whole world, — 1997.

The "young reformers" in the government

At the beginning of March 1997, Yeltsin took up office once again. It seemed as if the steps taken by his enemies had whipped him into action, and forced him to mobilize. He seemed energetic and businesslike, almost the same as he had been in the good old days. One of the president's missives to the Federal Assembly was headed 'Order in the executive means order in the country' Yeltsin admonished the government in strong tones: "I am not happy with the Government. The executive proved to be incapable of operating without having the president around to shout out orders. Most of the promises which were made to people, particularly on social issues, have not been kept."[975]

This was immediately followed by a reshuffle within the government: A.B. Chubais was appointed first deputy prime with the powers of the minister of finance, and B.E. Nemtsov was also appointed a first deputy to the prime minister. A.R. Kokh, Y.M. Urinson and O.N. Sysuev were all appointed deputy chairmen of the government. V.O. Potanin, A. Bolshakov, V. Ilyushin, O. Davydov, A. Zaveryukha, V. Ignatenko and A. Lifshits left the government.

The government put forward the program 'Seven top-priority matters', which included such tasks as reforming the tax system, adopting a Budgeting code, measures aimed at forming a class of effective property owners by means of privatization and bankruptcy procedures, reducing the rate at which prices were going up, land reform, reform of the utilities system, and reform of the social sector.

The new cabinet found it hard to work together: it was not a team of like-minded individuals. Yeltsin saw this and, sensing his responsibility for the government, tried to support the "young reformers" and iron out the differences between them. On 12th May 1997, addressing a meeting of the government, he openly declared: "It is time to stop the bickering, and attempting to grasp hold of a ever more powers. Each person must stick to their own affairs."[976]

Yeltsin was also required to defend the government against attacks by the State Duma: in the fall of 1997 the Duma gave a very critical assessment of the draft budget for 1998, and also raised some strong objections regarding the tax initiatives of the "young reformers" — the new Tax code, the reform of utilities services and numerous other measures. On 21st October 1997 the leaders of blocs in the Duma met the president, and after the meeting the two sides reached a compromise. Yeltsin revoked the Tax code and agreed to the requirement to amend Nemtsov's brainchild — the reforms to communal

---

975   Quotation taken from The Yeltsin era. P.727.
976   The Yeltsin era. P.729

utilities services. He also acknowledged the need to hold regular meetings with the leaders of the chambers in the Federal Assembly. A 'parliament hour' began to be broadcast on TV, and a parliamentary newspaper was set up, funded by the state budget. In addition, the president agreed to the creation of community supervisory councils, in which deputies would take part, for the two state TV channels — ORT and RTR. In response, parliament rejected the idea of holding a vote of no confidence in the government. Regular meetings began to be held between the president and the prime minister, on the one hand, and representatives of both chambers, on the other, in order to discuss important ongoing problems.

The prime minister's new deputies, dubbed the "young reformers", announced the start of a policy of active interference by the state in the economy. B. Nemtsov spoke on several occasions about the need to bring an end to "bandit capitalism". In effect he was talking about bringing under control the huge amounts of capital which the state was ting to use in its own interests. In an interview recorded in 1997, A. Chubais said: "Imagine a situation in which someone who has earned a lot of money, and thinks of himself as being the boss of the country, adopts the following line of reasoning: I was the one who elected the president, I was the one who appointed the government, and now the time has come to reap the rewards I am owed. To me, such an attitude is disgusting and unacceptable."[977]

The government declared war on the 'seven bankers' cable', and the first decisive battleground was the holding of an auction for the sale of the state's shares in the corporation Svyazinvest — the monopoly-holder in the Russian telecoms market. The Berezovsky-Gusinsky group was making a bid to buy Svyazinvest, but the government chose not to side with the group, as it had done in 1996. At the auction, held on 25th July 1997, Svyazinvest was acquired by V. Potanin, who had offered a high price for the company. Nemtsov and Chubais became a target for attacks in the TV and press, which were owned by B. Berezovsky and V. Gusinsky.

Yeltsin decided that he needed to get involved in the conflict in person. On 15th September 1997 he invited Potanin, Gusinsky, Khodorkovsky, Smolensky and Fridman to the Kremlin.

A huge row erupted in the media. At the deputy prime ministers' insistence, Berezovsky was fired from his role as deputy chairman of the Security Council on 4th November 1997 — a role he had held since 29th October 1996. A week later a struck back again Chubais. In an interview on the Echo of Moscow radio station, which was owned by Gusinsky, A. Minkin revealed that Chubais and four of his deputies had been given unprecedented royalties of 450,000 dollars in for a book about privatization. This occurred on the eve

---

977   Argumenty i fakty. 1997. No.47. P.3.

of the auction for Svyazinvest, and the money for the manuscript, which had not yet been written, had been paid to a business structure with close links to V. Potanin's ONEKSIM group. This was in effect an allegation of bribe-taking under the guise of book royalties.[978] A report on the as yet unwritten book lay on the desk of the minister of internal affairs, A. Kulikov.

The 'book affair' proved to be the banana-skin on which the team of young reformers slipped up.[979] Chubais lost his portfolio as finance minister and Nemtsov was removed from his post as minister of fuel and energy, but both men held on to the title of deputy prime minister.

Whilst the battle for Svyazinvest raged, a financial crisis was sparked off in Asia. Russia was not left unaffected by it, either. In the fall, the rate of economic growth in Russia slowed. On 27th October there was a dramatic drop in oil prices in the funds markets. This was the result of the instability of the Russian currency market, which was maintained primarily by means of an increase in the state's internal debt. In 1997 the cost of servicing the state's internal debt alone was more than twice as high as the tax revenue coming into the federal budget.[980] State-owned obligations were substantially more profitable than the manufacturing sector, and this led to an outflow of capital from the manufacturing sector.

The defence industry found itself in a particularly difficult position. Financing of defence orders was no higher than 40-45%, only about 34% of the sums indicated were allocated, and financing of academic and technical potential of defence industries was no higher than 5%. Companies' lack of funds continued the chain reaction of failure to pay. Experts declared that the crisis in the defence industry had reached the point where there was a genuine threat to the whole of the Russian economy and to national security.

The RF government tried on several occasions to take a series of measures designed to shore up discipline in the paying off and restructuring of debt, in order to increase the tax revenue coming into the federal budget. Nothing came of these efforts, however. The government, which contained both supporters of the path of liberal reforms and opponents of it, proved ineffective. Yeltsin recalled that towards the end of 1997 relations between Chubais and Kulikov soured (the latter was actively opposed to privatization and the entire liberal economy). At cabinet meetings, Kulikov accused the young reformers on numerous occasions of adopting a policy which was "enabling abuses, bringing the country down, and resulting in a multitude of impoverished citizens and criminals."[981]

978   Nezavisimaya gazeta. 1997. 13 November
979   B. Yeltsin. See above P.112.
980   Analytical gazette. No.20 (65) December M.,1997 http://www.council.gov.ru/inf_sl/bulletin/item/179/index.html
981   B. Yeltsin. See above P.114.

The President saw a potential way out of the situation which had arisen in the sacking of Chernomyrdin's government. All the more so given that he was worried about the issue of his successor, who would be able to take over the country in 2000, when his mandate came to an end. The post of prime minister took on a special significance in this regard: under the Constitution, if the president was unable to perform his obligations they were to be conferred on the head of the government. Chernomyrdin, having led the government for five years, had acquired political weight, and Yeltsin saw this as a threat.

His desire to assert himself before Chernomyrdin came across as rather childish at times. Yeltsin's aides tell of an amusing conversation which once took place between Yeltsin and Chernomyrdin. At the time, Yeltsin was taking a keen interest in the financial markets. One day he called the prime minister and asked him: "Viktor Stepanovich, what is the current trend in the market for short-term securities?" The prime minister laughed and asked for some time to prepare an answer. "There you have it — he's the prime minister, and he doesn't know. *I* know, though," the president observed, as he hung up the phone. He was radiant: he wanted to be the first in everything.[982]

On 26th February 1998 the President announced, in a short speech to an extended meeting of the government, that he intended to sack three members of his cabinet. The promised sackings followed a week later. Preparations were being made, meanwhile, for the sacking of the entire government. This move was announced on 23rd March 1998. Yeltsin would later write in his memoirs: "...at that moment I parted company with two of my strongest and most loyal allies — Chernomyrdin and Chubais. And as it transpired, I did so in almost complete political isolation."[983]

That same day, S.V. Kirienko was appointed to the role of Chairman of the Government. Kirienko had joined the government from the world of business in 1997 as the deputy minister of fuel and energy, and by 1998 had managed to climb the ladder as far as the rank of minister. When Yeltsin took the decision to appoint him, he was not yet a deputy prime minister, and in order to stick to the rules of hierarchy, he was firstly appointed first deputy chairman of the government, and then acting chairman. The emergence at the helm of the government of the young, little-known Kirienko, aged 35, who was dubbed 'kinder-surprise' by the public, came as a complete surprise and altered the political landscape. There was now a weak prime minister alongside a weak President. Yeltsin had high hopes for the new government, related to the latest breakthrough in the introduction of reforms. As the President's aides later recounted, the warm regard which Yeltsin usually reserved for his young favorites was now transferred to his new chosen one; he talked about Kirienko in a warm, fatherly tone of voice — one which would have been difficult to fake.[984]

982   The Yeltsin era. P.734.

983   B.N. Yeltsin: The Presidential marathon P.124.

984   The Yeltsin era P.732.

It took around a month for the appointment of the new chairman of the government to be rubber-stamped. On 27th March an introduction to the new prime minister was sent to the State Duma. In his address to the Duma, Yeltsin urged its members to approve the candidate he was proposing, hinting that the lower chamber might be disbanded if it rejected the President's proposal three times. The deputies took the hint. They voted against Kirienko twice (the number of people who voted against him went up in the second vote). But the President was in a decisive mood, and at the third time of asking, facing the threat of a disbandment of the Duma, the deputies voted to accept the new prime minister.[985] That same day the President issued a directive regarding the appointment of Kirienko as Chairman of the Government of the RF.

B.Y. Nemtsov, V.B. Khristenko and O.N. Sysuev were appointed Deputy Chairmen of the Government, and the following joined the government: Y.M. Primakov (minister of foreign affairs), I.D. Sergeev (defence minister), S.V. Stepashin (minister of internal affairs) and M.M. Zadornov (minister of finance). Of the 26 members of the Government appointed, 15 had been in V.S. Chernomyrdin's cabinet. On 29th May 1998, the head of the State tax service of the RF, B.G. Fedorov, was appointed to the new role of Minister of the Russian Federation (he was made a deputy chairman of the government on 17th August). Thus the new parliament had become more liberal than it had been in the past.

After agreeing to a liberal government, the Duma had been humiliated. All the more so given that the President made no secret of the fact that he had paid off the deputies. In a televised address, Yeltsin announced that he had issued instructions to the president's director of affairs P.P. Borodin "to decide the deputies' problems after a vote". The only concession to the opposition blocs in the Duma was the appointment of Y.D. Maslyukov, a member of the CC CPRF, as minister of trade and industry in July 1998. On this issue there followed a correspondence between the new minister and the CC of the communist party, during which Maslyukov told of the circumstances which the chairman of the Government had set in exchange for agreeing to let him become a minister.[986]

On the road to financial ruin

At the beginning of 1998 the State Statistics Commission presented a report to the Government about the socio-economic situation in Russia. For pretty much the first time since 1990, it contained some cautiously optimistic

---

985   For the results of the vote see: http://www.politika.su/prav/pr6.html
986   For the texts of the documents see: http://www.politika.su/prav/pr6.html

assessments of the state of the economy. GDP was up slightly — 101.3% compared to January 1997. The statisticians had recorded an increase in certain branches of industry — the ferrous metals industry had grown by 104.7% in a year, and the non-ferrous metals industry had gone up by 117.4%. It was significant that the upturn had been seen in those sectors of industry which were focused not on export, but on domestic consumption — in light industry (109.5%), and in the medical and polygraphical industries.[987]

The slight upturn in industry was unable, however, to reverse the generally negative trend in the Russian economy. Oil prices — an important source of extra income for the state budget — fell constantly throughout 1997. They fell from 23 dollars a barrel in October 1996 to 16 dollars at the end of 1997.[988]

State investment in 1997 was financed to the tune of 27.7% of the approved budget, which pointed to a failure on the part of the state's investment program. Rumors of a serious budgetary crisis in the government and the Central Bank began to spread in the fall of 1997. Various measures were proposed in order to prevent it, including the idea of acquiring around 2 billion dollars from strategic investors in the West as an advance payment for participation in privatization tenders for Russian companies. The tenders would be scheduled to take place at a later date. Yeltsin rejected this idea as illegal. Addressing a meeting of the government in December 1997, he talked about the miscalculations he had made: "You're all trying to explain it by citing the global financial crisis. Naturally, this 'financial hurricane' did not leave Russia untouched. Equally, it did not begin in Moscow. But there was another reason, too: the sorry state of the Russian budget. And the only people we can blame for that is ourselves."[989]

There was, nevertheless, a possible way out: to seek money from the West, if not via privatization tenders, then in the form of debt. Emissaries from the government and the Central Bank set off to Washington, to look into the possibility of Russia securing emergency assistance from the IMF in the event of a serious worsening of the financial situation. In February 1998 Yeltsin met the Managing Director of the IMF, M. Camdessus, and reached an agreement on a loan, but the payment of the loan was delayed.

In 1998 the Russian economy rapidly slid into crisis. On 9th January 1998 the quotes for the February contracts for crude oil on the NYMEX fell sharply, to $6.63 a barrel. Simultaneously, the price of gas also fell — another important component of Russian exports.[990]

987   Russia's socio-economic status. January 1998. Goskomstat, M, 1998. P. 10-11

988   For more details see: K.V. Zhilyaev: An analysis of the structure and dynamics of Russian exports, 1994-2000 //Anthology of academic works Institute of National Economic Forecasting, Russian Academy of Sciences. M., 2003

989   Quoted from The Yeltsin era. P.737-738.

990   Y. Shakhova: Iraq renews its supplies//Russky telegraf, 13 January 1998. P. 9

The situation regarding tax revenues worsened. In the first quarter of 1998 the plan for the collection of taxes was thrown out. In February, almost 20% less tax was collected than in the same period in 1997. This had a knock-on effect on the entire system of financing the state's expenses. The budget faced costs of 20 billion rubles in March, but had only 12 billion rubles paid into it. In April, 12.5 billion rubles had been paid in, as against 14 billion rubles in April 1997.

Against this backdrop, hidden unemployment was growing, as was the shadow economy and illegal forms of employment. The situation in the social sector was extremely serious. The social support programs were extremely ineffective. It was a well-established fact that the ideal ratio between the earnings of the poorest and richest sections of society (which accounted for ten percent of the population), developed countries with market economies, was no higher than 1:4 or 1:5. In Russia, this ratio had reached 1:12-13.

The commencement of work by S.V. Kirienko's government came at a time when the country faced numerous internal and external problems, chief among which was the budget deficit. The statements made by the new prime minister's program were no different from the program of Chernomyrdin's government. Kirienko once again highlighted the need to implement a balanced financial policy not only in Moscow but in the regions, to introduce a ban on taking decisions for which there was not sufficient funding, and the need to collect taxes and alter the nature of privatization.

One of the key aspects of the program was an expansion of the administration's powers: the government was relieved of the obligation to have its decisions approved by the President's Administration (with the exception of strategic decisions related to the economy). This testified to the complete trust that was felt by the President. On the other hand, this was related to the reshuffle within the Administration, which was carried out by its new director, V.B. Yumashev, who had replaced A.B. Chubais in the role.

The government's main focus of attention was on work aimed at financing stabilization and organizing the taxation system. Work with debtors gained ground. Kirienko emphasized on several occasions that he was not afraid of companies changing hands; the challenge consisted in making sure that the company was transferred from an ineffective owner to an effective one. In addition to profits, the issue of costs was also looked into. Serious attention was put into reducing the direct costs of the state apparatus, and strengthening the state's influence in natural monopolies.

In spite of all the government's efforts, the chronic budget deficit led to an increase in national debt, on both the domestic and foreign fronts. The cost of servicing this debt was going up, and in 1998 were higher than the tax revenues coming into the budget. In May 1998 the President described tax reform as the government's top-priority task in his speech on the Budget. Taxes, which were too high for those who paid their taxes honestly, were too high, and this had made it impossible to develop manufacturing, and often had a bankrupting effect, in a very literal sense. A significant proportion of companies evaded paying tax using all sorts of arguments, some true, others made up. The legal method of doing this was to receive tax breaks from the state, which widened the scope for corruption. The tax system prompted growth in the 'shadow economy' and a 'flight of capital' out of the country, and laid the basis for corruption.

The artificial dividing up of the regions into donor-regions and subsidized regions did not fit in with the principles of a market economy: it was not the regions that paid taxes, but the administrative subjects. The central government and the regions were carving up between them the same sources of tax, and this created real tension in the whole system of federative agreements.

The reform of the tax system which was proposed by the government strengthened the tax burden on people's earnings. It was proposed that tax on the sale of goods be increased, that income tax be collected on insurance payouts and interest on people's savings, and that the taxable basis for contributions to the state's non-budgetary funds be expanded by means of insurance payments. Against the backdrop of the economic crisis that was unfolding, these sorts of measures led to an even bigger fall in people's ability to pay their debts.

The implementation of the financial program was accompanied by brutal social pressure. In May 1998 a 'railway war' began in the country — miners in a whole range of regions (the Kemerov Region, the Rostov Region and the Komi Republic), unhappy over the fact that they had not received their salaries, blocked the railway lines. The conflict was brought to an end one week later. The government required the regions, too, to assume responsibility for the payment of salaries. Specifically, a directive from the President of the RF was signed 'On additional measures to ensure that salaries are paid to staff in the subsidized sector and to improve the health of state finances', under which the government would only assist the regions with the payment of salaries if measures were taken in the regions to bring about financial stability. This only served to make relations between the Kremlin and the regions more tense. The Federation Council, in which the heads of the regions had seats, insisted that urgent measures be taken to increase the role played by the state in regularizing the market economy, which went against the government line.

In an effort to find resources for the budget, the Bank of Russia began to entice commercial banks into making short-term deposits using their rouble resources. The interest rate was lifted to 22% per annum, leading to an increase in the lower threshold of the ruble's value on the lending market. On the eve of the auctions of state obligations, the rates on ultra-short loans rose to as much as 40-45% per annum.[991] State short-term bonds, known by their acronym GKO — OFZ, were released. The high returns offered by GKOs, which was achieved through all the hikes on interest payments, transformed these financial instruments into a contradiction in terms. Instead of ensuring that resources were paid into the budget, the GKOs turned into a method of obtaining money from the budget. The returns in the GKO — OFZ market were never lower than 40%.[992] The returns on state securities often shot up to 100% or even 300% per annum. The exchange rate for the ruble remained high thanks to the incredible efforts of the Central bank, which spent over a billion dollars a week to this end.

The political instability in the country and the unfavorable climate as regards foreign trade exacerbated the growing economic crisis. The sacking of Chernomyrdin, so unexpected in many ways, and the appointment of a new prime minister, Kirienko, fuelled the concerns of those in the markets and the expectations as regards inflation. Western investors saw the attempts to secure loans in the foreign market as a sign of impending catastrophe, and this resulted in capital flight.

The President was nervous, and kept on asking what was needed in order to prevent a financial crisis. On 2nd June he met Russian business leaders. Yeltsin was frank with them — he described the situation as extremely serious and told them what the government and the central bank were doing. The financial experts heard him out politely. In an interview in *Nezavisimaya gazeta*, one of the people present at this meeting, M. Khodorkovsky, declined to reveal exactly what was said in these talks with the president.[993]

In his memoirs, Yeltsin goes into great detail about a meeting between Kirienko and key representatives of Russian business held at the old government boarding house Volynskoe. According to Yeltsin's memoirs, the businessmen gave a fairly harsh assessment of the government. He would not have to rely on getting financial support from the West. Who on earth would be prepared to engage in talks with the little-known vice-premier Khristenko, or with the other young men in Kirienko's government? At this meeting it was decided that something akin to an economic council would be set up within the government, which would include all the representatives of the biggest banks and companies. It was proposed that Chubais be appointed Russia's special representative in talks with international financial organizations. Yeltsin describes this as a compromise by Kirienko, who did not wish to

---

991   Russia's socio-economic status. January 1998. M., 1998. P. 189

992   The Yeltsin era. Sketches from a political history. M., 2001. P.735-746

993   Nezavisimaya gazeta. 1998. 3 June.

contact the economists in the Gaidar school of thought or the 'oligarchs'.[994] In fact, though, he was the one who had resorted to compromises.

Yeltsin could not help but take cognizance of the approaching danger, and did what he could to try and prevent it. First and foremost, his role was to defend the government before the Duma. The condition for the loans being awarded was that brutal measures had to be introduced to stabilize the budget. Pursuant to the demands made by the IMF, an Anti-crisis government program was prepared and presented on 23rd June at a meeting of the State Duma called at Yeltsin's initiative. The deputies heaped criticism on the Anti-crisis program, however, saying it had been 'imposed by the West' and would only worsen the social situation in the country, which was tense enough already.

In mid-July 1998 it was reported that the IMF, the World Bank and Japan were going to give Russia a stabilization loan worth 22 billion dollars. Since receipt of this loan depended on those same conditions being met, Yeltsin once again asked the State Duma to accept the Anti-crisis program as a matter of urgency. The deputies only agreed to pass a few of the measures, however, and categorically refused to support a rise in taxes for citizens — a move on which the IMF was insisting. Against this backdrop, Yeltsin, despite resistance from the State Duma, signed presidential edicts which increased the taxes paid by individuals. Strictly speaking this was an illegal act, since federal taxes could not be altered without the consent of the State Duma or ratification by the Federation Council.

Nevertheless, thanks to the strong will shown by Yeltsin in taking this decision, Russia received the first portion of the loan promised by the IMF, which amounted to 4.8 billion dollars. Despite this, the whole of the first half of August was marked by the collapses which periodically befell various sectors of the financial market. The situation was made worse by rumors of an inevitable collapse in the value of the ruble.

On Friday 14th August, in response to a question from the Interfax agency, Yeltsin announced live on air, to everyone's surprise, that there was no cause for panic and no need for the president to cut short his holiday and return to the Kremlin: "Let me put it clearly and firmly. There will be no fall in the value of the ruble in Russia, and I am not just inventing this, or imagining it. It has been thought through, it is my work and I supervised it."[995]

What was behind this statement? Was it a misguided understanding of the situation? It hardly seems likely. The President had good knowledge of financial issues and was up to speed with the latest developments in the financial markets. Was it that he wanted to quell the rumors, which might

994   B.N. Yeltsin: Presidential marathon P.209-210.
995   Nezavisimaya gazeta 1998. 15 August.

accelerate the financial crisis on their own? Perhaps. Another probable factor was his belief that miracles did happen, and that this would all blow over. Whatever the real reason may have been, this speech on 14th August was interpreted as a direct deception, and certainly did not lead people to have more faith in the president. On the contrary, people remembered what he had said as they stood in line at the banks, hoping they would be able to get their savings back.

The very next day, on 15th August 1998, the radical decision was taken to announce a default. On the afternoon of 16th August the heads of the government and the Central Bank visited Yeltsin asking him to approve the measures they were planning to introduce the next day. The President agreed to do so.

The default and its consequences

On 17th August 1998 it was announced that the country was in effect bankrupt. The Central bank declined to fulfil its obligations as regards GKOs. Trading in state securities was halted. Restrictions were introduced on the carrying out of currency operations by Russian investors. Foreigners were forbidden from investing money in ruble assets which were due to mature in a year or earlier. A moratorium was declared on the charging of interest on debt repayments, including charges by foreign creditors; on the payment of insurance payments for loans provided as guarantees for securities, and on payments related to urgent currency transactions. Meanwhile the Central bank refused to keep the exchange rate for the ruble at its previous level. The upper limit of the 'currency corridor' was put up from 6 rubles to 9.5 rubles to the dollar. This did not prevent a subsequent fall in the value of the ruble, however.

The August default had serious political and economic consequences. The government was sacked, and Yeltsin's adviser on economic issues, A. Lifshits, and the chairman of the Central bank, S. Dubinin, both left office. Relations between the President and the Duma worsened dramatically. The State Duma was against Yeltsin's proposal to appoint Chernomyrdin prime minister and demanded that the president himself step down. 248 deputies voted in favor of a resolution calling on the president to resign. This was a majority of the deputies, but it was not enough for the decision to be passed. When the Duma rejected Chernomyrdin's candidacy on two occasions, the president found himself facing a dilemma: if he appointed Chernomyrdin, he would have to disband the Duma and call an election. Against the backdrop of the rapidly growing financial crisis, one could quite easily imagine that the new Duma might be far worse than the old one.

Yeltsin pulled hard on the steering wheel once again. The Duma was offered the Y.M. Primakov as a candidate. Primakov, who had been minister of foreign affairs since January 1996, had managed to earn the trust of society and support from the opposition blocs. On 11th September 1998 his candidacy was accepted. The role of first vice-premier went to the communist Y.D. Maslyukov, whilst the minister of finance was the Yabloko member M.M. Zadornov; several academics and economists who had been strongly critical of the economic course steered by the Yeltsin-Gaidar-Chernomyrdin trio — L.I. Abalkin, O.T. Bogomolov, N.Y. Petakov and D.S. Lvov were appointed as consultants to the Government. I.S. Ivanov was appointed minister of foreign affairs, I.D. Sergeev was named minister of defence and S.V. Stepashin was appointed minister of internal affairs.

Following S.K. Dubinin's departure, V.V. Gerashchenko was appointed chairman of the Central Bank. Gerashchenko had never made a secret of his refusal to accept the "monetarist policy" of his predecessor. The speeches made by Primakov, Gerashchenko and the minister of finance, Zadornov, indicated that the government considered gold, a revitalized economy, the printing press and the battle against financial crime as sources of money.[996]

Whereas the crisis in government had been overcome, the banking crisis was only just starting to get going. Many private banks, including the biggest ones — Inkombank, SBS-agro, Most, Oneksim and many others, which had held sizeable assets in the form of GKOs, began, taking their lead from the state, to refuse to make payments to their customers from out of their own pocket. Some of the banks passed on their obligations to private savings account holders to Sberbank, which was owned by the state. The collapse of the system of private banks dealt a blow, in turn, to the proper functioning of payment systems in the country.

Panic set it, and the exchange rate for the dollar at currency exchange outlets rose to 20 rubles, which led to the cost of imported goods going up and resulted in them disappearing from the shelves. The response to this unexpected shortage of goods was stronger demand among the public. In September almost all cash earnings were spent on buying goods and paying for services. As a result, prices shot up by 38.4 percent that month, although the total amount of money in circulation grew smaller as the year went on and by the start of September had fallen by 10 percent by comparison with the start of the year. By the end of 1998, the debt owed by regional and local authorities as regards staff salaries in the subsidized sector amounted to 16 billion rubles. There payments were delayed by an average of 2.6 months throughout the country. In the Altai region staff had to wait 7 or 8 months, and in Chukotka payments were delayed by 4 or 5 months. [997]

---

996   http://www.vybory.ru/sociology/polit_2half1998_vlast.php3
997   Y. Primakov: Eight months plus...M: 'Thought', 2001. P.50.

Amid the growing economic crisis, however, some light had appeared at the end of the tunnel — or to be precise, two factors combined and acted as a driver for growth in the Russian economy. For the first time since 1985, a favorable set of economic circumstances was taking shape in the country.

The collapse of the ruble led had at least two immediate consequences. Firstly, the cost of goods fell sharply, primarily through a reduction in the weight of salaries. Looking at it objectively, the fall in the value of the ruble therefore served to stimulate industry in Russia and made the country more competitive in both the domestic and foreign markets. The second consequence was a reduction in imported supplies. Almost overnight, imported goods became expensive and uncompetitive by comparison with Russian products. The volume of imported goods fell, and in 1999 stood at just 66.2% of the figure for 1998.[998] That said, Russian manufacturers now had some customers to sell to. The fall in the value of products which resulted from the collapse in the value of the ruble meant that Russian commodities — steel, pipes, non-ferrous metals etc. — could be purchased in the global market. This stimulated manufacturing, and for the first time there was growth in output. The total volume of industrial output went up 108.1% between the end of 1998 and the end of 1999. A rate of growth such as this was truly unheard of in the last twenty-five years, even taking into account the consequences of the collapse in production over the preceding ten years. Evidence of green shoots in the economy could be seen in the 118.1% increase in the amount of freight transported by rail.[999] At the end of 1998 and in early 1999 there was an upturn in the engineering sector and in the processing of raw materials. The fall in GDP was halted.

Primakov's government presented to the Duma its budget for 1999, in which there had been significant cuts to all state expenditure and revenue was due to exceed costs, resulting in a surplus. This was something that was fundamentally new in the economic history of the new Russia. The fact that there was a surplus ought to mean that steps could be taken to pay off Russia's debts, which amounted to approximately 170 billion dollars, including the debts of the former USSR.

As for people's living standards, things were worse. By the end of 1999, people's real-terms salaries stood at 76.8% of the figure for the preceding year, people were spending less in the shops (retail was 92.3%), and unemployment was up. By the end of 1999, 9.2 million people were out of work, up 6.8 % year-on-year.[1000] According to the World bank, between 1997 and 1999 poverty in Russia rose from 24.1 % of the population (35.3 million people) to 41.5 % (60.5 million).[1001] The poor in Russia are mostly accounted for by people

---

998   http://www.gks.ru/script/free/1c.exe?xxxx514F.2.1.1/13000R

999   http://old.polit.ru/documents/96808.htm

1000   See: http://www.gks.ru/script/free/1c.exe?xxxx514F.2.1.1/13000R

1001   www.ereport.ru. Experts from the World Bank and Russian statisticians use various

of working age in villages and small towns who have children. The number of people living below the official poverty line among people employed in education, culture and healthcare is very high.

One of the political consequences of the crisis in 1998 was that the differences of opinion between the various branches of power were exacerbated. A Temporary Commission, set up by the Federation Council to investigate the reasons, circumstances and consequences of the decisions taken on 17th August 1998, came to the conclusion that the main reason for the financial crisis was that the legal regulations governing the processes of preparing and taking state decisions, as set out in the Constitution, was extremely inadequate. According to the experts, the powers and instruments for management of the branches of power set out in the primary law were too vague. The status of President of the Russian Federation, and his ability to take decisions on all issues related to the life of the state without a clear description of the procedures and responsible bodies within the executive meant that all decisions could be taken and covered for using the name of head of state.

According to the senators, the decisions taken on 17th August 1998 had been taken in a way that featured gross violations of the procedures adopted, without any economic or juridical analysis having been undertaken or an analysis of the likely consequences. The drafts of the decisions had not been approved by the relevant ministries and had not been discussed in meetings of the Government of the Russian Federation or the Board of directors of the Central Bank of the Russian Federation. The question had been raised as to whether Kirienko, Dubinin, Zadornov, Aleksashenko, Chubais and Gaidar ought to be held personally accountable for the consequences of the decisions they had taken.[1002] The Federation Council proposed that amendments be made to the Constitution concerning a redistribution of powers between the federal bodies of state power, as well as amendments regarding the accountability of those in positions of power for the results of their work.

Operation successor

The default of 1998 left the president a broken man. He was deeply disillusioned, withdrew into himself and was frequently ill. It was no secret that he was in poor physical condition. Each appearance the president made

---

methods of defining poverty levels. The Russian experts assess the percentage of poor people based on monthly earnings. The World Bank does not feel this is the right approach, and proposes that poverty should be assessed not based on the level of earnings (about which people do not always tell the truth), but on the level of consumption.

1002   Analytical gazette No.10 (98). May 1999. The causes and consequences of the financial crisis in Russia in the late '90s. Material from the Temporary commission on the investigation of the causes, circumstances and consequences of decision-making on and after 17 August 1998.

on the TV news provided incontrovertible evidence that he had thrown in the towel. In October 1998, during a trip to Kazakhstan and Uzbekistan, the leaders of these two states and members of the security services were called upon to hold Yeltsin up, lest he fell. At the end of November 1998 the president was once again taken to hospital with inflammation of the lungs. He had no choice but to greet the Chinese premier, who had arrived in Moscow on an official visit, in the hospital, rather than engage in full-scale talks with him, as it would be unseemly to postpone the official visit yet again. In the mirror held up by the press, Yeltsin had been transformed into the subject of constant mockery at best, and furious insults at worst.

The matter of who would succeed him was becoming more and more pressing. The successor would have to satisfy at least two key criteria: he would need to be someone who could continue the political course being steered to develop the country, and guarantee the personal security of the previous President. The latter requirement was no small matter. Way back in 1992 the call had been heard in the opposition press and at rallies: "Put Yeltsin's mob in court!" There were a fair few people who espoused this view in the Duma, too. The task of finding a successor was made all the more urgent by the fact that the President's health was in such a state that he might at any moment stop being able to perform his duties. Under the legislation, if this were to happen he would have to be replaced by the prime minister, who would become the acting president until an election was called. Thus the Chairman of the Government became not only the President's successor but also one of the most likely candidates for the role of president.

In parallel to the search for a successor, Yeltsin also sought to strengthen his own Administration. In 1997-1998, Ryurikov, Baturin, Lifshits, Krasnov, Pikhoya and various other advisers and speech-writers who had worked for him since the early '90s, all left Yeltsin's team for one reason or another. The so-called 'family' — the people in Yeltsin's inner circle — had consolidated their position in the Administration. This group included the President's daughter, T.B. Dyachenko; the future head of the Administration, V.B. Yumashev; B.A. Berezovsky, the financier who had played an active part in the election campaign in 1996, and had successfully made use of his proximity to power to implement his business projects; and representatives of the 'old' Administration, who were "willing to play by the rules of 'family' policy (such as S.V. Yastrzhembsky and A.S. Voloshin)."[1003] It must be said that for all the appeal that lies in trying to identify Yeltsin's interests with those of the 'family', the president had in no way become an obedient puppet, with his inner circle pulling the strings: he still had a tendency to take unpredictable steps and was capable of asserting his character.

1003   The Yeltsin era. Sketches from a political history. M., 2001. P. 778-779

True to his political tradition of creating 'checks and balances', Yeltsin did not rely on the 'family' alone — he also strengthened the Administration with men from the intelligence services and the security structures, counting on the older generation's good discipline, efficiency and ability to carry out instructions to the letter. In December 1998 General N.N. Bordyuzha, the Secretary of the Security Council, who had previously been the director of the Federal border service, was appointed director of the President's Administration in place of V.B. Yumashev.

In his new role, Bordyuzha proved to be, in the opinion of the 'family', excessively independent. He insisted on restricting the influence of lobbyists, including Boris Berezovsky, Roman Abramovich and a number of other figures from big business, on the Administration's activities. Having failed to receive support, Bordyuzha tendered his resignation.

A.S. Voloshin was appointed as his successor. Voloshin had had experience working within commercial structures close to Berezovsky. He had worked in the Administration since 1997, as an adviser on economic issues and then as deputy to the then director, Yumashev. An ally of the 'family', he proved to be an extraordinarily good organizer who was adept at improving relations with the various blocs in the State Duma and using behind the scenes maneuvering to manipulate the actions of politicians, including members of the opposition.

The black clouds of the approaching elections hung in the air. The next election for the State Duma was due to take place in 1999. It was set to be a "political rehearsal" for the Presidential election in 2000. Yeltsin announced on several occasions that he would not be standing in the election. Few believed him. Although he was only entitled to hold the office of president for two terms, he nevertheless had a constitutional right to take part in another election campaign. Strictly speaking, he had only been elected once since the 1993 Constitution took effect — in 1996. And his ability to triumph even in the most unlikely of conditions had become part of Russian political folklore.

The Prime Minister, Primakov, had stated on several occasions that he did not harbor ambitions for the presidency, but his approval rating had gone up, and he began to be seen as a potential candidate for the elections due to be held in 2000. In order to ensure political stability during the campaign, Primakov suggested to the president and the chairmen of the two chambers of parliament that he could assume voluntary obligations: until the next presidential election was held, the president would not disband the Duma, would not exercise his right to disband the government, and the government would not hold a vote of no confidence, which might lead to the disbandment of the Duma. In its turn, the Duma undertook not to go down the route of impeachment. The Prime minister deemed it necessary to pass a law on guarantees of immunity for those who have held the role of President.[1004] This initiative was interpreted as a manifestation of ambitions for the presidency by the Kremlin, however. The State Duma did not heed Primakov's proposals, either.

Back in May 1998, in response to demands from striking miners, the communists and Yabloko launched a petition in the State Duma to remove the president from office. In two months they collected more than 225 signatures, and this was enough for impeachment procedures to be initiated. On 19th July 1998, under a directive from the Duma, a special commission was set up to assess whether the allegations made against the president of the Russian Federation had been made in compliance with the rules of procedure and were grounded in fact. The Commission was led by a former member of the Committee for constitutional inspection of the USSR, V. Filimonov (CPRF), and his deputy was Y. Mizulina (Yabloko). The President and his Administration were not unduly bothered by this, since attacks on the president in the Duma were a common phenomenon, the allegations made were of a political nature and the impeachment procedure was complicated.

The Commission set to work and by May 1999 had compiled five accusations against the president: 1) destroying the Soviet Union and weakening the Russian Federation by signing and implementing the Belovezha agreements; 2) carrying out a coup d'état in September 1993; 3) commencing and conducting military action in the Republic of Chechnya; 4) weakening the security of the RF and the country's ability to defend itself; 5) genocide against the Russian people.

The expectation that the prime minister, by making use of the support of a number of parties in the Duma, would be partially able to get rid of all the problems in the relationship between the President and the Duma, had proved unfounded. Primakov was either unable or unwilling to influence the deputies in any way, and persuade them to back down on their plan. In the event that Yeltsin was forced from office as President, Primakov would be the most likely candidate for the role.

Events took a different turn, however. The President seized the initiative. On 12th May 1999, on the eve of the impeachment vote and to everyone's surprise, he sacked Primakov. The Duma found itself facing a dilemma. It would now be asked to approve the new prime minister, and that, in turn, would enable the President to disband the Duma in mid-term, if it voted against the candidate he proposed three times. On 15 May, in an open vote in which voters' names were added to the voting slips, none of the allegations made against the president secured the 2/3 majority of the vote that was

---

1004   Y. Primakov: Eight months plus...M: 'Thought', 2001. P.179.

required. The results of the vote were as follows: the allegation of betraying the state: 284 for, 77 against; organizing a coup d'état: 263 for, 60 against; exceeding his authority: 284 for, 43 against; assisting foreign states: 241 for, 78 against; genocide: 237 for, 89 against.[1005]

Thus the majority of the deputies were against the president, and a considerable number of them abstained. Only 10-20% of the deputy corpus voted in favor of the president.

On 19th May 1999 Yeltsin proposed that the Duma approve General S.V. Stepashin as Prime Minister. Stepashin had formerly been the minister of internal affairs, and before that — the director of the Federal counter-espionage service.

This appointment was symbolic: the President was continuing to strengthen the 'security services component' in his governance of the country. General Stepashin was appointed to a post which the President's Administration had intended for the minister of communications lines, N.Y. Aksenenko. Aksenenko was traditionally thought of as a member of the 'family'. Reports emerged in the press about disagreements between Stepashin and the Administration, stating that Stepashin was insisting on an expansion of his powers, in particular in his management of the economy and industrial policy.

A new delineation of powers was gradually taking effect in the country. Yeltsin now had some new people within his field of view who were practically unknown among Moscow's political elite. One of these men was V.V. Putin. A staff officer in the KGB, he had worked as an adviser to the mayor of St. Petersburg, A.A. Sobchak, then as chairman of the Committee for external relations at the mayor's office. Following Sobchak's defeat in the 1996 election, he had had to leave St. Petersburg.

In Moscow he started out in the President's Directorate of affairs, then in the Administration; in 1997 he became head of the Chief supervisory directorate, and in 1998 — first deputy head of the Administration, in charge of the country's regions. In 1998 he was appointed Director of the Federal Security Service and, concurrently, secretary of the Security Council. By making use of his right and obligation to report to the President on a weekly basis, he had secured a place in the President's 'inner circle'.

Yet another crisis in the Caucasus accelerated the events taking place in Moscow. In the summer of 1999 the Wahhabis began to increase their influence in Dagestan, and there were clashes on the country's border with Chechnya. Stepashin, after visiting some Wahhabi villages, delivered a reconciliatory speech. Events in the North Caucasus took a dramatic turn

---

1005   The Yeltsin era. P.759.

for the worse, however. The insurgents' terrorist activities increased, and Chechen military divisions launched attacks on Dagestan. It became clear that the Khasavyurtovsk peace accords, agreed between the federal powers and the leader of the Chechen separatists, Maskhadov, in the summer of 1996, had collapsed.

On 9th August 1999 the President proposed that the Duma approve a new Prime Minister — V.V. Putin. The energy demonstrated by the new premier and the tough line he took in his statements about the terrorists led to a rapid rise in his popularity. The Chechen insurgents who had entered Dagestan began to be forced back out, and federal forces launched military action against separatists in the territory of Chechnya.

Battles of a different kind — political ones — were unfolding in the elections for the State Duma. This time, the main contender for a majority in the Duma and, consequently, the main rival for the post of President was Y.M. Primakov, in an alliance with the mayor of Moscow Y.M. Luzhkov. This powerful alliance, which made no secret of its intentions — to revise Yeltsin's political legacy — was opposed by the Unity party, which had been created with the direct involvement of the President's Administration and whose leader was the Prime Minister, V.V. Putin. Two old men against a young man. It was less a battle of political manifestos than a struggle between two political generations. Fifteen years had passed since the start of perestroika. People were tired of the constant economic hardships and the constant power struggles at the top; they were tired of the fact that in recent years the country had fallen ever deeper into a morass of regional conflicts, local nationalism and separatism on a local and regional basis. Hopes of change for the better were bound up in the election of a new leader.

Throughout the second half of 1999 Putin's approval ratings rose constantly: he was seen as someone who could restore order to the country. On the eve of the election for the State Duma, the sociological center at the Russian academy of state service conduct a study of opinion among the electorate. The results showed that V.V. Putin was the clear leader.[1006] In response to the question: "Which of the following statesmen and political figures do you tend to trust rather than distrust?" the following answers were given.

1006   V.A. Boikov: Establishing the level of awareness and political preferences of the electorate. (A sociological analysis three weeks before the elections for the State Duma)//A sociology of power. 1999, No. 4. P. 30. (The number of responses was over 100%, because under the system used for the opinion poll several answers were possible. The answers are stated in descending order in terms of the number of people who responded). Putin's lead in the poll is confirmed by data from the Russian independent institute of social and national problems (RNISiNP), although on the whole the results of the poll vary significantly. See: M.K. Gorshkov Russian society in a state of transformatin (sociological analysis). – M.:ROSSPAN, 2000. P.337

V. Putin — 54.3%,
Y. Primakov — 34.5%,
G. Zyuganov — 24.6%,
S. Shoigu — 24.2%,
G. Yavlinsky — 20.3%,
Y. Luzhkov — 20.1%,
S. Kirienko — 13.8%,
V. Zhirinovsky —11.1%,
V. Chernomyrdin — 10.1%,
G. Seleznev — 9.1%,
V. Ryzhkov — 8.0%,
V. Anpilov — 6.4%,
Y. Stroev — 5.5%.
Don't know — 13.3%.

On 19th December the elections for the State Duma took place. These were the third elections under the Constitution adopted in 1993. The votes were distrubuted as follows: CPRF — 24.29%; Unity — whose informal leader was Putin — 23.32%; the Fatherland — All the Russias (OVR) (led by Luzhkov and Primakov) — 13.33%; the Union of just forces — 8.52; the Zhirinovsky Bloc — 5.98; Yabloko — 5.93 %. The real-terms distribution of power in the Duma turned out to be even more advantageous for Unity, however. Having become the 'party of power', it joined forces with its recent adversary — the movement 'The Fatherland — All the Russias' and secured an absolute majority in the Duma.

This alignment of political forces meant that the communists had lost their majority in the Duma. For the first time, the State Duma became loyal to the Government.

Against this backdrop, B.N. Yeltsin made what was probably one of his most important steps of all during the final years of his presidency. He carefully thought through and brilliantly executed the task of ensuring the continuity of power.

Putin described the incident as follows: "Two to three weeks before the New Year, Boris Nikolaevich invited me into his office and said that he had decided to leave. I was thus going to be made acting president. He looked at me and waited to see what I would say. I sat there in silence. He began to fill me in on the details — that he wanted to announce his retirement before the year was out...When he finished speaking, I said: 'You know Boris Nikolaevich, to be honest with you, I don't know whether I am ready for this, or whether I want it, because it is a fairly difficult fate.' I wasn't sure whether I wanted such a fate...But then he replied: "When I came here, I had other plans, too. But this was the way life turned out. I was not striving for this position, either, but it so happened that I would even say I was required to fight for the post of President due to many circumstances..."[1007]

On 31st December 1999 the President arrived at the Kremlin at 10 am. He summoned the Prime Minister to his office. TV crews had arrived at the Kremlin to record the President's traditional new year message. At midday the President appeared on the nation's TV screens.

In his televised address, Yeltsin explained to the country's citizens the reasons which had forced him to take the decision to stand down from the most senior position in the Russian state — a first in Russia's thousand-year history. This meant that the acting President, until a new election was held, would be the prime minister, V.V. Putin. Yeltsin said that Russia would never again return to the past, and that Putin was a "strong man, who was worthy of being President, and with whom practically every Russian citizen today associates their hopes for the future! Why should I stand in his way? Why wait another six months?"

Summing up his stormy decade as president, he asked forgiveness "for the fact that many of the dreams you and I had did not come true. And for the fact that what we thought would be straightforward turned out to be tortuously difficult. I ask forgiveness for the fact that I failed to justify some of the hopes of the people who believed that by a single breakthrough, a single blow, we would be able to make the transition from a dreary, stagnant, totalitarian past to a bright, wealthy, civilized future. I too believed in this. It seemed as though with a single bound we would be able to overcome all the hardships. It did not quite work out with a single bound. Somehow I proved to be too naive. ...I am stepping down. I did all I could. ...I am going to be replaced by a new generation, a generation of people who can do more, and do things better."[1008]

1007   The Yeltsin era. P.790
1008   B.N. Yeltsin: The Presidential marathon. P.422-424.

Chapter 12
The president in retirement

Boris Nikolaevich Yeltsin spent the evening of 31st December 1999 with his extended family. Naina Yeltsina recalled: "everyone was feeling overjoyed. To begin with we saw in the New Year in the traditional Yekaterinburg way, then we did so the Moscow way. We watched the televised message made by the new head of state. We drank a toast and opened our presents. Boris Nikolaevich was always Uncle Frost in our household. He would wear a red hat and everything, but the grey hair was his own. It was all very moving and fun. It was a special New year, in that it was stress-free. In previous years, everyone had always felt some hidden tension during our celebrations — you never knew what might happen. But this time we were able to relax. We were even smiling in a different way from normal. Everyone was feeling glad. There was the sense of a calmness of some sort. There was the feeling that even if something were to happen — God forbid — the country now had a new leader to take decisions."[1009]

Yeltsin saw in the new year, 2000, as a pensioner. He had been the first head of state in Russia to be elected by the people. He was the first and only head of state in Russia who voluntarily stood down.

In the '80s and '90s there probably wasn't a single newspaper or a single political scientist who did not write or talk about Yeltsin's "thirst for power", and state that the desire for power was the essence of this man's character.

They were mistaken. In this regard, too, Yeltsin proved to be unpredictable. In everything, Yeltsin set a precedent.

He was the first President of Russia to retire and take up a pension.

The latest changes in his personal fate set a precedent for the political system in Russia. His departure meant that the status of former President now had to be created. On the day he left office, an Edict from the new President, V.V.

1009   http://news.mail.ru/society/3215746

Putin, was released, 'On the guarantees made to a president of the Russian Federation who has ceased to perform his duties, and to the members of his family'. A year later, this Edict was transformed into a special Law dated 12th February 2001.

Presidents of the Russian Federation who had ceased to perform their duties were assigned a state security detail, special means of communication and personal transport, medical treatment, immunity, and the right to use one of the state-owned dachas for life.

They were also entitled to keep a team of advisers, with the cost paid for using resources from the federal budget.

Yeltsin chose to keep by his side Vladimir Nikolaevich Shevchenko, who had created the presidential protocol for the USSR and for Russia and accompanied the President on all his trips around the country and overseas visits, and was extremely experienced in diplomacy and international relations; and Anatoly Ivanovich Kuznetsov, who in June 1996 had been appointed head of the Security Service of the President of the Russian Federation.

For Boris Nikoaevich Yeltsin, a new life was beginning — the life of a President in retirement.

A journalist from *Izvestiya* later asked V. Shevchenko, who was with Yeltsin on a daily basis:

- "How has his typical day looked in recent months?"

- "He does everything in accordance with a strict routine." He retired on 1st January 2000, and wherever he and I went afterwards, a program was always drawn up, and at this moment one would hear him asking: what's up next then? And he would look at his watch. He always had lunch at one o'clock on the dot. That never changed. No matter what.

- What time did he get up in the morning?

- He always got up early. And latterly he has hardly been getting any sleep at all. But getting up early is a habit you get into. When he was still in the job, he might call me at 5 in the morning, for example.

... But lately he had grown very fond of literature. He had huge boxes of books brought to him. He was a voracious reader. ... He read practically all the memoirs that were out there. He read Karamzin's *A history of the Russian state*, and Solovieva's history of Russia. Then he read about Peter the Great — whatever he could get his hands on. He read a lot about France and

Napoleon. He took an intense interest in everything, right down to which wine he was drinking."[1010]

Yeltsin read Checkhov, Murakami, the Strugatsky brothers, Nabokov, political memoirs — Albright's, Thatcher's, Clinton's, books about the history of the Second World War...

Naina Yeltsina began insistently getting her husband to take an interest in the theater. The theater *Sovremennik* (Contemporary) became a particular favorite, mainly due to the friendship between the President's wife and the senior director Galina Volchek.

He had more time for sport, too. He was a passionate spectator at sporting events. He watched a lot of televised sporting contests, and took pleasure in doing so. "We had a schedule that showed which tournaments were taking place where, and what time the broadcast started," Vladimir Shevchenko revealed. "And sometimes we would watch matches back-to-back: a live broadcast from Argentina would end, and then the Australian Open would begin immediately afterwards, then something else.

At his initiative, an international tennis tournament began to take place each year in Yekaterinburg, and he tried his best to attend it regularly, and present the trophy to the winner in person. He also travelled to international sporting events overseas, including the French Open at Roland Garosse. He went to watch his beloved volleyball team in Yekaterinburg — Uralochka.

His family — his daughters, grandsons and great-grandsons began to take up a lot more of their head of the family's time. "I began to cherish the comfort of home, family, the remarkably warm and loving relationship between Naina and myself," Yeltsin told the editor-in-chief of Izvestiya, Vladimir Mamontov. "I'm always delighted when Lena comes to see us with Vanechka, or Tanya comes with Mashenka. It's a real pleasure, sometimes I can't help myself and I give them a call: 'Come on Tanya, bring Gleb and Mashka and come over for dinner!' A few days ago we had another bit of good news: my granddaughter Masha, who is 22, gave birth to a little boy, his name's Misha. That means I've now got two grandsons. The first of them, Katya's son Sasha, is six, he's an engaging, talented little whipper-snapper. I was surprised to discover that my loving family — that above all else — represents true human happiness."[1011]

Yeltsin had left his former life, when he lived each day under the watchful eye of the mass media, and consciously moved away into a quiet field. As a

---

1010   Y. Grigorieva: The Chief of Protocol for the first President of Russia, Vladimir Shevchenko: 'I thank fate for the work I did with Yeltsin' //Izvestiya, 1 June 2007.

1011   Izvestiya, 2 February 2006

matter of principle he refused to give a verdict on his successor, refraining from expressing any views.

It immediately began to be suggested in the press that this approach had been part of the agreement reached with Putin.

We shall take the liberty of disagreeing with that assertion, though. Above all, Yeltsin acknowledged his *personal responsibility* for appointing Putin as his successor. To criticize the decisions made by the new President would be tantamount to saying that he had been wrong to choose him. Yeltsin's memory of the start of his political career in Moscow, when he had been 'stabbed in the back' by M.S. Gorbachev, who had promoted him to the Politburo and appointed him first secretary of the Moscow City Committee of the CPSU. To Yeltsin, 'media attacks' against one's former coworkers were not acceptable.

It should be noted that B.N. Yeltsin and V.V. Putin maintained a good relationship, on both a personal and professional level. The new President would from time to time come and visit his successor, particularly during his first term in office. The two men would have long *tête-à-têtes*, the subject of which was known only to them.

Yeltsin, meanwhile, wrote articles for the press in which he scrutinized his own political legacy. He was willing to discuss the difficult chapters from that part of the nation's history in which he had been the protagonist.

In a lengthy interview with the editor-in-chief of *Izvestiya*, Vladimir Mamontov, on the eve of his 75th birthday, he was required to talk not only about his life in retirement, but also about his understanding of the most recent period in the country's history.[1012]

When asked to assess Russia's place in the modern world, he said: "For a long time we were the only country that was warning the West about the real threat in today's world — terrorism. Politicians in the West pretended they couldn't hear us, though, and continued to hold firm on Chechnya, on peoples' right to self-determination and independence, and on violations of human rights and so on. Then terrorists attacked New York, Madrid and London, and the world finally grasped the fact that war had been declared on the civilized world. And that only through the coordinated efforts of all countries would it be possible to counter this threat to mankind in the new century."

When the journalist asked Yeltsin to name the five politicians he considered to have been the most significant in the last century, he replied: "I don't like

---

1012   Izvestiya, 2 February 2006

lists like that. They are based not on a genuine assessment of the role played by one person or another in history, but on interpretations created by the media themselves. The only thing I can say with any certainty is that my list would not contain either Lenin or Stalin, whom some of our politicians continue to idolize. For me that is one of the great mysteries. After all it is such a simple thing to do — to read the historical documents, and understand how many victims there were in the country, how many millions of lives were taken away because of the barbarity and inhumanity of those politicians. But nothing changes — Stalin is still high up in the ratings, and Lenin still lies in the Mausoleum on the Red Square."

Pondering over the question: which qualities, in his view, were important for a politician, he disputed his own answer and added to it. "Two things matter above all else. Intelligence and a strong will. No, three: intelligence, a strong will and humanity. Intelligence, so as to move in the right direction and take the right decisions. A strong will — in order to implement these decisions. A true politician cannot afford to be weak. Weak politicians brought down empires, gave away their territories and sacrificed their own peoples. And when I sought someone among the young generation of politicians with precisely these character traits, someone who could take charge of Russia after my departure, Vladimir Putin naturally caught my attention. He has both intelligence and a strong will. And at the same time he understands the meaning and depth of interpersonal relations in politics."

The journalist touched on a painful topic for B.N. Yeltsin — the flow of criticism aimed at him in both the foreign press and the Russian press. This gave Yeltsin an opportunity to express his opinion about the reasons for this criticism, and to talk about his attitude towards the press, including the critical articles.

He recalled the election that was anticipated in 2000, when "there was an intense battle raging as to who would take charge of Russia following my departure. Other than the communists, who were forever trying to return to power, hoping to secure the votes of the elderly and the discontented, another powerful force had emerged. Two elder statesmen[1013] joined forces and decided to take charge of the country in 2000. They were supported by some of the oligarchs. This group owned national TV channels, major newspapers and magazines. They put all their resources into discrediting the incumbent president and, by definition, everything he was offering the country. Then that term, the 'family', was used on NTV — and all those stories came out about villas in France, Germany, London... The more this nonsense appeared in print or on the TV screen, the easier it was for people

---

1013   This was a hint at Y. Primakov and Y. Luzhkov, who were actively preparing for the election campaign in 2000

to believe it. These same 'comrades' had financed a similar campaign in the West, using a huge budget."

At this point Yeltsin remarked that "I too became a victim of freedom of speech, which I had defended throughout all my years as president." He recalled that within the President's Administration there had been some who were against the idea of handing over the channel NTV to Gusinsky. In Yeltsin's opinion, though, "television that is independent of the state is one of the things on which civil society is founded. Yes, it has to be suffered, endured, and it can be tortuous, but we must preserve independent media...

For that reason I did not file a single lawsuit against the media, nor make a single call, nor did a single director of a TV channel or print medium ever receive a single request from me."

"Free media resources," Yeltsin said, "are one of the key components of a free, civilized country. I do not regret for a moment the fact that we destroyed censorship.

In 2003 Yeltsin gave an interview to the newspaper Moskovskiye Novosti, in which he gave his appraisal of the political leaders of the '90s. As Lyudmila Telen, the newspaper's assistant editor-in-chief, put it, "we had a one-on-one talk for the one hour allotted, plus an extra twenty-seven minutes over the limit. He did not demand to see the full list of questions in advance, nor did he complain when we went off on a tangent, nor did he ask his advisers to record the interview on a dictaphone. In a word, he behaved as if it was still 1991."[1014]

"Who introduced Yegor Gaidar to you? L. Telen asked Yeltsin. —

"Various people mentioned his name to me. After that I read some of his articles. Then I invited him to come and see me. We had a long conversation, about all sorts of things. But above all — about what he imagined Russia's future to be."

He recalled that when he held meetings with the new members of the Government, "Everyone disputed what I said. The president's council would meet, for example, and each of them would argue with me. But I would reply calmly: "Thank you..." Although on the inside I was seething. I realised: I mustn't hide away from this.

- Why was that?

"So that they wouldn't be afraid to express their opinions. On a few things, it later transpired, it was not me that was in the right, but the people who

---

1014   Moskovskiye novosti, 21 October 2003.

had disagreed with me. That meant that I must be able to listen, so that I could then think it over, take in what they had said and only then make my decision."

"Are you aware," the journalist asked, "that Gaidar was against the idea of you standing for election in 1996?"

"He wasn't the only one, my family was against the idea too. I had serious reservations about it myself. But I later realised: I was up against Zyuganov, and I was the only person who could defeat him. Can you imagine Zyuganov being president of Russia? I even said to Gaidar at the time: "Which of you is capable of defeating Zyuganov? Stake your claims." No-one put themselves forward. And at that point Gaidar gave me his support, too.

Yeltsin gave his assessment of Chubais, Nemtsov, Fedorov, Stepashin and Yavlinsky as politicians.

He said that since retiring he often met up with Gaidar, Chubais, Nemtsov, Voloshin, Chernomyrdin and Kasyanov, "and with many others we did not have time to discuss today. I have a constant line of communication with our governors and with the presidents of our republics. And also with the presidents of the CIS states, of course."

Meetings continued to take place between B.N. Yeltsin and his advisers, with whom he had lived through the incredibly difficult '90s. Relations between the President and his staff had not always been straightforward.[1015] But friendly, personable relations had been preserved, as had their deep respect for one another. For that reason the likes of Baturin, Ilin, Ilyushin, Korabelshchikov, Kostikov, Krasnov, Pikhoya and Satarov would visit him each year on his birthday.

These meetings were always warm occasions. This by no means meant that they did not continue their arguments of old and their discussions about day-to-day events. Yeltsin would listen to them and give his assessment of the past. Any attempts to get him to discuss current affairs proved fruitless, though. He followed his rule of never discussing his successor at almost all times.

When asked whether he had meetings with V.V. Putin, Yeltsin not only confirmed that he did, but also said that after his retirement he was "not entitled to remain a public politician. I vowed never to comment on what the current president was doing. I tell him what I like and dislike when we are alone together.

- But do you really tell him, you might ask?

1015   For more details see: The Yeltsin era. Sketches from a political history. M., 2001

- Yes, I really do. There must always be some opposition voices in society — it won't do in life not to have them. I said as much to Vladimir Vladimirovich, too."[1016]

On the eve of the 15th anniversary of the signing of the Belovezh Accords, Yeltsin gave some in-depth answers to questions from *Rossiskaya gazeta* about perhaps the most dramatic problem in the nation's history in the second half of the 20th century — the break-up of the USSR[1017]. He argued convincingly that this had been an inevitable process. In his opinion, the break-up of the Soviet Union had been the result of the collapse in the economy, when "the strategic stocks of foodstuffs ran out and the fast-approaching failure of the state's financial system."

The nationwide movements taking place in the country, and the events in Karabakh, the Baltic States and Georgia testified, in Yeltsin's opinion, to the mistakes that had been made by the leaders of the Union, which had on the one hand failed to self-evident facts, and on the other used excessive force.

The attempt to create a new Act of Union, which, according to Yeltsin, "probably would have been signed, had the coup not taken place in August '91, the attempted coup, which was led by people extremely close to the president of the Soviet Union. The coup ended in failure. But more than that, it also laid to rest any agreements on the creation of a new Union. Ukraine, Moldova, Kazakhstant and Georgia — all the republics in the Soviet Union, which was still in existence at the time — proclaimed their independence, and that they were creating their own states, within a matter of weeks."

Yeltsin objected furiously to the claims that "in Belovezh the leaders of three national republics had suddenly come together and signed some agreements, a few sheets of paper, and after that the mighty Soviet State had come crashing down. That is nonsense, of course. These days, however, this nonsense is increasingly being peddled, including by politicians and political scientists whom one would otherwise think of as right-thinking people.

In his opinion, "when they created the CIS, the leaders of the republics attempted to lessen the impact of the consequences which might be felt by people living in the former Soviet Union as a result of the collapse of the state. It was for precisely this reason that visa-free entry rules were announced for people travelling between the newly-formed countries, there were no customs barriers, and there was free movement of capital, and so on. We attempted to create something akin to the model of today's European Union, only with less bureaucracy and centralization... I grew up in the Soviet Union. I spent almost

1016   Moskovskiye novosti. 21 October 2003.
1017   Rossiskaya gazeta, 7 December 2006.

my entire life in the USSR, so to a certain extent I feel some nostalgia for it. And I think that is only natural. At the same time, however, I understand perfectly well that all empires are destined to fall.

The Alexandrine Empire didn't last forever, nor did the Roman Empire or the Ottoman Empire. All the empires we know about throughout history have come to an end sooner of later. This is a historically inevitable process, and the USSR was always destined to go the same way. As for exactly how this was to come about, that is another matter. If the process had come about spontaneously, there might have been a civil war. After all, we set ourselves the goal of preventing such a turn of events, and preserving, wherever possible, our economic and social ties. And preserve them we did. Nor did we allow a civil war to break out. As for my heartfelt nostalgia for the USSR, though — there's no escaping that."

In Yeltsin's opinion, the problem of 'unrecognized states' was not something that had been brought about by the CIS. It was the result of the national policy of the USSR, which had divided the people up into different levels, in the legal sense.

And he immediately added some information which, it seemed, was not directly related to the subject of the interview but concerned a far bigger range of issues directly related to his activities as President. "In the first few years of the existence of the CIS, Russia had hardly any gold reserves left, oil cost 8 to 14 dollars a barrel, and we had the pressure of debts of many millions weighing down on us, yet despite all this we kept the CIS going — for fifteen years now we've been unable to 'divorce' one another."

These words contained a veiled response to those who were accusing Yeltsin of making mistakes in his economic policy, and contrasting it with the economic successes of the first decade of the 21st century. Understandably, with oil prices at 70-80 dollars a barrel, the Russian Government now had the kind of resources available to support the budget which they could only dream about in the '90s!

Yeltsin did not seek to avoid journalists. In his responses to their questions he tried to find answers to questions about why things had happened the way they did — both for his own benefit and that of the country's citizens. He went to considerable lengths to avoid giving an appraisal or criticism of his successor, however. In his public statements, moreover, he spoke highly of V.V. Putin.

There were, however, some unfortunate exceptions. In late 2000, Yeltsin announced that he was "categorically against reinstating the anthem of the USSR as the national anthem. Khrushchev had got rid of the bit about the 'father of the peoples', but kept the same tune. Under Brezhnev they made another change to the words — but now, it seems, the words are going to be changed completely? No, such things are not to be toyed with."[1018]

It befell Yeltsin to create a new position, 'President in retirement', in Russia's political process during the first decade of the 20th century. This included what are referred to as 'protocol events', and events related to a new tradition in Russia — the international activity of a retired President.

On 6th January 2000 Yeltsin led the Russian delegation to Bethlehem, for the Orthodox Christmas, where he had meetings with the Israeli and Palestinian leaders.

Russia's first President was present at the inauguration of President V.V. Putin in May 2000 and again in 2004.

In 2001, on the day when Russia's state sovereignty was proclaimed — 12th June — B.N. Yeltsin was presented with the medal "For services to the Fatherland' of the 1st degree.

Boris Yeltsin's 75th birthday celebrations were held in the White Kremlin palace, in accordance with state protocol. The new President showed great respect for his predecessor.

The press took pleasure in writing about Yeltsin's meetings with his colleagues both at work and in retirement: the Japanese prime minister, Ryutaro Hashimoto; the German chancellor Helmut Kohl, the French president Jacques Chirac, the Chinese president Jiang Zemin; the president of Ukraine, Leonid Kuchma; the president of Kyrgystan, Askar Akayev; the president of Belarus, Alexander Lukashenko; the president of Latvia, Vaira Vike-Freiberga; the president of Kazakhstan, Nursultan Nazarbayev; King Abdullah of Jordan...

This is by no means a comprehensive list of the heads of state — both current and in retirement — with whom Yeltsin maintained contact.

The reports written by journalists about the retired dignitary's meetings with current or retired colleagues failed to cast a light on the secret, sacred essence of these meetings. Often they were informal, unofficial discussions of complex inter-state and international relations, which it was the job of the official diplomatic channels to monitor. "Helmut Kohl and I have become very close," Yeltsin told one journalist. "We still meet up nowadays, now that both of us have left office. ... The French president Jacques Chirace and I still enjoy warm relations, as well. When we meet it feels like a family get-together, and we remember events of yesteryear, and of course discuss current affairs as well."[1019]

1018   http://www.newsru.com/itogi/10dec2000/gimn_epoxa.html
1019   Izvestiya, 2 February 2006

Each time these meetings were held, special preparations had to be made. The retired President was allowed to discuss things which neither the minister of foreign affairs nor the current president were allowed to mention. He came up with a formula to describe his role, which is not without a certain elegance: "As a pensioner, I shall do everything in my power to ensure the continuing rapprochement between our nations." [1020]

Laying the groundwork and then reaching agreement are the informal, hidden parts of diplomacy, the diplomacy of the political elites, who devised the conditions for official diplomacy.

And it was not without good reason that all these meetings were prepared by V.N. Shevchenko, a worldly-wise and very experienced diplomat.

The health problems which had become part of the political biography of Yeltsin's second term as president remained, naturally, even after he retired. Discussing the health risks of his profession, Yeltsin told a journalist: "Being President is the kind of job in which you think about the problems weighing down on you both night and day. You are in a permanent state of tension, constantly analyzing the situation, and the cost of errors is so great that it can be felt even after many years have passed. And this constant pressure naturally eats away at your health — even at the strongest constitution. Ronald Reagan suffered a severe illness, Ariel Sharon's heart attack, the heart operation Bill Clinton had immediately after leaving office, the serious disease suffered by the French president Mitterand; there are countless other examples. As regard myself I can say that immediately after I stepped down as president it was as if an almighty, incredibly heavy burden had been lifted from my shoulders, and I could breathe freely."[1021]

Yeltsin gave a sigh. In the space of just a year he seemed to have grown younger. He had lost weight, and he no longer suffered from edema. He said he had begun to monitor his weight strictly, and imposed a ban on eating after four pm. Every year he was required to go for a check-up in Germany in connection with the heart bypass operations he had undergone.

He now had the opportunity to take vacations. He went on vacations to Issyk-Kul in Krygyzstan, the Crimea in Ukraine, China and Italy. He met up with his fellow classmates from university at the Bor health resort outside Moscow in 2002, and in Kislovodsk in 2005.

The life of B.N. Yeltsin, which on the face of it was so successful, had another side to it which never fully went away. This was the ongoing rabid criticism of him — coarse, mocking and often unjust — in the press and on the television, and the cruel puns about the 'wild nineties'. It was forgotten that the entire

1020   Izvestiya, 1 June 2007
1021   Izvestiya, 2 February 2006.

so-called 'political elite' was a product of these self-same '90s, and the criticism itself became possible thanks to the new opportunities which had arisen in the press under Yeltsin.

For Yeltsin, who had always had a keen sense for people's mood, a sad truth had become clear: people had not become happier as a result of the reforms putting food in the stores, or because the seemingly unthinkable had happened: the age-old Soviet problem had disappeared — the problem of providing people with food, clothes and shoes — the items of which there had been a deficit until so recently. The lines outside the stores and the 'on-site commissions' in the district committees had disappeared, and the comic Zhvanetsky's old line about going to Paris on Friday was no longer seemed so funny. Paris, Istanbul, Cairo and London were all accessible to people now, and holidays in Egypt and Turkey could be bought in any district town.

However, these changes, which essentially touched everyone's lives, also brought new problems of their own. There was now clear inequality in the country. The battle against special privileges had ended in a struggle for wealth. This struggle had been won by the few, and the rules in accordance with which it was waged — privatization, share auctions — were not deemed to be just by the majority of the population.

Yeltsin, with his political intuition and ability to identify with people, felt this, and it pained him. His constant desire to make life happier clashed with new challenges which could not possibly have been foreseen.

2006 was a difficult year for B.N. Yeltsin. It was the year of his 75th birthday, and that is never easy from a psychological point of view, although it is a very happy time. Triumphal celebrations were held to mark his birthday. There was a reception in the Georgievsky Hall in the Grand Kremlin Palace. The ceremony was attended by Russia's political elite at the time — ministers from the State Duma and Federation Council and the leaders of these institutions, the former prime ministers Viktor Chernomyrdin, Sergei Kirienko and Sergei Stepashin, and many governors. Among the guests invited to Moscow were the president of Belarus, Alexander Lukashenko, the former leader of Ukraine, Leonid Kuchma, the former president of Kyrgyzstan, Askar Akayev, the former Chancellor of Germany, Helmut Kohl, the former US president Bill Clinton, the president of Kazakhstan Nursultan Nazarbayev, and Yeltsin's actor friends Kirill Lavrov, Galina Volchek and Oleg Basilashvili.

The birthday celebrations prompted a new wave of arguments regarding the results of B.N. Yeltsin's activities. On the eve of his birthday, the editors of the newspaper *Novye izvestiya* published the following data from pollsters: 70% of Russians felt that more harm than good had been done during his era.[1022] The editors asked M.O. Chudakova, a literary historian and a member

---

1022   *Novye izvestiya*. 1 February 2006.

of the President's Council and the Commission on charitable matters in the '90s, to comment on these reports and answer a question about the final legacy of the Yeltsin era.

Below are a few of the answers she gave. "Yeltsin," she said, "is an individual of huge historical magnitude; it would be absurd even to mention various populist games that were played, although there are more people keen to cut anything important down to size than can fit in this country. He understood and sensed his historic opportunity — and did not let it slip: Russia returned to the map of the world in its former guise, as Russia. Here was a second, even more important step that he took: Yeltsin stole a march on literally all the other democrats of the day, and all those involved in the broad movement that was engaged in *perestroika*, by grasping something: there is no such thing as socialism with a human face. Behind his personal conflict with Gorbachev — a bitter one which played its role in the country's history — was this fundamental difference in their understanding of Russia's past, present and future. In the last six months of Gorbachev's tenure, when Gorbachev had told eagerly of how his grandfather had opted for collective farms, and said he would never betray this decision, the country had got stuck in a historical crevice. In August 1991, with an almighty effort, Yeltsin pulled the country out of that rut... ..."

I saw in him an inquisitive, curious man, who took a lively and genuine interest in the colorful characters he had assembled around him, so as to listen to what they had to say, rather than try to teach them anything. This was a very un-Soviet trait, something one would not associate with the *nomenklatura* at all. ... And as for the myths about him being a puppet, whose strings were being pulled by someone, they're ridiculous: they are put about by people who didn't know in their own lives what it was to make a decision..."[1023]

Other views were expressed as well, however. "President Yeltsin's era was for Russia a time of losses and failures." "That era brought Russia a great deal of negativity," said Luzhkov, who took charge of the city in 1992.[1024] This assessment — one of the few negative ones that were expressed — must have hurt Yeltsin.

According to V.V. Shevchenko, "in late 2006 Yeltsin was seized by depression — life isn't all sweetness and light. He even stopped grumbling — he would fall silent increasingly often. Only when he danced with his grandsons and great-grandsons in the swimming pool would his soul find comfort, and even then it was not for long. He began complaining about his heart more and more often. He got no sleep, his appetite got worse... It was as though he had

---

1023   Same ref.
1024   2006, NR2.Ru, Novy Region, 2.0

begun to do the summing up, and was checking whether or not he'd forgotten anything," recalled Vladimir Shevchenko. "Suddenly he remembered the book he had written back in 2000: had he forgotten anyone, when he gave out copies of it? I had a premonition even at that stage: Boris Nikolaevich was not thinking the right things, his thoughts were not in a very happy place. And he began to talk about Jordan with increasing frequency: I ought to take a trip there, he would say..."[1025]

A trip to Jordan would have a deeply symbolic significance. This was a part of the Middle East which featured in the Bible, where the history of the Old and New Testaments was present as an underlying reality in its geography, and where a special spiritual atmosphere of proximity to eternity is created. Jerusalem, Bethlehem and Jordan, places divided by new borders, but united in their sacred histories, were important and attractive to Yeltsin, who had undergone a complex spiritual transformation, from conforming with official atheism to acknowledging the importance of religion, and Orthodoxy in particular, and then — personal religion, and acknowledging himself to be a man of Orthodox faith.

For Yeltsin, Jordan was also associated with the dramatic events of his own political life. In 1999, whilst he was sick, he flew to Jordan to attend the funeral of King Hussein. Over forty heads of state and leaders of the world's governments had gathered there. Yeltsin's presence at the funeral ceremony not only signified the deep respect he felt for the memory of King Hussein (something that meant a great deal to his son, King Abdullah the Second). It testified to the fact that Yeltsin, in spite of his poor health, was carrying out his state functions, in spite of reports in the press which claimed that power had in effect been put in the hands of the Prime Minister Y. Primakov.

In the first week after his retirement, Yeltsin visited Bethlehem and Jerusalem.

In the spring of 2007 he intended to go and see the River Jordan, where, according to the gospels, John the Baptist christened Christ.

"That was our last foreign trip," said Vladimir Shevchenko, who had spent 16 years working with Yeltsin. "We came home on 3rd April. A few days later Boris Nikolaevich felt poorly. Then he began to get worse and started complaining of pains in his heart."[1026]

Below is an excerpt from the newspaper article: "They took Yeltsin to hospital but after spending two days there, he did a runner. They persuaded him by force to go back to hospital again, for a week at least - that was on 16th April,

---

1025   Izvestiya. 1 June 2007
1026   Same ref.

a Monday. And on the Sunday, after lunch, he wanted to go home again: "Right, it's been a week — I'm leaving now." Heart problems accompanied by a desire not to be in hospital — this was a bad sign. As any experienced doctor will tell you, this is how people behave when they sense their days are numbered and wish to spend their final moments not at hospital but with their loved ones.

His wish was not granted. The hospital staff convinced Yeltsin to stay in hospital at least until Monday — and to see what the medical council had to say.

He did not live to find out, however. At 8.20 he asked an orderly to help him get up so that he could get washed, and the next moment he lost consciousness. None of his loved ones were by his side in these final moments..." [1027]

On 23 April 2007 Boris Nikolaevich Yeltsin's life in this world came to an end.

1027   Same ref.

EPILOGUE

Boris Nikolaevich Yeltsin was born on 1st February 1931 in the village of Butka in the Urals Region. He died on 23rd April 2007 in Moscow.

Between these two dates lay the life story of a peasant's son,

- the first member of his family to get a degree;

- a talented engineer and civil engineer who became secretary of the regional committee of the CPSU;

- a man who reached the summit of political power in the USSR, a candidate member of the Politburo of the Central Committee and first secretary of the Moscow city committee;

- a man who left the Politburo of his own accord;

- who led a movement for democracy, won the election, became Chairman of the Supreme Soviet of the RSFSR and the first person to be elected head of state in Russia — the President;

- who in August 1991 warded off the attempted coup by the KGB, the Central Committee, the army and the Ministry of Internal Affairs, who had seemed so all-powerful, and who consigned the Communist Party of the Soviet Union and the Soviet Union itself to oblivion;

- who, through the use of armed force, resisted in October 1993 those who supported Soviet power in Russia's Supreme Soviet and opened up a way out of the political and constitutional crisis;

- who insisted that a referendum be held and that the Russian Constitution be adopted in 1993;

- who used the bargaining power of his extremely high approval rating among the people, to bring in difficult market reforms which consigned to the past the seemingly ineradicable concept of a 'deficit', but which created a new set of problems for a new society;

- who rescued the peoples of Russia and the former Soviet Union from the threat of civil war but was unable to avoid ethnic conflict in Chechnya;

- and a man who, it is worth reiterating, was the first person in the history of Russia to leave office voluntarily, and relinquished the office of President of Russia on 31st December 1999.

"Even now there are plenty of people who decry Yeltsin," wrote his adviser V.V. Kostikov. "There will be huge multitudes of them when he begins to grow weak. However just the criticisms made of him might have been, though, even his enemies will never be able to wipe from their memories what he actually managed to achieve: together with Russia, he took the first, most difficult steps toward democracy."[1028]

He was a man of change.

Changes in his own personal biography and in the fate of Russia and the world. He was a Russian political figure whose every step, given the unique nature of his biography, was conditioned by the traditions and political ideas of the people — both the ones that changed and the ones which remained the same.

Yeltsin was a flesh and blood man of the people. He heard the call of time, and understood what was expected of him. He strove to do this bidding. And it pained him when this task proved impossible.

1028   V.V. Kostikov: A love-story with the president. Notes by the press-secretary. M.: 'VAGRIUS', 1997. p.335

INDIVIDUALS MENTIONED

Belkin I.P.
Beloglazov
Belyakov Y.
Belyankin G.I.
Berezovsky B.A.
Berestova V.
Beria L.P.
Bersenev I.
Beryukhov
Beskov B.
Beshlyuss M.
Bignov R.I.
Bievets N.L.
Biryukov A.P.
Biryukov V.A.
Belov M.
Belov V.
Bezrodny I.
Belavin L.T.
Biryukov N.K.
Blokh B.
Bobykin L.F.
Boffa D.
Bogdashin P.M.
Bogomoov O.T.
Boiko M.
Boikov V.A.
Boldin V.I.
Boldyrev Y.
Bolshakov A.
Bondarchuk S.F.
Bondarev Y.
Bonet P.
Bonner E.G.
Bordyuzha N.N.
Borodin L.A.
Borodin P.P.
Bostandzhiev E.N.
Brakov E.
Brandt W.
Bratischev I.M.
Brezhnev L.I.
Brutents K.N.

Buchelnikova R.
Bulganin N.A.
Burbulis G.A.
Bush G.
Bushkov V.
Bykov L.P.
Bykov V.

Chakovsky A.
Chebrikov A.N.
Chebrikov V.M.
Chechenin N.K.
Chelnokov N.Y.
Chernenko K.U.
Chernomyrdin V.S.
Chernushkin V.S.
Chernyaev A.S.
Chernyak A.
Chiang Kai-Shek F.V.
Chikirev N.S.
Chivilikhin V.
Chubais A.B.
Chudakova M.O.
Churakov V.

Danilov V.P.
Davydov O.
Degtyarev
Demidov L.
Denisenko B.
Dneprov A.D.
Dobrovolsky V.G.
Dobryden A.A.
Dobrynin A.F.
Dolgikh V.I.
Dorofeev V.
Doronina T.
Dorosinsky G.P.
Dovgy I.
Dubchek A.
Dubenetsky Y.
Dubinin S.K.
Dudaev D.M.

Dundukov A.
Dvoryanov V.F.
Dyachenko T.B.
Dyakov A.
Dybcho G.
Dymshits V.A.
Dzhanenko N.S.
Dzukkono V.

Falin V.M.
Falk P.P.
Felgenhauer P.
Filatov S.A.
Filatova I.
Filimonov V.
Fomichev V.
Fominov
Foyo S.
Fridman M.
Fyodorov B.G.
Fyodorov V.

Gaidar E. T.
Gaisin O.D.
Galazov A.
Gantemirov B.
Garnak A.E.
Gdlyan T.
Geraschenko V.V
Gidaspov B.V.
Girenko A.N.
Girina N.
Giscardd'Estaing V.
Glebov A.A.
Glebov V.S.
Golubeva V.N.
Golushko N.M.
Gonchar N.
Gorbachev M.S.
Gorbacheva R.M.
Gorbunov Y.A.
Gorshkov M.K.
Goryacheva S.P.

Goryushkin L.M.
Govorukhin S.
Gozman L.
Grachev A.S.
Grachev P.S.
Grafov
Granberg A.
Granin D.A.
Grechko G.
Greshnevikov A.
GreshnevikovA.
GrigorievL.M.
Grishin V.V.
Gromov B.
Gromyko A.A.
Gryaznov B.A.
Gulyaev Y.
Guschin N.Y.
Gusinsky V.A.
Gutiontov P.

Hendricksen P.
Hoffman D.
Hurd D.

Ignatenko V.N.
Ilin A.
Ilin B.
Ilyushenko A.
Ilyushin V.V.
Imshenetsky V.
Ionin L.
Isaev B.M.
Isakov V.B.
Iskhakov A.B.
Israel Y.A.
Ivanov I.I.
Ivanov I.S.
Ivashko V.A.

Jenniger F.

Kadannikov V.V.
Kadatsky V.F.

Kadyshev V.D.
Kaeta G.
Kaganovich L.M.
Kalashnikov V.V.
Karabasov Y.S.
Karaganov S.A.
Karasik M.L.
Karlina T.
Karpukhin V.
Kashpurov V.S.
Kazannik A.I.
Khabarov A.I.
Khakamada I.
Kharin G.N.
Khasbulatov R.I.
Khazanov G.
Khodorkovsky M.
Khodov S. B.
Khokhlov V.
Khomyakov M.I.
Khonina A.P.
Khristenko V.B.
Khrushchev N.S.
Kinilev V.G.
Kirienko S.V.
Kirilenko A.P.
Klepikova Y.
Klepikova Y.
Klyuvgant V.V.
Kobets K.
Koivisto M.
Kokh A.R.
Koksharov F.M.
Kolbin G.V.
Koluga Y.
Kondratov Y.N.
Konotop V.I.
Konstantinov I.V.
Kopachev A.A.
Kopylov Y.V.
Korabelschikov A.I.
Korzhakov A.V.
Korolev A.M.

Korolev O.A.
Korotich V.
Kostikov V.V.
Korovitsyn A.I.
Kostromin Y.N.
Kosygin A.N.
Kovalev S.A.
Kozhokin Y.M.
Kozneva A.
Kozyrev A.V.
Kozyrev-Dal F.F.
Kraiko Y.
Krasnov M.A.
Kravchuk L.
Kryuchkov V.V.
Kudrin A.
Kukushkin V.
Kulikov A.
Kunaev D.A.
Kutsyllo V.
Kutsyllo V.
Kuzin V.
Kuznetsov M.
Kuznetsov N.I.
Kuznetsova P.Y.
Kuzyk B.

Labazanov R.
Lagunov K.
Lantseva V.
Lapshin M.I.
Latsis O.R.
Lavochkin A.
Lebed A.I.
Leidermann N.L.
Leschenko L.
Letov A.I.
Levada Y.A.
Levicheva I.N.
Lifshits A.Y.
Ligachev Y.K.
Likhachev D.S.
Lipatnikov V.

Lisovsky S.
Litvin A.L.
Litvin A.L.
Lobov O.I.
Lodkin Y.
Logunov V.
Lukin I.S.
Lukin V.P.
Lukyanin V.P.
Lukyanov A.I.
Luzhkov Y.M.
Lvov D.S.
Lyubimov I.I.

Magomedov M.
Makarkin N.P.
Makarov N.
Makashov A.M.
Makashov V.
Makhmutov I.S.
Maksimova K.
Malashenko I.
Malenkov G.M.
Malov V.
Malykhin A.
Malyshev A.V.
Malyshev N.G.
Malyshkin V.V.
Mamodaev Y.
Manyakin S.I.
Manyukhin V.M.
Marenich A.
Markov V.
Markushkin B.M.
Martynova V.A.
Maschits V.M.
Maskhadov A.
Maslyukov Y.D.
Matkovsky A.
Matveenko N.A.
Matveev L.I.
Mazav V.D.
Mazurov N.N.

Mazyrin V.P.
Medunov S.
Medvedev P.A.
Medvedev S.
Medvedev V.A.
Mekhrentsev A.A.
Mesyats V.K.
Migranyan A.M.
Mikhailov A.Y.
Mikhailov N.
Mikhalkov N.S.
Mikhnik A.
Mikushin G.K.
Minaev B.D.
Mingalyov P.D.
Minkin A.
Mitrofanov S.
Mitterand F.
Mityukov M.A.
Mogilnikov A.N.
Moiseev M.A.
Molchanov B.
Molchanov S.F.
Molotov V.M.
Molchanov B.
Molchanov S.F.
Moroz O.
Morokin V.I.
Morschakov F.M.
Muzykantsky A.N.
Muravlenko S.
Mukha V.
Mukhamadieva T.
Mukhamedeev K.A.
Mukhin G.A.

Naboichenko S.S.
Nagibin Y.
Nazarbayev N. A.
Nasedkin V.
Neverov I.A.
Nevzlin L.
Nemtsov B.N.

Neumin M.I.
Nizmutdinova L.
Nizovtsev A.A.
Nikiforov K.V.
Nikolaev A.I.
Nikolaev K.K.
Nikolaev K.N.
Nikolin V.
Nikonov V.
Nikonov N. G
Novikov I.T.
Nudel V.S.

Oblasov F.N.
Obolensky A.M.
Ovchinnikov G.E.
Okudzhava B.
Olbik A.
Orlov V.P.
Osintsev I.A.
Oslon A.

Paverman M.
Pavlov V.S.
Pavlov N.
Pavlova A.E.
Pavlovsky G.
Pain E.A.
Palm V.A.
Pamfilov A.
Panov D.A.
Pasternak B.
Patrakeev
Pekar G.S.
Peretrutov S.I.
Permyakov Y.A.
Petrakov N.Y.
Petrenko V.A.
Petrov L.V.
Petrov Y.V.
Petukhov D.
Pimenov R.I.
Pisarev I.D.

Pikhoya D.G.
Pikhoya R.G.
Plekhanov F.
Podoprigora V.N.
Pokrovsky N.N.
Poleschuk M.D.
Polozkov I.K.
Polozkov I.K.
Poltoranin M.N.
Ponomarev L.A.
Popkov V.
Popkov V.
Popov G.K.
Poptsov O.
Porotnikov A.F.
Porotnikov M.V.
Potanin V.O.
Potapov I.I.
Preobrazhensky A.A.
Primakov Y.M.
Prokofiev Y.A.
Promyslov V.F.
Pugo B.K.
Putin V.V.
Pyatygin B.S.

Quayle D.

Raevskaya N.
Raifschneider A.
Rakhimov M.
Rasputin V.
Razdyakonova R.
Razumovsky G.P.
Repenko M.P.
Resin V.I.
Rice C.
Rogitsky S.A.
Rodionov I.Y.
Rodionov I.S.
Rodionov S.
Rozhdestvensky R.
Rozhkov Y.P.

Romanov G.A.
Romanov G.V.
Rutskoi A.V.
Ruchev B.
RyabovN.G.
Rybakov P.D.
Rybkin I.P.
Ryurikov D.B.
Ryzhkov I.Y.
Ryzhkov N.I.
Ryzhkov Y.A.

Saenko G.V.
Saikin V.G.
Saikin V.T.
Sakharov A.D.
Samokhvalov S.K.
Samsonov N.
Sanochkin F.Y.
Satarov G.A.
Savchenko A.I.
Savostyanov Y.
Scherbakov V.P.
Scherbitsky V.V.
Schroeder G.
Schwartz Y.
Scowcroft B.
Seleznev G.
Semenov N.N.
Semenchenko V.
Semukhin I.
Sergeev A.
Sergeev D.
Sergeev I.D.
Sergeev M.A.
Sergeev P.I.
Sergeev V.V.
Sergeev Y.
Shabad A.
Shabunin T.P.
Shakhmanov I.V.
Shakhnazarov G.
Shakhnovsky V.

Shakhova Y.
Shakhova Y.
Shakhrai S.M.
Shaposhnikov Y.
Shatalin S.S.
Sheinis V.L.
Shelov-Kovedyaev F.V.
Shenin O.S.
Shevardnadze E.A.
Shevchenko V.N.
Shevtsova L.
Shevtsova L.F.
Shilin V.A.
Shilov A.
Shimaev L.
Shiryaev V.V.
Shmelev N.P.
Shoigu S.K.
Shokhin A.N.
Shtoff E.
Shtokolov B.
Shtyashev V.
Shubin A.V.
Shulzhenko K.
Shumeiko V.F.
Shushkevich S.
Silaev I. S.
Sitaryan S.A.
Skokov Y.
Slobodkin Y.
Slovtsov P.
Slyunkov N.N.
Smirnova S.A.
Smirnyagin L.V.
Smolensky A.
Smolsky P.A.
Sobchak A.A.
Sobyanin A.A.
Sogrin V.V.
Sokolov V.S.
Solomentsev M.S.
Soloviev V.
Soloviev Y.F.

Solovieva V.
Sorokin A.Y.
Soskovetes O.N.
Sotnikov K.A.
Spektor S.I.
Spiridonov L.N.
Spiridonov Y.
Stalin J.V.
Stankevich S.B.
Starovoitova G.V.
Starygin A.
Starygin V.E.
Starygina K.V.
Stepankov V.G.
Stepanov S. L.
Stepanov V.
Stepashin S.V.
Sterligov A.
Strakhov A.
Stroev Y.
Sukhanov L.
Sukhanov S.
Surat A.
Suslov L.
Suslov M.A.
Sutyrin V.
Sviridov G.
Syrovatko V.S.
Sysolyatin P.Z.
Sysuev O.N.
Sytnikov M.I.
Sytnikov N.I.
Syukosev V.D.

Talalaev N.A.
Talbot S.
Tarasov B.V.
Tarpischev S.A.
Tatianicheva L.
Telminov I.Y.
Timofeyev
Titov V.A.
Tiunov O.I.

Tikhomirov V.P.
Tikhonov N.A.
Tikhonkov
Tishkin N.M.
Tokarev M.
Tolpezhnikov V.F.
Tomashev Y.A.
Tosunyan G.
Travkin N.
Trenikhin V.F.
Tsaregorodtsev A.N.
Tsepennikov V.I.
Tsoi V.
Tuleeva A.M.
Tutviler M.

Ulyanov M.
Urazhtsev
Urinson Y.M.
Urmanov A.N.
Urnov M.
Usmankhodzhaev I.B.
Usmanov G.I.
Utyosov L.

Vavilov A.P.
Valenta I.
Varennikov V.
Varlamova N.V.
Varov V.K.
Vasiliev B.
Vasiliev V.K.
Vavilov A.P.
Vedernikov N.T.
Vertinsky A.N.
Veshnyakova A.A.
Vidineeva L.A.
Viks M.
Vilesova N.A.
Vinogradov A.I.
Vinogradov S.A.
Vinogradov G.
Vlasov A.V.

Volkogonov D.A.
Volkov V.A.
Volkov L.B.
Voloshin A.S.
Volynsky A.A.
Vorobyov A.
Voronin Y.
Voronina E.V.
Voroshilov K.E.
Vorotnikov V.I.
Voschanov P.
Vyzhutovich V.

Yablokov A.
Yakovlev A.N.
Yakunin G.
Yanaev G.
Yandarbiev Z.
Yarov Y.
Yarov Y.
Yaroshenko V.
Yasin Y.G.
Yastrzhembsky S.V.
Yavlinsky G.A.
Yazov D.T.
Yegorov N.D.
Yegorov S.
Yelokhin F.M.
Yeltsin N.I.
Yeltsin A.I.
Yeltsin A.S.
Yeltsin B.N.
Yeltsin V.P.
Yeltsin D.I.
Yeltsin Y.I.
Yeltsin I.Y.
Yeltsin I.I.
Yeltsin I.I.
Yeltsin I.M.
Yeltsin K.S.
Yeltsin M.N.
Yeltsin N.I.
Yeltsin P.S.

Yeltsin S.D.
Yeltsin S.N.
Yeltsin F.V.
Yeltsin F.Y.
Yeltsin F.S.
Yeltsin Y.M.
Yeltsin A.M.
Yeltsina K.V.
Yeltsina M.I.
Yeltsina N.I.
Yeltsyn A.M.
Yeltsyn V.E.
Yeltsyn Y.S.
Yeltsyn Y.S.
Yeltsyn I.Y.
Yeltsyn I.L.
Yeltsyn M. Y.
Yeltsyn M.G.
Yeltsyn N.I.
Yeltsyn P.L.
Yeltsyn P.M.
Yemelyanov A.M.
Yemelyanov S.
Yemelyanova P.
Yerin V.F.
Yerina M.
Yevstafiev A.
Yevtushenko Y.
Yezhov A.
Yezhov V.B.
Yumashev V.B.
Yuzefovich A.N.

Zadornov M. M.
Zagladin V.V.
Zaidel R.
Zaikov L.N.
Zakharov V.G.
Zakharov M.A.
Zakharov M.L.
Zakharov M.M.
Zamyatin L.M.
Zamyatin V.V.

Zarubin N.P.
Zasukhin A.
Zatvornitsky V.A.
Zavertkin I.S.
Zaveryukha A.
Zavgaev D.
Zavidiya A.
Zemerov A.P.
ZemerovD.V.
Zemerov I.F.
ZemerovD.V.
Zemerov I.F.
Zharov V.A.
Zhdanov S.A.
Zhdanovich A.G.
Zhilyaev K.V.
Zhirinovsky V.V.
Zhitenev V.A.
Zhukova R.
Zimyanin M.V.
ZinovievaS.A.
ZolotukhinB.A.
Zorkin V.D.
Zverev S.
Zykina L.
Zyryanov A.N.
Zyuganov G.A.

Glagoslav Publications Catalogue

- *The Time of Women* by Elena Chizhova
- *Sin* by Zakhar Prilepin
- *Hardly Ever Otherwise* by Maria Matios
- *The Lost Button* by Irene Rozdobudko
- *Khatyn* by Ales Adamovich
- *Christened with Crosses* by Eduard Kochergin
- *The Vital Needs of the Dead* by Igor Sakhnovsky
- *METRO 2033* (Dutch Edition) by Dmitry Glukhovsky
- *METRO 2034* (Dutch Edition) by Dmitry Glukhovsky
- *A Poet and Bin Laden* by Hamid Ismailov
- *Asystole* by Oleg Pavlov
- *Kobzar* by Taras Shevchenko
- *White Shanghai* by Elvira Baryakina
- *The Stone Bridge* by Alexander Terekhov
- *King Stakh's Wild Hunt* by Uladzimir Karatkevich
- *Depeche Mode* by Serhii Zhadan
- *Saraband Sarah's Band* by Larysa Denysenko
- *Herstories*, An Anthology of New Ukrainian Women Prose Writers
- *Watching The Russians* (Dutch Edition) by Maria Konyukova
- *The Hawks of Peace* by Dmitry Rogozin
- *The Grand Slam and Other Stories* (Dutch Edition) by Leonid Andreev
- *The Battle of the Sexes Russian Style* by Nadezhda Ptushkina
- *A Book Without Photographs* by Sergey Shargunov
- *Sankya* by Zakhar Prilepin
- *Wolf Messing – The True Story of Russia's Greatest Psychic* by Tatiana Lungin
- *Good Stalin* by Victor Erofeyev
- *Solar Plexus* by Rustam Ibragimbekov
- *Don't Call me a Victim!* by Dina Yafasova
- *A History of Belarus* by Lubov Bazan
- *Children's Fashion of the Russian Empire* by Alexander Vasiliev
- *Empire of Corruption – The Russian National Pastime* by Vladimir Soloviev
- *Heroes of the 90s – People and Money. The Modern History of Russian Capitalism*
- *Tsarina Alexandra's Diary* (Dutch)
- *Everyday Saints and Other Stories* (Dutch) by Archimandrite Tikhon

More coming soon...